In disquisitions of every kind there are certain primary truths, or first principles, upon which all subsequent reasonings must depend.... Of the same nature, are those maxims in ethics and politics, that there cannot be an effect without a cause.

> Alexander Hamilton 1754–1804
> Revolutionary, first U.S. secretary of the treasury
> *The Federalist* No. 31

The ultimate result of shielding men from the effects of folly is to fill the world with fools.

> Herbert Spencer 1820–1903
> Philosopher, essayist

The place had an overwhelming presence of literature, and you couldn't help but lose your passion for dumbness.

> Bob Dylan 1941–
> Songwriter

There are some ideas so wrong that only a very intelligent person could believe in them.

> George Orwell 1903–1950
> Novelist, social critic

There is not one of our simple uncounted rights today for which better men than we are have not died on the scaffold or the battlefield. We have not only a great treasure; we have a great cause.

> Winston Churchill 1874–1965
> Prime Minister of Great Britain
> 1940–1945, 1950–1955

History is mankind's painfully purchased experience, now available for free, or merely the price of attention and reflection.

> Thomas Sowell 1930–
> Economist and social critic

Man cannot make principles; he can only discover them.

Government, even in its best state, is but a necessary evil; in its worst state, an intolerable one.

An army of principles can penetrate where an army of soldiers cannot.

> Thomas Paine 1737–1809
> Revolutionary, essayist

FIRST PRINCIPLES

Self-governance in an Open Society

FIRST PRINCIPLES

Self-governance in an Open Society

Thomas N. Tripp

Black Sheep Farm Press
Wilson, Wyoming

Copyright © 2008 by Thomas N. Tripp

All rights reserved under International and Pan-American Copyright Conventions. Published in the United States by Black Sheep Farm Press, Wilson, Wyoming.

No part of this book may be reproduced in any form or by any electronic or mechanical means, including information storage and retrieval systems, without permission in writing from the publisher, except for a reviewer, educational professional, or student, who may quote brief passages in a review, treatise, article, etc. Members of educational or other institutions wishing to photocopy or otherwise reproduce part or all of the work for classroom use, or publishers who would like to obtain permission to include the work in an anthology or who would like to use extensive portions of the book, should send their inquiries to Black Sheep Farm Press at the e-mail address available at www.firstprinciples.us.

Cover and book design by Cox-King Multimedia, website www.ckmm.com.

ISBN: 978-0-9814967-0-2
LCCN: 2008900489

First Edition, Second Printing

This book is dedicated to the American soldier.

Without the devotion and sacrifice of each dogface, swabbie,

leatherneck, flyboy, and coastie nothing would be as it is.

Cherish those alive, honor those departed.

Contents

Author's Note: The Wildebeest Effect . . . . *xv*
Foreword to *First Principles*, James A. Baker, III . . . . *xix*

Welcome to *First Principles* 1
Self-governance in an Open Society: First Principles 13
A Note on Organization. 55

Section I: Part 1: The Architecture of a Free Society 57
Chapter 1: *The Second Treatise on Civil Government*, John Locke 59
Chapter 2: *Common Sense, The Rights of Man, and Other Essential Writings*, Thomas Paine 65
Chapter 3: The Declaration of Independence of the Thirteen Colonies, Thomas Jefferson 71
Chapter 4: *The Roots of American Order*, Russell Kirk. 77
Chapter 5: The Constitution of the United States, James Madison, et. al. 87
Chapter 6: *The Federalist*, Alexander Hamilton, John Jay, James Madison 109

Section I: Part 2: Case Studies 117
Chapter 7: *The Law*, Frederic Bastiat 119
Chapter 8: *Democracy in America*, Alexis de Tocqueville. 129
Chapter 9: *Essays in the History of Liberty*, Lord Acton 139
Chapter 10: *In Defense of Freedom*, Frank S. Meyer 147
Chapter 11: *Property and Freedom*, Richard Pipes 155
Chapter 12: *Wealth of Nations*, Adam Smith 175
Chapter 13: *The Road to Serfdom*, Friedrich A. von Hayek 187
Chapter 14: *The Constitution of Liberty*, Friedrich A. von Hayek. . . . 197
Chapter 15: *On Power*, Bertrand de Jouvenel 205

Section II: Part 1: The Twentieth-Century American Experience . 225
Chapter 16: *The Conservative Revolution: The Movement That Remade America*, Lee Edwards 227
Chapter 17: *Up From Liberalism*, William F. Buckley, Jr.. 233
Chapter 18: *The Conscience of a Conservative*, Barry Goldwater. . . . 241
Chapter 19: *What It Means to Be a Libertarian*, Charles Murray . . . 249
Chapter 20: *Let Us Talk of Many Things*, William F. Buckley, Jr. 255
Chapter 21: *Promised Land, Crusader State*, Walter A. McDougall . . 259
Chapter 22: *Modern Times*, Paul Johnson. 269

Section II: Part 2: Government and the Free Market. 279
Chapter 23: *Economics of the Free Society*, Wilhelm Röpke 281
Chapter 24: *Economics in One Lesson*, Henry Hazlitt 295
Chapter 25: *Capitalism and Freedom*, Milton Friedman 303
Chapter 26: *The Roots of Capitalism*, John Chamberlain 311
Chapter 27: *Wealth and Poverty*, George Gilder 319
Chapter 28: *The Ethics of Redistribution*, Bertrand de Jouvenel 335
Chapter 29: *The Commanding Heights*, Daniel Yergin
 and Joseph Stanislaw. 349
Chapter 30: *Reclaiming the American Dream*, Richard C. Cornuelle . 359
Chapter 31: *In Pursuit: Of Happiness and Good Government*,
 Charles Murray. 369
Chapter 32: *Socialism*, Ludwig von Mises. 381
Chapter 33: *A Humane Economy*, Wilhelm Röpke 389
Chapter 34: *The Theory of Money and Credit*, Ludwig von Mises . . . 403

Section III: Fundamental Inquiries 415
Chapter 35: *Ideas Have Consequences*, Richard M. Weaver 417
Chapter 36: *Selected Works of Edmund Burke, Volume 2:
 Reflections on the Revolution in France*, Edmund Burke
 The Portable Edmund Burke, Isaac Kramnick (Ed.) 425
Chapter 37: *The Conservative Mind: From Burke to Eliot*,
 Russell Kirk 437
Chapter 38: *Capitalism, Socialism, and Democracy*,
 Joseph A. Schumpeter 445
Chapter 39: *The Open Society and Its Enemies*, Karl L. Popper 455
Chapter 40: *Human Action*, Ludwig von Mises. 469
Chapter 41: *Witness*, Whittaker Chambers 479
Chapter 42: *Killing Pablo*, Mark Bowden 487

Section IV: The Future. 495
Chapter 43: *Fewer*, Ben J. Wattenberg 497
Chapter 44: *One Nation Under Therapy*,
 Christina Hoff Sommers, Sally Satel 507

Afterword. 515
Index of Subject Matter 533
Index 539
A note regarding particular editions of
 the books synopsized in *First Principles* 555
Acknowledgements 563
About the Author 565

Books Alphabetically by Title

A Humane Economy, Wilhelm Röpke 389
Capitalism and Freedom, Milton Friedman. 303
Capitalism, Socialism, and Democracy, Joseph A. Schumpeter 445
The Commanding Heights, Daniel Yergin, Joseph Stanislaw 349
Common Sense, The Rights of Man, and Other Essential Writings,
   Thomas Paine. 65
The Conscience of a Conservative, Barry Goldwater 241
The Conservative Mind: From Burke to Eliot, Russell Kirk 437
The Conservative Revolution: The Movement That Remade America,
   Lee Edwards. 227
The Constitution of Liberty, Friedrich A. von Hayek. 197
The Constitution of the United States, James Madison, et. al. 87
The Declaration of Independence of the Thirteen Colonies,
   Thomas Jefferson. 71
Democracy in America, Alexis de Tocqueville 129
Economics in One Lesson, Henry Hazlitt 295
Economics of the Free Society, Wilhelm Röpke 281
Essays in the History of Liberty, Lord Acton. 139
The Ethics of Redistribution, Bertrand de Jouvenel. 335
The Federalist, Alexander Hamilton, John Jay, James Madison 109
Fewer, Ben J. Wattenberg 497
Human Action, Ludwig von Mises 469
Ideas Have Consequences, Richard M. Weaver 417
In Defense of Freedom, Frank S. Meyer 147
In Pursuit: Of Happiness and Good Government, Charles Murray . . . 369
Killing Pablo, Mark Bowden 487
The Law, Frederic Bastiat. 119
Let Us Talk of Many Things, William F. Buckley, Jr. 255
Modern Times, Paul Johnson 269
On Power, Bertrand de Jouvenel 205
One Nation Under Therapy, Christina Hoff Sommers, Sally Satel . . . 507
The Open Society and Its Enemies, Karl L. Popper. 455
The Portable Edmund Burke, Edmund Burke, Isaac Kramnick (Ed.) . . 425
Promised Land, Crusader State, Walter A. McDougall 259
Property and Freedom, Richard Pipes 155
Reclaiming the American Dream, Richard C. Cornuelle. 359
The Rights of Man, Thomas Paine 65
The Road to Serfdom, Friedrich A. von Hayek 187
The Roots of American Order, Russell Kirk 77
The Roots of Capitalism, John Chamberlain 311
The Second Treatise on Civil Government, John Locke 59

Selected Works of Edmund Burke, Volume 2: Reflections on the Revolution in France, Edmund Burke 425
Socialism, Ludwig von Mises 381
The Theory of Money and Credit, Ludwig von Mises 403
Up From Liberalism, William F. Buckley, Jr. 233
Wealth and Poverty, George Gilder 319
Wealth of Nations, Adam Smith 175
What It Means to Be a Libertarian, Charles Murray 249
Witness, Whittaker Chambers 479

Books Alphabetically by Author

Acton, Lord: *Essays in the History of Liberty* 139
Bastiat, Frederic: *The Law* 119
Bowden, Mark: *Killing Pablo* 487
Buckley, Jr., William F.: *Let Us Talk of Many Things* 255
Buckley, Jr., William F.: *Up From Liberalism* 233
Burke, Edmund: *Selected Works of Edmund Burke, Volume 2:
Reflections on the Revolution in France* 425
Burke, Edmund; Isaac Kramnick (Ed.): *The Portable Edmund Burke* . 425
Chamberlain, John: *The Roots of Capitalism* 311
Chambers, Whittaker: *Witness* 479
Cornuelle, Richard C.: *Reclaiming the American Dream* 359
Edwards, Lee: *The Conservative Revolution: The Movement
That Remade America* 227
Friedman, Milton: *Capitalism and Freedom* 303
Gilder, George: *Wealth and Poverty* 319
Goldwater, Barry: *The Conscience of a Conservative*. 241
Hamilton, Alexander; Jay, John; Madison, James: *The Federalist* . . . 109
Hayek, Friedrich A. von: *The Constitution of Liberty* 197
Hayek, Friedrich A. von: *The Road to Serfdom* 187
Hazlitt, Henry: *Economics in One Lesson* 295
Jefferson, Thomas: The Declaration of Independence of the
Thirteen Colonies. 71
Johnson, Paul: *Modern Times*. 269
Jouvenel, Bertrand de: *The Ethics of Redistribution* 335
Jouvenel, Bertrand de: *On Power* 205
Kirk, Russell: *The Conservative Mind: From Burke to Eliot* 437
Kirk, Russell: *The Roots of American Order*. 77
Locke, John: *The Second Treatise on Civil Government* 59
Madison, James, et. al.: The Constitution of the United States 87
McDougall, Walter A.: *Promised Land, Crusader State* 259
Meyer, Frank S.: *In Defense of Freedom* 147
Mises, Ludwig von: *Human Action*. 469
Mises, Ludwig von: *Socialism*. 381
Mises, Ludwig von: *The Theory of Money and Credit* 403
Murray, Charles: *In Pursuit: Of Happiness and Good Government*. . . 369
Murray, Charles: *What It Means to Be a Libertarian* 249
Paine, Thomas: *Common Sense, The Rights of Man, and
Other Essential Writings*. 65
Pipes, Richard: *Property and Freedom*. 155
Popper, Karl L.: *The Open Society and Its Enemies*. 455
Röpke, Wilhelm: *A Humane Economy*. 389

Röpke, Wilhelm: *Economics of the Free Society* 281
Schumpeter, Joseph A.: *Capitalism, Socialism, and Democracy* 445
Smith, Adam: *Wealth of Nations* 175
Sommers, Christina Hoff; Satel, Sally: *One Nation Under Therapy* . . 507
Tocqueville, Alexis de: *Democracy in America* 129
Wattenberg, Ben J.: *Fewer* 497
Weaver, Richard M.: *Ideas Have Consequences* 417
Yergin, Daniel; Stanislaw, Joseph: *The Commanding Heights* 349

A NOTE ABOUT FOOTNOTES:

The reader will observe there are few footnotes or annotations in this book. *First Principles* is not a university dissertation, but a primer. As the manuscript was composed the intention was that quotations and references would come from the books that are the subjects of the synopses. In the few cases where mention of other works is made, or where quotes are derived from other sources, direct attribution is contained in the text itself.

Author's Note

The Wildebeest Effect

WHILE WRITING *First Principles* I was sometimes questioned as to my goal in undertaking this project. The answer is fairly simple; my intent is to define square one, the place from which one launches any attempt at self-governance. What I have often observed in the real world is the disconnection between the fundamentals of human nature and experience, and the results obtained when notions of idealistic governance overtake rationality. None of us should deny the value of idealistic musings; all of us should when necessary recognize their improbability—and act accordingly.

As I watch those elected to represent the citizenry I find that logic is sometimes present in their action or inaction, but common sense often is not. I want to describe that rational manner of governance history has taught us but that now seems to be absent, mostly as a result of the effects of politics and the media.

Americans, in particular but not uniquely, have only a superficial comprehension of self-governance and the fundamentals of economics. We understand democracy generally, but the object and workings of representative government and the free market on which it is based we grasp less well.

This is in part the Wildebeest Effect. The wildebeest is a large grazing animal that dominates the Serengeti Plain in eastern Africa. They are counted in the millions and roam in herds large enough to stretch beyond the horizon. But the wildebeest is fodder for the lion who hunts these massive beasts without fear of opposition or even confrontation. The reason the victims are such easy prey, of course, is their inability to organize or communicate. They are picked off one by one as they ineffectually run from the predations of their adversary. But, with the simplest turn of the smallest portion of the herd, and the stomping and stamping of the easily surrounded lion, the wildebeeste could almost effortlessly control their own destiny.

The modern democratic electorate can be seen as the wildebeeste— literate of course, but wildebeeste nonetheless. We are cowed by the theoretical insignificance of the individual, comforted by the security of the herd, and ignorant of our own power. We should not be; the system under which we operate is designed to take advantage of exactly that power by using the knowledge at each elector's fingertips.

What this volume intends is to bring to the fore the common sense of self-governance that we knew so well in the past, and to encourage understanding of the simplicity of successful human interaction, of successful self-governance. Creating the perfect society is hardly the goal for many relatively obvious reasons, but rediscovering a workable model of governing, and then executing that design is.

The wildebeeste should rule the African plain; the electorate should govern itself in a rational and just manner. That the wildebeeste will not rise to that level is clear—nature has not endowed them with either reason or courage. The question remains: can and will the people refute their wildebeest existence in the modern era, will they take on the lions in the government mansions and turn them back hungry and defeated because with their power that is an easy thing to do? Or will they trudge along in the hope that the lion won't come to their door more than he already has; will they continue in failing to recall that the greatest fear of the elected is the massed will, and sense, of their constituents?

The political class often espouses ideas about economics and self-governance that may seem appealing in the abstract but which disintegrate upon being exposed to fresh air. These flights of rhetorical fancy are their primary tools for obtaining or continuing in power. The bigger problems arise when idealistic concepts are given solid footing in legislation, or bureaucratic rule-making, or in court decisions, before their inadvertent effects can be assessed—often before they are even considered. In this volume there is an attempt to discuss and explain some of the good and bad ideas of governance that have evolved over the centuries.

While government is necessary, its role in the United States has expanded beyond the Founders' intentions and history's prescriptions. Time has taught us that government is to arbitrate among citizens while not devolving to directing or controlling them, and to encourage both opportunity and discipline. In order to be successful in this effort, our public actions (or restraint) must rest on a platform of relatively universal social comprehensions and agreements—the freedom to choose, the obligation to take responsibility for those choices and to perform concomitant duties, and the necessity of respecting one another's rights. We must understand that without an ability to trust one another, in a societal sense, without a mostly uniform sharing of methods and means, and yes, values (which is not a code word here), no system of governance can be functional.

Our intention is to distill from the political carnage that exists today the original design of the American version of representative democracy. That system is founded in a written Constitution that protects the rights of the individual, ensures his liberty, and gently directs him toward his duties—that it is hoped will be assumed without need for public intervention.

The books that comprise this colloquy contain core explanations, those first principles necessary to achieve what was intended beginning in 1776. The goal is to see what can be accomplished in a real-world setting by looking beyond romantic political idealism. We also consider the secondary and tertiary effects of public actions—better known as the law of unintended consequences—to evaluate everything that might occur on the way to our objective.

History has shown us repeatedly that freedom is the foundation upon which any society is best organized—mankind is too complex and too idiosyncratic to be governed in any detailed sense. The human condition prohibits such regimentation save only on very basic levels. Even at that level, organizing a free society is not easily achieved, for there is often a grand temptation in each of us to tell the next person what we've learned and then, with sometimes messianic fervor, to ensure they proceed in a manner of which we approve. This tug between freedom and control is the core issue with which society must continually deal.

My pursuit of square one, a habit more than a compulsion, has resulted in what is submitted here. It is an attempt to put things in perspective, then in order. Each synopsis in *First Principles* essentially self-selected its inclusion. What social imperative came first as culture and governance developed, what elements were necessary before the next step could be taken, what negative consequences were experienced that had to be superseded before further progress could be achieved are the substance of what is presented here.

Perhaps what this book offers will help the reader achieve a sense of understanding and satisfaction as to his or her place and methods and goals. What I've noticed over time is that people who realize what they stand for are often willing to stand up as well.

—Thomas N. Tripp

Foreword to *First Principles*

James A. Baker, III

THE COLLECTION of writings that has been compiled in this volume comes at a crucial time in the history of our relatively young country. With the end of the Cold War, which left the United States as the only global superpower, we occupy a pre-eminent position in world affairs—militarily, politically, and economically. At the same time, our country must confront the menace of terrorism. Paradoxically, at a moment when America is strongest, she is perhaps also most vulnerable to terrorists who don't value human life.

This contradiction of American power provides us with a challenge that can only be met with the type of leadership that has been America's good fortune for more than two centuries.

The terrorist threat is global in scope and may last decades. It will take a toll on our patience, our pocketbooks and, more importantly, our resolve. There have been and will continue to be critics and doubters as we travel the many pathways to confront terrorist activities. But as Winston Churchill observed in the dark hours at the outset of World War II, "without victory, there will be no survival."

Make no mistake, history will judge this country by the quality of its leadership as it resists the menace of stateless anarchists. But, it is not just the leadership of our elected officials, because in the United States the measure of leadership does not start at the top. It is imperative that each of us understand that leadership comes from the ground up. That is where our strength lies. This is something that our adversaries have not been able to grasp and that at times we take for granted.

I refer to leadership in daily life—in doing what is best for our families, our places of worship, our businesses, and, of course, our communities and our nation. Some say that leadership is a rare thing, found only in the dusty books, the private preserve of extraordinarily talented individuals and out of the reach of ordinary men and women. But I don't believe that. Don't tell that to the police officers and fire fighters who rushed into the Twin Towers on September 11, 2001. Don't tell that to the passengers who rushed the highjackers on United Flight

93 that same fateful day. And, don't tell that to the allied troops, who, throughout our history have liberated oppressed peoples; in Europe in 1918, and again in 1945, while they also freed people smothered by the Japanese everywhere in the Pacific and on the Asian mainland, and, most recently, in releasing Afghanistan and Iraq from the grasp of murderous regimes.

We must never forget that in order for our country to function as our forefathers intended, our citizens, each of us, must perform the duties of leadership for which we are destined. We cannot surrender to pessimism, especially the fashionable kind that expresses itself in a cynical or sarcastic spirit.

Instead, we must focus on our possibilities, not our limitations.

Each of us can realize our full potential only when we are committed to something larger than ourselves. The historian James MacGregor Burns called it "a commitment to values" and to "the perseverance to fight for those values."

Leadership is not a complicated concept. It's simply knowing what to do, and then doing it. This is what President Theodore Roosevelt meant when he said, "The first requisite of a citizen in this Republic of ours is that he shall be able to pull his weight."

What is offered in *First Principles* are the tools with which every American can make his or her civic participation useful, and meaningful. This book is a blueprint for understanding freedom and democracy, and then implementing them. Reading this volume will not only help each citizen understand how their country operates, but how to refocus their own lives. Each of us can make a difference, we only need to make an effort.

This volume provides a unique survey of writers who understand that personal responsibility and leadership are the pillars of both democracy and the freedom on which it depends. Our country's survival hinges on citizens who grasp that concept. As Friedrich August von Hayek observed in *The Constitution of Liberty*,

> Liberty not only means that the individual has both the opportunity and burden of choice. It also means that he must bear the responsibility of his actions. Liberty and responsibility are inseparable.

Our never-ending struggle against tyranny—whether disguised as Nazis or as Stalinists or as Islamic terrorists—will be won only if Americans continue to realize that liberty and responsibility, indeed, are inseparable.

—James A. Baker

James A. Baker, III was the 61st Secretary of State, 1989–1992, and the 67th Secretary of the Treasury, 1985–1988.

Welcome to *First Principles*

PUT MOST SIMPLY, this book looks at how we view ourselves as citizens and how we organize as a society. The content—an ordered, guided reading list—aims to explore the relationship between the individual and the social, governmental, and other entities that surround him. The beliefs and connections and arrangements that develop from our cultural constructions lead to political activity, but politics is not our focus, first principles are.

If you wish to gain a useful comprehension of the history, philosophy, economics, and political theory that led to the creation of Western Civilization and the founding of the American Republic—this should be your primary resource.

If you wish to serve your community—or more ambitiously, your country—in the political realm by becoming better and more usefully informed, or through public activism, you should start here.

Those who use this book to its full extent will see that it is not for Everyman. It doesn't try to be. We've attempted to be engaging and moderately comprehensive, and to be helpful. Some of the readings are demanding, most are not. They are simply practical and relevant. If you do engage, we believe that your reward will far exceed your effort.

Those of you who absorb the books offered here can make a difference in the world—somehow, somewhere, sometime. Ronald Reagan and Margaret Thatcher, Bill Buckley and David Keene made these works part of themselves. Many, many more unsung citizens have left their marks on the world after grasping the essence of what these books offer.

Margaret Thatcher observed in 1991, shortly after relinquishing her office as Prime Minister of Great Britain (and equally shortly after the demise of the Soviet Union), that the democracies of the West were not quite done on the world stage. It was her contention that we needed to make the moral as well as the practical case for representative democracy, the rule of law, and free-market capitalism. Little did anyone know at that point how prescient Lady Thatcher was, and little did anyone doubt the accuracy of her declaration after September 11, 2001.

The practical effects of democracy supported by capitalism are self-evident, but they can become distorted. What we have learned over time is that when they are skewed we need to fix the problem, not discard the system. This is what Lady Thatcher meant by her call for making the moral case—so that when we got to fixing whatever problems we encountered we might do so by a return to the noble foundation and fundamental value that experience has constructed in this arena.

Lady Thatcher understood as well that this economic and political system, which guaranteed individual freedom and offered a road toward self-sufficiency for its participants, also had to support those who cannot cope by themselves. This is the ever-present tug on the free market; where the obligations, opportunities, and results for each of us are equal neither in size nor import, judgment is required to help sustain community. The authors and theories offered here address these issues, and although the answers may change somewhat from generation to generation and culture to culture, there is a base line from which any society needs to operate. Here we attempt to define and order that social commonality.

Our book's secondary goal is to help clear away the clutter—the intellectual, emotional, political, economic, philosophical, and psychological obfuscation that surrounds the subject of government—usually caused by the machinery of politics coupled with the effects of mass media. We start at square one in an effort to make comprehensible the basic pieces, and outline how they fit together. What the authors represented here seem to know well is that the job of governing appears easy for those who don't do it. The difficult part is in understanding how actual, not idealized or simplistic governance, is best accomplished. The conclusion is that human nature must be given its due.

A society based on capitalism and freedom could be perfect—except for the human condition: man's imperfectability. In order to make the best of what's possible after taking into account our limitations, the authors we study in *First Principles* note what should work and then define what actually does.

Exploring and explaining the who, what, why, where, when, and how of those who developed the concept and practice of freedom in an open society is our goal. Through investigation of the books that embody and trace the course of mankind's efforts to govern we hope to create an intelligible framework that leads to understanding, and then action.

The Information Age

BECAUSE OF BOTH the insufficiency and growing corruption of "politically correct" public education, and the rising 24/7 information glut—via print, radio, TV, and the Internet—those not grounded in first principles may become unwitting victims of demagogues, charlatans, or their own uncertain judgment. The books offered here are a lifeboat back to the basics, a method to debunk the politically effective but ever-dishonest free lunch we are sometimes tendered.

While we cut through the information maelstrom and try to reduce the polarizing effects of rant radio and telemongering, we're guessing there will initially be snickers that this effort will simply add to the confusion. But our intent is to take a scalpel to the chaos and the bloated rhetoric of boast and demand.

Media, especially that which is electronically distributed, is obviously a major part of life. This condition is something new for those who grew up before television became not just ubiquitous, but dominant in the formation of public opinion. Media changes things for the better, and the worse.

In today's climate we oftentimes don't know what to believe. Sadly, we have too many tools and standards, and seemingly insufficient time to digest what appears before us. Perhaps the best solution to this problem is to rediscover some of the basic mechanisms and guidelines necessary to do this job. Instead of searching for a magic bullet or one-sentence theory to explain our world, we should reexamine the time-tested and proven philosophies of the past to see where they might help us clarify the modern era.

A note of caution is in order: if you are going to learn and use these ideas, you must understand them in some detail. None of the components of *First Principles* was an immaculate conception; each was derived through intellectual, and sometimes more bloody struggle. History brought us to the depths of nuclear destruction and the heights of freedom in the twentieth century and the roots of these titanic conflicts go back millennia. The analysis and deconstruction of some ideas and the crafting of others truly means something. Taken together the books summarized here leave few stones unturned—they start at A and go carefully to Z. When you finish you will have the basis of a rational and consistent political theory of how the world has been proven to work.

Finally, it must be observed that any effort to distill five-hundred-page books into five-page synopses necessarily requires that corners be cut and concepts be condensed. We have attempted to be true to the authors' observations, theories, and themes; however, it may be contended that some of what is presented is at variance from what any given author said. We realize the writers who are represented in this volume developed their philosophies in exquisite fashion in book-length odysseys for a reason. Our efforts to distill the essence of those efforts will omit some nuance, some reasoned logic, etc., but we believe the synopses are still true to what is contained in the authors' original works. We welcome comments or queries on the substance of this book if our effort leaves questions in the reader's mind.

We are not offering an ideology in a box, only the tools for becoming a coherent citizen. We hope that you will eventually use what you learn for civic involvement—from writing letters-to-the-editor or blogging, to feeling more confident in casting a ballot; from becoming involved with the campaign of a political candidate, to becoming that candidate yourself.

Ideas—The Tools

> Do not doubt that a citizen can alter the world. In truth, that is the only place where change begins.

THIS ANONYMOUS sentiment, often expressed (but equally often forgotten when we hear the public lament: "What can I do, I'm only one person?"), is basic to the suggestion that what you will learn in this book can make a difference. Ideas motivate people and inspire them to believe that somehow things can be better—and that they can make them so.

An understanding of the need for discipline in maintaining a free society likewise animates us. An example: it isn't just that the free lunch of the modern state is hard to sustain; it is the unrestrained sense of entitlement it breeds that makes governing difficult. Thus, when distortions such as this become apparent, when our methods seem sound but our results appear less so, when negative effects are taken to their logical conclusions and found to be not just discomfiting but dangerous, that's when individuals become active—no matter the cost—and ultimately make a difference.

Many of the ideas and much of the fervor demonstrated by those who would help correct contemporary errors, even irrational impulses, first appeared in the books summarized here. When today's activists are asked how they became involved in things political most look back to see their path was lit by these authors. And that is true not just now, but across the more than two hundred years of our American experience and earlier in Europe before the United States was even imagined.

What these books meant to various individuals was often of great import, and what they portend perhaps cannot be overstated. They are offered not only because they were consequential to specific efforts in the past, but also for their intrinsic value that must be tested by succeeding generations. The concepts in these writings are critical to carrying on the complex business of governance in a free society. As Alexis de Tocqueville noted in 1835,

> There is nothing more arduous than the apprenticeship of liberty. It . . . is generally established with difficulty in the midst of storms; it is perfected by civil discord; and its benefits cannot be appreciated until it is already old.

The books offered here embody the concepts and theories of what is termed conservatism or classical liberalism (which are not synonymous but which, for ease of reference, are often used interchangeably in this compendium). Our authors, many of whom wrote before today's labels were invented (or distorted), address the core ideas of freedom and justice, rights and duties. Rising above mere politics, every one of our writers exhorts his contemporaries to guard these values.

There is an important lesson here about labels. It must be understood that the modifier "conservative" is not as important as the subject: government and the social compact. Conservatism is not an ideology; it is a movement, and it is a way of thinking. The vitality of the subject is far more important than the political efficacy of the modifier. This book aims to present the foundation—the first principles of government and social interaction—in a manner that will be useful for today's discussions and defining for tomorrow's leaders.

Understanding and Action—The Methods

> He who endures what he could change acts no less than he who interferes in order to attain a different result.
> —Ludwig von Mises

MANY PEOPLE BELIEVE that the most important book of the twentieth century is *The Road to Serfdom* by Nobel Laureate Friedrich von Hayek. This work clearly and concisely explains why socialism and collectivism lead to slavery. Margaret Thatcher and Ronald Reagan both read the book and were changed by it. Each subsequently made decisions and took actions that transformed the modern world. The converted Thatcher and Reagan are examples of an observation by economist John Maynard Keynes, an advocate of government intervention in the marketplace. Keynes, whose star rose and then fell in the early and mid-twentieth century, understood the force of ideas:

> The power of vested interests is vastly exaggerated compared with the gradual encroachment of ideas.

Ironically, Keynesian interventionism itself was undermined, discredited, and largely discarded through the power of ideas and their influence on human action.

Ideas define square one. However, it must be observed that the principles enunciated and investigated within this book will not be immediately and uniformly applicable in all places and all times—there are preconditions to any attempt to implement them. If the cultural base of any given society is not similar to that of the West, then the creation of a free society will not be as elementary a process as it otherwise might be. Freedom must be allowed to compete with whatever is extant before its value will be accepted—or not. As well, the universal utility of a free society can only be learned; the gates cannot simply be opened for freedom to be understood, or to work successfully. For example, freedom is not self-executing, the rule of law must accompany liberty, or freedom will result only in anarchy. Without the rule of law the only way to control men is through violence.

But freedom, once planted, does allow the flowering of initiative and incentive. When those are present, as day follows night people begin to build lives. Once life is seen as an idea rather than just an existence, as opportunity rather than endurance, then consensual political institutions will thrive in order that the newly free populace can protect its gains—tangible and intangible, political and economic. They will discern the vested interest they have in the common weal, and democracy and duty will grow as secondary steps after freedom is established and law is implemented to protect it.

What conservatism represents was not inscribed on a tablet in an ancient era. This manner of thinking is made up of guidelines. Life is too complex and too varied to be reduced to very many rules. The fact that people will discern the ideas of conservatism, and then adhere to them as they institute self-government, requires something additional, something quite intangible—a leap of faith, not religious in nature, but spiritual nevertheless. It is a faith in those who travel with us and who will follow us, a faith that each of us will not only ensure everyone else's rights, but will voluntarily, and generally without need for conscious intention, fulfill the obligations those rights imply. The connection between rights and duties is *the* indispensable component in the practice of freedom and democratic government.

While society may suffer from some elements of the human condition, it also benefits from the inspiration embodied in the human spirit. It is this latter characteristic that defines us (and it is the former that sustains the media; beware the media). Being ever mindful of our duties keeps the human condition in check. Being ever aware of our opportunities fuels our spirits. Through both we can wend our way to a rational endpoint, as we have for so many thousands of years, improving with each century, each decade.

FOLLOWING THE eighteenth century's industrial revolution, as capitalism blossomed and free societies progressed to modern abundance, the economic and social authoritarians came to the fore. The authors who investigate the history and economics of this era and ours, and who were not afraid to comment upon human nature (an undertaking that is sometimes considered politically incorrect today) make clear the folly of this cadre. They shed a revealing light on the relationship between the twentieth century's despotism, collectivism, and socialism and the twenty-first's welfare state.

Our examination of these eras studies everything from the history of political theory (the first raw steps of which confronted equally raw power) to modern nuanced administration that deals with the common denominator of political efforts: the aforementioned human condition. We seek to enable people to understand the societal ties and interactions that result in government. Public administration, being the sum of how we conduct our social and political policy, can then be judged—and accepted or altered or entirely reconstituted. But it cannot be eliminated—thus our enduring endeavors to grasp the principles that underlie sound governance.

The authors of the books synopsized here dissect and refute the goals and theories of myriad monarchists, collectivists, socialists, and, of course, thugs and other less-than-benign despots who advocate imposing government on free people—imposing being the operative word. Sometimes the authors themselves were able to watch authoritarian attempts self-destruct because of the actions of a small group of committed citizens, sometimes these changes took many years.

As Hayek observed more than a half-century ago,

> What to the contemporary observer appears as a battle of conflicting interests decided by votes of the masses has usually been decided long before in a battle of ideas confined to narrow circles.

The job of assessing and improving every government is an ongoing effort. Collectivist theory (collectivism is universalist government that is imposed, supposedly for the good of the governed, by an unelected and arbitrary ruling class) will always remain seductive to some because of its superficial equalitarian promises. Reality makes these ultimately empty assurances look petty. The fact that collectivism's primary twentieth-century mechanisms—socialism and its ugly stepsisters, communism, Nazism, and fascism—have been discredited and discarded seems no impediment to this phoenix. Less overt collectivist impulses persist in the garb of state welfarism, and they are somewhat more insidious than their predecessors. They employ an emotional subtlety in the guise of public guilt or false duty. Authors Daniel Yergin and Joseph Stanislaw point out in *The Commanding Heights* (Chapter 29)—their survey of twentieth-century economic history—the draw of collectivism and government intervention in both the marketplace and the lives of citizens. This lure persists in spite of the obvious and enormous public consequences of such schemes, and is reducible to a natural emotional response:

Idealism, morality, justice, human sympathy, the shock of confronting poverty, the vision of a better world—all these brought people into the [collectivist] crusade.

Many perceptive Western intellectuals have observed this impulsive aspect of welfare-state governance and have understood the emotional appeal of collectivism and its egalitarian goal. Because our emotional faculties are invariably more developed than our intellectual capabilities, and because we first respond emotionally in almost every situation, the appeal of the apparent fairness of egalitarian results can overwhelm the compelling evidence that such goals have not and never can be achieved; the effort to do so, as is amply demonstrated by both history and our authors, is not only futile and unfair, but inherently unjust. This comprehension is investigated in-depth in the chapters that follow.

Once the notions of collectivism and egalitarianism were deconstructed (an effort that demonstrated such programs created more injustice and poverty than they alleviated and were equally inept in producing a utopian society) the question of what should replace them naturally arose. The answers that were offered ultimately influenced the world-wide social, political, and economic revolution of the second half of the twentieth century, and comprise most of the remainder of the book.

Intentions and Consequences—The Results

THE SYNOPSES PRESENTED in *First Principles* are the book's core. The authors and their writings cover the landscape of political, social, and economic reasoning and experience. The resulting combination of ideas—presented and dissected, compared and modified, discarded or etched in stone—has come to be known as conservative thought.

First Principles is organized to allow one to proceed from the basic tenets of governance to an in-depth investigation of the complexities of modern democracy. This allows the reader to look at the relationship between the individual and society, with particular reference to the reciprocal rights and obligations of each.

Around the time of the American Bicentennial a national newsmagazine published a letter to the editor commenting on the various festivities and celebrations extolling liberty. The writer was a newly minted U.S. citizen, a Russian immigrant, who simply noted that while studying for his citizenship test he was initially curious and then somewhat surprised to learn that there is a Bill of Rights appended to the Constitution, but no Bill of Responsibilities.

There are responsibilities, of course, but they are not codified. And perhaps that is a great failing in the design of our system. We emphasize freedom without making sure everyone understands that their freedom ends where the next person's begins, that their freedom also encompasses duties. If we focused on the equation between responsibility and liberty there might be less misunderstanding among us—and far less need for government. The synopses we present explore all aspects of this equation. However, it must also be noted that to understand the totality of both freedom and duty in a complex and shrinking world discovering the books themselves, not just our condensed overview, is necessary.

THERE IS A PRICE to be paid for all progress. What the free societies have attained and kept has been costly. In 1984 President Ronald Reagan observed the 40th anniversary of D-Day at the American cemetery at St. Laurent, France. (D-Day was the massive June 6, 1944 Allied military invasion of Europe to regain the continent that Hitler's Germany had conquered earlier during World War II.) Walking among row after row of the almost ten thousand grave markers, and remembering the same scene earlier that week at Arlington National Cemetery in Washington, D.C., he intoned with quiet emotion, as he faced the enormity of that field of lost soldiers, that their headstones "add up to only a tiny fraction of the price that has been paid for our freedom." A tiny fraction.

Reagan had observed previously, during his 1981 Inaugural Address, that not only is there a price to be paid for freedom, but that the cost is borne through individual dedication and devotion—not through a superficial or faceless patriotism. At that time he spoke of Martin Treptow, a young American killed in World War I in July 1918 at the battle of the Marne Salient in France. After the war young Treptow was buried in Arlington Cemetery. His diary was found on his bullet-riddled body when the battle was won. He had written on the flyleaf:

> My pledge: America must win this war. Therefore, I will work, I will save, I will sacrifice, I will endure, I will fight cheerfully and do my utmost, as if the issue of the whole struggle depended on me alone.

That sense of individual and solitary purpose must transfer whole from battlefield to back yard for a free society to be successful. James Wilson (1742–1798), an American born in Scotland, was one of the few men who participated in both the American Revolution in 1776 and the months-long Constitutional Convention in 1787. As a signer of the Declaration of Independence and the Constitution he understood the pristine simplicity of the personal determination that each citizen must feel in order for a free society to work. On July 4, 1788 he told those gathered at Philadelphia to celebrate the ratification of the new Constitution:

> Let no one say that he is but a single citizen; and that his ticket [ballot] will be but one in the box. That one ticket may turn the election. In battle, every soldier should consider the public safety as depending on his single arm. At an election, every citizen should consider the public happiness as depending on his single vote.

These sentiments, which are far from sentimental in their import, are the reason *First Principles* has been written. Our country, our society, and ourselves depend on our individual understanding of the values presented in Wilson's words. It is the *obligation* of each of us to be willing to ensure freedom in equal measure to what we receive; freedom is not free. The drafters and signers of the Declaration of Independence understood this as they began their treasonous course to liberty. At that time they made a pact with one another, and they closed the Declaration of Independence with this commitment:

> [W]e mutually pledge to each other our Lives, our Fortunes and our sacred Honor.

Today, as citizens who benefit so greatly, can we offer anything less? Contemplate for just a moment how much these men risked (and what they lost: many gave up their lives, many more their fortunes; but none saw their honor sullied) and then think about how much less each of us needs to do to preserve what they created.

Take a step back from the public declamations regarding this or that politicized event of the day. Find the tools to cut through this often mindless and directionless chaos by discovering the first principles of sound government in an open and free civil society.

We submit this final note: what is presented here is one judgment, illuminated by the details of experience. When Martin Luther received a reply from the pope in 1521 to his 95 theses that launched the Protestant Reformation, he burned the document in the public square. As the pages were engulfed in flame he observed: "It is an old custom to burn bad books." If you find deficiencies or anomalies or are critical with regard to the substance presented here, we welcome your thoughts—incendiary or not. Please voice your concerns by contacting us via e-mail at <editor.firstprinciples@gmail.com>. If you find merit in what you read here, please contact anyone else you know and commit to your own participation in the ongoing global experiment in self-governance.

Cordially,

Thomas N. Tripp

Self-governance in an Open Society: First Principles

> The struggle [for social order] will be decided in the minds of the rising generation—and within that generation, substantially by the minority who have the gift of reason.
> —Russell Kirk (1952)

Why First Principles?

First Principles offers a synopsis of the theory, history, and philosophy of self-governance. We try to place in perspective how we got from history to here while simultaneously making estimates of how best to get from here to history.

In beginning we attempt to define the common ground we share—irrespective of our political views. Those agreements come to the surface as the authors we present talk about human nature, the human condition, the human element, or the human spirit. Without a relatively uniform perception regarding both the variations and the commonalities of our character, our abilities, our goals and most importantly, what motivates us as individuals, it is unlikely consensus will be achieved with respect to governing paradigms. Appreciating, in a relatively coherent manner, where human consistencies and idiosyncrasies work either for us or against us is not difficult but it is crucial to arriving at agreement as to where and how government is likely to work. These comprehensions are not only the first hurdle in political or social or economic conversation, they are the most important—thus the many points where references to the human condition or human spirit independently come to the surface.

The next hurdle is to voluntarily determine the manner in which we will be governed, and to realize the consequences of each assumption made in the course of investigating and designing political and economic relationships. The authors we discuss attempt to define what has been proven to work, and why, and what has not, and why not.

The synopses we offer are just that—brief surveys; they suggest a focus to guide readers along paths that lead from the first questions of earlier times to the relevant inquiries, reasoning, and alternatives that arise as we govern ourselves today. *First Principles* presents an overview of the basics of modern political and economic thinking.

The books we discuss are ordered in four sections;

    A. The Architecture of a Free Society
    B. The Twentieth-Century American Experience
    C. Additional Fundamental Readings
    D. The Future.

The lists are an attempt to achieve logical groupings based on subject matter, the era in which each volume was written, the degree of challenge each poses, and its historical significance. We offer the synopses in the general sequence in which we recommend they be read.

A Note About Terms

To UNDERSTAND the story told through these synopses requires a clarification of terminology. Today in America the word conservative denotes someone who believes in a number of interrelated elements: a basic set of moral values and historical truths; free-market economics; minimal government intervention in the lives of citizens; significantly decentralized government composed of separate parts that check and balance one another at all levels; the practical qualities of self-reliance and personal accountability; and a strong national defense. An American conservative wishes to conserve, or restore, the self-government envisioned by our country's Founders. Until the 1930s in America however, and still today in Europe, the words liberal and liberalism were employed to locate American conservative philosophy on the political spectrum. It is necessary to understand these terms in their various environments and eras in order to appreciate their use by the authors we review.

During the nineteenth and early twentieth centuries when capitalism was expanding and the swift accumulation of wealth was notorious, socialism and equalitarianism gained an intellectual cachet. The fact that there was "poverty in the midst of plenty" caused more reaction than understanding. As a result, there arose an equally swift political attempt to redistribute this new wealth simply because disparity existed. There was little effort to discover cause and effect or the consequences of dismantling the system that had created both economic success and the rise in living standards for all.

As free enterprise seemed to falter during the Great Depression of the 1930s, liberalism, which is also the political cousin of capitalism, was semantically bastardized, intentionally, by a movement that proselytized "liberal populism." Populism refers in part to an effort whereby a more "equitable" allocation of society's wealth is achieved—that is, one based on essentially equal economic redistribution—without consideration of economic tenets that are based on innate human characteristics and real-world economic truths.

The movement is termed populist because its myriad equalitarian aspects are deemed popular with the citizenry—or at least the portion of it that is on the receiving side of the equation. Thus, liberalism in the original sense—which was associated with far-reaching economic progress—became distorted by the addition of equalitarian goals; the fact that populist methods were an attempt to spread liberalism's (meaning capitalism's) wealth without regard to any social or economic measure was initially not widely discussed, certainly not by those doing the disbursing. That group was reaping political advantage they didn't want to dilute with discussions of fiscal reality or human psychology.

The point is this: beyond understanding what the words liberal or conservative mean in any given context at any particular time it is necessary to comprehend how ideas and terms have evolved during the last century and a half—most often intentionally, but not always consistently. As author Paul Gottfried observed in *After Liberalism* (1999):

> The history of liberalism in the twentieth century has been one of growing semantic confusion. . . . [L]iberalism has not been allowed to keep any fixed and specific meaning. It has signified dramatically different and even opposed things at different times and places . . . from a defense of free-market economics and of government based on distributed powers to a justification of exactly the opposite positions.

Creating a common framework and uniform terminology is necessary to allow for simple communication—but that goal isn't always politically beneficial, thus the battle of words continues unabated.

In America, what today is denoted as liberalism Europeans generally call democratic socialism. Because this phrase is both an oxymoron (discussed in Chapter 38) and a public policy lever, its use makes comprehension of political goals difficult from the outset. Its original intent was to mislead the electorate for political gain by convincing the citizenry both that democracy was still in effect and equalitarianism was possible. That the latter was indeed not feasible no matter what political machinery or distorted nomenclature was in place was buried in the soaring rhetoric of possibility.

Frank Meyer, one of the authors reviewed in this book, outlines how the word liberal was informally transposed in the United States by the political use of language during the 1932 presidential campaign between Herbert Hoover and Franklin Roosevelt.

Roosevelt used the term liberal in a manner opposite of what he knew it meant, understanding that the public might not recognize the difference—that they would listen to the words and the promises and not think too deeply about the disconnection between the word's meaning and the political rhetoric being offered. As this election occurred in the middle of the hard times of the Great Depression, Roosevelt's political calculations were more than advantageous for his purposes.

Liberalism had earlier been shorthand for describing American freedom and responsibility. It represented that people were liberated to pursue their own goals, without government intervention. Roosevelt offered, in contravention to that definition, that *government* should be liberal in helping people. The political effectiveness of his effort is unquestioned. It is even somewhat accurate to say that his conceptual obfuscation would have been fine if government hadn't helped too much over the ensuing decades—to the point where some people not only stopped helping themselves, but were told and shown how they were really not capable of self-sufficiency. Roosevelt moved the country from employing a social *safety* net to deal with life's hardships, to effecting the beginnings of a cradle-to-grave social *welfare* net.* It was a purely political calculation that caused the country to suffer greatly from the law of unintended consequences.

---

* A social safety net takes care of those who cannot help themselves; the chronically ill or disabled or the unavoidably indigent. It also helps those who are temporarily in need and have few options other than short term public assistance. If properly designed these efforts do not operate as a disincentive to self-help or self-esteem.

A social welfare net is implemented for political purposes. These are programs available to everyone, irrespective of capability or need (e.g., Medicare, federal aid to education, Social Security), and often do not contain incentives within their design that encourage restraint in their use or the duration of eligibility. Although citizens pay for some of what they receive, usually at a flat rate, general tax revenues eventually support the bulk of the cost. Over time, benefits expand, politically, without any significant increase in user contributions. Additional general tax revenues are then redirected to make up the difference. The programs become state-controlled income redistribution, or state welfarism.

Eventually his brand of liberalism was taken too far; it made children out of many citizens, and unwitting parents out of all taxpayers. Because Roosevelt was successful in the 1932 election and three more after that his rhetoric became ingrained in political discourse. Liberalism in the U.S. became identified with an expansion of government. As a result, later authors coined the word "conservative" and the phrase "classical liberal" to regain some control of the nomenclature of political, economic, and moral debates. In the rest of the world, however, liberalism still means the opposite of what it nominally means in America—that people are liberated to control their lives without legislative or bureaucratic interference.

Humpty Dumpty noted awhile back "When I use a word it means just what I choose it to mean." That may be a convenient approach for fictional characters, high school sophomores, or YouTube adherents, but it is quite useless in the real world. Unfortunately, the perversion of language is a formidable and ubiquitous tool in politics. Today words are often Humpty Dumpty–like moving targets, sometimes used to inform, sometimes to mislead. When linguistic integrity is compromised and substance is changed through political manipulation rather than rational evaluation, we all lose.

And, just so we don't heap too much blame for any of this on one person, we recognize that Roosevelt's twisting of the meaning of liberal was not the first instance in America where language was turned on its head for political purposes. At the time the U.S. Constitution went through its bruising ratification process in the late 1780s, the word federalist was equally turned about by no less a democratic icon than Alexander Hamilton. Originally, a federalist was one who believed in the Articles of Confederation (drafted 1777, ratified 1781), the precursor to the U.S. Constitution of 1787, where the government was a *federation* of sovereign, or *independent*, states.

In *The Federalist* (Chapter 6) Hamilton used the word federalist to represent his idea of a strong *national* government—most importantly, one with the power to tax (a power not contained in the Articles of Confederation). But, to those reading his arguments, the word *federalist* meant what it always had—one who believed in limited federal power and autonomous self-governing states in charge of their own administration and taxation. By the time the ratification process was over, federalists were those who supported a strong central government and the word came to mean the obverse of what it originally signified.

As you read through some of the early books by Europeans like

Friedrich von Hayek, Ludwig von Mises, and Wilhelm Röpke, understanding the authors' use of the term liberal is important because the word conservative was not in their lexicon until near the end of their careers. And, just to make matters a little more complicated, the term classical liberalism—instead of conservative—is now used by some authors to define what liberalism meant prior to its being politically hijacked during the Roosevelt years. However, as the meaning of these terms did change gradually, and because the context in which the words are used will almost always tell you what the author intends, it will not be difficult to keep them straight. The caution is offered only to make the words stand out, so the reader can be watchful.

———

WHAT ONE TAKES away from either *First Principles* or the texts on which it is based will depend primarily on two things: how well one appreciates the concepts that underlie the stories presented in each volume, and how one relates that appreciation to the real world in which we now live. This is no small feat. It requires paying attention and acting with political and intellectual integrity, two components of self-governance that are often lacking today.

It also requires recalling that the precise use of language remains as consequential in the political and philosophical battles being waged now as it was in those fought over the centuries. It behooves the reader to recognize the nuances, gradual changes, and the sometimes intentional blurring effected for political purposes. The writings and speeches of William F. Buckley, Jr. are the most helpful in this arena. He makes clear some of the instances of political deception and electoral temporizing founded in dishonest rhetoric. His dissection of these distortions underscores equally the importance of fidelity to linguistic integrity and the need to expose its absence.

At the end of this section we offer definitions of various words, concepts, and movements in order to assist the reader's comprehension of what is being presented. At the conclusion of some of the synopses there are additional definitions to help facilitate comprehension. Further clarifications are available through our companion web site, <www.firstprinciples.us>, or through your local print or Internet dictionary.

The Ideas

THE AUTHORS in this symposium do not always agree with one another, and every author is not always "right" in all he offers. The discussion is better because of their disagreements. The range of inconsistency varies from conflict regarding fundamental understandings and conclusions to mere differences in approach. Some authors expand on the theories of others by applying them to the real world. However, when Frank Meyer took issue with Russell Kirk in the twentieth century or Thomas Paine with Edmund Burke in the eighteenth, the disagreements were deep. One can learn much from these and other classical discussions; indeed, one may not be able to comprehend the long developmental process of modern self-governance without having most of them as background.

Our authors often go beyond postulating, defining, and defending basic truths to the recognition that failures are as much a part of life as successes. In other words, no matter how true a theory may appear to be, when human beings become involved pretty much anything can happen. When theory is exposed to reality and errors are found they are mostly useful—by demonstrating what won't work—although the results can sometimes be devastating. This seemingly cannot be avoided, for human beings are not only imperfect, they are imperfectable. In spite of our authors' uniform conviction that the human spirit in each person should be its own guide (so long as it does not trespass on the rights of others) sometimes that spirit does go awry, thus the need for some form of regulation and redress.

There is an inverse relationship between the size and power of government and the extent of individual freedom. Some legislators and bureaucrats err grievously when succumbing to an apparently innate need or desire to tell other human beings how to lead their lives (the same need that probably drove them to "public" service in the first place) and impose blanket rules and programs without accommodating geographic, economic, and/or social—much less innate human—differences. The authors dissect and discredit the immodesty of demagogues who seek to control men, supposedly for their own good. The exercise of the liberal's fatal conceit—as Hayek termed it—diminishes our lives by destroying the essence of individualism.

The books reviewed here evince a marked emphasis on goodness, morality, and to a limited extent, religion. To remain free, a people must be good to and for one another. The Golden Rule (whether considered in a religious context or more prosaically) must come into play. If people do not observe various societal necessities, then as Hayek noted, "every act of dishonesty or violence, whether violence to person or to principle, will result in the call for more law, more regulation." The resulting outcry—"There oughta be a law!"—grows, and the idea of freedom isn't just diminished, it is simply lost in the competing claims that the "other guy" should somehow be constrained or punished. We forget we are to control ourselves, that that is *our* responsibility.

The authors rightly emphasize that a moral underpinning is necessary for freedom to exist among individuals. The freedom that results also allows individuals to protect themselves from an overweening government—a moral act as well. Ultimately it may be as simple (and utopian) as this: If we have a moral society it doesn't much matter what type of government we have (a moral citizenry will correct its own mistakes). If our society is not moral, it equally doesn't much matter what type of government we have (an immoral society will not follow the lead of decency, and it will not be cowed by the force of government). Of course, individuals typically exhibit both moral and immoral behavior (e.g., many of the Founding Fathers were slave owners); thus what type, and what extent, of governance we choose does become important.

In the United States we are fortunate to have not only a remarkably moral society, but also a fundamentally religious one. In our culture, government only becomes necessary on the individual level when the human condition forestalls "goodwill toward men." Government is also useful in other circumstances, such as protecting us from foreign interference, or in fulfilling public needs that individuals cannot easily accomplish alone. These are considerations that affect the body politic *after* we establish a moral framework. And if that moral framework is not established, then governing is a matter of much greater difficulty.

Corruption—whether individual or organizational, financial, moral, artistic, social, or intellectual—is not new. What is new is the public's inability, if not refusal, to constrain behavior on the grounds that there is no valid standard by which to judge it. This attitude is termed "moral relativism" and it holds that most choices are of equal value; in other words, because all individuals are philosophically equal each opinion, interpretation, and judgment should be considered to have equal value. This reflects a step away from understanding the interdependence of morality and governance—and the hard-won reality that some choices *are* better than others, demonstrably better. In today's world, by way of example, the media's portrayals of a moral society (or less than moral society) help create forces that sometimes work against the universal lessons learned during thirty centuries of social evolution. Competition for listeners, readers and viewers is so intense that intellectual, and thus moral integrity is often substantially compromised in the process of bringing content to the public.

Margaret Thatcher's recent book, *Statecraft* (2002), addressed the need and expectation of morality in American (or any free) society:

> The Founding Fathers believed that although the form of republican government they had framed was designed to cope with human failings, it provided no kind of substitute for human virtues. For them American self-government meant exactly that—government by as well as for the people. James Madison knew that democracy presupposed a degree of popular virtue if it was to work well. In Number 55 of the *Federalist Papers* he wrote:
>
>> As there is a degree of depravity in mankind which requires a certain degree of circumspection and distrust, so there are other qualities in human nature which justify a certain portion of esteem and confidence. *Republican government presupposes the existence of these qualities in a higher degree than any other form.* [Emphasis added by Lady Thatcher]

The loss of that higher degree of virtue in society endangers the opportunity for a viable democratic republic. Our everyday world rests on a foundation of reciprocity that is largely unstated, but is equally universally understood. If that commonality is not present, a free society can exist, but it is more likely to be anarchic than angelic.

Finally, we turn to the words of John Adams, the Founding Father who (after Benjamin Franklin) probably understood the most about human nature as it intersected with the new government:

> [T]he foundation of our national policy should be laid in private morality; if individuals be not influenced by moral principles, it is vain to look for public virtue.

MANY OF THE WORKS presented here were written in the middle of the twentieth century when socialism, not just liberal populism, was ascendant and the entire world tilted toward collectivist policies and programs. These were almost universally enforced through totalitarian rule. Today, with socialism debunked and freedom ascendant, some may question the need for our focus on these old books and those former times. The answer is simple: collectivist and totalitarian policies and goals have morphed, not died. To combat these new and varied challenges requires vigilance and education. As author George Santayana (1863–1952) noted in suggesting that people must help themselves: "Those who cannot remember the past are condemned to repeat it." Repeating the twentieth century's mistakes would not be pretty.

In his introduction to *The Constitution of Liberty*, Friedrich von Hayek observes:

> [I]f old truths are to retain their hold on men's minds, they must be restated in the language and concepts of successive generations. What at one time are their most effective expressions gradually become so worn with use that they cease to carry a definite meaning.

By way of example, although parts of socialism are virtual anachronisms (such as state ownership of the means of production or state control of resource allocation), many of socialism's ideals retain their allure. Modern liberals know they cannot successfully control enterprise through confiscation of, or excessive rules regarding private property, or command production in a direct manner. Nevertheless they are unrelenting in their efforts (and sometimes their inventiveness) to reinitiate these ends indirectly through tax and regulatory measures. The goal of such efforts, like the goals of socialism, is nothing more than the redistribution of private property.

Liberals still endeavor by these new means to attain the equalitarian society sought by Karl Marx (1818–1883) in *The Communist Manifesto* (1848): "From each according to his ability, to each according to his needs." The fundamental question, which interferes with these liberal tendencies, is how to define needs, or encourage abilities. If it is suggested that someone doesn't have something he "needs," the first issue becomes how and by whom is need determined?

Assuming the need is valid, the second issue is to determine if government is responsible to fulfill that need for the individual, or if government is to foster an atmosphere that allows the person to meet the need for himself. If it is to be the latter, then freedom *from* government is the only model that will achieve the goal. If it is to be in large measure the former, then collectivist, totalitarian government is the eventuality; there is little room for adjustment in the middle. The consideration of when and how government is to act reflects much of the substance of the discussion offered here.

Liberals often feel good about what they are trying to do and are ignorant of what they destroy in the process—the American virtues of liberty, individualism, and self-reliance. The inability, or even coarse refusal, of populists to take their ideas to logical conclusions and put them to the test of history and the human experience allows socialist liberalism to remain both theoretically attractive—as state welfarism—and socially dangerous.

As James Madison noted,

> I believe there are more instances of the abridgment of the rights of the people by the gradual and silent encroachments of those in power than by violent and sudden usurpations.

His understanding has not become stale with age.

A Very Brief History

Freedom

AS NOTED EARLIER, until the Great Depression (1929–1941) liberal—on both sides of the Atlantic—generally meant an approach to government and social life that implied a very limited central authority and few controls on people. Citizens were routinely supposed to manage their own lives; they were "liberated" from the pre-nineteenth-century command of monarchy and church. The sixteenth century's Protestant Reformation, combined with some aspects of the eighteenth century's Enlightenment (both of which are defined below and dissected in several synopses) had fostered much of this "public" freedom.

In Great Britain, the Reformation resulted in the birth of the Puritan (or Reform) wing of the Church of England. When various adherents to that group emigrated from England in the 1600s they became the founders of the American experiment. From the 1600s until the first third of the twentieth century liberalism evolved to embody the modern ethos of personal responsibility and minimal government. Then, in the political and economic climate of the 1930s the meaning of liberalism was reversed in America, and the new words previously discussed—conservative and classical liberalism—were put in place to describe old liberalism's philosophy.

The hallmark of classical liberalism is that individual freedom is a *natural* right, not a government or societal grant. Co-equal with the primacy of individuality is the recognition that an open society cannot, by definition, become tyrannical. If ideas and information are never censored or punished, the foundation for a free society exists. Classical liberalism refers to a society in which human imagination enjoys free reign.

Democracy became the starting point for the governance of such a society. It facilitates continuous changes in leadership and is conjoined with abiding respect for the principle of civic rule by law (versus authoritarian rule by men). This assumes, of course, that the laws are enacted within a philosophical framework where government takes little from us, manages only those social necessities that we cannot efficiently obtain for ourselves, and leaves us alone to shape our own lives, communities, and futures. To protect the fundamental rights of the governed, Thomas Jefferson (who feared men as much as he admired mankind's ultimate rationality) wanted written recognition of basic rights, contained in a document that could not easily be altered by a tyrannical majority:

> In questions of power, then, let no more be heard about confidence in man, but bind him down from mischief with the chains of the Constitution.

Along this line Madison remarked in *The Federalist*,

> All men having power ought to be distrusted to a certain degree.

But statists allege that society cannot run itself; instead they contend that the needs and economic prospects of the people have to be organized so that decision making resides in an executive elite—not in individuals, or in their community, or in their representative legislature. In other words, statists insist the public is too ignorant, or even too stupid, to govern itself. For these men freedom is simply intolerable—because it results in inequality and inconsistency. They cannot embrace the reality that inequality is endemic, unresolvable, and central to human existence and *progress*, no matter what form of social construction is in place. They contend they can outsmart or outgun reality.

The history of the statist movement teaches us that socialist ideas lead to government that becomes despotic for two reasons: First, those who actually wield power invariably wax confident in their delusional omniscience that they can create a society of equal results. Second, collectivist ideals do not just invite, but they require totalitarian controls simply because human beings will not voluntarily submit to the wholesale authority of others that is the necessary result of equalitarian goals. The individual, family, and community—the essential ingredients of society—are reduced by statist regimes to having only the freedoms that government allows. In collectivist societies people are required to act as part of an overall social order, and individuality is viewed as anti-intellectual, if not seditious. Human nature will not long suffer the indignities or controls of such an arrangement.

Opposing this dominant trend—which continually gained momentum through the middle of the twentieth century—were a few classical liberals who stood against the socialist tide. A reversal of course became necessary in the minds of those who understood the power and the utility of freedom; who understood that life is not just unequal, but that inequality brings the best of humanity's efforts to the greatest portion of society; that inequality not only doesn't hold people down, it lifts everyone up. Most importantly, it was clear that without life's inequalities nothing would be created that was worth arguing about *other* than—because of its absence—freedom. For these classical theorists, people and history (and history's prescriptions) became the reference point.

Although totalitarian socialism is leaving the world's stage, quixotic collectivist ideas are far from consigned to the trash heap of history. There remains a twentieth-century legacy of statist rhetoric (sometimes offered with an intellectual smugness masquerading as political correctness or social wisdom) in American and Western European media and academia and in the politics of the Third World. Idealism is still the common language of socialist cant, particularly in Europe where Judeo-Christian philosophy (which harbors the origins of individual freedom) is nearly irrelevant.

The battle against socialism's falsehoods never ends, because there are always well-meaning (at least in their own view) individuals who feel they know better than we do how to live our lives and how to distribute society's means and products. Our would-be guardians still seek to protect us from ourselves and each other; ever more intrusively they demand the right to dictate our interactions pursuant to standards of political correctness—an ill-defined, constantly-changing, emotional contract on which they claim society must be based. In the wry view of Stanley Johnson, a British former Member of the European Parliament, there is a worthwhile battle to be fought "against the crooks and nannies looking into nooks and crannies."

The foundation of a politically correct society is one in which an equalitarian distribution of its products and conditions is the goal. Government's neosocialist schemes of regulation and taxation are part and parcel of what we now call the "therapeutic state" or "nanny government." Within this government the bureaucracy grows ever more burdensome and economically and morally corrupt. Statist equalitarianism—which takes form in a social welfare net that removes individual responsibility (and thus individual opportunity and incentive) for life's everyday cares—represents philosophically and politically one of the main battlegrounds of the twenty-first century.

On Being Politically Correct

As noted earlier, there are often public attempts to place constraints on our ability to enjoy our individuality, private space, and personal preferences; this type of repression comes in the form of political correctness. The gender, race, national security, religious, or even fashion police make disproportionate and inappropriate calls for diversity, multiculturalism, pluralism, affirmative action, or other social controls, where the state is to dictate societal interaction. A commitment to the individual, or even to excellence, is termed inappropriate when there are alleged emotional or equalitarian needs to be met. As we step onto this slippery slope we must carefully balance two overriding considerations: our public nurturing of universal civil, social, human, or other rights, versus our fundamental individual rights. Achieving a balance in this instance has been ignored in many circles as the presumptions of those who understand what is politically correct become dictatorial.

Perhaps at base, the difference between the views of liberals and conservatives in these cases relates to their respective beliefs regarding human rights, or natural rights. Liberals view such rights in a contractual light, the result of various cultural or societal agreements, and thus as a social construct or a political choice. Viewed in this manner such rights are negotiable, and understandable only in relation to the times and the circumstances. Conservatives view these same rights as either God-given or natural, not subject to alteration to meet the fad or fashion or whim of the day. When liberals deny the existence of immutable natural rights, they use the terminology of rights in a capricious manner. When right and wrong become relative terms, political correctness takes over—and social coherence becomes wholly at risk.

In order to enforce the views of those who see society's members as controllable (and therefore entitled to less freedom than they might otherwise be), there has arisen a modern fealty to the managerial state. This particular management is not the type that directs traffic or collects taxes to fund public administration, but aims to superintend the people themselves. It is an intentionally camouflaged and modernized implementation of a supposedly more benign, collectivist totalitarianism. Collectivists formerly intoned, "Just do it." They insisted on compliance by fiat, unsupported by reason or even agreement. Today's governmental managers say, "Do it. It is good for you and for everyone else."

In this manner the public administrators create a moral imperative rather than just a social necessity that claims the right to guide society. However, it is only *their* morality and *their* imperative, despite its claimed universality. It is not consensually arrived at, but determined through social science—in other words, through opinions that have been selected, not proven. These opinions do not meet with uniform agreement or acceptance; their implementation thus denies freedom of choice, action, and debate, and man's individuality, when it does not conform to the liberal overview, is labeled dysfunctional.

How did we go backward so quickly after the defeat of socialistic totalitarianism was secured? As freedom paired with capitalism showed the way to solve the mechanistic problems of life—food on the table, clothes on our backs, shelter over our heads—the idealists were left with thoughts that actual paradise could be achieved. They were driven from the economic battlefield, where life's necessities are hard earned, by capitalistic freedom, while they claimed they knew all along how to procure these necessities. But once the basics were deliverable to everyone the welfarists entered the evanescent arena of perfect human comity and equality. To this group what can be still should be. These thoughts are likely the result, to put it charitably, of too much time, too little understanding. The rest of society pays for the consequences of this naïve idealism by being forced to reinvent wheels that are already carrying society along. It is ever thus.

The politically adept managers of the new utopia assert they can fix what ails us; and they intend to use the state to enforce their conclusions. The behaviorists abet the political class and aver scientific verity for their contentions. They claim "expert" status in spite of the lack of evidence, factual or otherwise, that they are experts. These equalitarians intentionally mount their politically correct assault through selected courts and legislatures intimidated by threats of political reprisals. A fawning media is used to validate their views. The prescriptions of historical experience are now held to be passé; understanding the imperatives of the human condition is dismissed; and all decisions are henceforth to be made "scientifically," in spite of the decidedly unscientific methods being employed. This ephemeral milieu, where society's faults and inadequacies are to be repaired by statistics and opinion, is yet another political and intellectual battleground of the present century.

Economics

Property and Government

TRADITIONAL EUROPEAN liberal doctrine (now classical liberalism or conservatism in America) has been associated philosophically and politically with capitalism since at least the time of Adam Smith and the eighteenth century's Scottish Enlightenment. At that juncture the need for the free market to be inextricably intertwined with free political expression (which results in the rule of law) became clear. If people were not free to choose in either venue, then both systems broke down.

The underpinnings of economic freedom—stable, enforceable laws; a free market; private property—are a sub-set of political freedom. Economic freedom is the essence of capitalism, but without legally protected property rights and impartial public authorities to enforce the law there is no foundation for incentive, initiative, or imagination (there is only anarchy). These elements are the mechanisms that drive human progress. The political principles that ensure our economic liberty are elemental; they cannot be divided or implemented fractionally. They embody what is called "ordered freedom."

Modern political contests often center upon who will determine what can or cannot be taken or constrained or encouraged by public authority—generally through taxation or regulation, or a lack thereof—for the ostensible greater good of society. Far too frequently, however, a concern for the public is declared by a candidate for office (irrespective of political affiliation), but after electoral success that person offers only shop-worn and tired programs designed to do little more than make everyone feel good—and, of course, see to that official's reelection. These programs are customarily accomplished with newly raised tax dollars or newly written regulations that most often actually work against the candidate's campaign assertions.

Unfortunately, politicians often do not know what they are doing—they have studied neither history nor economics and frequently have little or no marketplace experience (this is especially true today as politicians find electoral employment a good career choice). But often they *are* dazzled by what they can be: a darling of the media, or the recipient of a special interest's accolades and financial support, or simply the social consummation of their own vainglorious and fatal conceit. The consequence is that the country pays for ignorance when it is forced to operate an economic engine on empty rhetoric.

On the administrative side of governance, bureaucrats commonly look upon the alleviation of society's "ills" (many of which are not universally viewed as problems) solely as *their* mission—not in any fashion the obligation or opportunity of either the individual or the community. They rarely find an occasion to help foster personal initiative or private assistance, especially if they can create some administrative mechanism that will serve as a substitute for these options. They allow, by their very actions, palpable distortions of government purpose to arise. Practically speaking, if bureaucracies actually solved problems, those employed there might work themselves out of a job—clearly not something in the bureaucrat's best interest. Instead, as noted by author C. Northcote Parkinson in his 1957 book *Parkinson's Laws*, if their franchise begins to wane, bureaucrats tend to seek out or invent additional areas of need so government can provide another "service" which then justifies their continued employment.

When programs found ineffective are reduced by executive or legislative authority, bureaucrats (and their private sector partners) often attempt to achieve through the obscurity of regulation and/or stark administrative power that which they could not win in the political arena. Or they simply ignore what they've been told by the electorate and find ways to do what they "know" to be right by expanding other facets of their franchise.

Ultimately, the primary difficulty with government programs is there is no market discipline. When bureaucracies fail they don't face bankruptcy or liquidation, they use their failure to push for bigger more intrusive programs (a program's small size or the inadequate reach of the bureaucrat's power being used to excuse their failure to achieve results in line with their enabling legislation). As well, of course, politicians and bureaucrats don't spend their own money—thus accountability on either the practical or intellectual level is not part of their fiscal equation.

Most importantly, the philosophy and repercussions of governmental good works that seek immediate relief for the downtrodden are invariably not followed to their logical conclusion. Oftentimes these emotionally satisfying but socially and economically inappropriate impulses are found to do more harm than good. As Charles Murray noted in his book *Losing Ground* (1984):

> When welfare reforms finally do occur, they will happen not because stingy people have won, but because generous people have stopped kidding themselves.

What Murray was referring to was the public's eventual recognition of the negative consequences of giving a handout instead of offering a hand up. Murray's primary point was made by the 1996 legislation that effected massive welfare reform in America (discussed in Chapter 31). Unfortunately, the social welfarists persevere with their efforts in spite of the ignorant public's voted preferences; for example, by administratively expanding other "entitlement" programs that have not been modified or eliminated to take the place of what has been legislatively rescinded in the primary arena. Specifically, they have done this to work around and take the place of the now-discredited direct welfare payments reformed in 1996. This is a dishonest solution and openly retards progress toward the stated goals of both citizens and legislators.

The consequences of welfare reform are frequently fought in the courts, to everyone's further detriment, because legalistic decisions are often narrow and inflexible. In almost all cases, legal battles in this arena are little more than rearranging the batting order of a last place team. Implementation of the public's electoral statements is not only the honest response, it is the logical one. If the electoral preferences do not work, reversion to welfarist solutions will be greeted warmly with liberal "I told you so" rhetoric. But if the directions of the voting public are successful, then everyone is better off—except, perhaps, a few soon to be out-of-work public employees.

If private property is secure, if the people and their governmental representatives (whether or not elected) ensure incentive is in place to allow the public to act unhindered in their economic and social decisions, then society can be free and prosperous. When property is jealously protected, demagogic politicians cannot take advantage of social change or even crises to implement feel-good policy that is politically and/or economically bankrupt. Many of the books reviewed here were written by economists who understand the direct relationship between the limitations of law, the benefits of recognizing free-market economic reality, and the human condition. Their insights into how government can achieve its legitimate goals while keeping human freedom and dignity in view have enabled many to see that liberty is more than a political concept. Unfortunately, in order to get elected, politicians often offer the voters happiness (usually in the form of a free lunch), not a promise to protect their liberty. If the political class is to deliver a free lunch, it must have power—which means the citizen will have less freedom. That is the Faustian bargain by which the citizen gives the Devil his due.

Government cannot be used to protect individuals from the results of their own actions. It cannot strive for a particular distribution of economic resources, promote any particular region or group, or dictate a conduct code without becoming oppressive and destroying individual freedoms. To do so would end America as we know it and put into question the validity of individualism itself. Many contentious issues in our politics today involve areas of life that are wrapped up in some form of government intervention or desire for government intervention. This is usually at the behest of a group that is trying to force its own agenda on other groups. Controversial ideas must be tested in the marketplace, not imposed by government.

Edmund Burke commented two centuries ago, "All that is necessary for the triumph of evil is that good men do nothing." Forgiving

Burke his seventeenth-century gender insensitivity, his point is that *we* must prevent intellectual and moral corruption and ensure the implementation of good policy based on sound reasoning or no one will. In the synopses that follow you will see references to the fact that the only true protection for the citizen is vigilance; laws, leaders, and institutions alone cannot shield us from perfidy, dishonesty, infidelity, deceit, or disloyalty. In the fields of economics, taxation, regulation, and social policy, the attitude of vigilance, not deference, must always be the foundation of our relationship with those whom we elect to govern.

Capitalism and Capitalists

A TANGENTIAL JOURNEY from Adam Smith's nascent capitalism (explicated in *Wealth of Nations* [Chapter 12]) may be helpful at this point. *First Principles* is not intended to offer a detailed comprehension of capitalism's machinations; it is designed to foster an understanding of capitalism's unambiguous ties to freedom and the consequences that flow from that relationship. If capitalism's salient features—freedom of action *and* consequence—are not fitted first in the world that surrounds us, then the remainder of our efforts will be more difficult. Once the case is made regarding the organic link between capitalism and freedom, then investigation of all matters regarding the minutiae of a free-enterprise system may proceed as the reader's interest leads.

In the eyes of some, a twenty-first-century battle still rages over one of capitalism's foundations: freedom of action for both those who produce and those who consume. These individuals maintain that capitalism is at best immoral because its results offer only inequality; because inequality is unfair in this group's view both the system and its participants must be controlled. This group attacks what they allege is immoral economic freedom using the unequal results of capitalistic enterprise as the weapon. Ultimately, however, capitalism as an economic *system* is not moral, amoral or immoral; only the people who operate within it can have those characteristics. But the more important consideration is that capitalism's unequal results have nothing to do with morality; they are simply what drive human activity; they reflect nothing more than human incentive and capability. The claim of immorality—and even inequality—exists only in the hands of the demagogues. When freedom of economic enterprise, measured by the actual results we obtain, is balanced against the demand for some condition of human parity, equality as an issue of morality is reduced to a political conversation only. With freedom as our operating platform the world's progress is astounding; if equality were used as our fuel, the state of the world would be much, much different, and less, on all levels. Many of the authors presented here speak directly to these issues.

However, on the smaller stage and much to the chagrin of many of capitalism's promoters, there are bad, immoral, and thieving people who find the free-enterprise system's minimal controls useful for their nefarious purposes. For myriad reasons—not the least of which is media exploitation—this infamous group, and the consequences of their activities, occasionally form the basis of public perception of capitalism's essence. Thus a defense of capitalism in this book isn't one designed to advance its fundamental validity, but to deconstruct the self-serving and dishonest diversions of its detractors—who mostly contend that because life is not perfect under capitalism, capitalism must be at fault. What they really mean to say is that if life is not perfect within a free society, then a totalitarian construct, under their control, will be.

Capitalism's value, in broad terms, is ascertained by simply observing the progress of humanity under its auspices—and comparing that with the results obtained by means of other systems. The middle social and economic ground—between a society that is perfectly able to foster the well-being of its inhabitants (utopia), and one rife with thieves and frauds (anarchy)—was the true field of play as capitalistic freedom began to spread and succeed. In the nineteenth and twentieth centuries (once the English Industrial Revolution had become the Dow Jones Industrial Average), additional revolutions—in the myriad laws that aimed at rationally and fairly aligning people and the economy so they could work together functionally—brought the system mostly in balance (but never perfectly and never permanently). When the system was able to operate without substantial restraints the standard of living and dignity achieved through its mechanisms was unmatched, even *unimagined* by any previous generation or model. But the bad guy persona enjoyed by the nineteenth century's capitalist caricature, the result of that era's capitalistic excesses, has never melted away—first, because it is too convenient for the coarse media or the politically crass not to exploit it, and second, because that person, albeit in inappreciable numbers, still exists today.There will always be people who engage in fraudulent or dishonest behavior—no matter what economic system is employed. This fact relates to human nature, not to economic paradigms; the bad guys in collectivist and dictatorial regimes excelled in the creation of misery and depredation far beyond what selfish mock-capitalists might have conjured up in their heyday. What to do with capitalism's miscreants is discussed in several of the synopses that follow, but the basic premise is this: people who distort the system are not capitalists, they are still just thieves or villains. To alter or discard the system that they misuse is neither necessary nor desirable; instead we must remove them from the equation. Yet, even when that happens, the perception often remains that it is the *system's freedom* that is flawed, not the person. Thieves still break into our homes, but we don't abolish private property to thwart their efforts—we put them in jail.

In order to obtain a rational view of capitalism and its participants, we must counter myth with reality. For example, as *Forbes* Magazine publisher Steve Forbes observed, one common myth is that those who succeed in business "owe" something back to the community. The allegation is that only business owners profit from their businesses. Ignored entirely are the benefits obtained by the public (that receives new products or services), investors (whose risk is financially rewarded), employees (who receive wages, health care, retirement, etc.), and the rest of the economic community that benefits from the multiplier effect of private enterprise. This, of course, is not to forget the other conspicuous beneficiary—the government—that procures revenue by means of taxes levied on the profits that are earned. If there is no enterprise, and profit, there is no government, simply for lack of fuel.

While a voluntary charitable impulse is laudable, social pressure that the entrepreneur "return" something to the community for his success is in error. As Forbes observed, it leaves the impression that something has been "taken" in the first place. Business ventures are attempted at great personal and financial risk for the entrepreneur, his investors, and his employees. However, if the public perception that something is owed remains, it encourages the idea that capitalism itself is wrong and that engaging in it can only be atoned for by a return of its ripened fruits.

The breakdown in logic comes when the harvest of the capitalistic process is to be distributed and the effort of planting, growing, and tending is forgotten. Some think everyone should end the day on equal footing—regardless of any obvious inequality of contribution or capability. In the minds of this group, if one person *receives* more than another, then oppression (not just inequality) has occurred. The fact is that if equality of result is preordained, incentive is destroyed. There is no happy middle ground between equal result and equal opportunity. Either freedom of action and consequence exist or they do not, for by its very nature, anything in between must be arbitrary. It is human *inequality* of contribution and capability that allows us to imagine what can be and helps us to create what will be. It was Jean-Jacques Rousseau (1712–1788) who observed that ability should be rewarded for the advantage of the community.

A healthy capitalist society looks positively on what has been achieved and eagerly greets the thought of what else can be accomplished. This capitalism does not look enviously on the successful, but admires their achievement while benefiting from their effort. When great or small things are attained, most people are inspired, not resentful. (For an expanded discussion of this topic see *Wealth and Poverty* [Chapter 27].)

After three centuries of free-market achievement, debate on various economic systems continues only because of public misperceptions or demagogic disingenuousness. Potential misgivings about capitalism—crudely and cruelly manipulated by the popular press and liberal idealists—are what allow this "contest" to persist. Capitalism is sometimes seen in a light that does not take into account both its moral foundation and its fitness for the job at hand. This is because politics or idealism—not fundamental economic issues—are often allowed to drive the debate.

As Ludwig von Mises intoned almost a hundred years ago, the battle is not between capitalism and socialism (or now welfarism), but between capitalism and chaos. Resolving these perceptions and the issues yet extant in this arena is the focus of many of the efforts that follow.

The Human Condition

AMERICAN SOCIALIST LIBERALISM failed mostly because its purveyors misunderstood human nature. To be sure, liberals have always found sympathetic voters—people who wish to live in an imaginary world receptive to their passion to achieve perfection by proclamation. But efforts in this direction are undermined by the reality that governs our interactions: the human condition, man's imperfectability. As Wilhelm Röpke observes in *A Humane Economy*:

> It is the precept of ethical and humane behavior, no less than of political wisdom, to adapt economic policy to man, not man to economic policy.

Liberals tend to be parentalists and apologists; they believe that because they imagine what *could* be, they must tell us what *should* be. As Röpke notes, we cannot use government to force people to be different from their essence. Sadly, liberals often think man's essence is selfish and dark—thus their insistence on attempting to control us. But the essence of humanity—*humanity*, not any given individual—when considered in a social context, freed from oppression and supported by the rule of law, is decency, honesty, and fairness. That these traits and intentions are not in perfect sync for every individual every moment is a reflection of our imperfectability. Yet even if mankind cannot be perfect, it can, and does, strive to be so. In nature, certainly man is anarchic, not out of venality, but out of self-protection. When refuge is offered by means of a moral and ordered liberty, the better part of our nature surfaces for one simple reason: being good to one another in the fashion of enlightened self-interest achieves more for each of us, and all of us, than does acting in any other manner. In other words, courtesy, honesty, integrity *are* contagious. This theme is explored in greater detail later in this volume.

Ludwig von Mises addressed another real world fact that confronts today's politically correct equalitarianism head-on; Mises knew that social cooperation cannot rest in egalitarian authority where everyone's opinion is valid and no one is allowed to be in charge. He understood that human inequality (in our respective abilities) placed within institutional hierarchies is what allows society to work and progress. Although such views could fatuously be termed antidemocratic or even condescending and oppressive, Mises understood that individual inequalities are natural. To ignore those natural characteristics in ordering the economic or social aspects of any society is a formula for failure.

Further, because *someone* must be in charge Mises argues that human interaction ought to be primarily managed locally, rather than in distant government. He reasons that government should be simple, so those over whom it rules can understand it. The less complex government is, the more obvious corruption and incompetence are when they arise and the more easily they can be corrected. When the power of those in charge becomes too great, or corrupt, or intrusive, or just wrong, the governed can see these things, and take action.

Observations and Considerations

WHILE ECONOMY of words is always desirable, you will nevertheless find some ideas and concepts appearing more than once in this book. Occasionally these redundancies may seem pedantic, but the points iterated are core to each author who makes them. Many find the foundation of what they observe or conjure within the small orchard of principled thought, others are forced to act or react by the bright light of harsh experience. To not pay homage to their square one—and to the many authors who arrive at virtually the same square one over so many centuries past—would do a disservice to the remainder of what each individual has to say, and to the overall observations to be made here.

Some of these foundations are nearly universal. An example: a point made equally often and stridently by the political observers and economists represented in this book is that the many varieties of socialism, which seemed possible to eighteenth-century idealists and became a theoretical obligation in the nineteenth, morphed in the twentieth century into a singular obsession termed state welfarism that remains in the twenty-first a social, fiscal, and national danger. As Jacques Barzun notes in *From Dawn to Decadence* (2000), when John Stuart Mill opined in the nineteenth century that "the national product [of England] could be redirected at will and that it should be so ordered for the general welfare," the battle—not between capitalism and socialism, but between capitalism and chaos, as Ludwig von Mises termed it—was joined. When future president Franklin Delano Roosevelt uttered similar thoughts as he regarded the Prussian-German economic model in 1912, it was apparent socialism was seen by him as something good, and the State as something better: "The [Prussians] passed beyond the liberty of the individual to do as he pleased with his own property and found it necessary to check this liberty for the benefit of the freedom of the whole people" he announced to the People's Forum of Troy, New York. Lord Acton's contention that "liberty is not a means to a higher political end, it is itself the highest political end (Chapter 9)" was found wanting in Roosevelt's eye.

That socialism assumed its place on the world stage in the twentieth century, undaunted by either logic or common sense, "taking," in Barzun's words, "the twin form of Communism and the Welfare State, either under the dictatorship of a party or under the rule of democratic parliament and bureaucracy" was so audacious an idea in the face of reality that many of our authors remained astonished. They felt evermore obligated to expose sequentially the insanity of socialism and its theoretically more benign but equally untenable progeny, state welfarism. As well, many of their acolytes were forced to action. To observe with what common certitude these authors held and voiced their views in spite of equally vehement opposition, inures to the benefit of anyone who sees in these pages not just sense, but a reason for passion.

We hope through the recognition of the universality of many of these principles—whether in economics, governance, the protection of rights, or the necessity of performing duties—to achieve an appreciation of their extensive serviceability. Much as the foundations of most buildings share common engineering principles while supporting manifold architectural options, the first principles that underlie modern society's forms and relationships are equally simple and universal. It is essential that we recognize these foundations as the sometimes repeated substructure in varied applications and origins.

Finally, as was observed by historian Forrest McDonald when he wrote *E Pluribus Unum* (1965), his history of the formation of our republic at the time of the American Revolution:

> If I have stated the obvious I do not apologize, for it is the obvious that is so often most difficult to see.

The intention of *First Principles* is actually to do just that—state the obvious, note how each author uses the obvious to make more nuanced or broad points, and finally, to use the obvious to give credence to the principles that underlie both the origins and functioning of a democratic republic supported by a free-enterprise economic system.

As you explore the materials presented in *First Principles* we hope you will appreciate the intellectual integrity of the authors and their works, and the freedom of discussion our society affords each of us. We unreservedly believe that ideas have consequences. Bad ideas have bad consequences, bad government is still a distinct possibility, and acting even with the best of intentions can have unintended, often harmful, consequences.

As John Adams was fond of observing, "facts are stubborn things."

As you peruse the fundamentals presented here, try to keep both an open mind and a commitment to traveling all pathways to their logical conclusions. In this manner you may sharpen your own understanding and help solidify freedom and virtue in a more dependable and public fashion. You may even discover new approaches and methods to deal with particular problems of government and human relations, or help resurrect old ones.

Learn, then act. In that way our system and our society are made better.

Definitions

THERE ARE SOME words and phrases that appear throughout the books reviewed in *First Principles* that are difficult to decipher, or for which exact meanings are not readily apparent, or that have a historical significance with which the reader may not be familiar. The following definitions will go some distance toward explaining what these words and phrases mean to conservative writers. The list appears here, and not in an appendix, because understanding these words and concepts before reading either the synopses or the underlying books will make the journey much easier.

authoritarianism: the suppression of the freedom of individuals, and control of individuals without considering or soliciting their wishes or circumstances: government by force rather than consent.

Benthamism: the moral doctrine of Jeremy Bentham (1748–1832) that posits the greatest happiness of the greatest number as the ultimate goal of society and the individual. Closely related to Utilitarianism, the doctrine that the worth or value of anything is determined solely by its utility, its usefulness. Benthamism is anti-individual and anti-individual rights.

bourgeoisie: the social class between the aristocracy (the very wealthy) and the proletariat (the working class); the middle class of small business owners. In socialist doctrine the *bourgeoisie*, or capitalists as a social class, is antithetical to the proletariat.

Calvinism: (named for John Calvin [1509–64], theologian and religious reformer, lawyer) Calvin's religious pronouncements had a practical, temporal side and his quest for civil order was a blend of both law and theology. His amalgam of the Ten Commandments and cultural admonitions to perform civic duties, such as paying taxes and bowing to the authority of government, brought civility to bear as society perfected itself after the Middle Ages. Religion was recognized as having a secular side in that it is a necessary adjunct in the fight against anarchy. Calvinism, represented today especially by Presbyterians and some Baptists, but also members of the broad Reform tradition, offers a dual, practical approach to social organization. Calvinist precepts—universal (male) suffrage, equality in church self-government and other church matters, resistance to oppression, the obligations of civic duty, and ideals of personal liberty—were transferred almost in their entirety (from 1620 forward) into the nascent American experiment.

capitalism: an economic system in which most of the means of production, distribution, and/or exchange are privately owned and operated for profit. Initially capitalism was to be an open competitive system but government intervention and controls have developed over the centuries to counteract the economic power created by the success of the capitalism itself, and to deal with issues of national defense and public safety, health and well-being as they are affected by capitalistic practices.

classical liberalism: limited and decentralized state power, a free-market economy, freedom for the individual, and personal responsibility; now generally a part of conservatism in America.

collectivism: government control of most spheres of social and economic life; similar to socialism but without direct ownership of the means of production.

communism: an economic theory and system that takes socialism as its basis with regard to production and distribution. Communists assert that all means of production and distribution belong to the community as a whole (this tenet is the core of socialism), with the ownership of all other property also resting in the community; communist doctrine holds there is no need for private property. Distribution to individuals is "from each according to his abilities, to each according to his need." (See **Marx, Karl** following.)

conservatism: a social movement espousing minimal government intervention in personal lives, maximization of individual liberty coupled with personal responsibility, economic freedom with reliance on the market and decentralized decision making to order social/economic relationships, adherence to tested institutions and methods as described in the American Constitution and the writings of America's Founders. A more comprehensive definition assumes the existence of an objective moral order based on historical evidence. Within that moral order the individual is primary and the power of the state minimal. The individual enjoys certain freedoms and rights, but assumes certain duties and responsibilities. Conservatism is anti-utopian; it understands mankind's inequalities, and the benefits that derive therefrom, and acknowledges human imperfectability.

Deism: the belief that God exists and created the world but thereafter did not interfere with or assume any control over it. Reason is sufficient to prove the existence of God, but Deism rejects both revelation and specifically, religious authority. Deism holds that the universe, once created by a benevolent God, operates on rational rather than supernatural principles. (See also **Reason, Age of.**)

demagogue: a leader who uses the passions or prejudices of the populace for his own interest; an unprincipled agitator. "Demagoguery is the use of hyperbole and misinformation for political advantage by exaggerating either one's own virtue or the villainy of others"—Dick Armey, Majority Leader of the U.S. House of Representatives, 1994–2002.

despot, despotism: despotism is government by a singular authority, either an individual or a tightly knit group, which rules with absolute power. The word implies tyrannical control; a form of government that exercises exacting and near-absolute dominion over all of its citizens.

dialectics: the art or practice of examining opinions or ideas logically, often by the method of question and answer, so as to determine their validity; logical argumentation. Used by Friedrich Hegel and Karl Marx in their theories of social action. It is based on the concept of contradiction or opposites (thesis and antithesis) and their continual resolution (synthesis).

economics: economics is the study of acts of choice (causes) and their results (effects). Economics is not about things but about people's actions and reactions to their world. Economics itself does not have an ethical or moral base; economics is only about choices and actions. Economics is indifferent to the goals of actions; it is a science of means, not ends.

Note: most dictionaries treat the words egalitarian and equalitarian as synonymous. In classical liberal and/or conservative theory and writing, however, the words are not interchangeable, and are, in fact, essentially opposites. The following definitions capture this fundamental difference:

egalitarian: a belief in equal opportunity and equal rights for all people.

equalitarian: a belief in equal results or status for all people, irrespective of individual effort, capability, or opportunity.

Enlightenment, The: the eighteenth-century philosophical movement characterized by rationalism, learning, and a spirit of skepticism and empiricism in social, educational, religious, and political thought. The movement was centered in France and was founded in the blossoming of scientific understanding, often giving it anti-religious overtones. Its goal was the transformation of civilization on purely rational principles to achieve human perfection. Many of the Enlightenment's hopes were dashed with the disastrous reality of the French Revolution of 1789 that left unchecked power in the hands of a self-selected group in a legislative format. This was found to ensure no more fairness and justice than leaving such power in the hands of one person. Friedrich Nietzsche [1844–1900], a nineteenth-century German philosopher, captured the Enlightenment's failure succinctly when he observed "Man, instead of using reason to understand reality, tried to use it to master reality." The subsequent appreciation of man's imperfectability guided most of the ensuing rationalistic attempts at order and social construction. To control men's worst impulses when they exert dominion over others, mechanisms such as the separation of powers, checks and balances, frequent democratic elections, and a written constitution alterable only by the people, were implemented.

epistemology: the branch of philosophy that investigates the origin, nature, methods, and limits of human knowledge.

essentialism: the study of both economics and society through the use of base definitions of terms that embody their empirical or observable meanings. (Examples: a hammer is a heavy object used to exert force; taxes are revenues collected and used by a governing authority.)

fascism: a system of government characterized by a rigid one-party dictatorship and forcible suppression of opposition, the retention of private ownership of the means of production but under centralized government control, belligerent nationalism, and claims to racial purity. First appeared in Milan, Italy (1919), under the *Fascisti*, founded by Benito Mussolini. The *Fascisti*'s ostensible purpose was to oppose and then suppress all radical political movements in Italy, but their leaders—the Black Shirts—eventually established an ordinary dictatorship under Mussolini. Germany's National Socialism, a variant of fascism named for the National Socialist German Workers Party, or Nazi Party (1931–1945), was an amalgam of fascism and socialism created by Adolph Hitler, but taken to greater extremes than the Italian version.

free market: a set of circumstances and suppositions where the activities of the participants are not subject to coercion and where all individuals may exchange their products, services, or ideas voluntarily. A market, of whatever nature or subject matter, from education to economics, from government to social interaction, in which the terms of exchange are set and re-set by supply and demand in open competition, and are otherwise unregulated. In a free market, decision making devolves to those closest to the activities involved, who have the greatest knowledge of what is occurring and how to achieve whatever goals are desired. Free-market activity is the opposite of centralized control, where distant decision makers, often operating largely on theory, cannot comprehend the myriad factors that affect entire systems. A free market allows individuals to learn what they do not know, and then act on what they learn, by providing theory with an open laboratory.

historicism (determinism): a theory that holds that the future is determined by what happened in the past; the belief that historical inevitability makes studying the past a way to predict the future.

human condition, the: a reference to the totality of the experience of being human. As imperfect, and imperfectable beings, the manner and content of our individual and group actions and reactions (both good and bad) as we experience life's realities are the substance of this condition.

inflation: rising prices caused by an increase in the amount of money and credit circulating in an economy with no equal increase in the supply of goods or services. Prices rise as the supply of money increases because more dollars are chasing the same amount of goods; when people have more money, they are willing to pay more for any given object, causing its price to be bid up. The increase in the amount of money is the result, primarily, of government printing more currency. When the supply of money increases, the value of each unit of money decreases. In general, governments print more money in order to balance their budgets. An unbalanced budget arises when governments spend more money than taxation brings in. Inflation, allowed to continue unchecked, causes the monetary system to collapse and the currency to become worthless, as happened in Germany in 1923 and in America in 1781.

Jacobins: from the Hebrew: one who seizes by the heel, a supplanter. Politically radical French democrats during the revolution of 1789, ultimately led by Maximilien Robespierre, who favored extreme change in France's social structure. So called because their meetings were initially held in the Jacobin friars' convent. The Jacobins instituted the Reign of Terror in 1793, their intention being to bludgeon opponents—through mass and summary executions—into acceptance of and conformity with their views. Refers today to political radicals, especially persons with equalitarian impulses.

jingoism: boasting of one's patriotism and favoring an aggressive, threatening, war-like foreign policy.

Labor Party (English): a political party organized to protect and further the rights of workers, or professing to do so; originally a democratic socialist party, it is now evolving away from that stance.

liberal: in politics, a word or label denoting views with essentially opposite meaning in Europe and America. Historically (and yet today in Europe) a political viewpoint developed during the nineteenth century that stressed personal freedom, limited state interference in the individual's life, and the importance of constitutional rule. In mid-twentieth-century America, *liberal* came to denote those who favor largely opposite goals such as "reform" of current conditions or perceived problems through the creation of new social patterns or values; change is to be achieved by means of direct government intervention and programs. Personal freedom and preference is often to be controlled by the state; the stated and sought-after "community" good is valued over personal freedom and individual choice.

liberalism, or collectivist or populist liberalism (American): the opposite of classical liberalism; state economic control, various intrusive interventionist state actions that limit individual freedom and expand welfarism, with highly progressive and redistributionist tax structures.

Liberal Party (English): formerly the Whig Party in England; a party of no fixed principles today.

libertarianism: a political doctrine that supports the freedom of people to act for themselves so long as they do not interfere with the rights of others, and that favors government action only if it is confined to those activities that the members of a society cannot efficiently and voluntarily perform either individually or collectively at the local level; generally opposed to legislation involving deviant personal conduct of any kind, for example, legislation against narcotics use.

macroeconomics: The study of any national economy, the global economy, or other whole economic systems through the accumulation of continually changing economic information, such as the rate of inflation, of unemployment, of production, of price levels, etc. The effects of government actions on these large markets are also a key part of market analysis.

Manifest Destiny: the nineteenth-century doctrine that it is the destiny of the Anglo-Saxon nations, especially the United States, to dominate the entire Western Hemisphere.

marginal utility: the minimum degree of utility (usefulness), below which any activity (including everything from manufacturing to social controls) is not profitable enough to be continued.

Marx, Karl: (1818–1883) nineteenth-century political economist and social philosopher. His concept of economic justice was mathematical, and taken to its logical end resulted in a pure uniformity of existence for mankind. Marx's theories, based on his assumption that the history of society was a history of class struggles, were tested in a pragmatic manner as a result of the Russian Revolution of 1917 and the imposition of communism—Marx's brand of socialism—on the Russian people. Neither the experiment nor Marx's theories were able to pass the "real world" test and Russian (Soviet) Communism collapsed in 1991 when the Soviet Union ceased to exist as a political and economic entity. Marx's labor theory of value (that because all value was created by labor, all value should be returned to labor) was discredited as capitalism matured and the benefits and economic value of its various components (management, capital formation, imagination, incentive, etc.) was recognized.

meliorism: the belief that the world naturally tends to get better, and especially that it can be made better by human effort.

microeconomics: the branch of economics concerned with the behavior of and decisions made by individuals, households, and firms and how these decisions interact to form the prices of goods and services and the factors of production and distribution.

monetarism: the theory that economic stability and growth are determined primarily by the supply of money.

moral relativism: the belief that moral propositions do not reflect absolute or universal truth, that ethical judgments emerge simply from social customs and personal preferences; the belief posits that there is no single standard by which to assess an ethical proposition's truth. This term reflects a view that morality is personal and self or socially-defined. When used as a foundation for public interaction it can evolve to complacent irresponsibility, social futility and self-indulgence.

multiculturalism: a philosophy or theory based on the view that society works better if people feel their cultural beliefs are respected and that they do not have to abandon their values to be considered good citizens. This view holds that several different and distinct cultures (rather than one national culture) can coexist peacefully and equitably in a single country and that laws, customs and behavior are subject to citizen preference rather than unifying cultural norms that evolve sustainable values. A contrary view holds that overt or mandated cultural individuality breeds unnecessary conflict and jealousy and impedes citizen comity. This form of multiculturalism can devolve to pluralism (see below). Those who hold the contrary view argue that a basic national uniformity is essential (particularly in terms of language), but do not oppose informal recognition and tolerance of limited individual cultural heritage.

nominalism: a doctrine of the late Middle Ages that all universal or abstract terms are mere necessities of thought, or conveniences of language, and therefore exist as names only and have no realities corresponding to them; the opposite of realism. The idea that man's opinions are of greater consequence than truths gained by experience.

normative: of or establishing a norm or standard; pertaining to what ought to be, in contrast to a "positive" analysis, that is, analysis which determines what is.

opportunity cost: when one is choosing between two options, an opportunity cost is what is incurred because something else is chosen (i.e., any choice "costs" one a different choice). The opportunity that is lost is the next most valuable end, after the one chosen, toward which one could apply one's resources.

paradigm: the set of common beliefs and agreements about how problems should be understood and addressed; a coherent understanding of cause-effect relationships; the predominant view that defines what exists in the real world.

pluralism: A condition in which members of diverse ethnic, racial, religious, language, or social groups maintain their traditional cultures or special interests within a common (shared) culture. Pluralism is a framework of interaction in which groups show sufficient respect and tolerance of each other that they fruitfully coexist and interact without conflict but also generally without significant assimilation. Pluralism is more separatist than its cousin multiculturalism. In a pluralistic setting often mutually exclusive and contradictory religious, moral and/or political doctrines are held to be equal in status—though equality in merit or value are not universally accepted. Strident pluralism, such as when two languages cause intra-country conflict is called Separatism (Canada, Belgium).

political correctness: a term used to describe efforts to discourage recognition of various political or other views that are not in sync with equalitarian (and related) criteria. While it frequently refers to a linguistic phenomenon, it also extends to describe a non-economic, emotionally based political ideology and behavior. When the state decides what is "correct" for the society, the state's decisions evidence a "political" correctness, arbitrated by those in the government and supposedly, but not necessarily, expressing the general will. Those seeking a politically correct society strive for equality or social justice (from a particular viewpoint not necessarily universally accepted) through suppression of thought, speech, or practice they deem antithetical to achieving that goal. Questioning the morality or validity of various viewpoints that are not universally accepted is not permitted in a politically correct milieu; it is deemed "incorrect" speech.

(political) diversity: diversity refers to all of the characteristics that make individuals different from each other. In a political/sociological sense diversity reflects a respect for and accommodation of racial/ethnic, gender, cultural, disability, sexual orientation, and social differences. Political diversity, however, is often seen as a goal to be imposed (with all the difficulties of legislating morality or cultural norms), rather than as a byproduct of evolving social interaction.

populism: a political philosophy directed to the needs of the common people and advocating a more even distribution of wealth and power, without specific regard to classical economic tenets. Also: containing or advocating nativist or nationalistic tendencies, such as high tariffs and a restrictive immigration policy

positivism: a rationalist philosophy based solely on positive, observable, scientific facts, and their correlation to one another. It rejects speculation on or search for ultimate origins. It is an inductive method of reasoning that attempts to prove theories via evidence. Also called logical empiricism.

pragmatism: the theory that we learn best from experience, from what "works." Pragmatism leads to tolerance of others and their views; that is, for what works for them. Pragmatism became popular with the advent of the modern age when there arose many belief systems from which to choose. Skepticism about the authority or finality of any particular set of beliefs—out of the many available—led to pragmatism.

proletariat: the working class, especially the industrial working class; the class above serfs, peasants, or others bereft of freedom or property.

Puritan: A term first used c. 1570 for English Protestants who wanted to "purify" the Church of England of ceremony and ritual not found in the Scriptures. At first they simply wanted to reform their church, but by 1620 many were separatists who wanted to start their own churches. They felt reform was hopeless. There were never many separatist Puritans in England because they tended to emigrate to America. "Puritan" described a tendency, not a denomination; thus many sects evolved from Puritanism, depending on the parts of the Anglican (Church of England) service with which they disagreed. Puritans often defied human authority (religious or secular) in order to follow or rely solely on Scripture.

rationalism: the principle or practice of accepting reason as the only authority in determining one's opinions or course of action. The theory that reason, or intellect, rather than the senses, is the true source of knowledge. A rejection of revelation or the supernatural as explanations for temporal matters.

Realpolitik: foreign policy based on calculations of actual power and national interest.

Reason, Age of: a loosely defined period which began near the end of the eighteenth century, where rationalism was to define human experience and existence; also the title of a book by Thomas Paine whose thinking was archetypal of the age. Paine was a deist (see **Deism**). He vehemently rejected the authority of Judeo-Christian tenets and scriptures. In *The Age of Reason*, Paine outlined his objections to theism and his belief in deism, and he dissected the miracles and inconsistencies in the Old and New Testaments in an effort to bolster his view that God is less palpable than the adherents to conventional religions claim. Paine used reason, which he called "the most formidable weapon against errors of every kind," to point out problems and expose contradictions within various religions. Paine was so sure of his own reasoned conclusions that he thought the collapse of "revealed religion" was imminent as mankind entered the new Age of Reason.

redistribution (economic): a political effort to shift a substantial portion of society's wealth from the entrepreneurial class to the remainder of the population. This is accomplished by means of high rates of taxation whereby income, profits, estates, etc., are reallocated to the less well-off through law and regulation (such as Social Security and Medicare), direct transfers (in the form of various subsidies), and implementation of other public welfare measures. Generally considered to achieve ends opposite of the intended goal by undermining the incentive that created the wealth that is to be redistributed. Redistribution also depletes the pool of capital that is the fuel of economic activity thus making the entire nation poorer.

Reformation, or Protestant Reformation: the sixteenth-century movement initiated by Martin Luther with the nailing of ninety-five theses to his parish church door in 1517. The theses sought to expose religious inconsistencies and apostasies. The movement was aimed at reforming the Roman Catholic Church and resulted in the establishment of Protestantism—a group of Christian churches not aligned with, and often opposed to, the Roman Catholic and Eastern Orthodox Churches. Luther, a priest, contended that the Roman Catholic Church was corrupt and in need of reform. He favored the translation of the Bible into contemporary languages because most people could not read Latin. Luther strongly opposed the selling of forgiveness by church functionaries, which sale he considered to be immoral, especially when the sale was of forgiveness for future sins. The idea behind the Protestant Reformation was simple: the Church should be changed, or reformed, so that it would be less greedy, and also fairer and accessible to all people, not just the rich and well educated. Luther held that the only religious authority was the Bible, not the Church hierarchy.

Renaissance: the period of European history from the early fourteenth to the late sixteenth centuries. The term is derived from the French word for rebirth, and originally referred to the revival of the values and artistic styles of classical antiquity, especially in Italy. The word later acquired a broader meaning. Voltaire in the eighteenth century classified the Renaissance in Italy as one of the great ages of cultural achievement. In the modern age the Renaissance is considered a distinct historical epoch characterized by rejuvenation of the arts, the rise of the individual, renewed scientific inquiry and geographical exploration, and the growth of secular values.

scientism: the philosophy that scientific methods can and should be applied to all fields of knowledge.

Scottish Enlightenment: the period from c. 1740 until 1800 when the intellectuals of Scotland—most notably David Hume, Adam Smith, and Frances Hutcheson (Hume's antagonist)—defined and explored the changes wrought on society by capitalism. The Enlightenment in general, an eighteenth-century phenomenon, was a movement characterized by rationalism, an impetus toward learning, and a spirit of skepticism and empiricism in social and political thought. Appraising the newly born division of labor and its impact equally on economics and society, Scottish intellectuals began a centuries-long contemplation of modernity's moral foundations as they are affected by economic and social realities. Modern scientific processes based on the understanding of evidence, experience, and causation were developed in this period. Hume elaborated many principles of the scientific method—in addition to modern attitudes toward the relationship between science and religion, while Smith expanded on the logical consequences of capitalism's initial phases.

secularism: a system of doctrines, philosophy, beliefs, and/or practices that rejects any form of religious faith and worship; the belief that religion and ecclesiastical affairs should not enter into the functions of the state.

social contract; social compact: the voluntary submission of free people to the authority of government in order to secure their rights. If the government violates those rights, it breaks the contract and the people are free to organize themselves in another manner—by the use of force if necessary. The protection of rights and the enforcement of duties are the functions of government, but if government exerts power beyond that agreement, then the right of defiance is manifest. However, there are shades of citizen justification for self-determination, for no government is perfect or perfectly administered. If government fails the populace, there is a right of resistance; if government oppresses the people, there is a right of revolution. A continued theft of rights or enforcement of slave-like duties is no more justified in government than it is in private matters.

socialism: a theory and system that holds that the ownership of the means of production and distribution shall be by society as a whole rather than by free individuals. Everyone is to share equally in both the work and the product. In communist doctrine, socialism is that stage coming between capitalism and communism; a dictatorship—theoretically of the proletariat as a class, but normally of individuals—is required to bring about the eventual transition to a communist society.

sovereign state: a state independent of all others; a political entity not controlled by outside forces.

Soviet Union; Union of Soviet Socialist Republics (USSR): the former communist country in Eastern Europe and northern Asia; established in 1922; it included Russia and fourteen other socialist republics. The Soviet Union was the political entity that came into being after the 1917 Russian Revolution and the following Civil War of 1918–20. It was the home of a worldwide effort at socialist revolution by means of both stealth and force. The government and the country were run by a totalitarian political entity, The Communist Party of the Soviet Union. For most of the half-century following World War II, the Soviet Union vied with the United States for political and ideological domination of both populations and countries in what was termed the Cold War. The USSR ceased to exist politically in 1991, but its disintegration began in 1989 with the initial breakdown of its economic and political structures. When the USSR collapsed, its constituent parts became fifteen independent countries, many of which were loosely aligned in the Commonwealth of Independent States. Soviet is the Russian word for council. Soviets were councils of workers' deputies and organizationally began to be formed during the 1905 Russian Revolution (the deputies were those who represented the workers in the councils; the term deputies reflects their subordinate, in theory, position to the workers themselves); the term took on greater political meaning subsequent to the 1917 Revolution.

statism, statist: a term used to describe any economic system where a government implements a significant degree of centralized economic planning, which usually includes a comprehensive welfare system and state ownership of the means of production, as opposed to a system where economic planning occurs at a decentralized level by private individuals in a free market. A statist is one who believes in or implements this form of governmental control.

tautology: needless repetition of an idea in a different word, phrase, or sentence; redundancy; adding nothing to the sense of a subject.

Tory: the political party in England labeled today as Conservative. Also applied to those Americans who sided with Great Britain and opposed the American Revolutionary War.

totalitarian, -ism: a form of government in which one person, a dictator, or a political party exercises absolute control over all spheres of human life, and opposing political parties or ideas are prohibited.

utilitarian, -ism: the notion that the greatest happiness of the greatest number should be the aim of all social policy (regardless of individual rights and freedoms). (See **Benthamism**.)

Utopia, utopia: an imaginary island described as having a perfect political and social system, from a book of the same title by Sir Thomas More (1478–1535); any place, state, system, or situation of ideal perfection, especially social perfection.

Whig: the English political party that sided with the Americans during the Revolutionary War and opposed maintaining American ties to Great Britain by force. The party championed popular individual rights. Also the name of the U.S. political party (1836–1856) that supported protection of industry and limitation of executive power.

A Note on Organization

THE BOOKS we discuss are grouped into four sections and are ordered from basic to advanced within each group. These volumes represent an historical overview of the intellectual philosophy and practical implementation of a free society. In understanding the history and rationality of that system the citizen will be in a better position to apply its lessons in the modern world.

Books in Section I Part 1 offer an investigation into the foundations of constitutional representative government. Those in Part 2 discuss free governance in a real-world setting.

Books in Section II Part 1 are current in the broad sense and discuss history and political philosophy as they progressed, primarily in America, since the turn of the twentieth century. Books in Part 2 address the basics of economics in a free society.

Books in Section III are slightly more sophisticated and nuanced. They explore and explain governance and the need to consider, in some detail, the effects of the human psyche on the body politic.

Books in Section IV relate to what is to come. These volumes investigate matters that will directly affect the future of self-governance.

The Declaration of Independence and the Constitution of the United States are offered directly in the reading materials, not in an appendix. To be both fully appreciated and placed in context these two documents should be read where they appear, not as related reference works or just an afterthought. Familiarity with each text will offer a benefit going in both directions; viz., the synopsized books will be a little more comprehensible and the Declaration and Constitution will be a little more meaningful for having read all of them together.

Section I

Part 1

The Architecture of a Free Society

1

The Second Treatise on Civil Government

John Locke

Originally published: 1690
132 pages

INFORMATION OVERLOAD is a modern phenomenon that distorts the big picture and erodes our understanding of first principles. In the maelstrom of fact and opinion, many are the critics who attempt to define liberty for us, almost always with a political slant; yet we seldom find individuals who can clearly articulate the essence of their freedom and understand its attendant obligations. The danger is that taking freedom for granted or ignoring its accompanying responsibilities are the two surest ways to lose one's independence. It is disquieting that comprehending the indispensable conjunction of freedom and obligation is increasingly rare.

John Locke's *Second Treatise on Civil Government* brings us back to the basics of liberty and duty, to first principles. He offers a cogent look at what we seem to have lost sight of today. Since Locke investigates freedom at the inception of modern times, when problematic aspects of its nature were still relatively simple, his conclusions are among the clearest and most persuasive.

To a degree, Locke writes in opposition to fellow-countryman Thomas Hobbes (1588–1679), his predecessor in time and theory and author of *Leviathan* (1651). Hobbes holds that the state is a necessary evil, a beast-like Leviathan that is crucial to controlling men's self-interest. For Hobbes, the state is the sole antidote to anarchy. He saw that religion had failed in its efforts to bring peace among men, that religion had actually caused more conflict than it resolved. Hobbes thus relegates religion to a separate and secondary role and contends that men must submit to government because they ultimately fear one another more than they fear a central authority. This suspicion later received some validation in the aftermath of the French Revolution of 1789 when "citizens"—who were expected to respect one another once the monarchy was destroyed—proceeded to treat each other in an utterly barbaric and lawless fashion. Their behavior remained unchecked by the predicted but failed advent of reciprocal good will.

Hobbes understands mankind's individualistic and often self-serving nature and feels the need to restrain that with a Leviathan—in his case, a monarchy. But Hobbes's solution doesn't sit well with either Locke or Adam Smith, whose *Wealth of Nations* (Chapter 12), published almost a century after Locke wrote, elaborated an alternative, more practical and positive view of human nature. For Smith and implicitly for Locke, mankind's true spirit flourishes in the inducements of *enlightened* self-interest and *ordered* liberty. This proved to be a more accurate and helpful understanding of human nature, as was seen when America and its foundation of freedom came into being. Without denying the venal aspects of the human condition, enlightened self-interest posits that we can do well for ourselves by doing well for and with others (mutual cooperation, the division of labor, the advent of interpersonal charity, the creation of community). In other words, doing well for ourselves while engaging others in like-minded activities is not a selfish or negative concept; it is quite the opposite.

Locke and Smith view society as a largely cooperative venture rather than a continuous power struggle. Their outlook became the foundation of self-government in the centuries following the publication of both *The Second Treatise on Civil Government* and *Wealth of Nations*. Of course, certain freedoms that bring out the best in some men also bring out the worst in others. There thus remains the need for authority—but not absolute authority. Whoever holds absolute authority (whether as a monarch/executive/bureaucrat, a legislator, or judge) still suffers from the human condition. The tendency is always toward self-aggrandizement and self-interest at the expense of others when power is conferred. The practical result requires that there be checks and balances on those given power to prevent them from over-reaching. It also requires a separation of church and state to prevent religious edict from becoming civil tyranny.

The value of Locke's insights became self-evident after the implications of Hobbes's speculations (unrestrained power) were taken to their logical endpoint. In contrast to Hobbes's abstract and theoretical approach, Locke draws his conclusions from evidence and common experience. His first premise—that liberty is not a license—recognizes that freedom is a real-world equation, not just an intellectual concept. For Locke, before cultures or civilizations evolved, each man was in a "state of nature" and individually responsible for protecting his own natural rights to life, liberty, and property, and controlling, even punishing, those who violated those rights. When people agreed to form a civil society or community for the purpose of collectively protecting life and property, rules were piled on top of rules until we were left with modern attempts at government. The problem of how to contain the ever-proliferating rules and those who exercise power remained.

For Locke, the supreme authority in a social/governmental undertaking designed and controlled by its members (called a commonwealth) is the legislature; this body creates laws in a public forum that are to be made known to the populace in advance and applied with equal force to all individuals. In Locke's view this "social contract"—a contract *among* the people, and *between* the people and their government—requires the sort of definition that comes from a representative assembly, made up of the people themselves. In this democratic format legislators create the rules by which everyone (in a communal, majoritarian sense) is willing to be governed. Locke is equally aware of the need for amendability, for change such that when the majorities or the realities are altered the rules necessarily are mutable. Society's fluid nature is recognized from the outset and this fosters confidence in the fairness of the legislative process.

These rules, by which and through which agreement was achieved on most matters involving human relations, were neither black nor white, nor did they always fit foursquare with human activities. There was a need for impartial judgment in applying, or enforcing them, thus the executive branch of government was born. And for those times when the citizens disagree with the executive or the legislature Locke creates a judiciary for the interpretation and interpolation of laws, to arbitrate when the governors and the citizens arrive at odds.

In designing his system, Locke takes into account man's inherently contradictory nature—which is alternately generous and self-centered. He argues that a rational tension between centers of authority is needed in order to protect not just the people, but the system itself; in this manner he seeks to reduce the effect of self-interest. He views a separation of power between all three governing entities as indispensable to controlling potential errant human impulses.

The *natural* right to private property is central to Locke's vision, for private property is the institution essential to dividing one person's labors from another's. For Locke, property rights are the counterpoint to (limited) government. Indeed, people secure in their property rights experience only a minimal need for government to direct their activities, or the activities of those around them. (For a complete look at the development of the concept and reality of property from the very, very beginning, Richard Pipes offers a definitive assessment in *Property and Freedom* [Chapter 11].)

Locke's development of the concept of property takes up much of his energy, and many of his conclusions are sound and applicable today. However, some require nuance to fit into a modern capitalistic economic model that did not exist when Locke wrote. Understanding property is essential to understanding first principles, yet property is so basic to humanity's existence few people take the time to consider its implications or imperatives. Any distance from comprehension of such a core element of freedom and self-governance makes it difficult, if not impossible, to fit the whole together.

Concomitant with his equation of freedom and responsibility, Locke understands the necessity of enforcing our rights—whether property or personal—and recognizing our obligations to one another. The Golden Rule may be divine, but it is not self-executing in an imperfect world; thus Locke's next step, after discussing aspects of our rights and our responsibilities, is to expand his discussion of the "executive":

> No law is of value without an ability to enforce it.

Locke severely limits his executive's unilateral ability to affect the rights and circumstances of each person, but his executive also has to possess the power necessary to allow effective fulfillment of the legislature's enactments and the relationships created thereunder. This essentially delicate balance required of Locke a somewhat detailed consideration of how an executive should act and how those actions must be limited.

Fidelity to a rational assessment of human nature complements Locke's strategy of commencing his investigation of civil government at the point when human beings were in a state of nature. The fact that Locke was writing in 1690 when a government such as he described was only a vision (and historically still a century away) made his arguments both unique and revolutionary in the face of two millennia of monarchy and despotism. Watching Locke dissect human nature and human interaction at their most basic levels offers a comprehension that is fundamental to understanding most of the subsequent development of freedom in an ordered society.

Locke, of course, does not operate in a vacuum. The ideas he formulates are really an amalgam of thoughts and practices and customs that had been developing throughout the two thousand years that preceded his efforts. His work reflects history—first of the Greeks and Romans, then ranging through that of medieval Europeans in both England and on the Continent, and finally in the British colonies in America. According to author Richard Pipes, Locke's grounding in English common law was his most important historical resource. Often misunderstood, English common law was the aftermath of various struggles—as Pipes observes in *Property and Freedom*—between rulers and ruled, between church and state, between sects within religions, and between the well-off and the less well-off. Over long periods various traditions had evolved that became the common law. These helped avoid the necessity of starting with a blank slate each time a repetitive issue of governance arose. Such traditions allowed, as Edmund Burke noted, wisdom to prevail without need for continued reflection, investigation or argument.

Locke wrote when the law's evolution had come to accept considerable freedom of thought and action for Englishmen; thus his amalgam of precedents into a "new" whole was neither unexpected nor—for everyone but English and continental monarchs—unwelcome. The law had come to acknowledge governance based upon the mutual obligations and promises between the governed and the governing authority; in other words, that governance was contractual in nature. Breaking the promises encompassed by this contract would, as a matter of course, require a new governing paradigm. The ability to change the contract became the key to England's—and eventually America's—quest for sensible, workable government.

Russell Kirk's *The Roots of American Order* (Chapter 4) offers useful historical insights into what was known by Locke at the time of his writings. Kirk's overview acquaints readers with the origins of our modern political arrangements and offers a survey of how complex their evolution was. Locke's encyclopedic approach to the study of governance, coupled with his understanding of human nature, make his book the first among equals; yet none of Locke's work would likely have been accomplished without all that passed before. Although Locke did not describe each facet of representative government's "square one" attributes as they exist today, he came presciently close to crafting an almost flawless whole. Appreciating how Locke got where he did, described in Kirk's book, is equally important, for his accomplishment is not as easily understood without all of its foundations.

About the Author

JOHN LOCKE was born in 1632 into professional wealth and society. His education was extensive, as would befit someone occupying his station in life. Interestingly, he eventually took up the study of medicine in order to escape entry into the priesthood of the Church of England that his parents wished for him. Locke's mind was inquisitive and his ultimate avocation, epistemology, seems almost inevitable. When one considers the times in which he lived—revolution, counter-revolution, civil war, all as a result of the willfulness of the monarchy—one can readily comprehend how natural was his overtly logical, intellectual path. His association with the Earl of Shaftesbury—a mentor and powerful political figure who weathered almost all the vicissitudes of seventeenth-century England—not only benefited Locke's study of human relations but also gave him a living example of political intrigue and machinations from which to draw persuasive extrapolations regarding how the English system could be improved. John Locke died in 1704 after long service to the government and fidelity to the philosophical insights explicated in his writings.

2

Common Sense, The Rights of Man, and Other Essential Writings

Thomas Paine

Originally published: 1776, 1783, 1791
287 pages

THOMAS PAINE took life personally. Much of the world he saw in 1774 offended him and as a result he became an author and patriot simultaneously. His first publication, in 1775, dealt with the subject of slavery and its immorality. Later he wrote in support of the two great revolutions of the eighteenth century in America and France. His intent in both cases was not simply to engage in an intellectual exercise, but to stimulate direct political action. Thus, while trying to help his compatriots in the Colonies defy tyranny and the suppression of human dignity (first and foremost by enlisting in Washington's army) Paine also formulated the theoretical tenets of a government respectful of its citizens and their rights. He was an unusual critic; he did not just tear down what he felt was wrong, he also offered solutions to make things better.

Paine's first major effort, *Common Sense*, published in February of 1776, so roused the American public and so deftly put forth what the Colonists wanted that its principles found expression in the Declaration of Independence. *Common Sense* is unpretentious but was profound for its day. Because of its simplicity its ideas are nowadays often regarded as obvious. Thomas Jefferson and George Washington did not think so at the time, however, and they were influenced by what Paine wrote.

Paine observes that

> [a] long habit of not thinking a thing wrong gives it a superficial appearance of being right and raises at first a formidable outcry in defence of custom.

Jefferson, Washington, and much of the American population were awakened by this simple thought and many were moved to action because of it.

Paine's objective was to create a government responsive to the people and based on their consent, one that could not act arbitrarily. One part of the design he offers is a method to control government through regular elections. Paine argues that government can be justified only through consensus and can be practiced only under the dominion of the governed. "Nothing but heaven is impregnable to vice," he writes.

It is to be noted, however, that there is a subtle, even obscure point about Paine's electoral franchise. He offers it in a negative form as the Romans had; the election process was initially intended not as a method of *selecting* leaders but as an assurance of the public's ability to *remove* those in power who became corrupt or proved themselves incompetent. Choosing those who might be the best leaders through a democratic process was thought to be an important yet only secondary consideration. Of course, choosing the best leaders would theoretically reduce the need to later replace officials because of incompetence or dishonesty. But as Bertrand de Jouvenel points out in *On Power* (Chapter 15) corruption—whether intellectual, political, or personal—is embedded in human make-up; thus, as Paine was aware, it pays to plan ahead in designing institutions.

Paine hoped to keep government uncomplicated as well. In this respect his style of prose matches his preference in administration. As a result his writings have recently fallen victim to academic pretentiousness with the accusation that he was simplistic. The scholarly and better-educated Jefferson, Madison, and Franklin are allegedly more worthy of attention. But readers with a fundamental understanding of Paine's accomplishments, who recall his times and circumstance, do not deprecate his talents simply because he could (and did) clearly distill the issues.

Paine's second effort, *The Crisis*, is comprised of sixteen articles written during the Revolutionary War. The text begins with his most famous quotation, "These are the times that try men's souls," and later continues "Tyranny, like hell, is not easily conquered." *The Crisis* supports the righteousness of the American Revolution and spurred both the public and the fighting men to remain true to the cause. It accomplished this through the simple force of Paine's rhetoric.

Paine had experienced the war firsthand. He began writing *The Crisis* while at the front with Washington's army during December 1776 and he continued to make his views heard for the next six years. Paine's fervor and the substance of his exhortations provided a focus that held the revolutionary movement together (intellectually and emotionally) across the countryside. What he wrote—a mix of propaganda, history, political and military analysis, homespun philosophy, and finally a demand for fidelity to the bigger cause—offers a concise review of what he and his compatriots experienced during the war. Its greatest value was the encouragement to action by patriots.

The Rights of Man, written while Paine was in France during the revolution of 1789, was his final political effort and a forceful argument calculated to expose the bankruptcy of hereditary monarchy. In *Reflections on the Revolution in France* (Chapter 36) Edmund Burke had defended hereditary government, but Paine in his rejoinder reduced the issue to its basics. His argument that each succeeding generation has the sacrosanct right to choose its own form of government won the debate. Despite Burke's justified reverence for the wisdom of the ages, Paine believed that the right to choose must remain in the hands of those being subjected to control; that government could not be handed down as an immutable legacy. He understood that government was simply a necessary evil, one needed to restrain ourselves when we fail one another. He argues, however, that governmental restrictions must be conditioned on the approval of those living under them.

The cataclysmic method of the French Revolution—government by guillotine (which Paine witnessed firsthand)—distorted contemporary French understanding of government's premises and intentions. Therefore, getting a clear view of the implications and possibilities of government without a monarchy was difficult for the French. Burke was understandably rooted in the past, but Paine's ideas carried the philosophical day as they had in America. In the face of the horrible reality of mass and murderous equalitarian insanity, a disgusted and disillusioned Paine did join Burke in decrying the French Revolution's excesses, but that is about the only point where the two men reached agreement.

The Rights of Man provides a history of the first days of the Revolution including the destruction of the Bastille—the infamous Parisian fort and prison—and the march on Versailles, the king's palace. Interestingly, Paine's reply to Burke reflected a modern-day problem—distortion by the press for political purposes. As one reads Paine's description of the revolutionary movements which he experienced day by day, and recalls Burke's exaggerated recitation of these same occurrences in his later writing, one realizes the need for objective measures to determine the significance of any event. The excesses at the beginning of the Revolution were exploited by Burke (who was not present) in his defense of hereditary government. Factual distortion to prove a point was hardly novel in Burke's time and is hardly anachronistic today.

Ultimately for both men the difficulty of melding principle with mob action was patent. Deducing what course of action made the most sense and attempting to come to rational conclusions could only be achieved with time. The excess of mayhem just before peace was restored in Paris was disastrous and neither author tried to defend it. In the end, and regardless of its horrendous consequences for the many who were involved, Paine holds that the causes of the Revolution were legitimate; it was a necessary evil (as an antidote to tyrannical government) no matter the devastation it produced or the distortion of its goals along the way. Based on the exigencies of the situations in both France and the American colonies Paine saw each revolution as inevitable, in the Machiavellian sense of the ends justifying the means.

Paine's last authorial effort, *The Age of Reason*, which is not part of this edition of his works, brought an ignominious end to a brilliant political life. In an era of fervent religious belief *The Age of Reason* sought to denigrate what Paine saw as religious superstition, and substitute in its stead the deistic beauty of a world built in God's image. The reaction to *The Age of Reason* was a sad denouement to a life of accomplishments. Although the book had little effect on the secular success of Paine's political efforts it had a great effect on him during the years following the French Revolution. His was a life devoted to making sense of the world. His intent in *The Age of Reason* was to expose what he saw as the folly of then-entrenched religious dogma. His manner was too cynical—if not blasphemous—for his contemporaries and they shunned him for it. At the end of his life, Paine was a social and religious outcast in the freest society on earth—the one that he had helped to create.

About the Author

THOMAS PAINE was born in England in 1737, the son of a Quaker. After a brief education, he worked for his father and then for the British government in a tax office. In 1774, after several incidents that left Paine's government career in question (he was twice dismissed from public employment) he met Benjamin Franklin in London who gave him letters of introduction and suggested that he immigrate to America.

Paine began writing immediately upon his arrival in the colonies, and the following year, 1775, he published *African Slavery in America*—simultaneously condemning the institution and establishing himself as a social critic and philosophical investigator. A polymath, Paine read, digested, and distilled from the writings of others his philosophical foundation. Upon this base he passionately constructed his own ideas and conclusions, formed from what he himself knew to be right and valid.

Common Sense, which initially sold more than 150,000 copies, and ultimately passed the half million mark (the equivalent today of 40 million or more books) established Paine's influence on the evolving rebellion against England and became a core resource for American revolutionaries during the events of the next decade. Paine's dedication to the cause was unquestioned—he donated all profits from the sale of *Common Sense* to the sometimes ill-equipped and undertrained American army—and he served in the front lines of George Washington's forces from the summer of 1776 until the spring of 1777. It was during this period that he wrote the first section of *The Crisis*, the last chapter of which appeared in 1783. After his military service Paine worked as secretary of the Committee of Foreign Affairs in the national government. He lost that position, however, again through bad judgment; in spite of those difficulties, he subsequently served as a clerk of the Pennsylvania Assembly for almost a decade.

In 1787 Paine traveled back to England but two years later became engrossed in the revolution in France. His third political manifesto, *The Rights of Man* (1791), a denunciation of Edmund Burke's critical *Reflections on the Revolution in France* (1790), evolved from his belief that Burke was wrong in forcing monarchy on each new generation. *Rights* further elucidates the ideas Paine had formed during the American Revolution. Paine was elected to the French National

Convention in 1791 but was imprisoned in 1793 during the regime of Maximilien Robespierre (1758–1794), leader of the Jacobins who had taken over the government subsequent to the fall of the monarchy. Paine's jailing came because he had voted against the execution of the dethroned king Louis XVI (so much for free speech and democratic sovereignty in France). He was scheduled to die on the guillotine, but because of a clerical error the mark on his open cell door was incorrectly observed and he was spared execution. (Robespierre was not so lucky, falling to the guillotine in 1794.)

The Age of Reason was published during Paine's imprisonment. A steadfast attack on what Paine described as the Bible's primitive superstitions, it was written in praise of the achievements of the Enlightenment; it was because of this book that Paine was accused of being an atheist. But he was not; he was a deist who sought after a religion of reason and of intellectual integrity. After his release from prison he stayed in France until 1802 when he crossed the Atlantic yet again. In the United States he was faced with the charge of being a heretic. What he had done for the American Revolution was ignored. He was mystified that the reputation he had made as a patriot had been superseded by his infamy as the author of *The Age of Reason*. After his death in New York City on June 8, 1809, the newspapers read, "He had lived long, did some good and much harm," but Paine's importance and reputation have deservedly undergone substantial rehabilitation since that time.

3

After reading John Locke and Thomas Paine, the next logical step in understanding the construction of the American experiment is to digest the Declaration of Independence itself. For this reason, the Declaration and, a little later, the Constitution of the United States both appear in the text where their presence is most needed—not at the end as part of an appendix where they most likely will not be read. The posting of these documents within the text is done to emphasize that they do not just hold an iconic place in our history, but that both are yet living parts of our world. The distillation of Locke's and Paine's contentions (and that of many other authors) into the words of the Declaration and the Constitution gives the reader the opportunity to grasp what drove the thoughts and actions of men of the mid-eighteenth century.

Once becoming familiar with the intensity of their comprehensions, a declaration of independence becomes the logical end-point to what they were experiencing. The final sentence of their declaration should magnify the current reader's understanding of the dedication of the participants and how much they put at risk. It should also bring forth a stark awareness of what has been done for, and given to, those of us today who enjoy the freedom these men so clearly understood.

The Declaration of Independence of the Thirteen Colonies

In CONGRESS, July 4, 1776

The unanimous Declaration of the thirteen united States of America,

When in the Course of human events, it becomes necessary for one people to dissolve the political bands which have connected them with another, and to assume among the powers of the earth, the separate and equal station to which the Laws of Nature and of Nature's God entitle them, a decent respect to the opinions of mankind requires that they should declare the causes which impel them to the separation.

We hold these truths to be self-evident, that all men are created equal, that they are endowed by their Creator with certain unalienable Rights, that among these are Life, Liberty and the pursuit of Happiness. —That to secure these rights, Governments are instituted among Men, deriving their just powers from the consent of the governed, —That whenever any Form of Government becomes destructive of these ends, it is the Right of the People to alter or to abolish it, and to institute new Government, laying its foundation on such principles and organizing its powers in such form, as to them shall seem most likely to effect their Safety and Happiness. Prudence, indeed, will dictate that Governments long established should not be changed for light and transient causes; and accordingly all experience hath shewn, that mankind are more disposed to suffer, while evils are sufferable, than to right themselves by abolishing the forms to which they are accustomed. But when a long train of abuses and usurpations, pursuing invariably the same Object evinces a design to reduce them under absolute Despotism, it is their right, it is their duty, to throw off such Government, and to provide new Guards for their future security. —Such has been the patient sufferance of these Colonies; and such is now the necessity which constrains them to alter their former Systems of Government. The history of the present King of Great Britain [George III] is a history of repeated injuries and usurpations, all having in direct object the establishment of an absolute Tyranny over these States. To prove this, let Facts be submitted to a candid world.

He has refused his Assent to Laws, the most wholesome and necessary for the public good.

He has forbidden his Governors to pass Laws of immediate and pressing importance, unless suspended in their operation till his Assent should be obtained; and when so suspended, he has utterly neglected to attend to them.

He has refused to pass other Laws for the accommodation of large districts of people, unless those people would relinquish the right of Representation in the Legislature, a right inestimable to them and formidable to tyrants only.

He has called together legislative bodies at places unusual, uncomfortable, and distant from the depository of their public Records, for the sole purpose of fatiguing them into compliance with his measures.

He has dissolved Representative Houses repeatedly, for opposing with manly firmness his invasions on the rights of the people.

He has refused for a long time, after such dissolutions, to cause others to be elected; whereby the Legislative powers, incapable of Annihilation, have returned to the People at large for their exercise; the State remaining in the mean time exposed to all the dangers of invasion from without, and convulsions within.

He has endeavoured to prevent the population of these States; for that purpose obstructing the Laws for Naturalization of Foreigners; refusing to pass others to encourage their migrations hither, and raising the conditions of new Appropriations of Lands.

He has obstructed the Administration of Justice, by refusing his Assent to Laws for establishing Judiciary powers.

He has made Judges dependent on his Will alone, for the tenure of their offices, and the amount and payment of their salaries.

He has erected a multitude of New Offices, and sent hither swarms of Officers to harass our people, and eat out their substance.

He has kept among us, in times of peace, Standing Armies without the consent of our legislatures.

He has affected to render the Military independent of and superior to the Civil power.

He has combined with others to subject us to a jurisdiction foreign to our constitution and unacknowledged by our laws; giving his Assent to their Acts of pretended Legislation:

For Quartering large bodies of armed troops among us:

For protecting them, by a mock Trial, from punishment for any Murders which they should commit on the Inhabitants of these States:

For cutting off our Trade with all parts of the world:

For imposing Taxes on us without our Consent:

For depriving us, in many cases, of the benefits of Trial by Jury:

For transporting us beyond Seas to be tried for pretended offences:

For abolishing the free System of English Laws in a neighbouring Province, establishing therein an Arbitrary government, and enlarging its Boundaries so as to render it at once an example and fit instrument for introducing the same absolute rule into these Colonies:

For taking away our Charters, abolishing our most valuable Laws, and altering fundamentally the Forms of our Governments:

For suspending our own Legislatures, and declaring themselves invested with power to legislate for us in all cases whatsoever.

He has abdicated Government here, by declaring us out of his Protection and waging War against us.

He has plundered our seas, ravaged our Coasts, burnt our towns, and destroyed the lives of our people.

He is at this time transporting large Armies of foreign Mercenaries to compleat the works of death, desolation and tyranny, already begun with circumstances of Cruelty and perfidy scarcely paralleled in the most barbarous ages, and totally unworthy the Head of a civilized nation.

He has constrained our fellow Citizens taken Captive on the high Seas to bear Arms against their Country, to become the executioners of their friends and Brethren, or to fall themselves by their Hands.

He has excited domestic insurrections amongst us, and has endeavoured to bring on the inhabitants of our frontiers, the merciless Indian Savages, whose known rule of warfare, is an undistinguished destruction of all ages, sexes and conditions.

In every stage of these Oppressions We have Petitioned for Redress in the most humble terms: Our repeated Petitions have been answered only by repeated injury. A Prince whose character is thus marked by every act which may define a Tyrant, is unfit to be the ruler of a free people.

Nor have We been wanting in attentions to our British brethren. We have warned them from time to time of attempts by their legislature to extend an unwarrantable jurisdiction over us. We have reminded them of the circumstances of our emigration and settlement here. We have appealed to their native justice and magnanimity, and we have conjured them by the ties of our common kindred to disavow these usurpations, which, would inevitably interrupt our connections and correspondence. They too have been deaf to the voice of justice and of consanguinity. We must, therefore, acquiesce in the necessity, which denounces our Separation, and hold them, as we hold the rest of mankind, Enemies in War, in Peace Friends.

We, therefore, the Representatives of the united States of America, in General Congress, Assembled, appealing to the Supreme Judge of the world for the rectitude of our intentions, do, in the Name, and by the Authority of the good People of these Colonies, solemnly publish and declare, That these United Colonies are, and of Right ought to be Free and Independent States; that they are Absolved from all Allegiance to the British Crown, and that all political connection between them and the State of Great Britain, is and ought to be totally dissolved;

and that as Free and Independent States, they have full Power to levy War, conclude Peace, contract Alliances, establish Commerce, and to do all other Acts and Things which Independent States may of right do. And for the support of this Declaration, with a firm reliance on the protection of divine Providence, we mutually pledge to each other our Lives, our Fortunes and our sacred Honor.

The signers of the Declaration represented the new states as follows:

New Hampshire
Josiah Bartlett, William Whipple, Matthew Thornton

Massachusetts
John Hancock, Samuel Adams, John Adams, Robert Treat Paine, Elbridge Gerry

Rhode Island
Stephen Hopkins, William Ellery

Connecticut
Roger Sherman, Samuel Huntington, William Williams, Oliver Wolcott

New York
William Floyd, Philip Livingston, Francis Lewis, Lewis Morris

New Jersey
Richard Stockton, John Witherspoon, Francis Hopkinson, John Hart, Abraham Clark

Pennsylvania
Robert Morris, Benjamin Rush, Benjamin Franklin, John Morton, George Clymer, James Smith, George Taylor, James Wilson, George Ross

Delaware
Caesar Rodney, George Read, Thomas McKean

Maryland
Samuel Chase, William Paca, Thomas Stone, Charles Carroll of Carrollton

Virginia
George Wythe, Richard Henry Lee, Thomas Jefferson, Benjamin Harrison, Thomas Nelson, Jr., Francis Lightfoot Lee, Carter Braxton

North Carolina
William Hooper, Joseph Hewes, John Penn

South Carolina
Edward Rutledge, Thomas Heyward, Jr., Thomas Lynch, Jr., Arthur Middleton

Georgia
Button Gwinnett, Lyman Hall, George Walton

4

The Roots of American Order

Russell Kirk

Originally published: 1974
477 pages

OF ALL THE NECESSITIES of social construction, order comes first. It is the foundation upon which all organization is built. We strive for justice, we attempt to balance opportunity and obligations, and we expect to enjoy our rights. But without order we cannot do any of these things. Humankind has been seeking order since prehistoric hunters and gatherers discovered that cooperation (or in modern economic parlance, the division of labor) increased success.

Russell Kirk, a magnificent historian of ideas, describes the development of the concept and practice of order. This effort is not just a recounting of history useful though that would be. Kirk provides something more: his explanation of not just what works, but why.

The "why" most interested and defined Kirk. His explication of how the roots of civilized freedom came to exist rests on a simple notion, that of a transcendent moral order. The positive consequences of a moral social context appear almost limitless; the negative consequences of a society where ethical behavior is not suffused throughout are barbarism, anarchy, and ultimately totalitarianism. The differences are as stark and as simple as that. However, it must be understood that achieving a "good" society is not even remotely as easy to do as it is to describe.

Kirk, like the figures whom he discusses in his book, delved into the machinations of human society and came to comprehend square one: the imperfectability of man. With that as his starting point, Kirk investigates how we can nevertheless make society operate at its highest potential. He argues that although man is not perfectible, and although we cannot successfully legislate morality, we can understand it, teach it, and practice it. When we do, we generally achieve our societal goals. If society falls to the point of quagmire where it seems necessary to mandate morality by means of laws we are essentially fated to failure.

It becomes clear that order is something more than just rules or laws. Order consists of individuals voluntarily fulfilling their various societal duties and enjoying the concomitant rights that ensue. Today we hear incessant talk of rights, but Kirk proposes that the first business of a social order is the willing and voluntary performance of *duties*, almost as if we are bestowing gifts (not on one another, but on society as a whole). From duty fulfilled we become settled enough to begin to enjoy rights. Along with the paired reality of rights and duties Kirk notes that order comes before freedom by necessity and before justice by design. Without order there is no freedom, for unfettered freedom is nothing but anarchy; without order there is no justice, for there are no agreed-upon and common rules by which to judge.

Around 500 BC the Greeks recognized the idea of rights and duties as an interdependent whole. Gaining this understanding was a long journey; it did not occur seamlessly or as a product of benign logic. As Kirk notes, however, with the advent of the Greeks' awareness of mutuality a sense of public morality arose that was distinct from religiously based morality.

Rights are what we imagine, then create. Although in due time we may see them as self-evident, the Greeks understood the invariability of duties in payment for rights. As these two concepts developed in social and personal thinking an ethical if-then equation was created: if we do not meet our obligations then we jeopardize our rights—eventually to the point of rendering them meaningless, or absurd.

The austere concept of duty unadorned has been literally and universally captured in a familiar and quite un-legalistic form: the Golden Rule. Kirk offers that this rule is so utterly logical that it became the foundation of human interaction and interconnectedness in almost every society predating Christianity. The Hebrews had it long before Christ; the Chinese, Hindus, Buddhists, Islamists, Greeks, and Romans all embodied some form of it in their respective societies. The Golden Rule cannot be codified for mankind has too many facets, follows too many pathways, has too many views; this precept can only be lived. Kirk made the latter point as he traced the rule from its discovery and followed its application across the centuries. He explains that societies are living entities, continually judging, adjusting, and compromising to make our constantly evolving civil world work. Only some basic premises can be written; only the most common aspects of human relationships can be controlled by the state while the rest of life has to proceed by informal but readily apparent agreement.

In *Roots* Kirk analyzes the development of several other religious and secular principles that have been the foundation of social order. He examines the thinkers involved and their theories in seeking to understand which hypotheses worked when, and why, and which didn't. He pays particular attention to the rise and fall of Greek and Roman societies. The Greeks understood and practiced many forms of government—from direct democracy to despotic oligarchy—and they understood that any form can work so long as both the rulers and the ruled are moral. From the time of the Greeks this simple comprehension led humankind on a journey more toward morality than to perfect governance (of imperfect people). How our species probed, tested, and understood that simple truth the last three millennia is the story presented in *The Roots of American Order*.

After considering the various Greek designs Kirk proceeds to examine Roman law and society:

> Certainly the Roman understanding of the rule of law still lives in the modern world, restraining destructive impulses. This Roman concept of law and obligation . . . is permanently embedded in the American Constitution.

As he follows the success of Rome and the fall of Greece Kirk comments that the integrity of the Romans gave rise to their public impulses: "[T]hey were virtually incorruptible. The Romans may have been inferior to the Greeks in imagination and artistry, but they were a race of strong practical endowments, tireless administrators and organizers." Yet most of all, they were men of law who understood its value not just its utility. That comprehension allowed Rome to last a thousand years and to pass its lessons down to the Middle Ages frayed but understood.

The Roman strategy for order rested on a separation of political functions and a system of checks and balances between the aristocratic Senate and the people's representatives, called tribunes. Kirk notes that Roman government did not derive from abstractions but developed out of circumstances and the times. During the drafting of the U.S. Constitution the esteem of the Roman example was so high "that the framers ... would emulate the Roman model as best they could." Of course, the question immediately arises: if Rome was so good, and great, what caused its downfall? The answer, simply put, was that Rome became full of itself; it forgot its worthy separation of powers and checks and balances, and it suffered ultimately from the universal solvent—the human condition.

Kirk observes that Roman society declined into fatuity and luxury when envy displaced integrity as its defining feature. The downfall of Rome began when Julius Caesar was elected and then ruled as a dictator, with the initial approval of all involved. But autocracy was not Caesar's goal—that was cheap—he wanted to be revered as a god; an assassination soon followed.

Eventually, as the centuries ensued and as the emperors became overbearing, to combat public envy a false equality of all citizens (achieved through vain or stealthy political intrigue or sheer power) became the rule. This "equality" of citizens later (in eighteenth-century France) was transformed into the "general will," where citizen need and desire were supposedly expressed through legislative fiat. That all or even most citizens agreed with such pronouncements was often questionable, and the antidote to the imposition of legislative mandates, reflective of the alleged general will, was to limit what the legislature could do in the first instance. This was achieved by various means and ultimately found its written expression in the restraints that are core to the American Constitution These issues are discussed at length in Bertrand de Jouvenel's *On Power* (Chapter 15) and in several other synopses as well. The agglomeration of power fostered by centralized government—which, again, is supposedly an expression of the general will of the citizenry—is the primary mechanism by which citizen control of government is defeated. That this is still the case in the twenty-first century is readily apparent.

Rome collapsed as a result of the hubris of government by fiat. As Kirk explains, what the Romans came to forget was that the aim of power was not self-aggrandizement but public virtue; the prudence of respect and the reciprocity of obligation. Following Rome's demise, over the course of the Middle Ages this lesson had to be relearned again and again. The return of its salutary effects were seen most notably in the construction of the American experiment and as the missing ingredient in the French Revolution of 1789. (On this point see Friedrich von Hayek's discussion of the French Revolution (1789) in *The Constitution of Liberty* [Chapter 14].)

The path from Rome to the eighteenth century is the story of a fight for control of society between church and state and between both of these and the citizenry. These battles began with the Protestant Reformation, a reaction that flowered in the sixteenth century. The Reformation was a contest between God's law and man's, between priestly and secular rulers. It had become obvious that the church leaders of that era were more interested in temporal success than salvation. The disconnection between what the church propounded and what it practiced eventually toppled it from pretensions to authority.

But, in Kirk's phrase, there was still "a reserve of genius in Christianity," something that ensured its self-preservation by making it a counterpart to temporal society. This aptitude came to the fore in the person of John Calvin, a Swiss lawyer and theologian. Kirk contends that Calvin—probably more than any other person during the thousand years between the decline of Rome and the founding of America—created a climate where church and state could complement rather than compete with one another. His intellectual feat was the joining of religious obligation of fealty to church and clergy and Scripture with equally valuable social and civic obligations—pay your taxes, obey the civil rulers, adhere to legal precepts, etc.—and he thereby helped make a functioning society possible.

The application of the idea of responsibility to civic duty, which grew out of religious obligations, caused people to understand how order was to be achieved in both secular *and* religious affairs. Calvin's influence was so fundamental and practical that he can be credited with having helped to make order pre-eminent in the theory and the practice of Western civic construction. His reality was the antithesis of the religious corruption of the Middle Ages when dispensations for any sin could be purchased from the clergy. The incongruous and sinister religion that Christianity had become was intolerable to those who witnessed the disjunction between the words in the Bible and the conduct of priests in the public square.

Once religious corruption was made a public issue during the Protestant Reformation and the clergy were "forced" to resume pious ways, freedom of thought (that is, the clergy and the church were no longer controlling minds through religious terrorism) allowed the flowering of the Renaissance. The Reformation's intellectual revolt against thieving religious administrators (in both their temporal and spiritual aspects) became open conflict between the reformers and the clerisy. As Kirk explains the history of this era he observes that people no longer cowed by religious bullying could perceive a profound insight:

> Truth was knowable; order was real. Truth was obscured by man's follies and passions, and order was broken by man's appetites and desire for power. Yet right reason might disclose truth to men's eyes again, and order might be regained by courageous acts of will.

Kirk arguably provides too much detail in this treatise on the development of the concept of right reason from the Middle Ages through the seventeenth century. His motivation, though, was itself rational. He sought to establish an unassailable position from which to denounce the abuse of reason by the *philosophes* (the Paris "intellectuals" of the eighteenth century) during the peak of the Enlightenment. The utopian rationalism of this era was extreme; it relied upon mere abstractions—often intricately convoluted—to the detriment of an appreciation of real-world constraints. The *philosophes* focused almost exclusively on what might be, not on what was, and Kirk paints in vivid colors their myriad failed and chimerical efforts.

Kirk observes that intellectual abstractions always offer a perfect design. The problem is that man is not perfectible, only malleable. The difference between what we should do and what we actually do is measured by the yardstick of self-interest. Thus, humanity's goal over the centuries became not just to control self-interest but to direct it in a positive manner. In seeking this end, philosophers and theorists often went further intellectually than humanity's overall character could achieve. Additionally, of course, there were the *beneficial* effects of self-interest to be considered; for virtually all material progress (and much spiritual progress) has been achieved by humanity *because* of self-interest, not in spite of it.

Adam Smith, in *Wealth of Nations* (Chapter 12), defines this latter concept as "enlightened self-interest." The gist of his argument is that a person will do well for himself if he does well by others. The daily operation of enlightened self-interest in the totality of social interactions is so utterly complex that no one, not even Solomon, could write the rules for all people in all their circumstances. Accordingly, individual conduct must be largely self-regulated. And, in order for each of us to accept everyone's self-governance we must act wisely, with an enlightened self-interest that allows for the same self-interest to be practiced by those around us. This is the definition of a moral society. As Kirk demonstrates with his 2,500-year overview of human striving it is the only kind of society that can work.

Kirk's investigation of the philosophy of the Enlightenment and the Age of Reason (c. 1750–1800), when utopian ideals began to be formulated, is a prominent theme in this book. As pure reason began to be applied to human circumstances people began to imagine what could be, as opposed to what was. Utopian thinking seemed inevitable. Reason, however, cannot ultimately overcome the human condition and thus the Age of Reason could never fulfill its promise.

The boldest abuse of "reason" occurred with the French Revolution of 1789. As Alexis de Tocqueville observed, what happened at the time of the Revolution was that the idealists ran down the stairs toward equality for all but jumped out the window halfway there to get to the ground more quickly, with predictable consequences. It is important not to confuse the utopian Age of Reason with reason itself and with rationality and logic. These latter tools help us negotiate the steps from anarchy to sane civil government while navigating the human condition, and they comprise the crucial engagements with reality that the French *philosophes* tried to skip in their rush to unattainable human perfection.

The philosophies of John Locke and David Hume (late seventeenth and mid-eighteenth centuries respectively) also drew Kirk's scrutiny. Although he shared Hume's critical view of Locke's rationalism, a calm reading of Locke's *Second Treatise on Civil Government* (Chapter 1) allows a sense of just proportion to surface. Locke did not reason out the only blueprint by which humans could govern themselves. But he did study the human condition and discovered general principles with which to guide human action by means of a social framework. His goal was not to define a results-oriented system, but rather to describe a method of governance that would accommodate all the facts of human existence.

Locke was primarily rational—not formulaic or simply idealistic. Readers need to recall his time and place, his fight against monarchy, and his clear understanding of what wasn't working in order to fully appreciate Kirk's approach to Locke's achievements. A tolerance of Locke's intellectual meandering, a tolerance that Kirk regrettably didn't fully share, will perforce arise. It may be educational to pick apart historical thinkers in light of today's knowledge and understanding of history, but it may be more edifying to watch their genius advancing among the realities and the interrelationships with which they had to contend when they first deliberated.

The various social compacts or contracts of Jean Jacques Rousseau, Thomas Hobbes and Locke and others—all of which Kirk clearly analyzes—have never existed except as ephemeral visions, unattainable in practice but still useful as guides to evolutionary political interaction. In contrast, it becomes clear via Kirk's investigations and comparisons that the real-world social compact embodied in the conciseness of the Golden Rule and the enlightened self-interest of Adam Smith is the contract that we must sign with one another for any social system to function. Some theorists may attempt to convolute these simple observations with typical intellectual hubris but when they are put to the realities of life it is somewhat obvious how well they work.

The utopian goals of the Age of Reason, despite the anomaly of its name, were rationalized visions untempered with factual considerations. Such visions eventuated in the massive destruction embodied in the socialism and communism of the nineteenth and twentieth centuries. These and other totalitarian constructs suffered foreordained failure because they made allowances for neither economic incentives nor intractable vices that have ever motivated human behavior. The rationalists, whom Kirk rightly criticized, denied progress as a goal and focused only on a supposed equality of result. While immediately attainable in theory a utopian equality of result can no more be brought into existence than can Merlin, the medieval sorcerer, bring the sun to a stop in its track.

In *Roots*, Kirk stresses historical personalities and their understanding of their own times. He singles out specific individuals for the good or ill that they accomplished. Kirk's studies enabled him to weave the story of government and morality with factual reference points; he considers the ethical behavior that is at the base of any formulation of governance and he finds the seeds that ultimately blossomed into a coherent political theory and platform.

As Kirk reveals humanity's history of government he hits a core note:

> [T]he lust for power is rooted in the corrupt nature of mankind. If that lust is not restrained by morality, then it will be kept in bounds only by force and a master.

His generally dim view of human nature, or the human condition, should not mark Kirk as a simplistic thinker. He saw the failings of our species as less than inevitable yet more than mischance. This was why he studied order as the basic condition of social existence. He contends that a justly ordered society can be established only through a truly universal ethical insight, almost inevitably grounded in a strong religious experience. Significantly enough, although the migrants who ventured to America did so for myriad reasons, all had firm religious underpinnings and this foundation allowed an ordered society to develop. As Alexis de Tocqueville concisely observes of America's first immigrants:

> They all differ in respect to the worship which is due to the Creator; but they all agree in respect to the duties which are due from man to man.... While the law permits the Americans to do what they please, religion prevents them from conceiving, and forbids them to commit, what is rash or unjust.

This volume presents a study of the development of the understanding of order: common, rational, religious, and ultimately unbending. Kirk describes a continuum that is a bright spot in the human story. His rendition of this tale recounts important events that transpired and elucidates why. As Kirk succinctly comments, apropos of history, we need to "judge this path by its successes rather than its failures." The combination of liberty and law is not easily achieved. To ensure the best chance for both conditions, the founders of the American experience leaned toward the side of order bolstered by guided self-control of the human condition. Today, as Kirk observes, there may be too much importance attached to laws and too little to mores. The modern, historically unknown demand for proliferating "rights" could be better served by greater understanding and adherence to one's own duties and the rights of others.

If one takes only a single concrete idea away from this work it should be that although order is the foundation of a successful social construct, order cannot be defined by words—much less laws. Order is truly founded in the reciprocal understanding of how we all fit together; it operates on a willingness to extend trust to others, that they will do unto us as they would have us do unto them. Kirk intones that such order, as signified by the preposition "unto," implies that we serve one another willingly, out of mutual gratitude, not solely because of duty.

A society as economically, socially, and psychologically complex as ours, with its myriad and ephemeral relationships, cannot be described adequately in any single manner. Nor can it be reduced to statute. Indeed, as is obvious, the more government tries to proscribe the bounds and limits of our conduct the less free society becomes. If we cannot achieve a free society on our own perhaps it cannot be done, for all modes of public constraint eventually accede to virtually totalitarian demands for comprehensive politically correct administrative refereeing and judicial finality. Ultimately, this results in an intolerable smothering of both the good will and the necessary voluntary cooperation that allow a society to work. There is an inverse relation between the written rules, statutes, and injunctions that exist and the free society toward which we strive.

About the Author

RUSSELL KIRK was born in 1918 in rural Michigan, an area he called home throughout his life. He was a consummate thinker, acknowledged as such by the media of his day and of ours. Recognition of his talents and lessons came early and continued throughout his life. He received his education at Michigan Agricultural College (reconstituted later as Michigan State University) and Duke University. He wrote about so many subjects in so many disciplines that to list them all would risk losing the forest for the trees. He wrote fiction as well as insight and commentary and he received awards in both fields. *The Conservative Mind* (Chapter 37), his best-known work, changed thinking about political reasoning in the mid-twentieth century. It still ranks as one of the key books of the conservative canon. Vindication for his life's work, in the elections of Margaret Thatcher and Ronald Reagan, made Kirk's early years of political philosophical struggle seem prescient.

Kirk was a professor at Michigan State University until the decline of educational standards led him to return to his home in the northern part of the state, the place where he was most comfortable and productive. Kirk died in 1994 but not before completing his autobiography, *The Sword of Imagination*, a book through which interested readers can begin to appreciate the breadth of his knowledge and understanding.

5

The U.S. Constitution is a legal document but its precepts are simple, and easy to understand. The reader should not be daunted by its magnificence or the reverence in which it is held. Most important, it should be read start to finish. Almost all of what First Principles *discusses is based on the contents of this document and the Declaration of Independence. It is reprinted here not for decoration, but so the reader can acquaint himself with its contents and thereby understand the political battles of the ages and the political necessities of any society. To obtain full-value from reading* First Principles, *comprehending the Constitution itself, before the rest of the synopses are read, is essential.*

The Constitution of the United States

We the People of the United States, in Order to form a more perfect Union, establish Justice, insure domestic Tranquility, provide for the common defence, promote the general Welfare, and secure the Blessings of Liberty to ourselves and our Posterity, do ordain and establish this Constitution for the United States of America.

Article I

Section 1 All legislative Powers herein granted shall be vested in a Congress of the United States, which shall consist of a Senate and House of Representatives.

Section 2 The House of Representatives shall be composed of Members chosen every second Year by the People of the several States, and the Electors in each State shall have the Qualifications requisite for Electors of the most numerous Branch of the State Legislature.

No Person shall be a Representative who shall not have attained to the Age of twenty five Years, and been seven Years a Citizen of the

United States, and who shall not, when elected, be an Inhabitant of that State in which he shall be chosen.

Representatives and direct Taxes shall be apportioned among the several States which may be included within this Union, according to their respective Numbers, which shall be determined by adding to the whole Number of free Persons, including those bound to Service for a Term of Years, and excluding Indians not taxed, three fifths of all other Persons. The actual Enumeration shall be made within three Years after the first Meeting of the Congress of the United States, and within every subsequent Term of ten Years, in such Manner as they shall by Law direct. The Number of Representatives shall not exceed one for every thirty Thousand, but each State shall have at Least one Representative; and until such enumeration shall be made, the State of New Hampshire shall be entitled to chuse three, Massachusetts eight, Rhode Island and Providence Plantations one, Connecticut five, New York six, New Jersey four, Pennsylvania eight, Delaware one, Maryland six, Virginia ten, North Carolina five, South Carolina five and Georgia three.

When vacancies happen in the Representation from any State, the Executive Authority thereof shall issue Writs of Election to fill such Vacancies.

The House of Representatives shall chuse their Speaker and other Officers; and shall have the sole Power of Impeachment.

Section 3 The Senate of the United States shall be composed of two Senators from each State, chosen by the Legislature thereof, for six Years; and each Senator shall have one Vote.

Immediately after they shall be assembled in Consequence of the first Election, they shall be divided as equally as may be into three Classes. The Seats of the Senators of the first Class shall be vacated at the Expiration of the second Year, of the second Class at the Expiration of the fourth Year, and of the third Class at the Expiration of the sixth Year, so that one third may be chosen every second Year; and if Vacancies happen by Resignation, or otherwise, during the Recess of the Legislature of any State, the Executive thereof may make temporary Appointments until the next Meeting of the Legislature, which shall then fill such Vacancies.

No person shall be a Senator who shall not have attained to the Age of thirty Years, and been nine Years a Citizen of the United States, and who shall not, when elected, be an Inhabitant of that State for which he shall be chosen.

The Vice President of the United States shall be President of the Senate, but shall have no Vote, unless they be equally divided.

The Senate shall chuse their other Officers, and also a President pro tempore, in the absence of the Vice President, or when he shall exercise the Office of President of the United States.

The Senate shall have the sole Power to try all Impeachments. When sitting for that Purpose, they shall be on Oath or Affirmation. When the President of the United States is tried, the Chief Justice shall preside: And no Person shall be convicted without the Concurrence of two thirds of the Members present.

Judgment in Cases of Impeachment shall not extend further than to removal from Office, and disqualification to hold and enjoy any Office of honor, Trust or Profit under the United States: but the Party convicted shall nevertheless be liable and subject to Indictment, Trial, Judgment and Punishment, according to Law.

Section 4 The Times, Places and Manner of holding Elections for Senators and Representatives, shall be prescribed in each State by the Legislature thereof; but the Congress may at any time by Law make or alter such Regulations, except as to the Place of Chusing Senators.

The Congress shall assemble at least once in every Year, and such Meeting shall be on the first Monday in December, unless they shall by Law appoint a different Day.

Section 5 Each House shall be the Judge of the Elections, Returns and Qualifications of its own Members, and a Majority of each shall constitute a Quorum to do Business; but a smaller number may adjourn from day to day, and may be authorized to compel the Attendance of absent Members, in such Manner, and under such Penalties as each House may provide.

Each House may determine the Rules of its Proceedings, punish its Members for disorderly Behavior, and, with the Concurrence of two-thirds, expel a Member.

Each House shall keep a Journal of its Proceedings, and from time to time publish the same, excepting such Parts as may in their Judgment require Secrecy; and the Yeas and Nays of the Members of either House on any question shall, at the Desire of one fifth of those Present, be entered on the Journal.

Neither House, during the Session of Congress, shall, without the Consent of the other, adjourn for more than three days, nor to any other Place than that in which the two Houses shall be sitting.

Section 6 The Senators and Representatives shall receive a Compensation for their Services, to be ascertained by Law, and paid out of the Treasury of the United States. They shall in all Cases, except Treason, Felony and Breach of the Peace, be privileged from Arrest during their Attendance at the Session of their respective Houses, and in going to and returning from the same; and for any Speech or Debate in either House, they shall not be questioned in any other Place.

No Senator or Representative shall, during the Time for which he was elected, be appointed to any civil Office under the Authority of the United States which shall have been created, or the Emoluments whereof shall have been increased during such time; and no Person holding any Office under the United States, shall be a Member of either House during his Continuance in Office.

Section 7 All bills for raising Revenue shall originate in the House of Representatives; but the Senate may propose or concur with Amendments as on other Bills. Every Bill which shall have passed the House of Representatives and the Senate, shall, before it become a Law, be presented to the President of the United States; If he approve he shall sign it, but if not he shall return it, with his Objections to that House in which it shall have originated, who shall enter the Objections at large on their Journal, and proceed to reconsider it. If after such Reconsideration two thirds of that House shall agree to pass the Bill, it shall be sent, together with the Objections, to the other House, by which it shall likewise be reconsidered, and if approved by two thirds of that House, it shall become a Law. But in all such Cases the Votes of both Houses shall be determined by Yeas and Nays, and the Names of the Persons voting for and against the Bill shall be entered on the Journal of each House respectively. If any Bill shall not be returned by the President within ten Days (Sundays excepted) after it shall have been presented to him, the Same shall be a Law, in like Manner as if he had signed it, unless the Congress by their Adjournment prevent its Return, in which Case it shall not be a Law.

Every Order, Resolution, or Vote to which the Concurrence of the Senate and House of Representatives may be necessary (except on a question of Adjournment) shall be presented to the President of the United States; and before the Same shall take Effect, shall be approved by him, or being disapproved by him, shall be repassed by two thirds of the Senate and House of Representatives, according to the Rules and Limitations prescribed in the Case of a Bill.

Section 8 The Congress shall have Power To lay and collect Taxes, Duties, Imposts and Excises, to pay the Debts and provide for the common Defence and general Welfare of the United States; but all Duties, Imposts and Excises shall be uniform throughout the United States;

To borrow money on the credit of the United States;

To regulate Commerce with foreign Nations, and among the several States, and with the Indian Tribes;

To establish an uniform Rule of Naturalization, and uniform Laws on the subject of Bankruptcies throughout the United States;

To coin Money, regulate the Value thereof, and of foreign Coin, and fix the Standard of Weights and Measures;

To provide for the Punishment of counterfeiting the Securities and current Coin of the United States;

To establish Post Offices and Post Roads;

To promote the Progress of Science and useful Arts, by securing for limited Times to Authors and Inventors the exclusive Right to their respective Writings and Discoveries;

To constitute Tribunals inferior to the supreme Court;

To define and punish Piracies and Felonies committed on the high Seas, and Offenses against the Law of Nations;

To declare War, grant Letters of Marque and Reprisal, and make Rules concerning Captures on Land and Water;

To raise and support Armies, but no Appropriation of Money to that Use shall be for a longer Term than two Years;

To provide and maintain a Navy;

To make Rules for the Government and Regulation of the land and naval Forces;

To provide for calling forth the Militia to execute the Laws of the Union, suppress Insurrections and repel Invasions;

To provide for organizing, arming, and disciplining the Militia, and for governing such Part of them as may be employed in the Service of the United States, reserving to the States respectively, the Appointment of the Officers, and the Authority of training the Militia according to the discipline prescribed by Congress;

To exercise exclusive Legislation in all Cases whatsoever, over such District (not exceeding ten Miles square) as may, by Cession of particular States, and the acceptance of Congress, become the Seat of the Government of the United States, and to exercise like Authority over all Places purchased by the Consent of the Legislature of the State in which the Same shall be, for the Erection of Forts, Magazines, Arsenals, dock-Yards, and other needful Buildings; And

To make all Laws which shall be necessary and proper for carrying into Execution the foregoing Powers, and all other Powers vested by this Constitution in the Government of the United States, or in any Department or Officer thereof.

Section 9 The Migration or Importation of such Persons as any of the States now existing shall think proper to admit, shall not be prohibited by the Congress prior to the Year one thousand eight hundred and eight, but a tax or duty may be imposed on such Importation, not exceeding ten dollars for each Person.

The privilege of the Writ of Habeas Corpus shall not be suspended, unless when in Cases of Rebellion or Invasion the public Safety may require it.

No Bill of Attainder or ex post facto Law shall be passed.

No capitation, or other direct, Tax shall be laid, unless in Proportion to the Census or Enumeration herein before directed to be taken.

No Tax or Duty shall be laid on Articles exported from any State.

No Preference shall be given by any Regulation of Commerce or Revenue to the Ports of one State over those of another: nor shall Vessels bound to, or from, one State, be obliged to enter, clear, or pay Duties in another.

No Money shall be drawn from the Treasury, but in Consequence of Appropriations made by Law; and a regular Statement and Account of the Receipts and Expenditures of all public Money shall be published from time to time.

No Title of Nobility shall be granted by the United States: And no Person holding any Office of Profit or Trust under them, shall, without the Consent of the Congress, accept of any present, Emolument, Office, or Title, of any kind whatever, from any King, Prince or foreign State.

Section 10 No State shall enter into any Treaty, Alliance, or Confederation; grant Letters of Marque and Reprisal; coin Money; emit Bills of Credit; make any Thing but gold and silver Coin a Tender in Payment of Debts; pass any Bill of Attainder, ex post facto Law, or Law impairing the Obligation of Contracts, or grant any Title of Nobility.

No State shall, without the Consent of the Congress, lay any Imposts or Duties on Imports or Exports, except what may be absolutely necessary for executing it's inspection Laws: and the net Produce of all Duties and Imposts, laid by any State on Imports or Exports, shall be for the Use of the Treasury of the United States; and all such Laws shall be subject to the Revision and Controul of the Congress.

No State shall, without the Consent of Congress, lay any duty of Tonnage, keep Troops, or Ships of War in time of Peace, enter into any Agreement or Compact with another State, or with a foreign Power, or engage in War, unless actually invaded, or in such imminent Danger as will not admit of delay.

ARTICLE II

Section 1 The executive Power shall be vested in a President of the United States of America. He shall hold his Office during the Term of four Years, and, together with the Vice President chosen for the same Term, be elected, as follows:

Each State shall appoint, in such Manner as the Legislature thereof may direct, a Number of Electors, equal to the whole Number of Senators and Representatives to which the State may be entitled in the Congress: but no Senator or Representative, or Person holding an Office of Trust or Profit under the United States, shall be appointed an Elector.

The Electors shall meet in their respective States, and vote by Ballot for two persons, of whom one at least shall not be an Inhabitant of the same State with themselves. And they shall make a List of all the Persons voted for, and of the Number of Votes for each; which List they shall sign and certify, and transmit sealed to the Seat of the Government of the United States, directed to the President of the Senate. The President of the Senate shall, in the Presence of the Senate and House of Representatives, open all the Certificates, and the Votes shall then be counted. The Person having the greatest Number of Votes shall be the President, if such Number be a Majority of the whole Number of Electors appointed; and if there be more than one who have such

Majority, and have an equal Number of Votes, then the House of Representatives shall immediately chuse by Ballot one of them for President; and if no Person have a Majority, then from the five highest on the List the said House shall in like Manner chuse the President. But in chusing the President, the Votes shall be taken by States, the Representation from each State having one Vote; a quorum for this Purpose shall consist of a Member or Members from two-thirds of the States, and a Majority of all the States shall be necessary to a Choice. In every Case, after the Choice of the President, the Person having the greatest Number of Votes of the Electors shall be the Vice President. But if there should remain two or more who have equal Votes, the Senate shall chuse from them by Ballot the Vice President.

The Congress may determine the Time of chusing the Electors, and the Day on which they shall give their Votes; which Day shall be the same throughout the United States.

No person except a natural born Citizen, or a Citizen of the United States, at the time of the Adoption of this Constitution, shall be eligible to the Office of President; neither shall any Person be eligible to that Office who shall not have attained to the Age of thirty-five Years, and been fourteen Years a Resident within the United States.

In Case of the Removal of the President from Office, or of his Death, Resignation, or Inability to discharge the Powers and Duties of the said Office, the same shall devolve on the Vice President, and the Congress may by Law provide for the Case of Removal, Death, Resignation or Inability, both of the President and Vice President, declaring what Officer shall then act as President, and such Officer shall act accordingly, until the Disability be removed, or a President shall be elected.

The President shall, at stated Times, receive for his Services, a Compensation, which shall neither be increased nor diminished during the Period for which he shall have been elected, and he shall not receive within that Period any other Emolument from the United States, or any of them.

Before he enter on the Execution of his Office, he shall take the following Oath or Affirmation: "I do solemnly swear (or affirm) that I will faithfully execute the Office of President of the United States, and will to the best of my Ability, preserve, protect and defend the Constitution of the United States."

Section 2 The President shall be Commander in Chief of the Army and Navy of the United States, and of the Militia of the several States, when called into the actual Service of the United States; he may require the Opinion, in writing, of the principal Officer in each of the executive Departments, upon any subject relating to the Duties of their respective Offices, and he shall have Power to Grant Reprieves and Pardons for Offenses against the United States, except in Cases of Impeachment.

He shall have Power, by and with the Advice and Consent of the Senate, to make Treaties, provided two thirds of the Senators present concur; and he shall nominate, and by and with the Advice and Consent of the Senate, shall appoint Ambassadors, other public Ministers and Consuls, Judges of the supreme Court, and all other Officers of the United States, whose Appointments are not herein otherwise provided for, and which shall be established by Law: but the Congress may by Law vest the Appointment of such inferior Officers, as they think proper, in the President alone, in the Courts of Law, or in the Heads of Departments.

The President shall have Power to fill up all Vacancies that may happen during the Recess of the Senate, by granting Commissions which shall expire at the End of their next Session.

Section 3 He shall from time to time give to the Congress Information of the State of the Union, and recommend to their Consideration such Measures as he shall judge necessary and expedient; he may, on extraordinary Occasions, convene both Houses, or either of them, and in Case of Disagreement between them, with Respect to the Time of Adjournment, he may adjourn them to such Time as he shall think proper; he shall receive Ambassadors and other public Ministers; he shall take Care that the Laws be faithfully executed, and shall Commission all the Officers of the United States.

Section 4 The President, Vice President and all civil Officers of the United States, shall be removed from Office on Impeachment for, and Conviction of, Treason, Bribery, or other high Crimes and Misdemeanors.

Article III

Section 1 The judicial Power of the United States, shall be vested in one supreme Court, and in such inferior Courts as the Congress may from time to time ordain and establish. The Judges, both of the supreme and inferior Courts, shall hold their Offices during good Behavior, and shall, at stated Times, receive for their Services a Compensation which shall not be diminished during their Continuance in Office.

Section 2 The judicial Power shall extend to all Cases, in Law and Equity, arising under this Constitution, the Laws of the United States, and Treaties made, or which shall be made, under their Authority; to all Cases affecting Ambassadors, other public Ministers and Consuls; to all Cases of admiralty and maritime Jurisdiction; to Controversies to which the United States shall be a Party; to Controversies between two or more States; between a State and Citizens of another State; between Citizens of different States; between Citizens of the same State claiming Lands under Grants of different States, and between a State, or the Citizens thereof, and foreign States, Citizens or Subjects.

In all Cases affecting Ambassadors, other public Ministers and Consuls, and those in which a State shall be Party, the supreme Court shall have original Jurisdiction. In all the other Cases before mentioned, the supreme Court shall have appellate Jurisdiction, both as to Law and Fact, with such Exceptions, and under such Regulations as the Congress shall make.

The Trial of all Crimes, except in Cases of Impeachment, shall be by Jury; and such Trial shall be held in the State where the said Crimes shall have been committed; but when not committed within any State, the Trial shall be at such Place or Places as the Congress may by Law have directed.

Section 3 Treason against the United States, shall consist only in levying War against them, or in adhering to their Enemies, giving them Aid and Comfort. No Person shall be convicted of Treason unless on the Testimony of two Witnesses to the same overt Act, or on Confession in open Court.

The Congress shall have power to declare the Punishment of Treason, but no Attainder of Treason shall work Corruption of Blood, or Forfeiture except during the Life of the Person attainted.

ARTICLE IV

Section 1 Full Faith and Credit shall be given in each State to the public Acts, Records, and judicial Proceedings of every other State. And the Congress may by general Laws prescribe the Manner in which such Acts, Records and Proceedings shall be proved, and the Effect thereof.

Section 2 The Citizens of each State shall be entitled to all Privileges and Immunities of Citizens in the several States.

A Person charged in any State with Treason, Felony, or other Crime, who shall flee from Justice, and be found in another State, shall on demand of the executive Authority of the State from which he fled, be delivered up, to be removed to the State having Jurisdiction of the Crime.

No Person held to Service or Labour in one State, under the Laws thereof, escaping into another, shall, in Consequence of any Law or Regulation therein, be discharged from such Service or Labour, But shall be delivered up on Claim of the Party to whom such Service or Labour may be due.

Section 3 New States may be admitted by the Congress into this Union; but no new States shall be formed or erected within the Jurisdiction of any other State; nor any State be formed by the Junction of two or more States, or parts of States, without the Consent of the Legislatures of the States concerned as well as of the Congress.

The Congress shall have Power to dispose of and make all needful Rules and Regulations respecting the Territory or other Property belonging to the United States; and nothing in this Constitution shall be so construed as to Prejudice any Claims of the United States, or of any particular State.

Section 4 The United States shall guarantee to every State in this Union a Republican Form of Government, and shall protect each of them against Invasion; and on Application of the Legislature, or of the Executive (when the Legislature cannot be convened) against domestic Violence.

ARTICLE V

The Congress, whenever two thirds of both Houses shall deem it necessary, shall propose Amendments to this Constitution, or, on the Application of the Legislatures of two thirds of the several States, shall call a Convention for proposing Amendments, which, in either Case, shall be valid to all Intents and Purposes, as part of this Constitution, when ratified by the Legislatures of three fourths of the several States, or by Conventions in three fourths thereof, as the one or the other Mode of Ratification may be proposed by the Congress;

Provided that no Amendment which may be made prior to the Year One thousand eight hundred and eight shall in any Manner affect the first and fourth Clauses in the Ninth Section of the first Article; and that no State, without its Consent, shall be deprived of its equal Suffrage in the Senate.

Article VI

All Debts contracted and Engagements entered into, before the Adoption of this Constitution, shall be as valid against the United States under this Constitution, as under the Confederation.

This Constitution, and the Laws of the United States which shall be made in Pursuance thereof; and all Treaties made, or which shall be made, under the Authority of the United States, shall be the supreme Law of the Land; and the Judges in every State shall be bound thereby, any Thing in the Constitution or Laws of any State to the Contrary notwithstanding.

The Senators and Representatives before mentioned, and the Members of the several State Legislatures, and all executive and judicial Officers, both of the United States and of the several States, shall be bound by Oath or Affirmation, to support this Constitution; but no religious Test shall ever be required as a Qualification to any Office or public Trust under the United States.

Article VII

The Ratification of the Conventions of nine States, shall be sufficient for the Establishment of this Constitution between the States so ratifying the Same.

done in Convention by the Unanimous Consent of the States present the Seventeenth Day of September in the Year of our Lord one thousand seven hundred and Eighty seven and of the Independence of the United States of America the Twelfth.

IN WITNESS whereof We have hereunto subscribed our Names.
Go. Washington – President and deputy from Virginia
New Hampshire – John Langdon, Nicholas Gilman
Massachusetts – Nathaniel Gorham, Rufus King
Connecticut – Wm Saml Johnson, Roger Sherman
New York – Alexander Hamilton
New Jersey – Wil Livingston, David Brearley, Wm Paterson, Jona. Dayton
Pensylvania – B Franklin, Thomas Mifflin, Robt Morris, Geo. Clymer, Thos FitzSimons, Jared Ingersoll, James Wilson, Gouv Morris
Delaware – Geo. Read, Gunning Bedford jun, John Dickinson, Richard Bassett, Jaco. Broom
Maryland – James McHenry, Dan of St Tho Jenifer, Danl Carroll
Virginia – John Blair, James Madison Jr.
North Carolina – Wm Blount, Richd Dobbs Spaight, Hu Williamson
South Carolina – J. Rutledge, Charles Cotesworth Pinckney, Charles Pinckney, Pierce Butler
Georgia – William Few, Abr Baldwin

Attest William Jackson, Secretary

Amendments

Congress of the United States
begun and held at the City of New York, on Wednesday, the fourth of March, one thousand seven-hundred and eighty nine

THE conventions of a number of the states, having at the time of their adopting the Constitution, expressed a desire, in order to prevent unconstitutional or abuse of its powers, that further declaratory and restrictive clauses should be added: and as extending the ground of public confidence in the Government, will best ensure the beneficent ends of its institution

RESOLVED by the Senate and House of Representatives of the United States of America in Congress Assembled, two thirds of both Houses concurring that the following Articles be proposed to the Legislatures of the several States as amendments to the Constitution of the United States, all, or any of which articles, when ratified by three fourths of the said Legislatures, to be valid to all intents and purposes, as part of the said Constitution, viz.,

ARTICLES in addition to, and amendment of the Constitution of the United States of America, proposed by Congress and ratified by the legislatures of the several States, pursuant to the fifth Article of the original Constitution.

Amendment I
Congress shall make no law respecting an establishment of religion, or prohibiting the free exercise thereof; or abridging the freedom of speech, or of the press; or the right of the people peaceably to assemble, and to petition the Government for a redress of grievances.

Amendment II
A well regulated Militia, being necessary to the security of a free State, the right of the people to keep and bear Arms, shall not be infringed.

Amendment III
No Soldier shall, in time of peace be quartered in any house, without the consent of the Owner, nor in time of war, but in a manner to be prescribed by law.

Amendment IV
The right of the people to be secure in their persons, houses, papers, and effects, against unreasonable searches and seizures, shall not be violated, and no Warrants shall issue, but upon probable cause, supported by Oath or affirmation, and particularly describing the place to be searched, and the persons or things to be seized.

Amendment V
No person shall be held to answer for a capital, or otherwise infamous crime, unless on a presentment or indictment of a Grand Jury, except in cases arising in the land or naval forces, or in the Militia, when in actual service in time of War or public danger; nor shall any person be subject for the same offense to be twice put in jeopardy of life or limb; nor shall be compelled in any criminal case to be a witness against himself, nor be deprived of life, liberty, or property, without due process of law; nor shall private property be taken for public use, without just compensation.

Amendment VI
In all criminal prosecutions, the accused shall enjoy the right to a speedy and public trial, by an impartial jury of the State and district wherein the crime shall have been committed, which district shall have been previously ascertained by law, and to be informed of the nature and cause of the accusation; to be confronted with the witnesses against him; to have compulsory process for obtaining witnesses in his favor, and to have the Assistance of Counsel for his defence.

Amendment VII
In Suits at common law, where the value in controversy shall exceed twenty dollars, the right of trial by jury shall be preserved, and no fact tried by a jury, shall be otherwise re-examined in any Court of the United States, than according to the rules of the common law.

Amendment VIII
Excessive bail shall not be required, nor excessive fines imposed, nor cruel and unusual punishments inflicted.

Amendment IX
The enumeration in the Constitution, of certain rights, shall not be construed to deny or disparage others retained by the people.

Amendment X
The powers not delegated to the United States by the Constitution, nor prohibited by it to the States, are reserved to the States respectively, or to the people.

Amendments to the Constitution after the first ten amendments, which are known as the Bill of Rights, follow:

Amendment XI
The Judicial power of the United States shall not be construed to extend to any suit in law or equity, commenced or prosecuted against one of the United States by Citizens of another State, or by Citizens or Subjects of any Foreign State.

Amendment XII
The Electors shall meet in their respective states, and vote by ballot for President and Vice President, one of whom, at least, shall not be

an inhabitant of the same state with themselves; they shall name in their ballots the person voted for as President, and in distinct ballots the person voted for as Vice President, and they shall make distinct lists of all persons voted for as President, and of all persons voted for as Vice President and of the number of votes for each, which lists they shall sign and certify, and transmit sealed to the seat of the government of the United States, directed to the President of the Senate; The President of the Senate shall, in the presence of the Senate and House of Representatives, open all the certificates and the votes shall then be counted; The person having the greatest Number of votes for President, shall be the President, if such number be a majority of the whole number of Electors appointed; and if no person have such majority, then from the persons having the highest numbers not exceeding three on the list of those voted for as President, the House of Representatives shall choose immediately, by ballot, the President. But in choosing the President, the votes shall be taken by states, the representation from each state having one vote; a quorum for this purpose shall consist of a member or members from two-thirds of the states, and a majority of all the states shall be necessary to a choice. And if the House of Representatives shall not choose a President whenever the right of choice shall devolve upon them, before the fourth day of March next following, then the Vice President shall act as President, as in the case of the death or other constitutional disability of the President. The person having the greatest number of votes as Vice President, shall be the Vice President, if such number be a majority of the whole number of Electors appointed, and if no person have a majority, then from the two highest numbers on the list, the Senate shall choose the Vice President; a quorum for the purpose shall consist of two-thirds of the whole number of Senators, and a majority of the whole number shall be necessary to a choice. But no person constitutionally ineligible to the office of President shall be eligible to that of Vice President of the United States.

Amendment XIII
A. Neither slavery nor involuntary servitude, except as a punishment for crime whereof the party shall have been duly convicted, shall exist within the United States, or any place subject to their jurisdiction.
B. Congress shall have power to enforce this article by appropriate legislation.

Amendment XIV

1. All persons born or naturalized in the United States, and subject to the jurisdiction thereof, are citizens of the United States and of the State wherein they reside. No State shall make or enforce any law which shall abridge the privileges or immunities of citizens of the United States; nor shall any State deprive any person of life, liberty, or property, without due process of law; nor deny to any person within its jurisdiction the equal protection of the laws.
2. Representatives shall be apportioned among the several States according to their respective numbers, counting the whole number of persons in each State, excluding Indians not taxed. But when the right to vote at any election for the choice of electors for President and Vice President of the United States, Representatives in Congress, the Executive and Judicial officers of a State, or the members of the Legislature thereof, is denied to any of the male inhabitants of such State, being twenty-one years of age, and citizens of the United States, or in any way abridged, except for participation in rebellion, or other crime, the basis of representation therein shall be reduced in the proportion which the number of such male citizens shall bear to the whole number of male citizens twenty-one years of age in such State.
3. No person shall be a Senator or Representative in Congress, or elector of President and Vice President, or hold any office, civil or military, under the United States, or under any State, who, having previously taken an oath, as a member of Congress, or as an officer of the United States, or as a member of any State legislature, or as an executive or judicial officer of any State, to support the Constitution of the United States, shall have engaged in insurrection or rebellion against the same, or given aid or comfort to the enemies thereof. But Congress may by a vote of two-thirds of each House, remove such disability.
4. The validity of the public debt of the United States, authorized by law, including debts incurred for payment of pensions and bounties for services in suppressing insurrection or rebellion, shall not be questioned. But neither the United States nor any State shall assume or pay any debt or obligation incurred in aid of insurrection or rebellion against the United States, or any claim for the loss or emancipation of any slave; but all such debts, obligations and claims shall be held illegal and void.
5. The Congress shall have power to enforce, by appropriate legislation, the provisions of this article.

Amendment XV

1. The right of citizens of the United States to vote shall not be denied or abridged by the United States or by any State on account of race, color, or previous condition of servitude.
2. The Congress shall have power to enforce this article by appropriate legislation.

Amendment XVI

The Congress shall have power to lay and collect taxes on incomes, from whatever source derived, without apportionment among the several States, and without regard to any census or enumeration.

Amendment XVII

The Senate of the United States shall be composed of two Senators from each State, elected by the people thereof, for six years; and each Senator shall have one vote. The electors in each State shall have the qualifications requisite for electors of the most numerous branch of the State legislatures. When vacancies happen in the representation of any State in the Senate, the executive authority of such State shall issue writs of election to fill such vacancies: Provided, That the legislature of any State may empower the executive thereof to make temporary appointments until the people fill the vacancies by election as the legislature may direct. This amendment shall not be so construed as to affect the election or term of any Senator chosen before it becomes valid as part of the Constitution.

Amendment XVIII

1. After one year from the ratification of this article the manufacture, sale, or transportation of intoxicating liquors within, the importation thereof into, or the exportation thereof from the United States and all territory subject to the jurisdiction thereof for beverage purposes is hereby prohibited.
2. The Congress and the several States shall have concurrent power to enforce this article by appropriate legislation.
3. This article shall be inoperative unless it shall have been ratified as an amendment to the Constitution by the legislatures of the several States, as provided in the Constitution, within seven years from the date of the submission hereof to the States by the Congress.

Amendment XIX

The right of citizens of the United States to vote shall not be denied or abridged by the United States or by any State on account of sex. Congress shall have power to enforce this article by appropriate legislation.

Amendment XX

1. The terms of the President and Vice President shall end at noon on the 20th day of January, and the terms of Senators and Representatives at noon on the 3d day of January, of the years in which such terms would have ended if this article had not been ratified; and the terms of their successors shall then begin.
2. The Congress shall assemble at least once in every year, and such meeting shall begin at noon on the 3d day of January, unless they shall by law appoint a different day.
3. If, at the time fixed for the beginning of the term of the President, the President elect shall have died, the Vice President elect shall become President. If a President shall not have been chosen before the time fixed for the beginning of his term, or if the President elect shall have failed to qualify, then the Vice President elect shall act as President until a President shall have qualified; and the Congress may by law provide for the case wherein neither a President elect nor a Vice President elect shall have qualified, declaring who shall then act as President, or the manner in which one who is to act shall be selected, and such person shall act accordingly until a President or Vice President shall have qualified.
4. The Congress may by law provide for the case of the death of any of the persons from whom the House of Representatives may choose a President whenever the right of choice shall have devolved upon them, and for the case of the death of any of the persons from whom the Senate may choose a Vice President whenever the right of choice shall have devolved upon them.
5. Sections 1 and 2 shall take effect on the 15th day of October following the ratification of this article.
6. This article shall be inoperative unless it shall have been ratified as an amendment to the Constitution by the legislatures of three-fourths of the several States within seven years from the date of its submission.

Amendment XXI
1. The eighteenth article of amendment to the Constitution of the United States is hereby repealed.
2. The transportation or importation into any State, Territory, or possession of the United States for delivery or use therein of intoxicating liquors, in violation of the laws thereof, is hereby prohibited.
3. The article shall be inoperative unless it shall have been ratified as an amendment to the Constitution by conventions in the several States, as provided in the Constitution, within seven years from the date of the submission hereof to the States by the Congress.

Amendment XXII
1. No person shall be elected to the office of the President more than twice, and no person who has held the office of President, or acted as President, for more than two years of a term to which some other person was elected President shall be elected to the office of the President more than once. But this Article shall not apply to any person holding the office of President, when this Article was proposed by the Congress, and shall not prevent any person who may be holding the office of President, or acting as President, during the term within which this Article becomes operative from holding the office of President or acting as President during the remainder of such term.
2. This article shall be inoperative unless it shall have been ratified as an amendment to the Constitution by the legislatures of three-fourths of the several States within seven years from the date of its submission to the States by the Congress.

Amendment XXIII
1. The District constituting the seat of Government of the United States shall appoint in such manner as the Congress may direct: A number of electors of President and Vice President equal to the whole number of Senators and Representatives in Congress to which the District would be entitled if it were a State, but in no event more than the least populous State; they shall be in addition to those appointed by the States, but they shall be considered, for the purposes of the election of President and Vice President, to be electors appointed by a State; and they shall meet in the District and perform such duties as provided by the twelfth article of amendment.
2. The Congress shall have power to enforce this article by appropriate legislation.

Amendment XXIV

1. The right of citizens of the United States to vote in any primary or other election for President or Vice President, for electors for President or Vice President, or for Senator or Representative in Congress, shall not be denied or abridged by the United States or any State by reason of failure to pay any poll tax or other tax.
2. The Congress shall have power to enforce this article by appropriate legislation.

Amendment XXV

1. In case of the removal of the President from office or of his death or resignation, the Vice President shall become President.
2. Whenever there is a vacancy in the office of the Vice President, the President shall nominate a Vice President who shall take office upon confirmation by a majority vote of both Houses of Congress.
3. Whenever the President transmits to the President pro tempore of the Senate and the Speaker of the House of Representatives his written declaration that he is unable to discharge the powers and duties of his office, and until he transmits to them a written declaration to the contrary, such powers and duties shall be discharged by the Vice President as Acting President.
4. Whenever the Vice President and a majority of either the principal officers of the executive departments or of such other body as Congress may by law provide, transmit to the President pro tempore of the Senate and the Speaker of the House of Representatives their written declaration that the President is unable to discharge the powers and duties of his office, the Vice President shall immediately assume the powers and duties of the office as Acting President. Thereafter, when the President transmits to the President pro tempore of the Senate and the Speaker of the House of Representatives his written declaration that no inability exists, he shall resume the powers and duties of his office unless the Vice President and a majority of either the principal officers of the executive department or of such other body as Congress may by law provide, transmit within four days to the President pro tempore of the Senate and the Speaker of the House of Representatives their written declaration that the President is unable to discharge the powers and duties of his office. Thereupon Congress shall decide the issue, assembling within forty eight hours for that purpose if not in session. If the Congress, within twenty one days after receipt of the latter written declaration, or, if

Congress is not in session, within twenty one days after Congress is required to assemble, determines by two thirds vote of both Houses that the President is unable to discharge the powers and duties of his office, the Vice President shall continue to discharge the same as Acting President; otherwise, the President shall resume the powers and duties of his office.

Amendment XXVI
1. The right of citizens of the United States, who are eighteen years of age or older, to vote shall not be denied or abridged by the United States or by any State on account of age.
2. The Congress shall have power to enforce this article by appropriate legislation.

Amendment XXVII
No law, varying the compensation for the services of the Senators and Representatives, shall take effect, until an election of Representatives shall have intervened.

6

The Federalist

Alexander Hamilton, John Jay, James Madison

Originally published: 1787–88
652 pages

The Federalist, a collection of newspaper articles first published in 1787–88, had a single purpose: to convince the freshly independent colonists, particularly in New York where a ratification battle was looming, that the just-drafted Constitution was the best possible design for governing the new nation.

Ever since their initial dissemination these essays have served as a guide to interpreting the Constitution's provisions and intentions. Written individually by Alexander Hamilton, John Jay, and James Madison under the joint *nom de plume* Publius, the essays expressed opinions that were far from universally accepted at the time (and many of which are equally far from universal acceptance at this time). In fact, *The Federalist* consists in large measure of responses to serious doubts about the proposed Constitution set forth by opposition writers as part of the debates over ratification in New York and other states.

Although it may appear that the arguments and points made in *The Federalist* are an old story they are quite the opposite. It is the core explication offered in these documents that is a major part of the square one *First Principles* means to explore. These eighty-five essays achieve a full explanation of what representative democracy was to be.

In 1787 newspapers, pamphlets, and books were the best tools available for communicating with literate citizens. Public speeches were useful, but reached only a small audience. It was newspapers that offered the best vehicle to engage in the war of words that ensued subsequent to the

1787 Philadelphia Convention. In New York, Governor George Clinton was vehemently opposed to a "national" or centralized government and strongly preferred a continuation of the confederated, or "federal" government embodied in the Articles of Confederation. Two of the three New York delegates had been absent from the Constitutional Convention almost from its beginning (a spurious and ineffective political ploy by the anti-federalists to devalue, even belittle, the drafting effort). The third delegate, Alexander Hamilton, spent much of the summer of 1787 in New York where he felt laying the groundwork for the upcoming ratification battle more important than efforts he might expend at the convention. In fact, in Philadelphia his views of the need for an even stronger national government than what was ultimately embodied in the Constitution were not well received. As a result of the absence of their delegates to the Constitutional Convention the people of New York had become, by default, bystanders to the whole process. Yet, at the close of the convention the state's newspapers were full of zealous and barbed rhetoric espousing the views of various vested interests. As the ratification process began the battle lines were sharply drawn.

The Federalist eventually transcended its role as propaganda and came to be regarded by many as a masterful analysis and interpretation of the Constitution, as well as a compelling overview of democratic representative government. Indeed, *The Federalist* today is known as the fourth founding document along with the Declaration of Independence, the Constitution, and the first ten amendments appended to the Constitution during the inaugural Congressional session, collectively known as The Bill of Rights. However, it is also a given that *The Federalist* neither adequately foresaw nor honestly presented all of the arguments surrounding the proposed Constitution. That it did directly explain the fundamental tenets of a new paradigm is accepted, and therein lies most of its usefulness.

Although many participants at the time *The Federalist* articles were written saw actual and potential flaws inherent in the construction of the new government, Alexander Hamilton reminded the populace that nothing anyone could design would be perfect—especially in the face of any overwhelming moral, economic, or other conflagration that could tear the country apart. That the Constitution might not withstand such an assault he found as no impediment to accepting what had been drafted. In *Federalist* Number 17 he succinctly proclaims,

> [I]t would be idle to object to a government because it could not perform impossibilities.

Although it is now well understood that the American experiment created a democratically controlled federal republic both empowered and restrained by a written constitution, this was far from clear in 1787. Of course, the concept of democracy was hardly new to the world. But the form of government created by the men of Philadelphia—with its separated powers, civil authority over the military, frequent elections, and checks and balances (between the branches of the federal government, and between the national administration and individual state governments)—created a system of shared power and equity the likes of which had never before been seen. In *The Federalist* the intentionally spare words of the Constitution are given life and meaning readily accessible to the average person. The guidance suggested by Publius was offered not only as propaganda but also truly as an explanation. Writing *The Federalist* was an intellectual exercise as much as a political one. The essays were written by the men who had been thinking and planning and discoursing on these matters for more than a decade, some for most of their lives. What they wrote was not just a news story; it was more accurately an explication of a philosophy and a system.

Few, if any, of the participants at Philadelphia were so naïve as to believe that the document they had created would control human beings. They understood an underlying factor—that the government they contrived would be no better than the citizens who were elected to administer it. It was also a given that if the citizens did not defend their rights and perform their duties the issue of the Constitution's powers or limitations would be irrelevant.

One of the most remarkable aspects of the American constitutional experiment was the youthfulness of the men who had assumed the task of creating a new country. Alexander Hamilton was only thirty years old and James Madison was thirty-six. The breadth of their political thought and their understanding of human nature enabled them to achieve something their predecessors had tried in vain to create: a system of government that allowed human spirit and ingenuity to soar while simultaneously attempting to keep in check inevitable expressions of human perfidy.

Not everything that *The Federalist*'s authors anticipated has come to pass. One of the intents of the Founders was that Congress would be populated by knowledgeable, educated, and thoughtful members—forming a sort of mirror image of the Constitutional Convention's delegates themselves. Wisdom in deliberation was the intent but such sagacity has often been absent over the ensuing centuries. When Madison wrote that the people should elect to Congress the best and wisest men—not just those of whose policies voters happened to approve—he was perhaps forgetting his own admonitions about human frailties; Madison's hope for sage Congressional discourse may have been doomed to failure by the essence of human nature and in spite of the desire and optimism he expressed during the drafting and ratification process. Even so, *The Federalist* almost always provides concise and clear interpretation of the Founders' intentions. As the years have passed these explanations have often proved defining. Without this tutelage our federal system might have taken a much different course as it matured. Reading these essays today gives each of us an opportunity to put our comprehensions to history's test and to step back from a consideration of political goals to an appreciation of political wisdom.

IT IS OF VALUE to place the Constitutional era in perspective. While the Founders sought philosophically to embark on a new venture in governance the authors of *The Federalist* and those who would be the members of the first government had to achieve the Constitution's ratification and implementation in troubled, often dangerous, times. There were many competing interests with which the citizenry had to deal. At the end of the War of Independence the country was far from unified—physically, emotionally, politically, or economically. Trade, both national and international, was disorganized; self-inflicted inflation had destroyed the currency; an economic depression existed; armed insurrection was a reality in some quarters; taxation of any type (with or without representation) was abhorred by many. Yet the national government was deeply in debt as a result of the war and required a way out of its fiscal catastrophe. If the country was to be economically or politically viable on the international stage it had to honor its financial obligations. Undermining the ability to achieve that goal were widespread factionalism and insistent claims of state sovereignty that were both constant threats to national cohesion on even the most fundamental level.

Adding to the internal woes, the Spanish government had blockaded the Mississippi River, the outlet for almost all commerce west of the Allegheny Mountains; the English had stopped traffic on the St. Lawrence River; and the treaty with Great Britain was being ignored by both sides. That the times were unstable is an understatement. The hurdles facing ratification and setting up the new government were towering. Conflicting opinions on almost every practical consideration were the rule and seemed a far greater impediment to agreement than the visible intellectual battle addressed by authors in *The Federalist*.

The overall discussion in *The Federalist*—after a core explication in the early essays of strong resolve regarding the sanctity of liberty and property—was the proper scope and role of the federal government's authority. The sovereign entity created by the Constitution was not designed in the abstract; it had in mind the America and the people of that era, and it recognized their history, their make-up, and their habits. Hamilton's resolute desire for enlarged national powers—somewhat muted in *The Federalist* but expressed more vocally at the Constitutional Convention—was vigorously and publicly opposed by others who feared the loss of local autonomy. The apprehension of the unknown in this equation hindered the forward movement the Constitution offered. At the beginning of the twenty-first century, it is still easy to feel the depth of concern extant in 1788, as today we experience the ill-effects of lost local rule, while centralized, homogenized, and aggrandized government becomes increasingly more common and steadily less effective.

There was also a great practical difficulty facing the Philadelphia Convention. The convention's charter allowed only for amendment and repair of the Articles of Confederation under which the country had operated since 1781. The specific instructions to the delegates for amendment of the Articles also held that no proposed revisions were to take effect unless the legislatures of all thirteen states agreed. As debate began, a majority of the members of the convention came to understand that no repairs to the Articles would make them work—regardless of any unanimous ratification difficulties—and that a whole new document and system of government was needed.

The core contentious issue at the convention was taxation—just as it had been at the time of the Declaration of Independence. In the ensuing eleven years it had become apparent that funding national obligations by means of voluntary state contributions, as existed under the Articles, was untenable. States either temporized on their promises of fiscal support or frankly disavowed them. The result was the devastating inflation that was inevitable when the federal government simply printed money to obtain the materiel it needed to prosecute the war.

The inequality of state contributions to the revolutionary effort—financially, materially, and in terms of manpower—had caused both envy and disdain to arise in various legislative and executive quarters, threatening union from the outset. Of course, there were many other issues that needed resolution as well, yet most of them proved capable of compromise. But two questions presented no middle ground: slavery and affording the national government the power to tax. Ultimately, each was accepted as part of the Constitution, but agreement on these two issues, and others, wasn't easy. In the end a small number of the convention attendees were so dissatisfied with the power consolidated in the new national government that they refused to sign the Constitution.

With vocal dissent among the delegates in evidence and a successful ratification process looking more dim, convention attendees reduced the number of states that had to approve the new document to nine (from the previous unanimous thirteen). They also changed the assembly in which the states would determine their approval from state legislatures to state conventions. This allowed circumvention of vested political interests that inevitably reside in legislative chambers and offered direct access to the citizens. Any state not ratifying the Constitution was free to remain an independent entity not answerable to, or protected by, the fledgling government.

The Founders ultimately created a system that was wholly new and untested. The aim of *The Federalist* was to impress Americans that this document and the government that would ensue were workable for all sections and factions within the country. Delegates to the Convention had exceeded their authority in creating the Constitution and they had to convince everyone that this course was not only the best avenue, but the only avenue.

The fact that the new document was to be subjected to approval by popularly elected state conventions—allowing the people to maintain a veto power over the efforts of the drafters—was a significant risk. These state assemblies, consisting of delegates who were far more directly responsible to their publics than are legislators today, had to be convinced to support all that had been done in the convention. Ratification was to be a straight up or down vote, no state could alter what had been agreed upon. With further compromise not possible, the all-or-nothing approval mechanism made supporters and opponents more extreme in their claims. While the tenor and the goal of the eighty-five essays of *The Federalist* in some ways matched the desperation of both the people and the times, these commentaries also had a calming effect through their well-reasoned expositions.

If one seeks a comprehensive shortcut (which we hope is not an oxymoron) to understanding the U.S. Constitution, reading *The Federalist* is that avenue. Both the wisdom and shrewdness of the Founders is on display in these essays. To understand how our government was designed to work—before the intrusion of politics—and to see how to apply governing responsibility in the face of human nature, reading *The Federalist* is truly a necessary and certainly a profitable effort.

About the Book

THE LIBERTY FUND edition of *The Federalist* is intended as a study text as well as an historical reproduction. This volume contains the main documents of the Revolutionary era, namely, the Declaration of Independence, the Articles of Confederation, and the Constitution itself. Of equal value to the text is the cross-referenced guide between *The Federalist* essays and that portion of the Constitution which any particular essay investigates and defends.

About the Authors

ALEXANDER HAMILTON (1757–1804) was a distinguished New York lawyer and revolutionary war hero, an astute businessman, and a vigorous proponent of a strong national government. The basis of this need, he believed, was the difficulty of war, trade, and finance being conducted separately by the individual states. Although Hamilton wrote more than half *The Federalist* essays, he had little input during the Constitutional Convention because his colleagues did not trust his advocacy of expansive federal power. Nevertheless, when it came time to fight for adoption of the finished product there was no one more tireless in this enterprise. Indeed, Hamilton voiced the opinion, in spite of how little the final draft reflected his own views, that the Convention should unanimously approve the completed document.

James Madison (1751–1836) was a constant member of the legislative and constitutional bodies that met and guided the new American nation throughout its formative years. Madison, as opposed to Hamilton, played the greater role at the Constitutional Convention and the majority of the final document is his work. His profound knowledge of both history and politics often, but not always, helped convince the other members of the Convention of the value of his grand outline. Once the convention concluded he too was tireless at securing adoption of the new Constitution. As a member of the House of Representatives he was instrumental in drafting and adding the Bill of Rights to the Constitution in the first congressional session—a not uncontroversial battle itself.

John Jay (1745–1829) was an experienced and influential New York attorney when the Revolution began. Although he initially sought conciliation, once the course of the new nation was set he devoted his energies entirely to the success of the effort. His experience in international affairs and his post as foreign secretary (equal to today's secretary of state) under the Articles of Confederation secured his participation in all aspects of colonial foreign relations, including the negotiation of the Treaty of Paris in 1783 which formally ended the War of Independence. During his career Jay was president of the Continental Congress and governor and chief justice of New York. He also drafted the New York Constitution in 1777. Although Jay wrote fewer of the essays (five) than did Madison or Hamilton, his prestige at the time exceeded either of theirs and so his contributions to *The Federalist* added significance to the enterprise, especially for those working behind the scenes. When the new nation was finally launched, John Jay became the first chief justice of the United States Supreme Court.

Section I

Part 2

Case Studies

7

The Law

Frederic Bastiat

Originally published: 1850
76 pages

FREDERIC BASTIAT was a pragmatist:

> See if the law takes from some person what belongs to them, and gives it to other persons to whom it does not belong. See if the law benefits one citizen at the expense of another by doing what the citizen himself cannot do without committing a crime....

> Life, liberty, and property do not exist because men have made laws. On the contrary, it is because life, liberty, and property existed beforehand that caused men to make laws in the first place.

The Law is the forerunner to Henry Hazlitt's *Economics in One Lesson* (Chapter 24) written nearly one hundred years later. These two books intersect on a broad and practical plane. *The Law* was written at a time of great upheaval in France when economic and societal paradigms were discarded wholesale without a concrete mechanism to replace what was being removed. *Economics in One Lesson* faced a similar situation, but the change was being accomplished by means of politics and legislation rather than revolution. Both authors saw the same effects from their respective observation points—negative effects that were far broader than mere economic considerations—and each tried to bring his readers back to square one so that a rational analysis could be made of what was happening.

As seen in the quote opening this synopsis, Bastiat was unhesitant to dissect "acquired rights." He anticipated by more than a century the launching of U.S. President Lyndon Johnson's Great Society—a massive, mid-twentieth-century welfare program born of these "rights." This program was a logical extension of President Franklin Roosevelt's largely ineffective New Deal, an economically destructive social engineering effort in response to the devastation of the Great Depression of the 1930s. Today, the media and Congressional liberals call these acquired rights "entitlements," an effective political disguise for what Bastiat and others saw as much less benevolent or benign.

Bastiat discusses how well-intentioned but not necessarily well-thought-out economic programs create vested interests in a few to the detriment of all—including those whom the programs are specifically designed to help. He writes of false philanthropy as the often-harmful act of giving something of value to someone who has not earned it in any meaningful sense. Yet, like all political philosophers who consider the totality of society Bastiat was never averse to aiding the truly needy, those who cannot help themselves. He was opposed to the same narcotic we so often see dispensed by Congress and the states in modern times, namely, give-away programs that bear no relation to need, capability, or self-esteem. Such programs do, however, tend to have a strong correlation to political expediency. Bastiat talks about these things as being "legal plunder."

Modern social welfare programs (often based on governance by emotion) aim principally to eliminate significant differences in individual circumstances. Similar programs in Bastiat's day were the bane of his very existence. He saw them as a primary source of governmental and even societal corruption. Taking from some and giving to others (as has become obvious over the course of the ascendance of the welfare state) is more than just destructive of economic and political truths known for centuries; it is a political and social trivialization of foundational natural rights—and duties. Bastiat argues that as legislated rights, guised as "entitlements," come into being a public devaluing of natural rights and obligations will be as inevitable as night following day. Bastiat finds the basis of these alterations in the creation of the state:

> The state is the great fictitious entity by which everyone seeks to live at the expense of everyone else.

It is worthwhile to observe that Bastiat was hardly the first in his strong reaction to the long-term consequences of creating immoderate rights in whole classes of people. In 1835 Alexis de Tocqueville published a short essay titled *Memoir on Pauperism*. His pessimism regarding the charitable impulse that devolved into political entitlement was conspicuous:

> Any measure that establishes legal charity on a permanent basis and gives it administrative form thereby creates an idle and lazy class, living at the expense of the industrial and working class....

Tocqueville recognizes the need for charity, but he believes it can take only one form:

> [b]eneficence must be a ... reasoned virtue, not a weak and unreflecting inclination. It is necessary to do what is most useful to the receiver, to do what best serves the welfare of the majority, not what rescues the few. In practice this means that charity should never be made a right, to which the "needy" are entitled, but should instead always be considered to be a gracious gesture on the part of society. This is necessary because rights must be based on the idea of equality of individuals, while a "right to charity" would be based on the inferiority of certain individuals. When I assert a right to speak, or to own property, or to worship my God, I am stating that I am the equal of any man and so am entitled to be treated equally under the law. But to assert a claim upon my fellow men for assistance is to assert my own inferiority and my dependence upon them. This would degrade, rather than uplift, the supplicant.
>
> I am deeply convinced that any permanent, regular administrative system whose aim will be to provide for the needs of the poor will breed more miseries than it can cure, will deprave the population that it wants to help and comfort, will in time reduce the rich to being no more than the tenant-farmers of the poor, will dry up the sources of savings, will stop the accumulation of capital, will retard the development of trade, will benumb human industry and activity, and will culminate by bringing about a violent revolution in the State.

Tocqueville goes a step further as well; he presents an equally bright alternative to the gloom he sees in forced charity, known today as the welfare state. While raising a consciousness of the nineteenth century's alms giving he defines the relationship not just between the giver and the recipient of such charity, but between each person and his own comprehension of ethical and interpersonal verities:

> Individual alms-giving established valuable ties between the rich and the poor. The deed itself involves the giver in the fate of the one whose poverty he has undertaken to alleviate. The latter, supported by aid which he had no right to demand and which he had no hope to getting, feels inspired by gratitude [and some desire to then earn the generosity he has received]. A moral tie is established between those two classes whose interests and passions so often conspire to separate them from each other, and although divided by circumstance they are willingly reconciled. This is not the case with legal charity. The latter allows the alms to persist but removes its morality. The law strips the man of wealth of a part of his surplus without consulting him, and he sees the poor man only as a greedy stranger invited by the legislator to share his wealth. The poor man, on the other hand, feels no gratitude for a benefit that no one can refuse him and that could not satisfy him in any case.

The human element in all of these relationships is far more important than the economic. This will be further explored in the synopsis of *Reclaiming the American Dream* (Chapter 30) where Richard Cornuelle dissects how government drives private charitable efforts out of social intercourse.

The long-term effect of improperly judging human dignity is what underlies so many failed "intellectual" efforts—efforts that address conditions but not people and thus fail in both their design and execution. The imponderables of human pride and capability are the real subjects of the observations made by these authors. These are not things well-crafted in committee hearings or pontifical speeches, but in unfeigned activity in neighborhoods. In other words, people on one side are not so needy and those on the other not so aloof as demagogues would have us believe. Government intervening between the two becomes a false moral imperative and an economic disaster.

The well-intentioned contend they are giving hope but in reality they are suffocating it.

Bastiat states that the first purpose of government is to ensure our individual ability, by means of the rule of law, to *defend* our person, liberty, and property. These are the essentials of life. The signal point of government is to prevent anarchy and chaos in the population and thus to foster justice. Bastiat does not see government functioning primarily as an active purveyor of equity; he sees government operating in a negative fashion, that is, government's function is to stop injustice so justice itself remains. In a reciprocal way, in order to be secure *from* government, laws exist to protect the public from perfidy and corruption emanating from the governors or a tyrannical popular majority. We see in Bastiat an echo of Thomas Jefferson's imprecation: "In questions of power, then, let no more be heard about confidence in man, but bind him down from mischief with the chains of the Constitution."

For Bastiat the law created by men was merely, and only, an extension of a natural right:

> The law is the organization of the natural right of lawful defense. It is the substitution of common force for individual forces. And this common force is to do only what the individual forces have a natural and lawful right to do: to protect persons, liberties, and properties.

Bastiat is a mid-nineteenth-century Frenchman who deals with both the demise of the monarchy and the reality of socialism's growing popularity subsequent to the French Revolutions of 1789 and 1848. He addresses issues that became a constant source of conflict in the following century. He rails against socialism because its proponents found it necessary to use force not only to institute its equalitarian goals, but also to perpetuate them. Socialism goes against the basic instincts of humanity; it destroys incentive and ingenuity and its victims must be compelled to accept it. Moreover, because socialism is economically inefficient it robs the community of what it could achieve were it not being victimized by ignorant officials or artificial governmental controls.

Unfortunately, collectivist impulses are still present in the twenty-first century albeit in a more oblique and beguiling fashion. Foreseeing the growth of state welfarism, effected by shrewd political maneuvers, Bastiat warns that such welfarism is simply a more insidious form of socialistic thinking, created and enforced by means of demagoguery and legislation rather than tyranny and despotism.

Bastiat's concern is two-fold: First, the governmental act of taking property from one group and giving it to another is an inappropriate denial of the first group's natural right to the fruits of its labor. Second (and probably more important to Bastiat), there is a negative effect on society and the individual recipients as a result of such a coerced transfer of wealth. Although he doesn't use a phrase such as "the culture of dependency," that is what he foresees. He also foresees to where such distortions of the social fabric will lead—to the wholesale destruction of the culture of those to whom benefits are given.

Bastiat sees the potential for degrading social conflict if redistribution of wealth grows out of proportion to its justifications. He sees the cultural destruction of human dignity and the devaluation of human incentive when there is wholesale government intervention in the marketplace. The notion that dependency changes people has long been comprehended, even by those supplying the means through which dependency is supported.

When George Washington became convinced that slavery could not be countenanced in view of the premises underlying the American experiment, he made plans to free his slaves—and pay them at least some of what they were owed for the work they had given. Washington felt that sudden freedom for his slaves was not tenable—politically, socially, economically, and particularly individually—so he devised a plan for gradual emancipation. As Benjamin Hart observes in *Faith and Freedom* (2004), the execution of Washington's design took several decades. As late as 1833 (Washington died in 1799) his estate was still forwarding wage and pension payments to former slave families. Washington himself understood the culture of dependency he had created, and that his soon-to-be-former slaves needed some protection prior to emancipation. He felt, as Hart comments, that "a slave had no need to learn skills of self-reliance, entrepreneurship, and no means of cultivating the competitive instinct so vital for survival."

The modern victims of our largesse—the recipients of state welfarism—are in the same unenviable position. We insist that the less well-off be continually treated as children, and when they do not embrace the tools of responsibility, we blame them rather than our own excessive pride or intellectual inconsistencies.

On the "taking" side of the public experiment, it is clear from his text that Bastiat's concerns are not about taxation, per se. Simply presented, his anxiety is about the uses of power to achieve something legislatively that would be otherwise illegal—taking from one to give to another. While this form of stealing is immoral philosophically, it is often advantageous politically. In order to fully comprehend Bastiat's use of forceful language, we have to remember his proximity to violent and deadly revolution. In his era, if groups of citizens did not appreciate what was happening, they were as likely to take up a gun as a pencil, as likely to build barricades as ballot boxes. Thus Bastiat wants to be clear so there is no mistaking the perilous course on which he sees his contemporaries embarking.

Bastiat, as might be expected, was an activist in addition to being a theorist. He was outspoken in defense of his views and was politically involved in continued efforts to define, debunk, and destroy the dangers he saw; collectivism and its corollary, coerced conformity by government fiat. Bastiat remains important as a reminder to recognize and then expose the often demeaning and invariably disguised collectivist compulsions of modern "progressives." This group attempts to expand social welfarism through ignorance, naïveté, or even political deceit, to the detriment of the economy and the citizenry. Today, the welfare state is nothing but the repackaging and refining of socialistic goals. Bastiat contends that the alleged altruistic impetus behind such thinking seems benign until its full effects are observed. Opposing the false goal of equality of result is Bastiat's stark declaration of how the equalitarians succeeded politically where force failed:

> The law has been perverted by the influence of two entirely different causes: stupid greed and false philanthropy.

Bastiat views the popular law of his time (law also currently present in a slightly different form) as politically, intellectually, and economically corrupt. Its perverse results are an embodiment of the general will supposedly being divined by a legislative majority acting on its own, not with the intellectual or voting consent of the electorate. In writing this slim volume he seeks to define why this is so. In large part the political success of equalitarians lies in nascent political correctness where a cowed populace is condemned for suggesting thoughtful investigation of government programs that are aimed at helping the less fortunate. Those who should ask for demonstrated positive results of such programs don't out of fear of being labeled insensitive, uncaring, self-absorbed, or even bigots or racists. They are silenced by the glare of the politically correct and the fear of public excoriation in the media while the construction of new "rights" for the less fortunate proceeds unabated.

By returning to the era in which Bastiat wrote it may be easier to understand why he saw so clearly what he did. The politics in France subsequent to the revolution of 1848 were the antithesis of the then-ongoing American experience. In Bastiat's observations we see the first overt development of the battle between freedom (as expressed in the free market in the United States) and economic slavery (founded in the socialism of Europe). Because the differences were both unmistakable and simple, Bastiat's celebrated explication of this war of ideas is the most helpful from this era. Although it became clear during the second half of the nineteenth century that American capitalism needed controls, it was the series of adjustments that were effected in response to capitalism's excesses that made the system in the U.S. work. Abandonment of American capitalism in the face of its faults was never more than a proposition—and then only from a few radicals. But France was full of radicals. Many U.S. and European economic theorists and political figures of that period, including Bastiat, understood capitalism's imperfections and acted to correct them. The European political community was not so fortunate in its response to the intemperances of capitalism. As a result, they have struggled with socialistic intentions ever since—to their geopolitical and geo-economic degradation.

Politics is the art of the possible. Unfortunately, in Bastiat's time (as now), many more things were seen as possible than actually are. This was especially true in those whose intellectual or emotional musings conjured utopia. Fueled by the Enlightenment's rationalism, they did not realize that what could be thought of by human ingenuity could not necessarily be achieved by human striving. Their speculations devolved into legislated rights that required state confiscation of private property to be given to others. Both the proposition and the means resulted in a social battle that yet endures. Bastiat's solution for the ongoing "civil" war is simple:

> The safest way to make laws respected is to make them respectable. When the law and morality contradict each other the citizen has the cruel alternative of either losing his moral sense or losing his respect for the law. . . . There is in all of us a strong disposition to believe that anything lawful is also

legitimate. This belief is so widespread that many persons have erroneously held that things are "just" because law makes them so.

Bastiat was not one to simply criticize; he also offers solutions. By way of example, he denounces the philosophy of Thomas Hobbes who writes in *Leviathan* in 1651 that men submit to government because they fear one another more than they fear a central authority. Hobbes thus is contending that man craves security more than freedom; accordingly oppressive government control is necessary, even welcomed. Bastiat sees mankind in an entirely different light. He holds that there is a naturally harmonious order to the social world, an order that emanates from the free exchange of goods, services, and ideas between human beings driven to satisfy unlimited wants with limited resources. This exchange is essentially self-regulating as a result of the enlightened self-interest described in Adam Smith's *Wealth of Nations* (Chapter 12). The outcome is a steady progress in the material well being of all. Bastiat explains that interference with this freedom (and its corollaries of unfettered competition and secure property rights) leaves people poorer and ultimately oppressed as further government action is imposed in an attempt to remedy what the last program distorted. Citizens are driven away from the creative actions in which they would otherwise engage. The fruits of this unused creativity remain unripe because of government intervention.

The illusory collectivist (or welfarist) goal of economic equality is a corollary to Hobbes's centralized government. Bastiat fought against this not solely because it was undesirable from many points of view, but because it was (and is) unachievable. It is unachievable because the human spirit is not rooted in equality (or subservience) but rather in unlimited imagination and striving. The self-ordering success of these characteristics is evident in the free-market's almost fabled raising of the standard of living around the world across the centuries. Actions speak louder than words. And in this case, they simply overwhelm political rhetoric.

Bastiat emphasizes that the illusion of equality conferred by fiat isn't just destructive of what has been achieved. It ultimately destroys the very system that allows government largesse to exist in the first place. If there is no incentive to create, to imagine, to produce, because the fruits of one's labor are taken through taxation and regulation, then eventually there will be no production, no creation, and nothing to tax.

Interestingly, Bastiat saves some of his sharpest barbs for the political writers and social philosophers of his own day. His descriptions of their arrogance and condescension (applauding the imagined possibilities of Enlightenment thinking while ignoring the obvious potential of humanity's enlightened self-interest) could be reprinted in the present with equal effect and accuracy. But he does not just rail against this arrogance itself; he also denounces its evil fruits as the media of his era refused to present any views containing rational assessment. Here, too, Bastiat and Hazlitt were partners.

Bastiat laughs at the foibles and riddles of the self-appointed, those who look on the masses of society as inept, incapable, and ignorant of what is best for them. He notes that these self-same pontificators nevertheless defend (through equally uninformed circular reasoning) the inalienable right of the "ignorant masses" to elect those who will tell them how to live their lives.

We detect no hesitancy in Bastiat's writings to pronounce the emperor without any clothes. For Bastiat, the collectivist parade was not just flawed; it was sinister. In his view our obligation is to point this out in plain words and then to give our words force through strong actions.

About the Author

FREDERIC BASTIAT was born in 1801 in Paris and lived only to the age of 49. He died of tuberculosis in 1850, the same year *The Law* was published. Orphaned at age nine, he studied economics by choice and was fluent in several languages. The depth of his reading, especially in foreign languages, made his knowledge more extensive than that of most of his contemporaries. The great impetus for much of his writing was the revolution of 1848 when France turned wholly to socialism, an event from which it has yet to recover. Bastiat was a deputy in the French legislature and also an economist who understood both humanity and the imprecations of Adam Smith. The force of his logic is inescapable although to many in mid-nineteenth-century France it was inexcusable. Time has proven Bastiat correct much to the pleasure of those who today benefit from his clear thinking and profound understanding of human nature and the value and strength of free markets.

8

Democracy in America

Alexis de Tocqueville

Originally published: 1835 & 1840 (two volumes)
317 pages (abridged)

AMERICA, in all its guises, has fascinated Old World intellectuals since well before 1776, and French nobleman Alexis de Tocqueville was no exception. As a young man he was particularly captivated by the allure of our nascent democracy. Though his 1831 visit to the newly formed United States, when he was but twenty-six years old, lasted only nine months, his account of that journey continues to provide intriguing insights into the challenges inherent in a Jeffersonian democracy. There are few men who are more often or more widely quoted than this connoisseur of the American experiment.

When Tocqueville arrived in the New World the United States had recently celebrated its fortieth anniversary as a nation. The last of the Founders were passing into history and the focus was no longer solely on the new government but on the new country and the new citizenry. The states were yet mostly equal partners with the administration in Washington and economic and social relationships were beginning to form patterns. The free market was still the wild card. As would become clear over the years, capitalism itself (as much as the citizens) needed rules to constrain its darker impulses. But most Americans were too close to their own world to see what they had wrought. It took the independent and quite sophisticated view of a foreigner to comprehend all the potential—good and bad.

Tocqueville's own aristocratic family had suffered greatly during the liberty, equality, and fraternity of the French Revolution of 1789 yet he held no enmity toward the egalitarian effects of majority rule or democracy. Instead, he was fascinated by the question of what a democracy could be now that he well understood from his own country's revolution what it shouldn't be. And although the ostensible purpose of his trip to the New World was to study the American prison system his ultimate goal was to view constitutional government firsthand:

> It is not, then, merely to satisfy a legitimate curiosity that I have examined America: my wish has been to find there instruction by which we may ourselves profit. . . . I sought there the image of democracy itself . . . in order to learn what we have to fear or to hope from its progress.

What is unique about Tocqueville is his ability to get over the giddy feeling that the fraternity of democracy, coupled with the rule of law, is designed to foster. As a result of the French Revolution he plainly understood that human beings do not always strive for the good of their fellows. No matter what system of governance is chosen it has to be designed to restrain man's sometimes dismal nature. Tocqueville also opines that the well-being of any society achieved by equalitarian (as opposed to egalitarian) efforts is at risk if its citizens do not recognize the corrosive effects of too much equality, or equality that is forced, not earned. Finally, Tocqueville understood the nature of power (even if achieved by democratic means) and its effect on those who suddenly find themselves in a position to wield it.

In America, Rousseau's theoretical tyrannical majority (a majority that could make decisions without considering the rights of, or its duties to, a mostly powerless minority) is hypothetically stymied by the Constitution. The design offers protection for most of the citizenry's natural rights and puts forward some political guarantees. But that document does not dictate human *character*; that is, citizen individuality or morality. In other words, Tocqueville sees the first chinks in the practice of American freedom. They relate not to the documents or their direct governmental functioning but to the effects of massive uniformity and the striving for an intellectual notion of equality. Tocqueville is troubled that a social or corporate conceit might arise vis-à-vis the value of equality that could destroy individuality. As equality's leveling effects (intellectually) insist on uniformity the ultimate result can be complaisance bred of felt individual impotence or unimportance.

A corollary to this concern lay in America's vast commercial potential. Tocqueville sees the titanic American economic nation earlier than many others. Yet in that national possibility—encompassed in unimagined expanses of land and natural resources and pure enterprise—he also sees a tendency toward leveling that might command a repressive political/psychological unity in the name of progress. Tocqueville sees a uniform intention to achieve material success and thus an American society where its economic goals become increasingly both homogenous and overwhelming. Tocqueville fears a populace bereft of intellectual, cultural, or social diversity if all are solely focused, as they seemed to be, simply on profit and temporal abundance. What he didn't witness and therefore didn't count on was what could be done with those profits by private citizens, which as the years passed became a massive amount of individual activity not directed at further material success but aimed at fellow-citizens and society as a whole, and at sheer personal enjoyment, which is notably unequal.

Tocqueville worries further how America will ameliorate the potentially harmful effects of a constantly encroaching commercial power on both the freedoms and the rights of the minority. He sees that an overt but potentially false majoritarian intellectual or philosophical hegemony by those in positions of power, commercial and political power together, is possible and is thus a concern. Tocqueville warns of a "government for and of the people, but not by them." It should be remembered that Tocqueville visited America in the midst of Jacksonian democracy's flowering when ideas of egalitarianism and majority rule were approaching their apogee. However, the representative facet of governing, where wisdom is to be interposed between citizen democracy and laws, he sees as potentially being subverted. He foresees commercial interests clinching the social and economic bit in their legislative teeth to impose supposedly majority concepts that do not necessarily have majority backing or real majoritarian interests at heart.

And Tocqueville's fears did come to fruition to an extent by the turn of the twentieth century when the so-called robber barons seemed to operate by their own rules. At that point a counterforce arose in the form of Teddy Roosevelt's trust-busting efforts. The checks and balances worked, albeit slowly as they must, first, because the society is so large and fluid, and second, because when action is taken too precipitously the law of unintended consequences comes into play. Often that law brings forth results that are more destructive than the ill that is to be cured.

On another front, as Tocqueville also anticipates, some ideologues were extending the idea of majority rule and its egalitarian intentions to irrational conclusions that had nothing to do with democratic representation and everything to do with politics. Tocqueville predicts that if "intellectuals" can posit that our equality before the law also creates an expectation that we will treat everyone's talents and capabilities as equal, then someone would do so. Equalitarian elitists do not stop with the premise that the citizen's vote or opportunity is to be equal. They contend that the usefulness or value of a citizen's capabilities is to be determined, to a greater or lesser degree, not by the free market but by the state. Ultimately, this social equalitarian view embraces the charge that we should strive for equality of result—particularly economic result—and not just equality of opportunity. This call for equal result is a dishonest distortion of the Constitution's specific call for equal treatment and equal opportunity. Yet this demand continues unabated when demagogues posture as the supposed friends and guardians of human dignity. (James Madison, primary author of the Constitution, foresaw the probability of a call for equal result by means of the Constitution's insistence of equal opportunity, and addressed this directly in *Federalist* #10.)

In pursuing this long train of suppositions and possibilities Tocqueville comments at length upon the dynamic relationship between equality and individuality. He repeatedly suggests that individuality is at risk of being reduced to a mere concept by the leveling effects of majority rule. He sees not just the tyranny of the majority but the hegemony of the median—a social attitude *against* exceptionalism or excellence or even just the right to be different. For Tocqueville, the danger is one of fostering a docile citizenry that will ultimately come to accept an equalitarian dictatorship formed out of intellectual pretensions simply because it doesn't know any better, or is afraid to challenge it.

To bring this concept forward to the twenty-first century, one might consider the effects of political correctness or its cousin moral relativism. A society where differences are seen as merely opposite sides of various coins and right and wrong essentially do not exist can ultimately lead to anarchy, or meekness in the face of despotism. As emotionally satisfying as social homogenization may seem at first, progress is never grounded on sameness but rather on unique and valuable differences.

As fearful as some of Tocqueville's premonitions are he also argues the other side. He sees that an ability to ameliorate coercive majority rule (to ensure it would not become majority tyranny) rests in three uniquely American factors: strong and independent local government, the advantages of a socially mobile society, and the benefits of unfettered economic opportunity used to achieve self-sufficiency. As Tocqueville predicts, the ever-expanding grasp of federalism still fights for intrusive control at all levels of local and state government. He sees it as up to the citizenry to resist this intrusion into local and state affairs and incursion into the lives of individuals. He isn't sure the populace is up to this task because of its timidity in the face of idealized equalitarianism. Tocqueville is not so much pessimistic in these musings as realistic. He could not foresee how Power could be controlled by the populace but he is encouraged that in America's design there was at least a mechanism for allowing that to happen.

In America's early years Tocqueville did observe a social structure that was fluid, a condition which served as a bulwark against class jealousies and warfare both then and now. He found that the vast majority of the people were "sufficiently well-off to desire order, but not so well-off to excite envy." With respect to government he states that the American electorate is not degraded by habits of subservience to laws and officials, especially to the nobility and a king as was the case in monarchical Europe. He sees that this condition could continue so long as the public, through its right to vote, chooses the laws and people to whom obedience will be due. In other words, Tocqueville sees democracy as potentially self-correcting with regard to most of the indignities and insanities that exist when power is concentrated, but only if the populace remains vigilant, as citizens, and does not become complacent, as subjects. His theories of what *could* happen, on the positive side, however, do not leave him sanguine. His understanding of human nature is his overriding concern thus he expresses anxiety about majority rule.

Tocqueville considered local administration a powerful safeguard against corruption and oppression by either the national or state governments. He knew that a centralized administration simply couldn't run the whole country, even a nation as yet as uncomplicated as the United States was in 1831:

> However enlightened and skillful a central power may be, it cannot of itself embrace all the details of life. Such vigilance exceeds the power of man. And when it attempts unaided to create and set in motion so many complicated springs, it must submit to a very imperfect result, or exhaust itself in bootless efforts.

These comments are inevitably an oblique denunciation of the ultimate authority over every facet of life claimed by the French socialist state that had evolved in the aftermath of the Revolution of 1789.

Tocqueville sees a partnership in America that was lacking in Europe:

> When the [American] state seeks to act, within its own limits, it is not abandoned to itself . . . the duties of private citizens are not supposed to have lapsed because the state has come into action: but every one is ready, on the contrary, to guide and support it.

Yet, irrespective of any real or imagined citizen/government partnership Tocqueville still predicts the accretion of federal power through the "need" for policy to be guided in areas such as defense, transportation, and commerce that are inevitably national in scope. He expects these activities of the national government to proliferate and expand into control of ever more minor and local aspects of governance in order to achieve political or economic goals. It is an incontrovertible fact that bureaucracy feeds on itself. When we see today's federal government reaching down to the local level on issues such as welfare, health care, and education, and achieving ever smaller results, it is clear Tocqueville's fears were well founded.

Tocqueville, remembering the excesses of Rousseau's idealized omnipotent democracy, expresses his own intellectually healthy fear of the majority:

> If it be admitted that a man possessing power may misuse that power, why should not a majority be liable to the same reproach? Men do not change their characters by uniting with each other. The power to do everything, which I should refuse to one of my equals, I will never grant to any number of them.

Today, following the lode opened in Tocqueville's observation, we have seen those who wish to govern too often simply demand of the voters "Trust me." We hear the media or candidates themselves speak of "mandates" when an office-seeker wins 55% (or even less) of the vote. Gaining 55% of the vote still leaves a substantial minority not necessarily in agreement with any supposed mandate. Although the intentions of those elected are often "good," Tocqueville knew there is too much risk in granting to any majority a blank check uncoupled from fiscal, personal, or corporate responsibility. This result was seen at the beginning of the twenty-first century as the newly majoritarian neoconservatives engaged in political sleight-of-hand that resulted in fiscally capricious programs such as the Medicare prescription drug benefit or the No Child Left Behind education mandates.

Following this vein Tocqueville comments on the potential for excessive legislative and executive reach and the means by which such excesses could be curbed. He observes that his fear of the legislative majority or the electoral mandate is somewhat attenuated by the power of the judicial system. He views the ability of both elected and appointed judges to determine a law unconstitutional as one of the most powerful barriers that had ever been devised against the tyranny of politicians and political assemblies. Tocqueville and others were correct in viewing the judiciary as an antidote to oppressive legislative or executive grasp. They foresaw judicial control of extreme insults to the Constitution as a given; what they did not foresee, however, was the gradual debasement of Constitutional tenets through judicial interpretation and activism, and an omnivorous bureaucracy.

The compulsion of some in the judicial establishment to make judgments based on a "new era" or a new understanding often amounts to nothing more than the promulgation of law from the bench. In the end such actions are just as effective in changing the plain meaning of constitutional protections as would be any amendment to the document itself. This is primarily a twentieth- and twenty-first-century phenomenon that has yet to be resolved and can only be addressed by an informed and active electorate.

As observant as Tocqueville is about so many negative possibilities he nevertheless sees an oppressive majority and an ever-intrusive federalism coming to fruition only in stages. In his view there is ample opportunity to employ counter-measures to retain what might be lost. For Tocqueville there is as much hope as gloom in all of this. If the inherent effectiveness of citizen activism is realized it will act as a check on the potential oppressions of the governors; the people can maintain control of their own destiny and Tocqueville's fears of the slippery slope to electoral or actual tyranny can be abated. Unfortunately, in significant measure the course and consequences he presciently predicts have come to pass. On paper we still retain a democracy but as always the devil is in the details. In America, many today feel the need to reassert the importance of Tocqueville's countervailing "details" to lessen the hegemony of base equalitarianism fostered by an increasingly centralized government.

To a large extent the ability of the citizenry to control its government rests on what the people know. Tocqueville understood this correlation and dissects his era's media—newspapers and pamphlets—and their ability to encourage debate by spreading the word. He sees writers and editors as capable of creating groups of people who "will never meet, talk, study, or explore together, but who will nevertheless act as political blocs," (often today through political blogs). His observations are probably even more germane in the twenty-first century when the Internet and the media—much proliferated in terms of variety, numbers, and availability to citizens—operate so as to create even larger groups of unconnected but like-minded people. Ultimately, as Tocqueville foresees, we have created "mass civilization."

Tocqueville opines regarding the media: "The evil they produce is much less than the evil which they cure." Some today would disagree, arguing that the immense amount of information—along with concomitant misinformation and disinformation in quantities Tocqueville never imagined—actually has a negative effect. The sheer volume overwhelms the individual's capacity to comprehend even a portion, much less all that is available. A resulting inability to decide what is true, or truly best, ensues. The ultimate effect of this mass of media may be closer to intellectual paralysis than the systemic practicality Tocqueville hopes for.

Tocqueville ultimately recognizes the power of ideas to thwart government compulsion, especially in cases when the media fails the public or even joins the tyrannical majority:

> Force is never more than a transient element of success, and after force, comes the notion of right.

Ideas Have Consequences (Chapter 35), *The Commanding Heights* (Chapter 29), *The Road to Serfdom* (Chapter 13), and other books reviewed in following chapters repeat this theme and offer myriad examples of its truth. Ideas are the salvation of the worried, the tool of the oppressed, and the bane of the powerful. They ultimately right our wrongs.

The latter portions of this abridgment of Tocqueville's *Democracy in America* deal to a large extent with observations of the effect of majority rule and democracy on the personalities, habits, outlooks, achievements, and goals of American society. Tocqueville goes a considerable distance to demonstrate the direct relationship between the extent of democracy and what we would call today the "dumbing down" of citizens. Tocqueville predicts that as both democracy and commerce proliferate the individual can become marginalized with population growth and the need for overarching government uniformity in an increasingly diverse and complex society. On one occasion he discusses the potential for people to relinquish their individual character and thus, ultimately, their intellectual franchise:

> When neither law nor custom professes to establish frequent and habitual relations between men, their intercourse originates in the accidental similarity of opinions and tastes. In democracies, members of the community never differ much from each other, and naturally stand so near that they may all be confounded in one general mass.

In juxtaposition to this, however, is the dynamism Tocqueville sees in American ambition and, especially, in its commerce. Without excessively belaboring the obvious, it remains true that his sometimes schizophrenic approach makes one wonder whether we are as monotonous and bland (and perhaps doomed) as he sometimes describes us. Is it true that ever-pressing majorities homogenize us and cause our differences to be trivialized, or is our individual freedom of choice and action always the antidote to mass society taking over?

Tocqueville's overall observations on the differences between democratic freedom and democratic despotism—the latter expressed as the leveling effects of democracy gone too far—are as cogent and vital today as they were when he wrote them:

> There is nothing more arduous than the apprenticeship of liberty. It is not so with despotism: despotism often promises to make amends for a thousand previous ills: it supports the right, it protects the oppressed, and it maintains public order. The nation is lulled by the temporary prosperity, which it produces, until it is roused to a sense of its misery. Liberty, on the contrary, is generally established with difficulty in the midst of storms: it is perfected by civil discord: and its benefits cannot be appreciated until it is already old.

Tocqueville warns that the greatest danger to a failed democracy is not anarchy, as would seem natural, but totalitarianism. "Nations are led away [by the principle of equality] to servitude, without perceiving its drift." Although anarchy is what appears to be happening initially, totalitarianism eventuates because the people's will is broken by anarchic actions; they give up and give in, in order to obtain security. In the face of anarchy security is more valued than freedom.

As noted previously, Tocqueville foresees two great dangers for democracy: the accretion of central power because of administrative necessity, and the self-censoring fear of speaking up in an equalitarian society because we judge our opinions as no more valid than anyone else's. Here are the seeds of today's political correctness. These forces inure people to docility, and often strike them mute. Tocqueville proposes active freedom of expression as the remedy for this disease. He ultimately conveys confidence in the power of ideas and in the vehicle that carries those ideas, the human spirit. This is a lesson that, two centuries later, still transfers well from Tocqueville's musings.

Tocqueville introduces us to a thousand truths about a democratic society. All are tied up in the details of self-government exercised with care and corruption, fidelity and perfidy, by a people continually redefining and reinventing themselves. His time-honored observations on the human condition and its antidote, individual liberty, still define a practical framework.

About the Author

BORN IN 1805 into the French nobility, Alexis Charles Henri Clérel de Tocqueville was precocious, aggressive, inventive, and self-sufficient. His family was exiled after the revolution of 1830, but Tocqueville stayed in France, swearing allegiance to the new government. He obtained a French government grant to study the prison system in America and traveled around North America for three-quarters of a year during 1831–32. Publication of his preeminent work, *Democracy in America*, in two volumes in 1835 and 1840, made him both famous and sought after. Subsequent to the success of this book he led a rather quiet life, marrying an Englishwoman and accepting a series of minor posts in the French government. He forewarned of revolution in 1848 and endured the massive upheavals of 1848–49. He retired from public life in 1849 because of his poor health, suffering from a disease of the lungs. He moved south to a more temperate climate on a doctor's orders. Alexis de Tocqueville died in 1859.

9

Essays in the History of Liberty

Lord Acton

Originally published: 1860–62, 1877, 1899–1901
530 pages

LORD ACTON'S most enduring intellectual contribution to the study of society and its evolutionary processes was his effort to transform the consideration and recording of history in two ways: first, to elevate it to the level of rigorous scientific exercise; second, to cause it to be used as a method of achieving moral progress through judgment and discrimination. He notes, "Political progress is a process of adaptation, not a result of speculation; this distinguishes reform from revolution." He strongly asserts, as does Edmund Burke (Chapter 36), that history plays a role of paramount importance in any society and in any political process: "As growth is one of the laws of life, reform becomes one of the principles of government."

A member of the aristocracy, Lord Acton had the leisure to view the world from his perch at the pinnacle of society. His understanding of liberty and the place of government in the life of any people lead him to conclude,

> Liberty is not a means to a higher political end, it is itself the highest political end.

He argues that the state should intervene in the lives of its citizens only to the extent that it fosters the ability of individuals to secure their liberty; that is, their freedom from oppression, injustice, despotism, tyranny. Liberty is a concept that, in order to be understood, needs context to define it. The intention of the materials contained in *First*

Principles is to offer a definition of liberty under law. Lord Acton sought the same end thus his views are a primary resource.

As a close student of the New World experiment Lord Acton applied his considerable experience and judgment to the American model to see how well words matched deeds. Because the country had been formed out of whole cloth woven from threads of historical experience, judging the outcome of its efforts in relation to its stated goals allowed for both practical and philosophical utility. There was uniform European interest in America in Lord Acton's time; he took the lessons taught by American ingenuity and political freedom and postulated the full potential of a free society's social and governmental causes and effects for European consumption.

For Lord Acton morality was the foundation of social interaction, whether in the halls of government or between individuals or among nations. His introduction of moral judgment into the writing of history in the nineteenth century was probably his most direct contribution to the fight against totalitarianism in the twentieth century. Lord Acton saw history as more than just facts. He viewed it as a drama with a noble end and he believed that the story it told must not be ignored lest it play out over and over again, to no avail. His opinion of the importance of virtue and rectitude in making judgments on history is reflected in his writings. In *Essays*, when discussing the American Revolution, he writes of "principles which override precedents." With regard to the U.S. Civil War (which he watched develop) he notes, "The absolute subjection of the individual to the State is against the laws of political morality...."

Melding historical judgment with historical precedent yields progress by reducing the likelihood of recurrent mistakes. In order to learn the most from the study of history Lord Acton urged his followers to "Take up a problem, not a period." In this manner the student can see more than facts, he can discern conditions and influences not just actors. Lord Acton felt that progress is imbedded in the recognition of errors as much as in the discovery of new methods. In fact, without the former, the latter has often been delayed for decades, if not centuries. As the American democratic republic was the newest of mankind's inventions Lord Acton found fertile ground for observation and comment.

Although his investigations, through his essays, cover the history of the evolution of government, he was especially intrigued by the American Civil War: first, because it *was* a war between citizens; second, because its subtext—human slavery—would suffer no compromise;

and third, because American government was founded on the English system of equity and therefore one would expect a certain outcome as a result of that history. (It is important to recall that the Civil War was not fought over slavery; its subject was the legitimacy of the secession of the Southern states from the Union, though slavery was resolved as a result of the conflict.)

Lord Acton viewed the victory of the North as inevitable for practical reasons (manpower, industrial capability, resources—financial, human, and natural). Yet he also saw it as antithetical to liberty—to the right of self-governance under law—because the Constitution did not prohibit secession. In his analysis this glaring omission not only justified secession, but reflected the essence of the American form, that is, government by the *consent* of the governed. If the governed no longer concurred in whatever was extant how could they be compelled to remain?

Lord Acton argues that the North's approach, which forced a nation to exist, was a form of state despotism. His conclusions had broader implications than just the effects and outcome regarding the specific cause of the war. It was clear to him that if the national government could rule the states it could just as well rule the citizens. This undermined liberty not just collectively but fundamentally.

The issues he discerned then are the same issues with which we deal today. How much liberty can the citizenry demand while recognizing the need of the body politic to compromise widely differing views? How much cohesion can we enforce while not destroying the individuality to which each person is entitled? To try to answer some of these issues Lord Acton went back centuries.

He began his investigation of liberty with the Greeks—whose society he saw as incomplete. Essentially, he found that within the Greek polity democracy was born but justice was not. And justice was the goal—but it was the result *and* the means of attaining it that were equally paramount—thus began his view that judging history was as necessary as reporting it.

In his essays he discusses the development of the free exercise of government. The crowning moment for his own country came by means of the English Revolution (c. 1642–1651):

> [I]t is the greatest thing done by the English nation. It established the State upon a contract, and set up the doctrine that a breach of contract forfeited the crown. . . . Parliament

gave the crown, and gave it under conditions.... The king
became its servant on good behaviour....

After this revolution, Parliament, with some fits and starts, became supreme in overseeing both the administration of government and the legislation that set the rules that would judge everyone's conduct. But, again, this revolution was not whole, for there was still the potential of the "oppression of class by class, and of the country by the State." In order to achieve a more equitable balance as time passed and real life intruded upon the misty visions first imagined, the need for continued adjustment, conciliation, and compromise surfaced. As history has born out, these methods did work to help effect a more perfect union of government and citizens, and therein lies their enduring value—and that of Lord Acton.

This volume is a compendium of Lord Acton's most important essays on freedom. While freedom is itself timeless, we must consider the times in which the essays were written, as well as the man who wrote them. While we contemplate Lord Acton's moral understandings and judgments (formed in the era of Victorian England, 1840–1900) we will also find that Edmund Burke's philosophy of liberty (formed 1750–1790) is reflected in Lord Acton's reporting of history. The long chronicle of monarchical domination experienced by European nations caused Lord Acton to comment on the effects of statism—which is democracy/bureaucracy gone too far. His remarks were recorded as a democratic Parliament became supreme in Britain. He echoes the concerns of Alexis de Tocqueville (Chapter 8), in addition to those of Burke, regarding the leveling consequences of majority rule:

> [D]emocracy, like monarchy, is salutary within limits and fatal in excess.

He also predicts, with a prescience that must be noted, the tendency toward socialism inevitably bred by equalitarian (versus egalitarian) goals formed in a democratic setting:

> Socialism, [is] the infirmity that attends mature democracies.

His dissection of the progression from liberty to oppression, as it developed in the democratic nations of Europe, presaged much of the politics that evolved as socialism was imposed again and again in the first half of the twentieth century, and as we see happening in the modern welfare state ascendant in most Western nations.

Lord Acton spent the latter part of his career formalizing his method and his philosophy of history which he intended to publish as the *History of Liberty*. Although he never finished that project the pieces he did complete captured the essence of his thinking. Many are included in this volume. The foundation of his intended narrative is condensed in the oft-expressed idea that democracy can just as easily become a form of despotism as can monarchy because "popular power may be tainted with the same poison as personal power." Thus, coming to a moral judgment as to the goals and effects of any particular majority was as useful and valid as judging the effects of oligarchy or monarchy, where either may be benevolent or dictatorial. As Lord Acton succinctly observes,

> The will of the people cannot make just that which is unjust.

America's solution to this dilemma—a solution that Lord Acton views as wise and effective—was twofold: first, there is the system of checks and balances embodied in the separation of powers (he was especially enamored of the power of the courts to hold the other two branches in check); second, there was the citizenry's constant vigilance exercised through frequent elections to both test the government's power and, if necessary, change its personnel or policies. Alexander Hamilton, in *Federalist* No. 70, first enunciates specifically the duties of the polity under the proposed Constitution to protect both itself and the country:

> The ingredients which constitute safety in the republican sense are a due dependence on the people, and a due responsibility.

This theme is iterated often by the authors in *First Principles* and is repeated in various texts herein because of its paramount import. No matter how well our systems and institutions are designed, no matter how precise and pointed our laws, those who participate in and those who benefit from these systems need to recall that the primary check against public abuse of any type is a political one. Vigilance and action are *required* if these democracies are to work in the manner contemplated. If the people are not watchful, then, by default those in power will exercise diligence for them with almost invariably predictable results.

Because his ideas were not willingly embraced during his lifetime Lord Acton considered himself both an intellectual and professional failure. Nowadays, however, his insight, foresight, and methods are universally embraced in a world that enjoys more freedom than it otherwise would were it not for his intellectual contribution. Reading these essays and watching Lord Acton develop the foundation for assessing history as more than just facts is a valuable exercise in today's world where moral relativism is undermining our ability to form valid or practical opinions about our social and political foundations and interactions.

About the Book

IN ADDITION TO the essays themselves, the Liberty Fund's presentation of Lord Acton's writing contains several shorter pieces that are either reviews of contemporaneous publications or accounts of concurrent events. The reader is advised to focus on particular sections of this book for an understanding of what Lord Acton's writings bring to our comprehension of liberty. Obviously, the remaining sections may be read as well, but they are not necessary to complete the essential picture of this author's contributions. The most relevant pages are: 2–97, 189–367, 377–88, 409–33, 505–30.

About the Author

JOHN EMERICH EDWARD DALBERG-ACTON was considered by many to be the most educated man of his era. He was both an historian and a political philosopher. Born of English parents in Italy in 1834, he was educated in Germany and England. He never earned a formal degree because, as a Catholic, he was barred from English universities. His faith initially played a strong part in guiding his career. He later broke with the church politically, though not religiously, because he felt it was too mired in both the past and the idea of papal infallibility. He was the founder and editor of two widely read periodicals in which his views appeared. He wrote and commented on history and social progress throughout his life as an essayist and reviewer. In his later years, he became a professor at Cambridge University, an institution from which he had been barred as student forty years earlier because of his Catholicism. Lord Acton was a member of Queen Victoria's court though he was also elected to Parliament for a short time in the 1850s. He acted as a personal advisor to Prime Minister William Gladstone (elected British prime minister four times between 1868–1894) and helped guide Gladstone's liberal programs (using the classical European definition of the term "liberal"). Lord Acton died in 1902.

10

In Defense of Freedom

Frank S. Meyer

Originally published: 1962
229 pages

LIKE ALL POLITICAL constructions, conservatism has many facets. As was noted in the introduction to *First Principles* conservatism is not so much a philosophy as it is a movement, and a way of thinking. Over time—several centuries—the various methods and foundations of conservative thought have been tested in the political marketplace. Ultimately, two approaches to governance evolved, both of which embraced truly conservative thinking and each of which supported the other. The first was called conservatism, the other libertarianism. But there were differences; some were significant variations regarding what government should and should not be able to accomplish. These variations required cross-pollination, or at least mutual recognition, in order to make both processes serviceable and to allow them to be applied to everyday realities. They also needed the restraints each faction forced the other to consider. The two were far better off together than separate.

In the 1950s Frank Meyer blended these two approaches in one of his signal philosophical achievements. This melding was called "fusion." Classical liberal traditionalists, the philosophical descendants of Edmund Burke (known today as conservatives) and Libertarians had been partially at odds for many years, and Meyer knew that their methodological and substantive differences needed to be resolved before the theories both represented could or would be a force in philosophical, economic, or political conversations. Meyer's fusion helped make the American conservative movement intellectually and politically viable.

Meyer starts, as Lord Acton does (*Essays in the History of Liberty* [Chapter 9]), with the Libertarian premise that an individual's freedom, not the needs of society, is the "decisive criterion" of good government. The conservative heirs of Edmund Burke had taken a slightly different tack; they posited that society was an organic or living reality to which the individual's subordination, within limits, was necessary in order for the whole to function. For the followers of Burke defining exactly the dividing line between individual and societal rights was where a philosophy of governance served a purpose.

Meyer's fusion reflects his understanding, in line with Burke's, that the lessons of the past, which had coalesced into rules of human behavior and interaction (traditional or "classical" liberalism), could not be minimized for they were hard fought and logically established. As well, however, the imperative of change and the needs of each individual (Libertarianism) could not be eschewed at the behest of government no matter how much tradition was involved and no matter how important society's claimed preeminence. Through the generations since Burke's time the West experienced a continually evolving world where government expanded for no other reason than it could. The individual's need and right to protect himself from that ever-encroaching Leviathan had become, for Meyer and the Libertarians, a given. As Meyer observes, the necessity of controlling government both intellectually and actually, is simply a continuing obligation of the governed. They cannot rely on the governors to do this for them.

The philosophical conjunction of traditional or classical liberalism and Libertarianism was achieved through Meyer's process. This was not because the followers of either viewpoint necessarily felt they needed the each other but because their philosophies were mutually sustaining. The classical liberals understood the need to value history's lessons (its "prescriptions"); the Libertarians expressed the need never to lose sight of man's first goal—his freedom. It was, and still is, a good fit. The Libertarians continually remind us to control government to protect the individual's freedom; conversely, government, from the classical liberal viewpoint, is to continually strive to order society to protect everyone's individual rights. Liberty under law on one hand, freedom from unnecessary or arbitrary control of any ilk on the other. That, in Meyer's hands, became the paradigm. How well it actually works is up to us.

As he defines the two branches of conservatism Meyer dissects government and contends in opposition to the thinking of Enlightenment-era liberals that there is no "deified will" embodied in the state. The liberals insisted otherwise; that the state, not the individual, was the supreme "good." For Meyer the state has no purpose that can be exalted above mankind; the state is an empty vessel that only the people can fill, idiosyncratically, based on the vagaries of life. He maintains, with obvious validity, that truth can never be achieved with finality. Instead, each generation must test the truths of the past and, in so doing, find its own verities and discover its own errors. Man's relation to man and to society never ceases to evolve and it is thus a given that the test of truth is not logic or authority but experience.

The bulk of Meyer's commentary on the freedom he observes embodied in the fluid relationship between tradition and individualism appears in the main essay of this abbreviated collection of his publications. Because of his personal history it was almost imperative that Meyer go through the intellectual exercise that was to result in his contribution to conservative practice. That journey greatly benefited all conservative thinking.

Meyer came to conservatism and his concept of freedom through the same fanatical mid-twentieth-century communist route as did many of his intellectual contemporaries, and his ultimate anti-communism, anti-utopianism, and anti-totalitarianism were equally fervent. Meyer's earlier philosophy, before he enunciated the imperative of liberty, is relatively easy to comprehend. The rationalist goal of all the collectivist intellectuals (that they could judiciously design and forcefully implement a perfect society built with imperfect humanity) led them to authoritarianism and, for some, communism. But their intellectualism and the results that many of them eventually saw in the totalitarian marketplace brought those grounded in the real world to understand their basic mistake; that is, their failure to accurately account for the human condition—both its positive and not-so-positive facets.

They ultimately came to grasp that neither equality nor human perfection could be attained by fiat. They also arrived at the understanding that human inequalities, as measured by virtually all criteria, were not only not bad but were the foundation of all advancement. These inequalities license progress and its consequent betterment of life for everyone. The real crime according to Meyer and his formerly collectivist colleagues is the stifling or extinction of man's freedom—not the fact that society is rife with inequity. For Meyer,

> freedom is no more nor less than the possibility—and responsibility—to choose. Freedom is the essence of the being of man, and since all social institutions are subordinate to men, the virtue of political and social institutions should be judged by the degree to which they expand or contract the area of freedom.

Meyer's point that "all social institutions are subordinate to men" is one found repeatedly throughout *First Principles*. It is one not to lose sight of as the various political creations, programs, and philosophies are encountered down through the centuries. The ease with which men can manipulate life for their own ends results in less confidence in the design of any governing *entity* and more concern regarding the open and enforceable *rules* put in place to constrain mankind's or its ruler's impulses and power.

Meyer's second step in his analysis of freedom is to determine the climate under which liberty can flourish. Like all classical liberals he understood that civil society must have as its first premise an ethical base. If there are no "understood" rules by which civil discourse can proceed with comity, then it is folly to try to write or legislate those necessary to govern human interaction. Conversely, if we live in a moral society, then the number of rules, the number of points where government needs to step in to officiate are minimized (but not eliminated, for human foibles always exist).

For Meyer, the creation of the "state," the ultimate referee, furthers the (very limited) governmental aim of ensuring an atmosphere of freedom in which people can choose and achieve literally anything they might imagine. The people have to act in a virtuous manner so that the necessity of any state intervention will be minimal; insofar as they do proceed in a moral fashion they need neither guidance nor control. Virtue, to Meyer, is a condition, a "state of grace" toward which humanity must always strive. Though ephemeral it is nevertheless the only rational goal of society. Virtue has religious, altruistic overtones, but it does not necessarily rest upon formal religious practices or any one faith. It really rests on man's relationship to man.

Finally, Meyer returns to the concept of equality, which to conservatives means both the protection of everyone from coercion (from being forced to do or be something other than what one's nature demands) and ensuring to everyone an equality of opportunity. For society, these two pre-conditions inevitably end in unequal results. Inequalities in individual attributes, performances, and outcomes flow from each person's genes, circumstances, and character. It is not within a government's capabilities to ensure an equal result for each individual and that surely must not become its goal.

Apropos of this principle, Meyer focuses on what he calls the Myth of Society: that man engages in political union to serve the whole. As noted above, Meyer contends that the relationship is the opposite: that political society's purpose is the maximizing of freedom for the individual through mutually accepted minimal limitations on personal actions. This stance, often called libertarianism, reflects a fundamental belief in both the individual's natural rights, and reason, coupled with experience, as the interpreter of those rights as they are translated into action.

Perhaps most important for Meyer, there is no morality attached to freedom. Freedom is not a vehicle toward good; it is a condition or status. Freedom used badly or for bad ends is no less freedom. If man cannot choose to use freedom for his worst ends there is no opposition of values enabling him to know what his best may be. Thus, society affords no prospect for progress without the freedom to choose, the freedom to act upon the choices made, and finally, to take responsibility for the consequences of our actions.

For Meyer, the state exists to preserve the individual's freedom to act and to be free from coercion by others, either collectively or individually. Therefore, the only legitimate uses of the state's power are to defend tranquillity from without or within and to pursue the administration of justice; i.e., the determination of where one individual's rights end and another's begin. To exercise these minimal powers, however, requires a dangerous concentration of authority; as a result the state must be limited in its range of power. Individuals or collections of individuals can and must commit themselves to performing virtually all societal functions not granted to the state thus keeping the state from growing simply through opportunity or convenience. The American educational system would be a prime example of what happens when the state initially becomes involved and then, by means of its gathered power, morphs into a Leviathan that can be stopped only through pitched battle.

The goal of society, once limits are set, is to maintain a free order while pursuing virtue; and virtue, in a social construct, is defined as little more than the Golden Rule. The two branches of conservative thinking—the traditionalist (which emphasizes evolved virtue [truths learned through experience and time]) and the Libertarian (which dwells on freedom), can thus meld into one because their foundations are complementary. Being free is not antithetical to virtue, and being virtuous is not destructive of freedom. For Meyer, the ability to choose good or bad is the only method by which we might freely achieve virtue. Conversely, of course, Meyer argues that virtue cannot be decreed—not by agreement, not by democratic mechanisms, and not by means of a dictatorial leadership. He writes of truth and virtue as metaphysical and moral ends, and freedom as the political prerequisite to achieve them. Truth and virtue can only be obtained by individuals—the "state" can only be virtuous if its members are, and it cannot be virtuous if the citizenry is not.

Following this reasoning, Meyer sees government as properly having a minimal role; that is, to deal only with essential aspects of a free society. The problem with this approach is that as admirable as it appears on paper it often does not adequately take into consideration man's innate ability to act at cross-purposes with himself. Our inventive genius for stupidity and/or inattention creates demands to expand government's minimalist role, especially in our current no-fault politically correct society. However, for Meyer, it is imperative that government not manage our individual lives just as we should not individually control others or allow them to dictate to us. Sometimes, though, the effects of human perversity become so intolerable that government, of necessity, must intrude. The unfortunate sequence of events that seems to inevitably follow, and the point at which minimalist intervention exceeds its proper bounds, occurs when government's role in any aspect of social intercourse becomes domineering and—worst of all—permanent. (Again, public education comes to mind, as does today's welfare model, and soon our healthcare system.)

The important point nowadays is that government's supposedly "essential" activities grow in tandem with the intellectually fashionable aversion to relying upon personal responsibility to ensure individual well-being and societal tranquillity. Meyer's reasoning relates to the fact that we have appended a Bill of Rights to our Constitution, but no Bill of Responsibilities. Meyer repeatedly notes that although a perfect society is obviously not within man's capability, getting as close as we can *is* one of our responsibilities. Even though perfection is unattainable, striving is not futile as there are many good by-products derived from our efforts. Giving up on individuals and instead placing controls on everyone by means of government proclamation leads to an agglomeration of government that becomes counterproductive, oppressive, and ultimately, totalitarian.

Meyer sets the stage for understanding why the individual is the foundation block of society and why individualism is the antithesis of the welfare state. In *In Defense of Freedom*, he describes the necessary political mechanisms that have been formed out of the American experience which have allowed us to partially weather the collectivist storm thus far. However, as one can tell from Meyer's premises, the war is far from over.

About the Author

FRANK STRAUS MEYER was born in 1909. He attended Princeton University and later Oxford College in England where he became a leader of student radicals and a member of the Communist Party. He worked within the party for fourteen years until he experienced his anti-totalitarian epiphany, the result of reading Friedrich von Hayek's *The Road to Serfdom* while serving in the U.S. Army in World War II. After the war Meyer broke completely with the Communists and spent time exposing their methods and machinations. He served as an editor and columnist at *National Review* for many years and was a leading force in the effort to bring to fruition what became known as "fusion"—the joining of the major elements of American conservatism. Frank Meyer died in 1972, an icon among American conservatives.

11

Property and Freedom

Richard Pipes

Originally published: 1999
292 pages

WITHOUT PROPERTY in all its forms there wouldn't be much need of law. As John Locke observes in *The Second Treatise on Civil Government*,

> The great chief end, therefore, of men uniting into commonwealths, and putting themselves under government, is the preservation of their property.

The existence of property leads to enormous social and legal complexity; the ability to possess property was established in prehistory—first by might, later by religious precept, and finally through civil authority. Of the Ten Commandments, two deal directly with ownership—"Thou shalt not covet thy neighbor's house" and "Thou shalt not steal." Neither would be proclaimed if there was no private right to some "thing" that should not be coveted or stolen. With the aid of philosophers, lawyers, politicians, academics, economists of every stripe, and, of course, clerics, humanity has tried to get its imagination around the concept of property for millennia. Most attempts failed because individuals sought to define and circumscribe property in order to make it fit into civil society. Many did not see the truth: to be viable a civil society must conform to the reality of property. The contrast between these antithetical approaches became palpable with the advent of the Enlightenment (c. 1750) and the implosion of property rights during the French Revolution of 1789.

Property is the basis of virtually all human interaction. Up to this juncture we have focused on human individuality and freedom, and how those two aspects of life are defined by means of formal social organization—mostly connoted as government and law. We have also investigated the relationship between our economic interests and efforts and government's ever-present (mostly political) "need" to regulate such. But essential to fully understanding all of these relationships is a concomitant cognition of where private property fits into public discourse. And to understand property's place it is essential to comprehend what property is and how it came to be, and then how property and politics became inextricably intertwined.

Richard Pipes explores these steps in *Property and Freedom*. In the space of a few hundred pages he cogently and compellingly explicates the seminal relationship between people, their possessions, their government, and society as it developed over millennia. At the same time he philosophically and chronologically addresses the maturing of human associations and goals that are the core subject matter of *First Principles*. *Property and Freedom* is simply one of the most valuable tools available to aid in comprehending how modern society developed and how it functions.

In prehistory, when man was attempting to order his relationships with his neighbors (in the era when might was giving way to right), the main issue revolved about who owned what, who had a right to what, etc. As law developed, the power of the state grew as well—both to enforce the law and to order society. But at this early point the object of social organization was to settle the relations between men. Over time as has been and will be seen the state took on a life of its own and *it* began to claim a right to the property of the citizenry in order to "improve" the lives of all over whom it ruled. In the modern era the questions of a person's right to his property are not largely questions to be resolved between citizens but between the citizen and the state. In other words, while questions of property rights among men have become mostly settled, the right to property and the right of disposition or use of an individual's property are contests between people and their governors. Issues of taxation and regulation of citizen property are now the main battleground of modern politics. As Lao Tsu (a countryman and near contemporary of Confucius) observed about government (c. 500 BC): "The more restrictions and limitations there are [by government], the more impoverished men will be."

In order to understand both the evolution (some would say devolution) of property rights and the growth of statist views of government's purpose, which views denigrate and devalue individual rights, it is productive to start at the beginning and follow the course of property and its social meaning and effect as it developed over the centuries.

Early in his book Pipes introduces his readers to Jean Bodin, Hugo Grotius, and James Harrington, three relatively obscure philosophers not often acknowledged in twenty-first-century political and intellectual discussions. Nevertheless, their contributions were crucial to the development of modern property and political hypotheses. Their theories evolved out of historical truths that when applied rationally helped successfully mold ordered social relationships. Because what these men described worked, their designs were restated in successive generations. The self-evident value and utility of these arrangements became accepted doctrine.

Most of the authors of modern political practice drew from their predecessors as they developed their own theories. The Hebrew, Greek, Roman, and Christian philosophers (like practicing democrats, republicans, and parliamentarians throughout modern history) did not bring forth a complete and comprehensive system of government. Each built on what had been tried before by modifying, expanding, or discarding the works and thoughts of previous generations. For example, one cannot read Cicero without thinking of Socrates or understand Thomas Jefferson without considering Thomas Hobbes. This is the beauty of the history of governance—what we have today works as well as it does because it has been tested from so many angles for so many centuries. John Locke did not create out of thin air the concept of natural law or property rights, or the ordered relationship that was necessary between the sovereign and his subjects. He was well versed in the lessons of history before he ever put the first pen stroke on foolscap.

The concepts forged by Harrington, Grotius, and Bodin at the beginning of the Enlightenment (when early thoughts regarding representative, democratic government were forming) were very, very new. Pipes gave these philosophers talking parts in his book to acknowledge governance as an evolving process guided by seemingly small but sometimes hugely consequential ideas. It is a truism that theories, no matter how well conceived in the mind, are of little value until tested in the real world. The hypotheses of these three men were necessarily subjected to the human condition and the law of unintended consequences once they entered the marketplace. At that point we began to have an idea of how effective they would be as tools of governance.

Beginning in prehistory and continuing for more than ten thousand years, people grappled with the idea of property—well before formal religion and organized states began to exert their influence on a person's relationship to his possessions. Most of that history is unrecorded but the evolution resulted early in unquestioned personal control of labor's products. Pipes observes that as civilization developed, initially by means of tribal formations, later in larger agglomerations of people, the story of property involved the increasing dominion over the people's resources by monarchs, oligarchs, dictators, and totalitarian rulers. Along with the rise to power of these sovereigns (who possessed widely varying levels of autonomy, authority, and control) there developed two antithetical circumstances with which these rulers had to deal: first, they had to raise "money" (in the form of diverse resources) to fight wars and protect their own possessions and position; second, they had to contend with the natural law principle that people are always reluctant to surrender the fruits of their labor to whichever strongman comes along.

These contrary factors compelled the leaders of myriad cultures to cooperate—negotiate really—slowly and ever grudgingly, with whatever tribal leaders or feudal aristocracy existed in order to gain the riches they needed to remain in power. Once the crack was opened so that the nobility's control over its own property was recognized as a right (not simply a fact) their leverage grew—because rulers needed economic support to achieve their ends. Ultimately, of course, the monarchies shrank and then folded. The nobility (and centuries later, the people) began governing themselves—*through this right to property*. The story of this transition by way of systematic fits and starts over the last two thousand years is as much the story of property as it is of the right of self-governance and individual freedom. *Property and Freedom*, like *The Roots of American Order* (Chapter 4), is fundamental to understanding how we got from history's anarchy to a workable, if imperfect, conception of civil society.

Jean Bodin, the first of Pipes's relatively unknown philosophers, lived in the mid-1500s. He established the idea that an absolute sovereign, though not limited by the actions of his/her subjects, *is* constrained by natural law. This concept gave both rights and power to the people in relation to their property because such was theirs through a mechanism *not* grounded in their relationship to the monarch. These possessions were their *natural* right.

In the early 1600s Hugo Grotius brought forth an even more profound change when he classified personal property as alienable or inalienable. The former encompassed "things which can belong to one person as well as another;" i.e., tangible possessions. Far more importantly, however, Grotius postulated that inalienable property includes all "those things which belong so essentially to one person that they cannot belong to another, such as a person's life, body, freedom, or honor." Thus was born the idea that's one's essence cannot be removed from one's physical being, that that essence, that dignity, is the *property* of each individual.

Finally Pipes comes to James Harrington, a mid-seventeenth-century scholar who was the "first political theorist to view political power as a by-product of economics, or, more specifically, of the distribution of property between the state and the populace." Manifest in Harrington's observations is the need to discuss taxation and the apportioning of power to determine issues of social control. These relationships are tersely summarized by Harrington's axiom: "he who controls the country's wealth controls its politics. . . ." Later, of course, as the sanctity of the individual and the concept of Grotius's inalienable rights became established and codified in the English and U.S. Constitutions, Harrington's equation underwent modification as people recognized that governance isn't just about property. However, his innovative premise, namely, that property and its control are the foundation of politics, is the important point to consider today.

Around the middle of the seventeenth century, Grotius's concept of personal rights, something "owned" in an intangible sense, began to significantly complicate the already contentious subject of property. As Pipes observes,

> [T]he term "property" underwent a metamorphosis, revolutionary in its implications, by being broadened to mean not only material objects but everything which the individual had a natural right to claim as his own . . . his life and freedom.

This conceptual triad of the person, the state, and the physical contents of each human being's life has been uneasy and unstable for much of the time since Grotius.

When we think about property we think first of the obvious—what might be in our pockets or under our feet. But our most important possessions are our life, our liberty, and our prerogative to do with each as we wish. The idea that we have a property right in our own lives was truly an epiphany, especially after thousands of years of subjugation in the form of institutionalized slavery and law without rights found in virtually every society. Henceforth, the insistence that a person's life belonged to him, that neither one's life nor the liberty to act freely (subject to not interfering with others) could be arbitrarily taken away by the state, changed relationships between rulers and the ruled. As Pipes comments, history arrived at the point where there were two sovereigns in the land: the monarch and the individual. The clash between the two is the modern history of the development of freedom and property—the essential elements of an ordered civil society.

Grotius's idea that human beings should be masters of their persons was an outgrowth of the concept of natural law, a law that Pipes defines as "rational, unchanging, unchangeable." Natural law, in other words, is above mankind and its machinations and cannot be altered by temporal governors. Pipes further notes that considerations regarding natural law as applied to physical property gave rise to two opposing opinions around the middle of the eighteenth century: proposition one: the unequal distribution of property resulting from human differences in ability, personality, and situation causes human oppression and strife; proposition two: property is the root of progress because its individual possession is the source of the alleviation of human suffering. The acquisition and personal control of property, founded in a quest for security and satisfaction, allows for a cascade of benefits to all, albeit in differing proportions. This enables property, because of, not in spite of its unequal distribution, to be a universal good.

Which judgment is correct? The answer is both. Or, as any good attorney would respond, "it depends."

Pipes comments that as these two propositions were forming there arose in France a philosophical movement toward "rectifying" life's earthly inequities—in other words, wholesale acceptance of proposition one. This impulse resulted in an obvious conflict between a person's freedom to control his life and property and the state's right to control the citizenry and its possessions—for the benefit of "all." French intellectuals of the mid-eighteenth century, known as the *philosophes*, advocated the abolition of private property through the equal distribution of all possessions. However, this effort to change human affairs by changing the basis of political, economic, and interpersonal relations utterly missed the point—and caused enormous devastation in its wake.

Inequality does not reside in property or its distribution, for property itself is neutral; it is only human activity that creates inequities that can be perceived as negative or positive. If one person accumulates more property than another, a perceived inequality can come to the fore. The accusation of oppression even arises. The allegation may persist until one investigates how inequality is defined, how the accumulation was achieved, and to what use the accumulation will be put, or what effect it will cause. It isn't the essence of property that causes this effect, but the essence of human nature, and human inequality, that is at work. The accumulation of property, or capital, is what allows the economic multiplier effect to occur. That effect usually results in two quite positive consequences—employment for an increasing number of people and a proliferation of products and services, and a rising living standard for all involved. If the incentive that allows progress is removed, if equal ownership of property is the goal, if success is taxed heavily, then progress of any kind is more difficult—and life is as well.

One example encompasses the core of proposition two: Consider the proportionally greater risks taken, effort expended, or genius applied by those who obtain more than others—because people want what is created by those few. Different levels of reward appear more "fair" when viewed from the perspective of how much went into the accumulation, and how much the citizenry as a whole benefited, rather than how much an individual ultimately gathers. In essence, the accumulation itself is often the result of unequal effort or talent and is not necessarily an "unfair" result (unless it is contended that the very differences between individuals are "unfair," even if natural—a calamitous suggestion, at best). How we reward the inventiveness, imagination, and risk-taking of those who improve the lives all (whether through airplanes, art or arithmetic) is not black and white.

There are numerous reasons for beneficial unequal results. When viewed in the larger context that encompasses all of society these factors offer a useful and workable clarification of how property is distributed in a modern setting. These ideas, which explore both human potential and social "designs" versus individual rights are investigated in several other chapters in this symposium (*Capitalism and Freedom* [Chapter 25], *Wealth and Poverty* [Chapter 27] are but two). Fully understanding these ideas is essential to gaining a comprehension of the larger picture presented by the existence of property and its sometimes allegedly unequal or unfair distribution.

When taken to its furthest point, the actual foundation of inequality is the person, and his or her ability to earn, produce, create, etc. The intellectual war, fostered by the misunderstanding or misrepresentation of the causes and often beneficial effects of unequal results, continues today as it has for centuries. This battle draws its energy mostly from the emotional reaction to physical differences in people's lives. Pipes's investigation of the permutations of this conflict and of the historical perspectives on the two views of the "problem" of property is comprehensive and more than marginally useful in today's political environment.

Pipes proceeds from his discussion of essential concepts (gleaned from both obscure and well-known authors who wrote before and during the Middle Ages) to address examples of how various political and economic theories of property have complemented or undermined one another in an evolutionary development that still continues. He then comments on the substantive contributions of famous theorists such as Locke, Rousseau, and Hobbes. Although Pipes clearly wants his readers to understand the breadth of the subject, the period of time, and the number of places out of which he drew his conclusions, he also expects readers to realize that political theorizing is never complete. He makes clear that his observations on the understandings of others are essentially only a way-station.

Pipes ultimately arrives at a consideration of the problems and opportunities of property theory in the modern era. Whether overt and wholesale (as in socialism) or covert and piecemeal (as in state welfarism) he concludes that equality attained through governmental redistribution of property is theoretically achievable, but obviously impractical and contrary to human nature. Communist schemes (an extreme example of anti-property movements, many of which are yet alive and well in the developing world) seek to eradicate personality in the belief that human beings, through sheer will and the guidance of their re-educators, can be made to dissociate themselves from their individuality.

What one gains in this fashion is (theoretically) equality of physical possessions; what one loses is the individual's essence and humanity, for when the psychological dimension of ownership is denied people change and their relationships to property and to one another also change on a fundamental level. Of course, none of this discussion even begins to address what happens to property itself—the destruction of its value—when the incentive to create it or possess it is abolished. Ultimately, the effects of modern redistributionist schemes (whether in the form of the welfare state or overt socialism, etc.) are the same—

frustration, eventual anger, and then dissociation. The redistributionists, as will be seen at several points in this book, want to redistribute wealth that, using their philosophy and schemes, cannot be created.

Pipes gives example after example of how much life is altered when property rights are denied. On the individual level, one crucial illustration is that the concept of privacy emanates from property. Privacy entails being able to withdraw to one's own space. But with no right to property no one can own anything or exclude anyone from any private space. Thus, in order to have privacy there must be private property.

Pipes observes that the modern state is an organization that theoretically defends the property and the rights of its citizens in return for the revenues it collects (taxes). The transition from the absolute monarch of prehistory to one constrained by the aristocracy to one eventually subordinate to citizens followed a logical course. In England, for example, the state became organized around the sovereign. As noted earlier, the king needed resources to maintain the monarchy and to wage war and he had to give up some control in order to gain consent to taxation of those who supported him. He ultimately had to abandon any claim to absolute power because the people began to value their possessions as much as they valued the protection of the king. Thus they began to resist his call for fiscal support.

More to the point, as the citizenry created property they understood that they could use their resources to protect themselves *without* the king; ultimately they found they could protect themselves *from* the king as well; the extreme means of protection from the king, of course, was revolution. It was the people's growing wealth and the king's increasing dependence on it that compelled the crown to grant his subjects rights and freedoms in order to get their agreement on imposts. This is the story of how private wealth came to restrain public authority. Resolute royal power faced the people's absolute property right in what they had created; the king blinked and property won. However, as gratifying as that relationship sounds and irrespective of how many centuries it endured the story does not end there.

Pipes explains that as the twenty-first century dawned the power of property had receded. Property itself could no longer claim easy precedence over government. Pipes refers here not to the reduction of power of the very wealthy, but of the ordinary citizen—who should be secure in his smaller venue. This was as remarkable a story as the one of how property itself became owned rather than just possessed. Pipes quotes a fellow student of property rights:

> Private property once may have been conceived as a barrier to government power, but today that barrier is easily overcome.... Under the present law the institution of private property places scant limitation upon the size and direction of government activities characteristic of the modern welfare state. (Richard A. Epstein, *Takings*, 1985)

This convolution occurred partially because there was so much private property created by capitalistic enterprise that liberal politicians saw it as an unlimited resource for doing "good." The harm their efforts caused—by encouraging a culture of dependency and hastening the erosion of personal responsibility, accountability, and incentive through the ever-increasing goods and services government could offer—for "free"—was either ignored or denied. In the last ninety pages of *Property and Freedom* Pipes discusses the progressive wearing away of property rights over the course of the last fifty years, especially in the United States.

In his dialogue, Pipes sees us confounded, even flummoxed, by the encroachments on our freedom evidenced in the growing obligations placed on the body politic. These constraints require taxpayers to work longer each year to support the welfare state—a palpable restraint on the citizen's resources, time, and right to the products of his own labor. The liberal establishment unflinchingly denies the necessity and utility of property to the social construct and the protection of such as a prime premise of governance. It has instead demoted property to a vehicle to be used to achieve equalitarian goals. Pipes sees organic harm done to society by the intentional degradation of property. This devaluation occurs when property is turned into something to which everyone is equally entitled in some substantial measure, no matter the circumstances. The liberals insist on the truth of their proposition in spite of more than a millennium of evidence to the contrary. By means of their inversion of the fundamental concept of property a public culture of "entitlements" has been substituted for an obligation of reciprocal duty.

One asks how the derogation of property rights (therefore personal rights and our personal freedom) has been so easily achieved. The simple answer is found in political manipulation of the public by both the ignorant and the feckless. Pretentious accusation by the "anointed" (those who claim to know better than we do how our lives should be run) was the tool of choice. The public was informed of how it had failed in its "duties" to the less fortunate, while the duties of the less fortunate were ignored or found not to exist at all. These denunciations were implemented by those whose motives and agenda ran the gamut from guilt to greed. Their misunderstanding or misrepresentation of basic economics and their absence of fealty to human dignity were clear, and in the larger picture simply sad. But, no matter their means, when combined with the public's gullibility or indolence, these demagogues cowed an unsuspecting and complacent citizenry into a line of thinking that could only be changed by massive evidence of failure.

Such was the case with welfare reform in the U.S. during the 1990s. Forty years and five *trillion* dollars after its massive implementation the welfare impulse was found not only to have not helped those toward whom it was aimed, but to have made matters much worse. Thus, policy was revised; welfare became "workfare" and limits were placed on how long the able-bodied could remain within the system. Making the welfare impulse rational, such as was achieved in that instance, was hard won. The effort required fidelity to purpose and facts in the face of deceptive, even false, opposition accusations of the citizenry's unworthy self-interest in their own lives; sometimes there were even charges of economic, social, racial, or cultural discrimination.

Pipes's quotation from U.S. Supreme Court Justice Louis D. Brandeis best captures how damage is wrought by sometimes well-intentioned but naïve politicians and their self-serving demagogue compatriots:

> Experience should teach us to be most on our guard to protect liberty when the Government's purposes are *beneficent*. Men born to freedom are naturally alert to repel invasion of their liberty by evil-minded rulers. The greatest dangers to liberty lurk in the insidious encroachments by men of zeal, well-meaning but without understanding. (Olmstead v. United States [1927])

In mid-twentieth-century America, as Pipes points out, men of supposed good will but "without understanding" did more to destroy freedom and property in the name of benevolence than had many totalitarian revolutionaries. When their policies failed the excuse of this cadre of ideologues was that they meant well, or that not enough had been done, that even more was needed. As Pipes notes, at least when a totalitarian ruler is dethroned his regime and rules go with him. Not so in a society of laws—once the laws are enshrined in the ledger book, no matter that those who enacted them are defeated electorally, the laws themselves present the utmost difficulty in their repeal.

The ultimate insult to the body politic, of course, is that those politicians who follow in the steps of the original malefactors often believe repeal is not feasible for social (meaning political) reasons. Thus they simply tweak the system in a futile attempt to make it work and create an even greater cascade of unintended, and untenable, consequences. The public is further misled because it believes that these new politicians, in not deconstructing the false state, apparently support the overall the system and believe it to be viable—even worthy. It is not. At that point one has to consider Barry Goldwater's campaign pledge in 1964, "My aim is not to pass laws, but to repeal them," (Chapter 18) regarding the kind of peaceful but intentional revolution that is needed to effect true change.

Pipes reviews the history of how and why the American governing impulse changed so dramatically during and subsequent to the Great Depression of the 1930s. He explains that the expectations of government did not simply evolve they actually morphed as the scope of governmental activity grew. By mid-century, concomitant with an ever-diminishing social role for individual responsibility, the Democrats had bought into the concept of President Lyndon Johnson's Great Society. The underlying philosophy of this system was that government was obligated to care for all who allegedly were not being cared for. However, there were two political fallacies in these programs: First, there was no proof that people *could* not care for themselves—there was only limited evidence that some *had* not. Second, not only was nothing asked from those helped at public expense, it was insisted that nothing was due. It was claimed that society had done this to its own members thus society would pay the bill. This was the dawn of political correctness—the crafting of a social view that people were not responsible for anything that happened to them; it was someone else's fault, or it was society's fault. All of these conversations went well beyond accepting the need for a social safety net; the arguments were much larger than that and much more political.

Prior to the enactment of the Great Society programs there had been a window of opportunity to recognize the difference between a "handout" and a "hand up." This window slowly closed, primarily for political reasons, during and after the Great Depression and Franklin Delano Roosevelt's years in the White House. The concepts of personal discipline and responsibility that are the foundations of self-actualization began a metamorphosis in the 1930s as Roosevelt grappled with the severe economic effects of the Depression. By the time of President Johnson's election in 1964 the notions of public obligation were woven into grand designs. The definitions of both responsibility and discipline were inverted and used as political weapons against those who espoused the traditional American value of self-reliance. It had become the *public's* responsibility to aid the individual; it was through *civic* discipline that those who failed to care for themselves would be cared for. This politically expedient (thus electorally successful) approach to social welfarism found its voice in Johnson's new, even more majestic Democrat agenda.

This philosophy was the culmination of three decades of political effort that had not reduced the effects of bad economic policy, which earlier had extended the consequences of the Depression far beyond what was necessary. This extension of economic malaise through the 1930s had profoundly negative effects on the U.S. economy and psyche for the following seventy years—and the last of the damage is yet unseen.

Along with many others, Pipes observes that the Depression itself could have been ended sooner with appropriate government action; i.e., decreased taxes, free trade, and reduced government spending. These measures would have encouraged the economy by means of basic free-market incentives to expand to re-employ the millions who were out of work. Instead, the times were made worse by exactly the opposite: higher taxes (the lowest bracket income tax rate more than quintupled between 1931 and 1941); the Hawley-Smoot tariff imposts (which caused retaliatory, deadly tariffs to be implemented around the world); and massive government expenditures (primarily by the Public Works Administration which built thousands of public buildings, dams, bridges that consumed roughly *one-half* of the Roosevelt Administration's mid-30s budget and caused it to balloon from $4.6 billion in 1932 to $8.2 billion in 1936 [including a $4.4 billion deficit in that year alone]) that had little, if any, economic multiplier effect. By the mid-1930s when their measures did not end the Depression those in power assumed government simply had not done enough and they proposed even more intervention. The truth of the matter was that government had already "done" too much and to do more would further increase market distortions and undermine any progress toward regaining economic equilibrium.

There was an additional, wholly unintended and more devastating consequence of the actions of President Roosevelt and his Brain Trust (as his closest advisors were known). When the free-market economies of the West came close to collapsing—and in the view of the leftists had collapsed—the contention was made that the theories and predictions of Karl Marx had been validated. Marx said that capitalism was rotten from within and that its vices—greed and dominance—would cause it to fail as power accumulated at the top of the economic pyramid and oppression grew at the bottom. Ultimately Marx contended that social and political revolution would become the only logical consequence. As economic matters worsened during the 30s and more and more inappropriate responses were crafted by the politicians an almost inevitable conclusion was reached and proselytized as capitalism faltered—that socialism and communism *were* the answers to human needs.

Obviously economically and socially the West not only recovered—through the unfortunate mechanism of the Second World War that put everyone back to work—its economies flourished in unprecedented fashion when the war was over. But politically the stage was set for a five decade Cold War that came close to eliminating civilization. In the U.S. and other Western countries the economic myopia that prolonged the Depression invited government centralization after the war (the theory being that the governors needed ever more control to fix what they'd already broken) and began to substitute the welfare state to counter (philosophically, politically, and economically) the free lunch that was being offered by the communists and socialists in European states. That there was no free lunch, that such was not economically possible over the long term could not be disproved by the example of the strident communist governments during this era because the communists had closed their books and their borders to ensure hegemony over both information and emigration. The philosophical recovery of not only free-market capitalism but freedom itself was much longer in coming because the supposed results socialistic enterprise was to achieve took fifty years to finally fail. But the foundation for the battle lay in the policies invented in an earlier era: the more government had meddled in the 30s the more inept it and the capitalistic system appeared; and the more succor and apparent validity that was given to the false claims of the socialists. It was this economically ignorant meddling the prevented the system from righting itself.

Thus what was so devastating for the West as a whole was the long-term political effect rather than just the economic failures of Roosevelt's policies. Socialism and communism could claim their half century in the sun because the contention that their counterpart—capitalism—was fatally flawed appeared to have merit. It appeared to have merit because bright, thinking, well-intentioned people thought they knew what they were doing in the 1930s. And what they were doing was reducing freedom and attempting to control a mechanism—the free market—that suffers no master in its infinite convolutions. In its thrashing about to find political answers to economic problems the Roosevelt administration's nascent welfare state began the downward bureaucratic/welfare spiral that is now the main battleground as twenty-first-century governing and economic verities are yet again tested and measured by false premises. To be fair, many of those in Congress and the White House during the decades that followed Roosevelt's term in office were more than complicitous (again, mostly for political purposes) and just as ignorant in constructing and enlarging the modern welfare state, so it is necessary to look at the whole picture in this arena before judging the actions of those in power in the 1930s and 40s.*

It is unfortunately easy to see how the Roosevelt era's responses were constructed out of whole political cloth. By the early 1940s when economic recovery was as far from achievement as it had been ten years earlier Roosevelt was trying ever harder to solve what his administration had made worse. "Freedom from want," a new and even more extreme gesture was the phrase that launched his 1941 State of the Union address. It was a sentiment that ominously found its footing in the continuing widespread poverty of the Depression. Initially, politically, it had seemed a not unreasonable claim (considering the climate that had already been created). That is, as Pipes notes, until the public realized that the only way to achieve this freedom was at

---

* Although scholars have treated President Roosevelt harshly as a student of economics, it would be unfair to leave only this impression of Roosevelt in the reader's mind. Roosevelt is also considered the finest commander-in-chief the nation has had during wartime. His strategic decisions, from his use of U.S. troops in North Africa at the beginning of World War II in order to divide Hitler's resources in Europe without expending human capital in unconscionable numbers, to his resolute support of the immense efforts to create an atomic bomb at the end, decisions that often went against his own military's best judgments, are seen today as both necessary and masterful. The political and policy mayhem that was extant during the years Roosevelt was president—the economy was in shambles, communism's allure was on the rise, Hitler in Germany and Tojo in Japan threatened to overrun the free world—forced him to juggle so many conflicting options that it was foreordained that both his detractors and his chorus would have many opportunities for judgment and conclusion. It is up to the reader to assess Roosevelt, but only after understanding all of the circumstances of his presidency—the complete range of which is not offered within this text.

the expense of those who had not relinquished their sense of self-discipline and responsibility, those who had not embraced "the notion of entitlement in the absence of contribution or sacrifice." Those who were termed by William Graham Sumner, the nineteenth-century polymath and philosopher, "the forgotten men" of political discourse. "The forgotten man . . . He works, he votes, generally he prays, but his chief business in life is to pay."

So that there is no misunderstanding about this situation Pipes clearly demonstrates it was not "the people" who demanded freedom from want; this was a political fabrication. During the Depression the citizens of the U.S. were *always* willing to work. They felt no sense of society's obligation to support them; they understood it was *their* responsibility to support themselves. That was not only our history, but our culture. They just wanted jobs. Despite this truth the political atmosphere at that time became such that citizens were told that the consequences of not being able to work would be remedied by the government. Thus was born the political (not social) culture of dependency. What *could* have eventuated was a return to a free-enterprise economy but as Pipes points out that was not politically profitable and perhaps not even economically comprehended.

As Pipes argues, the politically voiced assertion of a "right" to freedom from want was a supposed "right" to life's necessities at public expense. It was a "right" to something that was not one's own. A skeptical public accepted the political reality and the Rooseveltian handout because for many the times still seemed desperate. But the public was not convinced of the truth of the concept. Nevertheless, the camel had his nose under the tent. As elections came and went the right to "freedom from want" metastasized into calls by the politically astute (that is, those who sought power for its own sake) for redistribution of goods and services. This unearned redistribution (the range of which grew as new politicians were elected and felt the continual expansion of what government did was the purpose for which they were sent to Washington) was to be done at public expense, of course. Those doing the "giving"—the taxpayers—were berated as unsympathetic, or greedy, or bigots, or worse if they found these programs unwarranted; those on the receiving end became inured to the "failures of society" and the redress of those failures in the form of freedom from want and both groups voted accordingly. As might be expected, the implementation of the welfare state preempted any thought of what could be done with a hand up rather than a handout.

In Pipes's view the carnage is yet unfinished and will get worse if the lessons of the Kirks and Hayeks and Meyers and Mises and Friedmans are not heeded. The only solution is for the citizenry to take control of the electoral process *in toto* to insert rationality back into fiscal opportunities. Changes along these lines were begun in the 1990s but between political backsliding and the neoconservative electoral expediency in evidence since the turn of the twenty-first century steps toward progress have been less than hoped for. What Pipes explicates is that if *we* do not take action in our own defense and in the defense of our children, we will get the government we deserve.

A final note on these issues: Pipes does not imply criticism of a social safety net as he reviews the sequence of events America experienced during and since the Depression. He only offers reproach of state welfare that goes beyond need and lands directly in politics. He proposes that governmental involvement applied rationally (not emotionally or politically) would be workable if its provisions were tied to concomitant obligations. These obligations include the responsibility to take care of oneself to the extent possible, to better oneself as opportunity arises, to offer work for what one receives if one is able, and to not rely on state-sponsored beneficence beyond basic need. But, as Pipes observes, the liberal's care-for-all approach has operated to extinguish awareness of both obligations and opportunities with regard to those being helped. This was the result of a false political assumption: that every person who lived in poverty was there *not* through any action of his own and was *utterly* unable to help himself. In other words, the condition of poverty was completely a societal failure. This is the essence of political correctness.

Pipes's contention is clear: the liberals in America have lost sight of square one. They cannot see and even go so far as to refuse to acknowledge how our economic system and society actually function. Unfortunately liberals have used poverty as a political lever. But in so doing they have conveniently ignored the fact that poverty and relative poverty are as often stage-of-life related phenomena as much as they are social consequences. The young, in particular, are often less well off because of their inexperience and less developed comprehensions but they move upward through the economic scale as they work and age; the lowest economic class does not contain a static population. Of course, there are many factors at work in such investigations, the details of which are beyond the scope of Pipes's observations and conclusions. Additional resources can be consulted regarding these issues, and the validity of some politically motivated economic and social assertions can be analyzed. For an investigation of poverty see Thomas Sowell's brief review of this issue in *Fewer* (Chapter 43), and *Economics of the Free Society* (Chapter 23).

(With reference to economic misrepresentations and misunderstandings, especially as regards the manipulation of economic statistics, one should read *Basic Economics* by Thomas Sowell. This book is not part of *First Principles* but it exposes the methodological and statistical [and thus philosophical] exploitation of economics. It also explores politically motivated economic theory for those untrained in this field.)

As Frederic Bastiat notes in 1850 in *The Law* (Chapter 7),

> See if the law takes from some person what belongs to them, and gives it to other persons to whom it does not belong. See if the law benefits one citizen at the expense of another by doing what the citizen himself cannot do without committing a crime.

This perversion of law is exactly what is seen in the utopian mirage created sequentially by Franklin D. Roosevelt, Lyndon Johnson, and mid-twentieth-century Congressional Democrats. All of these players seem to have had little appreciation of rational economic foundations, the sanctity of private property, or individual dignity—primarily because these concepts were not politically useful. Pipes completes his explication of these modern conditions by discussing the corruption of governmental purpose:

> The notion that every need creates a "right" has acquired a quasi-religious status in modern America, inhibiting rational discussion.

Need one say more? Probably not. Need one do more? Without question.

About the Author

RICHARD PIPES, Baird Professor of History (now Emeritus) at Harvard University for more than forty years, was born in Silesia in 1921. He lived in Warsaw, Poland at the beginning of World War II and watched the city bombed mercilessly as the Germans invaded. He and his family escaped to America via Italy where he excelled in the world of academia after serving in the U.S. Air Corps and earning educational credentials. He is the author of numerous books and essays, including *The Russian Revolution, Russia Under the Bolshevik Regime*, and *Property and Freedom*. In 1981–82, he served President Reagan on the National Security Council as adviser on Soviet and East European Affairs—where policy decisions were anything but unanimous or insignificant. In 1992 he was an expert witness in the Russian Constitutional Court's trial against the Communist Party of the former Soviet Union. Pipes was a key anti-Soviet crusader in the 1970s and 1980s, and from 1968–73 he served as Director of Harvard's Russian Research Center. He is a member of the Council of Foreign Relations and sits on the editorial boards of *Strategic Review, Orbis, International Journal of Intelligence and CounterIntelligence, Continuity, Journal of Strategic Studies, East European Jewish Affairs,* and *Nuova Storia Contemporanea.* He lives in Cambridge, Massachusetts, and Chesham, New Hampshire.

12

Wealth of Nations

Adam Smith

Originally published: 1776
590 pages

ADAM SMITH is to capitalism as Thomas Jefferson is to freedom. And *Wealth of Nations* is to free-market economics as the Declaration of Independence is to American sovereignty. Smith's understanding of commerce and human nature and his conclusions regarding the structure and future of the British mercantile system (which was rife with protectionist fabrications in the eighteenth century) are as germane and applicable today as they were to the emergence of capitalism more than two centuries ago.

Modern economic life was born with the Industrial Revolution and virtually all of the elements of present-day commerce were in evidence in England by the 1700s. With as much accuracy as if he were a contemporary lecturer in economics Smith writes of markets, trade, incentive—all the ingredients of economic discourse—and the limits of government. He discusses taxes comprehensively delving into how, when, by whom and to what degree they could profitably be levied for both the government and citizens. Finally, he writes about people—the good and the bad of the human condition. Smith's goal was to establish why it is in the best interests of both the governed and the government that consumer sovereignty rule economic markets.

Although Smith did not enjoy our ease of access to information he cites commercial statistics and cost data (i.e., the costs of doing business) to substantiate his conclusions for England and the European continent. The wealth of detail, which Smith was thoughtful enough to use somewhat selectively, dates from as long as centuries before he wrote. This makes his work as exhaustive as it is easy to comprehend, not just in its logic but also in the value of his inferences.

Smith begins his exploration of economic substance one step beyond the infancy of human endeavor. He assumes that the existence of private property has been intellectually accepted and economically justified; thus he does not attempt to defend it as an institution. He found the investigation and explication of property in the works of John Locke both logical and rational. (Locke's template, from which Smith partially assembled his own theories, can be found in *The Second Treatise on Civil Government,* [Chapter 1]). With that foundation, Smith jumps directly into a consideration of human nature to discover why progress (literally the "progression of improvements") occurs. He sees the catalyst of progress in human dissatisfaction with any *status quo*. People's ingenuity moves them from the unsatisfactory to the better and toward the unattainable best. Without the achievement of perfection the process neatly self-perpetuates.

A small digression may be useful at this point. There is in the modern era an often-expressed complaint from the so-called intellectuals (who may over-think such things to a remarkable degree) that there is a malaise infecting the body politic. The suggestion is that our society has produced an overabundance of almost everything—except happiness. They claim there is a general dissatisfaction with life in spite of how much we have achieved both materially, spiritually, and intellectually. The logical conclusion for this group is that we have accumulated a lot but given not enough. Once they determined that our dissatisfaction results from the fact we have not offered enough of ourselves and our resources to make the world a perfect Eden (in spite of the fact that the United States is the most generous nation on earth—now or ever—and is considered the "can-do" society by almost any measure used) their solution is to take from those who have been successful and award that bounty to those who are not as well-off, their theory being that this will make both groups happy. They contend we have not given enough because we are too free to keep the fruits of our labor and that this freedom needs to be curtailed. The proof of this need, they claim, is in the pudding—we have all this success yet in the realization of happiness, emblazoned in the Constitution as our inherent right, we have failed.

The problem with this straightforward declamation is that it ignores three points; the first is that the allegations of discontent may, unfortunately, be politically not sociologically motivated and constructed (another result of manipulation by or by means of the media); the second is that the Constitution doesn't promise happiness, just the right to pursue it. And happiness *is* achieved in the pursuit, not only in the momentary attainment of something that pleases us. Jefferson and the other Founders knew this thus their intentional phrasing. The third reason that a distorted claim of unhappiness can be made but not substantiated is man's well-understood uneasiness; this element has nothing to do with parsimony.

Man is uneasy because he sees opportunity—constantly. It is his uneasiness that drives the progress we obtain. The problem is that our uneasiness doesn't disappear with any given success, at least not in the long run. It is in our very nature to be displeased with the *status quo* thus it can be claimed that we are unhappy when we are not, we are simply exhibiting the human genius for improvement embodied in curiosity, inventiveness, cleverness, and diligence. It is this aptitude for change and invention that pushes us to move on from even the most spectacular success. That is a human condition not the result of some systemic malfunction or failure. Thus changing the system without changing the underlying factors of human nature actually changes nothing. That people can be happy in spite of the fact that they are not wealthy, that they can be happy because *they* understand the benefits of inequality among human beings and *they* recognize that none of those inequalities stop them from aspiring is the starting point of human comprehension. If the rules of the game are changed so that to aspire becomes a bootless effort then lives change fundamentally.

When we see a psychosocial inquiry into why modern man, whose life is abundant, is "unhappy" perhaps we should question the question. What is certain is that the romantic prescription—that because we are alleged to be unhappy with what we have we might as well give it for the benefit of some other group—misses the point of man's journey by a wide margin. Man is not unhappy with what he has achieved, but he does get confused if not disgruntled when someone suggests that removing the fruits of his labor from his bank account will make him happy. He sees such an action making him quite the more unhappy from where he supposedly is in the first place. This of course does not even begin to deal with the question: if economic well-being does not make those who earned it happy what is there in the wealth itself that will make those to whom it is given any happier than those from whom it is taken? For the redistributionists life is seen only in terms of mathematics—never as human reality.

Freedom is the real issue in these discussions; it is freedom that scares the twenty-first century liberal as much as it did the eighteenth-century Jacobin at the time of the French Revolution. The fact is that freedom doesn't scare human beings in general, and that is the point of *First Principles*.

Let us return to Adam Smith's more practical contentions: In any economic paradigm, relationships are primarily defined and operate in terms of two human characteristics: striving for power (through competition, not as megalomania) and the power of aspiration. In a free market progress is achieved by human endeavor to remove dissatisfaction—the lure of our aspirations—and change is the only constant. Striving for power, to be "the best," creates continual competition—to surpass one's rivals. This can, but rarely does, result in excesses of one sort or another. The reason these excesses are rare is found in Smith's concept of "enlightened self-interest"—a brilliant leap of understanding and expression and the first part of Smith's definition of a workable economic model (the other part being the free, unconstrained market).

Smith's model for enlightened self-interest is the person who realizes and acts on the fact that he must satisfy his customer to ensure repeated patronage or garner a positive reputation to enlist new business. He must offer fair value at a fair price. Enlightened self-interest is nothing more than understanding that "I will do well for myself, if I do well by others." The philosophy of capitalism is that *both* parties to any transaction view themselves as being better off when the bargain is struck—and once the deal is complete both actually *are* better off based on their individual circumstances and goals. There is mutual benefit from and mutual consent to the transaction. The consumer has parted with his money, but received something more valuable—to him—some need is fulfilled that his money as a commodity could not satisfy. The producer has sold his product or service, paid his expenses, taxes and employees, the cost of which is hopefully less than the amount gained from the transaction, and is ready to begin the cycle again. The negative stereotype—that somehow the consumer is being short-changed by paying money for something he wants and only the producer profits is bogus and survives only in a demagogic atmosphere. The consumer profits by attaining his goal more easily by using money made engaging in some other effort. He then exchanges that money for whatever it is someone else makes that he desires more than his pocket full of earnings (and that he could not likely efficiently produce himself anyway).

The unplanned cooperation when engaging in economic self-interest becomes reciprocally beneficial, and those benefits are not unnoticed by human beings. Social progress is palpable in this paradigm and Smith's discernment and explanation of enlightened self-interest, though it was little more than observing what was happening on the ground, was nevertheless near revolutionary in his era. However, self-interest as a concept also needs to be taught, evangelized; it is not always either self-recognized or self-effecting. The carrot of gain is worthwhile, but the stick of forfeit for behavior that is counterproductive is necessary as well. In making his observations, Smith discusses all aspects of free-market discipline.

Theoretical systems postulating economic symmetry, equality, and presumed beauty don't change men from their nature no matter how much we'd sometimes like that to be the case. Men embrace useful versus futile behavior not by the implementation of arbitrary utopian direction, but through individually comprehending the benefits of the former and detriments of the latter while maintaining their intrinsic self-interest. This enlightened state—self-learned through experience and observation—is what encourages unplanned and mutually beneficial cooperation. Idealized systems that attempt to force an equalitarian goal with wholesale uniformity cannot achieve the flexibility to account for individual differences in personality and skill, thus for their implementation they require, first, constraints, then control. Unfortunately, the nature of human affairs, economic affairs in particular, cannot be remedied by government, or even more remotely, by politics. We can only design society to work within the constraints of human character and human nature. To attempt more is to reach for a fantasy.

In the end if free-market competition goes awry private or public counter-measures become necessary. If the problem becomes significant government is available to step in as a referee. But Smith notes how well the free market works, referencing the thousands and thousands of transactions occurring each *day* (in his time) without a hitch. When we compare that with the few misdeeds that make headlines each *year* it is easy to understand that people not only want a sound and fair system within which to operate but that they will make every effort to ensure that happens. The lawless confusion of previous eras was unpleasant and unrewarding and wholly without any security—thus the unpopularity of anarchy, whether commercial or civil, and the acclaim of its antidote, enlightened self-interest.

Underlying all of Smith's writing is his view of human nature, both how it works and how it does not. From his acceptance of the existence of property rights to the gains in economy achieved through the division of labor to the establishment of the marketplace (where the pieces and players can freely interact), his systemic logic remains unchallenged. The market is the stage upon which all activity takes place, but in Adam Smith's play the director is the invisible hand of voluntary and enlightened human interaction. Smith mentions the invisible hand only once in *Wealth of Nations* but it is the part of the equation necessary to understand why liberty and free markets work, and collectivism (or centralized control) does not. The vast interrelationships inherent in any economic structure cannot even be comprehended much less charted, and even less, dictated, by any single or group effort—such a feat is well beyond the power of any human mechanism. The alternative is free interaction. In a system of free interaction decisions are made based on each participant's view of his own well being and his personal desires. The invisible decisions and processes not only allow this unimaginably complex system to function but to work to the advantage of everyone.

Smith could assume nothing about his reader's intellectual or economic sophistication. Writing at a time when the market itself was in its infancy (although it should be noted that in 1720 London, more than fifty years before the publication of *Wealth of Nations*, there already existed over 20,000 privately owned shops [and thus Napoleon's later derisive sobriquet that England was but a nation of shopkeepers]) and universal education was still a century in the future, he addresses both the learned and the economically illiterate using a rigorously logical but necessarily pedantic approach. Put simply, Smith was composing from a vantage point not just unappreciated by even above-average individuals but actually unknown to virtually all of his audience. In today's often contentious political climate enlightened self-interest and the unplanned symmetry of the market's invisible hand can be distorted for electoral gain—and to the detriment of both the voters and the economy—thus the need to reconsider capitalism and the free market in the more elemental form that Smith describes.

At the end of his practical and philosophical investigation into capitalism, Smith arrives at "opulence" as the *result* not the goal of human ingenuity and interaction. (In his day, opulence meant personal and national commercial success, not gaudy over-consumption.) How one economic system or any class within an economic system arrives at opulence was grist for Smith's mill.

While explaining the intricacies of commerce Smith takes the road less traveled. His survey of human beings and their nature differs from the morally needy characterizations that were embedded in the darker notions and severe punishments of the religious dogma in vogue during the Middle Ages and in practice in Puritan England. He views mankind not as venal and sinful but as worthy of trust—both collectively and individually. His insight was simple: people would effect the common good through their recognition of common goals. In this respect, Smith expresses not social Darwinism (the charge of those who view capitalism as a predatory enterprise), but enlightened self-interest. In his estimation monarchical authoritarianism impeded man's ability to reach his full potential. Personal freedom coupled with economic freedom was the best guarantee of social progress.

While Smith believed in the need for government he saw government as the arbiter not the director of social interaction. Because human folly cannot be eliminated (no matter how much we've learned about right and wrong) Smith understood people should not set up government in an attempt to control every potentially negative human action. Rather, government should have mechanisms to deal with grand or petty aberrations when they do occur. Having a policeman on every corner to prevent human perfidy is neither achievable nor workable. In Smith's estimation the (free-market) playing field would be largely self-leveling—because of the effects of reciprocal self-interest. If certain individuals were hard to deal with the market would limit their success as recognition of their practices spread.

There was little anonymity in the eighteenth century—population was low and concentrated, travel limited. Reputation was of paramount importance. Admittedly, however, there was also significant innocence, even gullibility, as the era's new products were offered. But for Smith it was up to the people to sort all that out—not the government, for neither the government nor its functionaries were wiser in these matters than were the participants. The participants had far more incentive to protect themselves than did bureaucrats who, even in Smith's time, were alternately indolent and authoritarian—and you could never be sure whether Dr. Jekyll or Mr. Hyde would show up to perform his bureaucratic duties on any given day.

Smith's basic insight into economic life admits of a succinct summary: free activities and free relationships best guarantee that all economic elements (both human and commercial) will balance one another to maximize progress. If we let government or some other monopolistic force tamper with any aspect of free economic life (absent a direct need to protect the citizenry) there will be widespread side effects—generally to the detriment of those not doing the tampering. Furthermore, we cannot view economic activity in a vacuum; there is a cascade effect no matter how trivial governmental intervention may seem.

Smith's assessment of the role of government was as concise as his explanation of how the free market works. The time and place where government is beneficial is generally threefold: to protect citizens from foreign invasion, to establish a system of civil justice for relations between citizens, and to construct and maintain public works and institutions that individuals cannot effectively create on their own. A subset of these necessary institutions relates to dealing with fraudulent, destructive or dangerous economic activity, oftentimes (but not always) criminal in nature.

The universal bugaboo of capitalism and its essential freedom, whether in the time of Adam Smith or today, is the shyster or the charlatan. This is an area in which government plays an important but secondary role. The bad actor, who distorts the existing economic balance, is often held up as exhibit one in defense of government control or intervention in a free-market economy. But the scoundrel, the fraud and the cheat are not capitalists in the honest sense; each is simply a thief. (Sometimes, indeed, he is not even a thief for it is not gain that drives him but the adventure and use of his own faculties in outwitting his fellows, or in driving away his boredom, that is the impetus.) We need not alter capitalism to prevent their misdeeds; we alter their relationship with their fellow economic actors by removing them from the system. This allows capitalism to work properly. When a bad apple is in the barrel we simply remove it hopefully before it corrupts the other apples. To deal with fraud and its cousins Smith recommends only two remedies: individual responsibility and the government's enforcement of clearly defined criminal statutes.

Smith's position is that personal responsibility is the first line of defense in all economic relationships. "Let the buyer beware" is one of many familiar aphorisms coined to make people cognizant of their role in protecting themselves. It expresses the obligation of individuals to use good judgment. Smith argues that it is our duty to act on the fact that if something sounds too good to be true it probably is.

Smith observes an unfortunate but simple fact regarding human institutions: it isn't capital or capitalism or the free market that is bad. Neither is democracy or unbridled free speech deleterious. It is always individuals who create the distortions. Moreover, there is not even a hint that if the government were to control the economy or any other aspect of our lives that frauds, cheats, or even incompetents (who appear so innocent, but do so much harm) would cease to exist, or, more to the point, avoid government employment. There would simply be no way to prevent such people from worming their way into positions of authority. Both moral and intellectual failings are human, not institutional, and are as commonly found in government workers—especially government workers with great power and indubitable job security—as in corporate chieftains or local shopkeepers who have to answer in the marketplace. After all, each of us suffers in equal measure from the human condition.

Over time Smith's canny observations about human nature became useful in creating solutions to those instances when capitalism did, indeed, suffer from its own excesses. However, the focus on the difficulties and criticisms of the free market often ignore the obvious and incredible progress for the societies in which it operates. The aberrant minuscule part of the story of capitalism becomes the flea that wags the tail that wags the dog. The public perception of materialistic perfidy—because of the existence of capitalism's infrequent failings and the omission of its achievements—is intentionally created and encouraged by the few. Such a view is often fostered by unjustified and erroneous media and political tumult and results in ingrained and sometimes ubiquitous, arrogant hectoring. This negative campaign works for both the press (to increase its own profit by encouraging public conflict) and the political hand-wringers who view, almost wholly through ignorance and emotional misapprehension, any individual failure as total or systemic failure, and a demagogic opportunity to encourage their own political success. Reading Smith's views re-engages the citizen in the reality of free enterprise without politicizing the subject. That is fruitful today almost beyond measure.

The ultimate form of governmental economic intervention in the twentieth century and the polar opposite of Smith's investigations was pervasive socialism. In defending socialism its proponents claimed that government can best control the multiple and ever-more-complex forces of commerce and do so to create the greatest good. In fact, it turns out that just the opposite is true; the more complicated an economy becomes the more necessary is the freedom of individuals to act in their own interests. Any centralizing force becomes less able to direct all segments at all times in any efficient or productive direction.

Socialism was and is every free marketer's worst nightmare. Its horrible reality took root in those places where the most egregious forms of governmental monopolistic controls already existed and thus did the most harm where it could be least tolerated. These excesses, as awful as they turned out to be in the twentieth century, were a perfect counterpoise to the value and utility of the free enterprise system. The pendulum thus swung back and socialism suffered accordingly. Although Smith foresaw a glimmer of socialism's economic madness, its salient characteristic—state ownership of production processes and facilities—was far enough from his world of monarchy that its eventuality was not central to his investigation. However, its ultimate place in the potential chain of events was certainly evident in his logic.

Socialism's twenty-first-century progeny, state welfarism, is the subject of other chapters in *First Principles*. Welfarism's characteristics and effects are so similar to those of socialism that the consistencies become a continual theme. As will be seen, when the fundamentals of economic understanding are followed during the period between Smith's eighteenth century and our twenty-first neither the community of concerns nor the array of misapprehensions regarding government intrusion into the marketplace suffers any significant mutation. Nor does the discussion abate.

In *Wealth of Nations* Smith's relatively modest goal is to demonstrate the foolishness of many British tax and trade policies. The operational foundations of England's international exchange system had become gravely convoluted—often in response to the policies of other nations—and frequently accomplished the exact opposite of what was intended. In spite of his somewhat narrow focus Smith knew he had to build a foundation to make his case for change. In doing so he created a critical volume that has been effectively applied across the globe and across the centuries. Today the topic of trade couldn't be more timely. What Smith would think of modern international tax and trade policies becomes self-evident as one reads his criticisms; *Wealth of Nations* regains its status as a most effective primer. He understood that what might appear as national self-interest, which was far more rarely "enlightened" than personal self-interest, was an impediment to rational economic policy. This was true in his time and we see its effects yet today. Even though the jargon of Smith's era did not include our "law of unintended consequences" his insights reveal its timeless operation.

Certainly Smith wasn't the only bright or perceptive person of his era. But one must wonder why he was nearly alone in recognizing the pernicious quality of so much government intervention in the marketplace. Most of the answer lies in the rigor of his efforts, which when shaped by means of his intellectual acuity made Smith unique. He had an ability to discern and differentiate between those policies that were the causes of economic missteps and those that were just symptoms.

Wealth of Nations is difficult neither to read nor comprehend. Its truths have withstood the tides of more than two centuries of economic practice thus its value is well established. Applying Adam Smith's eighteenth-century understanding to the two centuries of economic battles following his era was accomplished in two thin volumes: *The Law* (1850) by Frederic Bastiat and *Economics In One Lesson* (1946) by Henry Hazlitt (Chapters 7 and 24 respectively). In these books the faith that is often placed in government supervision and regulation is exposed as invariably counterproductive and counterintuitive—but almost always politically useful.

Smith's detailed conclusions make *Wealth of Nations* illuminating reading especially when we recall that he worked and studied at a time when mass production and comprehension of the value of the division of labor were in their infancy. Each scene in Smith's play reflects a different segment of economic activity. Smith starts with the division of labor and the creation of the market and ends with basic concepts of international trade and national taxation. His investigation proceeds with uniformly meticulous attention to cause and effect so that the whole has a footing that easily supports the structure.

The timelessness and utility of Smith's observations may be seen in current political confrontations. It is also visible in the history of U.S. political battles from 1929—when the Great Depression began—to 1980 when the Reagan Revolution toppled what were thought to be American political and economic verities. These former "truths" turned out to be philosophical and psychological conceits that had little correlation to human incentive or self-sufficiency. As we re-read Smith in the twenty-first century it is obvious that the accuracy of his commentary and his apprehensions regarding human nature have not been tarnished since he first penned them. His lessons remain valuable today when silly and even dangerous utopian notions of economic equality or political direction of an economy can seem attractive, until their details and consequences become evident.

About the Author

ADAM SMITH, whose father died before he was born in 1723, was raised in his mother's world of Scottish gentry. He entered the University of Glasgow when he was 14 and was at Oxford by the time he was 17. He remained at Oxford for the next six years as a student and nascent professor. Upon graduation he returned to Scotland and the University of Glasgow as a lecturer. There he met and befriended David Hume (Scottish philosopher, economist, and historian, 1711–1776). Smith's career took him to France for several years as a tutor to the French court where he met many of Europe's economic and political thinkers, including Voltaire (French dramatist and historian, 1694–1778). Smith began working on *Wealth of Nations* in 1766. It was published in 1776 to significant scholarly and public acclaim. After *Wealth of Nations* Adam Smith intended to write two philosophical overviews, one on the theory and history of law, the other on the sciences and art. Smith did not complete either of these works, and shortly before his death inexplicably destroyed all of his manuscripts. After spending more than a decade on his unfinished treatises while working as a Scottish customs official, Smith died in 1790.

13

The Road to Serfdom

Friedrich A. von Hayek

Originally published: 1944
266 pages

NEAR THE END of the twentieth century Friedrich von Hayek lived to see the future he had predicted in 1944: the self-destruction of the socialist monolith that was almost everywhere ascendant as World War II was brought to a close. *The Road to Serfdom* explores and explains why this result was inevitable. But readers must understand that the demise of socialist collectivism and the implosion of the Soviet Union in 1989—the most significant event of the second half of the twentieth century—did not happen by accident or evolution. It was brought about through a series of intentional acts. Hayek's book, one of those acts, literally helped change the course of history because it was read by and underpinned the resolve of Margaret Thatcher and Ronald Reagan—the two leaders who hammered the final nails into Soviet Communism's coffin.

The path from Lord Acton's nineteenth-century *Essays in the History of Liberty* (Chapter 9) to Hayek's mid-twentieth-century declamation of socialism's inevitable collapse is easily negotiated. As was noted at the outset of this treatise the intention of *First Principles* is to define the rational foundations for governance and social organization as they have developed over the centuries, then to identify the means of their application to the real world. In other words, there are differences between perfect theory and our best efforts—because of the human element. The intended effect of this group of synopses is to look at the picture from afar to understand the subject, then to investigate the brush strokes that underpin the reality. Hayek's *The Road to Serfdom* is key to this effort. His book represents the culmination of a century of dissecting collectivism, totalitarianism, and especially socialism.

As the world experienced the failure of two centuries of the Enlightenment's utopian thought near the middle of the twentieth century it became incumbent to speak the truth about romantic or idealistic schemes—despotic socialism in particular. Hayek did that concisely and concretely. At the time Hayek wrote, his thoughts and theories were considered most politically *in*correct—in essence they were blasphemous.

Hayek begins by investigating the merits and appeal of collectivism versus individualism. In an introduction to the fiftieth anniversary re-publication of *The Road to Serfdom* Milton Friedman put it fairly simply: the argument for individualism is subtle and sophisticated and depends on rational thinking while the argument for collectivism is emotional. Because our emotional faculties are both more developed and more easily influenced than our rational faculties collectivism initially evokes a strong—even visceral—response that can overwhelm rationality. Ultimately, however, regardless of the rhetoric or slogans used in political discourse much of this emotional/intellectual conflict comes down to definitions and a logical application of theory to fact. What does "fair" mean? What is "equal" treatment? What is the "right" thing? What is a "just" result?

The attack on individualism during and after the Enlightenment was based on the idea that people should not be allowed to be self-interested or to act for themselves. Of course, as Adam Smith points out in *Wealth of Nations* (Chapter 12), self-interest is the *first* stimulus that motivates humanity. If people are not allowed to create for themselves it is simply impossible to inspire them to create for others. *Enlightened* self-interest, the heart of Smith's explanation of how a society functions, allows both of these things to happen.

Hayek argues that the core issue for government is the coordination or absence of coordination of the activities of the governed. Liberals, from about 1750 onward, saw no plan in the economic structure then developing—and that freedom frightened them. They were constitutionally incapable of believing Adam Smith's admonitions and were too used to monarchy at best, despotism at worst. Conversely, Hayek observes that a *lack* of freedom is even more frightening and destructive. He contends that central direction of our activities leads to serfdom. For Hayek, *only* individual action and voluntary coordination lead to freedom. The proof in this case is truly in the pudding. The free nations of the world brim with activity and successful living standards while the collectivist and/or totalitarian societies struggle to meet minimum human needs. Hayek sees governmental terrorism often associated with these latter societies compounding economic inefficiency with brutality. Brutality is invariably not a good motivator—except to foster change away from those doing the brutalizing.

Hayek had witnessed insidious government expansion during the first half of the twentieth century. These increases were partially the result of sheer growth in population but they were also the product of the efficiencies found in centralized control of economic processes necessary during both of the twentieth century's world wars. Hayek outlines the social and economic distortions created by government's growth outside a wartime setting and defines for the reader the decay which necessarily would eventuate when war-time centralization and its focused purpose was no longer an issue.

He observes that shortsighted politicians and bureaucrats see the solution to the failures of big government not in retrenchment, but rather in still more government. Instead of returning more control and responsibility for one's own life to the individual the liberal agenda was based on more centralized power and increased one-size-fits-all regulations. (Examples of such centralization today include federal No Child Left Behind educational mandates, Patriot Act coercion, and health care edicts where medical cost and treatment decisions are preordained irrespective of individual medical facts.) Hayek accurately predicts the current-day neosocialist obsession to cure moribund big government's ills by making it bigger.

In contrast to this mania Hayek's classical liberal thinking turned in the exact opposite direction. The lesson of the Soviet Union's rise and fall is clear: centralized planning and control causes more problems than it solves and decrees more inequality than it redresses. More to the point centralization stifles individuality and personal freedom.

As Hayek explains, authoritarianism was the mechanism by which the designers of the collectivist society ordained change. He finds the modern genesis of this effect in the socialist model created by the French Revolution of 1789. Freedom of thought was abhorrent to the revolutionists for free thinking led to freedom of action. Thus, the guillotine was installed in the town square and liberally used to enforce conformity and silence dissent. Today, as in the eighteenth century, social welfarists seek to achieve equality of condition or result through legislation that is as unrelenting as that of Revolutionary France (but with less use of the guillotine). That goal remains as impossible as it always has been. Beyond a base level (termed the social safety net) Hayek notes that redistributionist activities simply result in different inequalities—inequalities founded in politics and favoritism.

Hayek comments that collectivists want equality of result because they see that as the most viscerally "fair" condition for those at one end of the social spectrum. However, collectivists forget (or ignore?) how much others, who occupy different slots on the economic continuum, are denied through the mandates of economic conformity. Any attempt to control a society is not only unfair to all who individually strive but also to society as a whole. Collectivist control sowed the seeds for its own destruction when it suppressed innovation-generating incentives of every sort. People are not blind. While temporarily lifting some, collectivism and its modern cousin state welfarism hold most others down. Where would modern society be if expressing individual imagination and acting through incentive were illegal or were controlled solely by the state? Would we have the light bulb, the airplane, the Internet, or the CAT scan?

Classical liberalism (generally, but only generally, connoted "conservatism" in the U.S.) seeks equality of opportunity. And, because of the nature of man's inequalities—of intellect, of drive, of desire, of understanding, of will, of circumstance, and even of luck—the results of individual efforts must necessarily be uneven *regardless* of whether everyone has an equal opportunity to achieve. For Hayek, the myriad ways a free society utilizes individual differences reflect liberty's beauty and have allowed the creation of virtually all of the world's material success. This success is the point. What *might* be achieved if the world and all its inhabitants were perfect, or just acted in perfect harmony, is not germane because either perfection is not just illusory, but unimaginable.

The Road to Serfdom's core investigation concerns the political, social, and economic ramifications of the central control essential to socialism, but its lessons apply as well to state welfarism. Of course, the fundamental difficulty of central planning as Hayek observes, is that it cannot be achieved without a dictatorship in one form or another. We do not arrive at central planning through an agreement abdicating either our liberty or our democratic principles; rather, socialists implement authoritarianism because agreement among myriad individuals *cannot* be achieved. At that point, to solve the impasse, the intellectuals, the liberal "elite," demand control of decision making. They say in the maelstrom of conflicting options and reasoning "We will decide for you." Hayek comments on the morality of this approach:

> [T]he spirit of commercial enterprise has been represented as disreputable and the making of profit as immoral, where to employ a hundred people is represented as exploitation but to command the same number as honorable.

For Hayek, an open society allows everyone to choose his own path and make his own decisions so long as his course or his decisions do not impede others with an equal right to freedom. When idealistic philosophical rhetoric is used for political purposes this truth is often intentionally buried if the good of society can be claimed as a justification. It must be continually recalled, however, that the best "good" that can be achieved for society is freedom, not ever-expanding government control. The authoritarian means proposed by socialists (earlier) and welfare statists (today) deny humankind's inherent qualities and characteristics. Only man's frailties and faults are seen as relevant. Modern social and economic systems are so complex that only a combination of free, competitive motivations and imagination can work efficiently to self-order social and economic relationships. Hayek spells out for the reader why central planning, regardless of its techniques, cannot act and react to order society nearly as well as can myriad individual decisions, freely made and unhindered by authoritarian direction. The difference is found in a single word: incentive.

Hayek explains that how we get from collectivist goals (offering lowest common denominator social equality) to collectivist action and finally to totalitarianism is elemental. As was noted earlier, because agreement cannot be reached on most—much less all—goals, dictatorial powers must be ceded to the rulers in order to get the machinery of a state economy focused and moving in any direction. Regarding the individual, socialists and welfarists contend there is too much selfishness for the good of society when individualism is allowed, thus each citizen must submit to oversight. In particular, socialists deny Adam Smith's concept of enlightened self-interest in economic and other matters.

Human beings are surely flawed but that is hardly humanity's primary characteristic. Therefore, for Hayek, society's first concern is not to counteract people's imperfections but to ensure their freedom. Humanity's occasional venality must be dealt with individually for in a free society that flaw is the exception not the rule. Most importantly for Hayek it is imperative to remember that human flaws and frailties, especially the desire for power, are just as likely to exist at the top of any dictatorship as in one or another layer of a capitalistic system. The obvious problem with a dictatorship is that there is no form of redress.

To curb the worst of human impulses free societies have effected the rule of law. As John Locke noted in 1690 "There can be no liberty without law" for absolute freedom results in absolute anarchy. Where there is liberty under law we know the rules before we play the game and we know that there is a framework to enforce the rules, as well as to change them if necessary. We agree to the rules so long as they apply equally to all, *including* the government (in this vein think of all the special privileges members of Congress grant themselves and government employees, but think the citizenry unworthy of). We can adjust the rules by consensus, up to a point. We cannot alter natural law by legislation or wishful thinking. Individual rights (for example those embodied in the U.S. Constitution) can only be adjusted by the people themselves. The rule of law is the antithesis of the institutionalization of status, and status is the foundation of the socialist/welfarist form of government. Under the rule of law who you are does not matter; how you act does.

Hayek observes that once the rules are in place members of society can interact with one another efficiently and confidently. He notes that the economic basis of that interaction is private property; and the creation and protection of private property, concomitant with the preservation of individual rights, is the essential goal and effect of the rule of law. Where the state in a democratically consensual manner controls the rules (but not the results) of the game there is actual freedom. Hayek contends that we ignore these tenets of human interaction at the price of our individuality and then our humanity. As the title of his book implies, we must choose freedom or else embark on the road to serfdom. Ultimately there is no middle ground.

As is obvious from the history of the twentieth century, socialism is today universally discredited. Yet Hayek's generations-old insights as to why government intervention in people's lives is counterproductive still helps us address a perplexing modern question: if socialism was dismissed as not viable why does government become more pervasive and invasive each year? The answer is somewhat simple. There are those who think that government power is acceptable so long as it is used to do good; to them so long as their intentions are laudable, to achieve equality, or to create rights, government power is justified. These objectives seem valuable but as measures of security for the populace they are actually destructive of real values. Individual freedom is abolished when the state makes choices for citizens or evaluates what the content of anyone's life should be.

In essence, policies effecting "entitlements," to achieve equalitarian goals, masquerade as a charitable (emotional) way to protect some individuals who may have failed to connect responsibility and success (this group does not include the truly needy). It is not that these individuals are venal, quite the contrary, their behavior is learned, not innate. As Hayek observes,

> [a] movement whose main promise is the relief from responsibility cannot but be antimoral in its effect, however lofty the ideals to which it owes its birth.

Ultimately, as Hayek demonstrates, socialist thinking is self-evidently self-destructive. It *prevents* self-actualization by creating a culture of dependency and a climate of learned helplessness. Yet political missionaries use soaring oratory to promise what no one can deliver—a perfect world cocooned in perfect equality, for which the government, not the people, is responsible. Who wouldn't want to believe?

In *The Road to Serfdom*, Hayek's message, declaiming the necessity of a free society ordered by a *moral* government (not only a moral populace) was designed to expose the poverty of socialism and central planning as effective means to arrange economic relations and society itself. His comprehensions have become even more pertinent in the modern era because present governing methods and goals carry a patina of caring that is either false or fanciful when viewed in the context of real world individualism and personal accountability.

Today, liberal activists on both the political and bureaucratic fronts attempt to apportion wealth, not through state takeover of production or economic management but through income redistribution. They attempt to achieve this goal by more subtle procedures and through smaller steps than in Hayek's era. Taxation, rather than collectivist decree, has become the primary tool to effect redistributive policy and to work toward a "greater good." Although the mechanisms are obviously different from socialism's halcyon days the effect is the same—a diminution of individual opportunity and responsibility. The road to serfdom, and perdition, is paved with good intentions. The need for vigilance and rational action to combat the sought-after, but flawed end product—equality of result—has not diminished thus Hayek's continued relevance.

Certainly for Hayek, government has a role but it is as referee not overseer. While the goals of the welfare or nanny state can be presented as superficially admirable they are inevitably as illusory as the goals of socialism. More to the point, they fail because their social and intellectual intentions are founded in myth; they simply wish to ignore human nature. Ultimately, as was shown by Hayek and others, the goals of state welfarism are incompatible with the preservation of a free society. There is a simple reason why this is true—welfarism has no logical endpoint. When combined with an insistence as to what is politically correct (no-fault social equalitarianism) state welfarism can be convoluted to support assistance at any level, to any degree, for any period. Eventually society devolves into two camps: those who are "entitled" to public support and those who are to supply such. The unhappy social and economic result of this scene, taken to its logical conclusion, is self-evident.

It is our obligation today to comprehend government intervention and controls in their more sophisticated and canny—and emotional—guises. When Hayek deals with blunt totalitarianism there is no misunderstanding what is afoot. The state took over at the very beginning of economic activity and ordered everything thereafter. As the inefficiency of that process—demonstrated by more than a century of failed collectivism—became clear, the utopians reversed their methods, but not their goals. Instead of telling people what they will do, the welfarists let the free market continue (rather successfully as can be seen) and then confiscate as much of the product as they can for the alleged benefit of the whole. If the liberal "elite" had stopped at any rational point, had there been any sense of proportion, the system (free enterprise supporting a social safety net), by the agreement and cooperation of all, might have worked. But power begets the desire for ever more power, until all that is left is the argument about power itself—who will have it. The consequences of its application are taken for granted.

As the twenty-first century begins, the arguments for state intrusion into both the economic system and our personal lives are increasingly synthetic and distorted. They are often built on a foundation of supposition (as was socialism)—of what laudable results *could* occur if someone tells us how to live and what to do, and what terrible consequence *might* or even *will* happen if they do not. These ideas and methods are nothing more than a recalibration of the socialist ideals Hayek criticized in *The Road to Serfdom*. The modern liberal goal, social welfarism, is evidenced in overarching legislation and regulation designed to control a politically correct society and to redress its inequalities by means of "entitlements." This is a sophisticated but morally corrupt political device. Social welfarists pursue this agenda to the detriment of a rational vision of personal responsibility in a framework of opportunity. And, when welfarist legislators and administrators employ their utopian methods, merely imagined evils (of forced conformity and confiscation of labor's products) are dwarfed by the harm wrought on the other side of this equation, the side founded on core human values: freedom, responsibility, and discipline. Hayek points out that the pursuit of the illusory collectivist goal of equality is simply incompatible with individualism or any sense of intellectual integrity.

Along with a number of political/social philosophers before him Hayek contends that political freedom is inextricably intertwined with economic freedom and that each must exist for the other to survive. This insight, which seemingly needs to be rediscovered every two or three generations (or is it every two or three decades, or even years?) is basic to Hayek as it was to Adam Smith, Edmund Burke, Lord Acton, and Alexis de Tocqueville. As the economies of the world, and the governments, become bigger and more complex our understanding of how a free system operates becomes lost in the details. Our awareness of what is needed to keep the system working also becomes muted. In any society mistakes inevitably occur. Social programs and government intrusion into the marketplace to fix the aberrations always begin small—but the problems are often politically exaggerated so the solutions can be more grand; government size and intrusiveness grow in equal measure to the political claims on behalf of the allegedly abused and neglected.

Hayek shows that a free system's occasional malfunctions do not require its abandonment; he observes that it is only necessary to formulate adjustments to allow the system to work properly where it wasn't before. The solution to capitalism's missteps is not the welfare state but the rational state. (The idea of capitalism as one of the driving forces in the rationalization of human behavior is investigated in more detail in Joseph Schumpeter's *Capitalism, Socialism and Democracy*

[Chapter 38].) Hayek sees our economic system as an evolutionary process, not an immaculate conception. If society attempts to mandate actions in what is an evolutionary process, then, as night follows day, totalitarian measures will eventuate.

About the Author

FROM ECONOMICS (the field in which he won the Nobel Prize in 1974) to psychology, history, anthropology, and science, Friedrich August von Hayek amply demonstrated his intellectual abilities. In twenty-five books and numerous articles he established the breadth and depth of his insights and thoughts. Obviously he was no casual scholar. Born in 1899, he earned two doctorates at the University of Vienna by the time he was 24. Hayek met his intellectual partner, Ludwig von Mises, after his schooling was completed, although both were in Vienna while Hayek was a student. Along with others, Hayek and Mises eventually helped develop what became known as the Austrian School of Economics. This system of economic thought denounced and then intellectually dismantled socialism as a viable form of government or economics. Hayek taught in London (1930–50), at the University of Chicago (1950–62), and then again in Europe (1962–88) at the conclusion of his teaching career. Although an economist by training and interest, Hayek took a more fundamental view of the interconnections of society. His works, which initially concentrated on economic matters, broadened in later years to the point where he argued passionately for a liberal (free) society. In 1960 he published *The Constitution of Liberty*, his treatise on classical liberal political economy. Hayek died in 1992.

14

The Constitution of Liberty

Friedrich A. von Hayek

Originally published: 1960
411 pages

WHEN HE WROTE *The Constitution of Liberty* Friedrich von Hayek intended to create an encyclopedic overview of how liberty is achieved in the modern world. At the time he was composing, capitalism and socialism, the two opposing economic systems then prevalent in the world, were in a fight to the death. Individual freedom was inevitably tied to free-market capitalism while collectivism was paired with socialism, thus in his discussion of liberty he necessarily had to consider economic paradigms as well.

One of the methods used in his investigation was to encourage his readers look at common phenomena in a different light. He did this in order to demonstrate how the painfully obvious can be hard to grasp in an emotionally charged political atmosphere. He begins by examining the origin of modern ideas underpinning the liberal view (in its modern American, not classical European sense) of philosophy and economics. These novel consequences of twentieth-century political maneuvering, such as the development and power of the bureaucratic state, or legislation coined at the behest of special interests, he sees as part of the intellectual corruption of the governing purpose.

This volume is the second *First Principles*–reviewed book authored by Hayek. In *The Road to Serfdom* Hayek explains how and why collectivist socialist schemes of governance cut against normal human impulses and are doomed to failure by the very nature of their mechanisms. In the present treatise Hayek dissects the fundamentals of liberty itself. What, exactly, is freedom? It seems a simple enough concept but understanding *its* mechanisms requires more than a superficial perusal. Offering a defined alternative in the philosophical arena to what he had deconstructed in the political arena in *The Road to Serfdom* seemed necessary.

Beginning with an assessment of democracy as discussed by John Locke and David Hume in the seventeenth and eighteenth centuries, Hayek proceeds to examine its reality in the twentieth century. First, he explores the concepts of separation of powers and of checks and balances on the political side of the equation, and he finds that they are essential because of the foibles of human nature. Then he considers why these safeguards, which were designed to help remove arbitrariness from governing, are undermined in the massive and essentially unchecked modern bureaucracies that democracy has created. He argues that there are only two antidotes to the bureaucratization of government: an independent judiciary that can reign-in zealous regulators, and frequent open elections to keep politicians within the structural bounds that had been set in democracy's founding documents. Hayek states that an independent judiciary is essentially the last line of defense against an expanding and often arrogant bureaucracy. (In the twenty-first century we must consider if even this bulwark may be insufficient as the judiciary becomes more and more politicized, goal oriented, and as a result, increasingly disconnected from Constitutional restraint.)

Hayek believes that any government that continues to grow administratively and bureaucratically is merely trying to correct the negative results of its last effort at ordering society by proclamation. And in Hayek's view, democracies are only slightly less prone to using dictatorial tactics in creating and administering their laws than totalitarian societies are. The greatest danger is simply having good laws administered badly. Hayek calls for dismantling any portion of government that gets out of control either in terms of size or mission. He argues that this is one of the most effective methods of reorganization. Even if the department itself isn't abolished, when threatened with extinction bureaucrats (like human beings everywhere) often offer change and revision that make both good sense and good economics.

As well, Hayek takes a keen interest in ensuring the executive side of government has its best chance at being honest. He defines the necessity of a sharp separation of the law-making effort conducted by the legislature—not the courts—from the application of policy effected by administrative agencies. He conjectures that if the lawmakers set rules that are applicable across the population, then, in theory, administrators will not be able to apply those laws so as to discriminate against or in favor of subgroups or classes within the population. Correcting abuses or errors in the execution of laws that might result from an aggressive executive Hayek again sees as the province of an autonomous judiciary. But he recognizes that only individual integrity will ultimately allow the system to work. Corruption—especially the petty and frequently rationalized intellectual kind, not fiscal thievery—is a barricade to sound and fair governance. The U.S. Constitution and the American state were designed for a moral people. The country could not be governed without this foundation and Hayek sees individual morality, and action, as the antidote to state corruption.

Hayek also reminds readers of the inherent value of a written constitution: to express a body of rights that no legislature may infringe. These rights are so fundamental that only the people themselves may change them. With these basic rules embodied in a document, legislatures and courts have guideposts to keep both policy and administration within the bounds of equitable government. Hayek underscores the development of this concept through his investigation of the contrasting histories of the American and French Revolutions. He knew to fear temporary majorities (as did James Madison and Thomas Jefferson) and he consequently regarded a written constitution as essential.

Hayek observes that the differences between the American Revolution of 1776 and the French Revolution of 1789 were based upon each country's distinct views of mankind. These disparate conceptions led to quite different historical outcomes. The contrasts are so important and so core to understanding self-government that they are assessed in *First Principles* by several authors.

The American Revolution aimed to secure personal liberty; freedom *from* government as much as freedom *for* individuals. The Founders later made this standard their goal as they designed our written constitution. In France, the idea developed that power taken from the king and the upper class would be placed in the hands of the people, all the people, with the expectation that the people would naturally not abuse one another. But unfortunately that is exactly what people do in the absence of rules, no matter their station or education. They do this out of self-preservation, not out of venality. If there are no rules, it is every person for himself, thus we see self-protective, not simply selfish, behavior. The followers of Rousseau (the pure democrats) wanted to tear down established methods and institutions because they saw them as responsible for the corruption of human beings, not vice versa. In theory, if the institutions were demolished man's natural virtue would emerge. The French revolutionaries' unmodulated trust in the citizenry thus doomed their government to failure. In contrast, the American Founders' faith in a written constitution and laws better ordered natural human inclinations by keeping potential despots from unrestrained power and the populace from unrestrained self-interest. The people accepted submission to these rules, first, because *they* had written them, and second, because if the rules did not work they could be changed through a democratic process.

When the French revolutionaries wrongly assumed that people would treat one another fairly and equitably pursuant to some enlightened or utopian impulse to do so they were unfortunately only reacting to the rule of the monarchy; they knew what they didn't want. Through removal of their inept king they hoped to create in the people that which they did want—a flowering of true brotherhood—Liberty, Equality, Fraternity. However, man's first *unrestrained* (morally or institutionally or by law) impulse is generally not toward equality or generosity and thus the French model failed, gloriously and ignominiously. The French learned that reasoned behavior and the civic culture necessary for self-government must flow from set rules not facile assumptions or hoped-for human behavior.

After considering fundamental concepts of how government should be designed Hayek proceeds to examine equality—under the law and as an objective for individuals in a just society. He recognizes that unequal results in human achievement may tend to conjure simplistic notions of injustice, especially in the discourse of judgmental and self-aggrandizing demagogic politicians. In a society in which the dignity of each person—not one's station, or employment, or one's accumulation of goods—is the prime consideration, equality of opportunity can exist. Hayek understood that only those who exploit human differences will distort the idea of justice so that the goal of a just society is seen as equalitarian (with a desire for equal results) rather than egalitarian (with a goal of equal opportunity).

Hayek addresses individual inequalities from a different angle. He asserts that equality is as undesirable as it is unrealizable. Attempting to achieve the unattainable requires each of us to forego who we are and what we can do in order to create something in which no one ultimately believes—a society where everyone is the same and has the same. He eventually arrives at the point of admonishing us against equalitarianism not because people are selfish (although that is obviously a part of human nature), but because individuals so differ with respect to their talents and ambitions. The outcomes of their efforts will reflect their diversity and redound to the great benefit of everyone. Life is a group of facts and a series of choices. The former limits the latter. Hayek notes:

> Let us by all means endeavor to increase opportunities for all. But we ought to do so in the full knowledge that to increase opportunities for all is likely to favor those better able to take advantage of them and may often at first increase inequalities. Where the demand for "equality of opportunity" leads to attempts to eliminate "unfair advantages," it is only likely to do harm. All human differences, whether they are differences in natural gifts or in opportunities, create unfair advantages. But since the chief contribution of any individual is to make the best use of the accidents he encounters, success must to a great extent, be a matter of chance.

The core ideal of modern American liberalism is equalitarianism—a theoretically noble but freighted and ultimately futile goal. As no two human beings are equally fit for all tasks (and some are fit for few tasks) achieving equal results can be attempted by fiat, but with no prospect for success. As Hayek notes, because we cannot control any given outcome even by decree, society is better off letting individuals freely adjust. Expressing this without appearing anti-egalitarian (or, in the twenty-first century, politically incorrect) is difficult; it requires some attempt at discernment and sophistication by the observer. Often people won't come to the truth without help. They get stuck at the start of their reflections on inequality as they realize how putatively unjustly life favors some persons with better chances, better foresight, or better discipline. Plain old good luck is also a commodity that can no more be eliminated than can good sense. That there are differences in circumstances is a given: nature, planning, parents, and community have allowed some people better opportunities. Yet even when opportunity does knock, many cannot or will not open the door. Conversely, other people with seemingly no advantages and myriad disadvantages attain incredible success. We cannot take away the freedom to use the circumstances with which we are presented unless all of us become automatons.

We also cannot take away anyone's success, no matter how great or small, because to do so would be impractical, unjust, and foolish. Would we discard all human progress because it comes from humanity's unequal distribution of ambition, talent, and intellect?

Chance, whether genetic or circumstantial or both, determines the place from which all of us start, but often goes unnoticed in our day-to-day affairs. It inexorably operates as a social lever. As Hayek notes, this seems so obvious, yet so difficult to grasp:

> Liberty not only means that the individual has both the opportunity and burden of choice. It also means he must bear the responsibility of his actions. Liberty and responsibility are inseparable. Liberty, by definition, also produces almost nothing but inequality in life, while demanding equality of opportunity and treatment. From the fact that people are inherently different it follows that, if we treat them equally they will achieve unequal results, thus the only way to place them in an equal position would be to treat them unequally.

Part of Hayek's overview focuses on the concepts of Benthamism (utilitarianism—an attempt to achieve the greatest good for the greatest number of people) in addition to the equalitarianism of the French Revolution. He discusses the negative effects on liberty and democratic principles encompassed in both philosophies. With profound understanding he notes that it is "the French tradition, with its flattering assumptions about the unlimited powers of human reason, that has progressively gained influence." These assumptions about human reason versus human action and experience (which time has repeatedly shown are often not interchangeable) devolve into equally overconfident assumptions about the value and validity of specific products of human reason—socialism, equalitarianism, the welfare state. This is the theory: if we can think of a perfect society, we must therefore be able to implement it. It is the vanity of those who assume they know better than others (and want to control the lives of others for their ostensible betterment) that causes so much misdirection of the governing impulse.

Hayek observes that the English tradition is the polar opposite of Benthamism (in spite of the fact that Jeremy Bentham was British). English tradition was based on empiricism; that is, the practice of deciding issues such as how a society will be governed by reference to what works in the real world. Empiricism's opposite—rationalism—was the foundation of the French Revolution. Rationalism assumes human beings can think through a concept logically and then implement it in that form, irrespective of the human condition. As was obvious to Hayek, any society formed by imperfect human beings of widely varying natures, views, talents, and goals will not fit well into some intellectual's view of what an individual's life should be. The opposition of empiricism to rationalism has marked the fight for liberty for more than two hundred years. The philosophical battles raging today between American conservatives and their liberal and neoconservative adversaries is a continuation of this struggle.

To combat socialist and social-welfare impulses Hayek repeatedly emphasizes the importance of common democratic political tools: separation of powers, frequent elections, an independent judiciary, and checks and balances—all embodied in a written constitution. Hayek explains that the absence of these tools (or our failure to implement them consciously) enables the authoritarianism of planned societies and economies to exist. Doomed to failure, rationalist authoritarian government suffers from a fatal falsehood: its proponents deny the truth of the human condition, including our inherent differences (which have led to all of the world's material successes), and our intrinsic imperfectability. Rationalists, assuming a *perfectible* population, know that they can prove anything is possible, certainly anything as simple as creating the economic foundations necessary to a sound society. Hayek investigates the role government assumes in our economic relationships and how that involvement affects both the social fabric and our individual liberty. In *The Constitution of Liberty* Hayek explores every authoritarian fallacy. He calmly disproves the conclusions arrived at by people who fail to comprehend and deal with human nature as it is, rather than as they'd like it to be.

About the Book

THE THREE INDEXES at the end of this University of Chicago Press edition of Hayek's work are unique. One offers an index of subject matter, the second is an index of authors, and the third (the most useful) is an analytical index of the table of contents. The latter allows one to quickly scan the political and philosophical content of Hayek's thoughts, and then go directly to a discussion of particular interest.

About the Author

FROM ECONOMICS (the field in which he won the Nobel Prize in 1974) to psychology, history, anthropology, and science, Friedrich August von Hayek amply demonstrated his intellectual abilities. In twenty-five books and numerous articles he established the breadth and depth of his insights and thoughts. Obviously he was no casual scholar. Born in 1899, he earned two doctorates at the University of Vienna by the time he was 24. Hayek met his intellectual partner, Ludwig von Mises, after his schooling was completed, although both were in Vienna while Hayek was a student. Along with others, Hayek and Mises eventually helped develop what became known as the Austrian School of Economics. This system of economic thought denounced and then intellectually dismantled socialism as a viable form of government or economics. Hayek taught in London (1930–50), at the University of Chicago (1950–62), and then again in Europe (1962–88) at the conclusion of his teaching career. Although an economist by training and interest, Hayek took a more fundamental view of the interconnections of society. His works, which initially concentrated on economic matters, broadened in later years to the point where he argued passionately for a liberal (free) society. In 1960 he published *The Constitution of Liberty*, his treatise on classical liberal political economy. Hayek died in 1992.

15

On Power

Bertrand de Jouvenel

Originally published: 1945
421 pages

THE NUANCES, details, and conflicts of society cause government to expand not because it must but because it can. Although men could solve their problems and differences among themselves they allow the state to step in to do it for them, and they allow that because it is easy. As well, they often think they might be able to influence the outcome of government's efforts to their own benefit. Conversely, these same nuances, details, and conflicts become increasingly complex and convoluted as government waxes more intrusive (the law of unintended consequences). The symbiosis is self-perpetuating.

When the state becomes overbearing, by default, its relationship to the citizenry becomes almost wholly negative; it is based on a downward spiral of subtle or overt attempts at control on one side and growing defiance, self-expression, and individuality on the other. The latter eventuates when men find the ease of letting someone else solve their difficulties offers consequences they never meant or even contemplated.

Although it is difficult to accept, democratic government mainly functions contrary to the purposes of its design because it functions mostly as those in charge want it to. The complexity of governance works to the advantage of those who act with intention and to the disadvantage of those who trust in institutions, or laws. There is a simple reason for this: Power.

In this seminal work Bertrand de Jouvenel discusses government in terms different from those of other historians and theoreticians. Although we have considered Power primarily by reference to its form, de Jouvenel considers it in relation to its extent. The forms of Power (democracy, republic, monarchy, theocracy, oligarchy, or dictatorship) inspire various theories, but its extent refers to reality. De Jouvenel explains how Power, grounded in human nature, has ever been on the increase, aided by apathy or fear and in the modern world by technology and the treacherous allure of centralization and utopianism.

The Leader

DE JOUVENEL came to his conclusions regarding Power via a path somewhat different from that of John Locke. Entertaining no substantial disagreement with Locke, de Jouvenel took the earlier philosopher's comprehensions to their logical and darker outcome. As can be seen in *The Second Treatise on Civil Government* (Chapter 1), Locke develops his theory of governance through an understanding of how rights came into existence—both through a person's own being (which was something individually "owned" as a property right) and through the right to one's possessions (which had value because of personal effort). De Jouvenel explores how people gave up some of their freedom through banding together to protect one another's rights and property thereby establishing security. The resulting community of action which aimed at supporting liberty and securing its gains naturally gravitated toward a need for leadership; thus Power established its foundation as the protector of progress. De Jouvenel investigates how Power at first came to reside in an individual, and how that person enhanced his power by convincing other individuals and groups within society that he would represent their needs or aspirations or protect their families and thus he should be their leader.

De Jouvenel then analyzes historical Power as it evolved in social aggregations larger than the primitive band. His core contention is that in that past era someone always rose to lead by force—not by agreement or default. As the size and number of groups that gathered for security grew, the unstable might of a sovereign (because there were always those who wanted the leader's power for themselves) became subject to how many subalterns he could convince to support him and how much wealth they could bring to his treasury. Over time, as the gentry (who had the wealth the ruler needed) paid more and more for the privilege of ensuring the sovereign's place (and thus their own) they also began to demand more say in how their protection was achieved and how their gold was expended.

The relative strength of these partners varied over the centuries and more formal relations eventuated as the size of society grew. These new devices were in the form of constituent assemblies—groups that represented the people and spoke for them, first for their class, and ultimately for all citizens. These congresses were the precursors of today's legislative bodies. (To see additional details of the evolution of Power and its basis in property see Richard Pipes's *Property and Freedom*, [Chapter 11].) The power of these assemblies ultimately far exceeded that of the sovereign and the king at length became subordinate and eventually disappeared or was trivialized.

De Jouvenel explores the weakness of early monarchies, founded in the voluntary nature of the support and protection offered to them by their closest allies—the nobility. The particular example of how a monarch raised an army is instructive in understanding all the forces at work: A medieval king could never form an army by fiat or through the equivalent of a modern military draft. He had to buy his armies, and their services ended the minute their remuneration stopped or their enlistments expired. (Even George Washington was subject to this relationship between armies and the power to create and hold them together.) In order to conscript men and *require* that they fight, some greater authority was necessary. This ultimate master arose when "the People" took over governing via a parliament or some other democratic medium. Involuntary recruiting became possible when a publicly constituted legislature that theoretically embodied the "general will" of the people decreed conscription; this law was accepted as the ostensible choice of the populace. One of the most intrusive and overwhelming manifestations of Power—that those in power represented the public's general will—thus arose and then flourished. This Power was defined and implemented by elected officials and deified by democracy.

Individual Freedom vs. The General Will

DE JOUVENEL was skeptical of the general will, especially when such was supposedly determined by representatives—not the people themselves. A main thrust of de Jouvenel's effort in *On Power* is to expose and then debunk the myth that any representative body necessarily voices the general will. If it were true that the general will could not be divined by the few then the power of government should be severely limited. Under this circumstance, only the most obvious matters (where real consensus was probable) should be decided by a legislature. In fact, just the opposite was the case; the more difficult the question the more apparently prescient were the legislators.

De Jouvenel observes that both conscription and the power to tax arose as protective endeavors, as measures of defense for the people. Communal protection embodied broad, practical efforts at security well before the tools of conscription and taxation took on a utopian glaze in the twentieth century. But when conscription and taxation were combined with the advent of democratic institutions Power was almost complete; the people did not object. We did this to ourselves.

As de Jouvenel observes, Power perpetuates itself from inception. It justifies its expansion in the first instance by serving those over whom it rules—by protecting society against outsiders and keeping order within. Therefore, in the beginning Power was beneficial. Its first consequences were not viewed as negative or dangerous even though its origins and mechanisms were darker than its supposed effects.

When society became too complex for an individual to rule, the instruments of modern governance were put in place (administrative agents and bureaucracies and representative bodies). They were proclaimed a substitute for the Power of the individual. These institutions eventually became a complex of governing compartments that the people themselves had to administer, "thereby going through phases of both command and obedience." As the populace became accustomed to having their own agents rule, and as they came to rely upon such safeguards as the separation of powers, checks and balances, judicial review, and a broad electoral franchise, they relaxed their vigilance: "We rule ourselves . . . how can anything go wrong?"

The State

HOWEVER, when society became so large that not even one group (much less one person) could rule or manage it, the idea of *the state* was established. It was the entity to which all owed allegiance—because of its beneficence and the fact that it was constituted by the people themselves. We drove out the personal ruler (the king or emperor) and replaced that individual with representatives of ourselves who, as a group, were the physical embodiment of the old ruler's power. Ironically, the new rulers had much more Power than the old-fashioned king because we confusedly conflated them with ourselves and assumed an identity of their interests with our own. "They" and "us" were no longer separate. De Jouvenel finds this Power far from benign:

> It is making a fateful mistake to suppose ... that the major political formation, which is the state, was the natural product of human sociability. It seems a natural enough supposition, for society, which is a natural entity, is just such a product. But a natural society is a small thing. And for a small society to become a large one a new factor is necessary. For that there must be fusion, and this in the great majority of cases comes, not from the instinct of association, but from that of domination.

Thus the public servant (whether elected or appointed) was born—that person who had a patina of authority, a core of righteousness, and who told us how to live simply because he had the ability to act for us (not necessarily with us, almost certainly not at our behest). He did this by means of his role as a governor, and he did this because he contended either that he knew more than we did, or worse, knew better than we did; he knew better because he could see more from his lofty perch, could consider more from his wide experience, and could understand better through his personal obligation to look after those in his charge.

De Jouvenel describes the formation and the later sustenance of the early state as being dependent on this Power and the concomitant ability to act with intention when Power was possessed. Whether that Power was held by the king, the church, the aristocracy or nobility of earlier times, or eventually a representative body, his theory about the control of society holds true today—but for slightly different, and slightly more hazardous reasons. Those in Power now relish their positions not solely for base egoistic domination or even substantial personal gain but out of an increased and ever-growing sense of righteousness—Power's most dangerous ingredient. However, as de Jouvenel cautions, there is an antecedent aspect even to righteousness: the every action of the public servant is still designed to first retain their hold on power.

Once in control, the public servant's "will to Power" shows itself as a desire to do good. This is a "fatal conceit," in the words of Friedrich von Hayek, that trends in the direction of destroying society's chance for rational progress—rational progress being defined as progress that takes human nature and individual liberty into full account.

In democratic regimes where "we the people" rule, we theoretically obey no one but ourselves and we are therefore free. De Jouvenel, however, strongly disputes the notion that popular sovereignty ensures individual freedom. He resolutely states that

> [t]o identify those who govern with the people is to confuse the issue, and no regime exists in which such an identification is possible. . . . Those who govern are neither the people nor the majority: they are the governors.

This is especially true of the modern commonwealth (whether a nation or state or even a city), controlled by legislative bodies that are returned to office *en masse* in election after election. The politicians—who seem to see electoral success as affirmation of their efforts—become an elite "with a life and interest of [their] own." Practically speaking, however, their only real success is in fooling enough of the people enough of the time (on Election Day, to be specific).

In actuality the intentions of these legislatures are administered by a standing army of civil servants—in de Jouvenel's coinage, "the Agentry"—but as he explains, this bureaucracy is in no direct way responsible to the people (or often the legislative bodies who fund them or the executive authorities who supposedly oversee them). The bureaucrats extend their own franchise in a symbiotic conspiracy with the politicians, conveniently elevating themselves and justifying their (theoretical) bosses. They simply extend government by proclamation—termed administrative rule-making—with essentially no oversight, except citizen vigilance.

De Jouvenel observes that two additional developments helped make the state's power exceed the people's intentions. First, there arose the illusion that we have a government of laws and not men, even though "it is men who write, administer, and judge our laws." Second, technological innovations made possible enormous state Power; the Power to intimidate, to protect, to conscript, to tax, to direct, and to kill. De Jouvenel clearly explains why Power increases in spite of the supposed constraints the people can effect through their institutions:

> By all means let the people be an absolute sovereign in the hour of choosing its representatives, for in that way the representatives hold from it unlimited authority. But when it has conferred on them this authority, its role is finished and it is of no further importance: it is now the subject, and only the assembly [legislature] is sovereign. Only the assembly is

the place where the general will is formed, and consultation with the people is no more than a species of cookery.... The members of society are citizens for a day and subjects for four years.

On Power shows de Jouvenel perceiving these eventualities with seasoned logic. He also predicts their increase, as does Alexis de Tocqueville in *Democracy in America* (Chapter 8), but in a slightly different manner that seems more and more accurate with each passing decade. De Jouvenel uses the philosophical meanderings of Hobbes, Spinoza, Kant, and most effectively, Rousseau, along with the reflections of other less well-known theorists, to explain the conundrum of the sovereignty of the people versus the Power of the assembly. In this manner he explains that even the supposed protections written "in stone" are not very sturdy.

Earlier philosophers had claimed that when the people voluntarily gave Power to a ruler—whether an individual or a council—they gave it unreservedly. Locke disagreed, contending that people reserve their personal rights, rights established through natural law. When formulating the American Constitution the Framers recognized these natural rights, which were then codified in the Bill of Rights by the first Congress—supposedly protecting them in this form in perpetuity. The problems inherent in the formulations of the earlier philosophers were thus allegedly solved; Americans gave over to an assembly (Congress) the right to order their society in its myriad and ever-changing configurations while protecting individual rights by embracing them in the impregnable Constitution. It is a nice compromise, if it works. However, Plato understood how man's nature undermined such expedients from their inception. He contends that

> good is one thing in nature and another in law; that in regard to justice, absolutely nothing is just by [in] nature, but that men, always divided in feeling about it as they are, are for ever making fresh arrangements in regard to the same objects.

By way of example, if we believe the Bill of Rights is intact, try to express free speech by buying a campaign ad the day before an election; or enjoy the free exercise of religion in an educational venue; or appreciate the right of free association by defining membership in a private organization; or experience the right to bear arms by buying a weapon for your own protection; or find comfort in the sanctity of private property by resisting the state's taking of your home by means of eminent domain for some other person's private economic purpose. All of these things are supposedly *guaranteed* rights in the Constitution. But the guarantees have been watered down or simply trivialized to the point of uselessness. Jefferson's sanctified *written* constitution, intended to protect us from the mischief of men, has failed to do just that. It is the violation of this precept through nothing more than the accretion of power and institutions vested in the political class that de Jouvenel writes about.

Recognizing that modern Power is not as pretty as it should be (were it to effect modesty and self-control), de Jouvenel sees its underlying shabbiness cleverly disguised by an almost sacrosanct five-step process of circular reasoning. This is another law of politics and governance; the law of contradiction:

1. The people naïvely ascribe superhuman characteristics and expectations to their elected representatives—characteristics such as honesty, integrity, wisdom, impartial intelligence and judgment, and, supposedly, a vow of poverty—simply because they vote for them.
2. Since the people cannot watch the governors all the time (they have their own lives to live) the government becomes freer to do as it wills. In a smaller setting governors would be subject to greater scrutiny. (The accretion of power by default is the negative effect of centralization.)
3. When things do go wrong (from any personal or even general point of view) the people feel ignorant—for they have not paid attention—and individually helpless. So they lie down in the face of (mostly distant) Power. (Whatever meager information the people do have, gleaned via the media, they have learned to distrust. According to a June 2007 Gallup Poll only 22% of the public has confidence in newspaper reporting, while television's reliability rating is at 23%.)
4. When taking action the governors do not understand the true will of the people, often not even what has been reserved in the Constitution, for they too are ignorant of all that must be known. When not forced to pay attention they will avoid doing so and thus they simply act out *their own* will—believing that they have

no better measure in such a confusing world. At this point the "government" takes on a life of its own and, as Rousseau notes, there arises even an *esprit de corps* among the representatives that breeds first confidence, and then arrogance.
5. The people are largely politically and particularly economically illiterate and despite the fact that the *government* has done some terrible thing they feel that *their representative* has not, for two reasons: (1) he could not do such a thing because he is a demigod and we believe in him; or (2) he said that he did not do such-and-such, or admitted that he did so but only out of necessity as it was the *only possible* thing that could be done under the circumstances to protect the people. And we believe him then as well, because we have elected him and he is sincere, and we send him back to do more to us because of consideration 1. above.

Circle complete.

If it be thought that such philosophical and real-world conjectures are limited to ancient European and modern American thinkers, consider the intellectual wanderings of Libyan Muammar Gadaffi, a boy and man who has lived in a tent in the desert most of his life, who has limited schooling but a sharp eye and keen sense of humanity and power, and who took over as ruler of his African nation at age 27,

> In Western democracies the electoral system separates those who govern from the people they represent. [I]mmediately after winning their votes [the governor] himself usurps the [people's] sovereignty and acts instead of them. The prevailing traditional democracy endows the member of parliament with a sacredness and immunity denied to other individual members of the people.
> *Gadaffi: The Desert Mystic*, by George Tremlett, p. 211 (1993)

It is the sacredness and immunity that defines the disconnection between the governors and the people. But both characteristics are merely a convenience for the people, created out of whole cloth, so they have to take neither responsibility nor action.

The Citizen

DE JOUVENEL's solution? Essentially the same as Alexis de Tocqueville's and Jefferson's and Madison's and most of the rest of the authors presented here: question authority, limit power, deny centralization, remove political opportunity from those elected and confine them to the precepts of the written Constitution—be aware and diligent. We must individually review the five-step process to see where we can involve ourselves. We must not be awed or cowed by those in the place of Power. Our governors are only people, with the same desires and weaknesses and strengths that we possess. If we are their partners, not their subjects, essentially sound government can be achieved. The five-step process can be broken into manageable pieces and sound reasoning and principle can prevail over the intentions of Power.

But it takes time and attention. If the government "runs" ten percent of our lives then ten percent of our time and effort might collectively be spent to effect a government in which we can believe. These are not impossible requests of a polity that benefits so much from something so simple as the U.S. Constitution. It is important for the electorate not to be daunted by public responsibility or at least civic involvement. These things do not have to be done individually; groups can be joined or formed; communication and action are not so difficult that we cannot express our beliefs to those in power in useful enough form to ensure what we have achieved is what we keep. It takes intentional action—as we have so often witnessed in the works in *First Principles*.

Today we can see the results of what de Jouvenel contends is inevitable in modern representative governance. These ends have been reached primarily because of our inaction and inattention. As Edmund Burke noted more than two hundred years ago:

> All that is necessary for the triumph of evil is that good men do nothing.

In America it certainly cannot be said that we do nothing but it can be seen that we do not do enough or that what we do accomplish is often not relevant to the issues at hand. As de Jouvenel notes, the entire population cannot exercise the general will, irrespective of the fact that it still belongs to the citizenry; it must devolve onto someone or some group that then has Power. Once Power is delegated it can be lost, save *in extremis*, a rare condition (war, fiscal bankruptcy, political corruption) when the people have the opportunity and obligation to rise to meet whatever challenge faces them. However, when extreme times are extant the governors often find it convenient to assert that *they* are the only ones competent to act (they will fight the war, they will fix the tax and spend syndrome, they will legislate ethics codes that will reign-in the venal within their own ranks). Thus the myth of the omnipotent governors is born. The observation that the problems we face will usually not be solved by the minds that created them is seen, by those in power, as mere ignorance, or stubbornness. Of course, the ignorance and inadequacy and subservience of the people become necessary corollaries to the continuation in power of the governors. De Jouvenel's conclusion

> that popular sovereignty may give birth to a more formidable despotism than divine sovereignty

seems almost inescapable. It leads to only one additional conclusion: vigilance is the *only* protection for, and the *prime obligation* of, the citizen. Therein lies our liberation—if we only can grasp it.

De Jouvenel explores an additional concept that developed early in the evolution of democracy and complemented the citizen's need to exercise vigilance. This notion surfaces several times in the history of governance and is just as repeatedly forgotten: democracy's initial purpose was not to *establish* popular sovereignty—that is, to pro-actively select a ruler or leader—but rather to delegate to the people's representatives the obligation to *resist* the power of the sovereign. This was irrespective of whether the sovereign was an individual or an assembly, a president or an emperor.

Thus de Jouvenel observes that the original parliamentary function was a negative one, best exemplified in the Roman Tribunate, which could only arrest the action of the Senate and the Consuls in the name of the people. It was essential that "the people were defended by those who did not aspire to become masters." We see this negative democratic function philosophically expressed by Thomas Paine in *Common Sense* (Chapter 2) as American independence was being established. It can be utilized again to reverse the course of Power. Intentional action grounded in common understandings of how our government must function can serve to remove from Power those who no longer deserve our trust or even our confidence. The threat of removal from office, of the loss of an election, focuses everyone's attention on what is missing from the governing equation. It does this far more effectively than pointing out the philosophical or actual failure of a politician's tenure in office and thereby attempting to change his course solely through the force of intellect.

De Jouvenel, in observing modern political foundations, explains that the way constitutional government is undermined is not "to deny representation, which the people would defend; it is to absorb representation in[to] government," into Power. This has been particularly prevalent in the Western democracies over the past hundred years or so. The all-important result is that in "achieving" popular sovereignty (with the concomitant right of the governors to rule once the votes are cast) we have eliminated any place to stand in order to resist Power. Modern democrats would contend that the electoral franchise is one such protection and that the Constitution is a second. But a review of American electoral history vis-à-vis U.S. legislative, judicial, and administrative actions denies that such safeguards are effective if the people are not adamant.

De Jouvenel's point is made more directly as he notes that both the U.S. Supreme Court and the Congress have chipped away at constitutional protections and in a convoluted manner have determined that there are things that must be done to protect society *irrespective* of the Constitution (a single example: restricting speech in political campaigns—perhaps the most essential freedom needed for the citizen to protect himself. It is not without reason free speech is addressed in the First Amendment.). De Jouvenel contends that, in essence, society has become more important than the citizens who comprise it. This evolution is the antithesis of Lord Acton's conclusion in *Essays in the History of Liberty* (Chapter 9) that individual "Liberty is not a means to a higher political end, it is itself the highest political end."

The Courts

UTILIZING DE JOUVENEL'S comprehensions to dissect the modern democratic state during the second half of the twentieth century we find that the U.S. court system, in particular the Supreme Court, drifted toward a concept of citizen equality that is supposedly more meaningful and more fundamental than individual rights. It has devolved in this fashion because citizen equality is more emotionally satisfying in the short run (more politically correct)—but more socially devastating in the long run—than individuality or individualism. Power's arrogance has thus metastasized from the legislature to the courts. Since judicial sovereignty in nearly all countries is not subject in any practical manner to electoral restraint or review (in the U.S. federal judges serve for life), judicial arrogance and judicial activism can become entrenched. However, judicial activism is a two-way street.

James Madison declaimed as the Constitution's ratification was being debated that it was the obligation of the judiciary to stand as "an impenetrable bulwark against every assumption of power in the legislative or executive." Today courts can too often appropriate to themselves, in their decrees, the function of shadow legislature (such as ordering school busing or coercing taxation or tax distribution for one or another social purpose). As Madison noted, what our court system was designed to do was truncate the reach of overweening legislatures and elected executives and unelected bureaucrats, not find ways to get around the constrictions of government's limits founded in the Constitution. An activist court that does the former is the protection the Founders built into the system of checks and balances; an activist court that does the latter oversteps its bounds and undermines the individual and common protections that were intended to be inviolable.

To Americans it may seem that de Jouvenel's analysis mocks the U.S. Constitution, which divides the powers of government among separately chosen branches. But his intention is not to ridicule the document, it is only to describe its application in the face of Power, in the face of the human condition. There is unquestioned value in the separation of powers and de Jouvenel himself observes that L'Enfant designed the city of Washington, D.C. by locating the White House and the Capitol on opposing hilltops thus signifying the healthy rivalry between our "king" and our "parliament." Yet America, as noted in the court/Constitution conflict described above, has hardly avoided the dangers that exercised de Jouvenel.

One of the strongest barriers against a monopoly of Power at the center has been almost entirely eliminated over time; that is the competing Power of the fifty individual states to which (along with the people themselves), by means of the Tenth Amendment to the Constitution, all Power not specifically delegated to the national government is reserved. The undermining of the rights of the states, and the people, has been achieved via a judicial activism that ultimately insists on the value and validity of increased centralization. This is achieved by means of the tools available in Article 1, Section 8 of the Constitution—the commerce, general welfare and necessary and proper clauses. The courts interpret these phrases with an eye toward uniformity (which is a code word for centralization) and expand government's Power by claiming the right to decide any issue with even the thinnest veneer of national interest.

The Division of Power

THE IDEA OF refashioning the different American constituencies into something akin to a disciplined parliamentary system (a system with a single legislative body where the opposition cannot block action, they can only call for elections to oust the governors with whom they disagree)—because we need to "get things done"—has been the goal of progressive tradition since the presidency of Woodrow Wilson (1912–1920). But this desire, which obviously can cut in favor of either liberals or conservatives, Democrats or Republicans, has brought forth an opposite desire in the citizenry: the late twentieth-century public preference for divided government—where one party controls the presidency while the other controls one or both houses of Congress and all are thought to be less potent. Unfortunately this idea nicely demonstrates a widespread misunderstanding of the preconditions of freedom in a constitutional republic. The populace may profess a desire for bifurcated Power because they feel less will happen—to them—if those in office have to compromise on myriad goals. The reality is that citizen freedom and independence from government are as unprotected in this circumstance as they are when Power is concentrated.

De Jouvenel points out two truths: first, a government of political opposites does not work effectively to limit itself because Power is its own master. The citizen's Power—effected at the ballot box—is only a small part of the equation. The reserve of power found in the hands of administrators and bureaucrats and the judiciary is the more important stumbling block to citizen control of government, thus the failure of theoretically impeccable constitutional measures to work well in practice even when Power is divided becomes apparent.

Second, de Jouvenel notes that when Power is threatened with stasis or impotence it morphs with one final twist of irony—it acts in concert. This is so for the reason observed earlier: those in Power have as their first goal their retention in office. If either faction cannot impose what they profess is in the public's interest (in their effort to claim the mantle of the people's champion) they act collectively—out of self-interest.

Sound legislation and policy often come to the fore in this circumstance (various reforms of Social Security, of the welfare system, and of the tax system have all come about within the confines of divided government) and the confidence of Power waxes ever larger. Those in Power see themselves as having done even more good because they acted in a bipartisan fashion; this evidence that they effected the true general will causes them to think even better of what they've achieved; the greater likelihood of their reelection causes them to smile even more widely. The question always remains: was the citizenry protected or enabled or was it merely mollified?

Vigilance

DE JOUVENEL'S particularly dark view of human social development in the arena of governance is troubling in most of its implications but inherently accurate, thus it is difficult to simply dismiss him as a pessimist. It is easier and more grounded in our experience to accept his views as realistic while we try to protect ourselves from sanctimonious and zealous officials. Social change in de Jouvenel's view, as Power accumulates at higher levels in more concentrated form, is ultimately destined to arrive at the (very politically correct) welfare state that germinated when socialism was thought viable.

Human beings are afraid of neither laws nor inequality—as long as *opportunity* is equal; they have proven themselves willing to accept the real world because so long as opportunity is sacrosanct in all venues (including the opportunity to change, even reverse, government when it becomes oppressive) then the populace feels secure. But the governors who have evolved find the populace too weak or too selfish or too ignorant for such freedom. In this circumstance the individual is lost and "the people" are found.

De Jouvenel believes that attempts at equality of condition are doomed to failure in a free society because of the possibilities of the human spirit—because of what people can imagine. The failure first manifests itself socially, then economically. The attempts at equality of condition are equally doomed in an authoritarian society because of the opposite side of that same human spirit—what people will tolerate before they rebel. This does not, however, stop the governors from trying ever harder (even in the face of practicality and reality) to achieve equalitarian success. They dream that if we do just this *one* additional thing, pass this one additional law, give slightly more power to this one administrative agency, society will obtain a more perfect and impartial equality—thus government grows. De Jouvenel sees but a single beacon to light the path of true freedom—citizen action as the *sole* antidote to Power. The question for de Jouvenel as for all the rest of us is this: will that understanding find the people at the ballot box or the barricade?

Freedom-crushing dreamers ultimately believe that the state can do no wrong if it is nothing other than ourselves, in other words, that we are actually represented by those whom we elect to operate government. However, the philosophical goal of such an elected state has become the protection of society, not the individual, by means of a spurious guardianship. In either case, the harm to the individual is no longer a consideration, for individuality has ceased to exist as a governing concept. The state must decide what is correct for the society. This is denoted as a political correctness, arbitrated by those expressing, supposedly, the general will. The circle is again complete.

U.S. legislators routinely speak of the will of the American people; what the people will or will not tolerate and the specifics of the public largesse to which the public is "entitled." These fabulous assertions allow the real Power of government to be masked in sleight-of-hand and anonymity. The legislator contends: "I did only what the people demanded." But in fact, the legislator made the choice and implemented the action—the general will did not. He did this, as often as not, for his own electoral purposes (note how many pieces of legislation offer the names of Congressmen and Senators in their titles: the Smith Act to Protect . . . , the Jones Law for Reform . . .). The claim that government's acts are an expression of the general will is how legislators and executives justify their Power or their tyranny. These methods have not changed since the time of the Romans. De Jouvenel turns to Rousseau for succor to deal with life's (and government's) real difficulty:

> Putting law over man is a political problem comparable to that of squaring the circle in geometry . . . until you have solved it, be sure that *instead of enthroning laws, as you imagine, you are really enthroning men.* [Emphasis by de Jouvenel]

This gloomy perspective takes only modest solace from the electoral franchise, still held by the populace, and still recalled as the weapon of the people. It is sometimes used as it must be, as in the elections of

Margaret Thatcher in England in 1979 and Ronald Reagan in America in 1980. But even these forceful personalities, each of whom had and took the opportunity to effect significant change, were unable to materially reduce the mass infusion of government into our daily lives. A smothering effect on the populace is yet in evidence.

As becomes clear from the construction of his arguments, de Jouvenel recognizes that the foundation of the political claim to power in the modern era is a declaration of an intent to do good. But the intention to do good completely misses the point, for good deeds are solely in the eye and mind of the beholder. Liberty is ultimately the only important goal because from liberty will flow a resolution of the ever-changing ideas of good. For example, is it more worthy to give a man a fish or to teach him to fish? Is it more worthy for government to foster dependency or instill self-sufficiency? One is certainly easier, and equally as certainly more expensive in both economic and human terms. Which represents that elusive "good" for which we are looking? For de Jouvenel, liberty's essence

> lies in our will not being subject to other human wills. . . . [it] is not our more or less illusory participation in the absolute sovereignty of the social whole over the parts; it is, rather, the direct, immediate, and concrete sovereignty of man over himself. . . .

De Jouvenel holds that the citizen's illusory participation in the application of Power through the electoral franchise has skewed our understanding of the essence of liberty. He wonders how and why this occurred:

> How had the democratization of government become more precious than liberty itself?

How was it that the encouragement of government, through idealistic caprice and political egoism, led to more encroachments on liberty than any king ever dreamed of? How have we become so inured to Power that we have twisted the concept of our individual liberty to not being a *right*, but a *grant* from Power?

De Jouvenel finds his answer in the nature of Power itself not just in our own individual failure of action or will. The factors leading to our dilemma are each logical—our desire for individual freedom juxtaposed with an emotional inclination toward social good—but not always rational. Each step of the politician's course seems but the next stage from the last, it is pretty much as simple as that. First principles have simply been forgotten, ignored, devalued, and/or sidestepped by the governors, and human nature has been eliminated as a consideration in governing. At this point politicians, while acting for factions or even in grand ignorance, do not just *assume* perfect administration in effecting governance, but *insist* on its certainty. In this manner they claim the individual is protected by the government, which is the opposite of experience. This is not just a copy of the idealism of the Enlightenment and the French Revolution (if a solution to mankind's misery can be thought of all that is necessary is its implementation) but its twin.

The ever-more centralized modern state causes perhaps the greatest harm. (On the issue of how citizens are turned into subjects by the destruction of community and the centralization of authority, refer again to Alexis de Tocqueville's *Democracy in America* and Richard Cornuelle's *Reclaiming the American Dream* [Chapter 30].) The creation of a monolithic therapeutic state lends credence to the idea that government's politicians and bureaucrats will do everything more perfectly for us poor individuals than we can do for ourselves. Our representatives (elected or not), whom we never asked to nurture us, sustain a nanny state through *their* exercise of the general will. The therapeutic state has grown from its modest origins, when it sought to help only those who actually could not help themselves, into a monstrosity that helps all of us because it insists it must. It has the Power that we have bestowed upon it. As de Jouvenel notes,

> [O]nce Power is based on the sovereignty of all, the distrust [of Power] comes to seem unreasonable and vigilance pointless; and the limits set on authority no longer get defended.

Liberty vs. Security

THERE IS ONE additional factor behind the evolution of Power—and de Jouvenel observed its universality half a century before America and the world began to directly suffer the effects of global terrorism based on Islamic fanaticism. This human need is for security, which many individuals mistakenly consider to be far more crucial than liberty. Liberty's objectively more pressing imperative becomes intellectually and emotionally elusive where security does not exist. Humanity forgets that liberty must first be established before security is possible. When security *is* achieved, to whatever greater or lesser extent, then liberty, paradoxically, becomes lost in equal measure because to achieve security one must trade individual autonomy. But even understanding the priority of liberty does not make limiting the governors any easier.

There probably are no political or even philosophical limits to what government thinks it can offer, or what the populace increasingly thinks it should receive in terms of protection. As James Madison observed when commenting on how much power government needed, logically there can be *no limit* to the power of government if it is to do its job in attempting to deliver security (illusory as this fruit of statism must be). The government must be given power commensurate with the obligations placed on it. With this logic we can perceive how the people trend toward security and the state toward omnipotence. The result for the citizen becomes obvious—he is turned into a subject.

De Jouvenel's case against more government "is an argument for not letting necessity, the tyrant's plea, have all its own way" (John Milton, *Paradise Lost*). Given any thought can we deny the proposition that the burgeoning effect of government is to deny us our humanity by creating a society founded on an illusion of equality and security? Regrettably, those "in Power" *do* deny this truth because they fail to recognize (or is it accept?) that life is inherently uneven and unequal—wherein lies its beauty, not its failure. While aiming to give security and equality to everyone by forcibly constraining our individual freedom those suffused with the conceit of Power destroy the very differences, incentives, and impetuses that are the essence of human existence.

About the Author

BERTRAND DE JOUVENEL has been termed "the least famous of the great political thinkers of the twentieth century," but his fame, or lack of it, may be inversely proportional to the value of his insights. He was raised in a prosperous literary family who were intensely political and of ancient French aristocratic lineage on his paternal side. His father was the French ambassador to the League of Nations after World War I and was elected to the French senate; his mother presided over an important salon with a particular interest in France's relations with Czechoslovakia. Born in 1903 in France, de Jouvenel was strongly affected by the rise of Adolf Hitler's National Socialist Party, the Nazis, and the world war that followed as a result thereof.

Although de Jouvenel graduated from the Sorbonne in law and mathematics his career soon gravitated toward economic and political commentary. His interest in the United States led him to write *La Crise du Capitalisme Américain* (1933) [The Crisis of American Capitalism], one of the first interpretations of the Great Depression. At the time he favored a strong role for the state in economic matters.

De Jouvenel worked as a journalist specializing in international affairs for much of the 1930s. He gained worldwide renown for his 1935 interview with Adolf Hitler. After the outbreak of World War II de Jouvenel joined the French resistance but was forced to take refuge in Switzerland. There he prepared his most famous work, *Du Pouvoir: Histoire Naturelle de sa Croissance* (1945) [On Power: The Natural History of Its Growth], a harsh critique of the modern state's authority. De Jouvenel built upon this historically oriented and profoundly philosophical treatise with several other books over the succeeding decades.

De Jouvenel taught at the University of Paris and was a frequent visiting professor at British and American universities. He worked tirelessly to acquaint the French elite with Anglo-American economic thought and practices; he was the author of scores of scholarly articles and books on these subjects. De Jouvenel died in 1987.

Section II

Part 1

The Twentieth-Century American Experience

16

The Conservative Revolution: The Movement That Remade America

Lee Edwards

Originally published: 1999
341 pages

THE POLITICAL CLIMATE in the United States changed dramatically during the last quarter of the twentieth century; most of that change resulted from the reemergence and then rapid public awareness of historical values and economic verities that would combat what was skewing the results our political system offered. The foundation for the new face of U.S. politics began to form in the 1930s, amid the intellectual, social, and economic turmoil of the Great Depression and in response to the emergence of Russia and re-emergence of Germany as international enigmas. As a result of these developments a counter-movement took place among those who understood the government's fundamentally flawed economic reactions to the Depression and the illusory promises of Russian communism and German fascism. Over the following fifty years, by means of both political machinations and economic discourse, the intellectual leaders of this counter-movement shaped the resurgence of American conservatism, a movement whose name belies its close affinity to European liberalism.

The momentum of political and economic change in the U.S. accelerated exponentially in the decades after World War II with the almost radical divergence of conservative and liberal viewpoints and goals. From our current vantage point we could easily overlook how close postwar left-wing Eastern "intellectuals" were to fully embracing economically bankrupt socialist ideology, and how vehemently conservatives fought this drift. Lee Edwards charts the different course taken by American politics because of the bold ideas and intentional actions of a handful of determined individuals. That notion, because it is so important, bears repeating: the bold ideas and intentional actions of determined individuals saved us from political and economic mistakes of potentially unbridled proportions. The struggle to achieve this end sometimes required confrontations of the most resolute kind, but also involved intellectual sorties of admirable subtlety.

Edwards's first task is to analyze the decades of misinterpretation (even deliberate misrepresentation) of conservative politics and politicians offered by mainstream, mostly east coast media outlets. He next introduces the original minds behind the regenerated conservative movement and clearly spells out their ideas and principles. Finally, Edwards traces the unintended consequences of (theoretically) well-intentioned but (certainly) ill-conceived liberal policies—policies that ran aground on the reality of our immutable human nature. Edwards acknowledges that many unsung heroes have contributed to the insurrection that resulted in modern conservatism, but the presence of four men was crucial to the achievement of fixed goals: Bob Taft, Mr. Republican; Barry Goldwater, Mr. Conservative; Ronald Reagan, Mr. President; and Newt Gingrich, Mr. Speaker.

Taft fostered the political revival of conservatism in Congress, while Goldwater's importance was his popular enunciation of what had gone wrong with government's purpose in the wake of the unrealizable dreams of President Kennedy. Ronald Reagan brought conservatism to the White House, and Speaker Gingrich delivered it to Main Street. Each built on the propositions and political accomplishments of his predecessors. The culmination of their efforts changed the course of America's governing archetype by the end of the twentieth century.

As Edwards further explains, the contributions of foundational figures Russell Kirk, Frank Meyer, and William F. Buckley, Jr. were unmistakably important. Without these incisive theorists and activists the conservative program would have taken far longer to both flower and implement. Others who are today less well known also contributed, often indirectly and sometimes, as members of the opposition, even unintentionally (in this vein watch the consequences of liberal senator Daniel Patrick Moynihan's efforts in Chapters 18 and 27.) But perhaps of paramount intellectual importance were the members of the Mont Pelerin Society, who are represented in myriad chapters in *First Principles* and whom Edwards brings to life so many decades later.

Whittaker Chambers, a person whose notoriety is flagging with time and the ever more distant memory of Soviet Communism, was also a catalyst in this era. Chambers was a tower as both an actor in and a reporter of those times, and his story, contained in *Witness* (Chapter 41), was one of the struts that made the struggle easy to embrace and made the battle comprehensible. It still does.

Of the notables, Buckley, in particular, gave popular voice to this movement. He had the twin virtues of sound theory and dogged intention. His unrelenting efforts to be heard and to offer a place for conservatism's presence to be felt (through *National Review*, a weekly newspaper he established in the 1950s) may be one of the most important effects of the group frustration that was evident in conservative circles beginning in that era. It is hard today to capture the extremity of the public situation, as difficult perhaps as it is to understand the true emotions of 1776. But it is all there in the words of each of the participants whom Edwards brings to the fore.

An example of what America faced is offered in the travails of Whittaker Chambers. He writes of the times and the enormity of the crime of communism to Buckley when the latter was beginning to take action. Chambers knew whatever happened to change America's course would begin in a small way, but he also understood that it would be in a manner that meant a fight to the death. He expresses this starting point as an emotional caring, the kind of caring that drives men outside themselves. He writes of how reality would once more intrude on a melancholy world

> when a few men begin again to dare to believe that there was once something else, that something else is thinkable, and need some evidence of what it was, and the fortifying knowledge that there were those who, at the great nightfall, took loving thought to preserve the tokens of hope and truth.

In response to Chambers's recollection of his hopes, Buckley later recounts his concurrent thoughts:

> The tokens of hope and truth were not, he seemed to be saying, to be preserved by a journal of opinion, not by writers or thinkers, but only by activists, and I was to know that he considered a publication—the right kind of publication—not a word, but a deed.

It was the deed of Buckley's actions that cemented in the public forum a method, and ultimately the substance of this effort. The new/old conservatives knew what they knew, their thoughts and understandings needed articulation; Buckley supplied that. The utterances spoke for themselves, and then were echoed. Conservatism was brought first to the political clerisy who had been publicly dormant in the onslaught of socialism and communism, and then to the masses—through action. Public rallies took place, political commentary became ubiquitous, political figures took positions that they had previously only espoused in private. Everything happened through human action.

In contrast to conservatism on the rise, Edwards also outlines liberal populism—the precursor to the modern welfare state—and dissects its premises as an anomaly that collapsed of its own intellectual, then practical convulutions. But pushing that anomaly over the edge into oblivion still had to be done. He recounts in this story the efforts these people took to ensure that happened. Of course, like the cartoon character that falls over the canyon precipice toward certain death on the valley floor, populism and welfarism never quite die; they sprout wings or are caught by some wisp of wind and land gently on the earth below to rise and taunt again. Why? Because few are willing to decline a "free" lunch—no matter what its ultimate cost might be; sycophant politicians recognize this human frailty and use it to their personal advantage.

The modern conservative movement is rooted in a simple concept, articulated by Senator Taft in the 1940s: "Every right is married to a duty." The governed have a responsibility to attend to their own destinies while the governors must offer opportunities rather than impediments to individual success. Already by the 1990s the concept of duty was the hallmark of change, leading away from the indiscriminate generosity embodied in the American welfare system of earlier decades.

As Edwards recounts, the story of how we got from Bob Taft in 1948 to Newt Gingrich in 1994 starts not in the United States but at a meeting in Mont Pelerin, Switzerland in 1947. The leader at this summit of dedicated minds was Friedrich A. von Hayek who, along with his colleague Milton Friedman and several other future Nobel laureates, sought to bring ideas rather than emotions to the forefront of political and economic policy discussions. As Edwards comments, "socialism and statism dominated" the political landscape at that time, yet the people who convened in Switzerland shortly after World War II knew that their philosophy and framework were sound. They developed criteria for governing with the individual as the paramount element in any design.

Following their initial meeting the members of the newly born Mont Pelerin Society spread the word and fleshed-out their theories. They recognized that collectivism would inevitably fail but they also knew that its demise could potentially be devastating if there were no alternatives to allow a rational transition to freedom in economic matters. Their concern and their intention was to ensure that an economic awakening would not lead to upheaval, or worse, to chaos. But they were neither Cassandras nor scolds, offering only fear and doom if socialism was chosen as a viable economic paradigm. As Milton Friedman explained years later in recalling this era,

> I have long believed that we do not influence the course of events by persuading people that we are right when we make what they regard as radical proposals. Rather, we exert influence by keeping options available when something has to be done at a time of crisis.

Members of the Mont Pelerin Society found influential and thoughtful supporters who published facts and data substantiating conservative ideas in order to refute the utopian dogma of liberal collectivists. Taxation was a primary topic because burdensome levies were not just bad economics, they were psychological and philosophical disincentives that discouraged individual initiative. And individual initiative was what created the modern world and kept it running.

Edwards's book recounts an invaluable story about people and ideas and the power of their confluence to change the world. A logical starting point for the novice seeking to understand modern economics and political discourse, this volume is also a source of inspiration. The conservative principles that many people take for granted today (no matter what their political affiliation may be) were formed partly in passionate response to the actual and perceived political and economic threats during the last century. How inspired and disciplined by these principles we are today will determine what life will be like for succeeding generations. It is tempting to drift toward becoming overwhelmed when holding the course begun by these pioneers appears difficult for innumerable reasons. When that happens, just recall how much greater their responsibility was in 1947, and how much easier our efforts are simply because these people iterated first principles and did not shrink from insisting on what they knew to be right.

About the Author

LEE EDWARDS is a senior fellow at the Heritage Foundation in Washington, D.C. and is senior editor of the *World and I* magazine. Edwards has been published in most major newspapers and periodicals in the U.S. and serves as a professor of political science at The Catholic University of America in Washington, D.C. He was the founding director of the Institute on Political Journalism at Georgetown University and has been selected as a fellow at Harvard University's John F. Kennedy School of Government.

Edwards is the president of the Victims of Communism Memorial, built in Washington, D.C., and dedicated on June 15, 2007. The memorial commemorates the 100 million victims of communist oppression.

Edwards earned a bachelor's degree from Duke University and a doctorate from The Catholic University of America; he has published seven previous titles, including biographies of Ronald Reagan and Barry Goldwater. Mr. Edwards was born in Chicago and resides in Alexandria, Virginia.

17

Up From Liberalism

William F. Buckley, Jr.

Originally published: 1959
176 pages

> What all conservatives in this country fear is the loss of freedom by attrition.

THIS IS THE starting point for William F. Buckley, Jr.'s observations and commentary on the state of activist conservatism in the late 1950s. What makes this volume so valuable today is how accurately Buckley sees the future from his then-youthful vantage point. Moreover, he does not fear to submit his views to public inspection. Observing Buckley's success, which was far from assured when he began his quest, we see a quintessential example of why not to be reticent about expressing one's opinions no matter how far afield our views may seem when judged in the light of "common knowledge" or "accepted wisdom." Buckley demonstrates by exposing his own ideas to public scrutiny how flimsy the wisdom of entrenched ideas often becomes.

The global view of both politics and culture has changed dramatically in the half century since Buckley took center stage in an attempt to reorder not just American politics, but American society. To reduce the myriad changes he suggests to a single concept is relatively easy: most of what has been transformed or accomplished in the last fifty years revolves around the notion of responsibility. Most of what has been removed or refigured revolves about the notion of entitlement.

Buckley intends to have us look at our responsibilities if for no other reason than at the time this book was written we as a nation and a society of individuals were beginning not to do so. Conversely, then (as now) almost everyone was happy to talk about their rights. That political rhetoric and policy had been turned upside down since the turn of the twentieth century was apparent. These changes found their genesis in the economic disaster of the Great Depression. *Up From Liberalism* doesn't address everything that it might in these arenas, but its incisive delineation of how to move forward in a specific manner—what to challenge—is a starting point. The results of Buckley's conservative political efforts, of course, speak for themselves. But it is still very important to recall how it all began.

Buckley's title is a play on Booker T. Washington's (1856–1915) autobiography, *Up From Slavery*, published in 1901. Washington's life story is one of sheer determination and fortitude. As he was born into slavery just before the Civil War began, his achievements were attained in an era when society sought to hold him and his race down as a matter of principle. When his work was done Washington had accomplished more than his contemporaries would have imagined (he forged the Tuskegee Institute into the great university it became) but less than he might have had his race not been used against him. It appears, from the title reference in Buckley's case, that the progress and achievement evidenced by the manner of Washington's life was something Buckley wished to instill in the conservative cadre, who were contending with a different form of slavery—an economic slavery defined in Hayek's *The Road to Serfdom* (Chapter 13). By means of pure resolve and conviction, neither Washington nor Buckley would be smothered by prejudice or intimidation.

At the outset, Buckley sets himself up as an arbiter of language—out of necessity and unapologetically. To advance their contentions liberals choose to use not just words but emotionally crafted specters of social disasters or their remedial opposite, brilliant equalitarian fiscal options. In explaining why he dissects these flights of fancy in rather blunt fashion Buckley feels constrained to make one of his fundamental points:

> The compulsion to soften (words and meaning) can be seen elbowing out the desire to make oneself clear. . . . The modulated approach threatens to overwhelm reality and truth. The human impulse to be tactful evolutionizes into a tendency to refuse to recognize facts.

As John Adams noted two hundred years ago "facts are stubborn things," and Buckley is equally stubborn in recalling them when faced with self-righteous, impractical, or utopian schemes to make the world over.

While evincing much frustration with liberals who deny reality Buckley continues to argue with them in an attempt to make sense of things that exist only as a mirror image of truth. By way of example, he describes—fifty years ago—what today is known as political correctness. Being politically correct involves more than using emotionally neutral wording, which often obfuscates personal responsibility; it also entails the effort to camouflage behind such phrasing partisan political goals that invariably revolve around full-scale government intervention aimed at equalitarianism. This was something Buckley could not then and cannot now let pass unnoticed.

Another example of Buckley's foresight is his discussion of "entitlements," a word that did not appear in *Up From Liberalism* but the substance of which and its inexorable infliction on our society he clearly envisions. The concept of "entitlements" and their social effect was seen earlier in Frederic Bastiat's *The Law* (Chapter 7) and will appear later in Bertrand de Jouvenel's *The Ethics of Redistribution* (Chapter 28). Buckley takes the fears and consternation of these authors through the course in logic now well-defined by modern American political confrontations; in stating his philosophical opposition to this brand of welfarism he preaches the law of unintended consequences—of aid thoughtlessly given without consideration of its whole effect. Although some may not care to give Buckley credit for being a prophet, he pursues to their reasonable ends liberal tendencies in evidence at the time he wrote and in so doing comes to what now look like inescapable conclusions.

Buckley launches his investigation into social welfarism (a main thrust of this book) on a foundational level. He observes that at the base of a liberal's beliefs are assumptions that human beings are perfectible, that social progress is predictable, and that equality is attainable—all through the action of the state. The modern liberal still claims that reason alone will lead us to successfully effect these goals. This reflects a rebirth of the failed theorizing of France's eighteenth-century Enlightenment. In his perennial fashion, Buckley demonstrates that reason does precisely the opposite of what the liberals claim. Actually, a blind faith in reason incongruously combined with gushing sentimentality—unguided and unrestrained by intelligent thought, rationality, or principle—is what causes liberals to feel so strongly and yet be so wrong at the same time. Emotions and arrogance often drive liberals to think they know the answers and can implement them through the state—despite fact and experience.

John Dickinson, one of the drafters of the U.S. Constitution, puts it succinctly in 1787 when he describes some of the less-than-benign structures for national government that were being considered at the Constitutional Convention in Philadelphia:

> Experience must be our only guide. Reason may mislead us.

Denying faith in reason seems almost blasphemous, but that is not what Dickinson is suggesting. What he offers is that man can intellectually reason his way to seemingly rational answers that human beings cannot willingly embrace. Man's reluctance to live only for his fellow man is not based on selfishness—obviously a negative concept—but on self-preservation. This latter reality is grounded on the idea that we are responsible for ourselves and if each of us attends to that personal obligation (recalling always the equal rights of others) we will achieve a greater good. Thus reason is as beneficially applied in understanding human nature and psychology as it is in imagining utopian possibilities. In recalling that reason can take us to more than one answer Dickinson was standing firm in reality. In the modern era it is the fiction of idealism that Buckley desires to address.

At mid-century Buckley saw the liberal political leadership—for political gain—offering everyone everything that they might need or could want. Moreover, if someone was not imaginative enough to envision what he "needed," liberals would not hesitate to proffer what they thought he should have. All of this was to be at the expense of the government as though the government was some Midas-like entity separate from the citizenry. It must be continually remembered that we taxpayers *are* the government. Buckley argues that the continuing liberal largesse is a crime of unbridled proportions. It is a crime against the recipients as much as against those who are taxed to fund the irrational, but pseudo-emotionally satisfying giveaways. Buckley's answer to such nonsense is to note that

> there will not be a robust political life until people become convinced that it matters what they think.

Then they must put their thoughts into action. The difference in the views of conservatives and liberals can be found in the idea of how to encourage a rational society. While each understands the value of the rule of law there are different views of what those laws are intended to accomplish; that same difference reflects the underlying philosophies of how our governing is to be effected. Conservatives see law in its larger context, as something that has to be applied to human circumstances—to what is. Liberals see law as a tool, a lever, to force conformity to reasoned (in their view) behavior—to what should be. For the liberal, if we lose our sense of morality, rules will suffice. The human condition says otherwise.

In the second half of his book Buckley dissects liberalism in its economic misapprehensions. He offers that the planned economy was fostered by demagogic politicians and supported by an academic aristocracy that derided any who were so bold as to disagree. This derision occurs either through personal attacks or intellectual condescension (as noted by George Gilder in *Wealth and Poverty* [Chapter 27]). Fewer dollars should be spent by the people themselves the liberal says, while more tax dollars should be spent on their behalf because the good of the people is not to be decided by them but by the political and academic cognoscenti. This centrally planned arrogance is easy to debunk and yet it was and is so widely accepted in the liberal political world and mainstream media that it frustrates common intelligence (and all of this takes place irrespective of the enormous success free markets attained after World War II [see *The Commanding Heights*, Chapter 29]). That so many people could be so misguided by their own hubris is simply the human condition in its most ineffective guise. It is human reason gone down a self-destructive path.

From his 1950s perch Buckley sees the centralization of government as the looming problem of the twentieth century. He intones that the more concentrated government becomes the more mechanical our response is because government is too big and too far away to do anything about. Apropos of this matter, he notes that the easiest way for liberals to circumvent political obstacles—any hindrance that common sense moves people on a local level to put in the liberal's path—is to create the greatest possible distance between where a tax dollar is collected and where it is spent. Liberals in Washington cunningly disburse ever-growing tax receipts (or, worse, deficits) to localities where the question is not "Is this a good program?" but "How can we obtain maximum federal funding?" (Someone else is paying for it, right?) This changes the first question that should be asked on the local level: is it proper that we participate in this program at all, and if so, how do we attain locally set goals reflecting local conditions?

The second and broader local query is whether these tax dollars should go to Washington in the first place. Do we get revenue and other advantages back in equal measure to what we are taxed and what we truly need—even if considered in the broadest sense of the national public interest? By sending its money off to Washington the electorate suffers a loss from friction (the surcharge Beltway bureaucrats inevitably must levy as a handling fee before sending local dollars back, reduced in size and covered with regulatory gobbledygook) while being concomitantly subjected to the vicissitudes of politics that misdirects tax dollars based on political whims—or political power. The latter results in the "earmark" scandals that are central to twenty-first-century congressional corruption. (Earmarks are the application of Congressionally-appropriated funds to specific districts or states at the behest of individual senators or congresspersons.)

Liberal income redistribution schemes foisted on an unsuspecting and often naïve public are a target for Buckley's sharp pen and incisive logic. Everyone loves a gift, and when it comes from the government it is not only thought of as free it is actually touted as such. Buckley marvels, as should we, that people can so consistently and completely act as though the government actually has something other than what it takes from us. There is no government money; there is only *our* money. How it is used should guide our every public impulse.

In this vein, while he reviews the Social Security program Buckley explodes all the myths of what it isn't and he exposes it for what it actually is—income redistribution. The system will ultimately fail because its interior financial logic is that of a pyramid scheme, where the benefits for existing beneficiaries are taken from current workers—with the hope by these contributors that there will be new workers to support them as they retire. Social Security is an unfunded liability of the government. When those workers fail to materialize the program will suffer catastrophic financial collapse. It is a system that does social damage by fostering irresponsible financial security expectations. That fact has come home to roost in the twenty-first century as the U.S. Social Security program faces near-term insolvency.

Buckley's considerations, as a group, call for the reduction of federal centralization and aggrandizement, for elimination of the idea that one-size-fits-all government is possible, and for the retention of tax dollars locally whenever possible so that those who are affected see to the proper application of these funds. Citizens must be able to watch government as it watches them and this can only be done on a local level.

What riles Buckley most, as noted in the opening paragraph of this synopsis, is his fear of a liberalism that becomes more coercive and more direct with each passing year as "the social planners seek more and more brazenly to impose their preferences on us." The taking of a dollar for taxes reduces the taxpayer's freedom incrementally just as every other reduction of property rights does. (For a comprehensive exploration of the equation that defines the incremental loss of liberty as taxation rises, consult *Property and Freedom* [Chapter 11], and *Capitalism and Freedom* [Chapter 25].) In the end, Buckley asks how much we are willing to give in before we simply give up. It is not an idle question. In 1835 in *Democracy in America* (Chapter 8), after he details the long list of things government tends to do for us if left unchecked, Alexis de Tocqueville asks,

> [W]hat remains [for the people] but to spare them all the care of thinking and all the trouble of living?

Reading Buckley's now half-century-old reflections provides some cogent and thought-provoking answers to what happens to us when we surrender responsibilities for ourselves and allow our lives to be remolded in the liberal image.

About the Author

WILLIAM F. BUCKLEY, JR. was born in New York City in 1925 and raised in Connecticut. He attended Yale University and sparred with American liberals continually from his undergraduate days until his death in 2008. In 1955, he established and for the next thirty-five years served as editor of *National Review*, one of America's preeminent conservative publications. He was one of the founders of Young Americans for Freedom (YAF), formed in response to the liberal agenda of the 1960s. From 1966 to 1999 he hosted *Firing Line*, a program devoted to intellectual give-and-take that was television's longest-running show. He authored more than forty books of political commentary, autobiography, fiction, and philosophy. His thousands of speeches and less formal talks promoted his aim of getting people to think, then act. From 1962 until his death he wrote a column titled *On the Right*, syndicated in more than three hundred newspapers, where he attempted to make sense of the political and economic life of this country and of the world. Wrote the *New York Times,* "His most inimitable pieces are those that skewer the people he doesn't like, of whom there is no shortage."

18

The Conscience of a Conservative

Barry Goldwater

Originally published: 1960
127 pages

ALTHOUGH IT EXPRESSES his thoughts and philosophy and its premises guided his actions *The Conscience of a Conservative* was not directly written by Barry Goldwater. It was ghostwritten in 1959 by L. Brent Bozell, a prominent conservative thinker and speechwriter, at the behest of Goldwater's strong supporters inside the conservative movement. Bozell took Goldwater's syndicated newspaper columns as the basis for his effort; his intimate knowledge of the state of conservative thinking helped form the disjointed and diverse articles into a comprehensive discourse. When the book was ultimately published its fidelity to Goldwater's beliefs was patent.

At the time Goldwater was a second-term senator from Arizona who didn't think he was right for a presidential run. He was not well educated and although he had been raised Episcopalian he feared that his notably Jewish name would cause too many problems outside Arizona. He eventually allowed an unsuccessful draft-Goldwater presidential movement to proceed in 1960 despite the fact that he didn't really believe he could—or perhaps even should—be president. All that would change within three years.

By 1963 one hundred thousand hardback and four hundred thousand paperback copies of *The Conscience of a Conservative* had been sold. It was a watershed event in American political history because the book did something that hadn't been done as starkly before: it made flat statements, demanded specific action, and offered (in what would become the title of a later biography about Goldwater) a choice—not an echo. The reason Goldwater was able to do this and chose to do so lay in the fact that he did not aspire to the presidency; he sought truth and sense in politics and hence he was plainspoken and demanding. He was a person who wanted to do something, not just be someone. If what he said squashed his chances for the presidency—so be it.

The book, a manifesto more than simply a treatise, was whittled down from its rough draft of two hundred pages to just 127 by the time of publication. Goldwater's spare words and straightforward positions philosophically embrace alternatives to all that conservatives found wrong with Republican President Dwight Eisenhower's leadership in the 1950s, and more to the point, the socialistic foundations of the modern Democrat party crafted during the presidency of Franklin Roosevelt. It also presciently addresses what they would find even more wrong with President Kennedy's policies. It was Kennedy's indecisiveness in the Bay of Pigs fiasco that finally motivated Goldwater to take action. (The Bay of Pigs operation, which the U.S. supported logistically, was a failed invasion of Cuba in 1961 by Cubans domiciled in Florida. This incident occurred shortly after Fidel Castro succeeded in a military takeover of Cuba, also with U.S. support, following which he instituted a Soviet-style communist government.)

Goldwater saw a lack of courage in the mood of the American governing elite as his rallying point. There were historical forces at work, forces that Goldwater felt were undermining American character and independence. These were found in the drift toward an over-regulated, over-taxed economy and a demeaning welfare state that were unacceptable to him.

There were also national defense issues that Goldwater wanted to bring to the public discussion. He was not afraid to use them as props and further proof of the need for resolution in calling out the real danger: communism. Although that danger was authentic there were complicating factors in the mix of rhetoric. The Soviets had launched the first successful earth satellite, had put the first human in space, and allegedly held a wide edge in missile technology. This latter fact, which was a significant political issue in the five-year period between 1957 and 1961, was actually not true. President Eisenhower knew the political claim by the Democrats that we were falling behind the Soviets was false because he had in his quiver all the information from the U2 spy planes that were over-flying the Soviet Union on a regular basis. The Russians were anything but ready to claim technological superiority in rocketry regardless of their space successes. But Ike wouldn't release that information to Congressional Democrats (or Republicans) for fear of having the spy program compromised (a not unreasonable concern). To Ike the over-flights were more valuable than any political capital he was losing by not revealing them. When a U2 spy plane was shot down over Russia in 1960 and the intelligence gained through that program was revealed to Congress a lot of the political bluster was diminished by the news.

Based on the information available up until 1960 there was widespread discontent with Eisenhower; one of his critics was Goldwater. During the 1964 presidential campaign Goldwater's fearless and confrontational statements regarding the communist threat, founded in the missile gap allegations (which by then were somewhat exaggerated) and Soviet expansionism in the Third World, would cost him dearly. It was during this time when the country faced nuclear devastation at the hands of the Soviet Union that no one knew specifically what to do. These issues were the "third-rail" of national politics that Goldwater faced head-on. However, the same utterances twenty-five years later by Ronald Reagan from his bully pulpit in the White House caused dramatic changes in the world. By then Goldwater looked more perceptive than pretentious or paranoid. But this was not so in the beginning.

Goldwater's book was designed to make a conservative statement that would capture the country's attention. It outlines positions that he had often presented in small venues. He found his message appealed equally strongly to a wider audience when he came to the national stage. His western independence was an asset in getting his views across, even if his cowboy appearance, born of his Arizona roots, was not.

The book's key premise is that man is as much a spiritual being as a biological one. Goldwater appeals to the human spirit by stating that the material prosperity of our population is not the sole measure of life and should not be the first aim of our government. He avers that we must be able to care for ourselves personally to maintain both our dignity and our humanity. Goldwater and his fellow conservatives understood that legislators and bureaucrats were impeding progress on individual and societal levels by restricting or obstructing the opportunities for self-reliance and self-betterment. The aim of conservatives was to dismantle inappropriate government intervention in society but not government itself, a distinction that had not yet seen enough light in the early 1960s, especially in the liberal press, to be understood fully.

Anarchy was not the conservative goal. The movement sought to provide maximum individual liberty *within a framework of order* designed to ensure that one person's actions did not impinge on another's freedom. In other words, conservatives proposed a field of play upon which the government should act as referee to ensure individual liberty might flower but would not otherwise intervene in the outcome. Most importantly, Goldwater felt that politics had come to *neglect principles* while trying to care for individuals. He wanted the country to heed the warning of John Adams, that the greatest menace to society is the political individual who knows better than the people what is best for them. Such a person doesn't just offer, "Let me do that for you"—he insists on taking the reins; "get out of the way" is his demand. Goldwater contends that our government had fallen to that level.

Goldwater's second front, echoed so successfully by conservatives in the last quarter of the twentieth century, is that property and freedom are inextricably intertwined. He forcefully makes this point in his discussion of the government's power to tax. Although he recognizes the strong emotional appeal of welfarism, he sees its dangers equally clearly. He outlines his goals in brief form:

> I have little interest in streamlining government or making it more efficient for I mean to reduce its size. I do not undertake to promote welfare for I propose to extend freedom. My aim is not to pass laws, but to repeal them.

No matter the clarity and simplicity of Goldwater's words, it would still be thirty-five years before big government's give-away welfare antics would begin to be brought to heel. This change did not come about because liberal politicians saw their public charity was not working, not altering people's lives for the better. Change came because the American people eventually were bold enough to vocalize the bright side of an ancient proverb: give a man a fish, feed him for a day; teach a man to fish, feed him for a lifetime. When incentive was introduced into the welfare system positive news became routine. There was one area, however, where welfarism did achieve the purposes for which it was intended—those espousing the free lunch of then current programs were re-elected repeatedly based on their "good works."

Interestingly, criticism of the unwritten but manipulative alliance between the liberal press and liberal politicians—founded as much in politics, emotion, and pseudo-guilt as sensible and effective policy—was not used by conservative activists who sought to change the rationale of government. Instead of exposing the lofty language and equalitarian image for what it was—an empty promise supported by feel-good but vacuous idealism—they primarily approached the disconnection between good government and bad politics by the direct and simple use of facts—of which many examples appear in Goldwater's commentary.

After the 1964 Goldwater defeat, Daniel Patrick Moynihan unintentionally but honestly helped in the efforts of conservative realists; he was unafraid to face the facts that were coming to the fore. Moynihan, a contemporary of Goldwater, and in 1985 a well-known and popular liberal Democrat with both a conscience and a concern, voiced the opinion that the only party with ideas since mid-century was the Republican Party and that those ideas had allowed the Republicans to gain control of the levers of government via the ballot box. Moynihan was then a U.S. Senator from New York. He had watched as first Goldwater and then Ronald Reagan had risen to the top of the American political scene almost solely by the force of their ideas. He warned his fellow liberals of what they were seeing and virtually demanded they pay attention.

Back in 1965, when Moynihan was a member of Lyndon Johnson's administration, he had authored an assessment of what was happening in the black community—partially as a result of federal welfare policies—and had published a study titled *The Negro Family: The Case for National Action*. In this document he outlines the negative consequences of then-existing government paradigms and calls for alterations of public initiatives in order to save black family structure. His report was either ignored in liberal policy discussions, or disbelieved—and matters got worse as he predicted. However, it was Goldwater who had offered many of Moynihan's ideas well before Moynihan expressed his comprehension and his anxiety—or committed his thesis to paper. Goldwater found in common sense what Moynihan documented in common statistics.

The tactics used by the media to deride conservative positions regarding the importance of family and morality as alarmist, or even racist, ultimately backfired as Goldwater's views were later validated by liberals like Moynihan. During the last quarter of the twentieth century the political and social truth about bankrupt welfare policies could no longer be ignored. Not only did the U.S. Government's fish distribution system feed a man today but it ensured to his ultimate detriment that he would be back tomorrow for another free meal. As a result of these realities conservatism became first intriguing, then accepted, and finally politically dominant.

Making someone a slave to the state was anathema to Goldwater. With uncompromising passion, he loathed the destructive culture of dependency created via welfarism and its paymaster: uncontrolled taxation. (When Goldwater first ran for president the top personal income tax rate was 91%. As of 2008, it is 35%). Without his willingness to stand at center stage and bear the brunt of liberal castigations the course of U.S. history and the beginnings of change in both domestic and foreign policy might have been much, much longer in coming. And that also meant that the presidency of Ronald Reagan, or his like, would have been postponed or even eliminated with concomitant consequences for the end of the Cold War and the beginning of the reform of state welfarism.

Goldwater's views on foreign entanglements as well as his appreciation of the danger of submitting to fear made him seem warlike in the liberal press, but *The Conscience of a Conservative* crushed this aspersion and made it look small. The book dispels any suggestion of demagoguery and stands comfortably on principle. His media critics didn't present him that way because he made too much sense—his rationality scared them for the political success it portended. Rather, he was made to look combative, pugnacious; but what really frightened liberals were his logic and his passion. Their lack of cogent and effective counter-argument was what froze them in their tracks—they didn't know what to do with this truth-teller, and so, rather than discuss his positions on the merits they attacked him as a political and social monster.

Goldwater ultimately came to be regarded as an icon not because he meant to be but because his principles made him such. *The Conscience of a Conservative* is a plain book, stating unclouded truths. Although Lyndon Johnson handily won the 1964 presidential election it was clear over the course of the rest of the century that it was Goldwater's vision that was ultimately victorious. His ideas and his book have not lost any value because of their simplicity but rather have gained stature because of their merit. Re-reading about this crusade now that many of its goals have come to pass is both fortifying and edifying—and it makes much of the passion expressed throughout *First Principles* easier to grasp. Understanding both Goldwater and what the liberals of his time attempted to do to him is an important part of comprehending the progress and eventual success of the conservative movement; the liberal tactics of Goldwater's era arise again and again as political battles ever repeat themselves. In this case, being forewarned through Goldwater's comprehensions and actions is an important step in being forearmed.

About the Author

BARRY MORRIS GOLDWATER was born in Phoenix, Arizona, on January 1, 1909. After graduating from the University of Arizona he worked in the family department store, which he ran after his father's death in 1929. He served in the Army Air Corps in World War II and rose to the rank of brigadier general. Goldwater was elected to the Senate from Arizona in 1952. A resolute conservative, he became a spokesman for right-wing Republicans in their campaign against massive federal government, advocating the alternative of greater state and local powers. He vigorously opposed federal welfare appropriations as socialistic and sought to curb public ownership of utilities. A strong anticommunist, Goldwater supported the American military intervention in Vietnam and criticized efforts to achieve détente with the U.S.S.R. He was decisively defeated by Lyndon Johnson in the 1964 presidential election, largely because of the electorate's apprehension over his allegedly extreme position on the use of nuclear weapons. Goldwater was re-elected to the Senate in 1967 and served there until his retirement in 1987. He was credited with generating the conservative resurgence that resulted in Ronald Reagan's presidency, but he grew increasingly concerned and then critical of the influence of the religious right's social conservatism within the Republican Party. Senator Goldwater died May 29, 1998.

19

What It Means to Be a Libertarian

Charles Murray

Originally published: 1997
178 pages

OPENING A BOOK that aims to analyze the relationship between individuals and their government with a lengthy excerpt from Thomas Jefferson's first inaugural address seems almost necessary. As the new president spoke of individual freedom and our right to care for ourselves, he observed that these were not quite enough to bring happiness. He noted that a wise and frugal government was also necessary, one that "did not take from the mouth of labor the bread it had earned." Jefferson was thinking, of course, of the new government's power to tax (the power most hotly contested during the Constitution's ratification battle).

Jefferson's understanding of human nature was reflected in the precision with which he described the boundaries that separated and the interdependence that linked governors to the governed. That relationship is based upon the comprehension each must have of their reciprocally reinforcing rights and duties. In the view of Charles Murray and the Libertarian movement, fidelity to the Jeffersonian principle of rights *and* duties is not just a definition of government, but its very essence.

Murray begins his exposition of Libertarianism by defining the goal of the Founders of the American system of governing: limited central power and protection of individual rights. The dignity of the individual and the integrity of every person's property and opportunity are Murray's points of departure. He doesn't suggest that his readers will misunderstand these ideas; he merely seeks to set the stage. Murray takes particular interest in where government and the governed actually fit together at the dawn of the twenty-first century. From his perspective that intersection is best defined by Libertarianism; implementing an active libertarian philosophy in practice is his goal.

The difference between government and all the other aspects of an individual's life is that people give government some power, but not necessarily the absolute right, to use force to effect what appears to be the consensus of the governed. The problem, Libertarians emphasize, is that consensus is rarely reached. Murray asserts that the lack of such accord should mean a corresponding reduction of action or intrusion on the part of government. The logic of this conclusion seems in equal measure inescapable and ignored. (For more on this point see Bertrand de Jouvenel's *On Power*, Chapter 15.)

Politicians all too often act to the contrary of Murray's hypothesis both while running for office and once elected. They become infatuated with passing laws and/or implementing regulations that deny the individual the right to engage in voluntary and informed transactions. Those in power do this because of pressure from special interests or their own hubris. They think they have been chosen to lead, so they are going to do so; often they attempt to lead through their personal sense of justice (or pique), which is not always fully shared by the electorate at large. The bottom line for Libertarians, as reflected in the essays of Lord Acton (Chapter 9), is that the right of the individual to be free is a higher right than any purpose of government, even a noble purpose. The conflict often ceases to be a debate over whose nobility is more sacrosanct, that of the person or that of the collective. Instead, it becomes a struggle over power. In modern times, it is the collective that has the edge for it automatically has most of the power. Individuals are left with but one weapon—right.

Murray dissects government at its basic level. What is the minimum amount of government needed? (That should be the maximum allowed.) How may individuals best pursue that elusive concept of "happiness" so succinctly articulated in the Declaration of Independence? And, perhaps the most pressing question, what are our responsibilities to ourselves, to our neighbors, and to the body politic?

The dividing line between the Libertarian approach to governing and the more intrusive manner of today's liberal politicians is the concept of equality. Libertarians start from a point of equal opportunity and equal responsibility, whereas liberals aim at equal result or condition. For the liberal, obtaining this equal result is the responsibility of the political class. Thus, not only is the starting point remarkably different between Libertarians and liberals, their respective views of human nature and the goal of government are also different.

The result is that in the eyes of each group government becomes a notably different tool. In the one case, it is a minimalist effort embodying control of legislative and bureaucratic excess while leaving the individual free to live his own life. In the other case, government tends to be a substantially enlarged interventionist effort to ensure equality for all. The latter in its worst form moves toward a redistribution of wealth through a confiscatory tax system that can—only initially and only briefly—produce a more equalitarian society but which cannot produce equality. The eventual economic result of such intervention is the reduction of incentives via progressively higher taxes that then cause economic contraction, eventuating in reduced living standards for almost everyone because of reduced economic activity and opportunity. Obviously when market production declines the government receives reduced tax revenue. A vicious cycle of tax increases to offset lower tax collections repeats itself, with a concomitant reduction in market activity. These actions unfortunately throw more people out of work, which results in a call for even more government assistance, *ad nauseum*. Society eventually operates on the basis of the lowest common denominator rather than the highest. There is another unintended consequence as well: almost invariably there arises a privileged and generally corrupt arrangement favoring the redistributionist elite ensconced in government.

For Murray, the concept of freedom of thought, choice, and action is fundamental. A person seeking to fully experience this freedom must be responsible *for* himself and *to* others. Murray makes an interesting conceptual note early in his definition of freedom by stating,

> Responsibility is not the "price" of freedom but its reward.

He asks the reader to think about what his most enduring satisfactions have been. For most of us they will have been when we were true to ourselves, our principles, and our moral judgments. That, for Murray and all the Libertarians, is the essence of their philosophy. It is an appealing outlook, especially when taken to its logical conclusion that our socially relevant private activities (i.e., those that we individually do for ourselves to avoid burdening others) determine our personal satisfaction in life.

But Libertarians sometimes engage in a romantic fantasy, that personal responsibility, which is the foundation of ordered liberty, can be achieved across the population if government would just get out of the way. That this is beyond the full capabilities of human beings is self-evident, thus the tension between Libertarianism and government itself is a never-ending balancing act.

The assessments that Murray makes—using specific examples of current and past government intervention—remain instructive, thought provoking, and structurally helpful. His contention that in most instances the good intentions of government are not realized makes one wonder why we continue to tolerate so much government. Is the explanation found in habit, lethargy, or the continued allure of hope in the face of reality? Murray does not tell the reader how to act on these issues, but he does make one think. His intention, of course, is that at the end of that thought process we will arrive at the less government solution—the Libertarian solution.

Murray's Libertarianism brings his readers back to fundamental concepts and relationships. His program for more effective and responsible governing—less is more—cannot be dismissed as some utopian ideal because much of what he writes makes too much sense. For Murray and anyone who thinks about it for a moment, government is not "they;" it is "we." We must take responsibility for ourselves and the governing paradigm we seek to create. Murray's work dovetails nicely with the classic catch phrase, "We get the government we deserve." In other words, if we devote too little time to governing ourselves, and if we think that our responsibilities as citizens are completed when we put down our pencils after marking our ballots, then we get bureaucrats and politicians who do for us what *they* think we want and need, or worse, what they think we *should* want or need. Murray seeks to change this thought process and its results. A reordering of both government's publicly accepted goals and its means toward those goals, he avers, could occur pursuant to our return to the Founders' vision of minimal governmental intervention and maximum personal responsibility and opportunity. If we take away the *crutch* of government, then our society changes fundamentally for the better. That is the goal of Libertarianism.

About the Author

CHARLES MURRAY is a resident fellow at the American Enterprise Institute in Washington, D.C. Born in 1943 in Newton, Iowa, he earned his undergraduate degree from Harvard in 1965 and subsequently spent six years in Asia as a Peace Corps volunteer and then as a researcher. Upon his return home he earned a Ph.D. in political science in 1974 from MIT. His investigations into crime, poverty, and social programs led him to write *Losing Ground: American Social Policy 1950–80*. This book did much to set the tone of President Ronald Reagan's domestic policy.

Murray's career as one of the nation's most influential conservative thinkers is well established. He lectures and publishes widely and is a frequent witness before congressional committees. Murray's most controversial book, *The Bell Curve: Intelligence and Class Structure in American Life* (with Richard Herrnstein) posits that wealth and other positive social outcomes are a product of intelligence and that intelligence is an innate characteristic that it is foolish to pretend either isn't important or can be compensated for in some fashion (political or otherwise) that eliminates the need to recognize its existence. Published in 1994, the book caused a still-continuing social debate.

20

Let Us Talk of Many Things

William F. Buckley, Jr.

Originally published: 2000
477 pages

WILLIAM F. BUCKLEY, JR., scion of American conservative thinking and action, began his political quest while a college undergraduate in the late 1940s. He eventually blossomed into the movement's preeminent spokesperson and activist. His career has spanned more than five decades of political change, most all of it for the better. Hardly any part of modern American reality has failed to come under Buckley's historical, philosophical, fiscal, or social scrutiny—or has failed to elicit his distinctive commentary—sometimes acerbic, often witty, always refined.

Let Us Talk of Many Things, one of more than forty books that Buckley has written or edited, contains many of his speeches, beginning with one from his senior year at Yale in 1949 and culminating with his address at the Heritage Foundation's twenty-fifth anniversary dinner in 1999. Between the book's opening acknowledgments and the final note of thanks appear too many insights, observations, and historical lessons to recount in this brief overview in any significant way. The value here is in Buckley's knowledge, paired with his experience and his stark moral foundations, that bring all of us a little closer to wisdom. His speeches are also a succinct history of the second half of the twentieth century's most important political moments. Buckley applies theory to fact in these talks and his statements encompass sharp consideration of policy choices.

Readers have repeated opportunities to savor Buckley's best didactic technique, which is to simplify, to melt things down to their basics, and to start at the beginning—well before where the other fellow wants to begin. The simplicity of Buckley's approach is reflected in his remarks on former President Bill Clinton's minimizing of the need for or value of honesty in response to being caught in his White House liaisons which resulted in his depositional lies and the exposure of his failure of character:

> If what he has done is trivial, then much of what we think of as the infrastructure of civil society is also trivial, our commitments to truth, to the processes of justice, to the sanctity of oaths.

Buckley notes nearly everything of significance in his career in this volume—including some of his mistakes. Early in his philosophical journey he spoke strongly of the domino theory of geopolitical relations, thus discounting the will of individuals to act for themselves when their lives were, literally and figuratively, at stake. He wanted to isolate the U.S.S.R. in a fashion that did not take into account that country's power. But his very public moral and factual jibes at Soviet Premier Nikita Khrushchev's U.S. visit in 1960 were a perfect counter-point to the obsequies laid in Khrushchev's path by an alternately fearful and fawning coterie of press and politicians.

Buckley understands more than do most people in or outside of public life and he isn't afraid to take a position. He willingly observes that he has not been perfect over the years, that some of his pronouncements and actions may today seem to have been ill-formed. But such instances pale before the many times when Buckley's affirmations and critical eye have been tellingly accurate, as history has proven.

Buckley offers a special derision for the liberal penchant of not asking people to take care of themselves, and then insisting, as if they never needed to inquire in the first place, that the government knows better how they should be taken care of anyway. Buckley observes that such condescension is not only arrogance of thought and action but also undermining of the building of self-confidence in both individuals and the public. This goes on to harm self-esteem, the primary ingredient in getting people to think and act for themselves.

Buckley argues that our concern for deficiencies in America must not cause us to censure the principles that have allowed our country—its faults notwithstanding—to tower over the nations of the world as a citadel of freedom and progress. He often reprises this theme, noting that no individual imperfection in our society—a bad law, a bad foreign policy, a bad social experiment, a bad elected or appointed official, or just a misunderstanding of how to apply American principles to real life—should result in a wholesale indictment of the system. In investigating these aberrations Buckley falls back on rational assessment to determine what went wrong: "Reason may not save us," he avers, "but an absence of reason assures failure." To be sure, Buckley always ties his reason to experience—his is not the utopian version untethered to facts.

With his greatest display of vehemence, Buckley demeans "facile universalist ideas" in a world where the individual (not the state, not the "public good") is the only common denominator. These speeches reflect Buckley's strongly negative appraisal of how big social agglomerations, especially government, tend to discount or ignore small ones, and individuals. Buckley believes that only specious policy is created using the fallacy that the good of the many should overcome the dignity of the individual. Such ideas and others like them are destructive of the essentials of our freedom. Buckley always seeks to bring his audience back to the simple understanding that each person counts in a manner that cannot begin to be reflected in collectivist government action. And when he notes,

> It is the general disintegration of a shared understanding of the meaning of the world and our place in it that made American liberalism possible, and American conservatism inevitable.

he was simply observing in a broad manner the erosion of principle that always starts with a small decline. When the decline becomes too big, then ideas reassert themselves.

When it comes to the world stage, Buckley shows both his wisdom and his commitment to freedom. As the Korean War Memorial notes, in chiseled stone, "Freedom Is Not Free" Buckley is in the first ranks of those who know that we have to be willing to pay a price to keep the freedom that has been established through the American experience—at such great cost. He echoes an old truth, enunciated by George Washington in his initial state of the union address, but which traces back to Aristotle:

> We seek not to start a war but to avoid war, and the surest way to avoid war is by asserting our willingness to wage it.

Buckley occasionally quotes Trotsky and notes that the communist who was axed to oblivion said, "If you wish to lead a quiet life, you picked the wrong century to be born in." To the betterment of America, and the world of ideas, Buckley was both born into and relishes the twentieth century. He most assuredly does not choose to lead a quiet life.

Turn to any page of this book or read any speech and you will encounter something worthwhile. It may be something entirely new to you or something familiar made to be seen in a novel light. In any case it will be interesting. Buckley is especially adept at blowing up the "common wisdom" or "universal recognition" by reciting facts and figures conveniently forgotten by those creating the myths of the good of the group—those who champion big government. Buckley always makes his audiences think. His speeches still stimulate today's readers to contemplate the history of the last seventy-five years, the lessons we've learned and the past we dare not forget.

>   We shall seek the truth and endure its consequences.

This terse principle is Buckley's guiding light—and should be ours as well. Its first part is easy to contemplate. Buckley's opponents in public debate usually come to a special understanding of its second part.

About the Author

WILLIAM F. BUCKLEY, JR. was born in New York City in 1925 and raised in Connecticut. He attended Yale University and sparred with American liberals continually from his undergraduate days until his death in 2008. In 1955, he established and for the next thirty-five years served as editor of *National Review*, one of America's preeminent conservative publications. He was one of the founders of Young Americans for Freedom (YAF), formed in response to the liberal agenda of the 1960s. From 1966 to 1999 he hosted *Firing Line*, a program devoted to intellectual give-and-take that was television's longest-running show. He authored more than forty books of political commentary, autobiography, fiction, and philosophy. His thousands of speeches and less formal talks promoted his aim of getting people to think, then act. From 1962 until his death he wrote a column titled *On the Right*, syndicated in more than three hundred newspapers, where he attempted to make sense of the political and economic life of this country and of the world. Wrote the *New York Times*, "His most inimitable pieces are those that skewer the people he doesn't like, of whom there is no shortage."

21

Promised Land, Crusader State

Walter A. McDougall

Originally published: 1997
286 pages

AMERICA-BASHING has become a sport—if not a vocation—in the media. It seems no national imperfection, real or imagined, is too small to be a capital offense. What helps in sorting through some of the more vocal indictments is a referee. Walter McDougall's monograph regarding U.S. foreign policy offers guidance in assessing how much of this self-flagellation is justified, and how well we've done with the responsibilities thrust upon us simply because of our success as a nation and a culture.

Promised Land, Crusader State traces the broad evolution of American involvement in geopolitics; its primary objective is to dissect only a few of the particulars of any given era or incident and use them as markers, not necessarily object lessons. As McDougall explains his subject he certainly offers some recitations of historical events, but mostly as a means to reacquaint the reader with facts, dates, nations, or people. What McDougall has created constitutes an almost universally valid lesson about the confusions inherent in an open society buffeted by the vicissitudes of democratic action and political power struggles.

McDougall examines three key aspects of U.S. foreign policy over the past two hundred-plus years: the actions taken, the moral impetus for them (including our tendencies toward both "messianism" and isolationism), and the self-interest, or national interest, that motivates our efforts. Working backward, he explains how we arrived at our place in the world and suggests which policies implemented in the past and which lessons learned could be applied in the present day. Obviously, there is also a new aspect of international relations that has not been a factor before—stateless global terrorism.

For the last three millennia, and for myriad reasons, insurgencies have plagued nations around the globe. But the stakes have been raised dramatically in the modern era as technology has changed guerrilla warfare; nuclear, biological, chemical, or high-explosive weapons of mass murder can relatively easily now be delivered to almost anyone's doorstep. This reality of potentially recurrent terrorist attacks is not addressed by McDougall as he writes his survey before Islamic fundamentalists began, in earnest, their suicidal murdering of civilian populations across the globe. In the face of this potentially enlarging threat civilized nations as a group need to take stock. Particularly in the West, our history of sometimes naïve idealism and an often equal aversion (especially in Europe) to expressing power in the face of catastrophe, has become an ostrich-like denial of real world exigencies. In dealing with the new paradigm, however, all of us will find that it is more than simply instructive to understand history. In order to adjust usefully in the West, McDougall's assessment of America, its past, its place, its power, and its limitations, is highly profitable reading as we address global terrorism.

From the beginning of the republic (and for more than 150 years before we became independent) Americans had been accustomed to running their own affairs without needing to seriously consider, much less answer to others. We wanted to keep it that way but modernity made that dream impossible. As well, our material advancements over the last two hundred years have made the country remarkably strong, so strong that we now have no serious challengers in the rest of the world. Our worst enemy, as McDougall observes, is our occasional arrogance—born of righteousness, not greed. McDougall notes with irony that over the course of our history as a country the U.S. was most often wrong the more strongly we felt we were right. The impetus to this disjunction started early, in 1630, when Massachusetts Governor John Winthrop intoned:

> Consider that wee shall be as a Citty upon a Hill, the eies of all people are uppon us.

Our preeminence on the world stage makes us different, but not always in the good way Winthrop envisioned. Even so, we were not often as bad as we were portrayed to be. American leaders have occasionally forgotten the purpose of our foreign policy which has always been, in McDougall's words, "to defend, not define, what America was." When the memory of our officials lapsed, the country veered off course—to our own and the world's detriment.

McDougall notes that the U.S. has typically lost its way when our foreign adventures were attempts to create a world in our own (ideal) image. This was a consequence of our feeling of exceptionalism—that America was not just different, but as Winthrop observed, better. McDougall rightly points out that we are merely different, and sometimes so different that both our friends and our adversaries turn away in distrust or self-preservation. He recites the views of several of the Founding Fathers who worried that if we were not moral and did not remember how ordinary we were that we could not continue to exist, much less lead. McDougall explores our conduct and finds the U.S. to have acted in its national interest most of the time over the past two centuries. When we didn't, when we acted out of righteousness or pursuant to some base motive, he finds the indictments of our critics largely justified.

As time passed and the republic became engaged with the rest of the world we sometimes compromised our moral foundations. This was not because we were venal but because international power politics is a survival game which we had to play according to real-world rules, not our own moral compass. (This factor is especially difficult now, in the age of global terrorism.) McDougall doesn't excuse any of this, neither does he extol or resolve it; he explains it so that we can go forward making choices that are both rational and, one hopes, ultimately moral.

To that end, McDougall develops his thesis by dividing his analysis into eight books of what he termed his foreign policy "bible." Although he pulls biblical nomenclature into service, his dissection of America's first and second centuries by this means is convenient, and incisive; it has nothing to do with religious content. He finds that U.S. foreign policy in the nineteenth century reflects a coherent passion (McDougall's books for this era are: Liberty, or Exceptionalism; Unilateralism, or Isolationism; The Monroe Doctrine; Expansionism, or Manifest Destiny), but in the twentieth he sees less consistency because there is less agreement on what to do with our power (the titles for the twentieth century are: Progressive Imperialism; Wilsonianism, or Liberal Internationalism; Containment; and Global Meliorism).

McDougall's divisions remain exceptionally useful for understanding the phases and conflicts of our national psyche as we enter the twenty-first century. By examining familiar events and personalities over the course of our history, he investigates where we went wrong and where right, as measured by our goals and our interests. When we evinced sanctimony (not superiority) we suffered the worst consequences. But when we were rational (even if based in morality, for morality is not less for being rational) we achieved our greatest successes. As McDougall explains, the important point was that our achievements were not grounded in what we happened to gain in the material world, but what we didn't lose in our struggle with ourselves.

Contemporary readers may be most interested in McDougall's investigation of how the U.S. was transformed from being *a* world power to standing alone as *the* world power. Understanding this transition may help us avoid misjudging our place in the international milieu or abusing our advantages. As McDougall explains, the initial change in America's global status took root in the industrial and intellectual might of the country that began developing after the Civil War. Our increased prestige was cemented in our willingness, when international realities pressed upon us, to use our physical power in a political fashion. Certainly we had what can be viewed as imperialist moments but those never defined our national character. We didn't need to be imperialists; we were capitalists who preferred to trade and invest rather than conquer. Our capitalism was a good and extraordinarily beneficial feature of our national existence despite the denials of liberal pontificators who affect ignorance as to the true basis of their prosperity and our national power. When the perceived need arose to deploy the might bestowed by U.S. capitalism—primarily in the two world wars of the twentieth century—America arrived at a state of global preeminence.

That we were aggressive, not just responsive, when pushed or threatened meant that we were unlikely to be perfect in either our reactions or our comprehensions. Acting in an aggressive manner makes anyone prone to mistakes because one's eye is often on the goal rather than the means. Cuba has been an example of this for almost half a century. Equally as true, however, was that when we saw an opportunity—rather than a threat—we were less likely to make a mistake. Europe after World War II was a shining moment for America. In that case we seized the chance to eliminate a repeat of the mistakes made after World War I that ultimately resulted in World War II. Vietnam, unfortunately, represented both issues; i.e., we were threatened by the aggressive spread of Soviet Communism in southeast Asia while we also saw an opportunity to offer freedom to an oppressed people. The results in that instance unhappily speak for themselves. The realities of both Islamic fundamentalism and the many competing forces in the Middle East are and will remain for some time to come challenges equal to those we faced during the five decades of the Cold War. Whether we respond or just react to these threats will make a significant difference to both our friends and our enemies.

McDougall observes that in the course of the twentieth century there were many American political, business, and religious leaders, and movements that became influential and powerful and led us down some wrong paths. As a group, the First World War, President Woodrow Wilson, and the League of Nations, was the foremost example of what could intend so much and go so wrong. (At the end of the First World War the sad confluence of those realities led the world almost inevitably to the Second World War.) But, as McDougall points out, our mistakes were not foreordained by our form of government or our national psyche. It was our occasionally misguided politics and a sometimes messianic, righteous adherence to what was not possible that caused our foreign-policy debacles. This important understanding—that our mistakes of judgment did not result from systemic causes—allowed the U.S. to continue on a course of self-actualization within the confines of a real world.

Historical analysts must decide where to focus their attention to accurately discern where any history starts. Those who find America failing in myriad ways seem always to begin their critique where we have not been or where we are not perfect in our actions (a subjective judgment in any event). That's a tough standard, one sure to offer many avenues for criticism—criticism advantaged by hindsight and the noble certainty that a better course was obvious . . . after the fact. As McDougall points out, we often made good starts to certain foreign-policy measures that turned out badly because we responded unwisely to changed circumstances—again Vietnam comes to mind, as does now the war in Iraq. The self-flagellating America-haters, who blame our government for whatever has gone wrong, always seem to forget that like any other society, ours is an imperfect one, populated by imperfect beings, among whom there is almost always contentious disagreement. McDougall looks at motives, methods, and facts before judging—and when he does offer an appraisal, our foreign policy appears, over the long term, more rational and effective than not.

There was a point early in the twentieth century when America began to go wrong, or at least so it seemed. The word "wrong" in this context is awkward because it is freighted, as ever, with both baggage and nuances. Prior to and during World War I, what McDougall terms Progressive Imperialism became our "wrong" in foreign policy. This was the dark side of an expanded Manifest Destiny (the nineteenth-century doctrine that it was the destiny of the Anglo-Saxon nations, especially the United States, to dominate the entire Western Hemisphere) that America exported overseas—outside our hemisphere. It was dark not because national gain was sometimes an after-effect, but because it was arrogant, presumptuous, and severely shortsighted. Problems arose for a very simple reason: not everyone thinks like us, much less wants to be like us—especially at a cost of altering their national identity. McDougall writes,

> For at bottom, the belief that American power, guided by a secular and religious spirit of service, could remake foreign societies came as easily to the Progressives as trust-busting, prohibition of child labor and regulation of interstate commerce [did at home]. . . . The result in foreign policy was that a newly prideful United States began to measure its holiness by what it did, not just by what it was, and through Progressive Imperialism committed itself, for the first time, "to the pure abstractions such as liberty, democracy, or justice."

And we failed, sometimes miserably, as the twentieth century progressed. Reform is a parochial matter, based as much on history and culture as destiny. America's hubris that it could reform others or transplant the American experience anywhere else, much less everywhere else, was simply a dream that in some cases turned into a nightmare. As the Progressive Imperialism of the early twentieth century devolved into what McDougall terms Global Meliorism, the do-gooders in America the Powerful turned sour on most of our oversees adventures by the second half of the century. There was substantial confusion in our foreign policy establishment and thus among the electorate as well. We began to drift, especially after the demise of Soviet Communism in 1991. Unfortunately we drifted right into Iraq as the twenty-first century dawned. That it may have been the wrong answer to the right question (how and where do we attack stateless global terrorism?) will only be determined in the years to come. McDougall, writing before 9/11/2001, voiced caution in any attempt at nation-building, thus his analysis of events since the Coalition Force's invasion of Iraq in 2003 might reflect his skepticism of our Middle-East efforts. (A revised edition of *Promised Land, Crusader State* that will address the post 9/11 evolution of U.S. foreign policy is currently in preparation.)

What the twenty-first century holds for America is difficult to assess. The main arena is seen as China, but the global opposite of Chinese authoritarianism and emerging capitalism, democratic India, is easily as important, and seems equally ignored by American media and political figures. Add in faltering Europe (see *Fewer*, Chapter 43), the Middle East and Islamic fundamentalism, and a newly corrupt Russia and the mix is volatile at least. The sub-contexts of religion, politics, natural resources, combined with pure, simple mistakes and luck will determine whether we will repeat our twentieth-century errors or learn from them.

As an example of how uncertain the results of our most intentional acts can be, during McDougall's investigations he finds the success of some of our best efforts was perhaps due as much to happenstance as to design; the extreme examples being the Marshall Plan (the American effort after World War II to rebuild the economies of our former European enemies to thwart Soviet Communist expansion into the center of the continent) and the democratization of Germany and Japan after the war. Although McDougall may not give enough credit in these cases to either American initiatives as an intended catalyst for change, or the psychological impact on foreigners of Americans acting deliberately, the facts may nevertheless justify his inferences. In other words, it's always better to be lucky than smart. It is also often advisable to act forcefully (which does not always mean using the machinery of war). After surveying America's foreign policy since the Second World War, McDougall succinctly concludes, "force must sometimes precede reason." Of course, the extreme opposite can also be true—that force sometimes precludes reason.

When and then how force must be employed are always the sticking points, especially if one's country is the most powerful nation in the world—at least for now (think again of China's growing military as well as commercial sophistication). As a realist, McDougall recommends that we always act in our national interest (although he does not voice that either often or directly) which customarily, but not universally, coincides with the interests of others of like mind. World War II was an example of this, as was our constancy in the Cold War. Our intentions in the Middle East are yet to prove one way or another but their impetus seems to fit more of the good side of McDougall's paradigm than not. At the end, the character of the people involved will determine their own destiny—mostly in spite of rather than because of our actions, thus we must tread softly.

The ultimate caveat to all of McDougall's assessments, of course, is that some theories of our leadership are sound only in a rational world. As we have experienced, the world is very often *not* rational; that is when judgment becomes most important and history most valuable. In this vein, McDougall's investigation of our involvement in Vietnam, an ill-conceived, ill-advised, and ill-executed policy of the Johnson Administration that was carried on and on by its own institutional momentum, is exquisite. (His dissection of Robert McNamara, Secretary of Defense in the Kennedy and Johnson Administrations, is quite useful today. McNamara helped craft U.S. policy throughout much of the Vietnam War and showed himself to be perhaps the most naïve American official of the twentieth century [after Woodrow Wilson], and most assuredly the most damaging to American integrity. He appears almost as a caricature of hubris, folly, and ignorance.)

The books of McDougall's bible—from his investigation into our original concept of liberty to his skepticism about the effects of our global meliorism—form a cogent and compelling assessment of American foreign policy. As we confront the international terrorism of Islamic fundamentalists and the power of China and India and the rest of Asia we'll have to make new decisions, but it is unlikely that the foundations of those judgments will change much from what McDougall presented as the American paradigm. His assertions about using our past as much as possible to influence conclusions about our future are important in their own right; his efforts at understanding and explaining the first principles of foreign policy offer a useful guide to governance as a practice, not just a theory, in a world that has become less certain, and certainly more dangerous.

About the Author

WALTER A. MCDOUGALL is professor of history at the University of Pennsylvania. A graduate of Amherst College and a Vietnam veteran, he received his Ph.D. from the University of Chicago in 1974 and taught at the University of California–Berkeley for thirteen years before moving to the University of Pennsylvania to direct its International Relations Program. McDougall teaches U.S., European, and Asia/Pacific diplomatic history and is the author of many books, most recently *Freedom Just Around the Corner: A New American History 1585–1828*. In 1986, he won the Pulitzer Prize for *The Heavens and the Earth: A Political History of the Space Age*. He is also a senior fellow at the Foreign Policy Research Institute in Philadelphia and former editor of *Orbis*, its journal of world affairs. McDougall lives in Bryn Mawr, Pennsylvania.

22

Modern Times

Paul Johnson

Originally published: 1983, Revised 1991
784 pages

FRENCH IMPRESSIONIST Georges Seurat's most famous work, *A Sunday on the Island of La Grande Jatte*, was painted in 1884. It is a wall-sized scene of bathers, picnickers, and holiday strollers. It looks like an ordinary painting until one discerns upon close inspection that there are no brush strokes on the canvas, only tiny dots of color. Seurat's intent was to achieve an accurate sense of shading through the application of various hues one dot after another so that the tone would change subtly but precisely. This style of painting is termed *pontillism*. The effect of his composition is striking.

So it is with Paul Johnson's *Modern Times*. Combined with detailed observations—the dots of time and place, of personality and perception—his broad sweep effectively investigates the causes and effects and the consequences of twentieth-century history. Johnson's accumulation of fact, informatively analyzed by reference to the first principles offered in the works of the other authors found here, results in an articulate and practical explanation of how the world organized and disorganized itself during the last hundred years.

History is obviously the province of the professionals but it is of practical importance to all of us. While politicians and the media tend to use history selectively, the rest of us too often foolishly ignore these historical distortions and suffer the aftereffects generation upon generation. Johnson has taken twentieth-century history from before the First World War to the demise of the Soviet Union and crafted a fact-by-fact account with the same panoramic sweep and minute detail of a Seurat canvas.

Johnson's introductory chapter covers several overarching realities. Perhaps the foremost change that occurred in the early part of the twentieth century was the demise of divine right monarchs (who reigned through the grace of God) and the rule of religion over matters that were mostly secular. The power of these two elements was coextensive with the rule of what law existed at the close of the nineteenth century. The transition to democracy in some cases and totalitarian dictators in others appeared as a simple separation of state and church. The full consequences, however, spelled death to hundreds of millions of people primarily through the loss of both religious foundation as the guiding public impulse and the restraint of mostly benevolent modern royal families.

Religion is mystical and often totalitarian. When Friedrich Nietzsche (1844–1900), one of many famous and infamous nineteenth-century German philosophers, belittled religion's mysticism as being beneath the modern human intellect, and when science began to make religion look paltry by explaining its miracles, the totalitarian practices formerly cultivated by religion were reconfigured. Modern systems of governance became predicated on secular "principles," malleable principles at that, or, on the darker side, they were based on mere human desires, even whims. These systems replaced the authority of the church or king. As Johnson explains, the collapse of religion's hold (which people had understood as submission to God's guiding moral hand) often allowed the resulting vacuum to be filled by a "will to power" embodied in the force of men who were seen to control their own destiny. In the end, the replacements for totalitarian clergy were often totalitarian demagogues, vested only with the urge to control others and a confidence conferred by nothing more than self-interest in the guise of righteousness. The new messiahs were uninhibited by religious sanctions of any type; the results were both pre-ordained and deadly—intellectually, spiritually, and literally.

The eight hundred pages of this book remain captivating and unfailingly readable throughout because of how well Johnson weaves drama into his account. His essay has such range that readers must frequently pause to think about both its magnitude and the interconnectedness of its pieces. One is continually reminded of the need to keep a double focus—on the big canvas and on the smaller dots of color. The ability to maintain a binocular view is especially valuable in understanding the twentieth century's complicated history; Johnson's text helps to make this possible.

Johnson studies the causes of much of the last century's insanity—from World War I near the beginning, to the unavoidable first war in Iraq toward the end—and he not surprisingly finds them rooted in human failings. Observers are not sure whether to draw hope, because these antecedents are known, or to despair, because the previous century's horrors were the result of mundane and persistently repeated causes and effects. Too often we suffered an inability to make public judgments on what was good and what was unacceptable; we delayed making necessary decisions even as the potential consequences of those decisions turned into practical inevitabilities. The lesson of Neville Chamberlain, prime minister of Great Britain (who tried to appease Germany's Adolf Hitler in 1938 and instead allowed the conflagration of World War II to eventuate) is a stark example of what happens when people and nations don't act when they must. Of course, that judgment is hindsight, but it does not belie how the factual context of those times should have more easily allowed right to insist on the use of might. The lesson in that case, a slight play on Walter McDougall's admonition in *Promised Land, Crusader State* (Chapter 20) that "force must sometimes precede reason," was that force should have been used to induce reason. Today, America's actions in Iraq reflect more the latter sentiment than the former. In all cases, unfortunately, we only see how well we arrived at decisions after the fact.

Underlying twenty-first-century society are the same problems with which Johnson begins his comprehensive recalling of twentieth-century history. We find familiar his themes of racial and religious antagonism; ethnic discrimination that results in "cleansing," a euphemism for murder (why do we allow such misguided, sanitized, and reluctant language to obscure reality?); petty and grand jealousies and larcenies; and modernized and aggrandized versions of the seven deadly sins: greed, envy, sloth, etc. In other words, no matter how much we might learn from the past the future will still be populated by human beings who have not changed much. Thus history is likely to repeat itself no matter how much we insist that should not be true. The only solace is that we can affect the course of events even while understanding we cannot control them.

Perhaps Johnson's most damning investigation begins with the Treaty of Versailles which set the terms for the conclusion of World War I. The stupidity of politicians (with revenge on their minds and fear in their hearts) who controlled the peace process at the end of the conflict merely set in motion a chain of events that inevitably resulted in more warfare. U.S. President Woodrow Wilson was the most naïve and hence most dangerous of these men (the righteous are ever thus) while the British and French leaders were equally as destructive in their own and opposite ways. As Johnson observes, the wisdom of those who understood the human experience—from British economist John Maynard Keynes to American columnist Walter Lippmann to the ever present, ever observant Winston Churchill—was ignored or dismissed, to the peril of all. There followed the rest of the twentieth century's history which Johnson presents in fascinating relief, and with object lesson after object lesson to bolster his theses.

One of this volume's most interesting analyses is Johnson's investigation into the causes and depth of the Great Depression of the 1930s which was a worldwide phenomenon. Johnson succinctly demonstrates how the Depression was not the result (much less the necessary result) of leaving a self-regulating economy to its own devices. Unfortunately, exactly the opposite was true; it was government intervention, not *laisse-faire* economic practices that caused the economic and social destruction of the Depression. Johnson uses the example of the negative consequences inflicted by the 1930 passage of the Hawley-Smoot tariff act in the U.S. just as the Depression was beginning. This legislation caused retaliatory and destructive counter-tariffs to be enacted around the world, with a concomitant decline in international trade and national well-being. The result of this interference could have been avoided but only if facts had been allowed to intrude upon fanciful economic and social theology.

In defiance of the meddlesome collectivists and utopians throughout the twentieth century, Johnson shows why such presidents as Dwight Eisenhower, Warren Harding, and Calvin Coolidge (who are often remembered derisively by paternalistic intellectuals) were men worthy of a respect verging on veneration. They were great historical figures precisely because they seemed to do so little while clearly doing so much. Not only did they control government spending, bureaucracy, and regulations, they also kept in check the size of the social burden, which causes ruinous inflation when it becomes too great. A few examples from the Coolidge presidency serve to demonstrate just this point. Under Coolidge's guidance, unemployment was essentially non-existent (employers competed for workers), the cost of living went down 2.3%, the budget showed a surplus, and the debt from World War I was paid off.

When Ike was in office wages went up steadily while prices remained stable. The workday and workweek were shortened, yet productivity rose. Taxes were lowered and parents could send their kids to college and buy a family home, all on one income. As Eisenhower observed in his laconic manner, inflation must be controlled *before* social security is attended to because a stable government and a sound economy provide the only reliable form of communal safety at all levels of society. The non-interventionist presidents, Johnson notes, were not emotionally or intellectually distant; they merely understood the necessity of allowing Adam Smith's invisible hand to control the market. He observes:

> What is important in history is not only the events that occur but the events that obstinately do not occur.

Turning to the administrative side of governing, Johnson fully investigates corporate government. On the half of the ledger where he explores the world's open societies he uncovers the seeds of the now-endemic welfare state and sees their germination in the need for government power in a far different venue: at the peak of war efforts. As John Dewey, one of the modern era's scholars of socialism claimed:

> No matter how many among the special agencies for public control decay with the disappearance of war stress, the movement will never go backward.

However, Johnson observes concisely and in juxtaposition to Dewey that

> private property and private liberty tend to stand and fall together.

Liberty and property can be secure, even in extreme circumstances, only if citizens act with intention. If they do not, then both property and freedom are easy prey for the demagogues. The progression is thus: governmental controls over individual lives during wartime work well as emergency measures but they do not function benignly in the long run; most importantly, they are indeed difficult to reverse. Johnson notes that government expansion to meet the needs of war changes a population's character, rendering people compliant to the state's direction because they don't know where else to turn for guidance. Lingering docility after a war does allow the "intellectuals"—who fought for, or may have even caused the war—to contend that they are better equipped to manage the peace.

The historical progression is from a collectivist war-footing, to the intellectuals' socialistic answers in questions of governance ("we know best") when the war ends, and eventually, sometime after the peace, to totalitarianism at worst, or the welfare state at best. Because socialism does not and cannot work voluntarily force is necessary to both implement and sustain it. This is the collectivist side of the twentieth century's historical ledger. It can be stymied but only if citizens take responsibility for their society; that is, if they are wary. Those who recognize and then demand a return of control can and do dismantle some of the machinery of government. It is often two steps backward—during the war—and one step forward once the war is over, until socialistic collapse threatens society, as it did in Britain in the 1970s. Then citizens can begin to regain control and return to a free-market economy, as occurred under Prime Minister Margaret Thatcher during the 1980s.

Johnson's investigation and comparison of the political leaders of the twentieth century remains especially useful. The facts surrounding the rule of many elected officials who usurped public trust should make us cautious of choosing ordinary people to lead in extraordinary times. Too many leaders have been ordinary in the sense that they were incapable of a judicious comprehension of history, of sound theory and/or of competent execution, yet they suffered from messianic delusions of omnicompetence or even omnipotence. They had visions that were sometimes so flawed, or were on occasion so incoherently attempted, that Johnson's readers are moved at least to reassess history's judgments of both their personalities and their actions: de Gaulle (France), Hammerskjold (UN), Mao (China), Adenauer (Germany), and even Gandhi (India). Of course, the demonic murderers—Stalin (Soviet Union), Hitler (Germany), Pol Pot (Cambodia)—though in a class by themselves, were notable only for their ruthlessness, a non-universal competence, that had little to do with leadership and much to do with insanity.

Throughout his treatise, Johnson explains what went wrong and what went right in the twentieth century. There are ways, he recognizes, to destroy or to build a country. He comments:

> The collectivists dismissed the Western notion of freedom of choice and providing for oneself based on sound employment and replaced it with a paternalistic vision of compulsory and universal security.

Collectivist bureaucracies functioned to control not just their economies in a paternalistic fashion, but society in a totalitarian nightmare. As Johnson notes, in terms of economics, governments should be designed to issue regulations aimed at perfect competition not utopian fantasies. There is a role for the government, but as has been demonstrated by so many of the authors reviewed here it should have a minimalist cast. The ultimate success of governing comes down to economics, the dismal science, and its operative energy: human incentive working in an open society. The arrogance of government or individuals who think they are smarter and more powerful than something quite ineluctable—human striving—has inevitably resulted in failed policies and economies.

Over the course of the twentieth century the progressives and totalitarians experimented with governmental direction or confiscation of the engines of commerce. They thought this necessary to support their welfare states. The progressives crafted their design by means of insupportable taxation and economic regulation; the collectivists went further and physically seized productive property, an act that they called nationalization. In those cases the government simply took over the assets and operations of core businesses such as communication, banking, transportation, heavy manufacturing, etc., and ran them as state enterprises. But without the instrument of a free market that sets realistic prices reflective of real costs and offers incentive, the wealth necessary to support any government simply failed to materialize and each of these welfare states faced collapse.

In order to compensate for (necessarily) inadequate tax revenues as fewer economic activities occurred (economic activity having been depressed because incentive had been quashed) the collectivist central authority had only one alternative to support their bad social/fiscal habits: print more money. The result was classic inflation; an increased supply of money chasing fewer goods and services. In this circumstance a country can become decapitalized (meaning the value of its money is greatly reduced or even destroyed) in short order. To study the details of twentieth-century collectivist economic disasters, the companion volume to *Modern Times* is Daniel Yergin and Joseph Stanislaw's *The Commanding Heights* (Chapter 29), the story of how the free market, capitalism, and democracy evolved to change the world step by step, country by country, after the intellectual disaster of totalitarianism had run its course.

Taking a slightly different tack, Johnson reserves special enmity for what he termed the most destructive twentieth-century demon, the professional politician, and the era's most radical vice, social engineering. The professional politician, as Johnson comments, sees the masses in terms of votes, power, and control (for the good of the citizenry these "statesmen" will take the helm) while ordinary people see politicians much differently, as purportedly and properly serving the interests of their freedom. Johnson observes that for the "real" nation (the people) democracy ultimately matters less than the rule of law. This is a concept that has been remarkably important throughout history, particularly as nations develop, but less often observed by either politicians or historians. Law is the foundation of order; without law order has no definition. The best example of this equation is the contrarian Fidel Castro in Cuba. When Fidel proclaimed that "Revolutionary Justice is based not upon legal precepts but on moral conviction," Johnson judged this to be the end of the rule of law in Cuba. "Moral conviction" is too amorphous, too idiosyncratic and far too subject to both differences of opinion and, more importantly, corruption to be a standard. Where one person's morals or philosophy or convictions result in government by decree there is neither law nor any reason to expect justice. As the West deals with the twenty-first century's militant Islam and comes to understand why progress toward its own dual goals of peace and freedom in the Middle East have been slow in coming it will most likely arrive back at Johnson's foundational comprehension of both the utility and allure of order as necessary before democracy can be practiced with any degree of success.

As Johnson observes the twentieth century's *nouveau* totalitarian leaders and dissects their motives he finds that "men are excessively ruthless and cruel not out of an avowed malice but from outraged righteousness." And, of course, from greed. This was especially true in the political vacuum that began appearing during the 1950s in the so-called Third World. As colonialism waned and European governors withdrew in favor of indigenous despots—esteemed as saintly merely because of their **erstwhile subjugated status**—righteousness and entitlement in these countries ran rampant. Johnson details the African post-colonial experience in particular and describes the slow descent into continental lunacy.

This decline was fomented, Johnson argues, by the Bandung Conference in Indonesia in 1955 when the non-aligned nations (unaligned with either the West or the Communists) joined together to plan their own utopias but with even less skill and fewer tools than their former colonial masters. None of the post-colonial rulers or bureaucrats had any experience in creating wealth; they were pure intellectuals who, not surprisingly as Johnson explains, thought that they could tax the air to garner the resources for their economically vacuous master plans. Their failure was inevitable, of course, and we see the results still in the twenty-first century.

In spite of petty and idealistic claims that matters are changing there remains a dearth of rationality and a devilishly large portion of corruption in the emerging democracies that received their freedom before they were prepared for it. Johnson warns at the end of his dissertation of an equally dim prospect for Europe as a result of the European community's reach for universal government ruling over sects, religions, language groups, races and cultures that are far from ready to meld and disappear into a unified entity, or even a united economic system. It isn't that despots will emerge, rather, unity will be unattainable because of too many conflicting goals and histories. At that point enmity, Europe's worst bugaboo and most persistent emotional response, will prevail.

In spite of Johnson's observations about the foundation of good governance, there still is room left for his apprehension regarding the potential for future "mischief." Although mischief sounds benign for the devastation wreaked by human on human in the twentieth century, atrocious crimes always begin with misdeeds that are fairly trivial and correctable. We correct mischief in our children with mild rebuke and, if their unacceptable activity persists, with a stronger sermon, but when they continue to misbehave, we visit the force of consequence upon them. It was precisely the force of consequence, no matter how obvious its need, that was ever ignored in the adult world of the twentieth century. Will we do this over and over again? Or will we recognize and then act against those who "seek by force and achieve by cowardice" their selfish goals, the attainment of which requires the destruction of a civilized society?

At the end of his survey, Johnson concludes that there are no strict inevitabilities in history. That lesson learned and then practiced could set civilization on a path of sustained improvement. But difficult choices would have to be made. Human reality cannot take a back seat to vacuous and emotionally freighted political sensitivity—something of a current trend in modern politics. There *is* a difference between good and bad, and where that difference goes unrecognized or unobserved or uncounted, people suffer, sometimes hideously. Under the totalitarians of the twentieth century, the suffering didn't need to be imagined.

About the Author

BORN IN BARTON, Lancashire, England in 1928, Paul Johnson was educated at Stonyhurst, England's oldest Catholic boarding school, and at Magdalen College, Oxford. Early in his career as a journalist he worked as assistant editor of Paris-based *Realités* (1952–1955) and then at the London weekly *New Statesman* (1955–1970) where he was the editor during his last six years. Johnson has been a visiting lecturer at educational institutions around the world and has won numerous literary awards.

Since he edged away from journalism and began concentrating on history, Johnson has written nearly thirty books and an untold number of articles and other pieces. He is most famous for *Modern Times*, his stunning epic of twentieth-century tyranny. Prior to the publication of this work liberals commonly distinguished between bad right-wing totalitarianism (fascism and Nazism) and justifiable left-wing totalitarianism (socialism, welfarism and Communism). The crimes of the latter the liberals conveniently swept under the rug while saluting their utopian intentions. Johnson justifiably denounced all totalitarianism as evil. Obviously not the first to do this, he nonetheless made a great impact by holding one dictator after another systematically and openly accountable for their savage killings.

Johnson emerged as a herald of liberty in the 1970s. "I had once thought liberty was divisible, that you could have very great personal liberty within a framework of substantial state control of the economy," he reflected, "but I don't mind saying I was quite wrong. The thing that finally convinced me was the issue of compulsory unionism." He made his conversion clear in *Enemies of Society* (1977), an extended attack on what he called the "fascist left."

Modern Times has been translated into twenty languages and sold more than six million copies.

Johnson lives with his wife of many decades, Marigold Hunt, in Bayswater, London. They have three sons, a daughter, and five grandchildren.

Section II

Part 2

Government and the Free Market

23

Economics of the Free Society

Wilhelm Röpke

Originally published: 1937, revised 1962
288 pages

THE FIRST TRUTH that strikes one about this book is historical: it was suppressed and then banned in Nazi Germany at the start of World War II. The freedom it espoused and substantiated as necessary for the establishment of a viable economy simply frightened the Third Reich. The second verity is subtle: a political and social balance—sometimes exquisite, sometimes casual, never static—is necessary for a free economy to exist.

Achieving a free economy is not easy. As Wilhelm Röpke demonstrates in this volume, democratic governments often suffer from expansive and intrusive pseudo-melioristic impulses. These usually stem from one of several causes: righteous indignation, a Mother Theresa complex, "intellectual" arrogance, or just pure flights of economic fancy for which no basis can be found in reality but which offer very real political advantages. These inspirations always have some predictably negative effect on the free-market capitalism that supports overall societal success.

As is evident in other chapters of *First Principles*, the devil of economic truth lies in the details. Röpke offers in *Economics of the Free Society* what a free economy should look like—warts and all. Although it is easy to explain where overweening government goes wrong—as Frederic Bastiat, Henry Hazlitt, and Milton Friedman do in their efforts (Chapters 7, 24, 25 respectively)—it is not as easy to describe just exactly what free-enterprise capitalism *should* look like. Röpke sets the standard.

The lessons here are relatively simple, but like those of Ludwig von

Mises (Chapters 32 and 40) they traverse almost the entire landscape of economic reality to arrive at their conclusions. Röpke reduces the complex to the understandable by effectively explaining the interrelatedness of a free enterprise system's individual parts and how those segments interact with political freedom. When we understand those relationships we have an increased chance of avoiding the great pitfall of intrusive government: the law of unintended consequences.

A recurrent theme in most of the literature about man's attempts to govern himself provides Röpke's starting point:

> The great risks implicit in an extreme dependence of all individuals in society upon each other are tolerable in the long run only where an efficiently administered legal system and an *unwritten* but generally accepted code of minimum moral precepts assure to the participants . . . that they will be able to carry on their activities in an atmosphere of mutual confidence and security. Economic history is a constant illustration of the truth that the intensity of economic activity rises or falls in the degree to which these conditions are fulfilled. [Emphasis added]

We see here a reprise of Russell Kirk's narration of the history of morality in *The Roots of American Order* (Chapter 4). In that book, Kirk establishes that the unwritten rules of social interaction, which are too many and too complex to codify, must persist within everyone's understanding for a society to function. If these rules are not uniformly assimilated there can be no faith in the system, nor can people trust one another's judgment or integrity, nor, ultimately, can there be any system at all. The two props upon which such an arrangement is founded are enlightened self-interest and the Golden Rule (referring here, in particular, to its practical application, not directly to its pan-religious significance). These must guide human behavior. The political ramification, if these understandings are present, is that government can be quite limited. The people will turn only sparingly to the legislature and will infrequently need to seek judicial recourse to settle disputes. Most citizens will be able to resolve their controversies informally or, better still, avoid them in the first place—because all are grounded in the same reality.

After setting these moral foundations, so necessary for a free society to exist, Röpke proceeds with an investigation of the mechanisms that allow the free market to operate. His conclusions are instructive in that they reveal the weave of the social and economic fabric, the strength of which over centuries has proven capable of sustaining whole cultures. By way of example, one of his longer and more arcane but important chapters deals with money—the means of exchange and the structural foundation of any economy. Although that sounds obvious and perhaps banal, money is a complex entity and understanding its uses and effects is essential to understanding all economic relations. The credit, or monetary, system of any given economy can either stabilize or exacerbate inflationary pressures whether they arise from economic, social, or governmental actions. Controlling inflation is crucial to economic fitness. In the end, Röpke wants his readers to accept the rudimentary importance of the monetary system being used—that unless it is healthy there is no second step toward a sound government or a sound society.

Another particularly valuable lesson, because it is so current, is found in the way Röpke lays out the economics of a global marketplace. He explains the operation of borderless economics; that is, a free market that operates in the absence of a worldwide social and legal system. The creation and implementation of a uniform international system of laws, even one that relates only to commerce, is likely to remain a practical and intellectual improbability for the foreseeable future. The characteristics of a borderless system, on the other hand, are essentially the same as those of a market within a single country—in each case enlightened self-interest is always the key. Röpke observes that in the field of international commerce where the enforcement of contracts is less than certain and fraught with cultural (not to mention legal) obstacles, integrity becomes more important than law. A lack of integrity to one's promises results in commercial ostracism, probably a more devastating punishment than mere legal responsibility. Röpke predicts the future of international economic activity in the twenty-first century (which at the time he wrote was more than six decades distant) with a prescience that creates confidence in the remainder of his observations. Those who deride efforts to make world trade efficient and reliable—efforts that help all countries and all people—will benefit greatly from Röpke's explanation of the practical side of global wealth creation.

When Röpke dissects international trade, he brings the issue down to its core element: Global commerce is nothing more than a process where

> exactly as with internal trade it rests on the division of labor and on the exchange of goods resulting from this division of labor.... Foreign trade is similar to a labor-saving machine or to any other method of lowering the cost of production.

After observing isolationist tendencies in the less developed nations, Röpke opines, "Poor countries can afford even less than rich ones to shut themselves off from the world economy." An example: the division of labor, by means of which poorer countries can obtain and benefit from advanced technology that they cannot develop on their own, becomes a lever that operates in both directions. The less developed nations supply raw materials and labor in exchange for machinery and technology; both parties to the transaction profit.

In today's climate of globalization, which is the inevitable result of free trade and technological progress, applying the principles of the free enterprise system to international markets is hardly novel. After all, Adam Smith had discussed the benefits of global trade nearly two hundred years earlier, in 1776 in *Wealth of Nations* (Chapter 12). Röpke affirms and deepens Smith's insights, an important effort for today's readers who may be overwhelmed by protectionist cant and accusations of imperialist designs, accusations that are almost invariably contrary to good sense and common experience, but which are politically convenient and effective.

Because of the era in which he wrote, Röpke had to dislodge socialistic thinking while presenting the fundamentals of a free economy. Much of his book nevertheless still rings true in our time when state welfarism and nascent attempts at global (not just national) wealth redistribution offer trite and uniformly failed promises. As Röpke and many others observe, socialism is simply an excess of intellect over experience. For the modern reader the import of this old adage can be ignored only at one's peril, for utopian ideals are reborn with every generation. Although Röpke abbreviates his investigation of socialism for reasons of economy (socialism, he observes, had been minutely examined by too many other writers for him to iterate all its flaws), he often can't avoid enumerating some of its deficiencies in order to explain the permutations of capitalism.

In a later era, Ronald Reagan succinctly expressed capitalism's essence in 1987 when he spoke at the Berlin Wall:

Just as truth can flourish only when the journalist is given freedom of speech, so prosperity can come about only when the farmer and businessman enjoy economic freedom.

Röpke anticipated Reagan's insight with a penetrating question and its answer:

Who is charged with seeing to it that the economic gears of society mesh properly? Nobody.

And, of course, everybody. How much more simple could it be? Adam Smith's "invisible hand" and Thomas Jefferson's admonition "that government governs best which governs least" are both at work in a free society's mostly uncontrolled economic system. Although constraints against monopoly and against deceit, dishonesty, and corruption are indispensable, an otherwise free economic system (born of a free market where the division of labor is allowed to operate unimpeded) will bring the most of the best to the greatest number of citizens. While the consumer sometimes needs protection, such defense of his well-being must begin as his own personal responsibility. It cannot be sought exclusively in rules and regulations and legislation and judicial decisions. If individuals look to others for safety the resulting protective measures soon become prescriptions, then demands, and ultimately laws, which, of course, beget more laws because law is such an inefficient mechanism to guide human behavior. This is all to the detriment of freedoms, large and small. In spite of Benjamin Franklin's intention to address freedom in the context of government, the essence of his thoughts apply as well to ordinary economic life: "those who are willing to give up a little [economic] freedom to obtain a little [economic] security deserve neither."

If we ask the state to make us secure in our financial lives rather than taking that responsibility upon ourselves we give up our freedom on all issues that we abandon to the decisions, whims, or desires of government functionaries. The incremental loss of freedom eventually becomes a monumental, then a tyrannical loss. In the United States, think of OSHA (Occupational Safety and Health Administration), which tells us, as though common sense does not exist, how to use a ladder ("If you climb on this device you may fall and injure yourself.")

or the believable but sardonic and mythical twelve thousand pages of regulations on the planting, growing, harvesting, selling, distributing, and consuming of cabbage supposedly promulgated by the Agriculture Department. How and how aggressively our government will proceed from these two virtually insignificant (unless you are a cabbage farmer) but magnificently distorting intrusions only Rube Goldberg or the Devil can imagine. We may be certain, though, that the effects on our freedom will not be mythical.

In offering his overview of free-market economics Röpke discusses wealth creation, the distribution of income, and monopolies. The monopoly we call government actually means *we the people* since the government has nothing, neither money nor power, unless it first gets such from us. This monopoly causes the greatest distortions in any economy by spending money (redistributing income) to cure discerned social ills. Röpke sees this almost always as an exercise in welfarism. He holds that an economist's (as opposed to a politician's) assessment of any such activity would not pay attention to how worthy any particular ill is of being fixed or even if it can be better fixed by leaving the citizens to their own devices. Whether the ill is accidental, self-inflicted, or societally induced is of no import. The critical matter for the economist to consider (for that person is not a social engineer) is the creation of wealth. This wealth has two purposes: it can be taxed to allow for the very public expenditures that the political class thinks of as its own, while at the same time it decreases the need for public expenditures because as wealth is created there is increased employment, which means fewer government actions are needed to care for the populace that now cares for itself.

According to Röpke, if taxes are not levied on this wealth (or are kept low) then the gains to the individual (and thus the society) become a vehicle through which all types of additional private sector activity and solutions can occur. With this additional personal income the economy is able to more efficiently address ills in myriad ways—ways that the politician or bureaucrat often cannot or will not see—while still ensuring the market continues to function. Many private solutions to public issues (always voluntary in nature) are explored in depth by Richard Cornuelle in *Reclaiming the American Dream* (Chapter 30). Understanding Cornuelle's premise reminds us of what we *used* to do as a society and how the state has inappropriately co-opted the popular impulse toward charity or good works and driven out both citizen sense and citizen participation in the bargain.

Röpke sees most social engineers as oblivious to these facts. The righteous see something "wrong" and they want a remedy, usually through governmental intervention, meaning using someone else's resources. (Just as often they are interested in achieving some political end—either their own or that of their political party.) They begin their involvement with the problem some distance from its genesis. Röpke surmises that if they were to trace any given situation to its origin they would see that it is likely amenable to alleviation through private initiatives and at the local level where solutions can be tailored to specific circumstances and defined populations.

In pursuing the ill and its resolution via government action the social engineers will be faced with the challenge of structuring the solution so it actually achieves the desired effect to discourage the problem's persistence or recurrence. But the government's action will also have to take into account the strong possibility of unintended consequences from this new action that may unwittingly create further ills. Of course, the initial ill very likely was an unintended consequence of some previous government action. In the end, if those who see government as the solution to anything were to delve to a problem's roots they might humbly question whether the social benefit to be achieved by governmental intervention would not be outweighed by damage done to other parts of society. Structurally, government intervention (again, made possible only through taxation) universally discourages the creation of wealth and employment that in all likelihood could and would solve the problem privately if left to its own devices. Röpke raises these relevant questions as part of his study of the totality of economic, cultural, and governmental relationships so that some type of practical analysis can be brought to real-world problems.

In Röpke's hands, the topic of monopolistic practices (the alleged existence of which is the subject of ever-present assertions of the need for governmental intervention) seems less complex than it might. The biggest threat to the market is not private monopoly but government monopoly—almost no private monopolies exist except those that are founded in and granted by action of the state. Röpke finds the recommendations of some who wish to preclude potential capitalistic monopolies (by means of more government regulations and control) even more bizarre than the reasons given as to why the private tendency toward monopoly is so supposedly dangerous in the first place. In point of fact, monopolies don't tend to persist in a free market. As soon as someone attempts to establish a monopoly, others replicate, imitate, improve upon the product or service, etc., so that the monopoly disappears. In Röpke's hands, the discussion of monopolies is sensible, not emotional; rational, not distorted by accusation of public harm unfounded in fact.

As it was in Röpke's era, the question today is not whether the state will monopolize the means of production and distribution but how the fruits of production and distribution will be taxed—and then "used" for the citizenry. Taxation is obviously a government monopoly. As the levels are reduced or increased the monopoly (on claiming any given economy's wealth) issue arises: will the populace be free to order their own world—will incentive be allowed to work its magic at all levels of society?

The secondary issue stemming from Röpke's discussion of monopolies concerns regulation of the economy. Should it be regulated? If so, how and when? The answers in any given period define and redefine the size and effect of the state. In his detailed analysis of these phenomena Röpke investigates and exposes the myriad truths and myths of an ordered economy in an attempt to make sense of how the legitimate interests of the state and the individual should interact. (For an expanded discussion of these two issues, see John Chamberlain's *The Roots of Capitalism* [Chapter 26] and Charles Murray's *In Pursuit: Of Happiness and Good Government* [Chapter 31].)

Some of the most interesting and arguably most valuable few pages of this book present Röpke's reflections on the work of an outsized twentieth-century economist, John Maynard Keynes, as Röpke compares Keynes to the eighteenth century's Adam Smith. Keynes is probably the best-known if not most talented economist of the era stretching from the turn of the twentieth century to the end of World War II. He was at first the darling of macroeconomists and political leaders because of his espousal of inflationary deficit government spending as the antidote to devastating boom-and-bust business cycles.

Politicians loved Keynesian economics because they got to spend the public's money or to print money that had no justifiable existence other than through Keynes's theories, and then claim a mantel of care while doing so. Under the guise of doing a public good these politicians got re-elected for doing exactly the wrong thing. Keynesian economics was the politician's dream policy. Ultimately, though, he became the bane of some of these same admirers when it was seen that this tool's unintended consequences caused more problems than it solved. Röpke, finding Keynes's tenure on center stage bittersweet (recall, they were contemporaries, talking to the same audiences), also detected him getting full of himself (messianic is the word that Röpke uses) and in the process doing even more harm when he moved from theorizing in an academic manner to pontificating from political platforms.

Keynes and Keynesian economics crop up incessantly, even today, and Röpke's assessment of how Keynes went wrong makes for useful reading given all that we have learned about economics since his generation. And the admonition again arises that although Keynesianism, like many other -isms, may be defunct now, we must know it and recognize it as it is sure to revive at some future time. (How that happens is a two-fold process: first, there are still educational or theoretical materials in existence that people will find and mistakenly or naïvely believe are true, no matter how false they have been proven to be; second, there are few elected or bureaucratic officials who will not hear the siren song of the free lunch Keynesianism seems to offer. They are drawn to it as alchemists were drawn to the possibility of turning lead into gold in the Middle Ages.)

Röpke's goal was to offer comprehensive and comprehensible observations about the fundamentals of a stable economy. He describes a national economy in detail, then meshes that with international trade, and proceeds to show the effects of various policies on each. He explains the factors of production and takes pains to analyze capital (generally meaning money), always the most ephemeral and misunderstood element in any economy. His discussion of a country's fiscal assets and policies provides a useful perspective on capitalism's most valuable and pervasive and perhaps most maligned tools. He examines population size in relation to the division of labor, compulsory unionism versus the right to contract freely, speculators (a group about whom Röpke offers a particularly useful analysis), the monetary and credit system, the attention-grabbing problem of inflation, and many other factors common to all large, complex economies. In sum, he omits little in his coverage of economic realities.

Röpke's penchant for citing particulars and details facilitates his demonstration of how an amorphous yet interconnected system of production, distribution, and consumption works efficiently only when left to its own devices. Push in at one place and inevitably the system pushes back or becomes skewed in another. Hence, we have to be careful how we intrude. Understanding all of these details makes a citizen out of a taxpayer. Without the knowledge and experience offered in Röpke's full but simplified analysis, people often remain victims of government, and politicians, rather than masters.

In his overview, Röpke steps back to look at the then-ongoing war between capitalism and collectivism/socialism. He acknowledges that he didn't take socialism to task in a thorough manner, because this collectivist aberration was widely recognized as a failed philosophy, defensive of an insupportable economic structure. He concludes that

> these degenerate aspects [the arguments in favor of socialism] are so obvious to everybody, they are the subject of such an extensive and overly emotional literature, that it is the duty of the scholar to emphasize the other side of the picture and to lead the discussion back to an understanding of the *foundations* of our economic system.

If one is interested in the details, goals, and methods of socialism, Ludwig von Mises's *Socialism* (Chapter 32) is probably the most comprehensive (and understandable) critique of the scores and scores of books on the character of socialist philosophy. Mises wrote *Socialism* in 1922, yet the manner in which he covers the entire subject remains as alive and valid today as it was then. As has been previously observed, the reader needs to be versed in these matters because in the current era socialist thinking is the impetus behind the welfare state. The mechanics are somewhat different (and only somewhat) but the goal and the effect are not. The bankrupt logic of the welfare state is nothing but the same heedless understandings of socialism repackaged for the twenty-first century. A volume that meshes well with those of both Röpke and Mises is Richard Pipes's *Property and Freedom* (Chapter 11). Pipes's work provides an understanding of the necessary conjunction between the substance of capitalism (which is property) and freedom—the essence of the human experience.

Röpke evinces a belief that if people simply understood capitalism better they would reject socialism, and by inference the welfarism so popular with generous and self-serving politicians. We daily witness the undeniable harm done by a culture of dependency, by "entitlements," by the ubiquitous attitude that nothing that goes wrong is our fault, and by the quasi-religious faith that a lot more government will fix almost anything. Demagoguery along these lines—that the wealthy, the corporations, and the internationalists vex us with various afflictions because *they* are greedy—denies economic facts.

Although today's enemies of capitalism and freedom do not generally aim to overthrow our economic system they do advocate defiance of the principles on which it operates (and, in the bargain, common sense) thus adding further to a thorough misunderstanding of its capabilities. In the end, if the demagogues do enough damage they will innocently claim that they were just trying to do the right thing, without understanding in the least how they did exactly the wrong thing. The further Americans get from seeing through the misleading dogma of statist fanatics the greater the chance that they will make a wrong turn and find only a dead end as they seek a short cut to some supposedly quantifiable concept of "social justice," or even the proverbial free lunch.

The final piece of Röpke's explication of the free-enterprise system addresses the dangerous and widespread economic illiteracy he witnessed (one of the three motivating concerns of *First Principles*, the other two being constitutional illiteracy, and moral/ethical bewilderment and corruption founded in political correctness and moral relativism). Economic illiteracy allows simplistic and inadequate answers to complex social realities to seem credible. Röpke makes the point that people don't take the time to understand capitalism and its indispensable foundation, the open society. The polity seems to indulge in an almost willful blindness or laziness:

> The first duty of an economist [or a citizen] . . . is to establish an exact understanding of two things: the economic system which we have and the one which we would establish in its place . . . [so] we will have a full awareness of all that we would give up, and all that we would receive, in choosing the one or the other.

After exhorting both the teachers and the students to learn, to expel ignorance, Röpke notes a serious difficulty:

> It is, indeed, disquieting to find how small a minority in any country really understands the essence of our economic system. . . . That the number is so small is in itself a cause for concern, *since the overwhelming majority of those who*

are engaged in passing random judgments on our economic system seek to disparage the minority who do understand it as ignorant and biased—a spectacle to be met with in no other science. [Emphasis added]

The italicized clause speaks to a continuing problem manifest in the growing divisiveness when public debate regarding economic issues ensues. Specifically, the "passing random judgments" thought applies to two groups of people. The first group encompasses various activists, pundits, "experts" (whether or not they actually are), editorialists, broadcast news readers, and politicians—all of whom are often guilty, to one degree or another, of passing economic fallacy off as gospel. Some do this out of ignorance, some for ignoble reasons.

In the second group appear the victims, the often-duped voters who respond to the economic representations advanced by members of the first group that may or may not have any validity. The second group's economic ignorance is obviously the major contributing factor to the efficacy of the first group's designs, for economic ignorance allows demagoguery to flourish. The often fanatic speakers frequently pontificate in naïve terms of justice and fairness, neither of which is as easily achieved or as black and white as the lecturer would have us believe. Too many of us allow ourselves to be led, almost to the exclusion of making our own decisions, because we don't take the time to understand economic fundamentals. Without that understanding we can do little but accept the judgments visited upon us. At the most basic level this is often abetted by the repetition of false premises. As Vladimir Lenin, leader of the 1917 Russian Revolution observed "A lie repeated often enough becomes the truth." Thus is the circle closed.

While Röpke covers the essentials of free enterprise in a reasonably comprehensive manner, he intentionally leaves some gaps so as not to confuse the subject with too many details. The interested reader may complete an investigation of free market economics by reading Ludwig von Mises's *The Theory of Money and Credit* (Chapter 34). Although Mises's title sounds daunting, his prose is clear and expressive. His book remains surprisingly useful despite the fact that it was written almost a century ago.

Röpke's readers should be aware that he uses the words liberal and collectivist in their traditional European meanings as he juxtaposes his views and understandings in relation to various economic configurations. His is one of those books written by early twentieth-century

European authors that uses the word liberal in the same sense that conservative or classical liberal is used in the U.S. today. Röpke's use of "collectivist" generally corresponds to "socialist" in modern parlance.

About the Author

BORN IN HANOVER, Germany at the very end of the nineteenth century, Wilhelm Röpke—the man and the philosopher—was a product of twentieth-century excesses. The son of a physician, his upbringing was grounded in traditional Protestant teachings whose influence on his thinking appears over and over in his work. He fought as a soldier in the trenches during World War I; as a result of that brutal experience he sought to understand the causes of such devastating conflicts, thus he pursued the study of economics and sociology. (To understand how the same circumstances could lead to a completely opposite personal course that also had profound public consequences, see *Witness* [Chapter 41] by Whittaker Chambers, a contemporary of Röpke.) Upon receiving his doctorate Röpke became a professor in Germany.

Röpke's reputation as an individualist thinker was well earned. He was not afraid to look at first causes; his ability and drive to do so marked his career and works. He taught in Germany until he was forced to leave the country in 1932 because of his outspoken opposition to Nazism. He resided in Istanbul and taught at the university there from 1932 until 1937. He then returned to Europe and began a career at the Institute of International Studies in Geneva, Switzerland, where he embarked on a collaborative professional life with Ludwig von Mises. Although von Mises emigrated early in World War II, Röpke remained in Geneva throughout the Second World War and for the rest of his academic life.

Röpke, along with von Mises, Frederick von Hayek, Milton Friedman, and others who were ultimately awarded Nobel Prizes in economics, formed the Mont Pelerin Society in Switzerland in 1947. Their intent was to publicize the folly of collectivism and to decry socialist ideology as it caused increasing erosions of liberty. The philosophy of the Mont Pelerin Society succeeded in spite of the fears of its founders and exceeded even the most optimistic of its members' expectations. Röpke married in 1924 and raised three children with his wife, Eva. He died in 1966.

24

Economics in One Lesson

Henry Hazlitt

Originally published: 1946
214 pages

HENRY HAZLITT wrote *Economics in One Lesson* at the end of World War II because he was disturbed about the course of economic discussion inside and outside of government. What he knew to be economic fallacies were then so accepted they were skewing policy debates from the outset, thus making it virtually impossible to arrive at a rational and productive free-market paradigm. In his description of what he observed in 1946, Hazlitt uses phrases such as "false premises," "fantastic conclusions," and "economic absurdities." He so effectively, and timelessly, exposes the wrong-headed notions then prevalent in economic thinking that *Economics in One Lesson* has been in print for more than half a century and has sold millions of copies in more than half a dozen languages. His lessons are well worth revisiting.

Hazlitt takes the economic mis-assumptions of his era (which often exist in their mistaken glory yet today) to their logical conclusions to see if they make sense. In so doing, he pays close attention to the law of unintended consequences. He proceeds to lay bare the nonsense, unfairness, destructiveness, and even silliness of what often passes for sophisticated economic thinking. His observations, coming close on the heels of Friedrich von Hayek's *The Road to Serfdom* (Chapter 13), provided Main Street substance to Hayek's academic and psychological acumen. Hazlitt contends "the whole of economics can be reduced to a single lesson, and that lesson can be reduced to a single sentence":

The art of economics consists in looking not merely at the immediate but at the larger effects of any act or policy: it consists in tracing the consequences of that policy not merely for one group but for all groups. [Emphasis in original]

The question becomes: why do so many bad policies seem to have so much traction with both the public and political/governmental functionaries? Hazlitt observes: "The reason is that the demagogues and bad economists are presenting half-truths. They are speaking only of the immediate effect of a proposed policy or its effect upon a single group. As far as they go they may often be right." He notes that in the bigger picture, when bad logic is applied to all times and all groups it creates worse policy—which then causes economic distortion, if not disaster.

The beauty and readability of Hazlitt's prose lies in the commonsense simplicity of his explanations and examples. Hazlitt's purpose in investigating small-scale economics by means of these examples was to provide a frame of reference, to set the stage so the reader could consciously make the transition to large-scale considerations. What Hazlitt ultimately demonstrates is the loss to the economy through government intervention—by means of taxes, laws, and regulations—that cause distorted and reduced economic activity. The funds that might have been created if the economy was allowed the freedom under which it was designed to operate are lost to the citizen and ultimately to the government because the pie from which both can gain their resources is smaller. (George Gilder expands on this relationship in *Wealth and Poverty* [Chapter 27]).

Obviously some government is both necessary and valuable and if government controlled its spread and reach, as James Madison in particular designed it to do, the system would work to society's benefit. What Hazlitt comments on is that government not only does not effect self-control, it does pretty much the opposite. (To review the everyday realities of how and why this happens recall Bertrand de Jouvenel's five-step circular political process in *On Power* [Chapter 15]).

When Hazlitt expands his investigation to macroeconomics he begins with an observation he considers primary in then current circumstances: "There is no more persistent and influential faith in the world today than the faith in government spending." Such thinking, inspired by economist John Maynard Keynes, Hazlitt calls the most fundamental fallacy of his time. This judgment remains as apt today as when Hazlitt first expressed it. While Americans watch tax receipts continuously fall short of government spending the federal debt lurches toward ten *trillion* dollars. As this spending seems not to have had a substantial effect on the underlying problems toward which, decade after decade, trillion after trillion, these funds are directed, Hazlitt's commentary on the dangers of over-sized government remain more than topical.

For Hazlitt, the negative economic consequences of any government's interventions in the marketplace—whether through government spending or regulation or taxation, etc.,—are cumulative and self-perpetuating. The progression is thus: first, government procures its funds through taxation. Hazlitt observes that the value of those funds diminishes when they pass through the collecting bureaucracy because of the expense of the bureaucracy itself. This cost, which Hazlitt calls friction, significantly lessens the economic benefit to society of whatever government purpose is afoot. Then government uses the remaining tax dollars to set up an additional bureaucracy for each program it creates. All of these actions have a negative impact on both the freedom experienced by the public (it is less at liberty to dispose of its own wealth) and the free market's ability to perform its magic (it is less able to take advantage of the multiplier effect of ordinary economic activity because there are fewer resources with which to multiply). Of course, if the government simply spends money it has not collected in taxes, by means of deficit spending, the negative effects already described by Hazlitt are merely compounded by the inflation such spending causes and the additional interest cost thus created.

Economic dampening is the far more important consequence of intrusive government activity; the money diverted from the people by taxation precludes them from using those funds as they would have had they not been taken in the first place. But, based simply on the math, he further explains that

> for every public job created ... a private job has been destroyed. ...

These financial diversions directly skew the economy in a relatively straightforward manner. Since the people who act to create private enterprise end up paying more to achieve their goals—because they have to support the cost of their efforts *and* pay the cost of government endeavors simultaneously—the amount they produce decreases and the concomitant multiplier effect of their private effort is reduced. Because there is now less economic activity to tax government revenues decrease as well. In the worst case scenario the entrepreneur abandons his goals altogether because too many of the funds that would have served his private purposes have been taken for some public one. Taxation can actually eliminate a new wing on a factory or a new line of production or a new research effort and all the jobs (and additional tax revenues) that would have been created by either effort.

The cascade of negative effects caused by this cycle continues unabated. Hazlitt observes that public employment, which was a tool of choice and a substantial part of government enterprise in Hazlitt's time, does not bring to the economy what an entrepreneur might. In the aftermath of the government's failed efforts to combat the effects of the Great Depression of the 1930s it became clear that public largesse *suppresses* the economic initiative and even the capability of those who receive it. Such spending creates a perverse public dependency almost equal in proportion to the amount of benevolence it theoretically dispenses.

In Hazlitt's opinion it is also important to consider the bureaucracy itself. It is not benign—merely a conduit that extracts a fee for its service. It is created as an infant but grows into a behemoth for two simple reasons: first, because it can, and second, because it must. In the first instance a bureaucracy grows as it finds more and more clients who "need" additional assistance. These new avenues are ubiquitous and are also a form of job security for the administrators. The administrative entity begins to swell—because it can be more helpful than was initially thought, at least in the minds of the bureaucrats. It also serves a dual purpose of the legislators who seek to please the public through political entrepreneurship; not only do their bureaucratic efforts satisfy myriad constituencies, but of more value, the politician obtains re-election in the bargain because he appears to be doing so much that is good.

Later the bureaucracy grows because it obtains sanctified or even holy status—its job is no longer just to assist, but to deliver that to which the people have become "entitled." Thus it must be given more authority and money because it too does so much that is good. Once entitlement status is achieved then the protections offered by the originally benevolent agency are changed in character from help to obligations. Obligations create rights that are protected by further layers of bureaucratic or even judicial oversight. The cycle has become fully self-perpetuating at that point.

In order to learn how what he was experiencing in 1946 had come to pass Hazlitt goes back a generation; he explores and then explains why President Franklin Roosevelt was not able to tax and spend the United States out of the Great Depression. Indeed, as Hazlitt (and many others since then) makes clear, Roosevelt's policies extended the Depression's effects far beyond what was necessary. It was frequently stated that the country was "spared" (if one dares to voice that result considering the price paid for such an exemption) another decade of economic failure only by the advent of World War II and its massive calls for military production and national employment. His exposition vis-à-vis the Depression is one of the core lessons of Hazlitt's study. His explanation of the true cost of government's forced transfer of economic resources is a straightforward and commonsense approach to comprehending the negative effect and substantial expense—economic and human—of government intervention in the marketplace.

Hazlitt was especially disturbed by the notion that only government is large enough to tackle major projects, projects that private industry supposedly cannot afford or does not have the will to undertake because of the potential complications beyond financial woes. What the theorists and pundits often either miss or ignore, muses Hazlitt, is that the government has no money except what the private sector creates. It is an old saw that bears repeating as a mantra, "We, the people, are the government; the money of the government is our money." The necessary conclusion is that if the private sector cannot afford a project, the government cannot either. It is the coercive ability of government to force such efforts that allows them to happen. Whether that results in good or bad choices is usually a matter for posterity to determine.

Hazlitt brings forth at several points this core lesson: each dollar taken for a governmental purpose is one dollar less that is available for a private effort; and each private effort thus foiled has a cumulative negative impact on the whole economy. If the government has no money save what it takes from the citizens, Hazlitt inquires, why can't the citizens simply use their fiscal resources for *any* worthy purpose—and circumvent the added burden of government inefficiency and growth or claimed omnipotence?

It was just a question. Hazlitt, however, does not take these possibilities to the extreme conclusion that we need *no* government any more than do other conservative thinkers. But he does want to consider redrawing the arena in which government is primarily responsible—to make it smaller and more reasonable in all possible ways. Concomitantly, Hazlitt seeks to enlarge avenues open to the private sector by removing government monopolies and impediments to private activity.

In following economic fallacies through to their logical conclusions Hazlitt exposes some of the negative consequences of large government enterprises such as public housing and federal lending. He refutes the bizarre claim that there are purported economic benefits of such program's *in*efficiencies—that somehow inefficiency has a positive economic multiplier effect resulting in more jobs being created to do the same amount of work. Obviously, inefficiency is inefficiency. Government inefficiency is doubly insulting because it is the taxpayer's money being taken and those funds are being collected to allow more government and more government waste, which then requires more resources, ad nauseum.

In his analysis Hazlitt also explains the destructiveness of tariffs, price supports, rent control, and minimum wage laws among other legislative adventures. He clearly defines the risks we incur when we naïvely ask or allow government to take our wealth for ostensibly noble purposes. Government is no more capable than the people in this arena and, unfortunately, no less venal on occasion as legislators and bureaucrats serve their own purposes.

Hazlitt reserves his harshest criticism for the inflationary consequences of many of these government actions. In his view, inflation is the most dangerous repercussion of fallacious economic thinking. Hazlitt uses Depression-era Germany as an example of the extreme case. Germany could not both support itself and pay the war reparations forced on it at the end of World War I. The crushing economic burden was resolvable only through the German government spending money it did not have and could not raise. Eventually the country's currency became worthless—at one point it took a wheelbarrow full of paper money to buy a loaf of bread. It was then Germany threw off its guilt and became once again belligerent. The few steps from outrage to arms were easily taken in the hands of the demagogic Adolph Hitler. Hazlitt's comprehension and explanation of why all these things happen within any nation, not just the U.S., is not just instructive, it is literally a call to action.

Through Hazlitt's exposition it becomes clear that if each citizen does not personally engage in economic and governmental processes entirely predictable consequences will result. He concludes that our problems stem not so much from a lack of understanding of basic economics but rather from our society's political inability to own up to basic tasks. High-level government officials should not be ignorant when they come into office. Their experience and education should not allow them to act as they do, but their fealty to *noblesse oblige* (literally the "obligation of the nobility") or their own agenda seems to overwhelm what they should know to be true. The schemes they develop for the redistribution of wealth tend to smother incentive and foster a culture of dependence (as common understanding dictates they should realize) and these results lead to impoverishment at every level of society. That this happens again and again is the ubiquitous human condition in full flower.

It is this human element that Hazlitt brings to the forefront by emphasizing the inability of politicians to see both sides of the coin—not just the pain of the less able, but the dignity of the self-sufficient. Rather than using the lowest common denominator approach to bring the successful down in a futile attempt to create economic equality, Hazlitt proposes increasing and improving the available opportunities for the less prosperous. This would occur by removing government impediments in the marketplace, often disguised as government assistance programs, or more accurately, "entitlements." His views and methods bear repeating in each generation, and the simplicity of his investigation makes his exposition the most useful point at which to begin.

About the Author

HENRY HAZLITT was a journalist, literary critic, economist, philosopher, and author. Born in 1894, his life spanned the American Century and his interests mirrored our sometimes-fractured history. He lived to be 98, dying in 1993, and was still amazed at the end of his life that of all his works *Economics in One Lesson* was his most successful. His personal favorite was *The Foundations of Morality* in which he investigates why ethical behavior is so fundamental to human interaction.

Hazlitt received no training as an economist and did not graduate from either college or high school. Obviously self-taught, he demonstrates what can be done with a sound intellect and a commonsense approach to the facts. He was more inclined toward the fields of ethics and philosophy than economics but he profoundly affected world-wide economic practice through his straightforward attack on economic illiteracy. Hazlitt was probably the person most responsible for the fame of Ludwig von Mises and Friedrich von Hayek by means of his reviews of their books. (The works of both Hayek and Mises are presented elsewhere in this volume.)

Hazlitt published his first book before he reached the age of 20 and landed a job as a stenographer at the *Wall Street Journal* shortly thereafter. He traveled within literary and newspaper circles most of his career. His penchant for standing on principle earned him a reputation for integrity but cost him some of his more lucrative employments when his philosophy was faced with economic absurdities he could not allow to pass without comment, or even argument. Hazlitt wrote a score of books and millions of words in editorials, reviews, articles, and commentary pieces. His indefatigable devotion to freedom made his presence on the American scene a thorn in the side of statists and a boon to rationality in economic and political pursuits.

25

Capitalism and Freedom

Milton Friedman

Originally published: 1962
202 pages

MILTON FRIEDMAN was perhaps the most widely celebrated of the University of Chicago's eminent economists, one of the numerous Nobel Prize winners in the school's cadre of creative and penetrating economic thinkers. But Friedman was not just a theorist; he was an activist, a proselytizer.

Capitalism and Freedom, a title that expresses an equation basic to free-market economics, is a slim volume, almost a companion to Henry Hazlitt's *Economics in One Lesson* (Chapter 24). But whereas Hazlitt explores the fundamental relationship between government tax and spending policy on the one hand and Adam Smith's marketplace on the other, Friedman correlates the effect of the same governmental policies on individualism, that is, personal and economic freedom. In the preface he notes that his intention is to expose some of the myths of government intervention—including the failure of avowed collectivist policies to bring us closer to utopia. His purpose is to help us as individuals understand what we can do to protect and promote our personal and economic liberty. Throughout the book his encouragement to activism is patent.

Friedman observes that almost invariably it requires a crisis to energize human beings to act. His goal, therefore, is to provide tools to deal with economic crises so when something does happen to motivate us we will be able to address our problems more effectively. Based on an understanding of economics and human nature these tools could best be used, of course, to avoid approaching disaster in the first place, but Friedman recognizes that the human condition often gets in the way of such common sense.

Ultimately, Friedman sought to set a foundation so that what appeared politically impossible—freedom from overweening government—would eventually become politically inescapable. For example, when the socialist ideas of the 1930s and 1940s ultimately failed to bear any of the fruit that was promised, the need to return to the free market became palpable. Friedman and his academic cohorts from around the world provided the philosophy and programs necessary and enunciated some "rules" to ensure that the freed economic system could function efficiently. They wanted the system to be understood and embraced on a personal, a national, and an international level so that collectivist impulses did not again become the answer to the vicissitudes of economic activity—whether in a micro- or macro arena.

In order to effect their intentions, Friedman and his contemporaries gathered in Switzerland in 1947 and formed the Mont Pelerin Society. Once constituted, this organization and its individual members publicly called to account the fallacies then prevalent in economic thinking. They were successful, to the chagrin of their many critics, beyond almost all expectations, and to them the world owes a great debt—for they allowed rational economic thinking to re-emerge on the global stage.

Friedman opens his book by dissecting the results obtained when liberal ideas are put into effect and the reality of everyday living vis-à-vis these ideas puts a face on the law of unintended consequences. He finds that the implementation of the ubiquitous liberal notion of paternalism is almost always demeaning and destructive of self-confidence and self-sufficiency. Friedman asserts the obvious, namely, that we are individuals. Not only are we quite able to take care of ourselves, but we want to. We don't want to be told how or what to do, or be cared for by government in any measure if we can avoid it. The personal sense of shame felt by those who first find themselves in the welfare line is no less prevalent today than it was in the depths of the Depression. However, those inured to government paternalism and who have been told they are entitled to welfare are taught to lose that sense of personal dignity with which we are all endowed at birth. Thus is born, instead, the culture of dependency. This culture can be reversed—not only for the benefit of the taxpayers but for the individuals whose sense of life has been so grievously distorted.

Friedman understands the human impulse toward self-sufficiency; he comments that we would not normally allow or expect anyone else, much less everyone else (by means of government oversight and intrusion) to do for us that which we can better do for ourselves. He avers that those who call for a public effort in this vein do far more harm than good.

Welfarism simply induces people to postpone deciding when to become responsible for themselves. Friedman's understanding of these matters reflects his view of government as an instrument of people engaged in political action—not as an entity apart from them. Government, which is a continuing personal responsibility for each of us, is our way of arriving at and implementing policy. Conversely, government does not exist either to afford faceless bureaucrats the opportunity to meddle in our affairs or to allow politicians to actualize dreams of how *they* can better our lives, or assume responsibility for us (and obtain re-election in the bargain by means of their often feckless promises).

Central to Friedman's thinking is his largely successful effort to grapple with a simple question: how can we keep government bureaucracy and regulation from destroying the freedom on which America is based? Government can be a threat to freedom because of a combination of centralized power and the indulgent attitudes, efforts, and condescensions of misguided politicians and bureaucrats. Friedman offers two time-tested and effective suggestions to counteract these threats. First, we should limit the government's reach to those things that either should not or cannot be accomplished by the private sector. Second, we should design and implement government policies that directly assist individuals at the level closest to the citizen in order to avoid the inherent arrogance and inefficiencies of a distant centralized bureaucracy.

Although the attraction of federal pronouncements is that they can be uniformly applied across the country, Friedman notes that the country (much less the individuals within it) is not uniform and consequently a national system can implode upon local application. During the last quarter of the twentieth century private sector initiatives and government programs specifically tailored to local constituencies and circumstances proved far more effective than any national policies necessarily designed to address needs in a lowest common denominator approach. Wisconsin's revolutionary approach to welfare—welfare to workfare—reduced welfare rolls and brought self-sufficiency and personal dignity to tens of thousands and was copied on the federal level in the 1990s. This is a prime example of entrepreneurial and innovative government efforts that are possible when local entities are given the freedom to address local issues. National pronouncements attempting to resolve local realities produce uniform mediocrity at best—at great administrative cost.

On the macroeconomic side of his efforts, Friedman and his partners in the Mont Pelerin Society easily determined where then current (1940s and 50s) government policies were headed. They understood equalitarianism as the intended result of socialism and its latter day cousin, the welfare state. Both are antithetical to freedom. Friedman offers that people are unequal in diverse ways and their differences go far toward sustaining the essence and beauty of humanity—not to mention all human progress. Liberals, who wish to impose an equalitarian outcome, and who ignore these realities, do so at our peril, for their notions go against the human spirit and human experience. The dignity of all work and each life is something that liberals often seem to simply ignore or deny. Their conclusion, based on their false assumptions, is to *force* conformity and results. They thereby give proof that their fundamental premises are destructive, not just wrong.

Friedman posits that economic freedom does one simple thing, namely, it separates political power from economic power so that the two achieve a balance (similar to the balance between the executive, legislative and judicial branches of government). This is a sometimes uneasy equilibrium, but essential nevertheless. If the state (through the legislature and its attendant bureaucracies) subverts that balance and controls economic relations through political power, the state becomes a substitute for the people. In this manner the expression of individuality through free choice is curtailed. During the last half of the twentieth century it became apparent that legislatures and bureaucracies felt a need to express their power; the former to maintain their tenure in office (through the use of both carrot and stick), the latter to exercise the authority conferred by the former and thus to validate their possession of it. This exertion of power by political entities reduces the freedom of the citizen.

An economic model based on voluntary and informed transactions is what Friedman calls a free, private-enterprise exchange economy, or competitive capitalism. Friedman notes:

Underlying most arguments against a free market is a lack of belief in freedom itself.

Recognizing that humans are imperfect, governments mistakenly (and often brazenly) conclude that economic decisions and actions must be made and taken on behalf of individuals. This suggests not only that ordinary people are flawed, an assertion with which few would argue, but also that they are incompetent (until one looks at what human beings have *done*). Further, it suggests that politicians and bureaucrats, who are themselves ordinary humans until they get elected or hired, are more perfect. They are those human beings wise enough to run the government; they are the anointed or the chosen. They and their goals are the subject of George Orwell's 1948 novel and screed against totalitarianism, *1984*. Orwell effectively takes collectivism and totalitarianism to their logical conclusions and puts a conjectural but not unimaginable patina on Friedman's philosophical declamations.

Friedman, like his colleagues at the University of Chicago, was not against government; his goal was merely to rationally limit government's power. With respect to the free market, it is clear that someone is needed to referee its activities since human beings (subject to the human condition) will sometimes treat one another unfairly or dishonestly; however, it must be remembered that the vast machinery of government, in trying to rectify such idiosyncratic circumstances, is dealing with an infinitesimally small number of incidents when one contemplates the billions and billions of honest, open and unregulated transactions that occur each *day*. The people, by means of government, implement rules to moderate their interactions, but the governors often overreach while trying to rein in the few who are deceitful or dishonest. In so doing the scope of public authority must not become so enlarged that it affects or interferes with the 99.9% of life that is not its province. Of course, government also takes on tasks that are too big, or do need national unity to perform (such as defense, transportation services, and the monetary system) and are obvious areas where governmental oversight or coordination is quite useful. Friedman would be the last to deny the validity of these public efforts.

How all governing roles play out as well as how the policies we need to govern ourselves are chosen, in Friedman's view, reflects "a consensus reached by imperfect and biased [people] through free discussion and trial and error." With freedom, the biases and self-interests can be balanced out, the mistakes corrected. This is the reverse of what liberals attempt to force on the public, a programmed economy supported and regulated by intellectuals who are largely inexperienced in real-world economics but who think that government should play a greater role in economic (i.e., *private*) affairs. In the view of the liberal there is little room for discussion—and much need for obedience.

To Friedman, trying to affect our economic relationships through government intervention is to "make matters worse by introducing a largely random disturbance that is simply added to other disturbances." It must be observed that this additional random disturbance often has no *economic* basis, thus its effect on the free market has no rational foundation—it simply skews economic relationships and causes myriad unintended consequences. Finally, if the government's theoretical good intentions cannot be effected by means of political carrots, they can only be implemented with regulatory sticks. In the latter case the distortions that ensue are obvious. The economy is too large and too complex to respond rationally to repeated, rapid, minute course changes through government's intervention either by fiat or even pursuant to supposedly well-intentioned tax or spending policies. Thus, when government intervenes in the market the law of unintended consequences takes baneful effect. Unfortunately, each unintended consequence creates another of its kind, all to the detriment of free actions being allowed to have their intended results. The outcome is a descending spiral of interventions with the eventual goal of each successive government step being to correct the negative effects of its previous action.

Friedman recognizes the delicate balance that must be maintained between freedom and power. Political power, no less than any other kind, corrupts those who hold it. Therefore, politicians must be limited in what authority is delegated to them. Ultimate power must be reserved for the people, in whom it resides by virtue of their choices expressed through voting. If governmental power is exercised according to democratic principles and kept under control by a system of checks and balances and frequent elections the relationship between the government and the governed remains healthy. If governmental power, expressed by elected representatives, is used for social engineering then government tells people how they should live their lives. Interventionist ideas such as income redistribution—one of the fundamental tenets of collectivism and state welfarism—are often claimed by means of political power to be necessary to achieve "justice." But

Friedman holds that this justice (in the equalitarian sense that everyone should have the same life) is in direct conflict with individual freedom. For Friedman true justice resides in the individual, not the collective. That life is uneven precisely because we are all individuals is self-evident. Human beings do not voluntarily choose the same life; why would we want to be forced to?

To Friedman, none of this is to suggest that a social safety net is either unwise or unjust. But to use an equalitarian and/or collectivist economic system to achieve a measure of protection for the less well-off while *denying* freedom to those who do not need or desire such protection, is at best naïve and at worst intellectually bankrupt and socially pernicious. Protecting those who cannot protect themselves is not only worthy, it is a fundamental human response. But Friedman (and many others who give the concept more than a moment's thought) understands that people will freely care for one another in the absence of the state's directed and controlled beneficence. And they will be driven away from that care as the state intrudes and claims dominion over the less well-off. Friedman's point is that protecting the freedom of those who *are* self-sufficient is as laudable *and honorable* as protecting the lives of those who are not.

In *Capitalism and Freedom*, Friedman addresses a range of topics, including the education monopoly (a life-long focus of Friedman's efforts), employment discrimination, labor contracts, price and rent controls, the gold standard, licensing, and income redistribution. Although some discussions may now seem dated, the philosophy and comprehension behind them is decidedly not. Friedman's stimulating presentation of his main economic concerns—the tyranny of the status quo brought about largely by redistributionist tax policies and the poverty of imagination in liberal political circles—still encourage the reader to ponder not just the issues in the book, but how to participate in the "big picture" as individuals. Friedman's methods and conclusions regarding the functions and responsibilities of government remain as valid as we move into the twenty-first century as when he voiced them almost half a century ago.

About the Author

MILTON FRIEDMAN was a senior research fellow at the Hoover Institution at Stanford University until his death in 2006, and a professor emeritus at the University of Chicago (from which he retired from active teaching at the in 1977). He won the Nobel Prize for economics in 1976 for his part in the study and extension of monetarist theory. Friedman was born in New York City in 1912 and relatively early in life he came to view economic and social freedom—understood in terms of the free market and secure rights to private property—as intertwined inextricably with broader personal freedoms. His career followed the evolution of this field of study.

He began his professional life in economics after obtaining a BA from Rutgers University, an MA from the University of Chicago, and a Ph.D. from Columbia University. He was one of the founders of the Mont Pelerin Society, the group that re-focused on classical economics in the vein of Adam Smith and helped debunk collectivist ideas at the conclusion of World War II.

Perhaps most notable regarding Friedman's efforts was his lifelong intense interest in education and educational policy. Friedman viewed the educational monopoly enjoyed by public educators and their teacher union cohorts to be one of the great "crimes" of the American experience. That he devoted so much effort to this nearly half-century passion requires that anyone who considers his life and accomplishments in the field of economics must also investigate why education was an equal enterprise in his journey (see <www.friedmanfoundation.org>). This is more than a worthwhile tangential effort for anyone interested in where education has been, or is going—and everyone should be.

26

The Roots of Capitalism

John Chamberlain

Originally published: 1959
284 pages

AS HIS BOOK attests, John Chamberlain loved America. He devoted much of his professional efforts to an explanation of the philosophy and machinery of modern capitalism, the foundation of America's freedom and security, so his readers could appreciate what we have created—good and bad. He became an expert in dissecting the connection between government and the free market: how we legislate and adjudicate, how we accomplish our duties and expand our opportunities, and most importantly, how the excesses of government we visit upon ourselves affect everyday lives.

In *The Roots of Capitalism*, Chamberlain investigates the origins of the entrepreneurial economic model and the free enterprise system. But he considers that paradigm as square two; he starts his discussion at a point *before* the issues of government or the free market arose. Like so many others, he begins with the premise that a free society must be predicated on a moral framework and an understanding of man's free will. Without a moral foundation and the freedom to *choose* to make it work, citizens in their ordinary lives cannot trust the system, nor are they likely to trust one another.

> To make any sense of the idea of morality, it must be presumed that the human being is responsible for his actions—and responsibility cannot be understood apart from the presumption of freedom of choice.

For Chamberlain, like Frank Meyer (*In Defense of Freedom* [Chapter 10]), if human beings do not have the option to make bad choices they will not understand the content, and necessity, of good choices.

After setting the stage with these fundamental premises Chamberlain analyzes the market on which a free society must be based. He demonstrates that a free market exists when free choice is exercised in both the application of labor and the disposition or acquisition of property. Without these freedoms we reel toward collectivism—embodied first in control of economic life, then dominion over our personal lives.

Yet, even before these freedoms can work together there must be a physical foundation, for man is a physical animal. That foundation is private property. Chamberlain engages in a root investigation of property, which he found to be the basis of liberty. (For an expanded account of this essential relationship see Richard Pipes's *Property and Freedom* [Chapter 11].) It is beneficial, as many of the authors studied in *First Principles* recognize, to return to the foundations of modern social relationships before examining their more complex interactions. For Chamberlain, economics was the study of the significance of ownership—"the right to dispose of [or acquire] a good or service."

If there be any question of the human impulse to ownership and the right to the free exchange of property Chamberlain gives stark examples of what people have historically risked for these basic entitlements. What he offers is a sketch of the conditions that slowly, but inexorably, led to the freedom we experience today—a freedom attained only with blood.

Chamberlain's model is eighteenth-century France where freedom of action was essentially destroyed by the arrogance of the monarchy and the "intellectuals" of the period, and virtually inflexible economic rules were put in place. The French had implemented over two thousand pages of regulations covering the textile industry, with dire consequences for those who ignored the precepts of the government. Yet people would still risk all for their perceived right to economic freedom. As Chamberlain recounts,

> For breaking [textile] regulations some 16,000 people were either executed or killed in armed brushes with government agents. And ... on a single occasion, seventy-seven people were sentenced to be hanged for breaking economic regulations, fifty-eight to be broken on the wheel, and six hundred thirty-one were sent to the galleys. Yet for the sake of "natural liberty" men continued to break the rigid mercantilist laws.

These brutal statistics found their genesis in the Enlightenment—a label that becomes an oxymoron when some of its effects are considered. The Enlightenment's foundation was rationalism, a process distorted by an excess of logic over experience. Essentially, rationalism contended that if the human mind could define a practical solution to the difficulties of human interaction, implementation was the only impediment to a more perfect world. The problem, of course, is that human beings are not always rational. It is not that we are wholly irrational very often, but our thoughts and hopes frequently do not mesh well with the surrounding real world. While this may be a minor inconvenience, the more important issue is that what is rational to one person can be insanity to another. Thus there was not and cannot be agreement on what might be the best course in any situation. Far more to the point, no one can know which course of action will ultimately prove most advantageous. This simple fact led to freedom of choice being the only reasonable method to arriving at best solutions for whatever problems arose (these best solutions will, as well, change over time as facts, imagination, and outcomes determine additional course changes).

The masters of France did not see it that way. If the resolution to circumstantial social and economic differences was only a matter of making a choice those in power would make the decision (often in a corrupt fashion—after all, they were only human, and French). This, of course, was nothing more than a dictatorship, or perhaps more accurately, a kleptocracy. However, no matter how directly and surely choices were made there were always those who disagreed and believed in their right to act on their disagreement. Perhaps most importantly, there is a more subtle and far more remarkable point to be found in the murderous statistics cited by Chamberlain. It relates not to the simplicity of the penalties (death in most cases, implemented to encourage adherence to the regulatory decrees) nor to the authoritarian reduction of choices to only what was commanded by those in power; it was found in the massive resistance expressed by the people in spite of the lethal punishments. Freedom of choice and action were more important, more core, to these citizens than their very lives.

The American experience of this era was the opposite of the European. The Founders of the U.S. constitutional system were wise enough not to fashion a blueprint for all social arrangements. They understood that freedom would open a pathway to choices that would bring us to functional, but varied, conclusions about how to make economic and political decisions. Chamberlain voices concern regarding how this approach had been insidiously undermined in modern times. For example, he believes that the federal government's regulation of the private sector under the auspices of the commerce clause in the U.S. Constitution has resulted in far more negative than positive consequences. This has been especially noticeable in the twentieth century, where such intervention is often effected through the courts as well as Congress. This continuing battle between government and the free market has changed both American society and the business climate to such an extent that the whole struggles to be recognizable as a market capitalism model anymore.

Chamberlain's commentary in *The Roots of Capitalism* contends that a sense of equalitarianism and political correctness (long before that term came to the fore) underlies melioristic government intrusion into the marketplace. It is enforced by means of the legal system—a system that operates in an economic vacuum and is often arbitrary and rarely evidences an understanding of the existence of vast vertical and horizontal market forces. Unless this process is reversed, eventually the market will become so skewed we will experience nothing but increased government intervention as each special interest or constituency makes its case—to the point of substantial economic contraction or even social instability.

Milton Friedman's comprehension of the effect of these government actions, delineated in *Capitalism and Freedom* (Chapter 25) and written contemporaneously with *The Roots of Capitalism*, is equally stark and apprehensive. He observes that government's eventual authoritarian form results in continued attempts to rectify by further legislation and judicial and bureaucratic intrusion that which had already been warped by previous attempts to control market sectors. These results were the inevitable consequence of what the courts and Congress had incrementally (and in theory, innocently) constructed. Chamberlain, like Friedman, holds that followed to its logical conclusion, such programmatic excesses as he witnessed in the 1950s would simply result in the disappearance of the free market as any sort of effective independent mechanism. That this has not happened to the extent Chamberlain feared is more a testament to American economic ingenuity and the massive size of our economy than any reluctance on the part of bureaucrats or politicians to intervene in our economic relationships.

As a business realist Chamberlain helps define how human beings express their motivations in the marketplace. He focuses on the continued striving of individuals to upend any equilibrium in the world of commerce (to their advantage, of course, but then obliquely to the advantage of the whole system) as they try to better their products, their prices, their sales, and themselves. In order for this atmosphere to allow each person to act as he deems fit, even to chase his dream, freedom and a free market must exist—with a minimum of government's direct interference and indirect meddling via regulations and bureaucratic overseers.

Chamberlain saw politics as it is—a game of power.

> In point of fact, political power is correctly to be defined as interference with social power.

It may be even more useful to reframe his proposition at its basic level and change Chamberlain's observation slightly to say, "political power is correctly to be defined as interference with social *rights*." Stated this way, the juxtaposition is more palpable, and perhaps more accurate. It isn't just that free citizens have social power; it is their rights to freedom of action and freedom of choice that are more sacrosanct—no matter how much actual power they possess. For a quite profitable and detailed investigation of Power—a topic that must be understood in all political and economic contexts—Bertrand de Jouvenel's *On Power* (Chapter 15) covers this subject from serf to king, citizen to president.

Chamberlain reserves some of his harshest criticism for government regulators who do not understand competition (which is both vertical and horizontal) and how it functions in conjunction with the imperative of freedom of action. Writing in the 1950s, he cites the competitive challenges to then-corporate behemoth United States Steel as an example. Chamberlain notes that U.S. Steel did, at one point, control some two-thirds of the domestic steel market. Federal regulators took note and salivated at the opportunity to dismember the company because of its dominant position. They could not, however, alter U.S. Steel's corporate structure or operations at the time because of various political, economic, legal, and social realities. It was fortunate that the regulators (who as do-gooders did not look so much forward as downward from their exalted perch as *public* servants) found themselves thwarted. What they might have done, to the detriment of the system—through the precedent that could have been set—was instead accomplished as it should have been, based on the facts as they evolved in a free-flowing and open market.

Lacking business acumen, or patience, the regulators neither understood nor sought to comprehend that U.S. Steel faced competitive pressures from four sources. Each of these sources was individually more threatening than all the government interventionists combined. Big Steel, as the company was known, battled the other one-third of the industry; it fought foreign competitors; it had to innovate as fast as specialty producers, who were improving products as quickly as finished sheets rolled off U.S. Steel's lines; and most importantly, it faced vertical competition from wood, plastics, other metals, and the new composites that researchers were developing. Within twenty years of the peak of its power U.S. Steel was on the ropes as a major producer of anything; within forty years the company had disappeared from the corporate landscape and the New York Stock Exchange, all without government tampering. Whatever the company's complacent and even presumptuous executives didn't inflict on U.S. Steel by failing to manage its workforce or modernize its facilities, the free market did. Big Steel was held up to the light by its competitors and found wanting and the free market "dismantled" U.S. Steel more thoroughly and decisively than the government ever could have hoped to.

The governing impulse, somewhat curbed in an earlier time, today enjoys much freer rein. What is frightening to American business is the government's markedly increased regulatory and administrative power to meddle. And, perhaps more harmful, is the changing of tax policy or the regulating premises mid-stream, so that the business owner, the consumer, and the taxpayer are prevented from planning with any certainty. This causes economic caution and reduces the impetus of those on all sides of the economic equation to assume risks (the consumer doesn't purchase, the producer doesn't manufacture, the entrepreneur doesn't invest or invent, the innovator doesn't experiment, etc.). The stifling effect on the economy is palpable and, over the long term, dangerous. Finally, it should be ironically apparent that there is only a random and small chance that ignorant and inexperienced legislators or government regulators, or even judges will impose workable, much less salutary, restrictions on the market.

Considering these circumstances, the suggestion arises that before we ask the government to manage anything else, let us first look at the results of what it has wrought in the past: public housing, public education, public health, and public transportation to mention a few. Chamberlain notes that government has historically been quick to step in, but slow to understand the market and even slower to step back once engaged. After all, government regulators have jobs to do and if they don't regulate something they cannot justify their existence. So they act. How Chamberlain would have cringed had he seen the government's case against Microsoft in 1999 and again in 2003.

In his book, Chamberlain does not shrink from attacking the sweeping notions of the collectivist society. As noted earlier, he observes that one regulated sector of an economy inevitably begets another; the conceit of government becomes operative through incremental, ostensibly innocent or even theoretically beneficial regulatory steps, until liberty is lost. In an avalanche each snowflake claims innocence.

Chamberlain's commentary foretells of government potentially *in extremis* when it takes its "omnipotence" seriously—an act which is itself the highest form of intellectual corruption. In *The Roots of Capitalism* one can foresee the progressive destruction of a society by reason of government incompetence, then corruption—as it tries to cover its tracks and defend its failures—resulting in increasing paternalism and equally intense resistance thereto. Eventually, government becomes paralyzed because of misguided policies that largely work against one another. The effects of unchecked intellectual corruption—an administration's increasing insistence that it is right as the evidence is ever stronger that it is wrong—lead to government that cannot do good or prevent bad. It is reduced to picking up the pieces of its last fiasco or putting out the fires created by its never-ending remedial efforts to fix what *it* has already broken—while blaming the market, the business person, or the public for its failures.

The downward spiral begins—always—in intellectual hubris, based first in ignorance, then arrogance, then power, and finally presumed omnipotence. Lest anyone believe that omnipotence is not claimed in American government—simply review the tax code, our educational mandates, our commercial or environmental regulations, or any of the other 10 million pages of federal edicts.

Although the modern regulatory state is portrayed as harmless as it insists on helping those whom the bureaucracy says cannot help themselves, or stops those whom it contends are harming the public, the effects of its programs are larger than their material or even philosophical content. They concern how we govern ourselves and what we think of ourselves and our lives. Those who don't understand the potential for violence or catastrophe when a populace is denied its liberty and property—through the incremental destruction of freedom portended in the ever-increasing nanny-state—will pay a price that is not yet imagined in America. Corruption can take many forms: the intellectual corruption of statist or "therapeutic" liberal endeavors intends benevolence, but in terms of human behavior, achieves an end far different from its goal. Left unchecked, such intrusions can grow in devastation equal to that experienced in the revolutionary histories so well documented by the authors reviewed in *First Principles*. The future that is seen by these authors—particularly that of John Chamberlain—is not a predictive insistence, but it is a caution founded in history and facts.

About the Author

BORN IN 1903, John Chamberlain attended Yale University where he acquired a taste for literature and literary pursuits and thereafter spent his life writing about things important to him. In 1932 he published his first book, *Farewell to Reform*, the story of American enterprise from 1880 to 1920. During the bulk of the Depression, in order to make a living, Chamberlain wrote a daily book review for the *New York Times*. But his true love was investigating the permutations of modern free-market capitalism and its partnership with individual liberty.

Chamberlain came to classical liberalism through a personal process, which he revealed in his autobiography *A Life With the Printed Word* (1982). Like many intellectuals of the 1930s he briefly flirted with socialism, but he was brought back to his devotion to classical liberalism when he read Albert Jay Nock's *Our Enemy The State* published in 1937. From the mid-1930s through the end of his career, the book reviews he wrote—probably the part of his career for which he was best known—along with articles for *Fortune*, *Life*, and numerous other publications, were combined with the publication of several more books. He served on the editorial staff of both *Fortune* and *Life* between 1936 and 1950. *The Roots of Capitalism*, perhaps his finest effort, was published in 1959. He was a longtime member of the American Conservative Union's board of directors. Chamberlain died in 1995.

27

Wealth and Poverty

George Gilder

Originally published: 1981, revised 1993
282 pages

PRIMARILY BECAUSE OF some spectacular individual failures, and despite three centuries of inspiring success, capitalism does not always engender warm, soft feelings in people. George Gilder opines that capitalism's deficiency in creating a positive emotional response is as much the fault of the observer's knowledge as it is of the system's defects. As proof of that, when *Wealth and Poverty* was first published and extensively reviewed, Gilder noted that "the central theme of the book had not been grasped, even by my closest intellectual allies in the conservative movement. Indeed it was missed by all the book's reviewers. This failure was so widespread I was forced to conclude it was ... my fault." In a second attempt to achieve his original purpose—a useful explication of modern capitalism and its effects on society—Gilder offers the updated edition synopsized here. The point of Gilder's experience, that even the most precise and succinct explanation of any theory or philosophy can be misconstrued or even wholly misunderstood if the public's mindset is at odds with its premise, is something skeptics of all hues should keep close in mind as they are asked to consider taking a road less traveled.

The principal intent of Gilder's effort in *Wealth and Poverty* is to investigate two aspects of modern economics: the logic, machinations, and rationale of private enterprise, and the effect of government on a free market system (with particular attention to taxation).

For Gilder, as for Adam Smith and all those who have honestly investigated competitive free-market economics, the core of capitalism is inherently (but not exclusively) self-interest. It is not greed in a negative sense, for if this were the heart of our capitalistic interrelationships neither consumers nor producers would be very interested in participating. Self-interest's beneficial essence is a form of mutual sustaining; "I will do well for myself if I do well by others."

Capitalism's engine is the division of labor. Its fuel is profit. Essentially no one, except those who choose to live on a primitive level, can create a self-sustaining life. This results in a need for personal and commercial cooperation.

As Gilder notes, the necessary variety of objects and services required in a modern economy is well supplied through the division of labor. In a free enterprise system after each person acts individually to create something of value (whether working alone or under the umbrella of a larger enterprise) he or she engages in "marketing" their skill or product. The free interaction with others who offer different skills and products establishes an "open" market where exchange is (essentially) uncontrolled. Each hopes to *profit* (in the broadest sense) by means of that interaction—the goal being to achieve a personal level of independence. Each wishes to become self-sustaining through mutually beneficial but primarily self-interested exchange.

Gilder offers the following in explaining Adam Smith's comprehensions:

> [I]t is not from the benevolence of the entrepreneur that we expect to profit, but from the interaction of each of us with regard to our own interests.

Enlightened self-interest, Smith's concept and phrase, is what makes the system work. The division of labor basic to capitalism results in everyone organizing coincidentally—not intentionally—and that unplanned cooperation becomes reciprocally beneficial simply by default.

Unfortunately, in offering his explanation Gilder uses the word "altruism" to define and explain the mutual cooperation and profit inherent in a successful capitalistic system. This word's modern meaning and use, "the practice or philosophy of devotion to the welfare or best interests of others," when utilized as an explanation of the foundation of capitalism, somewhat confuses the topic. It makes Gilder's larger point marginally more difficult for some readers to comprehend. Ludwig von Mises, in *Human Action* (Chapter 40), dissects the motivations behind capitalism and suggests that, in a market economy,

> Everybody acts on his own behalf; but everybody's actions aim at the satisfaction of other people's needs as well as at the satisfaction of his own.

Gilder's attempt to raise these motivations to the level of altruism, a word that connotes self-sacrificing subservience to the greater good of others, creates some ambiguity, especially in relation to the concept of profit, an equally integral part of capitalism. It is enough off the mark that it can foster an unease in the comprehension of his unquestionably valid point. If we "lower" the definition of capitalistic enterprise to express it as a community of interests, one's own and those of others, the essence of everyone's mutual efforts may be better understood.

As was noted earlier in this book, capitalism sometimes gets a bad reputation because of the actions of that small minority who actually operate *outside* its boundaries. This is an anomaly that deserves some attention. It must be stressed that such deviants as the crooked financier, the dishonest salesperson, the slick huckster, or the outright thief not only do not typify free enterprise, they operate in opposition to it. These parasites abuse the open market by contravening it. That these charlatans get as much press as they do skews the impression of capitalism to the detriment of everyone who participates honestly. This is particularly obvious when one considers that on any given day there are literally billions and billions of free-market transactions, all of which are fair and open and mutually benefiting to the parties who participate. The number of honest transactions so dwarfs the dishonest players that their marginalization—within the *system*, not with regard to the individuals affected—should be recognized. However, much to the detriment of society such recognition and perspective would not serve the needs of the media (who know better but do not, like an insolent teenager, act as though they do), so the actual size of the miscreant population is largely ignored or buried and media exploitation of their mostly trivial acts continues unabated. (Regarding the issues of both criminal activity and legally permitted yet unethical behavior that can take advantage of the public's ignorance and/or greed see *Wealth of Nations* [Chapter 12] and the introductory section to this book "Self-Governance in an Open Society.")

The successful entrepreneur is the person who realizes and acts on the fact that he must satisfy his customer by offering good value for a fair price, thereby ensuring repeated patronage and a solid reputation that will draw others to his products. As Gilder notes, the often-widespread misunderstanding of how the system works leads to negative reactions when we view capitalism out of its context. And the *context* of capitalism is people, not profit.

After defining capitalism's foundations, Gilder changes directions slightly and brings to the fore a little-noted economic reality. His observation had widespread political consequences, thus its importance yet today. His contention is that naked consumer demand is not the force that creates the free-market sequence of foresight, invention, production, distribution, sales, and consumption. Instead, he maintains that the process begins with the conjecture and ability of the risk-taking capitalist to create supply. If a product doesn't exist there usually isn't voluble clamoring that calls for its creation (think of in-vitro fertilization, Internet dating services, international air travel, or the internal combustion engine). The public's imagination is usually not that inventive. Instead, a new product or service appears pursuant to the efforts of a visionary producer who often risks all in the hope of capturing the consumer's heart. Without the creativity, efforts, and expertise of the producer and the support of capital financing formed out of someone's previous profits, there is no supply. This understanding—called supply-side economics—came into focus during the presidency of Ronald Reagan.

Gilder notes that a supply-side economy requires that incentives be in place to encourage the entrepreneur to take the risk to create something novel, improved, less expensive, etc., while in the bargain creating new jobs and hoped-for profits. As a free-enterprise system becomes over-regulated and subject to high levels of taxation (remember, if not controlled, government grows inexorably) there comes a need for adjustment to the tax system and the bureaucracy to allow the capitalist to see the advantages and potential success of attempting something new or different. Mostly that simply means lowering tax rates to free up funds that formerly went into government coffers. It also means reigning-in regulators who stifle both invention and competition because they do not understand enterprise as a concept, and whose administrative franchise has expanded over time for too many reasons to iterate here.

When taxes are lowered and remain low and without fluctuation capital becomes available to finance industry; new products, services, and concepts abound. (With regard to an unpredictable tax structure: the business person thrives on the certainty of government intentions and is cautious when government roots about for small changes that are usually political, and mostly ineffectual in increasing real revenue.) With lower taxes the economy expands—to everyone's benefit, but especially to the benefit of the government because increased economic activity brings in greater revenues than were collected before at the higher tax rates. This fact is one that must continually be brought to the fore as it is misrepresented often—from the city desk to the broadcast booth, from the political stump speech to the halls of Congress. But it is also a fact that must be understood in its details.

A diversion to politics is worthwhile at this juncture. In the thirty years since Gilder first offered his theories, political rhetoric in this arena has gone to extremes in almost every direction possible; yet there is still just one distinct issue with which we are dealing, viz., which economic design will best allow the free market and government to work together. Arthur Laffer is an economist who in the early 1970s conjured the Laffer Curve and publicly re-offered the common sense notion that as taxes are lowered economic activity increases (his insight had first appeared in economic writing as early as the fourteenth century). This results in increased revenue for the taxing authority when a larger economic footprint is taxed at lower rates. In 1961, when John F. Kennedy began his presidency, the highest marginal income tax rate was 91%. That means that above a certain income level the government took $9.10 of every $10 earned. A Democrat Congress, at Kennedy's urging, reduced the rate to 70%, and over the course of the next 20 years the mark was further lowered to 28%, and then raised and lowered again in the ensuing 30 years. It rests at 35% today (2008). During that five decade period the American economy experienced periods of both boom and bust. However, what is obvious to anyone who looks at the details is that what occurred in the economy at any given time was not solely the result of tax policy but was buffeted by many elements such as crises in oil prices, the beginning of stateless terrorism as a global reality, the massive increase in federal spending as a result of President Lyndon Johnson's Great Society programs, etc.

At the turn of the twenty-first century the political conversations regarding this subject are once again about the actual effects of lower tax rates. However, these conversations are sometimes disingenuously attempted in a false economic vacuum and are often presented in simplistic, black and white terms, which is unfortunate for the discussions but convenient for the politics. The fact is that tax rates and their effects and consequences, like any other aspect of government policy, are subject to a vast array of forces. Here are three of the basic issues (in exactly that political vacuum noted above) that determine whether lowering tax rates brings in more or less revenue to the government:

A. The rate in effect at the time lower rates are proposed and how much of a reduction is contemplated. Lowering the personal income tax rate from 91% to near or just above a 28% level increases economic activity and brings a net gain to the treasury (absent any significantly changed government or social circumstances). The massive strength of the American economy, known as the engine that pulled the world along for much of the last half-century (abetted by continually expanding free trade policies), is example enough of this proposition. Lowering the rate from 35% to 31% generally will not induce the same effect in the same measure, thus secondary considerations will also affect what happens. Lowering it from 35% to a flat rate of 19% would likely expand economic activity and increase tax revenues to a significant extent because of both the lower rate and the disappearance of tens of thousands of pages of tax regulations that also stifle the free market.
B. What taxes are being lowered. (The federal government currently imposes hundreds of different taxes and fees.) The area where the tax applies will determine how economic activity is affected and thus whether there is a net gain or loss of revenue. If capital gains taxes are lowered from 28% to 15%, as was done during the last decade, economic activity in that arena will increase dramatically and there will be a net revenue increase *in that sector*. If they are lowered from 18% to 15% the effect may actually be a net revenue loss—that is, there may be some increased activity but not enough to offset the 17% decrease in revenue that was generated at the former level of activity.
C. To what purpose the revenue is being put. If Congress lowers taxes but increases spending (usually as part of the political bargain that allows the lower rates to be implemented) because it expects greater revenue as a result of the reduced tax rates, the effect on the actual revenue stream may be doubly negative; first because the populace sees that the increased revenue is being used only to enlarge government (something

of which the voting public does not approve) and is not being applied toward reducing previously created debt; second, because when the dual realization hits home that government is not only going to get bigger, but past excess isn't going to be paid back, people will understand that the reduction in taxes can only be temporary. Their incentive to increase economic activity only to have that activity taxed more heavily in a few years is thus itself reduced, if not flattened or even reversed.

The political games being played today regarding the issue of taxation are far too complex to fully investigate by means of Gilder's book. Briefly, however, the following factions are vying for control: There are those in Congress who want to "starve the beast" of government by keeping taxes low so there is simply less money for government to spend. A second group will not stop spending even if there *is* less revenue, for spending is their key to continued political power. Each group intends to overwhelm the other, and both simply allow federal deficits to grow—in unconscionable amounts—while each blatantly seeks to force the other to succumb to fiscal blackmail to reduce the deficits they both created. This battle is pure power politics in its ugliest form.

There is an opposite question here as well, one also too broad for any serious consideration in this volume but which needs to be addressed even if only superficially. It asks what effect *raising* taxes has on the people, the market they operate, and government revenues—although based on real history the answers seem somewhat plain. The point is that lowering taxes doesn't automatically raise revenues any more than raising taxes does because there are too many other (mostly political) factors that have a strong effect on economic activity.

What's a body to do? As Jean Bodin observed in the sixteenth century, Rousseau noted in the eighteenth, and Wilhelm Röpke commented in the twentieth, we must design economic policy to fit mankind, we cannot expect mankind to conform to economic policy. The latter demand is simply a fool's errand, but one often undertaken by those who understand little about the human condition and even less about the free market.

There is a quite legitimate conversation that must take place regarding levels of taxation and realized revenues before sound policy can be implemented. However, that dialogue cannot occur in a milieu of accusation, or disingenuous black and white statements regarding complex calculations that involve both human nature and fiscal possibilities, nor can it occur where political goals are squarely in the way of anything resembling fair economic discussion.

The truth for Gilder is both plain and simple: low taxes, fewer regulations and less government intrusion into the free market result in greater economic activity, which will increase government revenues. Conversely, more of any of these elements reduces economic activity, and more of all of them makes a significant difference in how well the whole operates—and how much revenue the government receives. Yet, in this arena what will work best for the citizenry and its goals is now almost solely and unfortunately a political question. That means distortion, exaggeration, and indictment will abound—to the detriment of everyone.

As was noted in the introduction to this book, there were those at the Constitutional Convention in 1787 who were opposed to allowing the national government the power to tax. From our twenty-first century perch it is easy to see how well they knew of what they spoke. If we had left taxation to the states the competition among them to keep taxes low and thus attract and build economic opportunity would have kept legislatures within the bounds of reality. We know this is true because we see it happening currently in the U.S. as individual states try to attract business with favorable tax rates and structures. With no competition and a virtually unfettered power to tax (essentially no check or balance), the national government increases the revenue it can collect and its equal (or greater) unfettered ability to spend. It has become an entity over which the electorate has no control except that effected at the (now mostly ignored) ballot box. Of course, what America would or would not have become without the power to tax at the national level is an entirely different and equally broad query. As noted above, all of these issues are far too extensive for this treatise, but they *are* necessary elements, foundational elements, in determining how we tax, and govern, ourselves.

The are two further and equally consequential pieces in this puzzle: the real need to regain control of and eventually reduce government spending in order to keep the system itself viable, and the effects of fiscal deficits (incurred increasingly as tax revenues do not meet legislative mandates) on near and long term economic stability. The citizens of the United States, particularly the next three generations, now face somewhere between $30 and $47 trillion (not million or billion) in unfunded retirement, healthcare and other liabilities payable to ourselves. That is an untenable burden, but it exists. The only options to resolve what has been created are higher taxes and/or fewer services. Further federal deficits/debt will not adequately address this circumstance. Here is why: debt can only be created within reason because the market where future debt is to be sold will ultimately not participate as it becomes obvious that the paper being offered by the government has little chance of being repaid. As Ronald Reagan humorously but entirely accurately quipped when asked about the size of the federal debt during his presidency, "I'm not too worried about the deficit. It's big enough to take care of itself." What Reagan was observing is that the national debt can only grow as far as the market will allow; it cannot expand to whatever level the political class demands. That means real answers to political and fiscal questions will have to be found.

Unfortunately for our future generations, how the politics, much less the payments themselves, will be accommodated are large questions that are yet being ignored. The longer we let them fester, the worse will be the treatment—including real economic disaster or revolution by other than law and negotiation. These fiscal issues are called the third rail of electoral politics (meaning that any politician who tells the truth about them will be defeated if not tarred and feathered as anti-American) thus the lack of political will to address them. In simplistic fashion, increased taxes (generally on the "unlimited" resources of the wealthy) will be the first (political) response. Gilder's point in all of this is that tax increases are counter-indicated and would be fully inadequate to solve the problems created by unrestrained growth in government.

To return to the sub-point of this discussion: the increased federal income raised by Gilder and Laffer's model is intended to be used to reduce previously incurred government debt, or at the very worst, to stabilize government activity at its current levels and keep inflation in check; the revenue is not supposed to further increase the size of government. However, if those with political muscle see matters differently then government grows yet again. If an increased (largely unrealistic but politically expedient) government intrusion into society on the spending side is the result of the increased revenues, lower taxes will eventually only result in further deficits. It is important to understand that in the hands of some politicians the *lower taxes* get the blame for this effect, but they are decidedly *not* the cause, obviously the increased spending is. That such a link between lower taxes and increased debt is made at all is political dishonesty of the first rank.

All his adult life President Reagan recalled something he learned during the Depression: "We cannot spend our way to prosperity." Winston Churchill observed a like reality: "I contend that for a nation to try to tax itself into prosperity is like a man standing in a bucket and trying to lift himself up by the handle." We would all do well to recall both men's observations as discussions regarding fiscal issues come to the fore.

GILDER'S EXPOSITION of supply-side economics is more than just an attempt to create a climate where more revenue finds its way to the federal treasury. His real goal is to define how to change the culture of government itself by changing its foundations. Gilder is obviously aware that since the Great Depression the legislative process has been controlled by the liberal redistributionists of the Left, as well as other hand-wringers whose concern for the have-nots often does not extend beyond public posturing largely aimed at claiming a mantle of virtue. Gilder looks at social inequities and sees the need for something more than liberal efforts to tax wealth to level the playing field to make all of life equal. He knows that such actions are intellectual attempts to subdue both society and the economy, but that they instead cause incremental economic contraction on a broad scale and endemic destitution on the individual level.

Gilder observes that modern liberals seek melioristic if not socialistic results bought with capitalism's wealth. The negative consequences of simply taxing wealth as a solution to life's inequities are candidly and eloquently discussed in Bertrand de Jouvenel's *The Ethics of Redistribution* (Chapter 28) and Frederick Bastiat's *The Law* (Chapter 7). But, Gilder independently builds on the substance of both authors' observations, which coincide with his own. After exposing meliorism's premises, and failures, he (like Hayek and Freidman before him) addresses the fundamental fallacy of liberal tendencies toward redistribution that simply substitute one form of inequality for another.

Ultimately, inequality is intractable, a fact that percolates to the surface in almost all of the books presented in this colloquium. But inequality is as beneficial as it is universal, something liberals refuse to recognize publicly but ceaselessly take advantage of in their political maneuvers. Inequality's beneficial effect comes to the fore in the genius, drive, imagination, fearlessness, and dedication of each individual who has created the world's wealth, raised the standards of living, and done all of the labor required to make dreams come true—from those in the mine shaft or on the shop floor, to those in the laboratory or boardroom. As these truths have gained public recognition, "solving" inequality in the twenty-first century has been less and less the object of surmise of social philosophers. These philosophers have begun to understand the benefit to society of recognizing inequality's overwhelming positive contributions, not just its sometimes-negative image in the wrong politician's hands.

Of course, using superficial allegations of inequality as a populist ploy has not left the repertoire of the politically starved or the demagogues who seek to achieve power by embracing specious economic policies and goals. Gilder precisely dissects the programs of these self-aggrandizers, while coincidentally giving substance to economic realities that will allow a rational approach to the benefits of a supply-side market economy.

Gilder's conclusion, that any attempt at redistribution of wealth always results in further inequity (especially for those whose resources are being redistributed) is inescapable. But he is equally ready to offer that some redistributive *assistance* is both justified and essential in the twenty-first century. For Gilder—as for most *First Principles* authors who address the economically less well-off—this assistance should as often as possible be privately constructed and administered, as it was during the ten thousand years prior to the mid-twentieth century. If aid is directly fostered by local agencies (where those who give and those who receive can observe what is working and what is not) the public component cannot as easily grow, nor can it as easily drive out private initiative—which is invariably more effective, nimble, and less expensive than government subsidies. Above offering help on a basic level, the premise that government redistribution is fairer than free economic interplay is simply false, despite its prominence in many a left-leaning political campaign. In the end, the only real commodity to distribute is opportunity.

Gilder takes this insight slightly afield from merely examining capitalism. He finds that any economic configuration—not just free enterprise—results in inequality. The nature of the free market and the foundation of its ultimate utility is that it is transparent. This allows everyone to equally understand its operations and make decisions in their own best interest. Natural cause and effect are overt and the inevitable inequality isn't simply the arbitrary result of bureaucratic or legislative caprice, political influence peddling, or even populist or dictatorial whim.

Gilder finds that after the market has met the essential needs of all members of society—sparingly and rationally abetted by various forms of both public and private social safety nets—each person must engage the system on his own. Government should only be allowed minimal intervention to ensure fair play. He notes that we are first *individually* responsible for what happens to us, so that government should not have to intrude in our efforts and relationships on more than a very basic level. Given a moment's thought, that's pretty much what all of us want anyway, because pride and self-esteem are basic components of human nature. In this vein see Charles Murray's *What It Means to Be a Libertarian* (Chapter 19).

Of course, determining where government should be further involved is where much disagreement arises. Conservatives argue that additional government interference beyond what is described above would simply recreate inequity. Liberals, through both their rhetoric and their programs, contend otherwise. They appear to purposely ignore the harm done to the whole system when the energy of capitalistic impulse—better termed the human spirit—is suppressed through redistributive taxation and ignorant or even foolish regulations. All of these skew the market, invite both the law of unintended consequences and corruption to blossom, and cause social devolution toward the culture of dependency in those oppressed by paternalistic government.

Wealth and Poverty arrived on the *New York Times* Best Sellers list and came to be called "the bible of the Reagan revolution." President Reagan had been telling the public that government could raise revenues by cutting taxes, thus freeing the economy from high levies while maintaining government services on an even level. At the time, as this seemed an inherent contradiction even though it was historically a given (every federal tax cut from Presidents Coolidge to Kennedy had resulted in increased government revenue by means of increased economic activity), people bought Gilder's book to have the riddle explained. The answer was simple and hardly revolutionary. In addition to what has been noted previously in this synopsis, Gilder also observes that as lower taxes revitalize entrepreneurship numerous additional changes occur, especially higher rates of employment. Gilder examines how capital migrates from tax shelters to more productive investments; why tax avoidance declines; finally, he observes that individuals previously disengaged from the job and capital markets re-enter them because opportunities abound. As a direct consequence of higher levels of employment, *a reduced need for government assistance* results. As government now costs less it needs to tax less.

This simple cycle has to be reinvented and reinvented and reinvented because liberal demagogues insist on penalizing the "rich" with high taxes (as though they had done something venal in creating the various aspects of our prosperity), thereby driving down tax revenues, drying up the supply of capital needed as fuel for economic activity, and creating exactly the reverse economic result from what they intend. One of the main reasons this result ensues is that although the tax rhetoric is aimed at the wealthy, the reality is that such schemes invariably must be applied to the top half of income earners—who currently pay 97% of all income taxes—in order to have their supposed effect. Clearly the liberal attitude of "let the wealthy pay for it" is both counterproductive and not what happens when tax rates are raised. As Gilder explains, the alternative offered by supply-side theory looks not just attractive, but obvious as well. If tax policy is to be discussed rationally it must be done in terms of economic activity, not individuals or a class of people, or social goals. Economics as a craft creates opportunity, politics as a methodology most often does the opposite—it wants to effect control.

American liberals beginning with the last half of the twentieth century were like their pro-Communist "intellectual elite" forebears of the 1930s and 40s who sought wholly equalitarian goals. In both cases, the mistake was that of arguing against human nature, especially the principle of individual incentive that is the foundation of economic success. This error was often not an honest one. Populist political speech, no matter how disingenuous or unsupported by facts, was simply too useful to demagogues seeking to be elected or re-elected. Sadly, the economic illiteracy of the citizenry abetted the office-seekers in this enterprise. This fact won't be changed easily—that is human nature—thus vigilance is the tool, if not weapon, of choice in the ongoing battle surrounding the free enterprise system.

In *Wealth and Poverty* Gilder is especially hard on the post-World War II liberal economists, particularly those who attempted to justify the free lunch of President Lyndon Johnson's Great Society. These "experts" pontificated in the service of liberal politicians who instituted programs that failed in the face of human realities. Gilder notes that populist and pessimistic economists such as Lester Thurow and John Kenneth Galbraith put forth a weak argument in favor of government control of the economy. Their premise was that the human race had "seen its finest hour and that the future looked bleak," and that government's centralized control was needed to create any chance of economic stability. To expose this kind of narrow pessimism one needs only to step back to secure an historical perspective. Optimists like Reagan did just that. Spurred on rather than daunted by modern challenges, they were optimists because they appreciated what people had done in the past and saw what they could do in the future. The history of the human spirit makes negative contentions such as those of Galbraith and Thurow look particularly paltry and even silly. The economic history of the world since they offered their views and theories at mid-century makes them look like something even less.

How and where wealth will originate (if only so it can be taxed) if there is no mechanism in place to create it is a question liberals never ask, much less answer. The question appears not even to have occurred to them. The political success of 1960s liberals bred hubris and led to an almost complete inversion of economic truth. They thought simply because they had been elected that their programs would work; however, voter validation is often a bad test of free-lunch economics. The destructive economic and social force of President Johnson's Great Society programs, and, by inference, the confiscatory tax policies and deficit spending necessary to support them, was individually deconstructed by former New York Senator Daniel Patrick Moynihan when he was assistant secretary of labor in the early 1960s. His 1965 report, *The Negro Family: The Case for National Action* (the premise of which was that welfarism did more to destroy families than encourage them), abetted the social sea change that culminated in the unprecedented political ascendancy of conservatives by the end of the twentieth century. Yet, as Gilder observes, such "intellectuals" as Galbraith are still given room for their diatribes in the popular press because liberals simply refused to brook any argument debunking their theories no matter how much experience has shown them to be bankrupt.

As he approaches the end of his discussion, Gilder dissects inflation, perhaps the most dangerous effect of bad government policy. Inflation has many elements, and the details and permutations of inflationary theory and practice cover a range too broad for substantive discussion in a synopsis such as this. But Gilder wants the reader to have more than a passing acquaintance with the subject. He devotes a chapter to the evolution of inflationary assumptions and follows inflation's history from John Maynard Keynes's assertions that tax increases don't cause inflation (they do), to the effects of deficit spending (also highly inflationary).

In the modern era it has become clear that inflation is caused principally by government's inappropriate expansion of the money supply, effected almost invariably to cover deficits created by legislative largesse. The unfortunate part is that fiscally illiterate politicians often do not see, or do not want to see, the connection between their actions and economic distortions, distortions that almost invariably act to the great detriment of the participants at the lower end of the economic scale. This, of course, fits nicely, albeit paradoxically, into the goal of raising taxes in the first place—so the government has more revenue to help the disadvantaged—a group the legislators have conveniently enlarged by their very actions. Unfortunately the pool of resources to aid this enlarged population has shrunk with equal vigor as tax increases stifle economic activity.

As Gilder makes clear, the government's deficit expenditures ultimately must be made good via myriad inflationary practices: generally new or increased or even hidden taxes; or through the expansion of the money supply; or through the sale of government debt (with accompanying repayment of principal and interest that requires even more inflationary tax revenues), or with bankruptcy. Government spending is not and has never been an effective answer to either a faltering economy or grand schemes of "social justice" because the expenditures must be paid back sometime, someplace, somehow. That requirement invariably generates a less, not more, robust economy.

A weak economy is made strong by increased economic opportunity, never by increased government; when an economy is strong, economic and social justice are achieved on their own terms, not by redistribution of society's income. Yet inflationary government policies are always a convenient political solution and are seen as a quick fix—which they might actually be in the short term and the narrow view—thus their siren song is ever-inviting to the political class. But, in the long term, the quick fix has to be paid for by otherwise productive dollars taken from the remaining citizens whose opportunities are thus reduced, as is the power of the economic engine those citizens drive. (For further discussion of the negative consequences of short-term solutions to long-term problems, see *Economics in One Lesson* by Henry Hazlitt [Chapter 24] and *The Theory of Money and Credit* by Ludwig von Mises [Chapter 34].)

Gilder's theories and prescriptions in *Wealth and Poverty* make sense because he bases them on human nature not wide-eyed and idyllic Enlightenment-era "rationalism." Human inventiveness and the economic rules of incentives and risks are his guideposts. Although no theory in its execution can be without side effects and dead ends, supply-side free-market economics seems more sensible and offers hope for more progress than does any rationalization for government intervention and control.

About the Author

BORN IN NEW YORK CITY in 1939, George Gilder attended Exeter Academy and Harvard University. While at Harvard he studied under Henry Kissinger and helped found *Advance*, a journal of political thought that he represented in Washington, D.C. after his graduation in 1962. Four years later he co-authored *The Party That Lost Its Head*, a profile of Republicans in turmoil. He later returned to Harvard as a fellow at the Kennedy Institute of Politics and as editor of the *Ripon Forum*. In the 1960s, Gilder served as a speechwriter for various officials and candidates, including Nelson Rockefeller, George Romney, and Richard Nixon.

In the 1970s, as an independent researcher and writer, Gilder began an inquiry into the causes of poverty; this research resulted in his writing several books, including *Wealth and Poverty*. He pioneered the formulation of the theories of supply-side economics while serving as chairman of the Lehrman Institute's Economic Roundtable, as program director for the Manhattan Institute, and as a frequent contributor to the A.B. Laffer economic reports. After the publication of *Wealth and Poverty* he consulted regularly with key figures in the Reagan and first Bush administrations. Gilder is presently a Senior Fellow at the Discovery Institute in Seattle.

28

The Ethics of Redistribution

Bertrand de Jouvenel

Originally published: 1952
91 pages

FUNDAMENTAL COMPREHENSIONS develop as people navigate the millions of words and tens of thousands of books, essays, speeches, and studies on the subject of self-governance. This doesn't guarantee that such knowledge will be uniformly applied, or perhaps applied at all, but one hopes it will continue to be part of honest, ongoing conversations.

By way of example, less than a decade after the Second World War ended, as the long-term economic and social consequences of the growing welfare state became plain, significant political and economic discussions ensued. Many treatises on this subject were written then, and during the next quarter century. Bertrand de Jouvenel's short study of the effects of economic redistribution on both society and the individuals of which it is comprised is an elegant and valuable contribution to this discourse.

Redistribution encompasses the welfare state in its greater form, but stops short of fully embracing socialism or communism. The redistributionists seek to achieve socialism's goals using capitalism's wealth. The progression is as follows: First, in the early stages of capitalism, free-market gains allow private enterprise and private charity to support those who cannot help themselves (the eighteenth century). Second, as an economy becomes more successful and means are found to tax that success, government programs come into being, and those who cannot see to their own care are supported by the state through a social safety net. This is a political act, as benign as it may initially appear (the nineteenth century). Third, as the social safety net expands, incrementally, into the welfare state—where public assistance grows beyond essential levels, primarily for political reasons—a culture of dependency is fostered, unintentionally at first, but eventually callously. As well, the welfare state drives private charitable efforts away thus opening the window even further for increased state beneficence (the twentieth century). Fourth, as the welfare state reaches its final stages, equalitarian goals are seen as possible, and redistribution becomes a barren political tool. The realities of fiscal, psychological, and overall social costs are pushed to the back and political meliorism becomes the only measure of value (the twenty-first century).

Extreme welfarism, termed redistribution, embraces high rates of taxation, leveled directly on the entrepreneurial class for the purpose of redistribution of profits to the less well-off. However, it achieves goals that are the antithesis of its intentions. It kills the geese laying the golden eggs (entrepreneurs creating profits that can be taxed) and destroys the character of the society it attempts to make better. Governmental redistribution of a free-enterprise economy's products is one of the particular cases where human folly is almost perfectly camouflaged as human compassion and ingenuity.

De Jouvenel does not attempt to support his criticism of redistributionist programs with a mass of graphs or charts. His point is not just that redistribution doesn't achieve its stated economic goal or its unstated emotional objective, but that it does something more significant—it changes society and its free-market underpinnings in an unseemly and ultimately untenable manner, through attempts to alter or even defy human nature. De Jouvenel discusses the morality of redistribution not just as it relates to individual incentive or self-reliance—this had been done by many authors—but as it affects human society and culture by distorting macroeconomic realities.

Since the Great Depression, government has gravitated toward a central role in the remission of poverty thanks to liberal political activity. This has often pushed out community-based, private efforts. De Jouvenel observes that over the same period liberals have disguised as an intellectual precept their quasi-religious judgment that economic inequality is "intolerably unjust." It should be noted, however, that contrary to the liberal assertion of capitalism's putative injustice, the free-enterprise system (when joined with an open society and the rule of law) actually generates a higher standard of living at its base than has any totalitarian, centrally-planned, or even redistributionist economy operating at its highest potential. And, although the living standard measure is certainly one of the pillars of a "just" society—it is not the only one. In other words, there is more proof of the folly of the redistributionists. There is the issue of a nation's character, the impetus of the people toward charity and assistance that is in effect until government efforts push such actions aside and trivialize them.

While a free system of economic interaction necessarily results in inequalities (as does any collectivist or other centrally directed system—and a redistributionist system must, by definition, be centrally directed), almost all of them are positive and beneficial as is demonstrated by the far higher level of social and economic advancement achieved by the free economies. These inequalities are a matter of degree and are based on intrinsic differences between human beings—in other words, they are the result of normal human interaction. Most important of all, these differences are accepted, even embraced, by society as individuals see opportunity for themselves, or especially their children; the variations are not judged to be destructive or demeaning. (For additional discussions of inequality itself—a heavily freighted and oft-abused term—see Friedrich von Hayek's *The Road to Serfdom* [Chapter 13], Milton Friedman's *Capitalism and Freedom* [Chapter 25] and in particular, Richard Weaver's *Ideas Have Consequences* [Chapter 35].)

De Jouvenel comments on those who would tax the wealthiest citizens, siphoning off their "excess" income in an essentially confiscatory fashion for redistribution to the less well off. These theorists assume that the "surplus" dollars in the hands of the affluent would bring little additional joy, comfort, or substance to their lives, but would substantially improve the existence of the less fortunate. In essence, they believe that skimming from the top of the economic scale to shore up the bottom would result in a more balanced distribution of essential comforts. However, giving to some what has not been earned by them is an effort fraught with far more bad consequences than good—as has been seen in Frederick Bastiat's *The Law* (Chapter 7). There is also in such distributions an inconvenient punitive reality for society's more productive members. As redistributionist efforts gained traction the discussion of this aspect of their plans was to be set aside for substantive consideration at another time—a time that has yet to arrive in liberal circles.

The problem with the liberal's equation, as de Jouvenel succinctly explains, is that redistributing the "excess" income of the rich would not begin to substantially improve the economic circumstances of the economically less well off, much less society as a whole. The mathematical reality is that while the wealthy have excess resources, as a group even they do not have a level of income that matches the designs of the redistributionists. The economic fact is that 97% of all U.S. income taxes (2005) are already paid by those in the *middle* and upper class (those who earn at or above the median income). Those who earn below the median income—50% of earners—pay only 3% of all income taxes. In order to make the lower half of income earners equal to the upper half virtually all income of the upper half would have to be redistributed.

De Jouvenel directly observes the point to be made—the redistributionists do not stop when they've helped those who cannot help themselves, they intend to level the fundamental economic circumstances of society *en masse*. Here redistribution diverges from the social safety net and expands broad-based welfarism beyond what is economically tenable. The reason for such expansive redistribution is simple—it is how the demagogues expect to get public approval for their plans and reelection for themselves in the bargain—by including everyone on the gravy train who isn't deemed "rich."

In the determination of the redistributionists, society's "excess" wealth is essentially all wealth above the average. Thus, the amount of money that would have to be collected to achieve this goal would mean increasing taxes all the way down the economic ladder to the heart of the middle class, a move that would change that group's lives in an ultimately unpopular manner. De Jouvenel comments,

> The idea that sums which pass out of the State's hands come from above is true as regards only a very minor fraction; and it serves to obscure the fact that for the most part the buying power which is redistributed comes out of the same social layers as receive it.

Aside from the fact that redistributionist math doesn't work, and neither the U.S. Treasury's calculations nor those of the most liberal Marxist accountant can change it, the lives of all members of a society—rich, poor, or middle class—are altered when economic equality is attempted through redistribution. De Jouvenel offers basic observations to explain these changes.

The first and most obvious effect is that when high incomes are substantially reduced through taxation, culture, the arts, education, public service and public charity essentially disappear as personal initiatives because there remains little or no discretionary income left to support them. The second and more important change is in regard to the depletion of capital needed for investment, or public improvements, or any other purpose. Capital and its resultant profit are what drive *any* economy. The third, and most profound effect on both the economy and the citizenry, is the destruction of incentive. If there is no incentive (no matter what level of society is being considered) there is—nothing.

If accumulated (or "excess") profit is taxed away and redistributed, the only alternative to replace private funding for entrepreneurial and cultural objectives—efforts that will not be given up easily by the public—is the government. But governmental intervention in either the market or cultural initiatives invites dire consequences. Without offering extended examples of what would eventuate in those circumstances one has only to consider the inefficiencies and intellectual corruption and incompetence of political/bureaucratic oversight already extant in our own federal and state governments to know what would eventuate if more power vis-à-vis the economy was turned over to public and/or political control.

Unfortunately, after tax rates had been raised to actually allow equalization of (lower) living standards, more and larger regulatory agencies would need to be established to manage the redistributionist mandates. This would require government budget increases, so taxes would almost immediately need to be increased again across all but the lowest income levels. This would even further stifle incentive, or the ability to act on opportunity because the capital that used to be created through private activity (largely from the savings of the roughly eighty percent of Americans who are the members of the middle class) would have disappeared, so additional taxes would be needed to create capital for investment. The capital pool, however, would be directed and controlled by bureaucrats, and the judgment, much less the competence, of government employees with so much power would justifiably be questionable.

The problem in any redistribution scheme is that extreme taxation suffocates initiative and entrepreneurial activity. When prospective gains from productive efforts face confiscation and redistribution, the entrepreneur's incentive is eliminated. Economic activity eventually comes to a standstill, for a time, and then it begins to reverse. We ultimately arrive at a terminal condition that is not just predictable, but inevitable: equality at the bottom. Real-world examples of this scenario were seen in the Soviet Union until it collapsed under fiscal burdens it could not support, are currently in evidence in North Korea (where the population has been reduced to mass starvation) and Cuba, and are equally observed in China, where a cultural battle (between a government that professes a belief in de-incentivized equalitarianism and a populace that does not) may eventually break into a civil conflagration.

De Jouvenel notes that governmental schemes for wealth redistribution maim and then subvert the sense of social responsibility and even the human connectedness that constitutes the social bond. As personal involvement in our own lives is degraded through governmental direction and control, our personal sense of worth is undermined, as is each person's sense of his unique value to society. The standard of living gets lower and lower because there is less and less income to tax so a greater percentage of income must be taken just to keep even. As de Jouvenel comments, not only do we *not* eliminate poverty through redistribution, we actually institutionalize it, and then expand it. Supervision of wealth's redistribution demands continued interference with individual freedom, with negative consequences too broad to enumerate—and the povertization of all aspects of life: economic, cultural, educational, social.

De Jouvenel comments regarding why redistribution retains any credibility in the face of hundreds of years of free-market economics and thousands of years of experience in the machinations of human nature. He notes that all of those who consider that income redistribution will work assume two facts: First, everyone will agree on the method and level of redistribution and the level and degree of taxation. Second, the level of productivity in society will not be affected by such redistribution. On its face, neither assumption is valid. And if neither is valid, the results obtained will be individually unjust in the first instance and calamitous to society's standard of living in the second.

At the outset of his discussion, de Jouvenel summarizes both the history of equalitarian economic methods and the goals of liberal thinking. He notes that redistribution is not exactly the stepchild of socialism for redistributionists do not want to dismantle capitalism or the free market; they do, however, want to achieve socialism's objectives. Their ambition is to take the profits from those who produce goods and services—and who presumably spend them frivolously—and give those profits instead to those who have not fared as well. This approach represents a purely emotional response to the inevitable inequalities of an economy based on free human activity—a response that attempts to make liberals feel better about some of the unavoidable, and valuable, differences among people in terms of talent, intelligence, and ambition, but succeeds only in making everyone feel worse about the results.

Perhaps more importantly, redistribution also denies the dignity of labor—all labor. It concentrates on fiscal results, not on the content of any individual's life. It fails to recognize, much less comprehend, that inherent differences in ability and gifts are the foundation of life—and that those differences are not "unfair." Even if they could be termed such, bureaucratically compensating for differences in every individual's life would involve judgment, not math. In that circumstance dissatisfaction with public intuition as to what is fair would be more certain than the existing presumed dissatisfaction with life as it is.

On the other side of the equalitarian coin, human beings are perfectly aware of the *benefits*, to themselves and to society in general, of the inequalities among people (otherwise why would they pay to hear someone other than their mother-in-law sing, or build them a car, or perform their open-heart surgery?). What the redistributionists forget is how we will feel when the desirable differences of society and culture are eliminated and economic opportunity overall diminishes simply for lack of fuel; as Wilhelm Röpke observed, the fuel of any economy is profit. When profit is debased through extreme taxation, it descends the path leading to its extinction. The end result is an ignoble existence for all of society.

A point should be noted as one travels through the "inequalities" of an open society: often, modern demagogic disquisitions on income variations focus on the "rich" and the "poor," and emphasize the gulf between them. These speakers, for political purposes, talk only in terms of black and white. What they intentionally ignore is that the vast majority of the developed world's population lives in society's economic middle ground, not at the extremes.

The intent of the social revisionists is to convince the middle class of two things—that they are poor, because they are not "rich," and that this circumstance is the "fault" of the wealthy. These tactics are mostly not well received by the largely educated middle class in America, but they can bear fruit among the less educated elsewhere. Class warfare, so often attempted as a tactic in U.S. politics, has never fared well because of overwhelming evidence that economic status is not static. In fact, there is unrestricted social and economic mobility, and the American standard of living belies any portrayal of most citizens as being poor. Finally, and perhaps most importantly, the American ethic of earning one's place, one's bread, and one's success is ingrained in our cultural experience and not easily dislodged by promises of equalitarianism.

De Jouvenel observes that redistribution can appear superficially attractive, in part, because of the media's distorted focus regarding the lifestyle of the wealthy. This small but now highly visible cadre of moneyed persons (allegedly given to cavorting in remote resorts, driving outrageously expensive automobiles or jet airplanes, and conspicuously consuming high-priced items in myriad variety) is the perfect foil for the demagogues. All of this, of course, is simply the media feasting on frivolity.

The focus on admittedly ostentatious displays of wealth conveniently ignores what the very well-off do with the vast majority of their income. The portion that they cannot spend, they *invest*. (And let us not forget, the spending and consumption by the wealthy has its own positive multiplier effect on the economy.) Whether in new companies or new ideas or in pools of capital that others may use to create more opportunity, the "excess" income of the wealthy is invariably put to work improving one thing or another. It also goes toward private funding of the cultural, public-service, and educational initiatives previously mentioned. This money does not sit idle inside some mattress. If this wealth, transformed to capital, is taxed away through redistributionist schemes, the reserve of assets available to the economy is less. At that point the economy simply produces less, and that changes everything—not just the comfort level of one group or another.

Apropos of the supposed case against the wealthy, de Jouvenel observes:

> It is well known that "the people" are less critical of the high-living than [are the intellectuals]. . . . [W]hile it still seems right to give [to the less well-off], the rightness of taking away [from the economically successful] is far less obvious.

When contemplating the media's exploitation of the superficial entertainment value of the whimsical minority of the affluent, it is seen simultaneously that the so-called intellectual elite experience a judgmental abhorrence of conspicuous consumption (other than their own). The basis for this is found in envy, or righteousness; the latter is sometimes even obliquely or inadvertently admitted by those intellectuals engaged in judging. The public does not often share the intellectuals' distaste, as de Jouvenel notes.

As was observed earlier, class warfare has never been a successful political tactic in America because parents in each generation expect their children to be more successful than they were, or at the very least, to have more opportunity. Therefore, to advocate eliminating the ability to move up in the world (through the roadblock of redistributive taxation) or even to imply that each generation cannot be more self-sustaining, more successful, and more secure, is antithetical to parental goals for their offspring. It is essentially an insult to parents and children alike—and is also contrary to the economic and social history of free-market economies the world over.

De Jouvenel's point that redistribution is not socialistic in means but is in terms of ends, merits emphasis. Redistribution's guiding light is meliorism. Under socialism ownership of private property is essentially to be eliminated, the good will of all people toward one another is expected, and eventually we are all to get along so well that the state becomes unnecessary and withers away. These were the premises of the 1789 French Revolution. But, under redistributionist schemes, the state has never withered away. It not only hasn't withered away, it has become more obtrusive (even though its intention was to become *less* necessary) in the private *and* public sectors as it strives to regulate the distribution of assets, presumably *without* the voluntary consent of all parties. The emotional foundation of the impulse to achieve equalitarian results, as de Jouvenel intones, rests on a simple theoretical precept:

> The rich would feel their loss less than the poor would appreciate their gain.

As long as the argument is presented in personal terms (that is, as long as we consider specific individuals whom some think have too much money, and some who do not have enough) this contention's immediate logic and appeal can appear obvious and to some individually arguable. But when the discussion moves to a larger forum, to the society itself, then as de Jouvenel points out, income redistribution proves to be immoral, for in practice it would erode the quality of life across all economic and social strata. The resulting government structure, essentially totalitarian in nature, would ultimately collapse of its own burdens for the simple reason that it is irreconcilable with human nature. At the point of collapse, we would start all over again, man versus man, for as de Jouvenel notes:

> democracy is a regime of well-regulated strife where force is made to prevail without violence.

But when democracy fails, because people no longer accept its redistributed fruits as a rational manner of governance or economics, then violence resumes, as it inevitably must whenever social life goes backward too far. Intellectual violence occurs initially, with something more serious following eventually. (For a discussion of governmental power in a democracy and how that power increases in the name of the people as participation in the electoral system becomes near universal, see de Jouvenel's *On Power* [Chapter 15].)

Interestingly, de Jouvenel initially acknowledges only in a footnote that what occurs first in the transfer of wealth is the redistribution of *authority*, not just resources, from the individual to the state; yet this is the essence of his intellectual calculations. If the state takes from some and gives to others, the state will have to arbitrarily make fifty economic, social, and political decisions with regard to what it (not the individual) now controls. The resulting fifty determinations will generate five hundred more questions, ad infinitum, all to be settled by bureaucrats who have no stake in their answers. These public servants work their hours, return home, and think (if they are arrogant) or hope (if they are humble) that they've made the right decisions. They won't know they've got things terribly wrong until they stand on the gallows in a social upheaval. They will suffer, not because they taxed away people's resources, but because they stole everyone's freedom.

What we witnessed over the course of the twentieth century, as de Jouvenel observes, was the corruption of political institutions by means of legislation that discriminated among citizens. When it is understood that redistribution will not work to effect the desired result, that it not only doesn't make life better, but makes it much worse, it will also be understood that

> [t]he error must then lie in the original assumption that incomes are to be regarded solely as means to consumer-enjoyment. . . . [and] the ideal of income equality is, then, seen to fail by the two standards: justice as between individuals, and social utility.

Income obviously has purposes other than for consumption, and to use it as the exclusive means to address raising the standard of living for some people—whose reason for being "disadvantaged" may or may not relate to their economic circumstances—seems a poor bargain. This is especially germane considering that simply giving people money has historically proven to have more negative (personal and social) consequences than positive. Income redistribution creates contradictory effects and costs that are incalculable except in hindsight. To ignore these results while aiming at emotional or even righteous satisfaction is why, for example, America's War on Poverty has failed to change virtually anything for society as a whole or the conditions of the social stratum at which it is aimed. It has only made government bigger—certainly not better.

De Jouvenel recognized that living is a social process, and that feeding, clothing, and housing oneself are merely support mechanisms. When the benefits of and the opportunities to engage in the social process are limited, the social life and the individual's vitality are diminished. The greater the economic opportunity, the greater is the social life, but that life is rife with inequality. This is a fact of existence, the reality of which we have accepted for millennia. To try to eliminate inequality through political maneuvering is to beg the law of unintended consequences to become the basis of social interaction. What we must continually recall is that most of life's inequalities are far more beneficial than derogatory of mankind's existence.

Perhaps de Jouvenel's most optimistic observation comes toward the end of his dissection of income redistribution schemes. While discussing the history of taxation and the typical insistence of rulers that they "know best the common interest, which the individual, sunk in his selfish pursuits, cannot perceive," he notes the silver lining in such arrogance:

> Indeed, the subject's dislike of taxation has been the means of turning him into a citizen.

Reflecting one of the themes of *First Principles*, de Jouvenel also warns that "[a] society of sheep must in time beget a government of wolves." We do, indeed, need far more citizens than subjects to ensure that the state, and the political class (by means of their own miscalculations or misunderstandings) do not destroy a social and economic structure that is the best chance for providing the highest standard of living for all of its citizens. In *The Roots of American Order* Russell Kirk succinctly states, "economic leveling is not economic progress." As the state becomes stronger, individuals become weaker, not only in relation to the state, but in real terms as human beings. This is because, as Kirk further observes, we no longer have those "habits of mind and action that self-responsibility teaches and which make us individuals;" we only react to the state.

De Jouvenel's dire forecasts of redistribution's endgame are not probable in societies where citizens remain vigilant, but they are certainly possible. Is de Jouvenel crying "wolf" too loudly? A quick look at Europe's continuing fiscal crises (founded in their social excesses and declining populations; see *Fewer*, by Ben Wattenberg [Chapter 43]), the economic mayhem practiced in Third World countries, and the U.S.'s looming insolvency based on the insupportable Social Security, Medicare and Medicaid programs, make a strong case that redistribution is alive and well—and not just in academic or political theory.

About the Author

BERTRAND DE JOUVENEL has been termed "the least famous of the great political thinkers of the twentieth century," but his fame, or lack of it, may be inversely proportional to the value of his insights. He was raised in a prosperous literary family who were intensely political and of ancient French aristocratic lineage on his paternal side. His father was the French ambassador to the League of Nations after World War I and was elected to the French senate; his mother presided over an important salon with a particular interest in France's relations with Czechoslovakia. Born in 1903 in France, de Jouvenel was strongly affected by the rise of Adolf Hitler's National Socialist Party, the Nazis, and the world war that followed as a result thereof.

Although de Jouvenel graduated from the Sorbonne in law and mathematics his career soon gravitated toward economic and political commentary. His interest in the United States led him to write *La Crise du Capitalisme Américain* (1933) [The Crisis of American Capitalism], one of the first interpretations of the Great Depression. At the time he favored a strong role for the state in economic matters.

De Jouvenel worked as a journalist specializing in international affairs for much of the 1930s. He gained worldwide renown for his 1935 interview with Adolf Hitler. After the outbreak of World War II de Jouvenel joined the French resistance but was forced to take refuge in

Switzerland. There he prepared his most famous work, *Du Pouvoir: Histoire Naturelle de sa Croissance* (1945) [On Power: The Natural History of Its Growth], a harsh critique of the modern state's authority. De Jouvenel built upon this historically oriented and profoundly philosophical treatise with several other books over the succeeding decades.

De Jouvenel taught at the University of Paris and was a frequent visiting professor at British and American universities. He worked tirelessly to acquaint the French elite with Anglo-American economic thought and practices; he was the author of scores of scholarly articles and books on these subjects. De Jouvenel died in 1987.

29

The Commanding Heights

Daniel Yergin and Joseph Stanislaw

Originally published: 1998
399 pages

The Commanding Heights is Daniel Yergin and Joseph Stanislaw's exhaustive global political/economic survey assessing why the free market is the solution to failed collectivist top-down economic policies known as "command economies." Collectivism saw its apogee primarily in Soviet (greater Russia) and Chinese totalitarianism during the latter half of the twentieth century. This parched scheme was also the template for control of the Soviet Union's satellites in Europe and the client states of both in the Third World. The collectivist model matured under Joseph Stalin in the Soviet Union and Mao Zedong in China, but it was guided through its adolescence in the early years of the twentieth century by Vladimir Ilyich Lenin.

Lenin (1870–1924) was a brutal dictator and the leader of the 1917 Russian Revolution. He believed as much in murder and terror as any revolutionary ever had; he was also an economist, but only out of necessity. Lenin understood what he needed to do—make newly communist Russia work in real-world terms—but he had not enough time and less expertise to achieve that goal because there was just too much to do. His grasp of at least a portion of the fundamentals of economic thinking was sure, but his understanding of how to build a viable *command* economy was far less so. There was no model to follow, and, of course, the fact that a command economy could not successfully be built by anyone was a reality that escaped his notice in the aftermath of the revolution. In other words, Lenin made the classic political mistake—he thought attaining power was the difficult step when it was the actuality of governing that was impossible.

Lenin suffered from the twentieth century's worst case of Enlightenment rationalism. He believed he could intellectually muscle his way through any problem. His successor, Joseph Stalin—less educated and less skilled at either governance or economics—was the century's premier megalomaniac. Between the two of them they caused the deaths of twenty, or fifty, or seventy-five million people—no one will ever know the real number. That fact alone is why these men and their theories must be kept in mind—decade upon decade.

After his take-over of the machinery of government in the middle of World War I (and his immediate withdrawal of Russia from the Allied war effort by means of a separate peace with Germany), Lenin's health deteriorated fairly quickly (although he had not yet reached 50) so that by the early 1920s he was ailing and frail. Aware of the short time he had left, he became desperate to save the revolution before its economic failings caused a counter-revolution. His brand of socialism—total control of both property and production—had not been economically successful in the early years after the Revolution and the Russian marketplace was in shambles. Lenin tried to reverse this course by introducing what he termed the New Economic Policy in 1921. This program brought back a small degree of capitalism in the form of petty trade and private agriculture. Because his grand vision of state control was not compatible with these modest but desperate measures, Lenin was criticized by his fanatical followers. He made an excuse for his approach by explaining that the government and the Communist Party would always control the "commanding heights," the high ground of economic power. Lower levels of the economy did not require, at least for the time being, the imposition of puristic socialism; they merely had to work. Lenin the Pragmatic.

Lenin's failure to make socialism viable was just one in a long string of collectivist fiascoes. Nevertheless, statist economic measures retained their political appeal, even in the United States, long after socialism had been thoroughly discredited philosophically and practically. U.S. president Richard Nixon, standing atop Washington's commanding heights in 1970, instituted wage and price controls when no emergency or threat to the country existed and when the economy was, with little question, healthy. Government's economic intervention in this case was widely thought to be good, even necessary. In reality, it was nothing more than an example of how warped economic and, especially, political theory had become because of the siren song of socialism's progeny: state welfarism.

Twenty years later (and seventy after Lenin's initial failures), when communism exposed itself as a futile philosophy amid the ruins of the Soviet Union, the free market was again on the rise as the antidote to the exorbitant fiscal and psychological costs of collectivist economic control. Capitalism and its market economy had governments shedding public businesses like liberals abandoning a Baptist revival meeting.

As Yergin and Stanislaw showed in their wide-ranging political/economic survey, none of this happened by accident. Although liberal Western politicians had long been preaching government control and paternalism—mostly because their pronouncements made them feel good and got them re-elected, not because they understood the issues—serious economists had been saying since the turn of the twentieth century that collectivism and socialism would not and could not work.

As the political cognoscenti realized that an ever-expanding welfare state was as unaffordable intellectually, psychologically, and economically as socialism was, the public began to understand that government was not the answer to every question. Simultaneously, the knowledge of those at government's center proved inferior in competing against the combined knowledge of all participants in the market. In the U.S., economic liberty brought prosperity; elsewhere government controls brought economic stagnation. At this point the pendulum began to swing back toward freedom in economic matters.

Yergin and Stanislaw explain where many of the free market's mid-twentieth-century economic problems began, with John Maynard Keynes. Keynes was the grand defender of the "prime the pump" theory of economic stability. He held that if governments would spend money to get an economy going (money those governments did not have, which was to be taken from taxpayers and/or printed out of thin air in classic inflationary fashion), the machinery of commerce would ultimately thrive on its own through the multiplier effect founded in the infusion of fresh dollars or credit.

There were several problems with this theory: it was wrong, in the first place, because money taken from the private sector in the form of taxes is that much less money in the hands of the individuals who actually make the economy work; thus government priming the pump actually slows an economy. Also, the multiplier effect of government employment/spending is miniscule compared with what those dollars do in the open market. Government spending, whether a one-time event to build a bridge or a persistent event such as providing a service must be continually (negatively) funded entirely through taxation or borrowing. In the private sector the business person spends money and then makes money, over and over, continually creating profits at each step, all of which, to the government's benefit, are taxable. Finally, money taken by the government and then redistributed back into private enterprise suffers from the "friction" of government intervention because a substantial portion of the money taken in is used up in administrative costs, increased red tape, and expansion of the number of government employees and employee benefits (federal employees are the best paid and best protected workers in America), all of which diminish government effectiveness and efficiency, and is therefore money that is mostly lost to the economy.

Ultimately the Keynesian program was untenable because it led to increased administrative intervention as politicians and bureaucrats decided exactly how to prime the pump. In other words, government didn't just throw money at the economy, or make credit more easily available; government decided that if it was "its" money that was going to do the work, then government itself would determine how the funds would be spent. Politicians and administrators began to believe they had an expertise they cannot and never will have, an expertise that only the market's invisible hand enjoys. Of course, the tendency toward corruption brought about because of the power of distribution further defeated any chance that real assistance would be effected.

Keynes made a comment that would explain the eventual demise of his own philosophy:

> Ideas are more powerful than is commonly understood. Indeed, the world is ruled by little else. . . . Sooner or later it is ideas, not vested interests, which are dangerous for good or evil.

It was the renewed understanding, after World War II, of why government must allow the market to work and why government was inadequate to order the economy that dealt the death blow to socialistic theory in all its guises. (However, socialistic *goals* are manifestly and unfortunately not dead.)

Although some economists—notably those at the University of Chicago, before, during, and after World War II—correctly appreciated the market's imperatives, these academics could not effect political change; they could only offer economic principles, coupled with a sound and useful understanding of human nature. This is the second theme treated at length in *The Commanding Heights*. As the authors explain, the importance of political leaders and leadership is so fundamental that pragmatic governing is not possible without both.

This systemic realization was a watershed moment in modern political/economic practices. Through the influence of liberal intellectuals it had become gospel that large economies could not run themselves. But it had become even more readily apparent in the real world that politicians should not run them either, to put it bluntly, because they simply didn't know what they were doing. This is true for a simple reason; economic interaction is far, far too complex to be ruled by anyone or anything. Additionally, because government officials approach economic matters from a political perspective, their goals become political goals, which do not necessarily match private goals or public good. Thus, the system could not and would not respond appropriately or effectively to political intervention. When politicians and economists alike grasped that there is a psychology, a human element, as well as a narrow economic method to making a free economy work, progress away from fear of the free market began—and the pendulum's journey back toward the center accelerated.

The authors note, with regard to the intention of government as it crafted mid-twentieth-century economic policy:

> [In matters of] economic regulation ... from the New Deal onward, market imperfections and failures became a dominating rationale.

In other words, government intervention to fix anything that was perceived to be broken became not just the watchword, it became the *raison d'être* of administrative activity. Fixing aberrations that found their way to the front page was clearly more politically profitable than pontificating about the value of government abstention on a big picture scale. Yet, almost none of the legislated regulations or bureaucratic intrusions worked to make things better. In most instances they complicated and made worse whatever minor irregularity had previously existed, and which would have most likely self-corrected in any event.

Hard economic realities experienced up to and including the twentieth century helped tip the scales dramatically toward free-market capitalism in the short twenty years from 1970 to 1990. Inflation had been a vicious malefactor for centuries, destroying whole economies, even nations, in matters of years; wise observers who realized the devastation inflation had caused in Germany after World War I didn't want that to happen again. Across the world's economic landscape at mid-century the fiscal burden of liberal tax and spending policies and of government control was becoming overwhelming, with no end in sight. Yet in almost all these nations there was little social progress as a result of these programs. There were just as many poor, backward, bankrupt nations and people as there had ever been, and just as many wealthy and corrupt dictators who sat atop these economic disasters.

Yergin and Stanislaw note as well that the regulatory burden, which was designed to protect the people from themselves, had become suspect for its rigidity and incapacity—particularly in collectivist societies. During this period governments began to understand both the role and the limits of regulatory effectiveness. None of this happened without the help of political figures and private sector economists who wished to effect free-market rationalism as the controlled economic measures of the collectivists proved not just ineffective, but destructive. As a result of these hard economic lessons, and the example of the free market economies that flourished after World War II, socialist governments began to collapse because of the internal factors and mechanisms by which they were supposed to operate.

The turnaround started small, most prominently in England in the 1980s under Prime Minister Margaret Thatcher, and grew into a global avalanche of change by the turn of the twenty-first century. In 1950 socialism was the ascendant form of government worldwide; by 1990 it had been buried. The gap between socialism's goals and its performance—and then its ultimate demise—spurred Yergin and Stanislaw's investigations. They engage in an encyclopedic overview of the world's economies; their examination of the leaders and the individual circumstances of each region or country follow what transpired in an effort to quantify those actions and comprehensions that worked and disassemble those that did not. This treatise, essentially an historical textbook without the pedantic touch of academic scolds, is striking by virtue of its details and the authors' skill at tying the facts, figures, and history together.

The book is divided into chapters that correspond to the economic points to be made and the history of their "discovery" and implementation. The authors observe that perhaps America's most valuable contribution to the world's economies was not only its example of free-market capitalism but its ability to change on the fly and to recognize the difference between procedure and substance. For example, in the U.S. the effects of the wartime planned economy, necessitated by the demands of World War II production needs, were not viewed as universally beneficial by war's end. In fact, as the authors note:

> Even liberals wanted, in the aftermath of the war, "to find a role for government that would allow it to manage the economy without managing the institutions of the economy." (Quoting Alan Brinkley in *The End of Reform* [1996])

Managed capitalism had produced mightily when the war came along—that fact was not lost on the Depression-era American public as it initially was in Europe. Our economic explosion after the war, however (when the economy was allowed to find its own level and measure without governmental guidance), ensured that domestic eyes would easily comprehend how much more the economy could do when freed from regulation and oversight. It was also thought that because of America's material success the public would not be easily blinded by melioristic equalitarian and socialistic paradigms that were in intellectual vogue in Europe at that time. And for a period, it was not.

The European reaction was different—governments there were still grounded in naïve Enlightenment-era ideals of perfect social organization and distribution. The physical and psychological devastation that remained after the war ended reinforced equalitarian impulses; thus government control grew. The contrary but expected economic results obtained on either side of the Atlantic—based on the differences in the respective economic principles used as blueprints—were easy for the authors to dissect.

As they did with Europe and the United States, Yergin and Stanislaw explore each instance of economic foolishness and genius experienced around the globe, primarily since the end of World War II. Their reach is one of the values of this effort; the reader doesn't have to wonder, well, OK, that's what happened in the U.S. and France, but what about Argentina or Indonesia or Rhodesia? All of the major players and regions are examined, then the whole is fitted together in practical form. The sweep of their survey is daunting because there are so many interconnected pieces and players, but the result leaves the reader with many comprehensions—and, as surely, many questions about the future.

Those seeking to still better understand the past century's sociopolitical movements that went hand in glove with fresh economic forces and philosophies, should consult Paul Johnson's *Modern Times* (Chapter 21). This companion volume to *The Commanding Heights* will enable readers to fit many of the twentieth century's puzzle pieces into their proper places. Johnson's comprehensive compendium fills in the political and historical details germane to Yergin and Stanislaw's economically oriented study. After reading both volumes, the complementary scope and value of each book becomes apparent.

The authors of *The Commanding Heights* recognize that the battle over economic sanity will never be ended. In the expression of George Shultz, former U.S. Secretary of State, Treasury, and Labor, markets are "relentless," and never-ending competition is sometimes harsh and often wearing. People not infrequently want respite, or protection, even from just having to work with diligence. There thus occasionally arises a clamor for government to do something *for* us or something *to* a competitor. It is the human condition that makes reality so difficult. Yergin and Stanislaw are not reluctant to point out this reality. Ultimately, they are optimistic; their confidence is based on thirty centuries of already achieved results. Today, in spite of some discontent with insecurity (often magnified by the media), we know for certain that government is neither the sole answer nor even the antidote to life's difficulties. The free market's possibilities, the potential for good and bad, and multiple chances to be the creators of our own economic destiny still make more sense than the certainty of socialism's negative and demeaning government dole.

Finally, in their treatise, Yergin and Stanislaw go to the root of some of society's most deeply ingrained frailties. They see corruption (intellectual, economic, social, and political) and inflation as the two most destructive forces for all economies and all societies. They also aver that government does have a role, but as investigator and arbiter of the myriad social and economic forces extant, not as supervisor. Their ultimate message is that government is not the court of last resort. The people's success will be determined by their willingness to do what is required of them—to be vigilant and steadfast, and free, and to be rewarded both personally and nationally for their efforts, as so many people and nations were after World War II.

About the Authors

DANIEL YERGIN was born in 1947 in Los Angeles. He graduated from Yale University in 1968 and thereafter received his Ph.D. from Cambridge University (England) in international relations. He won the Pulitzer Prize for non-fiction in 1992 as co-author of *The Prize*, a definitive study of the worldwide oil industry. He was the founding chair of Cambridge Energy Research Associates which, as its name suggests, studies and gives advice on energy issues. He is vice-chair of Global Decisions Group, a consulting firm that provides economic and political risk analysis for its clients.

Joseph Stanislaw is a graduate of Harvard University where he obtained his undergraduate degree. He received his Ph.D. from Edinburgh University (Scotland) and he is president of Cambridge Energy. Previously he taught at Cambridge University and for a time was senior economist for the European Union's Organization for Economic Cooperation and Development. He is a student of energy and other markets, and does consulting work in those fields.

30

Reclaiming the American Dream

Richard C. Cornuelle

Originally published: 1965, revised 1993
199 pages

ALL OF US at some point have asked ourselves where we fit in. Sometimes fitting in only means getting along in a small social group; the ultimate question for society, though, is how do we help each human being fit within the larger group that constitutes our culture? Without human connectedness life can be both difficult and solitary—and discouraging. When Richard Cornuelle wrote *Reclaiming the American Dream* his intention was to explain the role of being connected in the most direct fashion: by voluntarily helping one another. He felt he could turn his observations and comments into a "political" opportunity, to prove a point and offer a real-world example.

Yet there is also a legitimate sense in which Cornuelle intended his book to be apolitical, or more accurately anti-political. For him, the essence of volunteerism was to keep politics and the government *out* of people's affairs. With governmental intrusion comes money, bureaucracy, distant administrators instead of those who act directly, and arbitrary standards and statistical goals meant to establish a one-size-fits-all prototype. The bureaucratic attitude morphs into the prosaic jurisdictional and intellectual conceit of "we know best" that will brook no intrusion and no review. This immodesty becomes not just an assertion, but a fact. For Cornuelle, bureaucratic governance proceeds to the extreme detriment of the many services that we would voluntarily, and far more effectively, render one another in its absence.

As Cornuelle explains, with the bureaucratic model the essence of volunteerism—caring—is largely lost, and in its place is created obligation of the most perfunctory kind. Study after study has shown that those who successfully help the poor, the disadvantaged, the handicapped, or even those just ignorant of some portion of society's avenues, are those who care about them and engage in their efforts for concrete (and almost certainly to some extent, altruistic) reasons. On the other hand, those in this arena who instead see primarily a job, a paycheck, and secure retirement and health benefits, cannot effectively fulfill the needs of this sector of society by the very status of their relationship to those within it. They perform a service, surely, but their connection and thus their effectiveness is far less certain.

Conservatives, who were rising to intellectual prominence at the time of the initial publication of *Reclaiming the American Dream* in 1965, investigated many aspects of government's activities and saw a primary problem: volunteerism could not exist comfortably in a statist society where government was supposed to take care of all those who did not or could not take care of themselves. Aptly enough, these analysts saw government inhibiting or even driving private efforts out of the marketplace and felt the merit of Cornuelle's ideas and the practicality of their application; they integrated them into their own larger paradigm of less government that they hoped meant less distortion of private activities.

Cornuelle's concept is that big is not better in a society where grand designs are a political disease. He argues that millions of small efforts, made day after day, are what make the difference so that caring becomes second nature and self-help grows. The community existed before the state; the caring individual connection prevailed before the advent of the dispassionate and unconnected machinery of government.

The underlying problem for any public effort (that is, any political effort) is to decide when a given individual cannot take care of himself. But, because of the nature of government programs, which are supposed to be utterly egalitarian, policy has to be designed to reach out equally to everyone. That allows a lot of people to self-select, causing several relatively obvious detrimental consequences. It can also short-circuit the capabilities of others who are told they need help (often by those wishing to ensure the full reach of their bureaucratic franchise), and who unnecessarily and unfortunately succumb to those imprecations.

Inevitably, the definition of when someone was unable to help themselves expanded whenever any particular assistance program took shape and some people at the fringe did not qualify. Cornuelle saw new, more generous and more comprehensive programs become "necessary" to remedy the situation of those few who were left out; as programs expanded, there were more new people on the edges, and they were also incorporated in a never-ending circle of enlarging government "help." A culture of dependency was born. Government caring grew, unabated—simply because there was always someone left on the periphery, and always some political figure or bureaucrat who knew these problem citizens (or citizen problems) could be helped. To the mid-century liberal, seeing the world as it could be, there was nothing we could not afford, and there was nothing we could not fix. Life did not "happen;" and programs grew inexorably.

The value and success of government assistance began to self-destruct—in the broadest understanding of government's purpose—as a result of President Franklin Roosevelt's political offer of a "New Deal" in the 1930s. At that time, because of the debilitating effects of the Great Depression, the American people were told and began to believe that security was more important than freedom—that high levels of taxation and government control of the economy were necessary to protect their lives and livelihoods. This development limited the necessity and reduced the opportunity for us to take care of ourselves. It was the genesis of the culture of dependency. The growth of this culture conferred a spurious moral superiority on liberals who, because they offered the needy direct support instead of enhanced opportunities for self-help, eagerly claimed the mantle of compassion. (How great was the political motivation in this course is a question for another place, but one that might be profitably addressed from many points of view.)

Cornuelle takes an opposite tack. He writes that social problems that are cultural as well as individual are best addressed on an elemental level. Doing so involves making repeated assessments of and adjustments to measures of actual assistance while emphasizing the opportunity to those being helped to bolster their own situations and character, as argued in Richard Weaver's *Ideas Have Consequences* (Chapter 35) and Charles Murray's *In Pursuit: Of Happiness and Good Government* (Chapter 31). These are things that government (and particularly politicians) are less well equipped to do than might be hoped. As welfarism develops, intellectual/political conflicts of interest may arise in a most unseemly manner and a fatal intellectual conceit can arise. As well, a superficial compassion born of political habit and perfunctory judgment, not concern, can distort what eventuates.

In Cornuelle's view, volunteerism addresses social problems by serving as an alternative to, not an adjunct of, the state. He sees the advantages of a competition of ideas and actions (such as school choice advocates offer, who today challenge the entrenched public education monopoly). Bureaucrats do not care, do not see, and do not act as volunteers do. This is not to paint all bureaucrats as bad, only as different. Their power, their resources, their view, and their mandate are all different. The bureaucratic mindset developed into the mid-century Democrat method of government assistance: if there is a problem, the first thing to do is deliver money to fix it.

Cornuelle sees things differently: solutions that address causes should be the first order of business; in the government model they are generally the last. Regrettably, on the political stage wholesale problem solving is never personal and thus it is ultimately less effective (but much easier to implement) than local answers to local problems. Individual problems, it is most important to understand, have *specific* causes. The government, however, never starts at step one: rational assessment of the root of the problem and the development of some direct action to alter, reverse, or adjust the antecedent cause in order to obtain a different and hopefully more permanent result.

Cornuelle recognizes that dispassionate and doctrinaire government is most of the problem. Government, by its very nature, often *prevents* real solutions. He also understands that the political effect of more government, encompassed in proliferating programs, is always electorally appealing. Politicians find it hard not to offer or support "free" government services or handouts, especially once such programs are established and the public has become accustomed to them. The political answer to programs that are not working is to simply make them bigger—the reason for failure must be that we are not doing enough; it could never be that we are already, inappropriately, doing too much, or worse, simply doing something wrong.

Two observations as to why public administration goes awry: Parkinson's second law, that expenditures rise to meet income, and humorist Will Rogers's commentary that we are lucky we don't get all the government we pay for (government waste being good from at least this perspective). But neither offers effective countermeasures to big government, other than that matters will improve with the reduction of taxes and/or a reduction in spending—that is, by starving the beast or suffocating it. Cornuelle believes in both methods, but he also argues that conservatives have to offer viable alternatives in addition to the suggestion of reduced government involvement.

Cutting taxes, of course, often means cutting already existing services,

services the liberals are exceedingly clever at calling "entitlements." How many would vote to rescind something poor or disadvantaged people are "entitled" to? (These issues are discussed more directly in Wilhelm Röpke's *A Humane Economy* [Chapter 33].) This is where Cornuelle steps in with his observation that many government assistance programs are over-intrusive and, as a result, over-funded, and rarely accomplish what they were designed to do in the first place. If they did, as is somewhat obvious, both the programs and the bureaucracies that support them would self-extinguish. Cornuelle notes that to justify both their existence and the expansion of their franchise,

> [t]he government sector's boosters overstate public problems. They also say problems have causes only the government can remedy.

The usefulness of these claims, for political purposes, is self-evident, yet the fallacy of their substance is equally manifest. Reordering, which essentially means reducing, the efforts and the resources used to support the government's agenda was necessary. Here Cornuelle anticipates by forty years former Congressman Newt Gingrich's 1994 Contract with America and overt conservatism. Gingrich was Speaker of the U.S. House of Representatives in the Clinton Administration and one of the main architects of modern welfare reform. Gingrich's program, like Cornuelle's before it, intended to change the default mechanism of social assistance from the public to the private sector. As Friedrich von Hayek notes in *The Road to Serfdom* (Chapter 13), and James Madison observes two hundred years earlier in *The Federalist* No. 44 (Chapter 6), if we give government a job to do we also must give it the requisite power and money to achieve the goal. The incremental buildup of this power as we ask government to do more and more is not easily turned around when it becomes a monster. As every conservative since the time of President Franklin Roosevelt has grasped, the conservative movement has always stood for the idea (and ideal) that each of us is personally responsible for himself in far greater measure than government is or should or can be. That is something the majority of Americans still believe. How to turn this into an electoral reality is another matter.

Witness President Bill Clinton's assertion in 1996, when he signed the massive welfare reform bill (welfare to workfare), that "the era of big government is over." Despite Clinton's political rhetoric, the countervailing fact is that we are still experiencing untenable rising government expenditures for social purposes at the beginning of the twenty-first century, most directly within the presidency of George W. Bush, a self-styled "compassionate conservative," and his sycophant congressional toadies.

While liberals today scorn conservatives as heartless, even as conservatives point with dismay to the liberal's failed programs, government keeps getting bigger with the overt assistance of both parties. Cornuelle has an answer: volunteerism, a special brand of private-sector work that *competes with and supplants* government action or intervention. He shows how it can work and why it can work. Then he actually made it work.

Cornuelle calls for Americans to apply private-sector business practices to private-sector charitable impulses. His point is that the private sector can *displace* some of big government and be more effective while doing so. But, for this to happen the private sector has to change how it both thinks and functions in a public venue. It has to practice, when acting altruistically, what it preaches while engaged in business. Cornuelle notes that such considerations as accountability, responsibility, entrepreneurship, competition, graded performance, obtaining results, and living with consequences are equally applicable to charity and business (and most obviously should apply to government as well). American business is efficient and successful not just because it wants to be, but because it has to be to survive. If, as Cornuelle advocates, business applied its methods to private-sector charitable initiatives everything would change. With measurable results made mandatory private-sector initiatives would become successful to a significant degree. They could reduce the need for and replace government programs and accomplish what everyone would like to see: a truly compassionate system of help for the clearly needy that actually works.

Cornuelle finds the biggest danger in the fact, already observed by Alexis de Tocqueville, that we become numb to government running our lives in proportion to the extent that we let it do so. Robert Nisbet in *Quest for Community* (1953) and Bertrand de Jouvenel before him (*On Power*, Chapter 15) are both critical observers of modern social organization. They each note that when communities erode political power replaces them. And the more government does for us, the more it does to us. Without competition, bureaucrats won't make government more effective or efficient. As monopolists they have no incentive to do so. The most direct example of this maxim is public education in America—a monopoly that achieves less and demands more fiscal support every year. This system is the perfect foil for the competition offered through private entrepreneurship.

Cornuelle, as well, is especially harsh on private foundations that in his view abdicate their responsibility to show how the people themselves can remedy society's failings without more government involvement. The convolution here was and is truly amazing. Instead of understanding where charitable foundations could lead, these organizations simply identify problems, often detailing how they arose and what was happening in society, and then suggest that *government* fix them! Cornuelle's concomitant dose of scorn is for rubber-stamp boards, full of successful people who do not do their jobs of overseeing, but bow to the "professionals," and allow themselves to be talked down to by staff. They do not assess, they do not demand performance, they do not set policy, and they do not review with a critical eye; they abdicate their jobs, they just do not leave their seats.

Both in his book and in his personal life Cornuelle took on the burden of proving that the private sector can solve most, if not all, of our public problems. His intention was to show what could be done if the private sector *competed* with government and didn't just abandon a field when government stepped in. His demonstration vehicle was a private corporation he created called United Student Aid Funds, Inc. He picked a sector of society that needed attention and an area where government was already involved (but doing a poor job) through the federal student loan program. He addressed the relevant issues and then mapped out a solution, which he successfully put into action.

In its first year USA Funds raised (from private individuals) a few million dollars to lend to students, and signed up 944 banks to administer the loans and 37 colleges that wanted to participate. USA Funds generated 3,000 loans to students that year. This Cornuelle accomplished entirely with private money, talent, and time. By the third year, Cornuelle's operation was in partnership with 5,500 banks in 49 states serving 685 colleges and 68,000 students. USA Funds had but one office, with a small staff, to operate the entire *national* program. Cornuelle's thoughts and his actualization of those thoughts were the raw material with the potential to start a great movement and are, admittedly, the stuff of few people. Starting smaller, with less grand designs, is still more than realistic. The observers of Cornuelle's follow-through should not be daunted, but inspired.

In his book Cornuelle concludes that the private sector's resurgence as a force to solve social ills could reduce and redefine government's role, but only if the private sector's leaders come to see themselves as fundamentally different from the state—and as having a potentially more powerful franchise. The private sector cannot be successful until it both competes with government and decides not to accept government's power as final, or its pull as irresistible. Cornuelle observes, following Richard Weaver, Friedrich von Hayek, William F. Buckley, Jr., and so many others, that

> [a]bove all we need an intellectual revolution before its practical counterpart will have a chance.

Since first expressing those views in 1965, we have experienced the beginnings of both revolutions. But we still have far to go, and Cornuelle wants us to persist with intention. He identifies the overpowering force of government, which often stifles private initiative simply because those in the private sector are grateful to be relieved of the burdens of their exertions. But Cornuelle knew and acted upon the plain fact that government cannot, for too many reasons, effect social good or public welfare as successfully as the private voluntary actions of citizens. Most of all, in combating government's presumptions, its political intrusions, and the force of entrenched bureaucracies Cornuelle saw that

> in the end the only practical way to make a modern state less large was to starve it of responsibility.

Richard Cornuelle acted on his beliefs. His book is a primer on how we can do the same and change both government and America to reclaim them for ourselves.

About the Author

AS FOUNDER OF the Center for Independent Action, Richard Cornuelle is not shy about practicing what he preaches when he calls on the private sector to take action. From humble beginnings as a roustabout in the oil fields of the western U.S., to his post as executive vice-president of the National Association of Manufacturers, Cornuelle participated in all levels of American business and the private non-profit sector during the twentieth century. His investigations into the employment of the supposedly unemployable, privately funded low-cost housing, and private urban renewal have led to a rethinking of how the independent sector can reshape the American economic and governmental landscapes.

Cornuelle was born in 1927, and in the late 1940s was a research assistant to Ludwig von Mises at New York University. He learned from Mises the idea that the economic way of thinking (*praxeology*) could be applied to areas outside the market economy, to understand the societal forces at work that either lead to or hinder peaceful social cooperation. After leaving New York University, Cornuelle worked in various jobs, including as a Program Officer at the Volker Fund that in the 1950s and early 1960s was instrumental in helping establish the Thomas Jefferson Center for the Study of Political Economy at the University of Virginia, the *Journal of Law and Economics* at the University of Chicago School of Law, and a lecture series for students that helped produce such books as Bruno Leoni's *Freedom and the Law*, and Milton Friedman's *Capitalism and Freedom* (Chapter 25).

Cornuelle has a continuing presence among those organizations that tackle social opportunities with the idea of displacing less efficient governmental efforts while fostering private initiative. Cornuelle republished *Reclaiming the American Dream* in 1993 and in his review of the revised edition, John Chamberlain observes that the welfare state has become entrenched, as evidenced by Ronald Reagan's insignificant attempts and secondary successes in curtailing (much less disassembling) it. But Cornuelle is optimistic about the independent sector—and he may be right. The information age might just reduce both the hodgepodge and the staggering size of government, and social reform may be a logical opportunity to flow from those reductions.

Cornuelle's own research focused on the role that voluntary associations play in society. He coined the term "the independent sector" to refer to activity that was neither in the market sector nor the public sector. Philanthropic enterprise became the subject to which he devoted his intellectual energies and in so doing he drew inspiration not just from Mises, but also Tocqueville. Cornuelle understands the vital importance of a vibrant independent sector for the functioning of a free society. It is in the application of its aptitude for and the science of voluntary association and self-governance that a citizenry enables a free society to function and flourish. If the people lose this ability, the free society will be threatened. This is the meaning behind the often made statement by Cornuelle to the effect that "while we know much about the free economy, we still know too little about the free society."

31

In Pursuit:
Of Happiness and Good Government

Charles Murray

Originally published: 1988
272 pages

FOR HUMAN BEINGS happiness is an inherently elusive concept. To complicate that fact, we are sometimes prevented from seeking our own definition and level of bliss by the institutions of government we have created. Leave it to politicians to confuse both the meaning and measure of something as simple as happiness. The authors of the Declaration of Independence laid it out so ingenuously—that we are entitled to life, liberty, and the *pursuit* of happiness But we are not *entitled* to happiness itself—for a fairly obvious reason: happiness means something different to almost every one of us. It is thus up to each of us to create our own happiness, and not to expect such from someone else, much less everyone else in the form of government intrusion into our lives.

When Thomas Jefferson wrote his initial draft of the Declaration of Independence he did not use the phrase "pursuit of happiness" when defining mankind's inalienable rights. He talked about property, along with life and liberty. Jefferson and his revolutionary editors broadened his scope from the concrete "property" to the more ephemeral "happiness." And to an extent we've been arguing about the consequences of that change ever since.

Charles Murray aims to sort out some of these complications. He begins by asking what the goal of government should be. His conclusion, as evidenced by his book's title, is that government should help facilitate happiness by being "good." His next inquiry is to question if "good government" is an oxymoron or if there is something in relation to governing that we can do better than we have been doing so far. Troubles arise when we realize that the quality of government is much in the eye of the beholder, as most things are. Murray further postulates that one's view of human nature is also inextricably intertwined with one's concept of what government should be and do.

Murray contends that we have lost some control of our lives as the national government has inserted itself into matters that are more cogently understood from a local point of view—or are seen as not any of government's business at all. He asserts that Tocqueville was right when he looked at local government in the early 1800s:

> If you take power and independence from a municipality, you may have docile subjects but you will not have citizens.

Here is an explanation of why the percentage of people who vote continues to drop, and why there is more public sentiment of powerlessness in the face of government, and distrust and disillusion at its operation. Murray recalls that Jefferson and his contemporaries understood the interrelationships all people have, that they complement one another in community more than they compete. We naturally achieve that comity in both our private and our public lives. Murray seeks to rekindle the sentiments of interrelatedness even as he labors to determine how to reign in government.

Does this suggest that the local political/social entity is more capable of self-governance than are those at higher levels? For Murray, and many others, that inference is mostly correct. The recognition is that the agglomeration of power and administration on a grander scale and with increasing power over local considerations (and the idea that one-size-fits-all government actually works) is a less valid notion. But, with little room for debate in Murray's view, it is clear in spite of the real efficacy of local governance that we are drifting if not careening toward a scenario of extreme centralization.

Modern media helps foster this trend toward concentrated government. The press, for example, often takes what is an idiosyncratic problem that is emotionally appealing and visually simple, and tries to make it the rule; then it offers a fix (in a thirty second sound-bite or three paragraph editorial) that is equally simplistic but inappropriate, unhelpful, and even incorrect much of the time. Each media outlet, national or local, seeks to claim it was the one that found the problem and offered the solution—and then asks why the government is so slow to respond to such an obvious need. The legislators and executive branch officials, who fear looking inept or uncaring, take the lead and proffer solutions not just for that one place but for all, ad infinitum.

Largely ignored in the expansion of government at higher levels is each individual's dignity. Distant officialdom seems blind to the citizen and that person's place in the overall scheme of things. Murray asks, "When will government stop telling people what to think and start listening to who they are?" For Murray, quantifying the "success" of government through statistics and guidelines is not nearly as important as observing what government does to the concept of individualism (and, in the process, to real people). Here Murray reflects Milton Friedman's concerns voiced in *Capitalism and Freedom* (Chapter 25).

Perhaps the juxtaposition between expansive and contracted notions of government is as simple as this: is government there to give things to the governed, or is it there to allow each person to reach his own potential and ensure that others don't get unnecessarily or unfairly in his way (and vice versa)? The welfare state grows out of the misplaced notion that an equality of outcome is the goal of government, or worse, the goal of society. In contrast, the idea of self-sufficiency through individual effort suggests less government and more freedom to strive toward our own goals. Opportunity can be demanding, but that fact should not cause us to try to "protect" anyone, much less everyone, from the consequences and effects of their individual efforts. That kind of protection offers only a dependent, cocooned, and thus incapable and unproductive society.

An example: retirement security for the citizen. Protecting the worker from her "inability" to invest wisely what she does put aside, and do so without incurring excessive fees, risk of loss, etc., was one of the arguments used in 2006 in deflating the necessity of privatizing at least part of the Social Security system. The liberal view was that Jane Public couldn't do these things and thus we had to continue with the existing fiscally insupportable system (eventually reaching bankruptcy) rather than risk that some citizens might not be able to cope one way or another. The fact that there were additional options to that of private investing of individual Social Security deposits was ignored; a government-operated investment account, protecting any individual citizen's actual funds deposited therein from potential bogymen (including Congress's long reach) is one viable option for those who don't feel comfortable handling their own retirement assets.

The vested interests vetoed this as a consideration—but with growing intellectual and fiscal dishonesty.

Murray's larger point is that we should prevent retirement funds from falling into the hands of the government in the first place (meaning Congress) because the government does *not* protect the citizen's retirement; current politicians spend those revenues on non-Social Security projects (to help assure their reelection) and hope the next generation will willingly make up the shortfall via future increases in Social Security taxes and reductions in benefits. The responsibility and opportunity for self-protection in this instance and almost all others should rest with the individual, with paternalistic government oversight (which insists citizens are incompetent) and Congressional thievery truncated.

Government exists to facilitate self-determined, self-actuated happiness—in the sense of ensuring a level playing field where the rules apply equally to all. Government is not intended to deliver or guarantee equality, or most dangerous of all, to attempt to force it. Murray observes that in order for us to pursue happiness by our own efforts and in our own measure certain realities must prevail—individual freedom and personal responsibility are the two most important of these.

He notes there is a legitimate role for government in ensuring the fundamentals that allow human beings to achieve. At the most basic level, contending that all are free to pursue life as they see fit is not a defensible proposition if one is homeless or ill or hungry. Alleviating these limiting circumstances has become a justifiable aim of modern government. The administrative or bureaucratic response in this area, however, has become more political than substantive. It is the necessary obligation of the citizenry to ensure that governmental assistance is given in rational measure with regard to the human condition (both its capabilities and its constraints). Political accusations, on one side, of unfeeling or hard-heartedness, or on the other of moral poverty and intellectual hubris, are symmetrically distracting from the common effort.

Following this path, Murray makes an often forgotten point: while assisting citizens, the government has not just a right to ask those helped to exert themselves, but an obligation to do so. If government does not ask for individual responsibility in return for its assistance, it creates a dependent constituency. This is to the detriment of everyone (both those to be helped and those who pay for such assistance) except the politicians who thrive by "serving" the less well-off. Where the equities lie in the relations between the people themselves and their government is the stuff of modern social-policy debates. Murray's answer led him to his prescription for good government.

The nexus of the discussion regarding government's role has changed since the end of the Second World War, during the period when socialism rose toward the sun and then fell in disrepute. Disguised as "good government," the welfare state has risen to take socialism's place among the liberal's answers to life's differences. Economic history has repeatedly shown that a free market creates higher standards of living for those even on the lowest rung of the economic ladder than government intervention in the market has produced as a result of its best efforts. Nevertheless, this lesson, this wheel, must inexorably be reinvented. As Milton Friedman so succinctly points out in *Capitalism and Freedom*, each government intrusion in the lives of its citizens or their economic machinations, called the "therapeutic impulse," causes an aberration (known commonly as the law of unintended consequences). These distortions require further government meddling until the maze of regulations and prohibitions and simple largesse is incomprehensible. Politicians seem to reflexively respond with more official interference, simply because they can. This is decidedly *not* the proper role for government in Murray's view.

Murray is one of the rare essayists who crosses disciplines to get legitimate answers. Government, in Murray's judgment, is not to be studied in isolation (as it so often is) with the hope of discovering what it should do for people and in what measure. It is to be studied in a vortex of all human needs: social, psychological, intellectual, economic, and emotional. Murray holds that government should construct policy to facilitate people reaching their individual potential. That potential is both great and sacrosanct; our failure to address government policy and programs outside the specific goal of any given political agenda is why we achieve so little when we spend so much. It is why government interferes so often and accomplishes only frustration, distortion, and dislocation—not resolution.

There is a political lesson/problem inherent in this mix. The contingent in Congress that creates and expands the "entitlement" programs that are the point of Murray's discussion do only half their work. They generate political capital through righteousness and a stated belief in the programs they create. However, a refusal to acknowledge that the programs do not achieve their intended result is not part of the equation—it is only their belief in what they are doing that is important. Those on the other side of this equation, who believe that measuring results is important, are portrayed as mean-spirited—not honest brokers of ideas—if they question the efficacy of what has been constructed. In politics believing is enough. Questioning or even disproving beliefs (in an effort to achieve real results for the actual people whom we intend to help) is denoted as crass, tactless, and insensitive; in the hands of the worst demagogues it is sometimes even deemed racist.

Murray acknowledges that government can do much, but then it must get out of the way. Its goal should not be merely to make people "feel as if they are in control of events," but to ensure that they actually *are* in control. Then responsibility for all actions—their success or their failure—lies with individuals who act on their own behalf. Murray's confidence in the results that can be achieved when we let people control their own lives should be measured against the continued progress of free people over the centuries, and the lack of progress generated by most social welfare institutions.

For Murray, if government must intervene it should do so in a fashion that involves citizens as partners, not as children or charges. Will we waste some money and effort while we refine this approach? We likely will, but in miniscule amounts compared to what we already dissipate in ways too numerous and too voluminous to contemplate (without changing much at all in the lives of those to be helped). Murray states it is incumbent upon us not to be afraid to recognize that government, as much as any other aspect of our lives, is built on trial *and* error. Pandering political figures—whether elected executives or legislators or un-elected bureaucrats or judges—err in their faith that they can create perfect programs and achieve error-free results in the face of uncooperative reality. Not without reason have we come to distrust government and government's judgment.

Political handouts and attempts at a redistribution of the country's profits through the power of government to tax (or to spend money it doesn't even have, through deficit financing) hasn't made a difference in the ability of the less successful to help themselves in anywhere near the proportion of resources devoted to this venture (five *trillion* dollars spent on federal welfare programs between Lyndon Johnson's presidency and the advent of welfare reform in 1996, with only an increase in the number of recipients to show for these efforts during that period). Since government has instead often gotten in the way of its stated goal of self-help, Murray contemplates that it is time to change the paradigm.

As a specific example of his approach, Murray discusses volunteerism. To volunteer one's help is instinctive, reflexive. Volunteering brings social gains from myriad points of departure. Murray finds that volunteerism can be fostered by the government, even though few lawmakers recognize the advantages of doing so. Politicians want to denigrate volunteerism because it doesn't, they allege, accomplish enough, or isn't certain to solve each and every aspect of each and every problem (as though government programs do). The failure of government initiatives to achieve their stated goals easily evidences how little a bureaucracy can understand a community of problems.

Part of the larger picture is that government looks at volunteerism as a numbers game; for the bureaucrat, volunteer efforts cannot help *all* or even *enough* people. To an extent, this belief came to be the rule during the Great Depression of the 1930s when private volunteer efforts were overwhelmed by the masses of destitute people who needed help. Those economic conditions no longer exist and are not likely to re-emerge. It is time to let the pendulum of government assistance swing back. Murray contends that the view that the private sector cannot do enough is both false and facile, and that experience has demonstrated otherwise.

Volunteerism is a social perspective and psychological attitude, each of which fosters the success of private charitable enterprises. It is infectious and self-reinforcing for both the volunteers and those to be assisted. For Murray, volunteerism is built not just on the needs of those helped (the handout approach), but on the gains those in need can make for themselves when empowered in myriad ways (the hand up approach). Grasping this contrarian reality is fundamental to comprehending Murray's perspective. (For an in-depth understanding of volunteerism, both historical and practical, see Richard Cornuelle's *Reclaiming the American Dream* [Chapter 30].) That volunteer programs increase every year, that new non-profit organizations are more numerous every year speaks directly to the human spirit on which Murray and Cornuelle rely. That these programs demonstrate government ineffectiveness and failure as the impetus for the efforts of the people who create them tells us most of what we need to know about public administration.

In Murray's view, government function and individual happiness are conjoined only when the former creates opportunities for self-awareness, self-involvement, and self-help; they work at cross-purposes when government offers only idealized assistance from above that has no direct correlation to an individual's particular needs or potential. The assessment of a policy designed pursuant to Murray's perspective would focus less on the gross numbers of persons to be helped and more on what an *individual* could do based on the policy's goal, its resources, and the assistance to be offered. In other words, Murray's assessment is *results* oriented, not numbers driven. The numbers will take care of themselves if results—not programs—become the goal.

He recommends a strategy of building government programs from the individual up. Such programs, designed to help people rather than populations, would readily accommodate rational assessment of their efficacy. By instituting meaningful assessment we have an opportunity to at least arrive at more rational government. An example of this approach was federal welfare reform implemented as an effect of the Contract with America—a group of legislative goals developed by Republicans elected to Congress in 1994. This effort resulted in two changes to existing welfare programs: first, it sent welfare program design responsibility from the federal level to the states while instituting accountability for results; second, it placed a limit on the number of years anyone could receive benefits so long as they were able to work. The program focused on both training and assistance in finding employment. At the time there were concerns that people who were no longer eligible to receive benefits would flood private charitable programs—but that never happened. What did happen was an almost immediate significant reduction in the number of people on welfare and a significant increase in former welfare recipients becoming employed.

The question is not why was this reform so successful, but how did it happen so quickly? The answer is simple, and it flows from Murray's approach to public administration. People were given two things: an incentive to change (the eventual end to their benefits), and an opportunity to make a change for the better (employment and a beginning toward self-sufficiency). The public cost was well worth bearing this time, and both political parties engaged in substantive assessment and practical change—based on one elementary fact: human nature and its striving toward human dignity.

Murray counsels against ever asking how government can solve any social problem. He prefers to pose an entirely different question: "What in society is happening that is preventing people from solving the problem for themselves?" In most instances, we already know the answer, but we can't seem to get from A to B, much less from A to Z, often because it is actually *government* that is in the way. One of Murray's examples remains particularly germane. Since we know how to educate children (as people have done it for thousands of generations) why aren't we doing it effectively today? The answer is invariably not more money or more testing (we have thrown so much of both at the system it is embarrassing). The answer is more care, more attention, more time, more parenting, more choice, and more family involvement, regardless of whether the family is extended or blended or even fragmented. *No* government program and *no* cadre of education "professionals" can act as the substitute for those ingredients no matter how much money we pour into the effort.

The consequence of implementing these elements into education also requires that families have an ability to effect change when change is needed—that means they must be able to choose the educational venue they feel is best for their children. That competition will improve all schools, as it improves everything else in life, is patent. To continue to deny the efficacy of instituting competition in the educational process is simply insulting to both the electorate and the parents whose children are forced into failing schools run by self-protective teachers and administrators.

The more opportunity we have to do for ourselves, to grasp responsibility, the closer we get to taking care of ourselves. Although Murray is the first to admit that our best efforts cannot perfect the world, his contention that those efforts can make it better is virtually certain. Isn't that just what we've been doing for hundreds of centuries—making the world better through our own individual and group efforts?

Murray spends much time investigating the human spirit—the essential element of life—and human needs, the essential foundation of physical existence. Once basic needs have been met via the creation of what Murray terms enabling conditions, the most pressing issue is human liberty. Each of us ought to be unhindered to pursue happiness in any fashion that does not inhibit the pursuit of happiness by those around us. The challenge for Murray, as enunciated by Bernard Bailyn (in *The Ideological Origins of the American Revolution* [1967]), is to create an atmosphere

> where the use of power over the lives of men was jealously guarded and severely restricted. It was only where there was this defiance, this refusal to truckle, this distrust of authority, political or social, that institutions could express human aspirations, not crush them.

Having recognized the ugly phenomenon of how a person's conduct often worsens once he gains power, Murray argues for government not to be any more powerful than necessary. The individual's potential is regularly subverted by the authority of those over him. Therefore it is exceedingly difficult to justify the power supposedly transferred to the government by the governed. The governed vote and act as individuals, while government reciprocates by setting one-size-fits-all economic and social policy. As that measurement never actually fits well, the function and form of government should in all instances be as *limited* as possible. When a government assumes as little control over the people as necessary, and operates as close to those to be helped as feasible, then in Murray's view, we will come closer to good government. Government function and individual happiness are conjoined when bureaucracy creates opportunities for self-help. They are disconnected when government sees its role as controlling assistance—a condescending and paternalistic approach.

Murray looks at all the unmet promises of government and asks how many such failures must occur before those toward whom assistance is directed evidence a learned helplessness. This condition then "requires" an even greater governmental effort to remedy past failures. Murray wants to unlock the potential for human achievement—potential now smothered in governmentally controlled programs that tell people what they supposedly cannot do for themselves. Murray's approach is an honest presentation of his faith in individual effort coupled with minimal government. Murray's examples ring true to what each of us knows specifically about himself and about human potential in general. The prospects are endless when people are treated with dignity and the respect that recognizes what they can do for themselves when given the opportunity.*

---

* On the overall subject of "good government" it is more than valuable to observe what occurred in New Zealand when wholesale government reform was achieved in the late 1980s. The country went from welfarism/socialism to a free-market economy in just a few short years, reduced the size of government by staggering numbers, and changed the lives of New Zealanders in a most remarkable way. Their success at creating good government would be considered a fable if it was not so demonstrably real. Much of this was accomplished through the efforts of the Hon. Maurice McTigue and his New Zealand compatriots. Mr. McTigue has brought his approach and the lessons learned to the United States as part of the Mercatus Center at George Mason University in Arlington, Virginia. His programs and goals can be viewed through the center's website www.mercatus.org. But the real value of McTigue's experience can be gleaned from a CD titled "Making Government Accountable: Reform Lessons from New Zealand." Listening to Mr. McTigue describe what was accomplished during New Zealand's reform years offers sheer inspiration to those who are confounded and frustrated by government's ever-widening grasp and malfunctioning intrusions into the lives of citizens. The CD can be obtained or downloaded through the Mercatus Center's website.

About the Author

CHARLES MURRAY is a resident fellow at the American Enterprise Institute in Washington, D.C. Born in 1943 in Newton, Iowa, he earned his undergraduate degree from Harvard in 1965 and subsequently spent six years in Asia as a Peace Corps volunteer and then as a researcher. Upon his return home he earned a Ph.D. in political science in 1974 from MIT. His investigations into crime, poverty, and social programs led him to write *Losing Ground: American Social Policy 1950–80*. This book did much to set the tone of President Ronald Reagan's domestic policy.

Murray's career as one of the nation's most influential conservative thinkers is well established. He lectures and publishes widely and is a frequent witness before congressional committees. Murray's most controversial book, *The Bell Curve: Intelligence and Class Structure in American Life* (with Richard Herrnstein) posits that wealth and other positive social outcomes are a product of intelligence and that intelligence is an innate characteristic that it is foolish to pretend either isn't important or can be compensated for in some fashion (political or otherwise) that eliminates the need to recognize its existence. Published in 1994, the book caused a still-continuing social debate.

32

Socialism

Ludwig von Mises

Originally published: 1922
567 pages

SOCIALISM IS A WORD and concept that is ubiquitous in *First Principles*. We have repeatedly proclaimed that understanding socialism is tantamount to understanding the welfare state. While that is true philosophically, it is not always so transparently true in the real world. Consequently, we return to square one, to ensure the correlation between the two is comprehensible.

For several reasons, one of our intentions has also been to demonstrate that we cannot understand the twentieth century without understanding socialism. And although understanding the third or even the thirteenth century is not wholly essential to understanding the progress of humanity, for those of us in the twenty-first century it is more than necessary that we comprehend the twentieth. For the reader who has traveled this far in *First Principles* it must also be apparent that history has a pernicious habit of repeating itself. Thus we come back to socialism—as a fact and a factor and as the foundation of how liberal thinking got to where it did.

The best, first, and most comprehensive exploration of socialism was produced when the concept was relatively old but its effects were finally becoming widespread. Ludwig von Mises published his investigation in 1922 and what he offers is still a masterful exposition of the topic.

Unbridled capitalism and the Roaring Twenties were in full bloom in the U.S. when Ludwig von Mises wrote *Socialism*. But in his native Austria, the times were not good. His country suffered from a monumental World War I reparations debt, an economy that was struggling to stay afloat, and a national psyche that hadn't truly learned any lessons during the Great War except the main one: Don't lose. New paradigms were on the rise and Austrians desperately sought them. Some of those ideas, in the view of Mises, were invalid on the drawing board and unquestionably dangerous in the marketplace.

In trying to both explain and deconstruct socialism, Mises investigates the subject from every conceivable angle. His insights turn out to be accurate, for Mises understood how human nature plays its part in economics—even though his contemporary critics characterized his views as negative and myopic. The human condition is the sticking point that derails any scheme to make the world an instantly better place. Appealing solely to man's "finer" nature may be laudable in the parlor, but it's naïve on the factory floor or Main Street. For Mises, failing to take into account mankind's primary operative and energizing quality—incentive—meant simply that failure was inevitable.

The overall philosophy of social organization interested Mises to such a degree that in *Socialism* he delves into some of the arcana of generations and even centuries past. He goes so far as to explain how the philosophers Kant and Hegel prepared the way for the specific mindset that embraced socialism in the modern era. In the main, though, he endeavors to pick socialism apart piece by piece, because that was the rational thing to do. Mises basically takes the tenets and methods of this political/economic theory to their logical conclusions, and when those conclusions betray themselves as insupportable either practically or philosophically, he declares, "Just so."

The prime example of early twentieth-century socialistic fantasy was the conviction that human beings would willingly abandon the concept of private property in order to create a society based upon universal generosity—a hoped-for transformation expected to energize a new kind of economic system. However, when socially recognized property rights no longer motivated individual striving, and when ownership was abolished and rules were set in place for human action based on giving rather than earning, the social fabric became stretched beyond the limit of people's imagination and charity. The human condition rose up to overwhelm utopia.

Socialism wears a mantle of moral superiority to capitalism because of its attempt at equality of result rather than of opportunity. It is founded on the idea that all men are equal, and as such ought to fare equally well. But, obviously, we are not equal (in talents, skills, energy, drive, intellect, or anything else) and we do not achieve in equal measure.

Thus, socialism is a dream not compatible with either human nature or mankind's circumstances. In actuality, nothing other than our inherent *inequality*, as harnessed by our social genius to benefit from our differences, is the foundation of progress.

Karl Marx, whose work was in vogue at the time Mises was writing *Socialism* (primarily as a result of the political success of the Russian Revolution of 1917), had insisted that the struggle between capitalism and socialism—and ultimately communism—was a class struggle, not just an economic or philosophical one. Mises dissects and then dismisses the Marxist theory of class struggle by pointing out that the evolution of economic success "comes on waves of knowledge, experience, and trial and error," none of which is intentionally the work or idea of one class or another. As importantly, those who do improve human society through invention, imagination, or insight often start at the lower end of the economic ladder, but do not remain there for long. It is invariably their own incentive that drives their efforts, not the fact that they first appear at one level or another on the social scale.

Economics is the study of property (in its largest sense) and property's relationship with and among people. Mises explains that economics is not a philosophy although it contains philosophical considerations; it is an observational science. As he perceives the limits of socialism's importance, Mises understands that socialism captures the minds of the masses, not because it actually tends to their interests, but because the masses are led to *think* it does. Ultimately, reality steps in to make one look at his neighbor and remember that that person is not *entitled* to anything in particular. Human beings are built to compete and discern and they naturally look askance at any system of equal rewards. This is an essential feature of human nature and, on a more practical scale, human progress.

The fundamental appeal of socialism (and of its ugly stepsisters Nazism, fascism, and communism) was the aforementioned idea of equality of result. The rallying cry of the socialist movement to the workers (the proletariat) was to not let the owner-class (the bourgeoisie) take away the yield of their work. At its root, the idea was for each worker to keep the entire product of his labor, because anything less would mean that someone had engaged in a form of thievery, or slavery, and received something that was not earned. Socialism does not recognize either intangible labor—planning, management, organization and efficiency, invention, leadership, deploying capital, developing a reputation for integrity, etc.—or such non-labor factors of production as land, capital, supplies, and materials. In a socialistic scheme, everything that was not labor (narrowly construed), was to be supplied by the state. All intellectual components were considered valueless and easily achievable by the state, run by bureaucrats. The latter is a group for which Mises has the utmost unhidden contempt. The paucity of logic and the denial of human value and instincts (positive and negative) in socialism's plan are transparent in Mises exposition.

For Mises, there is no escaping the reality that owners (capitalists/bourgeoisie) must serve non-owners (workers/proletariat), or there will be nothing created for either the owners to sell or the workers to buy—nothing for either to labor toward. That is not to say that owners or workers get their interrelationships right every time; progress is achieved by trial *and* error.

Wholesale abandonment of the capitalist social/economic system would only become tenable if the system were to fail utterly—not if some segments of it were merely found to be flawed or if some individuals were to skew the system for their own ends. There is a symbiosis between the owners and workers on all levels because each owner and every worker has a social and economic investment in the whole system. Henry Ford (who knew that he had to pay his employees enough so that they could buy the products they built) got it right; Karl Marx, who thought Henry Ford was entitled to nothing, did not.

Socialists purport to deal rationally with the complex modern workplace where the division of labor is not just necessary, but fundamental. They elect to solve the dilemma of how to reward the worker (who produces only part of any product or crop or service) by declaring both that the state owns everything on behalf of the workers and that the state will decide reward and distribution issues. The statist solution could be fine if everyone were to agree on two matters: the state's determinations as to who should *do* what and the workers' acceptance of who should *get* what. Human nature is an insurmountable roadblock in both instances.

The patent absurdity of ignoring much that production requires—the intellectual and entrepreneurial inputs, the inventive/imaginative genius, the capital investment, and the skill of management—was Mises's field of play. He describes socialist redistribution schemes as quaint (i.e., possible in an agrarian society) but nonsensical and useless in a complex industrial and service environment. The division of labor (the foundation of economic and concomitant social progress) was marginalized in socialist schemes. Yet, the division of labor, whereby we become more specialized and thereby create more wealth, was the foremost tool that had allowed society to progress both economically and intellectually. This was Adam Smith's theme, if not mantra, in *Wealth of Nations* (Chapter 12).

By the middle of the nineteenth century, the effects of the industrial revolution caused socialists to renounce the redistribution of all a society's wealth since that was impractical. How do you "redistribute" a buggy factory and still make it work? In its place was put community ownership of the means of production, with the equal distribution of its fruits. Absent the personal incentive that only private ownership of property offered, however, common possession required intellectual, philosophical, and physical coercion of human beings. To Mises, that alone made socialism not just flawed, but indefensible. Although he does not use the word "incentive" often, his view of social order implicated incentives as the indispensable prompting necessary to elicit both the regular and the extraordinary efforts that energize a society. If society distributes all production in equal portions, yet takes away in unequal measure from those who achieve economy, or sacrifice for the future, or think creatively or wisely, or work harder and longer, why would anyone make that extra effort? Conversely, if the system accepts less from those who don't bring a fair share to the table, why would those who do work hard continue to do so? Socialism brings material and intellectual impoverishment to those under its thumb. It is a sentimental notion, unsupported by any rational argument, and advocated with transparent sophistry, which clearly irritates Mises.

Without much attempt at humility, socialism's apologists set themselves up as morally superior. Their invective of greed and self-interest hurled at capitalists was and is unrelenting and equally unproven. Mises eloquently defends capitalism, private property, and the division of labor, showing they are not only *not* morally bankrupt, as the socialist dogmatists insist, but that these economic elements form the genuinely moral foundation of a symbiotic relationship between owners, owner/workers, and workers. Mises dissects socialism, revealing that far from being morally superior it is intellectually vacuous.

Today, understanding how socialism and equalitarianism became ascendant during the middle of the twentieth century remains important. Pernicious and larcenous portions of the socialist agenda are ever present—as exemplified in the welfare state run amuck in many nations. Twenty-first-century equalitarianism doesn't attempt to create parity by nationalizing the means of production. Instead, the welfare stepchild of socialist thought takes away the fruits of capitalism through inventive means of taxation—often implemented at confiscatory levels—and redistributes them legislatively in the form of "entitlements." The creation of some "entitlements" gives rise to many more, so that the population eventually becomes accustomed to being entitled to many things—and obligated for few. The works of Mises retain their importance precisely because they allow readers to appreciate the many ways whereby socialist thinking hides its goals; e.g., by mendaciously seeking equality of results behind a façade of "politically correct" opportunism. In other words, the goals and methods of socialism are still worth studying, for the logic, agenda, and many of the methods of equalitarianism are identical with those of socialism's philosophy.

Modern day state-sponsored and state-run welfarism exudes the same overt moral superiority and internal moral bankruptcy of its ancestor. On a practical level there is an often unspoken partnership between the liberal mindset and the legislative and bureaucratic frame of reference; and an equally unspoken disconnect between those same bureaucrats and responsible legislation that recognizes and relates to a rational view of human nature. A bureaucracy can overcome the best intentions of any legislature, or can arrogate those intentions well beyond what was expected by the lawmakers, and institute paternalistic policies not readily amenable to reversal. For these reasons the vocal and pointed efforts of conservative political action in the second half of the twentieth century became necessary but ultimately only partially successful.

Ludwig von Mises preceded Barry Goldwater by fifty years and Ronald Reagan by seventy, but the cry for vigilance by the standard bearers of conservative thought was no more heartfelt, or more necessary, in their era than it was when Mises exposed the bankruptcy of socialist theory and practice in the early decades of the twentieth century. Neither the field of play nor the rules have changed much in the ensuing one hundred years. Reading the early views of Mises on the overall vacuity of socialistic thinking and on the necessity of rationally assessing human activity in order to logically create human institutions helps us keep in focus that our obligations as a society take precedence over misdirected, idealistic notions.

Definitions

ALTHOUGH MISES does not directly define any of the terms he uses context usually makes their meaning reasonably clear. Nonetheless, a distinct understanding of certain concepts will prove valuable. Some of the terms Mises employs, though in vogue in the early part of the twentieth century and therefore part of his vocabulary, have long since gone out of popular usage. The words that have been defined for the reader appear after the synopsis of *The Theory of Money and Credit* (p. 409).

About the Author

LUDWIG VON MISES was a product of antipathy to nineteenth-century European economic dogma; he became a prime creator of twentieth-century economic science. Born in 1881 in Austria, educated in Vienna, and chased to Geneva, Switzerland by the Nazis in the 1930s, he finally settled in the U.S. in 1940. His battles were never ending. Even in the United States, his views were so widely disputed by the ultimately discredited Keynesians that he could not secure regular employment. He eventually landed a job at New York University, but his salary was paid by outside interests not the school, and he never became a regular member of the faculty. During his career he wrote twenty-five books and hundreds of scholarly articles; his students changed economic thinking and policy in the twentieth century, literally around the world. Mises died in New York City in 1973.

33

A Humane Economy

Wilhelm Röpke

Originally published: 1957
261 pages

As AN ECONOMIST and a student of the free-enterprise system, Wilhelm Röpke understood, perhaps more acutely than most theorists, that the foundation of a free society is a moral one. This was a personal lesson initially learned in the deadly trenches of World War I's battlefields. Later, while enduring the Great Depression and World War II, his comprehension of this fact sharpened and became an imperative in his work. That did not turn him into a preacher, or a scold, but it did make him understand the dual necessity of encouraging man's potential while deflecting our darker side.

When Röpke writes of a moral society he doesn't just mean "Thou shalt not steal" must guide us; he sees a larger frame of reference wherein our institutions need to be morally designed and effected. He argues that if we (and that includes our government) are not encouraged and *allowed* to act in an honest, honorable, and humane manner, then our society must become burdened with rules and the power of government to enforce them. For Röpke, that which is humane recognizes human dignity and the integrity of human interaction unencumbered by ubiquitous legal or bureaucratic oversight as the starting point. Government intervention in individual lives, no matter how well intended, ultimately leads to both frustration and the insidious undermining of freedom. Government causes this reaction for one simple reason: it makes decisions for us—decisions that are almost always different from what our own choices would be.

Röpke deals with several concepts in this book. In the main, he discusses how government must adapt itself to man's inherent nature rather than rely upon man to conform to idealistic government. This does not necessarily mean giving in to our darkest impulses and then excusing them with a bureaucratic *c'est la vie* (such is life) nod and wink. In every way possible we must assist people in learning, and relearning in successive generations, the true foundations of a free community's social, economic, and governmental interrelations.

While politics is the art of the possible, two things are not possible: the perfection of human beings or the universal and precise assimilation of social imperatives by the individuals who comprise society. As we *aim* at the possible, according to Röpke, we ought to postulate two additional comprehensions: a clear understanding of how ethical behavior is fostered, and that it is necessary that government be designed around both our frailties *and* our potential. In other words, if there is too much government—to correct our failings—that same government will stifle our potential. The balance between too little government (anarchy) and too much government (collectivism and totalitarianism) is delicate.

An appraisal by Röpke of his previous work, *The Social Crisis of Our Time*, written shortly after World War II, appears early in *A Humane Economy*. Looking back, he intended to reassert in the present volume what he now saw was permanently valid from the body of his work, while using current examples to support his contentions. Even at that early date he was particularly interested in the economic, political, and social success of the open and free post-World War II West Germany, as contrasted with the closed and paranoid East Germany. (At the end of the war Germany was divided into two separate nations: the West was administered by the U.S., Britain, and France, the East by the Soviet Union.) Recall that *A Humane Economy* dates from 1957, twelve years after the end of the war but four years prior to the construction of the Berlin Wall. The Wall was the death zone built by the Soviet Union that physically enforced, by means of weapons, guards, concrete barriers, and barbed wire, a ban prohibiting all interaction along roughly 100 miles of the border between East and West Germany. It is estimated that 1,245 people were killed trying to flee from East to West Germany during the time the Wall was in place and roughly five thousand successful escapes were achieved. The clear separation the Wall imposed could not have been better designed to demonstrate the ultimate consequences of a closed society compared to an open one. The lessons learned from the juxtaposition of these two countries and their diverse economic systems (both before and after the Wall was constructed, and then once it was torn down in 1989) formed much of the template for both *A Humane Economy* and the twentieth-century political and economic success of capitalistic enterprise on one side and the failure of state socialism on the other. (For an in-depth discussion of this template, see *The Commanding Heights* [Chapter 29].)

As important to Röpke as the components of a sound economy are the ingredients in a sound government. In this arena reside his concerns regarding a broader and more ephemeral and emotional issue: impulsive and often naïve political reactions to some of life's inequalities. In particular, Röpke pursues a critical investigation of Christianity's charitable impulse, often misrepresented in public conversations about government's aim and its capabilities through a literal presentation of the Bible's narration. In the hands of the politically astute, it can be claimed that Christian charity directs us to socialist thinking that promises equalitarian results by means of an economic reordering. That this is a factual and philosophical misrepresentation of Christian tenets is one thing; that these concepts won't work over time, regardless of any religious foundation, is quite another.

Although equalitarian ends are simplistically presented as philosophically laudable and superficially satisfying in theory, Röpke intones that they can be achieved in a modern complex society only through ceding dictatorial powers to the government. This is primarily because citizens have shown they will not or cannot embrace literal Christian charity and its equalitarian vow of poverty on their own. This is not the result of an excess of self-interest but is a reflection of man's innate being—the need and drive for self-preservation. It is simply a given that Christian charity begins at home. If equalitarian authoritarianism occurs in the public sector it ensures that real social and economic progress that helps reduce the need for charitable efforts and increases the spread of human dignity will not be achieved. Put simply, freedom mostly eliminates the need for people to rely on the charity of others. And for those who cannot survive without such charity it is true they are more easily cared for when freedom creates resources and impetus to do this.

That only totalitarian government can effect equalitarian ends is clear from the manner in which human nature operates; human beings are simply not capable of voluntary social indulgence on a level that will achieve equal economic results for all members of society. Röpke's point is that to force that result by means of collectivist practices—whether comprehensive socialism or state welfarism—in the face of the human condition will result only in failure. Charity is and should remain a personal and private matter, not a government function. When charity is turned on its head and becomes a government mandate and is implemented through necessarily oppressive taxation to achieve its goals, not only does its character change (it can no longer even be termed charity), its effectiveness does as well. In this vein, Richard Cornuelle's *Reclaiming the American Dream* (Chapter 30) and Bertrand de Jouvenel's *The Ethics of Redistribution* (Chapter 28) explore public assistance as a government enterprise versus private benevolent initiatives. Both authors conclude, as does Röpke, that government drives out private care; government does so at such great cost that to pursue this course is to invite inefficiency at best and indiscriminate social dependence at worst—which was exactly the result achieved in certain sectors of American society at the beginning of the twenty-first century.

From a strict economic standpoint, publicly sanctioned and enforced equalitarian "charity" ultimately denies any fuel to its source. It inevitably consumes a greater and greater part of the public economy as more and more "inequalities" are found (since clearly, inequality is limitless). Eventually the self-sufficient stand up when the product of their efforts is taken in greater and greater measure. At that point the economic engine implodes and social repercussions grow. This result is not inherently uncharitable, there is no value judgment attached to it; it is intrinsic in human nature and the economic system that creates the excess wealth by which magnanimity is supported in the first instance. These two aspects of the human personality—self-preservation and charitable inclinations—are not mutually exclusive, but they are only complementary; they do not work in exact tandem. Most importantly, they work together only voluntarily. When excessive and compulsory generosity is introduced, real charity, and more importantly, real results, disappear.

AS HIS INVESTIGATION proceeds, Röpke takes a step back from dissecting the existing functions of government and contemplates the governed. He does this in order to determine how a government should be designed. He reaffirms what the Founders of the American system declaimed, that governance should begin at the bottom with the citizen and his freedom; not at the top with the ruling class and its control. As his title explains, he is attempting to formulate not just a free society, but one that is humane. To Röpke that means employing a government that looks after the citizen's best interests, mostly by leaving the populace to order their own lives; one that neither panders to humankind's inherent weaknesses nor stifles its most worthy capabilities.

Röpke understood that men can learn the lessons of a humane economy only through education *and* experience, through trial *and* error. To aid in the education of the citizenry, Röpke harks back to Edmund Burke's belief in the value of tradition as a learned and *tested* set of "rules" or prescriptions (Chapter 36). Writing from the perspective of the mid-1950s, Röpke was first offended and then disheartened by our tendency toward collectivist mass society, which seemed to deny all that we had so painstakingly discovered about individuality from the time of Burke to the defeat of fascism during World War II. He expresses his concerns regarding these lessons in strong language with vivid imagery, and he offers counter-arguments, based on individual freedom of choice and expression, that lead to a sound and moral society.

Once Röpke sets the stage, by first defining what we can learn from the past and next outlining the socialist construct then extant, he assesses modern economic thinking. He offers a comprehensive insight into the economic realities of a free or "liberal" society. (Note that Röpke, a European, uses the word liberal in the Old World manner, which equates with conservative or classical liberal as they are generally used today in the U.S.) When Röpke views the tension between a free society (that centers on the individual) and a controlled one (that focuses on the state), he observes:

> The rights of the community are no less imperative than those of the individual, but exaggeration of the rights of the community in the form of collectivism is just as dangerous as exaggerated individualism and its extreme form, anarchism.

In spite of the things he knew to be true and rational, as Röpke surveyed the mid-century social landscape he saw the path turning inexorably toward collectivism; first because socialist equalitarianism seemed to offer so much utility, and then because he thought society could not readily retreat once the path to socialism was chosen—no matter how economically absurd it was. Röpke seems guilty of Joseph

Schumpeter's error (expressed in *Capitalism, Socialism and Democracy* [Chapter 38]) of assuming that socialism and collectivist governmental policies would continue after World War II simply because they had worked during the war and people had become accustomed to them. They both felt that continuity was more likely than reassessment. Neither author was able to embrace the view that future circumstances could and would change people's methods and goals. In point of fact, once the citizenry had suffered the excesses and failures inevitably resultant from the collectivist progression during and subsequent to the war, they were willing to discard these methods and move back toward their core values—most notably those centered on individual freedom. Practically speaking, the war effort *was* collectivist, but out of necessity. Once the war was concluded, the individual again became the focus of social interaction. That individualism would revive after the collectivist urgency of wartime expired is obvious now, but it seems it was largely hidden from both Röpke and Schumpeter.

What is perhaps most interesting in Röpke's case is the value of, and the certitude with which he views the potential of the human spirit in some instances, and the destitution of hope he exhibits in others. As he considers the totalitarian impulses that sought to achieve an alleged greater good and then recalled the necessity of freedom to achieve such ends, he seems to become schizophrenic. On the downside, these see-saw feelings, certainly not novel in Röpke's era, were evidence of the paucity of fiscal and psychological integrity in most political discourses produced by the socialist intelligentsia, conversations that worked against rational thinking in economic matters. These maledictions were followed, almost inexplicably (even in England), by actual mass political movement toward collectivism—as if Tinkerbell had sprinkled pixie dust on everyone's oatmeal and then commanded fealty to a false equalitarianism. On the positive side, Röpke knew the power of ideas and facts, thus his pessimism may have been cautionary only; pessimistic but not really conclusive.

Röpke dissects the socialist/equalitarian impulse by seizing upon the arrogance and dissonance of the idealistic utopians who to him are

> people who pride themselves on their generosity at others' expense.

And when Röpke uses the word expense he means it in all senses, not just the obvious economic impact of forced collectivism and social welfarism, but the human cost as well. To Röpke, inflicting this damage on the citizenry in an attempt to reach a chimerical goal is inhumane. Röpke believes in the tested and proven methods of the free market, where the moral behavior so necessary to a sound economy is required for success at every level. It is not competition alone that guides the actors; it is also the recognition by each individual that he must seek his success by serving the market. A person subject to the free market's discipline will do well only if he meets the needs of others, not if he demands that others accept whatever he judges they should accept—as is the case in collectivist societies. The very act of serving the market necessarily requires any individual to commit himself to the market's rules—that pay back as much as they exact a cost. These rules apply (work) only in a *quid pro quo* society, a society that is morally grounded and founded in enlightened self-interest.

Obviously, such a society cannot require that integrity be enforced; people understand that an absence of integrity would leave them without a foundation on which to base their community, including its economy and government. Röpke argues that the state exists to enforce the fulfillment of commitments when they are violated, but this is necessary only infrequently. The state decidedly should not exist to determine what commitments are to be created in the first place. As many of the synopses in *First Principles* make clear, the foregoing truths must be learned by each succeeding generation. Readers may consult George Gilder's *Wealth and Poverty* (Chapter 27, written in 1981, twenty-five years after *A Humane Economy*) to see the same laments and hopes and rules as proffered by Röpke repeated in a more recent incarnation and from a U.S. perspective.

Once Röpke defines the primary issue—the psychological fallacy and human cost of collectivist government—he notes that there are two additional inevitabilities that result from collectivism and exacerbate its economic follies. The first is the monetary and human price of chronic inflation, the inevitable consequence of socialistic enterprise. The second is the size, distance, and disconnection of government centralized at higher and higher levels from the citizens to be served.

Röpke finds that the concentration of power at higher levels is often a consequence of collectivist-driven economic failure on the local level. When economic energy flagged in the socialistic setting, managers and politicians assumed (really hoped) that bigger enterprises would be more efficient. Larger, top-down ventures, of course, would not solve the problems of socialistic production because it was the stifling of human incentive that made collectivist enterprises fail—not some lack of efficiency or size. In this context, Röpke reprises age-old arguments against distant rulers, a necessity in the top-down governing requisite to socialistic endeavors. His conclusions, cogently framed in a modern context, remain as apt as when his predecessors drew them centuries before. It is a simple equation: the further a government is from the governed and perforce the greater its size, the more it can do to the people, often without the population even knowing it until well after the fact, and the less the people can do to protect themselves.

The consequence of the failure of collectivist enterprise—revenues that do not meet government obligations or the promises of utopian material abundance—results in a government need to print money to pay its bills. This new currency is mostly used to buy foreign goods imported to make up the shortfall in government managed production. This obviously causes runaway inflation and eventual economic collapse. Inflation is the bitterest thief of all, no matter the era, for it is insidious and relentless and no respecter of people. Röpke's portrayal of inflationary tendencies and problems and their causes and solutions is a core economic exposition in this book. Inflation, although not a complicated subject, is nevertheless often wholly misunderstood in its origins, its mechanisms, and its consequences. Röpke's analysis helps the average reader understand this problem, especially as he explains the need for independent monetary policies (such as the U.S. Federal Reserve banking system), which are unfortunately only a partial solution to combat government (legislative) irresponsibility in the welfare state.

RÖPKE TAKES a long look at social welfarism, the political heir of collectivist economic designs. He observes that welfare programs no longer function to help the weak and needy as a form of social insurance and public assistance. He comments that welfare was being increasingly used as

> a social revolution aiming at the greatest possible equality of income and wealth. The dominating motive is no longer compassion. . . .

This development still poses a decisive question in twenty-first-century America; i.e., what are the motivations and the objectives of the welfare impulses in our political arena? Is there an understanding of what welfare means and is to accomplish?

When Röpke dissects what he sees in the 1950s, he concludes, as so many economists of that era did, that welfarism is socialism under a new label. The welfarist paradigm eventuated to solve what liberals saw as an intractable problem, human differences, and the traditionalists saw as human nature simply using opportunity. Tendencies toward equalitarian government constructs are found at all levels of the welfare system. The biggest difficulty with welfarism is that the successful are required to sustain the unsuccessful in indiscriminant fashion, thus further impeding the chance the less prosperous will have any motivation or opportunity to help themselves. By using law, taxation, and bureaucracy to control social policy (rather than socialist confiscation of the means of production and distribution), the political leaders attempt to achieve by stealth what they cannot achieve directly at the ballot box or the point of a gun.

What Röpke fears most is the extension of public assistance to ever more classes of people and the eventual refusal of any such class to forego for any reason the largesse they have come to expect. He sees the middle-class as too timid to call the actions of the equalitarians to account; they fear that they will be seen as miserly, selfish, or narcissistic if they deny the needy something to which they might be "entitled." The liberal media seems happy to reinforce these thoughts.

On the other side of this equation, it is clear that extensive welfare is equally pernicious for the recipient because it almost irresistibly tempts people to become dependent on public assistance, sacrificing their integrity and self-reliance. As Röpke revisits these basic insights, he argues that it is far better that people and governments prevent the creation of entitlements in the first instance because they are too often morally harmful and economically unsustainable claims on the public coffers. Obviously this is easier to say than do because the creation of entitlements is so politically useful.

All of this goes to the core of what Röpke means by a moral society and a humane economy. A humane economy is one that does not destroy the essence and the dignity of the individual by conflating the difficulties of individual self-sufficiency with manufactured, destructive, wholesale social obligations. Social welfarism does just this; it takes the idiosyncratic difficulties of the individual and makes them the rule, and then visits the force of government on the "problem" to ensure this result can never be suffered by anyone again. It is truly the use of a sledgehammer to knock down the house to find the fly and then kill it. The paradox is that the impulse that drives welfarism achieves exactly the opposite of the end it seeks. It is inhumane to lock someone into a system of receiving something he does not earn (and may not need [a politically incorrect thought]), while preventing him from attaining it by his own efforts. It destroys both the individual and the society at once. According to Röpke, the danger of the welfare state is

> that there is nothing in its nature to limit it from within.

Thus the duty falls again to the integrity and intentional acts of the electorate and the control they exert over their representatives.

Röpke notes that the desire for security, whether economic security or social security or national security or personal security, is natural and legitimate. However, when it becomes an obsession, when an intention to *remove* risk is evident and when the quest for security feeds upon itself, it inevitably demands payment in the form of lost liberty and individuality on a personal level and lost economy on the public level. The inverse equation is patent: the more security we seek, the less liberty we have.

One of Röpke's most discerning and practical observations revolves around high taxes imposed on the most productive members of society. The demagoguery that was skillfully used for the alleged social purpose of helping the less successful he reveals to be merely misguided politics as usual:

> Very many people imagine that taxation of the higher income brackets merely implies restriction of luxury spending and that the purchasing power skimmed off from above is channeled into "social" purposes down below. This is an elementary error. It is quite obvious that larger incomes have so far mainly been spent for purposes which are in the interests of all. They serve functions which society cannot do without in any circumstances. Capital formation, investment, cultural expenditure, charity may be mentioned.

The first effect of personal consumption by wealthy individuals is that it provides fodder for the media and the liberal demagogues, who remain a significant source of economic misinformation (and unfortunately, disinformation). While personal consumption is overt and can readily be sensationalized, personal spending for non-investment purposes by the highly successful consumes only a small portion of their income, and even that spending obviously has broadly positive economic consequences. The wealthy invest, or keep invested, most of the remainder of their capital.

Somehow, somewhere, even if it's only sitting in a bank account, wealth serves to create something—jobs, opportunities, research, construction, culture, education, etc. It is the investment of excess income—above needs for food, shelter, clothing, health, and education—that drives any free-enterprise economy. And it is the chance for success that motivates the entrepreneur. If the opportunity to work toward and enjoy one's success is removed, progress wanes, then stops. It is a simple truth: capital formation sustains *every* economy—capitalist, socialist, communist, fascist. In capitalism, private investment resources are forged when income is allowed to exceed expenses (including the expense of taxation) through economic freedom. If profits are consumed for social purposes by means of excessive taxes on income, that capital is irretrievably lost. To replace this forfeited resource requires new, but redundant, effort. As is clear, human beings will not operate either long or well in a society that denies incentive.

The obvious result of predatory taxation, particularly in the case of the highly successful, is that of killing the goose laying those golden eggs. As Röpke notes, profit is necessary not as a *goal*, but as a *fuel*. If this elemental reality is not embraced by an open society, then that society will bankrupt itself within a generation and destroy itself within two.

As is equally obvious, if wealth cannot be created, there will be nothing to tax. If there is nothing to tax, there is not only no welfare state, there is no state at all—only residual anarchy. Thus, as most economists have recognized, taxation used for social engineering, especially confiscatory levies on higher levels of income, achieves exactly the opposite result than its proponents intend.

It is a well-established economic pattern: the higher the level of taxation, the more quickly negative economic consequences will present themselves, and vice versa. To offer a modern example of these economic realities: income and capital gains taxes were reduced in the United States beginning in 2003. During the next four years the American economy created just under ten million new jobs—an unparalleled rate of economic growth (*Wall Street Journal*, April 9, 2007, p. A13). The correlation between the incentive of lower taxes and the opportunity to create is inescapable. Concomitant with the creation of the new employment opportunities and business activities, federal revenues *increased* in that same period in spite of the lower tax rates (see *Wealth and Poverty* [Chapter 27] for an expanded discussion of these issues). The opposite inescapable conclusion is that if tax rates are now raised again, especially on the entrepreneurial class (which is *not* made up, in large measure, of only the country's wealthiest citizens, but as well consists of those in the middle economic strata), an economic downturn will occur. That downturn will hurt the entrepreneurs, certainly, but it will hit hardest those least able to afford economic distress—the people who work in those now at-risk ten million new jobs, and those who follow them who will be looking for work as well.

AT ONE POINT Röpke makes an intellectually interesting tangential journey: he defends the economist's professional worth after he notes that there is always a delay between

> some economic or social claim and its demagogic exploitation on the one hand, and the moment, on the other, when the price of its fulfillment can no longer be concealed.

This observation appears to be Röpke's effort to ask for serious consideration of what he and his fellow economists see. Essentially, he is contending that economists earn their keep when they expose political chicanery and explain the remedial measures necessary to achieve a sound economy. Although his call seems somewhat self-serving, it is not. His concern is for the larger effort, and it is an honest summons. He understands that the long-term consequences of short-term policy can be devastating. He is asking that that case be heard—publicly.

Toward the end of his book, Röpke attempts to offer definitions distinguishing liberals from conservatives, individualism from collectivism, and liberalism from socialism, but he finds these words already too freighted to be useful. He offers centrism versus decentrism as his dividing line. But, whatever the words the concepts change little. Röpke's characterization of the Jacobin republicans at the time of the French Revolution of 1789 and their spiritual heirs over the last two centuries went to the core of what he saw happening when democracy was used as a tool (or even a weapon) rather than a principle:

The idea of democracy is seen, not in a well-articulated state with balanced and therefore mutually limiting powers, but in centralized power of a kind which is unlimited in principle and can in practice be wielded all the more freely as it is supported by the fiction of the sovereign will of the people.

Democracy is but an instrument in governance, one part of a recipe that yields an elegant dish so long as all the ingredients are present in proper measure. Röpke's discernment of democratic components and how they must necessarily fit together in a logical economic construct is the theme of the latter portion of his volume. Röpke sought more than just a material benefit for society's citizens—he knew that was not enough. He also sought an understanding of man's higher being as it intersected with community. An important companion to Röpke's observations is Bertrand de Jouvenel's *On Power* (Chapter 15). In it the nature and consequence of unbridled fealty to democratic egoism and the mythical general will of the people (discerned by prescient legislators) is exposed. Taken together, these two works explain the balance necessary for a humane economy and society to exist.

About the Author

BORN IN HANOVER, Germany at the very end of the nineteenth century, Wilhelm Röpke—the man and the philosopher—was a product of twentieth-century excesses. The son of a physician, his upbringing was grounded in traditional Protestant teachings whose influence on his thinking appears over and over in his work. He fought as a soldier in the trenches during World War I; as a result of that brutal experience he sought to understand the causes of such devastating conflicts, thus he pursued the study of economics and sociology. (To understand how the same circumstances could lead to a completely opposite personal course that also had profound public consequences, see *Witness* [Chapter 41] by Whittaker Chambers, a contemporary of Röpke.) Upon receiving his doctorate Röpke became a professor in Germany.

Röpke's reputation as an individualist thinker was well earned. He was not afraid to look at first causes; his ability and drive to do so marked his career and works. He taught in Germany until he was forced to leave the country in 1932 because of his outspoken opposition to Nazism. He resided in Istanbul and taught at the university there from 1932 until 1937. He then returned to Europe and began a career at the Institute of International Studies in Geneva, Switzerland, where he embarked on a collaborative professional life with Ludwig von Mises. Although von Mises emigrated early in World War II, Röpke remained in Geneva throughout the Second World War and for the rest of his academic life.

Röpke, along with von Mises, Frederich von Hayek, Milton Friedman, and others who were ultimately awarded Nobel Prizes in economics, formed the Mont Pelerin Society in Switzerland in 1947. Their intent was to publicize the folly of collectivism and to decry socialist ideology as it caused increasing erosions of liberty. The philosophy of the Mont Pelerin Society succeeded in spite of the fears of its founders and exceeded even the most optimistic of its members' expectations. Röpke married in 1924 and raised three children with his wife, Eva. He died in 1966.

34

The Theory of Money and Credit

Ludwig von Mises

Originally published: 1912
526 pages

LUDWIG VON MISES was born in Lemberg, Austria, in 1881. From that year until his death almost a century later in New York City the world and its economic underpinnings was turned upside down. Mises, who never won recognition outside the intellectual and academic circles that were both his audience and the frequent targets of his criticism, fought difficult battles on the road to his (then) under-appreciated and under-recognized achievements. His fidelity to his work was remarkable in light of the derision, ignorance, and just plain stubbornness of less accomplished but more popular thinkers. Although a Nobel Prize was never in the wings, he changed the way that the world thought about money and commercial relationships. His understanding of the full impact of inflation and the boom-and-bust cycle of business, among other economic phenomena, were seen as unfashionable at the time he wrote. His enduring contribution regarding the nature of money—that it is a commodity like any other—initially caused consternation. It later elicited mere circumspection and eventually won acceptance.

Being out of step caused Mises to remain a peripheral figure among professional economists, thus limiting his personal prospects. He labored in the backwaters for many years, trying to establish a comprehensive understanding of all sides of economics, an understanding roughly analogous to physicist Albert Einstein's goal of a unified theory of the physical world. The approach of Mises demanded working on a broad range of issues in a complex agglomeration of disciplines: economics, history, sociology, and even scholarly methodology. His achievements, the scope of which is apparent from his major works, led to inescapable economic conclusions, which in turn caused a revolution in how governments are organized and how they approach economic planning and execution.

Mises had a great antipathy toward any attempt to control human behavior through governmental activity. The individual and his actions constituted the fundamental building blocks of the economic paradigm Mises describes. In his preface to the English edition of this work he notes that a deep knowledge of economics is not necessary to gauge the immediate effects of monetary or economic policy. The trick, and the substance of *The Theory of Money and Credit*, is to determine long-term effects

> so that we may avoid such acts as attempt to remedy a present ill by sowing the seeds for a much greater ill in the future.

Mises maintains that the answer to resolving any present ill lies in individual human action, not government direction or control. In his text he offers examples of long-term ills on both the micro- and macroeconomic stages caused by implementation of short-term (often politically expedient) solutions; for Mises the law of unintended consequences was ever in effect.

Relevant to the current debate on the globalization of most economic sectors, Mises long ago recognized commonplace misunderstandings of the international division of labor, that it is no different from the division of labor in any venue—whether that be in a factory or within a national economy. He also saw and described the negative effects of nationalism and protectionism. Economic specialization and the expansion of trade in the early twentieth century were a fulfillment of Adam Smith's comprehension of human economic activity as seen in the eighteenth century. Mises understood that governmental shoveling against this natural tide, in the guise of protective tariffs, was a formula for economic disaster of the sort that did occur with the Great Depression. Regrettably, the persons who could have made a difference were unable or unwilling to see the logic of Smith and Mises.

The policies of John Maynard Keynes that expanded public enterprise at the expense of the already overburdened private sector (through untenable increased taxation) were sold wholesale during the first third of the twentieth century. The world was much the worse off as a result. The autarky (nationalistic economic self-sufficiency) of the seventeenth century and before was seen by Keynesians as a goal rather than an anachronism. This goal was to be achieved through high tariffs and jingoistic monetary policy. The effect of these efforts was to extend and make deeper the economic depression those economists who followed Keynes had created in the first place. Mises makes several points about economics as a method of assessing or guiding human activity and how its functional attributes weren't always used to good effect in the years just prior to the Great Depression.

When Mises steps back to look at economics as a discipline (certainly more art than science) he finds that once economic activity passed beyond production for individual consumption, then economics—the dismal science—was invented. In reality, economics is not gloomy; it is the method that we use for predicting and then ameliorating the bad effects, or expanding the good effects, of human economic actions.

Economics as a methodology is scientific in its observations, but that which it observes is not scientifically organized. Human economic behavior is random and overall not wholly predictable, thus the dismal, or frustrating part—the non-science. Mises observes that economics is not prescriptive (that is, future economic results do not fit into rules that are immutable), it is projective (economists can guess at what will happen in the future based on what has happened in the past, but these are and always will be guesses); we see economic "rules" only after the fact, and the rules change as fast as the facts change. Governments and politicians get in trouble when they view the past as a formula for the future. Economic "laws" don't determine human action; human action determines economic laws. The chicken did in fact come before the egg in this instance.

A USEFUL AND significant portion of *The Theory of Money and Credit* is an investigation of money itself. As a medium of exchange, some tangible (or today electronic) monetary unit is necessary for any economic functioning above the direct barter system. Mises explains that money is that medium. But money's value lies in the eye of the beholder, and the same amount of money does not mean the same thing to two different people who are always in different circumstances. A million dollars on a deserted island is useless, while a hundred dollars to a single parent may hold a saving grace. Further, Mises comments on two economic verities: he demonstrates the failure of authoritative interference in the markets by governments, and he elaborates on the anarchic nature (because of human whims) of both production and consumption. He also levels a direct attack on inflationary governmental policies, which if left unchecked inevitably lead to totalitarianism because when inflation is not controlled, one failed policy after another leads to an insistence of even more rather than less government. He observes that as economic activity disintegrates in the face of inflation each section of the governmentally controlled house of cards is built. Government causes inflation with deficit spending or an unrestrained increase in the supply of money, then claims only *it* can control inflation by directing the economy, while simultaneously refusing to recognize that its actions were the basis of the inflation in the first place. A house of cards built on inflationary actions and government hubris that it can fix things often falls with great noise in spite of its slim construction.

Mises's investigation of inflation marks his transition from economist to political realist. He is adept at pointing out inflation's economic and political implications, one of which is the boom/bust roller coaster ride that overly regulated economies often endure. His ability to call things what they are and to discredit policies implemented solely to salve the body politic but which do not carry the seeds of successful course alterations make his economic discussion both readable and correlative to already-experienced political reality. As importantly, his observations on economics offer an accurate method of assessing political promises.

Mises lived through an era of dictators and collectivist governments. He observes that when the state moves to intervene in or govern the market, it takes the first step on the precipitous and slippery slope to economic conflagration. Mises contends that the state has only a secondary, political interest, in the economic activity of its citizens; it is the people who have the primary interest. Private property, in all its forms, belongs to them. This includes ownership of the means of production—which is the prime moving force of economic activity. Mises holds that so long as private property exists and the means of production are allowed their anarchic relationships, state intervention usually can only negatively influence an economy. The real-world examples of what Mises predicts (recall, this book was written in 1912) can be seen in the encyclopedic overview of socialism versus capitalism presented in *The Commanding Heights* (Chapter 29), Daniel Yergin and Joseph Stanislaw's review of this battle. Whichever volume one reads first, the two together form bookends to the economic history of the twentieth century.

The most severe indictment Mises issues is reserved for the folly of wage and price controls—government's solution to the inflation it caused in the first place. When a government begins to set wages and prices (including minimum wage levels), even in the smallest measure, its action constitutes an attack on private property and threatens its very existence. This is because fixing prices is nothing more than the taking of property without compensation. This is one of the long-term consequences of an imprudent intervention in the economy for short-term goals. It is a consequence that politicians do not care to face and thus ignore when implementing the very wage and price controls that will cause economic stability to disintegrate. These controls only ensure soaring inflation when they are lifted, or a free-fall to totalitarian solutions if they are not. In either case, their certain adjunct is a black market that further distorts an economy and undermines any government's success at economic oversight or tax collection. (It should be noted that these observations are global and do not often directly apply to the U.S. economy. The fruits of the actions described by Mises can grow any time, any place—thus the value of understanding these economic realities irrespective of what conditions or practices may exist in any given nation at any particular time.)

On the subject of economic regulation, Mises observes that every restriction of trade—whether by an excise duty, quotas, price controls, tariffs, government subsidies, or other mechanisms—creates vested interests in the beneficiaries thereof. From then on, the beneficiaries will be opposed to the removal of the initial restraint. No matter how allegedly laudable the immediate goal, economic interference inevitably results in cascading negative consequences. When these activities destroy lives, setting the market aright again often takes all the king's horses and all the king's men—sometimes literally.

An example of how the human spirit circumvents or abridges the edicts of economically illiterate governors can be seen in the later years of the reign of Tsar Alexander I of Russia (c. 1822), grandson of Catherine the Great. The tsar wanted to reduce Russian dependence on foreign goods so he set steep tariffs on much that was imported and banned the balance of these items in an attempt to encourage his subjects to engage in their own manufacturing. Soon the shops were flooded with goods bearing Russian labels—but there wasn't much else Russian about them. As Jason Roberts notes in *A Sense of the World*

(2006), making foreign goods expensive to buy was not the same as making production of native products affordable. It was more efficient to smuggle foreign goods in and change the labels than to manufacture such items at home.

The demands of the tsar did not change economic reality, they only fostered an illegal charade that covered the economic futility of his plan. What must be understood in order to place the tsar's incentives and the merchant's counter-actions in perspective were the penalties for disobeying the government's rules—these were not simply white collar crimes, punishable by a suspended sentence, a small fine, and momentary public censure. The price to be paid ended on the gallows; still the violations were rampant. We see in this example the folly of attempting to force man to accede to economic policy, and the need to design economic policy to man's inherent nature. Even the incentive to obey Alexander's laws (death for violation) was not enough to overcome everyman's need to act rationally in an economic milieu.

Mises devotes much of this treatise to refuting various existing economic theories prior to asserting his own. As the foundations for appreciating this work are self-contained, the reader needs to devote little effort toward preparation prior to reading it. Mises's logic flows so smoothly and simply that his account of historical facts virtually demands his theoretical and prescriptive conclusions. To properly appreciate the book it is best read as a whole for it does not lend itself well to being read in stages. That being said, the general reader need cover only the first sixteen chapters and the last three (21–23). A more detailed presentation of national and international monetary factors appears in chapters 17 through 20; this material requires close attention yet adds little to a general understanding of his theories.

This book represents Mises at his best. He is so logical, so unrelenting in observing the details (wherein the devil always lies) that despite its length and intricacies his effort is simply a masterpiece of analysis and cogent, conclusive prescription. Most valuably, the reader should recall—as current-day problems are investigated and weighed against their sometimes inane political solutions—that Mises wrote this book almost a century ago, yet the answers posited then are still valid today.

Definitions

ALTHOUGH MISES does not directly define any of the terms he uses, either in this book or the two others he wrote that are reviewed in this compendium (*Socialism* [Chapter 32] and *Human Action* [Chapter 40]), context usually makes their meaning reasonably clear. Nonetheless, a distinct understanding of certain words will prove valuable because some of the terms Mises employs, though in vogue in the early part of the twentieth century and therefore part of his vocabulary, have long since gone out of popular usage. The following definitions can be useful in comprehending all three of the Mises's texts.

aleatory factor: of or depending on chance or luck.
a priori: deductive reasoning, based on logic, without recourse to experience; prior to and furnishing a base for understanding experience.
autarky: economic self-sufficiency as a national policy.
bourgeoisie: the social class between the aristocracy and working class, or proletariat, made up of shop owners, manufacturers, service providers, etc. In Marxist theory, the capitalists (i.e., bourgeoisie) as a class are antithetical to the proletariat. In capitalism the bourgeoisie and proletariat complement one another.
catallactics: the science of commercial transactions.
chrematism: the science of wealth; the study of the manipulation of property and wealth.
chreotechnics: the useful arts, especially agriculture, manufacturing, commerce.
classical liberalism (now generally termed conservatism in America, liberalism in Europe): limited state power, free-market economy, freedom for the individual, personal responsibility, a society governed by the rule of law.
commodity money: that money which not only serves as money, but is also a commodity, i.e., gold and silver.
credit money: money, or a claim for money, issued by a government, entity, or person, but which cannot be converted into gold or some other valuable commodity on demand. Credit money refers to a government's ability to stand behind its obligations. The value to the citizenry is in using this money for exchange purposes. Today, money that is legal tender in almost all countries is actually credit money by classical definition.

division of labor: the incrementally smaller sphere of work each person does as specialization and cooperation make one more efficient.

epistemology: the branch of philosophy that investigates the origin, nature, methods, and limits of human knowledge.

etatism: the concept that the state is not only the center of political thought and action, but the only voice that should control. In monetary theory, the concept that money, and in particular an abundance of it and its value in relation to the money of another state, is the measure of the economic merit of any state. The more powerful and rich the state, the more valuable its money.

eudaemonism: the doctrine of happiness, or the system of ethics that considers the moral value of actions in terms of their ability to produce happiness.

fiat money: money simply created by the state that has certain legal characteristics. Fiat money has no correlation to any underlying value; the market establishes its value through supply and demand. Fiat money, when used as an economic tool, is created with the view that more money means more wealth. This, unfortunately, is a fallacious presumption because money's value is not static; its value is always in the eye of the beholder.

fiduciary media: notes and credits issued by banking or lending institutions that are not covered by cash on hand. The value of the notes and credits are founded in the reputation and subjective value and solidity ascribed to the institution itself. Fiduciary media enable monetary transactions to occur without the need for money. Fiduciary media multiply the economic resources of a nation.

Gresham's Law: bad money (cheap money, of less than par value) will chase good money out of the marketplace. In colonial times paper money drove gold and silver coins out of circulation (the coins were hoarded by individuals, not withdrawn by the government).

inflation: rising prices caused by an increase in the amount of money and credit circulating in an economy. Prices rise as the supply of money increases because more dollars are chasing the same amount of goods. Since people have more money they are willing to pay more for any given object, causing its price to be bid up. The increase in the amount of money is the result, primarily, of a government printing more currency. When the supply of money increases, the value of each unit of money decreases. In general, governments print more money in order to balance their budgets or to purchase foreign goods not available within the country because of the negative consequences of government policy. An unbalanced budget arises when governments spend more money than taxation brings in. Allowed to continue unchecked, inflation causes the monetary system to collapse and the currency to become worthless, as happened in Germany in 1923 and in America in 1781.

inflationism: any program that seeks to increase the quantity of money in an attempt to increase the economic well-being of a given society. An inflationary policy does not create more wealth; such a policy devalues the goods and services extant.

latifundia (plural of *latifundium*): large landed estates, as in ancient Rome.

liberalism or collectivist liberalism: in the U.S. and in socialist dogma, the opposite of classical liberalism or European liberalism; state economic control, interventionist state actions that limit individual freedom, a highly progressive tax structure.

marginal utility: the value of a commodity (or service) based on subjective considerations of the person holding or acquiring it. If one does not have an automobile, the marginal utility (and thus the value) to a potential possessor is greater than an automobile to a person who already has ten.

meliorism: the belief that the world naturally tends to get better, and especially that it can be made better by human effort.

mercantilism: the doctrine or theory that the economic interests of a nation as a whole are more important than the interests of the individuals who make up the nation, and that exports are desirable because the payments that come in over the cost of imports supposedly make the nation wealthier. In fact, such an imbalance changes nothing. The excess of exports over imports (though brought into equilibrium by an inflow of money) creates no new wealth; that is, the exports equal the imports plus the cash difference. Also known as commercialism.

metaphysics: the branch of philosophy that deals with first principles; the systematic investigation of the nature of first principles, and problems of ultimate reality.

Midas theory: in international trade, the fallacious notion that exports that exceed imports make a country wealthier.

nominal value: that value of money decreed by the state, e.g., a U.S. dollar is worth one hundred cents. Nominalism's opposite, commercial value, is the value established by the market when money is used for exchange.

nominalism: a doctrine that all universal or abstract terms are ephemeral, existing in name only. Nominalism is the opposite of realism.

normative: of or establishing a norm or standard, what should be as opposed to what is; the opposite of that which is positive, which already exists.

praxeology: the general theory of human action, rooted in economics. The foundation of economics is acts of choice (causes), and their results (effects). Economics is not about things but about people's actions and reactions to their world. Economics itself does not have an ethical or moral base; economics is only about choices and actions. Praxeology is the study of those actions. Praxeology is indifferent to the goals of actions; it is a science of means, not ends.

proletariat: the working class in socialistic jargon; in socialism, the antithesis of the bourgeoisie.

ratiocination: the act or process of reasoning; rational thinking; deducting consequences from premises.

romanticism: man's dismissal of or revolt against reason, as well as the conditions under which nature has compelled him to live. He uses his imagination to disregard the laws of logic and nature.

syndicalism: a theory and movement of trade unionism whereby the means of production and distribution are controlled by the workers. Workers achieve their goals by direct action, by striking. The general strike, akin to a revolutionary attack, is the workers' ultimate (economic) weapon.

tautology: needless repetition of an idea in a different word, phrase or sentence; redundancy that adds nothing to the sense of the matter under discussion.

teleology: the study of final causes, a belief that natural phenomena are determined not only by mechanical causes, but by an overall design or purpose in nature.

velocity of money: the speed with which money changes hands by traversing through the market. The greater the speed, the faster profits are created, the faster money is made available for continued economic activity, including taxation.

About the Author

LUDWIG VON MISES was a product of antipathy to nineteenth-century European economic dogma; he became a prime creator of twentieth-century economic science. Born in 1881 in Austria, educated in Vienna, and chased to Geneva, Switzerland by the Nazis in the 1930s, he finally settled in the U.S. in 1940. His battles were never ending. Even in the United States, his views were so widely disputed by the ultimately discredited Keynesians that he could not secure regular employment. He eventually landed a job at New York University, but his salary was paid by outside interests not the school, and he never became a regular member of the faculty. During his career he wrote twenty-five books and hundreds of scholarly articles; his students changed economic thinking and policy in the twentieth century, literally around the world. Mises died in New York City in 1973.

Section III

Fundamental Inquiries

35

Ideas Have Consequences

Richard M. Weaver

Originally published: 1948
187 pages

RICHARD WEAVER'S ATTEMPT to sort out modern society is perhaps the most difficult book to comprehend in the *First Principles* stable. There are several reasons for this, but the primary one relates to his insistence that a common understanding of man's ignorance (even in the middle of the twentieth century) is the essential starting point for any discussion of man's future. Ignorance, of course, represents a void. And comprehending a void is somewhat more difficult than addressing something—anything—more concrete.

In an attempt to lift the fog that blocks both the present and what is to come, Weaver asks the reader to think in a broad manner, not just observe. The concepts he presents are philosophical and require expanding one's horizon to fully understand his meaning. As a result, even many reviewers and commentators who tackle Weaver's analysis and admonitions do not always agree on what they see or what he says. However, having observed the opportunity for confusion and the potential complications, *Ideas Have Consequences* is still more than worth any labor devoted to its consumption.

To understand Weaver's approach, we can start with a specific instance of his fidelity to both precision and comprehension by investigating a solitary concept: discrimination. Discrimination is a word with many meanings. The negative connotations—suggestive of when human beings become bullies or racists—are invariably ugly. The positive connotations, which recall our attempts to separate what is good from what is better and strive for what is best, refer to some of life's beautiful moments. In *Ideas Have Consequences* Weaver investigates the upside of discrimination.

His core psychological comprehension is perhaps his most interesting: we Americans sometimes look upon excellence, which is the result of applied discrimination, with suspicion. We wonder whether excellence might somehow be undemocratic, or even unfair. This misunderstanding is usually the result of those who confuse our egalitarian passion (equal opportunity) with equalitarian expectations (equal results), and concentrate more on the latter than the former.

Writing after World War II, Weaver sees a small hope amid the massive physical and moral destruction of the war. His oblique optimism rests on the idea that critical, discriminating thinking is the necessary starting point for achievement in any endeavor, and is especially needed in making something positive out of the insanity of the world war just concluded. To be of value, such thinking has to proceed methodically from initial facts or premises to logical conclusions. Weaver's initial inquiry reflects author Karl Popper's maxim: "First, get the question right" (Chapter 39).

Weaver writes to dispel notions that transcendentalism, which calls for most things to be explained mystically, has any significant impact in the everyday world of human existence. Transcendentalism is important, he notes, but not as an explanation for temporal things (e.g., why the stoplight turns from red to green). In Weaver's opinion, mixing transcendental sentiments with real-world problems often causes fallacious thinking. An example of this might be combining too literally the temporal social safety net and biblical injunctions to care for the poor.

Weaver sees the degeneration of thought, action, and accountability, and the concomitant rise of materialism, as the causes of an increasingly amoral society. To Weaver, integrity in the system of relationships and accountability among individuals and organizations is of paramount importance to an ordered society. Without systemic integrity, hollow terms such as "situational ethics" become common coin. Society moves from entertaining a concept such as situational ethics, to testing it, to finally accepting it—to society's moral confusion and increasing detriment. The prime caustic example is the ethical carnage caused by former President Bill Clinton, who by his very actions denied that leadership, morals, and personal responsibility apply to all, regardless of their position. Although the electorate now apparently readily forgives the egregious personal misconduct of those who openly and freely confess it, this hardly repairs the damage done by such wrongdoing to the social web of trust in a moral society. In Weaver's view, it is patent that both ideas *and* actions have consequences.

Interestingly, while watching the explosion of commerce in the late 1940s, Weaver foresaw the future ubiquity of the media and its power to confuse as well as educate. He feared that the inability or unwillingness of people to sort through unmanageable amounts of information and misinformation (and even disinformation) would cause them to defer necessary decisions. Those decisions might then end up being made *for* them by others.

In 1948 (curiously the same year in which George Orwell published his uncanny futuristic novel *1984*) Weaver appreciated how the amount of available information (the ultimate quantity of which he had only a hint) confused or simply overwhelmed people. For Orwell's characters the solution was information control, which easily led to thought control. For Weaver, who lived and wrote in a real world, individual effort and fortitude were the tools necessary to get through the information muddle, so that first principles would not easily become masked. The minutiae and the fragmentation of whole paradigms had a tendency to obscure the truth. Weaver sought to clear away the obstructions simply by paying attention. Intellectual muscle, not magic, would bring clarity to confusion.

Weaver strives to unmask the integrity hidden inside the insidious growth of information; he seeks to rediscover the ideas that are foundational to our society, ideas that ought to guide our actions. He simply calls for the intellectual integrity that allows us to both understand what is good—and better and best—and then suggests that we set a course rooted in principle to get us there. Weaver ultimately sees no separation between morality and integrity and the everyday realities of our individual lives. How we live reflects the ideas in which we believe. As evidenced in both our experience and millennia of history, we ignore this logical relationship at our peril.

Skirting metaphysics and any direct appeal to religion, Weaver takes his bearings from a point of accepted and common understanding, namely, that each human being has an innate sense of what is right and how people ought to behave. At an early age, this precious understanding emerges from a sense of wonder that Weaver esteems as the spur driving human beings to think, assess, and then decide (discriminate). In the modern age, when our choices are supposedly unlimited, we can feel paralyzed by the stunning amount of information with which we have to deal—and the details and trivializations offered as substance. Eventually, we lose a sense of certainty in our ability to make judgments and set a course of action or a mode of behavior. Weaver puts it directly:

> We live in an age that is frightened by the very idea of certitude....

The loss of nerve as we face repeated demands for our immediate attention discounts reflection, destroys contemplation, and defames common sense. We become disengaged or—still worse—puppets who are manipulated by others. Our sense of wonder disappears as we are cowed by the need to make too many decisions based on a confusion of conflicting information. As noted by other authors (Alexis de Tocqueville, *Democracy in America* [Chapter 8] and Russell Kirk, *The Roots of American Order* [Chapter 4]), this confusion and information overload leads *not* to anarchy, as might be expected of people cut lose from expectations and purpose, but to an essential totalitarianism. The totalitarianism shows forth in cultural, political, and social arenas as citizens cede their responsibility for exercising critical assessment and judgment. This is where political correctness gains a toehold.

Weaver also looks at sentiment—his term to denote our feelings for one another, and for both past and future generations—as the way human beings connect with life. Lives lived purely in response to stimuli are mostly sterile and meaningless; a life must have points of reference to have any inherent value. Problems can arise when we recognize that our freedom allows us to abuse our freedom—to be free of even responsibility. We ultimately become free to ignore anything of value in human relations. When this happens, Weaver writes that we risk descending not into chaos, but loneliness—or worse, pointlessness. Weaver aims to bring us back to one another through shared values. Such values frame the sentiments that we have for one another; they help us to refrain from abusing our personal freedoms, and each other.

Weaver's next step involves analyzing how cultural and other authority emerges. He recognizes that any value system giving structure to a society must allow for a social hierarchy to maintain that structure. The essence of hierarchy is nothing other than a further effect of discrimination—the making of choices as to who will lead or make decisions, in concert with the people. That hierarchy is useful, and ultimately inevitable in a free society where *inequality* is unavoidable, is another recurrent theme in *First Principles*. Many authors deal with the effects Weaver's observations offer regarding hierarchical social relationships, but the core point is that a social entity cannot exist without hierarchical control—no matter how much the politically correct equalitarians might otherwise contend.

Granted, the idea of constructing various hierarchies conflicts with a naïve notion of equality and *unfettered* freedom (which, of course, is the definition of anarchy). In the wrong hands, adherence to a hierarchical model could be termed anti-egalitarian, anti-democratic, and even anti-intellectual, but it actually has no sinister implications. Much time has been devoted to this concept by many authors over the course of the last three centuries. This is because of the number of negative possibilities that can eventuate when the necessity to have *someone* in charge in any social configuration is realized. As Russell Kirk observes in *The Roots of American Order*, the first element of society is order, and the first elements of order are law and hierarchy. In simplistic theory, a just society is one in which there are no levels of distinction among individuals. However, a classless, leaderless society cannot work except in a most primitive setting. Even then, it won't work well, and it won't work for long. Human nature does not allow that.

Human beings are not and cannot be made equal, nor would they want perfect equality given the full measure of what that would entail. Likewise, it is simply not possible for each of us to treat every other person in equal measure. We would not choose the first person in line to pilot our airplane, perform our surgery, handle our lawsuit, run our country, or be our best and perfect friend. In terms of making qualitative choices, discrimination is only natural.

The core of Weaver's comprehension of human relations is the idea of individual dignity irrespective of personal capability or achievement. This dignity, Weaver stresses, can be maintained only through respect of and adherence to personal integrity. Discipline learned in this fashion spills over into social integrity—with all the positive effects of that transition. When *Ideas Have Consequences* is digested whole, it is seen that the entire thrust of Weaver's effort leads to an understanding of the importance of those first principles enunciated throughout the entire American experience—from the Declaration of Independence forward. The discipline to effect such understanding, and an active realization of the correlation between first principles and the real world, are responsibilities that devolve not on "the people"—but on each of us individually. To complete that circuit is not easy—it requires paying close attention to all that life represents. Yet, Weaver argues not only that it can be done, but that we all can do it—if we take the time to understand the importance of the whole.

In his recitation, Weaver is sometimes as pessimistic in 1948, when he ponders the future of America as a nation, as the communists and socialists of that time were optimistic about achieving their aims. Their goals seemed to be within their grasp. To some, socialism *still* seems potentially desirable, until one recalls that human beings vary so much in makeup, personality, and in their reaction to the human condition from which we all suffer, that an equalitarian solution is unworkable. That brings one full circle to Weaver's title premise—ideas *do* have consequences. Actions do, as well. It is the combination, and the integrity of our application of these two realities, that makes progress possible.

As knowledge was dispersed and wisdom often disappeared in the mass, Weaver's observation that what we know should tell us what we don't know, led him to call for an understanding of the humility knowledge brings. Unfortunately for mankind, in spite of the obvious validity of Weaver's concern, we may have ended up at the opposite end of the spectrum, being guided or even ruled by our pride in possessing so much information.

Weaver's thoughts from 1948 are antithetical to modern society's superficiality, and time has proven that his observations are probably more valid now than they were sixty years ago. Although many today believe that whatever is, is right, Weaver knew better—he knew in his heart of man's fabulous ability to careen off course. He contended that a ubiquitous relativism, to justify any personal philosophy, was essentially a disbelief in truth. Denying the existence of truth makes us skeptical of any notion of certitude and leads to a counterfeit interpretation of life's value and meaning. The shallowness of modern society's glut of information has eroded our confidence in determining the truth and acting upon it. Weaver believed in truth. Probably most importantly for Weaver, truth leads to morality—the two characteristics that must underpin our existence. He recognized our fear of sharing his belief, and he saw that we will come to ruin unless we discern truth and the existence of truth, and act accordingly. These are the consequences of which he warned.

About the Author

RICHARD WEAVER was not a politician; he was a teacher, an observer and, above all else, a writer. His roots lay in the South; he spent much of his life studying that region and attempting to explain its ways. After successive degrees from the University of Kentucky (BA), Vanderbilt University (MA), and Louisiana State University (Ph.D.), he taught English at the University of Chicago and wrote poetry, essays, and criticism. His investigations into rhetoric, culture, and composition were his professional milieu. He studied his surroundings and believed, whether he always stated it directly or not, in George Santayana's aphorism that those who ignore history are doomed to repeat its mistakes. As might be expected of such an intellectual, Weaver was reclusive and focused his attention on those matters that inspired him. He was born in 1910 and died in 1963.

36

Selected Works of Edmund Burke, Volume 2: Reflections on the Revolution in France

Edmund Burke

The Portable Edmund Burke

Isaac Kramnick (Ed.)

Reflections originally published: 1790
476 pages
Portable contents originally published: late 1700s
573 pages

[Note: These volumes are companions. *Reflections on the Revolution in France*, Burke's reaction to the excesses of the French Revolution of 1789, expresses his view of the proper role of government and the people who rule. These observations still define the foundations of conservative theory. *The Portable Edmund Burke*, which includes most of his essays, tracks Burke's evolving philosophy from the time of the American War of Independence (1775–1783) through the remainder of his public career. These books are presented together to provide an overview of Burke and conservative philosophy as both developed.]

Reflections on the Revolution in France

RADICAL IDEAS WERE ubiquitous in 1790. Americans had completed their revolution and had already lived for a year under a new constitution. The French Revolution was ongoing, and there was confusion and speculation among European intellectuals as to what sort of government would succeed the discredited monarchy. If a republican form of government (rather than a return to monarchy) was to be effected, Edmund Burke supported the American model. While most intellectuals deplored the waste caused by the French radicals, no one was sure what type of system would work or could work in France, given the disparity between the French and American circumstances and historical experiences.

The French populace had spoken, but they had done so with many voices. The conflicts among means and ends and between the masses and the leadership that had seized control had to be dealt with. That anyone had to "deal with" the people at all, or their concerns, was itself a novel concept in France. Burke, a royalist, recommended Britain's enlightened monarchy as an example of what could work. However, since he also understood and defended individual rights, he felt ambivalent in the face of French extremism that moved toward wholesale egalitarianism.

The principle, and radical, idea of the era was simple; i.e., that human beings are individuals endowed with natural rights. This view was in juxtaposition to Aristotle's largely accepted notion (up until the eighteenth century) that people are political animals meant to live in political society; for Aristotle, individuals were to act only in a manner that primarily benefited society. Any "rights" or individual opportunities that remained after society's needs were met could be exercised by the people themselves. As one can surmise, based on this less-than-easy relationship between individual and societal rights, there were many issues that needed resolution before social comity would ensue.

Burke was skeptical of governmental power. In his writings he opines that government should act only when it must, never just because it can. He felt strongly that individuals should transfer rights to government reluctantly, and government should assume jurisdiction only when necessary; that is, when there was conflict *between* individuals. For Burke, civil society was an artificial institution entered into by individuals who contracted with each other to organize their respective lives as they interacted. Where such organization was not essential, Burke felt an individual's rights were inviolate.

For Burke, the foundations of law are but two: equity and utility. Government must work; there is no utility in a perfectly designed government that exists in theory or in the abstract, but doesn't work in the real world. Further, liberty must be limited (through laws) in order to be possessed, since unbridled liberty is simply anarchy. For Burke, ordered liberty results in the greatest (but certainly not perfect) equality and opportunity. The degree of restraint to be imposed, by agreement of the governed, is impossible to settle precisely. For this reason, courts were necessary after legislative decrees were implemented. The circumstances of the time and place, and of the temperament of the people, must be a consideration in the process of governance. As well, Burke assumes that every man acts from motives relative to his own interests and not because of metaphysical considerations having primarily his fellow man's interests at heart. Thus there would be a need for malleable, but not definitive, societal controls.

Burke writes *Reflections* in reaction to the extremes of the French Revolution. He draws the conclusions observed above from what he saw and what he knew. These inferences, once stated, caused him to break with his own political party, the Whigs, and to develop a philosophical view of both man's nature and our obligations to one another that were different from what had been thought up to that point. Because he writes at the very time of the revolution his commentary includes not only a probing investigation into the meaning of various events, but also a necessary abhorrence of some of their effects.

Burke simultaneously developed into a monarchist and democrat; he believed in the historical good of a hereditary king, but he likewise cherished the equally inherited right of a legislature or parliament to exist because of past sacrifices made by the people to obtain such instruments of government. Burke portrays parliament as the antidote to the excesses and egoism of monarchy. He also holds that neither the king nor parliament could abdicate their respective powers in the face of the other—that the balance created between the two branches was essential, if ever difficult to attain, to protect not just the people, but the system itself.

> To make a government requires no great prudence. Settle the seat of power; teach obedience; and the work is done. To give freedom is still more easy. It is not necessary to guide; it only requires to let go the rein. But to form a *free government*; that is, to temper together these opposite elements of liberty and restraint in one consistent work, requires much thought; deep reflection; a sagacious, powerful and combining mind.

In opposition to Burke's dual concerns about the unwarranted mayhem of the French Revolution and the value of monarchical leadership combined with parliamentary restraint, Thomas Paine put forth *The Rights of Man* (Chapter 2). This effort was in support of the French Revolution, and exposes the bankruptcy of hereditary monarchy itself and France's in particular. As Paine analyzes (and Edmund Burke tries to defend the practice of) hereditary government, Paine wins the argument because he puts forth the conclusive consideration; i.e., the sacrosanct right of the governed to choose their own form of government in each succeeding generation or era.

Government is simply a necessary evil, useful, if not mandatory, to control ourselves when we fail one another. How we effect that control (and what additional restraints need to be governmentally supported) is for each age to decide. The important consequence for Paine was that no matter how much reverence Burke adduces to support the undeniably important wisdom of the ages, Paine asserts that those living now should not have to forfeit their right to pass judgment on choices made by those no longer alive. Both Paine and Burke decried the extremes of the French Revolution, and both were disillusioned by man's inhumanity to man, but both saw opportunity for needed change in the events unfolding in Paris. Paine's support of the revolution was founded in the insanity of the French monarchy. Burke's denunciation of the revolution was rooted in the insanity of the republic. Both were right.

Watching these two authors dissect what was good and bad with respect to the events of their day still teaches valuable lessons. The matters with which they were wrestling were novel and grew in opposition to a thousand years of history. The fact that neither man was wholly right in either his assessment or his prescriptions reflects not so much their inadequacy, but the difficulties of "squaring the circle;" that is, solving all the conundrums of governance in one scoop—it cannot be done. We still battle over the issues that first arose in their era, and it is more than useful to understand our difficulties by viewing theirs as representative government evolved during the eighteenth century.

The Portable Edmund Burke

THE TIMES in which Edmund Burke lived were unsettled. The role of government in people's lives was rapidly evolving into something quite different from what it had been only two or three generations before.

Burke had an incisive intellect and a historian's eye for the big picture; using these talents he became a prolific essayist, commenting on many of the topics that were so much on people's minds. As we travel Burke's path we see not so much political dogma as everyday practicality. As was noted in the introduction to *First Principles*, conservatism is not an ideology; it is a movement, and it is also a *way* of thinking. Burke's manner of thinking is the genesis of conservative practice.

The difference between forming an ideology and simply letting practical politics define self-governance is an important distinction to keep in mind; as one compares Burke with his contemporaries in America and those who followed him subsequent to the French Revolution, one can see practical governance develop and utopian design falter. A brief overview of some of the subjects he analyzed follows. This abbreviated slate is but a taste of his lifelong comprehensive investigation of man in relation to his government. All of these, and many more, are covered in depth in *The Portable Edmund Burke*.

Individual Rights

BURKE WAS a historian first, and history was his guide. He felt that people's rights, insofar as they had developed in his era, needed a precise definition for the protection of both the ruled and the rulers. Although he recognizes natural rights, he deals more with historic rights because natural rights, which he calls "original" rights, were a subject for speculation rather than experience, and such speculation could give rise to conflicting claims of inviolability. In Burke's understanding, natural rights, abstract and often ephemeral, relate to one's essence as an individual; social rights, on the other hand, relate to one's opportunities and responsibilities—while maintaining one's individuality—to those around us, and they to us. Although natural and social rights were complementary, they did not offer reciprocal justifications of their validity. They merely worked together, but each for its own reasons; they were not a whole except by necessity, not by design.

Most importantly and logically for Burke, natural rights could not extend beyond the state of nature; once the distant ancestors of the present generation developed civilization, natural rights gave way to social obligations and privileges. Burke felt that recorded rights—fought for and instituted by the direct action of the people, rights that had been defined and nuanced and that worked—were more defensible against government than were natural rights. The latter might reflect conflicting absolute claims, with the potential to cause social unrest as partisans asserted them.

From Burke's viewpoint there was practicality in the observation that if humans didn't develop or evolve beliefs over time and out of experience, they would have to make decisions as events unfolded—idiosyncratically, and most likely inconsistently, and thus with an invitation to anarchy as each day brought new, varied, and discrete circumstances. The prescriptions derived from experience worked to resolve these events, at least most of the time. These remedies ultimately became entrenched reactions to repeated situations; they achieved the status of prescriptive rights; that is, they helped prescribe how we might reasonably act today. Thus Burke defends historic rights not so much as an ultimate standard simply because they had evolved in the past, but as a reflection of solutions that had worked. Although they can always be questioned and compared—in order to allow for further development—they do not have to be discarded simply because they are old. A failure to comprehend the lessons of history simply makes current life more difficult.

Modern conservatives, as is their wont, refer to both history and reason as they wend their way through the myriad decisions we must make in everyday life. "If something is done a number of times it seems to be the result of a deliberate rational decision," wrote Saint Thomas Aquinas. To ignore that rationality is itself irrational.

Nowadays, the argument between those who believe in natural rights and those who argue that rights are the result of a social compact seems archaic some of the time (until political goals enter the equation), but in Burke's era such discussions were at the core of political discourse. In order to understand what has evolved to become the nucleus of today's governing standards, it is advantageous to comprehend the course of the political theology that matured as eighteenth-century philosophers considered governing options in the face of human needs and desires.

Human activities give rise to all sorts of complicated relationships, goals, and methods of dealing with one another. Burke's writing holds that it was not possible to define how we should interact before events unfolded. Accordingly, he doubts whether abstract principles of governance could be used very often to solve real problems. How we live together must flow from social experience and the gradual development of custom and law. Once established, such custom and law must be adhered to with fidelity, and changed only upon great cause:

> [The] choice [of government is] not of one day or one set of people, not a tumultuary and giddy choice; it is a deliberate election of ages and of generations; it is a constitution made by what is ten thousand times better than choice; it is made by the peculiar circumstances, occasions, tempers, disposition, and moral, civil and social habitudes of the people, which disclose themselves only in a long space of time.

Burke was a practical man who felt that the world works the way it does simply because it works. The question unresolved in Burke's time, as much as it is unresolved today, was how to prevent injustice while preserving individual rights. The limiting factor in achieving pure justice and inviolate human rights is, of course, the essence of our being—the human condition. Burke's recognition of this restricting element forced his solutions to always be practical.

Democracy

BURKE WAS the first to articulate a government design based upon a comparative study of two modern styles of democratic rule—the American and French models. In France, the rights of the individual were stripped of meaning and the mob prevailed—by means of the guillotine; in America, individual rights were exalted on paper but in such a manner that in practice (at least in 1790) no one knew how comprehensively individuals could actually be free. The harm to the populace, meted out because of overindulgence in individual rights, or, conversely, the restriction of one's own liberty in deference to others, represented both extremes. A balance needed to be continually struck; but agreement on the middle ground was not easy. Human nature, which is intricate and full of subtlety, and the complexities of social interaction demanded a thoughtful and malleable government. Good political leadership was an art admittedly founded on principle, but aware of circumstances as well. Burke ultimately decries the French Revolution as it occurred, but not most of its practical intentions. He was cautionary, not reactionary. Today we still see the effects of the conundrums that he faced.

Reading Burke in the twenty-first century, in light of the historical American experience—which is instructive by virtue of our piecemeal, gradual promotion of individual and social rights through democratic processes—is more than useful in gaining perspective. And perspective is the most valuable tool in understanding history and effecting government. If Burke were alive today, he would probably approve of our concepts and methods of governance as they developed. How he would look at our results is less certain, for twenty-first-century governmental power has exceeded its stated (Constitutional) bounds in many instances. We have often lost sight of individual rights in favor of massed rights embodied in the mob, contrived rights that serve no social need except the spurious one of rectifying the alleged victimization of parts of society. These mostly fictitious "rights" create further aberrations that seem to demand even more adjustments, resulting in additional anomalies, *ad nauseum*. Because of this, both society and government have become so distorted that picking a place for rational retrenchment becomes almost impossible. (Along this line of thought, it is valuable to read the latter portion of Richard Pipes's *Property and Freedom* [Chapter 11] to grasp the full import of the differences between individual rights and mob demands, and how we legislate in each circumstance.)

Today we talk of rights incessantly, and of responsibilities infrequently. Burke would not have approved of that. Since we do not live in some chaotic, pre-historic state of nature, Burke would argue our democratic manner of governance should reflect the duties we must individually perform to foster our collective goals. Therein lay the key to *ordered* liberty and good government.

The immorality and corruption of many politicians in Burke's day had left the people distrustful of government and anxious to have their say. (Sound familiar?) Burke's recognition of this condition, inflamed by the rants of fourteen daily London newspapers (compared to our own forty versions of talk radio and fourteen thousand daily Internet blogs), led him to think much about what people can do for themselves. Largely as a consequence, Burke developed his characteristic philosophy of individualism tempered by the citizen's obligations to his neighbor. The creation of "public opinion" through the newspapers of Burke's day left the body politic with a taste for what it wanted, but endeavors to satisfy public wants brought on the dramatic political conflicts of the eighteenth century. The battle then, as now, was the tug between majority rule and inviolate individual rights. In America this sometimes direct, sometimes subtle conflict was mostly resolved in the Constitution and its first ten amendments, the Bill of Rights. The former protects the right, and evokes the practicality, of majority rule, while the latter envelopes the individual in a cocoon of natural and prescriptive (earned over time) protections that no majority, certainly no tyrannical majority, should be able to affect. These are the essential compromises that allow modern government to work. But they *are* compromises and thus not perfect or perfectly acceptable.

Recognizing the reality of this evolution and its concessions, Burke holds that a state without a means to change itself is a state that will not survive. Burke's practicality is ever the essence of his lectures.

Voting

CONSIDERATION OF WHO should vote, and thus choose the government, rendered Burke ambivalent. Since he did not have significant faith in ordinary people because of their lack of both experience and education, he did not advocate full democracy as a viable means of governing. But he was in favor of limited democracy, much as Thomas Jefferson was in the U.S. In expressing his lack of confidence in the ability of the general populace to choose a "proper" path by means of the electoral franchise, Burke observes:

> The people should not be suffered that their will, any more than that of kings, is the standard of right and wrong.

In other words, Burke feared the tyranny of the (ignorant) majority, as did all others who understood the downside of democratic possibilities. To allow the "educated" will to prevail he thought the best compromise. As the proportion of society that was sufficiently educated to properly employ the electoral franchise was small, in Burke's view, voting rights needed to be restricted.

Equality

ON THE SUBJECT of equality, of what it means and how to achieve it, Burke and many other classical liberal thinkers discerned a natural order in which discrimination had a role. Discrimination effects a prejudice, not in the negative sense of being against something, but in the positive sense of favoring those things that are good. Burke further understood that there is scant equality in life, so little in fact, that to govern as if equality were an essential goal was doomed to failure. Burke was a realist committed to the principle of doing the best that was possible given real-world circumstances. He did not approve of sacrificing what was good, what worked most of the time, on the altar of perfection—the idea that if what was achieved wasn't perfect, it should be discarded.

Burke's works remain instructive because of their advocacy of principled political action. Even so, contemporary readers may doubt whether he really believed everything that he averred, some of which, to the modern student, may appear to have been a too-hasty reaction to his revolutionary times and the conflict between the results of the American and French Revolutions. Regardless, watching Burke develop his views on equality is valuable in understanding the worth of our current systems, which are designed to confer at least equal opportunity, if not something slightly more—the loosing of imagination.

Property

WITH RESPECT TO property, Burke, not unexpectedly, finds it to be the foundation of society. As had been obvious for centuries before Burke's era, without property rights and private property, anarchy prevails. Burke, who often takes a dim view of humankind, opines that it was not liberty and property that were so valuable, but "the lack of both that was so horrible." Burke considered the importance of property as he sought sense in the relation between the governors and the governed. He early rejected communism and collectivism (without so naming them) where property was held in common, as inconsistent with the natural rights of man and the natural congruities that allow a society to function. This view is perhaps the classic example of Burke's fealty to the limitations of the human condition (over fantastic notions of equalitarian social outcomes); equalitarianism appears exquisite in theory but works not at all on the ground. Thus private property—baneful, baleful, potentially divisive private property—for Burke, was not just the best solution, its existence was simply the only solution to the question of how to divide the spoils of society's success, and ensure there was an incentive to achieve ever more.

Public Morality

BURKE WRITES THAT in order for people to govern themselves, they must relinquish their "selfish will." He maintains this can only be done through fundamental adherence to religion; religiosity thus became basic to Burke's view of mankind's ability to govern itself. Today, when we separate church from state so dramatically and in such minute detail, as we emphasize we are a nation of laws, we must accomplish purging ourselves of selfishness in a more secular atmosphere. Our sometimes-intrusive civil laws, combined with our hubristic determination to watch over our neighbors, leads to confusion and sometimes contention in matters of morality. Since our species is adept at ignoring both religious injunction and secular laws, we must commit ourselves to acting realistically—meaning acting ethically, irrespective of the sources from which we gain our fundamental beliefs—in order for society to function. In America, we have found that we can adhere to religious or moral principle without being required to adhere to a state religion or any particular theology. This is a significant difference between Americans and much of the English populace of Burke's experience. Americans quite generally accept the adage that "we cannot have a just society if we are not a moral society." An American secular morality has become not a substitute for religion, but a complement to it in the public domain, where state and religion are required to be separate, yet occupy the same space. We are still a fundamentally religious people, and that, more than any other factor, certainly more than any secular factor, is what has made America what it is.

Conclusion

IN ALL OF BURKE'S work we can see a striving to meld political necessity with human reality. His solutions are not always perfect, but they are far more rational than those of the despots and demagogues with whom he contended. Reading Burke and watching his own evolution gives one an understanding of how difficult the path was that brought us to our nuanced and sometimes-contentious model of democratic governance. Understanding Edmund Burke is a first step toward first principles.

About the Author

EDMUND BURKE was born in 1729 in Ireland, the son of an attorney. In 1750, at the age of 21 he immigrated to London to attend school and remained there for most of the rest of his life. He began his career as an essayist, which led to his interest in things political, and was elected to the British House of Commons in 1765. Burke was a classical liberal in his political views and a supporter of four revolutions: the English, American, Indian, and Irish. But he recognized before anyone else the destructive power of the French Revolution, which was founded on the mutually exclusive doctrines of theoretically unlimited rights of the individual at one end, and the role of the centralized state as the sole legitimate protector of those rights at the other.

Burke spent much of the middle of his political life dealing with the revolution in America. He endeavored, mostly unsuccessfully, to ameliorate the effects of taxation imposed by Britain, which demonstrated British proprietary inclinations toward its colonies. In his later years, he fought the abuses of the executives of the East India Company, which had become a corrupt fiefdom of the British aristocracy. He spent most of his intellectual career writing about the theory of government and about the relationship between human nature and human action. Based on his investigations, Burke crafted a literary corpus that remains unrivaled in its exposition of the fundamentals of the individual's relationship to his society and his government. Burke left parliament in 1794 and died in 1797.

37

The Conservative Mind: From Burke to Eliot

Russell Kirk

Originally published: 1953, revised 1985
535 pages

RUSSELL KIRK was a religious man, not just personally but intellectually as well. He believed in a transcendent order and a body of natural law that should rule humankind, just as our properly formed individual consciences should govern our personal actions. Individualism, which he considered the essence of human existence, led him to his life's work, a quest for universal self-affirmation, personal responsibility, and a social order devoted to the realization of individual potential. Kirk saw man as capable of being self-governed through intellectual integrity and a comprehension of historical truths. Russell Kirk was Edmund Burke in the twentieth century. He was a man with the understanding and vision to see mid-century public policy for what it was: limiting, controlling, even de-humanizing—and doomed to failure.

Private property and the liberty to do with it as one pleases were Kirk's temporal talismans. He felt limited only by his conscience in his relations with the world. Government, essentially the antithesis of imagination and individual responsibility, frightened Kirk, and so he reflected often on government's role. "Government is intended [to allow us] to provide for our wants and enforce our duties," and that is it. The rest is up to us.

Kirk's importance as a conservative thinker, embodied in his myriad writings, was his ability to give conservatism a public coherence that it had lacked. As Kirk saw it modern American liberalism was failing, though the economic and public tragedy that would eventuate from its tenets went unrecognized by most political and intellectual leaders until well after World War II. The postwar period through the early 1960s was economically deceptive because so many resources were released from wartime application that we seemingly could afford anything we could imagine. But Kirk saw the law of unintended consequences looming large in the profligacy of government. He expounds his warnings and his postulates of public-management truths in the light of history's lessons.

In his own words, Kirk's goal in writing *The Conservative Mind* was "[t]o review conservative ideas, examining their validity for this perplexed age. . . . This study is a prolonged essay in definition." His ability to absorb and then cogently present those ideas—and to do so at a time when answers were needed before the cascade of liberalism, misplaced sympathy, and fuzzy logic overwhelmed public thinking—are what make this work still masterful and relevant. A failure to comprehend Kirk's history makes the confusion and contentions of the twentieth (and now the twenty-first) century even more confounding.

In making his survey, Kirk reviews the thoughts and writings of authors from Edmund Burke (1729–1797), British father of modern conservatism, to T.S. Eliot (1888–1965), American poet, critic, and editor (who lived in Britain most of his life) who was a sly arbiter of the first half of the twentieth century's exhortations and extremes. It would be futile to attempt to inspect and define the notions of the thinkers and theorists who appear between the bookends of Burke and Eliot—it takes Kirk 535 pages to do so, while he also offers a ten-page bibliography noting an additional almost five hundred books, articles and treatises that define and support his observations and assertions. What is useful in this synopsis is to observe Kirk's design in making his review, while at the same time understanding what he sees after the war when the first edition was published, and then later in this revised edition as conservatism became resurgent.

What Kirk witnessed is best captured through the voice of Lionel Trilling (1905–1975), American teacher, critic, novelist, and essayist. Trilling looked at the pontifications of the socialists of his day, as they publicly masticated on their intentions vis-à-vis the masses, and declared them imbued only with rhetoric:

> The "liberal intelligentsia," a rootless body of people intellectually presumptuous, on a European model, manifestly were incompetent to offer intellectual guidance to a people

for whom they felt either contempt or a condescending and unrealistic pity.

As much to the point is Kirk's observation, probably more cogent at the beginning of the twenty-first century than when he first made it:

> [T]he radical parties that detested tradition have dissolved successively, adhering to no common principle among them except hostility to whatever is established.

Those of a liberal bent are yet again at that crossroads (still looking for perfection) where they decry the principles of both common sense and commonality, but without a hint of what they would substitute in their place. Of course, the fact that those of a conservative mind find support in religion further drives the liberals over the edge, for the liberals see no answers in faith, or prescription (learning from the past), only in the long discarded and destitute rationalism of the Enlightenment (an era now clearly understood to have been misnamed, at least when it comes to human experiments in governance).

What Kirk offers in his investigation are the details of the development of conservative thought and conservative reaction to the ascendancy, first, of the Enlightenment's rationalism and then both American liberalism (a philosophy of sorts) and socialism (its political and economic foundation). Conservative theorists refused to accept contrived and artificial social conceptions (mostly collectivist utopian schemes where everyone would end up above average, as in Lake Wobegon, author Garrison Keillor's whimsical Minnesota enclave) and instead engaged in organized opposition to this protean and constantly expanding liberalism. They founded their criticisms on the brutality of coerced conformity embodied in universalist dogma, and in its place insisted that human dignity and individual *capability* be the basis of society.

Kirk writes that the means and ends of socialistic humanitarianism, evolved today as welfarism, are counterintuitive; they breed indolence and incapability. For Kirk, there is a more relevant and more useful human need—freedom—and its driving force, incentive, that are the foundation of human existence. Kirk finds that incentive can only be stifled by the requirements of then-current government design, which in Kirk's era meant a spreading socialism, planned equalitarianism, and the welfare state. Out of his reflections grew a rational view of egalitarianism: opportunity embodied in action. Kirk favored a self-ordering hierarchical society molded about the realities of human interaction and individual abilities, not government controls or edicts. He recognized that equality of result was a false god.

Like many conservatives, Kirk fulminates against the media's lack of restraint. The claim of the press to be a second sun disheartened him:

> The press supplies an endless stimulus to popular imagination and passion; the press lives upon heat and coarse drama and incessant restlessness. It has inspired ignorance with presumption, so that those who cannot be governed by reason, are no longer awed by authority.

Kirk wanted no part of mass media, but he did not decry its existence, only its mercenary goals and its methods of half-truths, exaggeration, and distortion used to attain pecuniary success. Like any other tool, he felt that the press could be and regularly was misused by those who wielded its power. For Kirk, therefore, it was up to the rest of us to put up a universal resistance to those of its means and ends that distorted, or worse, public issues. He would be further saddened today by the still more pronounced uselessness of the press for its intended purpose—to inform, even provoke, but only when integrity was at the core. At the beginning of Kirk's era television was the rising but not yet dominant medium. Even then, Newton Minnow, President Kennedy's Federal Communications Commission chairman, saw a "vast wasteland" in television—and that has not changed. Although TV remains potentially one of our most effective vehicles, it has become too trivialized and politicized to be taken seriously. That brings one back to Kirk's method—reason, founded in facts not emotion.

Kirk's readers would go wrong if they were to translate his thinking into dogma beyond his insistence that life's only certainty is change. Although he views people as imperfectable, he nevertheless believes that the search for the good and the great should continue:

> The twentieth-century conservative is concerned, first of all, for the regeneration of spirit and character . . . this is conservatism at its highest. . . . Recovery of moral understanding cannot be merely a means to social restoration: it must be its own end, though it will produce social consequences.

By temperament Kirk could not be a fatalist. The often-meaningless circularity of modern society was not strong enough to overwhelm him. Custom, convention, constitution, and prescription (making decisions today based on past experience), all malleable, all changing as life progresses and alters, are still the foundation of Kirk's conservatism. There is no single answer, and all answers are subject to review. Such review, though, must always be within reason, taking into account the enduring truths manifest in historical precedents of proven efficacy. Indeed, Kirk's most important contribution to conservatism is his contention that utopian politics cannot supplant historical reality—the reality that people suffer from the human experience of false starts, inattention, and failure, in addition to their successes and great acts. Against the evolving landscape of widely varying human interaction, conservatism's goal is to maintain a foundation of individual freedom.

Kirk fears the oppressive society and encourages all to rise against it intellectually and literally, if necessary. His grave concerns may largely have been a reflection of his times (the ubiquity of socialism's rising tide after World War II), but they were nevertheless genuine. Despite Kirk's fears, a society's ability to discern good governance from what is not is undiminished, for as we have seen since he wrote *The Conservative Mind*, the more oppressive the government the greater the number who ultimately rise against it. What Kirk also fears, however, and what William F. Buckley, Jr., enunciates in *Up From Liberalism* (Chapter 17) is the incremental loss of freedom evidenced in progressively more intrusive and overweening government. These fears always have been and always are well founded, thus vigilance is ultimately the citizen's first and last defense. This understanding is so core to all governance that it bears emphasizing: vigilance is ultimately the citizen's *only* defense.

What Kirk voices in opposition to the incremental loss of sense manifested in liberal rhetoric was as confounding to liberals as it was satisfying, even uplifting, to others. He simply declares that the emperor has no clothes:

> Conservative thinkers demonstrated that "intellectuals" enjoy no monopoly of intellectual power, and that intellectualism and right reason are not synonymous terms.

Kirk goes on to dissect the word "intellectual" and to recount its history. This leads him to discuss the value of precision in the use of language, as does Buckley on many occasions; Kirk is not reticent to call to account the misuse and misapplication of words. In this fashion, it was not just accuracy, but exactness (not only of language but with regard to subject as well) that became the calling card of conservatives—much to the benefit of everyone concerned.

Finally, Kirk believes in the continuity of human progress, that life becomes discernibly better century by century, if not decade by decade. He recognizes that the forces driving progress, such as the prompting of enlightened self-interest or the value of precedent, have always been greater than those of political opportunism, which tend to be anarchic. While he embraces man's natural impulse to strive for improvement he accepts that continuity is generally more dominant than change. Kirk knew that continuity provided a sense of certitude that allowed us to travel through life with enough comfort to be secure—but hopefully enough opportunity to make things better.

About the Book

TO BE FULLY appreciated, Kirk's treatise requires a certain amount of background, both philosophical and historical. Most of those details are presented in the volumes previously synopsized in this book, which is why Kirk's effort appears as late as it does while being so core to understanding conservatism. However, Kirk also discusses and makes use of the efforts of additional authors, theorists, and philosophers who are not represented in *First Principles*, thus it may be worthwhile for the reader to independently follow inviting tangents as they are brought to the fore while benefiting from *The Conservative Mind*. Of course, the Internet offers virtually instant and comprehensive access to what may be helpful in comprehending Kirk—so the opportunity for additional viewpoints, theories, experience, etc., is not so difficult to resolve, and the results of such investigations can be substantially rewarding.

About the Author

RUSSELL KIRK was born in 1918 in rural Michigan, an area he called home throughout his life. He was a consummate thinker, acknowledged as such by the media of his day and of ours. Recognition of his talents and lessons came early and continued throughout his life. He received his education at Michigan Agricultural College (reconstituted later as

Michigan State University) and Duke University. He wrote about so many subjects in so many disciplines that to list them all would risk losing the forest for the trees. He wrote fiction as well as insight and commentary and he received awards in both fields. *The Conservative Mind*, his best-known work, changed thinking about political reasoning in the mid-twentieth century. It still ranks as one of the key books of the conservative canon. Vindication for his life's work, in the elections of Margaret Thatcher and Ronald Reagan, made Kirk's early years of political philosophical struggle seem prescient.

Kirk was a professor at Michigan State University until the decline of educational standards led him to return to his home in the northern part of the state, the place where he was most comfortable and productive. Kirk died in 1994 but not before completing his autobiography, *The Sword of Imagination*, a book through which interested readers can begin to appreciate the breadth of his knowledge and understanding.

38

Capitalism, Socialism, and Democracy

Joseph A. Schumpeter

Originally published: 1942
425 pages

THE ABILITY OF a specialist to keep in mind the big picture while concentrating on his smaller arena is crucial to the overall value of his work. Joseph Schumpeter had such a talent, even though the conflicts he faced in the larger world sometimes caused him to doubt the conclusions to which his work led. His individual field was the economics of business; however, to make sense in that domain he had to understand how the public economy and the body politic broadly adapted to one another and to myriad additional considerations. His ability to comprehend both perspectives and dissect them for the reader is what makes his works so valuable on the broad plain of social discourse.

Schumpeter's discernment of business cycles and how they work—periods of stasis that alternate with growth or contraction—formed the basis of modern economic prediction and management. Though his ideas seem routine and even elementary today, in Schumpeter's era they were novel and untested. While developing his entrepreneurial economic paradigms, Schumpeter's talent for seeing the horizon led him to write *Capitalism, Socialism, and Democracy*. When he drafted his thesis, no one was sure, including Schumpeter himself, which economic system—capitalism or socialism—was more viable either practically or politically, and there was great debate within the social disciplines.

Schumpeter begins his analysis with an investigation of communism as envisioned by Karl Marx (1818–1883). Marxism, explained in *The Communist Manifesto* (1848), was still evolving at mid-twentieth century and just being tested in the real world. Schumpeter concludes that the Marxist system is chimerical, dishonest, and dissociative. Sharing President Abraham Lincoln's belief in the impossibility of fooling all the people all the time Schumpeter asserts that the economic folly of communism would cause it ultimately to fail—wholly, and with great noise. His real query is the other side of the economic question; whether capitalism could succeed and if its adjunct, democracy, could meet the challenge of governing the world's many interrelated minorities (whether that be one and half billion Muslims spread among 40 nations or 4 million Zulus as a population fraction inside South Africa). These were legitimate questions in the first half of the twentieth century and they continue to remain relevant in the twenty-first where the fledgling economies of the Third World (including rapidly modernizing China and India) are just beginning to enter the free market and freedom itself is still largely miscomprehended.

Schumpeter turns Marx and his economic predilections inside out; not just because it was easy to do but because it was necessary. Marx was venerated by the heirs of the Enlightenment—the newly minted socialist equalitarians of the twentieth century—but their veneration could not trump reality.

Schumpeter explains part of his critique of Marx by means of Marx's personal background and social environment which he then uses to dissect Marx's political and economic import. Schumpeter notes that Marx had no country having been displaced from Germany to France to England. Marx thus thought that no one else needed a homeland, or really, even a home, and so his utopian vision was largely a reflection of his myopian viewpoint. Yet Schumpeter finds that Marx felt unsettled in each country because of more than just personal experience. Marx was dissatisfied with the world because he, like Vladimir Ilyich Lenin after him (the leader of the 1917 Russian Revolution that resulted in the imposition of a communist state in the vast Russian landmass), found something wrong with everything. At the same time he quite incongruously insisted that perfection was possible, as seen in his idealized ordering of society by means of his communist fantasy. The disconnection between fact and fiction, their views and their goals, and the inherent futility of their means never seemed to bother either man.

Schumpeter, after offering his own summary of Marx's economic theorizing, directs his most derisive scorn at Marx's contention that socialistic democracy was of a different ilk than bourgeois, capitalistic democracy. The fact that "democratic socialism" was an oxymoron—both by definition and as a philosophical precept—was but a beginning point to dismember Marx's political assertions. That democratic socialism achieves oxymoronic status can be demonstrated in syllogistic fashion: the foundation of a free society is based equally in the individual's natural right to own property and in his right to freedom of thought and action. A free society is one democratically controlled by the thoughts and actions of the people. Socialist theory denies the validity of both private property and the concurrent right of the people to govern themselves; thus a society cannot be democratic and socialistic simultaneously.

The phrasing—democratic socialism—was a ruse to mislead and calm the public into thinking they actually had a hand in utopian constructions that would work in the real world. The ultimate proof of the anti-democratic nature of socialism was the fact that when elections did occur in a collectivist environment, only one name appeared on the ballot for each office, and that candidate was imposed on the people, not publicly selected. When this false democracy was offered it was purely and obviously a subterfuge, a means of deflecting reality. Of course, the fact that in a socialistic setting distribution of society's products must be controlled in a totalitarian fashion because public agreement on such matters is not possible (it must be remembered that individuals have *opinions*) deconstructs with finality any pretensions of freedom.

Once Schumpeter dissects Marxism he turns to a consideration of capitalism. One of his goals is to encourage his readers to think horizontally and vertically; to consider, for example, that the economic and social opening of India or Japan, a political feat, is perhaps less important than the conquest of the air or the airwaves. He wonders, as well, if geographic frontiers are less of an impediment to progress than economic boundaries. For example, does the lack of free-markets hold back an economy more than the unavailability of natural resources? (The answer is yes, and for illustration look at what free markets have done for resource starved Japan, Hong Kong, Switzerland or Israel and what a lack of freedom has accomplished in resource rich nations such as those in southern Africa.)

These were relatively sophisticated considerations that few economists up to that point had investigated. At the close of every great epoch, Schumpeter notes, it is rare that people can see the future, but the future is exactly where they should focus. His intention in this book is to expose the competing political and economic elements that he sees—the elements that define how the future will play out.

In looking forward Schumpeter sees capitalism as the propelling force in the rationalization of human behavior. Think about that concept: the rationalization of human behavior. He steps back a few centuries and observes that the commercial impetus to rational conduct was clearly operative in the Middle Ages when business transactions founded primarily but not exclusively in the division of labor were a key element in the demise of feudalism. The landed aristocracy slowly discerned they could make more money in "business," such as it was, than solely by overseeing their serfs' agricultural activities.

In his investigation Schumpeter underscores how pragmatic economics always and everywhere influences all facets of human endeavor. (Ludwig von Mises's much expanded philosophical and practical examination of this concept can be found in *Human Action* [Chapter 40]. The theories of both men are extrapolations that have an unstated but basic foundation in mankind's quest to ensure self-preservation—i.e., food, shelter, etc.—that causes human beings to act in a rational manner.) Schumpeter maintains that the viability of the capitalistic process, including freedom of individual action, must be included in any assessment of how far and how successfully a culture has progressed toward both liberty and sound economic behavior. For Schumpeter the important effect for social progress wasn't just capitalism's mandate of fundamentally rational activity, it was also capitalism's demand to measure everything that was happening that was so valuable. For example, capitalism brought logic and math into the lexicon of the ordinary sixteenth-century peasant trying to determine if he should sell his cow, and if what he was being offered was at least equal to the value of the cow—to him. The element of judgment in this small example and also in every aspect of capitalistic enterprise is a valuable tool for a simple reason: it fosters progress across the spectrum of human activity through the use of discrimination and critical evaluation.

After delineating his economic assessment of capitalism and socialism Schumpeter turns to the realities of practical politics and history's conventions. He hedges his denunciation of socialism's chance to become the world's dominant economic system. He does not equivocate with regard to socialism itself—he knows that it is not viable, but that simple fact in his view did not ensure that socialistic practice would soon die on the vine. (His temporizing on this subject led to his ambiguous standing among well-known economists for many decades.) As a result of the times (he was writing just after the Great Depression and during World War II) and the state of the public's less-than-benevolent perception of free enterprise because of the fiscal and social disaster that had transpired during the 1930s, he was concerned that even more government intervention in the economy would be seen as the answer to what had theoretically impeded economic recovery around the world during the twenty years prior to the publication of his book; i.e., too little intervention.

Schumpeter knew bureaucratic or political intrusion wasn't what was needed in a situation such as the Depression, indeed, he understood these were decidedly what was *not* needed. Schumpeter was more than aware that government intervention—meaning high taxation, burdensome regulation, trade barriers, and deficit spending—had caused the Depression to last longer and affect the world's economies more deeply than would have been the case if the free market had been allowed to independently regain its footing. Many economists were led to accept the political thought that socialism, with its wholesale government control of all economic fundamentals, could be seen as the answer to what didn't work in the 30s.

The fact that Schumpeter understood socialism's systemic failings, rooted primarily in the suppression of individual incentive and reward (and the obvious reasons for its political success—the free lunch it offered) did not, by default, make democracy the answer to the question: what system of government will achieve the dual goals of individual freedom and economic progress? In the real world, Schumpeter sees democracy as less than wholly successful exactly because of what many of the world's democracies had experienced over the previous century (ubiquitous economic depressions, civil wars, capitalistic oppression, etc.). He is especially concerned about the viability of democratic rule in the context of a "mixed" population or when the times create highly confrontational divisions:

> Whenever ... principles are called in question and issues arise that rend a nation into two hostile camps, democracy works at a disadvantage. And it may cease to work at all as soon as interests and ideals are involved on which people refuse to compromise.

The extreme possibility of suggesting civil war or political division arises infrequently in a mostly homogenous society; but in a blended commonwealth war has occurred more often than those who believe in democracy's efficacy like to recall. Schumpeter's recognition of this potential, in 1942 in the middle of a worldwide military conflict, is not unexpected but may contain more pessimism than was warranted. Yet what Schumpeter felt the world faced was the possibility of one of two very unpleasant eventualities: democracy would lead to civil conflict because various (ethnic, cultural, social, language, tribal) minorities could not agree on fundamental choices and would rather fight than give in; or, totalitarianism would be seen as the way to avoid internecine conflict but would destroy humanity's individual freedoms. (The effects of the minority intransigence that worried Schumpeter are seen most starkly today in those countries cobbled together by the Great Powers as political acts after World Wars I and II. The Balkans and Iraq, of course, come quickly to mind, but many of the countries in Africa and Asia mired in a Third World mentality fit this profile as well.) Schumpeter thinks socialism, which is ultimately totalitarian, might look better in spite of its destruction of freedom than ever-present, ever-recurrent conflict. He feels people might see this choice—security without freedom—as the eventual solution. Freedom without security—in light of both the Depression and World War II—Schumpeter thinks might be more than humanity could face.

Time has shown that having faith in the upside of the human condition (its continued striving toward change for the better, in other words, its ability to discriminate between what is good and what is not, what will work and what will not) rather than certainty as to its downside (human perfidy, fear, or selfishness) is more than justified. The pessimism that Schumpeter offers is more a reflection of his very unsettled and difficult era—perhaps the most contentious of the twentieth century—than long-term political reality.

What that observation refers to is this: throughout *First Principles* we have noted the negative effects of the human condition, how it can often work against well-intentioned and even good theoretical designs or some form of benevolent ordered liberty. We have done that only with the intention of explaining (in a somewhat shorthand fashion) why a mostly well-designed government doesn't always result in a well-oiled and smooth-functioning society. But in Schumpeter's case we also have to equally recall the beneficial potential of the human spirit—that it does covet order and freedom in a context of rationality. Conflict, confrontation, and war are sometimes necessary tools in an attempt to force rationality (recall Walter McDougall's observation in *Promised Land, Crusader State* [Chapter 20], "force sometimes precedes reason"), but are not conditions under which one can live permanently.

Thus the upside of the human condition, the human spirit, incites a drive to resolution and ultimately peace—so long as such are ultimately achieved through voluntary agreement and not by force.

At the end of World War II (which not only wasn't in sight when Schumpeter published his treatise but which was proceeding favorably for the Axis Powers [Germany, Italy, and Japan]) he expected the socialist order (or at least central planning if not centralized control of the economy) to be more entrenched than ever. Although he knew socialism's goals could not be achieved by socialism's methods, he bases his expectation of its ascendancy on the Great Depression's stimulus to enlarged government oversight and intervention in economic and social matters and the war-induced economic centralization in both the Allied and Axis camps. He sees the expansion of central planning and control that had begun in the 1930s as virtually unstoppable. Accordingly, he predicts the likely triumph of, at least, socialistic practices over capitalism—not because socialism was superior but because it was already in place to a considerable extent and because the times and personalities would allow its further entrenchment. In other words, Schumpeter comes to his conclusions based on practical expectations—a social or humanistic assessment—and foregoes his own well-argued faith in the demands of rationality in economic enterprise.

Schumpeter believes that a docile population cannot prevail against those in power who would implement the peacetime conversion (no matter which side won), demand primary control, and justify their actions by claiming that what had worked in wartime would continue to work in peace. He also believes that such leaders would frighten people into thinking they knew what they were doing by suggesting that no one would want to return to the chaos and poverty of the 30s. The prediction of socialism's dominance was based on "extrapolating observable tendencies" not on a lack of faith in our ability to formulate intellectual and practical arguments against such a system of governance.

Initially, certainly, Schumpeter's predictions were correct; at the end of the war Great Britain, the cradle of free democracy and market capitalism, not only installed a socialist government, but turned out of office Winston Churchill, their war-time prime minister, who was seen, literally, as the country's savior. Churchill had not only predicted the coming war as early as 1933, he had led England through its darkest hour; his exalted status achieved through respect for his prescient intellect and dogged determination in war should have been secure but he decried socialism in all its contortions—and the British public again ignored him and his advice as they had in 1933. At that point Schumpeter's expectations became reality.

However, in spite of the British experience Schumpeter's fears were ultimately proven ephemeral. In his examination of "observable tendencies" he seems to have overlooked the fact or even the possibility that what the citizenry was willing to cede to the government during times of war was not necessarily that to which it would acquiesce over the long term in peacetime. He also seems to have erred by focusing on humankind's single-mindedness in war, a mental state that broadens to become expansive, multi-faceted imagination in times of peace. People tend not to countenance interventionism when it is not mandatory for survival. One is reminded particularly, when reviewing Schumpeter's reasoned concern about the future, of John Maynard Keynes's injunction regarding the force of ideas:

> The power of vested interests is vastly exaggerated compared with the gradual encroachment of ideas.

Despite the sometimes pessimism and ultimate inaccuracy of his predictions, the breadth and depth of Schumpeter's investigations in this book and the supporting history he recounts are simply awesome. His exposition of socialism's weaknesses, and failures, laid a foundation for future writers and economists who studied the political centralization of public purposes in all its guises. Therein lay the continuing value of Schumpeter's investigations. It is not that widespread socialism is likely to revive anytime soon, but collectivism and totalitarianism *are* both still alive, and could gain acceptance—especially in the Islamic and Third Worlds where fundamentalist religious or social constructs are still the rule. With these possibilities extant, having knowledge of the past and pragmatically based counter-arguments prepared to stifle its repetition are necessary.

Understanding that someone as incisive and brilliant as Schumpeter won't get everything right every time, while appreciating the incalculable value of those things that he does predict accurately, is useful in approaching the comprehensive explorations of the authors who helped shape the modern world. It is not easy to convince human beings that freedom is first among equals and more necessary than security, that without freedom there is no security. If a society does not have the ability and the will to change what goes wrong—and invariably something goes wrong—then that society can only become totalitarian or anarchic. Watching all of the theorists and philosophers presented throughout *First Principles* struggle in the attempt to not only make that case but prove it is seen in the writing of Joseph Schumpeter.

For Schumpeter and others the seemingly overwhelming real-world facts of their times caused misjudgment of the capability of human striving. The long-term effect of distorted reality on human behavior and sound theory is still not as powerful as the human spirit. In spite of the fact that the real world is at intervals temporarily wrong, even insane, it generally rights itself although sometimes in devastating fashion. In other words, sometimes people die, and are willing to die, to recreate a rational world. And that is exactly what happened during the second half of the twentieth century. But that experience was not so clearly seen from the vantage point of 1942—thus Schumpeter's sometimes pessimism in *Capitalism, Socialism and Democracy*.

Schumpeter's work has an intellectual reach that demands the reader engage in the debate on every level and with respect to all particulars. Understanding Schumpeter's dark view regarding the ascendancy of socialism—in spite of that system's inherent and fatal failings—and then viewing the course of history subsequent to Schumpeter's stated fears, where freedom and individuality again became the norm, offers continued hope in the ability of human society to right itself—but almost always with great effort, constant vigilance, and many unintended consequences.

About the Author

HAVING EARNED a doctorate at a young age, Joseph Schumpeter became known as "the genius without a knack for success." Born in 1883 in what is now Slovakia, he was only four when his father died. Schumpeter went on to a brilliant early career in academia yet, in spite of many opportunities to succeed, he was unable to turn them into palpable accomplishments. Regardless of the fact that Schumpeter was a polymath and fluent in six languages, his intellectual talents failed to prevent his real-world dismissal from his post as Finance Minister of Austria and later as a private banker, mostly because he was in the wrong place at the wrong time. Yet his books on economics inspired others to investigate his subject matter on a broader scale than had been done before. During his career at Harvard University, where he began teaching in 1932, he formed the basis of his economic and more broadly theoretical works, thereby laying the groundwork for advanced investigations by him and others into economic theory and practice. Late in his career, when his academic accomplishments advanced his reputation, he served as president of both the Econometric Society, which he helped found, and the American Economic Association. Schumpeter died in 1950.

39

The Open Society and Its Enemies

Karl L. Popper

Originally published: 1943
Volume 1, 343 pages
Volume 2, 396 pages

TAKING THE STUDY of mankind's efforts at rational governance back to their origins and trying to build a sustainable paradigm requires consideration of the basic social conundrum any political theorist or author faces—how to make the world work for its inhabitants while recognizing our imperfectability; that human beings are prone to both mistakes and self-interest. In reality, unfortunately, it is a fact that we can only make the world work as well as the character of the individuals who inhabit it will allow.

Karl Popper begins this intense and penetrating investigation into social comity with the early Greeks. These men were the first to consider, in an organized fashion, the subject of government by the governed. Because they lived in relatively small societies, their assumptions and conclusions were somewhat skewed. But they conjectured on the possibilities—and became revered in many circles for their efforts, even their wisdom. However, some of that veneration was later thought to have been misplaced, and certainly not as useful for a large society as it might be for a smaller one (Rousseau was one of the first to comment on this disconnection). Popper was one of those who looked more closely at what had been and was unafraid to question what he saw in spite of the almost universal admiration of Greek society and what were thought to be its accomplishments.

In Volume 1 of *The Open Society and Its Enemies* Popper examines what Plato, the most thorough and intentional of the Greeks, designed as a prototype for governance. He finds problems with Plato's immoderate emphasis on security over freedom and on the elite over the people. (And we must recall that in Greek society, as in almost all early cultures, the People did not include an often substantial slave population, who had no rights at all.) In Volume 2 he investigates various political constructions as they evolved over the centuries and were then introduced into a modern setting; he finds as many inconsistencies and dead-ends in this era as he did within Greek society. In spite of these difficulties, however, Popper does find reasonable, if not perfect, solutions to the question of who shall govern, and how.

Volume 1

WITH RHETORICAL SUBTLETY Popper begins his discussion of the open society, where man's freedom and his individuality are sacrosanct, by asking why so many people with seemingly strong intellectual capabilities respond favorably to the siren song of collectivist utopian political theories. Although none of these idealistic hypotheses of government have borne fruit after hundreds of attempts over thousands of years, people continue to trust their false promises.

Popper seeks, as his first task, to explain why utopia is unachievable: humankind strives for a visionary, perfected condition, but fails because the very notion of perfection is a fantasy. That is a simple and straightforward answer, yet the prospect of an equalitarian and "just" society brings many people to the brink of rapture—thus the effect of hope over experience, as societies try again and again to achieve the unattainable. Fantasy is so much easier to embrace than the harsh reality of a constant struggle to sustain a real-world, functioning community inevitably marked by successes *and* failures. Put simply, a mirage is a powerful force.

The open society of Popper's study is one in which man relies on his reason and uses the power of criticism as he seeks improvement. It is a social setting wherein both personal responsibility and perforce, the community's responsibility, have as their goal the advancement of knowledge. The open society was originally created in the time of Socrates, when Athens became the first democracy, and was immediately denounced by those who were disappointed with the ensuing results. In other words, perfection was not quickly achieved (people had *opinions* and *desires*, and their *convictions* and *cravings* differed, one from the other) and discussion seemed never-ending.

Standing in conceptual opposition to the open society was the closed society, which took its cues from mysticism rather than rationality. In early closed societies, people were governed by magical rules delivered by shamans and derived from superstitions and fears of the unknown or the unexplainable. Modern closed societies are founded on the same proposition—that the rulers somehow know better than the ruled what is best for the population. This message is still delivered by shamans, albeit better dressed and more presumptuous than their pre-modern predecessors. These false prophets deliver mysticism—the kind that says they can create a path to the perfect society, one that is "unknown" to the people, and thus the mystic's guidance is necessary. The truth is that their perfect society is as unreachable as the ancient magical construct; both are utter myths. However, the concept is so fantastic that people *want* to believe and thus do so—or at least accept it (albeit sometimes when directed by cudgel or rifle).

As Popper explains, the evolution of the open society is the product of man's ability to reason deductively, to explain magic through investigation, and to employ the scientific method to discover the basis of our world in both its palpable and its desired or imagined forms. It requires effort to detect, comprehend, and institute. The closed society is just easier all the way around, for all knowledge and expectations of behavior are handed to the subjects. That is, it is easier at the start, but much more difficult to retain in the end. The human condition—of striving, hope, imagination, and critical assessment—ultimately gets in the way of the closed society's demands.

Since many modern utopian political theorists looked to Plato's pronouncements for guidance, Popper dissects Plato's writings to expose what he really intended to accomplish. To reconstruct the circumstances, we must recall that Plato wasn't writing directly for the ages; he was writing for his contemporaries and to address then-current realities. Popper argues that the reverence with which we esteem Plato is idealized and misguided if we wish to sustain political institutions suited to the real world. Popper goes so far as to aver that Plato must be proven unworthy of our respect before we can embark on a new course, one that does not venerate him as the founder of modern democratic principle.

Popper's disappointment in Plato is straightforward; Plato offers totalitarian answers to mankind's failures in self-government. Signal defects in Plato's thought, Popper contends, are his hypocrisy and his use of argument to conclude the obverse of what his argument supports. Plato's striking error is in placing too much trust in institutions.

He did not appreciate that they are mere tools by which we multiply our social powers, much as a lever multiplies the force of our muscles. Popper observes that institutions are only as good as the people who run them. He contends that social institutions are analogous to fortifications: they are of little value in protecting us because of their design alone; they must also be managed well.

Popper describes Plato's utopian thinking thus: although individuals are imperfect, if the state is under the control of certain "wise" individuals (as in a closed social order) it can render *society* perfectible even though its human components—real people—are less than perfect. In other words, if everyone were to do as he was told, everything would be fine. The problem, of course, is that ensuring full obedience to any set of rules or conclusions is quite impossible—not to mention the difficulty of ensuring full understanding and then agreement on the rules themselves. People reason differently and seek different goals; they find themselves in different circumstances and thus arrive at different conclusions. Conflict inevitably ensues. The best we can hope for is cooperation, not submission; utopian good will is seldom ever achieved, and when it is, it only remains for a limited time. (Recall the popular patriotic reaction in the U.S. after Pearl Harbor or 9/11 and the fights over the prosecution of each war that ensued.)

From Plato's society, which was founded in class distinctions, later philosophers following his line extrapolated a different, but also allegedly perfect society—the controlled society. In this manifestation the rulers not only decide what each of the ruled will do and be, but also what they will hear and see (the twentieth century's Soviet Union, the twenty-first's China, and to an extreme extent this thinking is seen in the last two pure Marxist enclaves, North Korea and Cuba). By restricting information, the rulers of a controlled society hope to prevent people from going astray. Of course, information control, which is difficult enough, ultimately aims at thought control. Obviously the latter is simply not conceivable—as George Orwell conjured when he wrote *1984*, his dark novel about totalitarianism. For Popper, the most important reality, irrespective of these totalitarian constructions, relates to the bankrupt intellectual presumption that if someone isn't "educated" to think (if what they know or see or hear is controlled), they can't and won't think—and will, therefore, obey. Reliance on this patently false supposition shows the design of a closed society was fated to failure from the outset.

Popper observes that Plato's charge—that justice must be in the best interest of the state, rather than the people individually—leads to a totalitarian result antithetical not just to the idea of individuality, but to its essence. If the individual must bow to the state, then collectivism is established. Plato's reasoning proceeds along the following lines: the state is the supreme good; necessarily, then, the individual must be subservient to the state; if all individuals are subservient to the state, then all individuals are unselfish; our lack of self-interest or self-action/aggrandizement frees us all to be equal. For Popper, it was clear that people were thus rendered "equal" only in the most restrictive, least individualistic, even least humanistic manner.

For Popper utopian dreams had run their course; it was time to deal in facts. The emperor had no clothes, but because the emperor was Plato, Socrates' pupil (yet thought a traitor to Socrates), no one could say such a thing. Yet Popper was unafraid to shoot at the king, in an eloquent and seamless dissection, and as the aphorism notes, "if you are going to shoot at the king, you'd better kill him." Popper does just that, but there was a caveat. The caveat explains the longevity and the continued reverence that Plato receives, while at the same time demonstrating the false premises and distorted logic of modern totalitarian constructions supposedly devised on the Platonic model.

Popper's caveat rests in the distinction between Platonic totalitarianism and modern collectivist totalitarianism. Plato's intellectual design intends stability for society, and public contentment. His society is not one intended to allow exploitation of the masses by a few. Platonic interpretation thus differs markedly from its evolutionary heirs. Of course, exploitation of the masses and corruption of Plato's system were inevitable simply because government must be operated by human beings; these leaders are weak and selfish and no more susceptible to perfection than anyone else. Actually, as Popper notes, they are especially prone to self-assertion when they encounter no one stronger than themselves to check their base or other desires. Plato looks to the good of the whole as he yields to his totalitarian impulses—and his good intentions save his historical reputation. But because he does not deign to leave the masses free to act in their own interests or even out of self-preservation, his closed society allows for dictatorial rule and thus the devastation wrought by those who claim his mantle. The people are disenfranchised, essentially, *before* they get the vote.

Plato's search for who should rule, which culminates in his assertion that only the best will suffice, results in his equally closed approach to selecting leaders. Popper states that the real search is for *how* we shall govern ourselves to ensure that our rulers do the *least* harm. The *person* who rules is not the answer, since all people are fallible and encumbered with frailties. Far more important are the rules put in place to prevent the fallible from perpetrating their own mischief. The rule of law serves this function far better than does any philosophical plan—let alone the cult of one personality or another, or the creation of one institutional form or another.

Popper concludes that Plato's whole approach to governing is fundamentally flawed because it focuses on the who rather than the how. Although Plato was sociologically astute in recognizing that only a few can rule, he was politically naïve in his proposals for finding or choosing those few or controlling the governors when one of the few good leaders was not at the helm. Popper asserts that a system can be designed to reduce the opportunity for the rulers to do wrong; but the reality is that no *institutions* can be devised to maximize the chance that all of their actions will be good. Only rules (including punishment for their violation) that proscribe behavior or limit the opportunity for evil can ultimately work to control the rulers. Popper recognizes how the possession of power invariably debases the ability to make reasoned judgments. In other words, individuals always have been and always will be corruptible; the people must be left free to correct that corruption.

Utopianism, and the totalitarianism to which it leads, Popper condemns as a failure for two additional reasons. First, utopian planning demands a perfect design, implemented in its entirety, such that the failure of any part of it leads to the disintegration of the whole. Second, totalitarianism fails not because men cannot agree on most things, but because they cannot agree on all things. They will not agree because they are individuals. Collectivism is appealing because life would be simple if everyone were to follow government's or the governor's directives. But, people cannot follow another's dictates in all instances; in most cases they should not have to at all—so long as they do not trespass on the rights of others.

Faith in reason funded by facts, an understanding of the meaning of freedom, comprehension of the value of prescription (what we've learned from the past), respect for the individual, and equal treatment for all are the foundations of a rational society, an open society. If man were perfectible, society would be as well; the truth of the matter is really as simple as that. The cry of the utopians and totalitarians (that if we want security we must give up liberty) is the opposite of the truth. When we abandon our freedom we experience no security at all, only subjugation often in its most malevolent form. There is no absolute security in life, no matter who is in charge. Security that is attainable must be achieved through watchfulness over ourselves—and in watching over the guardians who watch over us.

Popper notes that the law of unintended consequences is the biggest impediment to a rational society. Unintended consequences abound—even in the simplest economic choice of buying one loaf of bread rather than another. Thus, freedom of choice, an unfettered marketplace, and the liberty to be oneself are the only conditions that can enable a society to correct its occasional wrong turns—initially small and noticeable in an open society—before they become insurmountable and insufferable. Various features of totalitarianism (e.g., central planning, collectivist conformity, and choosing for others) eventually make life intolerable, and that leads people to demand change, most often at the expense of peace.

Volume 2

IN THE SECOND book of his treatise, Popper reviews the philosophers and philosophy of the modern era: Kant, Hegel, Schopenhauer, Marx, and others. He avers that progress since the Dark Ages has had so many fits and starts that we sometimes find it hard to tell the forward from the backward steps. In Volume 2 Popper attempts to give order to that history.

He commences with a comprehensive treatment of the "master criminal" of modern political thought, Friedrich Hegel (1770–1831), whose dialectics Popper demonstrates to be the foundation for spurious thought, moral turpitude, and boundless inanities. Popper observes that Hegel did not devise his philosophy independent of earlier thought. Indeed, he relied heavily on Plato, who, as Popper explains, feared the future and dwelled so much on the more secure past that he offered a plan and a justification for recreating it by reversing progress. Popper describes Hegel as having based his thoughts on the idea that mankind is here only to meet its fate and that the pre-ordination of future developments can be discerned from history, if one just looks at the record in the right light. This philosophy is known as historicism, or determinism. What was constructed, in part, from Hegel's theories in the twentieth century was Nazi Germany. For the Nazis, history led ineluctably to the rule of one man, Adolf Hitler, whose exactions resulted in the flight or prostration of all others.

Popper, who was a man of his times, scrutinizes Hegel and his progeny in then-current (World War II) Germany and finds them deficient in common sense, rectitude, and an appreciation of reality. He also finds the rest of the world to be timid and desperate to hide, which he was not. The black and white confrontational stance of the German followers of the distorted version of Hegel's historicism forced the rest of the world to fight them on those terms. Of course, the insane brutality of the Nazis ultimately made this choice easy. But viewed retrospectively, Hegel was probably not as simple to explain as Popper indicates. How relevant is this discussion today? When viewed in light of how often history repeats itself, understanding how the Nazis justified their efforts is still important. We have not seen the last Hitler, Stalin, Pol Pot, or Mao in this world take a relatively complex philosophical comprehension and simplify it for popular consumption and personal political aggrandizement.

Hegel's "historical determinism," by way of but a single example of Popper's condensing of Hegel's theory, can more accurately be seen as historical tendencies than historical certainty. Hegel's view is that what is real is rational; in other words, things happened in the past for a reason, mostly a rational reason. His critics find determinism in this; Hegel finds only ramifications in the past and possibilities for the future, not determinism. For Hegel, what one sees in the reality of the past determines how we should *view* the present, not what is going to happen now. These are important philosophical distinctions that help bring a greater understanding to what Hegel actually preaches. They are mentioned so that in reading Popper, as when reading any of the authors presented here, one can still avail oneself of skepticism vis-à-vis both the author and his contentions. Popper is harsh with Hegel because of the times and the intentions and actions of the Nazis and their use of Hegel to justify themselves; viewed in an historical light Hegel's supposed philosophical transgressions appear less malignant.

[Note: Readers who consume all of the authors who appear in *First Principles* will see that contradictions in authorial contentions exist. When this occurs, it is most important to recall that no one idea or theory or philosophy fits all situations perfectly in all circumstances and throughout all time periods, thus the diversity of opinion—and the need to comprehend many different ideas and circumstances. It is difficult to compare the thinking of an eighth-century philosopher with an eighteenth-century essayist. The times are very important in understanding various points of view. Hegel is one of those cases where his "bad press"—because of the Nazis' use and partial distortion through simplistic scholarly devices of certain tenets he espoused—is so overwhelming that he now serves almost exclusively as a bad example. To ferret out his constructive observations and essential thoughts is perhaps more than anyone other than the student of pure philosophical history wants or needs to do. These observations are offered here because assessment of Hegel's reputation is a very good example of the phenomenon that occurs when, in an overview such as *First Principles*, we paint only with a broad brush.]

Popper points out that the authoritarianism of the two thousand years between the flowering of Greek democracy and the American and French revolutions (the latter of which was set in motion partially by Plato's defense of the superiority of "elite" intellects over the knowledge and experience of the rest of society) began to die when economic individuality became a reality and when feudalism and serfdom faltered. Authoritarianism declined, in other words, as the world grew complex; exponential economic, social, (and equally important) technological progress was achieved when mankind was voluntarily left alone to act (or forcibly left alone through revolution). In the end, it became an article of faith that the road to freedom can be navigated only in an open society. Popper observes that Hegel, and then Karl Marx (1818–1883) after him, denied this truth.

The notion of citizen control of the governing, and thus economic processes brought Popper, because of the times and the circumstances, to a substantive consideration of Marx, who saw such freedom only as a danger to the ordinary citizen (to whom Marx offered wholesale protection). Marx witnessed the ravages wrought by uncontrolled capitalism, when power in the form of economic control over the workers' lives was often close to absolute. In Marx's view, capitalism was successful only in engendering the hopeless subservience and grim degradation of the people it oppressed. That this is not a fully accurate picture of eighteenth and nineteenth-century working conditions is another matter, and is addressed by modern research that aids in the deconstruction of stereotypes and anti-capitalism myths.

To a not insignificant extent, the workers in the early years of the Industrial Revolution were enamored of the money they were making. Small as that amount may seem today, it was infinitely more than they made before capitalistic employment was available—when they received no wages but were allowed to keep, out of their own work product, subsistence levels of goods. Thus, when it became possible to break the cycle of poverty some worked long hours in shops or factories, and had more than one job simply because their lives were so changed by the advent of real money in their pockets. The dawning of feelings of independence was an almost irresistible incentive to want more. That the portrayal of worker exploitation in those times, which no one suggests did not happen but which is also not the entire picture, is conveniently used to denigrate capitalism for twenty-first-century political purposes is still a given.

The reality is that during its early years capitalism was continually transforming itself. Obviously it was far from perfected in that era. Considered rationally, the need for reform and its subsequent implementation should not be used today to undermine or ignore the value of what has come to pass by means of these critical assessments—massive economic and societal advancement via capitalism's mechanisms. That is akin to holding a two-year-old's temper tantrums against him when he is 40. However, to those with an agenda, the crime once committed is a useful place from which to begin any and all assessment.

Marx's solution to nineteenth-century capitalistic excess was to scrap the system in its entirety. Popper, however, even though he sympathized with Marx's motives, recommends only continued piecemeal adjustments to free-market economics. Marx thought in one plane—what was happening to workers on the job in his time. But the benefits of increased and discretionary income and of improved living conditions because of economy-wide gains also need to be considered before a blanket indictment of the system ensues. Popper's melioristic approach takes into account all the fruits of capitalism—the good and the bad. Popper sees that adjustments to alleviate bad conditions allow the beneficial effects of capitalism to increase exponentially—which is exactly what happened over the course of the century between when Marx published *The Communist Manifesto* and Popper investigated its modern consequences.

Popper's basic recognition is that freedom for individuals is embodied in free markets, freedom of association, and freedom of action. These freedoms are manifest in the fundamentals of capitalism, and they interact in such convoluted ways that we cannot intellectually muscle our way through the maze of options and decisions in order to control mankind's economic interrelations. We have to travel the actual road to know how best to proceed. For example, capitalism's nineteenth-century owner class often denied basic rights to workers. This did not make capitalism as an economic system bad, although the extremes to which the capitalists of that era sometimes took their power were unreasonable. A real-world balance was both needed and achieved in late nineteenth and twentieth-century reforms and it was partially the province of government to act so that those with power did not use their dominance indiscriminately.

Popper uses that simple fact as vindication of his thesis and validation of his deconstruction of Marx. In the modern era, however, the power of government to make those adjustments also needs to be controlled. If it is not (by such simple means as observing Constitutional restraints) it too will travel to twenty-first-century extremes that are as inappropriate as were those of the nineteenth-century capitalism it formerly needed to constrain. Moving forward a century and a half from Marx's theories it is seen that government, which initially benefited the public with its powers and used them effectively, has since waxed confident, then strident, and finally omnipotent in its supposed expertise at guiding capitalism, and, more to the point, in remedying its alleged defects. It is no longer the power of the market that is to be feared, but the power of those who regulate and tax. This results from political inhalation of a witch's brew: an intoxicating combination of conceit and ignorance. This swill induces a euphoria that allows the first consequence of political hubris to grow unabated—that only government can protect the people and counter the supposed force of the market.

In his long polemic reducing Marx to a bad economist and a worse psychologist, Popper demonstrates Marx's paucity of human feeling in his solutions to the excesses of capitalism as the system visited itself on its mid-nineteenth-century workers. This deficiency, as Popper notes in fairness to Marx, was typical of his era. Marx accepted conventional wisdom in his conviction that things would only get worse because more and more power was being concentrated in the owners of production. He missed two classic points of industrial psychology; first, if one treats people better, they work better, thus allowing the excesses of developing capitalism to be self-curative as industrial barons found that they could make more profits through fairness than through exploitation. Henry Ford got it right, Marx did not. Second, as workers become more sophisticated, and are able to save a few dollars, they eventually strike out on their own—singly or in groups. The economic base thus expands rather than becoming concentrated. At that point working conditions become a bargaining chip for the workers, and conditions can only improve when this second tier competition (competition among producers for workers rather than for customers) enters the picture.

Popper notes that Marx also misses a fundamental point of governance, i.e., the importance of continuity. The rejection of an entire governing system, as Marx advocates, would create a vacuum that must be filled by the immediate establishment of a "whole" new one. Such a wholesale change is a monumental task that would engender many unintended consequences. We act far more wisely in political matters when we retain what we know does work even as we eliminate what doesn't. The basis for such wisdom is that we know less about what is true than what is not true. We should find it easier to be rid of the false than to search endlessly only for the absolutely true.

Although it is easy to dismiss Marx today and look upon reference to his writings, plans, and times as anachronistic, there is a valid point to be made: where might capitalism have gone—intermediately and over the longer term—without the juxtaposition of Marxist thought to push political and economic matters in the direction they took? That is to say, Marx didn't come out of the blue, with no justification and no valid reason to oppose capitalism in its nineteenth-century incarnation. Thus Popper's revelations and investigations are still worthy of consideration today, for history, as has been observed interminably, does have a tendency to repeat itself. And human beings persistently attempt to reinvent square wheels.

This is seen, by way of example as the twenty-first century opens, in dictatorships that are again in the forefront of Latin American politics. Claims for the validity of socialism and paternalism resurface. The reversion to economic fallacy in this instance is made possible for a simple reason: as a supposed antidote to corruption. Corruption is the operational foundation of both political and economic relationships in many Central and South American societies. Corruption is what distorts free markets and the political process so that neither works as it might and both work as those in power deem they will. It is endemic corruption in the supposedly free markets that allows untenable populist social sentiments to re-emerge.

When the markets are distorted by means of the thievery of the political and owner classes the masses are simultaneously disenfranchised and made poor. That corruption—both petty and grand—can have such an overwhelming effect that it can murder a society is analogous to a cancer—it cannot be stopped piecemeal because it takes on a life of its own inside its host. When the citizenry is promised change and offered a distribution of wealth through re-introduction of socialist tenets, initially the people cheer. That no redistribution will occur because of the further corruption of these new political promises is equally a given (the corruption is imbedded in the society, not in one particular economic system); that only the leaders and their cronies will profit is equally true, and that the nation's economy will again collapse, and that chaos and then reform will ensue is surely as certain. Nothing moves forward on square wheels, no matter how sleek the design of the vehicle they supposedly support.

THE PARADOX OF freedom, that freedom defeats itself if it is unrestrained, is central to Popper's understanding of both how the world works and why people need to govern themselves. Irrespective of Popper's appreciation of the self-contradiction of freedom, he is nevertheless reluctant to accept *government* intervention in the affairs of humanity when liberty's license goes awry. He recognizes that people throughout history have achieved most progress by themselves in spite of government rather than because of it. Formalized freedom (or ordered liberty) guided by democratic principles ensures the right of people to judge and dismiss their government, and is how the ruled control the rulers. Economic freedom, i.e., competitive and enlightened free enterprise founded in law, is what marks social progress. The freedom of choice embodied in economic autonomy (with true excesses controlled by government only when the people themselves have absolutely failed) brings the most benefit to a society. A government that begins to take either political or economic freedom away will eventually abolish both, in a supposedly benign and grand gesture.

Popper ultimately returns to the Greek question of how the citizenry will tame the rulers or hold them in check so that their purposes will remain the purposes of the people. Popper notes that universal laws, those that help ensure these purposes, are usually so ingrained in our nature that we unconsciously take them for granted (the Golden Rule, the salutary effects of honesty, integrity, discipline, and responsibility, etc.). Our predecessors over the last few centuries created sound, working governments, but only through a natural process of fits and starts. Between the starts and fits there was sometimes anarchy. When the dust settled after those times it was once again apparent that all progress was achieved only in open societies. In any era, the next question becomes, so long as society remains open, will the rulers react in the manner of these given, ingrained, and universal laws, or will they fail themselves and us—in a fit that will require a new start?

Karl Popper lived and thought in dangerous times. The breadth and the creativity of his scholarship are not just bold, but reflect a fundamental understanding that can get lost without a long view. His delineation of history's common threads is functionally core to a comprehension of modern democracy, and of capitalism—democracy's economic strut. The way in which he analyzes how both governments and economies work—considering learned truths—makes for substantive reading, a fact underscored by footnotes and almost necessary digressions that equal the length of his text. The reading is not light, but then, neither is the subject matter.

About the Author

KARL POPPER was one of the most important philosophers of science and the scientific method since Sir Francis Bacon, the sixteenth-century English pioneer in this field. Popper was born in 1902 in Vienna, Austria. He had a modest upbringing and worked as a cabinetmaker and schoolteacher before entering the world of academia and becoming one of the most influential economic and political theorists of the twentieth century. He left Austria in 1937 and immigrated to New Zealand where he taught at the national university until the end of World War II. In 1946 he traveled to England where his theories and teaching did not find favor within mainstream thinking (produced at Oxford and Cambridge Universities). He experienced difficulty securing employment until he finally found a home at the London School of Economics where he taught for twenty-three years. He lectured around the world during his career and was knighted in 1965. Popper died in 1994. As one of the most influential polymaths of our time he received accolades and honors from all corners of the globe both during his life and after.

40

Human Action

Ludwig von Mises

Originally published: 1949
885 pages

IN 1922, WHEN Ludwig von Mises published *Socialism* (Chapter 32), his exposition of collectivist government's fraudulent character, he made clear his strong convictions about the relationship between the two signal aspects of the human condition—our inner selves and our external, interrelated lives. Our societal relationships (governmental and economic in particular) reflect the interdependence of our public persona and our private character. Mises does not address these relationships in-depth in *Socialism*; however, in his *summa* work, *Human Action* (published almost thirty years later, following the Great Depression and a subsequent world war) he studies exactly these details: he investigates human society as a continuum of interactions, but without as much emphasis on government. *Human Action* is a compendium of observations and inferences from the fields of psychology, sociology, psychiatry, economics, history, anthropology, and evolutionary biology (before that field even had a name). Directly and often eloquently, Mises expresses basic and enduring comprehensions regarding human activity.

Mises contends that there is essentially no break between economic and non-economic motives in human choices; he contends we individually act as consistently as we do in all phases of our lives because of how we are constituted, not primarily in response to externalities that induce desires or goals. However, this is not a nature versus nurture argument because Mises places in abeyance the question of whether one or the other causes any individual to think or react in one manner or another. For Mises, the salient point is that our disposition makes our individual behavior generally predictable, but *only* generally.

Mises observes that economics is the foundation of all societal relationships, even though life obviously encompasses more than just material concerns. He suggests that before we act in any environment, we must recognize and account for the substantial demands of the economic (in the broadest sense of the word) aspects of human existence. Thus, whether we contemplate a new purchase, or marriage or having children, or a new job one or a thousand miles away, or moving closer to parents to help them later in life, or simply in deciding whether or not to go fishing—economics plays a strong role. In other words, we have to determine *how* we are going to do these things, not just that they are what we want to do.

As Mises defines it, the goal of human action is the reduction or removal of any "felt uneasiness," a phrase he uses to express why humanity progresses. Our attempts to improve our lives, in each and every way imaginable, are efforts to change whatever it is about which we feel "uneasy." Unfortunately in the modern era this uneasiness is sometimes portrayed as unhappiness; it is not. The uneasiness is a reflection of our nature; an interminable striving to make things, lives, better. Suggesting or even accusing the citizenry of being unhappy is to miss the point of human nature, but can be a facile method to exploit (especially politically) human vulnerability, ignorance, or insecurity. That the accusers may not even understand the mechanisms or character of human nature complicates matters further.

Unease can be present intellectually, artistically, emotionally, structurally, economically, etc. For example, the unease that drove Beethoven to compose was not something he saw that he didn't like or he felt could be improved, but something in his mind that made him uneasy, until he "said" it in the form of a symphony. His unease was that he had to express himself. Bill Gates, the founder of Microsoft, and Ted Turner, the originator of the Cable News Network (CNN), were both uneasy about what they knew in their fields—not in a negative manner but in the opportunity each saw—thus they sought change at least, improvement at best.

During the one hundred years preceding the publication of *Human Action*, philosophers, social scientists, politicians, and religious leaders had aimed at making the world a better place by either persuading people how they should live or, if they had enough power, dictating how they would live. The availability of the mass-produced printed word, and eventually rapid communication and transportation, afforded humankind's would-be benefactors opportunities to proselytize, even coerce action that matched their views. Social engineering came into vogue. The idea was to make people better and happier by causing them to behave in certain ways—mostly to the benefit of society itself, not directly for the benefit of any specific individual. The thought was that the individual would experience greater comfort if everyone else did. The theory fell apart with its first step because what makes one person happy won't ordinarily do the same for the next individual—particularly over the long term. The efforts were pure self-righteousness, conceit, and narcissism. With time it became clear that social engineering was nothing but thinly disguised totalitarianism and tyranny—no matter the alleged goal or the "good" intentions of the actor.

Mises observes that life offers neither stability nor safety; it is a ceaseless risk because it cannot be controlled. Each day brings only possibilities, including the simple possibility that things will remain as they have or that they will get much better or much worse. We must *continually* determine how we will act and react in this real but quite uncertain world. Social engineers seek to transcend these realities and transform life's vagaries into certainty and convert people into predictable, and presumably secure, automatons, who will unfortunately be bereft of individuality and humanity. However, history has shown us that human beings cannot be taught or forced to give up their individuality. Mises illuminates the myriad fallacies of the social engineer's intentions in regard to this truth.

He methodically attacks the utopians through his explication of how we organize ourselves in a human society. We do that not through theory, but through actions. Mises takes the "actions-speak-louder-than-words" aphorism a step further than normal. In his view, *only* actions speak. Praxeology, the study of human action, became the foundation of all of the investigations Mises pursued. Economics is action; it is not values or goals. Although those exist, especially on an individual level, economics itself is only about active relationships among people, and between people and things.

The primary tool Mises uses for explanation is freedom of choice. He focuses on how personal actions have consequences and create relationships such that the ensuing agglomeration of individuals and their behavior results in society. Since the unmarked beginning of human sociability, through the invention of tools and language, we ultimately arrived at the division of labor. Division of labor drove progress because people were better off through specialization and cooperation. When people collaborated society was born and man became a social animal.

Yet, for Mises, society exists only in the actions of its individual members. Society is not an entity; he observes that it can no more act than it can eat or drink. Society is the result and reflection of individual choices, nothing more. It follows from this axiom that society is subject to control only if individual actions are controllable. Because of the human condition, however, this is obviously not the case except in very proscribed circumstances.

Mises investigates the ideas and ideals of equality. He starts with the fact that although neither society nor individuals are controllable, they may be led to cooperate out of self-interest. Of course, the consummate American achievement is equality of opportunity—but not of results. The modern battle is recognizing the fundamental difference between these two antithetical goals. The great American liberal myth, the supposed embodiment of equality in our founding documents, miscasts the Founding Fathers' subtext of equal opportunity and forms a demagogic justification for equalitarianism—equal results. (James Madison, primary author of the Constitution, foresaw the probability of a call for equal result by means of the Constitution's insistence of equal opportunity, and addressed this directly in *Federalist* #10.) As Mises explains, the myth of equal outcome's desirability ends up as an intellectual conspiracy that gives birth to socialism and, when that fails to deliver on its promises, the welfare state ensues. These embody the idea that equality of result is not only desirable, but that it is attainable. As he demonstrates—and this was a crucial twentieth-century understanding—it is neither. Such an achievement would be paradoxical to the essence of individuality and the progress of humanity.

Mises notes that we attempt to achieve equal opportunity under civil law not because people are fundamentally equal (clearly they are not) but because this policy is beneficial to society as a whole and to all members as individuals. Equal rights to individuality lead to unequal results because of individual differences in talent, character, luck, family, intelligence, circumstance, etc. Liberals would take away the right to be who we are in order to make equal the oppressed, those whom they see as encumbered with disabilities because their innate talents and gifts are different. As a premise it is doubtful those who do not see themselves as Albert Einstein, Bill Gates or Dwight Eisenhower or someone even akin to them on a far smaller scale and in a local venue, do see themselves as disabled. The nanny state and political correctness—the twenty-first-century tools used to effect equalitarianism—were born of the liberal's disability thesis. Taking away the right to use our differences, which are not disabilities—they are simply differences, and appreciate the fruits thereof, no matter how small or great, makes society less than it could be. If a person can imagine or invent or create, everyone benefits from the product of that labor; if you take away some or most of the results of that talent through government intrusion into private lives, you also destroy the incentive to use it; everyone's life is smaller for that.

For Mises, the individual's ability to reason through facts is everything. Thinking precedes action. It is only the individual who thinks—not society, certainly not the government. Thus, only individuals can create society. Any and all change begins with the thoughts, followed by the actions, of but a single person. And each reasoned thought by each individual contributes to the social whole.

Mises's goal was recognition of not just the value of reason applied to facts, but the primacy of this relationship. Reason is man's unique tool. The problems of all social interactions are amenable to solution, but only through reasoned action that recalls man's innate characteristics. This is not the pure reason of the Enlightenment, but tempered reason that recognizes society's human element. The rub comes when demagogues shift problems of facts to fields of morality or ethics or even desire—in other words, to realms of subjective judgments.

Morals and ethics obviously are not bad elements, but they can be misused to distort or even deny the validity of rational responses. For example, the concept of Christian charity can be misrepresented to justify theoretical equalitarianism, by taking from those who have and giving to those who have not. However, when one citizen's property is reduced and another's is increased—by the hand of the government and not through the free action of the parties—there is little that can be termed equal treatment. Under this model there is a simplification of society and human nature that not only doesn't exist today, but didn't exist in the time of Christ or at any other time. Even the Bible offers the Parable of the Talents, where using one's capabilities is a valued and expected act. There is no moral or other demand in Christian theology that the abundance created thereby is to be equally distributed in an act of Christian charity. The demand for conformity to a mythical model of charity (enforced by government if such is not forthcoming voluntarily) is both dishonest and destructive of what society can create when freedom of action is the governing principle.

Uniform and unbending moral codes used to make universal rules in response to idiosyncratic behavior (to either prevent or force "appropriate" actions) work against social comity and common sense. Neither bad nor good behavior is universal, nor can either be prevented or promoted with universal rules. Bad behavior can only be proscribed, even punished, but it cannot be eliminated, no matter the foundation or breadth of the rules. Good behavior cannot be forced; it can only be offered and encouraged by example and by means of our innate humanity. For Mises, society is formed by means of choices that are made on no other basis than individual freedom. If we intend to constrain that freedom in some fashion, we must construct our rules from observed action; we cannot make them out of whole cloth; we cannot create them by theorizing alone.

From consideration of individual action, Mises broadens his investigation to contemplate how that activity affects social organization. Socialism was the blueprint for government and economic interaction during much of the twentieth century when Mises was addressing statist economic intentions. He begins this portion of his study by exploring the foundations of modern economic understanding. Mises contends that what started the study of economics was the observation that remote consequences of current action can be more important than that action's immediate effects. For this reason thoughtful planning and observation are important factors in economic relationships and activities.

The main achievement of modern economic practice was the discovery of the value of long-term and broad-based thinking with regard to human activity. Macroeconomics became not just important, but paramount in societal actions, particularly in governmental behavior. Economically oriented debates have been raging ever since, between the observers of ultimate goals (teach a man to fish, feed him for a lifetime) and those emotionally committed to immediate desires (give a man a fish, feed him for a day). What is sociologically interesting is those who want to teach fishing seem likely to understand the necessity of also offering sustenance as the process is learned. But those who see only the short term—the hungry man—too often don't seem to think about the longer term—how this person will be hungry again next week and next month and next year. In the terse view of Mises, economics opposes the frenzy and insistence of the apostles of the short term. In his view "History, one day, will have much more to say."

One of Mises more interesting observations is his contention that modern demagogues espouse an old error, one rampant in the ancient world, but whose modern incarnation arose from what Mises termed the *Montaigne dogma*. The view in Michel Eyquem de Montaigne's era (1533–92) was that economics is a zero-sum game, in which one can profit only at the expense of another. The theory holds that there are a limited number of resources available; therefore, what one person gains, someone else must lose. This notion, still as false and illogical as it has been since the division of labor created modern economic relationships, was part of the foundation of socialism. Socialist theory purported to "scientifically" recognize that limited resources allowed capitalists to gain additional wealth only if proletarians suffered an equivalent loss. If this is true, socialists contended, we have to institute a system of equal distribution so that none will be harmed or denied participation while others unfairly experience gains.

Of course, the fallacy of zero-sum game theory is obvious even to unsophisticated observers: if such a relationship did exist, how could one explain *any* material or social progress for one group without an equal povertization of others? How would we explain the unending improvement of the standard of living for all groups in all open societies? But the persistence of this error is so strong in contemporary economic thinking and liberal political dogma that equalitarian politicians still excoriate the exploiters and commiserate with the exploited, as though neither material nor social progress (let alone the comprehension of economic realities) has occurred since the Stone Age. The apologists for equalitarianism eventually resort to propaganda and indictment—rather than valid argument or a study of economic reality—to advance their objective of economic and social leveling in order to achieve "fairness." They couple their striving for equalization with some form of punishment for the exploiters (the entrepreneurs who actually created the progress the equalitarians use simultaneously as a springboard and a whip) to offer both an example of and to justify their concept of what is fair. All of these convolutions can only be termed *Alice in Wonderland* economics.

In *Human Action*, the efforts of Mises to explain both the fallacies of socialism and the necessity of taking all economic (human) actions to their logical conclusions does not always make for light reading, but it is methodical and clear. Because socialism isn't just a bankrupt ideology but also an impossible goal, Mises views the political choice as being not between capitalism and socialism, but between "capitalism and chaos." His insights remain cogent today, for socialistic tendencies and equalitarian goals are far from dead. They are present in statist administrative activities, bureaucratic regulatory interpretations, the judicial interpolation of statutory mandates, and politically correct approaches to "social justice." How, one asks, can the educated, the experienced, the studied be so naïve or so blind as not to appreciate how ordinary logic clearly explodes the welfare state's fallacious methods and goals? Mises puts it simply:

> In enacting . . . measures governments and parliaments have hardly ever been aware of the consequences of their meddling with business. . . . The statesmen who were responsible for the . . . policy were not aware of the import of their action. . . . The plight of Western Civilization consists precisely in the fact that serious people can resort to such artifices without encountering sharp rebuke.

Politicians think about elections, popularity, and legislative choices. When they do think more substantively, they often do not think logically or with a long-term view (they are far too often neither educated nor experienced enough to be able to do so). Sometimes they simply don't want to think that way because it might be (electorally) unpopular. They are not practiced in simple fiscal integrity, and the show of confidence with which they present the economically impossible as the socially feasible has become routine and is often declaimed by fawning media as virtuous.

The profound understanding of the human condition that Mises exhibits—actually his book could rightly bear the title *The Human Condition* as easily as *Human Action*—does not deter him from politely and sometimes impolitely railing against that condition when he observes how real people respond to real problems with wholly unreal answers. His investigations and dissections are detailed, persuasive, and ultimately irrefutable. However, it is worth noting that parts of his analyses are sometimes so professional and professorial that only the truly insistent will need to devour this whole work. For those who wish to indulge in the philosophy without seeing every proof, it is possible to skip chapters XVII, XVIII, and XX.

Definitions

ALTHOUGH MISES does not directly define any of the terms he uses context usually makes their meaning reasonably clear. Nonetheless, a distinct understanding of certain concepts will prove valuable. Some of the terms Mises employs, though in vogue in the early part of the twentieth century and therefore part of his vocabulary, have long since gone out of popular usage. The words that have been defined for the reader appear after the synopsis of *The Theory of Money and Credit* (p. 409).

About the Author

LUDWIG VON MISES was a product of antipathy to nineteenth-century European economic dogma; he became a prime creator of twentieth-century economic science. Born in 1881 in Austria, educated in Vienna, and chased to Geneva, Switzerland by the Nazis in the 1930s, he finally settled in the U.S. in 1940. His battles were never ending. Even in the United States, his views were so widely disputed by the ultimately discredited Keynesians that he could not secure regular employment. He eventually landed a job at New York University, but his salary was paid by outside interests not the school, and he never became a regular member of the faculty. During his career he wrote twenty-five books and hundreds of scholarly articles; his students changed economic thinking and policy in the twentieth century, literally around the world. Mises died in New York City in 1973.

41

Witness

Whittaker Chambers

Originally published: 1952
799 pages

WHITTAKER CHAMBERS wished to change the world; it was a conviction, not a crusade. *Witness* is his intensely personal account of a life that ceased to be his own because of his beliefs. All of humanity's frailties, foibles, and failures, as well as its integrity, goodness, and striving are exposed as Chambers tells his tale. The harsh light of his reality, to the fierce dismay of mid-twentieth-century liberal America, exposed a cancer within our government; the country did not see the death of this scourge until the collapse of the Soviet Union fifty years after Chambers began his struggle.

Chambers, a simple soul, grew up in a famously dysfunctional and poor family in pre-World War I rural Long Island. The conflicts and confrontations in his life make the reader pause. His travels were not black, then white; his life was a kaleidoscope of learning experiences, and even the shades of his evolution were always changing; his journey reflected the times in which he lived.

Like many of us, he was initially quite timid:

> I ran away from my first fight. In those days I did not know that courage is the indispensable virtue. Life had not yet taught me that, without courage, kindness and compassion remain merely fatuous postures.

For each of us these sentiments are worth contemplating—and reading again. Chambers's own reticence faded as he endured life, and what he presents in this recounting of his experience reflects the courage most of us wish for as we realize what life demands. Kindness and compassion are not effectively bestowed without a long view and direct action.

Chambers became educated almost as a last resort—he failed at most everything he tried up to the point of returning to school. He joined the Communist Party in his twenties and broke with it a decade later when he realized that communists were not engaged in communism, but in a conspiracy—the goal of which was power over all human beings.

As a communist, Chambers was devoted, committed, and active. His turn to this dark theology in the 1920s came as a result of the despair he felt after World War I. His was an intellectual and emotional act to make the world better. In a sense he was naïve and narrow; the opponents he ultimately exposed, who were once his compatriots, derided him for that, but from their perspective not his. (To understand how the same circumstances Chambers experienced could lead to a completely opposite course see the biography of Wilhelm Röpke following the synopsis of *Economics of the Free Society* [Chapter 23].)

Chambers was a thinker first, but also a revolutionist. For the reader's benefit, early in his recitation he asks how so many bright, involved, educated, and experienced people could have turned to communism. Of course, he was one of them. His answer reflects the time in which he lived: "A man does not become a communist because he is attracted to communism, but because he is driven to despair by the crisis of history through which the world is passing." As he explains his somewhat guileless youth, he elaborates: "Communism makes some profound appeal to the human mind" that the world can be a better, more fair, more livable place. Like Marx, his intellectual inspiration, Chambers and a particular cohort of the American liberal establishment were enamored of what communism offered. They thought (without thinking) "I can do that. I can live a life of communism, of utopian ideals." And they were right. These ideals *could* become actualized, but only if the world were not populated with people, who suffer from the human condition. What happened to communism is what happens to any system that requires for its success the demolition of the human spirit—failure in the face of reality.

Communism was ruthless. But, since it was justified—at least according to the thinking of its adherents—the barbarous path of terror and dictatorship leading toward it was also justified. This is Machiavellian, with the ends justifying the means. It is also adolescent nonsense, carried out by deadly force. Chambers's case for what he did during the 1920s and 1930s may cause readers to question his understanding, even his sense. In 1922 Ludwig von Mises had already published his massive work *Socialism* (Chapter 32), which debunked collectivism *in toto*. The arguments against communism didn't change in 1925 or at any time during the following six decades, at the end of which the Soviet Union ultimately collapsed of its own weight—as Mises and many others had predicted. But after World War I, naïve intellectuals the world over thought that *their* collectivism might be feasible. Chambers embraced these false hopes, which grew and were romanticized in his mind by their opposite, the disastrous social and economic experience of his earlier years. Most of all Chambers and so many others saw communism as the means to end war for all time. As time demonstrated, it was just the opposite—it threatened war continually.

The story of Chambers's life is as much about defeating totalitarianism in its most personal and intrusive form (i.e., as a pernicious force invading an individual's imagination with visions of glorious equality) as it is about Soviet Communism in particular. Regardless of how thoroughly Chambers rued his youthful errors, his country ultimately benefited from his principled repudiation of his erstwhile allegiance to communism. Chambers explains himself by noting that "the revolutionist cannot change the course of history without taking upon himself the crimes of history." In other words, Chambers's guilt for the world's condition underpinned his sense of responsibility—"he" made this mess and it was his obligation to right it.

This narrative is about one man and two cultures, the one in which he lived and the other where he secretly worked. In addition to this chronicle, Chambers provides an insight into his intellect. His asides, such as his commentary on the New Deal (President Franklin Roosevelt's program to revitalize America in the midst of the Great Depression), are stimulating, revealing, and still relevant today. The New Deal emotionally satisfied Chambers's generation even if it didn't resolve the economic disaster of the 1930s. He later understood that Roosevelt's program

> was a genuine revolution, whose deepest purpose was not simply reform within existing traditions, but a basic change in the social, and above all, the power relationships within the nation. It was not a revolution by violence. It was a revolution by bookkeeping and lawmaking.

Chambers's observations are still timely. He recognized that the power shift that occurred in the 1930s was a transfer of control from the world of business to the society of government. This was a revolutionary transformation for which violence was unnecessary given the grave economic failures of the time. The then-present disaster was falsely laid at the feet of the capitalists and the free market, thus the country undertook an oblique course to socialism and government control of the economy; Chambers ultimately saw it for what it was.

That similar arguments are made today by the welfarists for government control of more and more of our everyday lives and the economy to "protect" any particular segment of society evidences a second revolution. In this era power is taken from individuals and subsumed by government which will then rectify life, no matter the arena—employment, education, health care, retirement, personal safety, etc. Settling this much control in the society of government (and it must be noted that government, at all levels, is a society unto itself; those in government often act with more supposed power than we give them in order that they might do what is best for us) is the antithesis of the constitutional democracy created in 1776. The efforts of the government are always presented as a national obligation to repair inequality—a condition that has no limits.

The attainment of authority in political matters was and always is the goal because of the nature of human beings. To bring Chambers's observation forward, the same attitude can be seen in neoconservatives today, and for centuries past by liberals of varying hues. As a result of ego or false intellect, or plain naïveté, people may intentionally seek power and offer their good intentions—or something the population fears, such as terrorism—as their rationale or vehicle, or worse, their justification, to achieve control. In all events, the world seems to change very little in how it works. Thus the disconnection between the goals, the means, and the results of those who would control society for its inhabitants is ever present.

Chambers explains the bitterness of liberals of his era as he exposes the insufficiency of their thinking and their notable gullibility (and early on his as well, of course):

> The men in power at this time, who could not see that what they believed was liberalism added up to socialism could scarcely be expected to see what added up to Communism.

Do liberals tend toward political innocence in all generations, or do they refuse to face the reality of following their own course to its logical conclusion? Are they just intellectually lazy, seeing the goal but unwilling to face both the chimerical nature of their desires and the human values strewn along the path they travel to reach their idealized vision? As Chambers observes, every move against the communists was felt by the liberals to be also a move against them, for they couldn't or wouldn't distinguish between themselves and overt totalitarians. How they could either miss or refuse to see this was never explained by them after the fact—they dismissed the whole process of Soviet Communist infiltration of the U.S. government as something with which they really weren't involved, although the facts clearly demonstrated otherwise. Today liberals, who cannot see that what they believe is welfarism adds up to socialism, again miss or refuse to see the long-term effect of their policies on both the country and those they claim to want to help. And, just as facilely, they aver they are not involved in anything so nefarious as what they are directly doing.

The liberals of the 1940s understandably derided Whittaker Chambers as a traitor (to the country he was trying to protect, but what they really meant was that he had deserted their cause); that was the most convenient counter-accusation and explanation to minimize, or even dismiss his primary indictment. Their reaction to his assertion of communist infiltration in the government was one of feigned disbelief and ridicule. We now know that even the most innocent of them couldn't have been more wrong. And the most involved could not have been more deceitful both in their attempt to discredit Chambers and in their refusal to believe the intellectual reality of communist goals. As a cautionary tale, *Witness* remains pertinent today, more than a half century later.

What ultimately brought Whittaker Chambers to action was a core cognition of himself and his world. He found that indispensable courage he thought he lacked in childhood when as an adult his utopian blinders dissolved in the face of too many realities. At that point he understood that the force of words alone was not enough against the treason of communist ideas. Chambers intones that "acts were also required of a man, if he were capable of them." Thus, Chambers acted.

When telling his story, he neither excuses nor defends his past. Once World War II began, he felt compelled to rebel openly against totalitarianism and his own communist goals. He saw his role as that of a person who must bear witness to the evil ends and methods embraced by the communists and their liberal dupes. He thus exposed his friend and co-conspirator, Alger Hiss, a high State Department official, as a communist and an agent of the Soviet government. From the moment of Chambers's accusation, to the beginning of Hiss's jail term a decade and a half later, Chambers led the life of a figure in a fable.

The personal and public roadblocks he encountered when he turned informant make Chambers's journey through these darkest hours a story of heroic proportions. He wanted to understand those against whom he must testify, but he didn't want to harm them as individuals while exposing their communist infiltration within the U.S. government. That reticence complicated matters sorely. At the same time, he was forced to confront the Soviet monolith (which had almost perfectly protected communism's secret existence in America) and intellectual and emotional skepticism among the members of the Eastern Establishment that such a conspiracy could possibly exist. He describes his difficult path simply and eloquently, because he writes with his heart as much as with his head.

But even understanding all that transpired, all that he sought to change, Chambers felt an authoritarian collectivist society was the one that would ultimately rule the world. When he finally quit the Communist Party Chambers said, "I have left the winning side for the losing side." He acted against his expectations because he knew the monolith that was communism was wrong. He, like so many intellectuals of his era, had little faith in the ultimate rationality of human will or the power of individuals. Here again we see the pessimism, in spite of their own intellectual comprehension of the nature of the conflict, of those so deeply immersed in the middle of a battle, so battered by widespread but irrational or romantic conspiracies opposite of their knowledge. We saw earlier that no matter what they knew to be true, both Joseph Schumpeter and Wilhelm Röpke (*Capitalism, Socialism and Democracy* [Chapter 38] and *A Humane Economy* [Chapter 33]) also felt that the weak side of the human condition would allow totalitarian constructions to ultimately prevail over freedom. That all three men were wrong in their predictions is not so much a testament to their lack of faith as a reflection of the overwhelming force of the times in which they lived.

Chambers's story can be seen as dated. Politically and economically, communism is dead. But totalitarianism and collectivist assumptions are not (witness the resurgence of socialism in Latin America in the early 2000s). There were two dangers to which Chambers called attention sixty years ago: one was an immediate threat to the nation's security, while the other was the more pervasive threat of intellectual and political meddling with the human spirit. His observations in both these arenas still ring true. The Muslim jihadists of the twenty-first century find blasphemy in all things different from their view, and they, like the communists before them, want to impose their values and beliefs on everyone else—by force, not debate. Although global warfare over these issues is virtually unthinkable because of the freedom that has spread since the fall of the Soviet Union, the threat of conflict on a smaller scale is ever-present. And the threat of plain terrorism is a fact, not a conjecture. Thus the times, again, must make us recall the need to keep our responses rational in the face of those who intend us harm.

The debates of the day are becoming more intellectually intense because of the fact of stateless terrorism and its potential for more mass murder, and the scarcity of real-time solutions that have been offered. In appreciating these circumstances it becomes apparent there is a pristine beauty in *Witness*, primarily because its lessons are the same that apply to our current dilemmas. Chambers writes a personal study of governance and of the human personality. His insights, and most of all his demonstration of the inherent need of intellectual integrity and personal action, make his story still wholly readable and useful in today's political cauldron.

Unmasking the communist conspiracy in the U.S. was a lonely task for Chambers. He nonetheless persisted, and in the process exposed how American communists enjoyed protection behind a complicated weave of establishment intransigence, liberal psychopaths, political expediency, and war-time distractions and even disbelief (remember, the Soviet Union was our ally in World War II, and uncovering its duplicity in this era was a delicate matter). The conspiracy was so vast, subtle, and effective that its sheer size and audacity convinced all at the top to ignore it because claims about its existence seemed so exaggerated. Obviously they were not.

In the end fealty to the principles with which Chambers fought his battles will stand us in good stead.

About the Author

BORN ON APRIL 1, 1901, Whittaker Chambers lived a life of strong contrasts. His early years were hardscrabble as he worked in varied sectors of the American labor economy. He later attended Columbia University before working as a translator of foreign-language books.

Chambers eventually became a senior editor for *TIME* Magazine and, coincidentally, a farmer. The years between his youth and his departure from the Communist Party were spent initially as a paid and open party organizer for the American Communist Party, then ultimately as an underground conspirator/agent of the Soviet government employed to engage in espionage. His witness against the party and its members—his friends and fellow believers—began in earnest in 1939 and ended fourteen years later with the conviction and incarceration of Alger Hiss, Chambers's close associate and handler. Richard Nixon, then a congressman from California and the member of the House Un-American Activities Committee who was Whittaker Chambers's champion and believer, rose to prominence and ultimately the vice-presidency on the substance of the Hiss case. After the Hiss trial, William F. Buckley, Jr., befriended Chambers and gave him an editorial job at the newly founded *National Review* where he worked until he could work no more. Whittaker Chambers died in July 1961, after long struggles that had ravaged his body and his soul. In the end one can tell he rested in peace.

42

Killing Pablo

Mark Bowden

Originally published: 2001
272 pages

MOST OF THE TIME life gets better, or worse, incrementally. The move from one stasis to another is generally small, seemingly reasonable, mostly logical, and frequently unnoticed. The accretion eventually is not. As conditions gradually change, we often cannot see how a slow and ostensibly benign shift reflects not an idiosyncrasy or an aberration, but a new paradigm. In the end, when the totality is apparent, we all of a sudden wonder how we got there.

Colombia, a relatively small country from its beginning, was made smaller when President Theodore Roosevelt (in furtherance of his dream of a canal linking the Atlantic and Pacific Oceans) engineered the independence of Panama, Colombia's far northern province. This occurred shortly after the turn of the twentieth century.

The remaining national entity got over Roosevelt's amputation and was mostly stable and corrupt (in a rational way) and undistinguished among South American states for the next half century. In 1948, however, with the murder of Colombia's president, there began a period so devoid of anything rational that the times became known simply as *La Violencia*, The Violence. At that juncture, Colombians and their institutions entered an incremental but downward spiral, which is chronicled in this volume about the life and death of Pablo Escobar, an infamous cocaine lord.

Without reading this necessarily somewhat superficial recounting of the Colombian tragedy, one cannot grasp how fast life can travel back to the Dark Ages, which, with due respect to history, may not have been as black as Colombia during the reign of Pablo. The sheer madness continues today with corruption, bombings, murder, assassination, kidnapping and other crimes both grand and insidious. Even in its skimming of the surface of the chaos, Mark Bowden's recitation of the drug wars, and then *the* drug war against Escobar himself, is usefully comprehensive and quite pointed. The almost unimaginably grisly and widespread violence, the full horrors of which one must read between Bowden's lines to fully discern, is astounding.

Corruption, the cardinal human failing, underlies the world. It is the ever-present flawed fraction of the human condition. It also seems to be the most prominent characteristic that best defines Latin American governance and much of its society. Corruption has always been humankind's greatest difficulty, but in Colombia it was and is not just endemic, but a social cancer for which no surgery or medicine is effective. It is a disease of the somnolent and fearful, and only the awakening of everyone, at one moment, could possibly mitigate it or hope to cure its worst effects.

In Colombia the king of this scourge was Pablo Emilio Escobar Gaviria, born a year and half into *La Violencia*. He grew up middle-class, by Colombian standards, his mother being a schoolteacher who evinced middle-class insight and fervent Catholicism, while his father was a cattle farmer. His family was not corrupt and had no need to be, but the society that surrounded them was, and the corruption led only to violence of the gravest kind. This Pablo learned.

By 1983 Escobar was both a murderously prominent figure in the Colombian cocaine trade and a rising political aspirant—unfortunately, a not-incongruous duality. While controlling much of the massive exportation of cocaine to the United States, he had been elected to the national government as a shadow congressman; that is, an alternate who sits whenever the primary congressman is absent. But respectability proved elusive and his lawlessness finally overshadowed his striving for political power as an avenue to acceptance. The more he was denied respect, the more violent he waxed, and each step, each revolution of the downward spiral, seems inevitable in Bowden's story.

Some statistics demonstrate the gravity of Colombia's chaos at the time: between August 1989 and February 1991 (the period known as the First War) 457 police officers were murdered *in the city of Medellin alone*. After the national police committed two hundred men to the hunt for Escobar, thirty of them were assassinated within fifteen days. Escobar had offered a "reward" of five million pesos, about $2,500, for the execution of any police officer. The colonel in charge of the hunt for Escobar was offered, directly, a bribe of six million U.S. dollars to fail. This was corruption on simply the boldest scale of all.

Escobar was personally noteworthy for his calm and deliberation. Not a great intellect, he was nevertheless a master at understanding the human psyche both in isolated individuals and in groups. He became expert at publicly defending himself and his "business" by starting at square two, always a step beyond his own lawlessness. His tactic was to accuse the government of violating his rights, as he was officially pursued, thus deflecting attention from his crimes. The often crassly or fearfully sympathetic media tried to leave him alone, thus giving credence, however obliquely, to Escobar's claims. He was both generous and conniving; his attempts at bolstering his image through bribes, charity, or intimidation were regularly successful. These efforts brought not just acceptance, but acclaim and even adoration, especially in his hometown of Medellin. His admirers did not allow rationality to intrude upon their feelings, and without question, they accepted the cash.

Neither handsome nor imposing, Escobar was deadly. As Bowden observes, he was lethal in a sense and manner that has only rarely occurred in modern human society, especially infrequently outside of the political arena where a dictator controls an entire country through a compliant military, a corrupted national police, and command of the machinery of government (particularly the judiciary), thus making him immune to challenge.

Escobar styled himself a revolutionary, but Bowden portrays him as he was in reality—only a gangster. His personal exploits, the atmosphere he helped to create throughout Colombia, and the fact that he was just one of many drug thugs, makes readers wonder what the people of Colombia were thinking, or if they thought at all. Such explorations, except at the highest level of government, are a missing link in Bowden's book. Although the populace can understandably be seen as somewhat unnecessary to the tale (because this is a book about Escobar, the drug trade and its vast financial success, and the efforts to stop him), critical readers will be remiss in their responsibility to themselves if they do not read into Bowden's account a warning about the vulnerability to corruption of civilized life and economic, thus social stability if fealty to principle is lost.

As Bowden narrates the story, he explains how the Colombian and U.S. governments routinely acted ineffectually when they addressed the problem posed by Escobar. Potential missteps regularly became actual ones. The Colombian government's incompetence, the fear of officials for their very lives, and the pervasiveness of bribery and intimidation and kidnapping and murder were grievous flaws that first crippled and then almost wholly compromised law enforcement. Neither the will of Colombia nor the sometimes-clandestine intervention of the U.S. government could touch Escobar. Ultimately, "official" Colombia and the United States (the presence of which was, in theory, advisory only) were both brought to their knees.

Something bizarre, but logical, happened at the point of total failure. *Los Pepes*, a vigilante assemblage, arose like a phoenix. In retrospect, this development, which was only one of many lawless enterprises that occurred in Colombia's recent history, seems almost inevitable. *Los Pepes* engaged in Escobar's game by Escobar's rules; there were no options left, for the people and the government could not stand up to be counted. Escobar's relatives, associates and even his lawyer began to die in execution-style murders.

The ante continued to rise and Escobar ultimately was killed (note—not arrested, indicted, tried, convicted or punished—he was simply killed) as the title of Bowden's book reports, but the carnage and its aftermath were frightening. After reading this account, one looks around and feels assured that nothing comparable could happen here in our country. It probably cannot—at least not without enormous and almost incomprehensible change—but it can and does happen elsewhere, in Central and Latin America, Africa, Asia, and the Middle East. The ripple effect in the U.S. can be palpable in these circumstances, as it was on September 11, 2001.*

If the distance between Osama bin Laden and Pablo Escobar seems too great to draw the analogy, consider the underlying philosophy and actions of both before reaching that conclusion. Readers finishing Bowden's account should infer that incremental societal destruction, no matter how seemingly far away and no matter its underlying genesis, does affect us. Violent Muslim terrorism began to affect the U.S. directly when the American Embassy in Tehran, Iran was seized in

---

* Lawlessness and terrorism, founded in the $25 billion Mexican drug trade, are directly affecting the U.S. as gangs quartered in Mexico bring their murder and mayhem across the Texas border to both protect their traffic lanes and ply their products. The captains of these gangs are as ruthless and conscienceless and deadly as Pablo Escobar and threaten law enforcement personnel and citizens in equal measure. See "The Killers Next Door," *TIME*, 18 April 2005 and "The War Next Door," *TIME*, 20 August 2007.

1979 by Muslim ideologues, and the carnage has not stopped at any point since then.

That Islamic jihadists are attempting to force their views on the world as Escobar sought to do in Colombia through violence and intimidation is patent. How the civilized world will react is the issue. While the bombings and murder practiced by the Islamists are widespread, they are still, from a global perspective, small. Dealing with these terrorists by means of civilized law enforcement in Europe and the U.S. seems to be working for the most part but not on all occasions as was seen in London in 2005 and Madrid in 2004—but if our security efforts fail, as has been the case in Israel as it fights the terror of the Palestinians, what mayhem and vigilantism may ensue remains a very open question. Although it is unlikely the West will turn tail and run as Spain did in response to the Madrid bombings, the responses of any nation are complicated by many factors. There is a large Muslim population in virtually every country in Europe. The option for reprisal and vigilante action to future terrorist attacks in both Europe and the U.S. is real. The social cost of such a reaction would be enormous.

The world has become a very small place. Bowden's warning of what can transpire when terrorism occurs is muted by the fact that the story of Escobar's killing occurs within a single country with a homogenous population. Everyone breathed a sigh of relief when Escobar was dead and by that point no one much cared who was responsible. But that we must always be aware of what is transpiring beyond our borders that will eventually affect us is now obvious; that we need to act purposefully, when we can, where we can, to influence change in our favor is necessary. Those determinations are difficult and dangerous. But, if we cannot make those choices, we shall find ourselves validating George Santayana's famous admonition: "Those who cannot remember the past are condemned to repeat it." As well, we need to consider Walter McDougall's observation in *Promised Land, Crusader State* (Chapter 20), that we need to act when we cannot afford not to, and most assuredly when it is in our national interest to do so. That last dilemma sits atop the discussion pyramid as the currant conflagration in the Middle East falls dangerously into civil war, religious jihad, and a sink-hole of ethnic and fundamentalist hatred, with virtually no resolution in sight. The question of our response to non-state sponsored terrorism is one that will not be single-tiered or monodimensional. Under such circumstances the chances for misstep, bad judgment and worse execution are ripe.

More than just an account of a horrible circumstance, the question arises from Bowden's recitation, is *Killing Pablo* a cautionary tale with broad implications or simply a corrupt nation's anomaly? The Machiavellian destruction of the political process, it seems, can devolve to corruption of market processes, from which the next step is corruption of the social fabric. It has happened in Iraq by means of the fractured world of Islamic fanatics. In Colombia, Escobar did not steal money, not a dime—he stole lives. The terrorists of 9/11 did the same thing, and the Islamists of the twenty-first century seem to be repeating the process.

The response to terrorists, whether narco-, eco-, political, religious, or otherwise, according to modern thinking and planning, is to jail them or kill them. But how and under whose auspices is this to be done? The Colombian nation failed to protect itself and citizens felt they had to go outside the standards of civilized actions, or at least change the measure of what a civilized society can be allowed to do. If enough suicide bombers are recruited, if enough terror is rained upon a free nation on any continent, particularly in Europe where there are large, sympathetic indigenous Muslim populations, the reaction could be both dramatic and wide-spread as was seen in France in 2006 when Muslim youths went on wild sprees of vandalism in response to policies with which they disagreed. More importantly it could involve both individuals and government itself as frustration is magnified by a failure of containment.

The Israelis, who enjoy a modern constitutional democracy and a reputation for institutional integrity, provided their own answer to such circumstances. After the invasion by Black September (Palestinian) terrorists of the 1972 Olympic Village in Munich, Germany and the murder of eleven Israeli athletes in a botched rescue attempt, Israel's government ordered the systematic assassinations of the ten leaders of Black September who were thought responsible for the initial attack. These murders, which had the appearance of sanctioned vigilante actions, occurred in various Western nations, complicating the response even more. They began in Italy and included the execution in Norway of an innocent Moroccan waiter incorrectly thought to be a Black September leader. The government of Israel obviously felt pressured to go outside both the law and norms of international agreements, because they could not see solving their problems within those parameters. Years later it was claimed that these assassinations were not of the leadership of the terrorist organization, but others associated and within it, because the leaders had melted back into Islamic countries where Israel had little access—thus a message was sent by proxy murder. Israel's actions thus can be seen as at least one step removed from potentially quasi-justified retaliation, and are an equal distance away from civilized society. The question of how much free governments will tolerate one nation protecting itself with actions carried on inside another is an open and dangerous issue. The Israelis seem to do so inside Lebanon with impunity; where else will this be tolerated, much less approved?

In all cases, the thin line between an acceptable response to terrorists and thugs, and organized mayhem being used to theoretically finish an argument is easy to cross. Although the vigilante reactions of an organization such as *Los Pepes* are an ugly phenomenon, sometimes a civilized society (particularly those in Europe), even our own, may take similarly ugly measures to protect itself and to effect change. The end of Islamism is far from visible, thus our nation will be asked to answer many questions on the limits of our patience and our fidelity to being a nation of laws.

We do not always have the luxury of playing this "game" by our rules, and that is the core of Bowden's story. When abiding by those rules creates a certainty that we will incrementally continue to lose (as it did in Colombia), then the last resort is to play by the rules of our adversaries. Where will such measures take us, and more importantly, will we be able to stop employing them? The United States is a constitutional democracy that is threatened with mass murder, if not outright regional annihilation, by Muslim jihadists who may ultimately possess nuclear weapons or chemical and biological agents capable of widespread deployment against Western populations. These religious fanatics are Pablo Escobar's emotional and intellectual cousins. How shall we fight back, under Escobar's and the terrorists' rules or our own? Being forced to make these decisions is a hard pill to swallow—but the obverse, playing by our rules of civilized justice and losing too many battles, as we did on 9/11, is even harder to contemplate.

In today's interconnected global village, *Killing Pablo* is a most thought-provoking social commentary. The link between Pablo Escobar and Osama bin Laden, or anyone else like either of them, may be shorter and more direct than everyone imagines.

About the Author

MARK BOWDEN is a journalist and writer whose credits include newspaper articles, magazine features and books about human beings in action. Bowden contributes to *The Atlantic Monthly* and *The New Yorker*, writes a column for *The Philadelphia Inquirer*, where he was a staff writer for more than two decades, and is an adjunct professor at Loyola College of Maryland, where he teaches creative writing and journalism. He was born in St. Louis, Missouri, in 1951, and grew up in Glen Ellyn, Illinois, Port Washington, New York, and Timonium, Maryland. He graduated from Loyola College of Maryland in 1973 with a degree in English Literature. Bowden lives in southeastern Pennsylvania, is married, and has five children.

Section IV

The Future

43

Fewer

Ben J. Wattenberg

Originally published: 2004
241 pages

POPULATION IS A big-picture subject that is typically presented as a simplistic, short and long-term issue; specifically, that there are too many people already on the planet and there are likely to be a whole lot more. That that portrait is no longer true is the point of Ben Wattenberg's essay; he dispels the notion that this is only a numbers game:

> About modernity, then, think economics, not biology. . . .

Media pundits, non-profit population foundations, demagogic politicians and UN bureaucrats, all of whom have a vested interest in doomsday over-population scenarios, offer the public their traditional, generally monochromatic agendas concerning population. But there is something new in the air, different from what we've been hearing for so long, something quite striking. *Fewer* doesn't fit snugly into the *First Principles* grid, but it does have its place in an open-ended category: The Future. This book is not about political philosophy, but it does form the basis for long-term global economic and political reassessment.

According to Wattenberg, there are two key points about current demographic figures. The first is simultaneously mundane and far reaching: world population *growth* estimates, based on observable trends, have been officially and dramatically lowered—to the point where population *decline* will be a reality by the end of the this century. The second point is as interesting as it is important: almost no one is talking publicly about this shift. The lack of discourse is likely a result of the conception most people still have about population: that its growth is based on Malthusian theory, which posits the inevitable extinction of the human race due to over-breeding. This misperception is not helped by the media's short-term, profit-motivated tendency to peddle alarmist stories that support the Eastern Establishment's big-government model as the only solution to the supposed population crisis (perhaps, in their view, ultimately entailing forced sterilization, euthanasia, or other such outrages). The liberals don't want the fact that the world is getting better, all by itself, to become part of any new paradigm. Least of all can the liberal press admit that any of this is occurring through the mechanism of free-market economics in contravention of their accepted wisdom that only by government intervention can the world be made to work optimally.

Wattenberg, the U.S. Representative to the UN World Population Summit in 1984, presents in direct and concrete terms facts and figures to explain the slowing and ultimately declining population numbers. He cites known statistical resources and then offers a more probable estimate of population trends, based on a lifetime of study that allows him to observe how far behind reality (most likely because of political considerations) official sources inevitably are. *Fewer* provides a probably more accurate extrapolation of population trends than that which appears in any standard reference work—especially those published by the United Nations. Of necessity (if one is going to take on the UN) Wattenberg concisely explains why.

Of equal or perhaps more value than his observations and calculations on actual population trends is Wattenberg's overview of population issues from a combined political, social, and economic perspective. There is utility in knowing what is happening and there are advantages in realizing why, but what is of paramount importance is to grasp what it means going forward. Wattenberg addresses all three of these concerns.

Those who understand the import of population dynamics on all facets of economic, governmental, and national-security issues may find Wattenberg's data rather bleak for most European countries and Japan, Australia, New Zealand, and Canada, but more positive—with certain caveats—for the less developed countries. The U.S. sits in something of a middle position as one of the few exceptions to all the other rules. Wattenberg eliminates the standard euphemisms, qualifications, and dissembling in his presentation. His refreshingly simple language and concepts enable anyone to understand what is happening.

The reproductive numbers are simple: replacement fertility rates for most societies center at 2.1 children per woman during her core childbearing years; i.e., through age forty-one. In the lesser-developed countries, the replacement benchmark is slightly greater because infant mortality is correspondingly higher. These rates have been exceeded for centuries.

The startling fact is that the worldwide population explosion experienced since the Middle Ages (roughly the last five hundred years) slowed and then *reversed* during the second half of the twentieth century. To repeat, this reversal occurred in *just fifty years*. Comprehensible only with a long view, this transformation is extraordinarily significant. A trend of over five centuries' duration, a trend that had threatened an environmental disaster of biblical proportions, *stopped and then turned itself around within two generations*, with little prospect of reverting to the old pattern (for both social and mathematical reasons that are dealt with below). The change portends, quite simply, a truly new world order.

Population growth is calculated in terms of the total fertility rate (TFR), which is a measure of how many children are being born, per mother, at any given moment. In most Western countries (except for the U.S., where the TFR is just under replacement level at 2.01) fertility rates have plummeted. As Wattenberg observes, it isn't just that the TFR for developed countries has fallen below 2.1; it has actually collapsed—down to 1.14 in Russia, 1.15 in Spain, 1.17 in Korea, 1.23 in Italy, 1.32 in Japan, 1.35 in Germany, 1.47 in Canada, 1.60 in Great Britain, Sweden, and Australia, and 1.89 in France.*

The TFRs for the less developed countries, especially "the billionaires," as Wattenberg refers to India and China, are equally astonishing. China's TFR of 1.80 is already below replacement and India will reach a rate lower than replacement in the near future. (It is difficult to tell exactly what the rate is at any specific time in any given nation, but the trends are clear from ongoing surveys of birth records and other local statistics.) In Mexico, where the TFR was seven children per woman in the late 1950s, the rate is now close to 2.1 and will fall below the replacement rate within a year or two, if it hasn't already. (As an aside, the dramatic decline in the birth rate in Mexico may not only solve the illegal immigration flow from Mexico to the U.S. within the next twenty to thirty years—because there will not be enough young

---

* All figures in this synopsis are current as of 2004.

Mexican workers to run Mexico much less supply labor for the United States—but the demand to stop Mexicans from entering the U.S. may quickly reverse, to the point where the U.S. makes emigration from Mexico attractive to bolster our own declining labor force.)

The international fertility numbers do not mean that population will stop increasing this decade, for the earth's current inhabitants will continue to procreate, albeit on a decreasing scale. But it does mean that global population will drop meaningfully, before environmental or social catastrophe likely descends. In other words, Wattenberg finds sound reason for optimism in the statistics and their causes.

All of this is stunning, and in stark contradiction to the doom and gloom portrayed about the future of the earth by the population and environmental Cassandras. Instead of a world population of 15 billion or more, in less than two hundred years we face a potential global population of near 3 billion, *less than one-half what it is today*. Making an educated guess as to this number is not easy, since there are varying methods used to achieve high, middle, and low-range estimates. None of this is set in stone, but today's real numbers, as opposed to those concocted using archaic theories, tell us what is most likely for tomorrow.

Considering the messages of radical environmentalists and strident climatologists proffered by the media, it would appear that these "experts" are wholly unaware of the news. Perhaps they are ignoring these facts until they discern how to spin them to stay in business. Various ramifications that *Fewer* brings to the fore about the near-term effects of a declining population, though stark in their political, geopolitical, and economic implications, have also been largely ignored by media outlets. This cannot last much longer as neglecting the facts inevitably becomes unsustainable.

The first lesson to be gleaned about population decline is that almost none of this happened as a result of strong private or church sponsored family-planning efforts, coercive political/administrative methods (except in China), or any other form of direct governmental action. It has come about as a result of modernity and economics.

As modernization proceeds, populations manifest a shift from a rural-based short life expectancy and high birthrate, to an urban-centered increased life expectancy and lower birthrate environment. There are many reasons that explain the changed population paradigm, most are the result of changes in culture: broader urban educational efforts, especially for girls and women; paid (as opposed to in-the-home or in-the-field) employment for women; greater access to basic health care for all age groups; increases in the availability and use of contraception; greater personal wealth as free-enterprise becomes the norm (which allows mothers to think of and certainly to appreciate an enhanced quality of life for their children—a very important factor as the educational, healthcare, and economic levels of women also increase); and the mere move from rural to urban areas (in an urban setting children are more of a burden, in rural areas they are more of an asset). Additionally, as women become more equal with men in their ability to participate in modern society (with marriage thus coming later in life), and cohabitation becoming an accepted living arrangement, the socially desirable childbearing years for all women are reduced, thus the TFR declines across the board, through choice. In other words, as women experience the drive toward self-realization, children, *per se*, or at least large numbers of them, are not always their first priority, or sometimes a priority at all.

Of equal or greater importance to modern parents is the quality of life their children experience. There is a relatively direct correlation between the number of children in a family and the quality of that entire family's existence. As women become educated and urbanized this reality strikes home with great force. Even poor women who live in a remote setting are having fewer offspring, perhaps because of a modern communications system (think satellite TV and even a rudimentary electric generator) that simply allows them to see what is possible, both for themselves and their progeny.

Aside from the likely continuation of the foregoing fertility-inhibiting conditions, there are practical reasons why fertility rates will not be reversed yet again, at least not soon and not easily. One is the same Malthusian calculation that had predicted exponential population growth. Once population is substantially diminished, mathematical realities (how many children women can bear), constrained by the time involved to return to former population levels (how long it takes to mature each generation), dictate that it would take centuries to re-attain today's population level. It is unlikely that people would see that as a good thing having already experienced overpopulation once, and in this I believe we can be optimistic.

Additionally, government intervention in various countries to increase fertility rates (called pro-natalism), generally through monetary incentives and offering government child-rearing support such as day care, educational opportunities, and health cost relief, has not been successful, for purely economic reasons. Giving a couple ten thousand dollars (or even ten times that) to encourage having a child doesn't begin to cover the overall cost of child rearing in modern society. In other words, governments cannot afford to "buy" children, especially considering lower tax revenues going forward because there are fewer workers as population declines. While governments struggle to support the public costs involved in paying off the retirement and health care promises made to existing adult citizens very few funds will be available for pro-natalism. Most important, the basic reasons for population decline are the economic and cultural factors that have been developing for half a century; the genie that created them won't fit back in the bottle. All of this shows the law of unintended consequences (free-market capitalism creating the solution to overpopulation) in one of its most powerful and almost certainly irreversible manifestations.

The implications of the two-step process, first the decline in population growth, followed by a decline in population levels, are profound—especially for Western countries as their next two generations age. The unfunded, pay-as-you-go public retirement and health-care systems in place throughout the developed world, but particularly in the U.S., Europe, Canada, Australia, New Zealand, and Japan, are simply fiscally insupportable in the face of population collapse. This portends significant economic and political reconfiguration if not confrontation unless alternative solutions are embraced. Such solutions are feasible, but not always seen as desirable and thus are pushed off into the future where they become ever more difficult to implement.

The public's sense of entitlement to high, even untenable, levels of pension payments, subsidies, and health care indemnification—that populations bought into when spoon-fed such notions through political pandering—seems to grow in inverse proportion to fiscal reality. The idea that the older generations have somehow "earned" their "entitlements" through votes for a free lunch to be provided by pyramid-scheme social programs becomes more unreasonable each year. Almost all of these programs are going to collapse if dollars are not aligned with sense. If they do founder because of political naïveté or willful public ignorance, the consequences will be sudden, and the cures (and pain) dramatic.

Wattenberg notes that demographic changes also offer seldom-considered realities regarding national and international security questions. Who will fill the ranks of the armies of the future? One possibility is that armies will be less used, even if they will not be less useful. As world population shrinks and resources are freed up, while national territorial pressures are reduced, it may be that diminished proximity will simply decrease tensions in every direction.

The new demographic reality gives rise to myriad issues involving regional, religious, cultural, and ethnic considerations, as well as environmental, business, legal, governance, education, and immigration problems. The migration question, in particular, is one of the more controversial and complex. Wattenberg contends that immigration is the most likely antidote for the various declining labor forces and declining numbers of taxpayers facing developed countries. The problems of population decline in these nations are compounded by the reluctance of the native-born to engage in labor or work past quite early retirement as life expectancies expand, while these same citizens do not welcome the immigrants necessary to keep their economies going. Wattenberg doesn't discuss the apparent lack of appreciation in developed societies for the inherent dignity in all work, but this cultural attitude may change in the near term as the demographic situation forces a reappraisal of workforce needs. People are both more resilient and realistic than many pundits seem to believe, thus the future may not look as bleak as Wattenberg's book might suggest to some readers.

An additional consideration is that demographic changes in combination with technological developments will trend toward economic convergence, leading to a shrinking global community where wealth is more evenly distributed. Immigrants earn higher wages in their new countries, send excess funds home, and thus raise the economic level of their country of origin. In the home country these funds are often pooled as capital rather than just as income, thereby raising the economic base there.

Another example Wattenberg offers refutes the American myth (often promoted by the press and some politicians) that the rich are getting richer, the poor poorer, and that the gap between the wealthy and the less well-off is widening. This is a falsehood perpetuated by the misuse of both language and statistics. The rich are indeed getting richer, but so too are the poor, sometimes more quickly than the wealthiest sector of the economy. The wealth gap sometimes widens marginally, and sometimes shrinks, but the important fact is that all sectors of the workforce are doing better, with the least well-off improving their lot every year.

What is critically misleading, however, about exaggerated claims in this venue, is that people move through various levels of economic well-being as they age and gain experience; the "poor" at one statistical moment are not the same people who are "poor" twenty years later. Apropos of this matter, Thomas Sowell observes:

> Although people in the top income brackets and the bottom income brackets—the "rich" and the "poor" as they are commonly called—may be addressed as if they were different classes of people, often they are the very same people at different stages of their lives. An absolute majority of the people in the bottom 20 percent in income in 1975 were also in the top 20 percent at some later point. . . . Fewer than 3 percent of those in the bottom 20 percent in 1975 were still there in 1991, while 39 percent of them were now in the top 20 percent. Most of the "poor" of the 1970s had reached higher real income levels in the 1990s than most of the whole American population had in the 1970s. (*Basic Economics* [2000] p. 136–37)

In other words, the permanent underclass is much, much smaller than demagogues would have us believe, and the solutions to its problems can be much more modest than the massive government programs often recommended; that governments with declining populations will be less able to afford such largesse is becoming equally apparent. Although sometimes government assistance programs are popular because of politically calculated voter empathy for the poor, they are often wholly unwarranted and actually counterproductive for the economy, the cohort to be helped, and the society as a whole. Lower population levels will likely force recalibration of both what is needed and what can be supported in this arena.

The entrepreneurial/educational impetus of any given economy drives its fiscal realities. Yet, this positive, utterly factual attribute of social life is often painted in snapshot form and for political purposes as a greed-based negative. The demagogic pronouncements of today's welfare-state enthusiasts won't be discussed at length here because economics and capital, which underlie wealth creation in its various forms, are the subject of many other synopses in this volume. Some of these works also discuss the fact that a hierarchical system, an inherent result of human differences, allows for the exact result recounted by Dr. Sowell.

As Wattenberg observes, "Wars, like life, can be about several things at once." His intriguing and substantive presentation of the consequences of global depopulation touches on many issues that should be part of political and economic conversations regarding the near and long-term world outlook. Demographic realities must be faced by modern nations whose responsibility is to continue to provide sound economic foundations for their citizens. National leaders and voters would do well to heed Wattenberg's warnings and act sooner rather than later on the opportunities he foresees.

About the Author

BEN WATTENBERG is a prizewinning author and commentator, political activist, and recipient of various public tributes and appointments. He graduated from Hobart College in 1955, and was awarded an honorary Doctor of Laws degree from Hobart in 1975. Wattenberg was an aide and speechwriter for President Lyndon B. Johnson from 1966 to 1968. He served as an advisor to both Minnesota Senator Hubert Humphrey's race for the Senate in 1970 and Washington Senator Henry Jackson's campaigns for the Democratic presidential nomination in 1972 and 1976, years when Mr. Wattenberg also helped write the Democratic National Platform. Among his public service credentials are his appointment as a public member of the American delegation to the Madrid Conference on Human Rights by President Carter and a 1981 appointment by President Reagan to the board of Radio Free Europe and Radio Liberty.

Since the early 1990s, Wattenberg has hosted a PBS show that features discussion of topical matters with professionals, politicians, and experts, and he has written ten books, many of them on population issues. His most recent major TV/print project was *The First Measured Century*, an effort to understand, explain, and dramatize American life through the lens of social and economic data. He spends much of his time investigating demographic facts and trends. Mr. Wattenberg lives in Washington, D.C., where he is a Senior Fellow at the American Enterprise Institute. He was born in 1933 in the Bronx, New York.

44

One Nation Under Therapy

Christina Hoff Sommers, Ph.D.,
Sally Satel, MD

Originally published: 2005
307 pages

IN THE EARLY 1990s, an unpublished thesis discussed the emergence in modern society of a potentially maladaptive human behavior: the emotionalizing of life to the point of both personal and societal paralysis. The now ubiquitous emotional response and the transfer of "pathos to pathology"* according to the authors of *One Nation Under Therapy* is seen to be prevalent in the U.S. mental health and legal systems and the media. In the thesis this response is compared to the ever-elongating saber-toothed tiger's incisors. Eventually the tiger became so overburdened with maladaptive dental apparatus that his extinction was foreordained.

The same is suggested for Western society (in a political/social, if not biological sense), that we are becoming so emotionally over-involved in ourselves and our own inabilities that we will lose the capacity to act rationally or respond factually on either the small or large stage. Because the real world will fade into the background, self-destructive decisions—those that go against logical action based on authentic circumstances—will proliferate to some point where we actually might do ourselves in, or more plausibly, we will become so politically and psychologically weak that others will find it easy to save us from our misery. *One Nation Under Therapy* takes this theory off the drawing board and brings it to the street.

---

* pathos: a quality that arouses feelings of pity, sympathy, tenderness, or sorrow in another. pathology: a biological or functional (mental) manifestation of disease.

In their book, Christina Hoff Sommers and Sally Satel dissect the therapeutic state—a social entity that is the care-all and resolver-in-chief for what ails almost anyone who doesn't live in Wyoming or Burundi, places where people haven't been overexposed to their own inadequacies and fragility and know they are supposed to take care of themselves in spite of life. The growing dependence on therapy as the answer to life as it is, is often bewailed by rationalist pundits and politicians, and a small cadre of mental health professionals. These observers, grounded in a real world, remember three centuries of American resilience, capability, confidence, and character. From them, the question is put plainly: has "therapism" gone awry and taken on a life of its own? The authors' short answer is "yes," and their longer response is a reasoned explanation and investigation—based on myriad studies, surveys, and research efforts that use science rather than emotion, intuition, or anecdote—to explain and support why they come to this conclusion.

Although *One Nation Under Therapy* contains eighty-seven pages of footnotes, which exhibit detailed support of what is delineated in the main volume, that feat of professionalism did not cause the authors to use unintelligible jargon or rationalized gibberish in presenting their summary of the state of mental health care in America. This is a volume of clear, concise language and premises dealing with life as it is, and always has been; existence unmuddled by "psychobabble" or presumptions of frailty or pretensions of pseudo-psychological acumen claimed by the practitioners of therapism.

The authors present facts and a reasoned comprehension of human beings—and beg to have them tested against the claims of those who seem to have their conclusions written before the examinations begin. Most often Sommers and Satel detect the obvious flaws in the research and logic used by "professionals" who appear to have both an agenda and a stake in the outcome of their work and premises.

In its essence this book is akin to the simplicity of Friedrich von Hayek's dissection of socialism in *The Road to Serfdom* (Chapter 13), where Hayek concludes that socialism won't work because it defies human nature. Sommers and Satel contend that modern therapism defies human reality. They bring the trauma, loss, and inconstancy of life into focus—as real facts—and explain that real people have been dealing with such events idiosyncratically for eons. Why are Americans, in particular, and modern society in general, all of a sudden so weak, delicate, and incompetent to deal with life? The authors inveigh that modern psychology (probably more than psychiatry) has "pathologized [that is, made an illness of] normal human response to tragedy."

It is contended by the practitioners of therapism that trauma is not something an ordinary person can digest or respond to alone. In the words of the authors, by taking this tack the trauma "experts" have in all likelihood actually made matters worse than they might have been with a more nuanced, personal, and positive approach to human misfortune or even calamity. They conclude, based on the evidence,

> that most people are not clinically traumatized by extreme events.... The reframing of normal reactions to loss and tragedy as pathological—the notion that we are too often unfit to cope with adversity [has become] accepted wisdom.... [T]o presume fragility in the face of adversity [is to] forget how frequently survivors ... persevere nobly.

They further suggest that

> [c]ommon sense alone should tell us that a one-size-fits-all psychological approach to anything as complicated and varied as human reaction to [trauma or tragedy] is deeply misguided.

As well, the authors find the careless and often intrusive use of therapism, involving the negative power of suggestion, a large part of their diagnosis of amateurism. The imposition of outsiders into the lives of strangers to insist upon therapy as the answer to virtually everything that ails us is as offensive as it is inappropriate. Those in the "profession" cannot seem to see how disabling their own intrusions are. Even U.S. Supreme Court Justice Antonin Scalia, viewing the spread of psychological assessment practiced by everyone from school administrators to members of the Court, could not help commenting in *Lee v. Weisman*,

> [I]nterior decorating is a rock-hard science compared to psychology practiced by amateurs. A few citations of "research in psychology" ... cannot disguise the fact that the Court has gone beyond the realm where judges know what they are doing.

There is in the authors' findings a theme of professional failure in the therapy community. This is a deficiency those in charge refuse to recognize. The authors discern, essentially, more individual agendas and egoistic empire building in the ideas that permeate the assertion of massive psychological inadequacy in modern America than they detect actual therapeutic skill or understanding. What their research brings to the fore is the need for intellectual and social integrity in this arena—not just more training. In other words, it isn't just the professional ideas that are wanting; it is the people who practice them.

There is a necessity for a force of practitioners who are substantively dispassionate and independent, and capable of seeing and understanding what is before them in factual *and* psychological terms, rather than the amateurs, even charlatans, who adhere to quack-degree, simplistic, and universally applied formulations of dealing with human emotion. For many in the field of therapism, it may be as much about their own goals and their own wallets (an especially important aspect that the authors essentially leave alone), coupled with an almost unimaginable ignorance and lack of intellect that drives the practitioners of therapism ever more intrusively into our society. The America of this battalion of "trained experts" is one that could not possibly have created the America of the twentieth century, or the nineteenth, or eighteenth, or seventeenth; the America that is the focus of so much admiration and imitation. These "experts" see a nation of weaklings who cannot cope without their help, without the assistance of those who truly "understand their pain, and feel it."

Mass therapy being applied across major segments of society or in response to catastrophic events, such as the terrorist attacks of 9/11, or Hurricane Katrina along the Gulf Coast of the U.S. in 2005, the authors find to be inappropriate at best, almost universally counterproductive in general, and damaging at worst. In catastrophic circumstances the loss experienced by each victim can be substantial, long lasting, and most importantly, personal. But, as the authors comment, loss is also one of life's essential ingredients. If human beings hadn't developed an ability to deal with such things, then human beings would have evolved into something else—a branch of the wildebeest family, for example. And, yes, there are those who truly need therapy and psychiatric care, no one would deny this, least of all the authors, but their point is that those cases are the exceptions. To suggest otherwise, as many women's magazines and daytime television talk shows do, to suggest that almost no one can get through life without therapy whenever something goes wrong, is wrong itself.

Although Sommers and Satel address the often inappropriate, even incongruous, response of therapists to major tragedies, the same response on an individual basis in individual therapeutic practice can be just as dangerous and just as inappropriate—for the same reasons: lack of professionalism, lack of control, lack of ability, and worst of all, the greed factor. Although the authors don't directly bring their thesis and investigation down to the level of individual therapy, the questions they raise regarding the therapy brigade in major venues seemingly apply equally to the individual. Of course, it is likely that the mass response so decried in the book blossomed from the objects and conclusions of individual therapy in the first instance. The professional extension might have been thus: if our practice works for individuals, why, we'll just market this on a wholesale basis—because the same ingredients are present in both individual and society-wide situations. In other words, it may have been a "eureka" moment. Therapy became more business than profession.

The status of mental health practice today would be a bad joke if the subject matter, the victims, and practitioners weren't so ever present in modern media. The media effect is strong and relentless. The public is subjected daily to disasters large and small, and the more tears, the greater the wrenching anguish of the victims, the more close-ups the camera offers. *TIME* Magazine's Pictures of the Year for 2005 contained almost nothing but such images, as though nothing good, uplifting, successful or even comical happened for a whole year. The media offers that the world is a terrible place and then asks, how can anyone cope? But cope we do, and quite well, thank you. We wouldn't know that we could if we didn't actually do it; there are too many "professionals" telling us otherwise.

The omnipresent insistence of the therapy community that life is so bad we likely cannot endure it without "professional" help (and the spread of this story by their partners in inadequacy—the media) is sometimes taken literally, according to Sommers and Satel. This approach is certainly something politicians use no matter what they may believe themselves. We see the government response (mostly in the form of Congress and the White House each trying to outdo the other in empathy) in the face of adversity, that they will take care of everyone—whether everyone needs or wants their help, or, God-forbid, deserves it (a very politically incorrect question). This not only encourages all to seek succor in the arms of "the state," but also encourages many *not* to take care of themselves in the future, for they now believe that's the government's job. This political reaction is present even in circumstances far from real trauma, such as rising gasoline or food prices, that have less to do with true hardship than economics.

It is to be noted that while decrying the excesses and inappropriateness of much of therapism's agenda, the authors do not simply dismiss human response to tragedy with a cavalier "Get over it." What they do recognize is that human beings are *built* to get over it, but the thrust of therapism has been to undermine that reality and to assert that we are weak and incapable. The facts, of course, demonstrate otherwise. It appears that therapism, an essentially unregulated segment of business often heavily disguised as caring, has overstepped the bounds of common sense. Returning to a realistic and workable middle ground is all the authors seek.

Moving toward that end, Sommers and Satel ask, "Why . . . have so many mental health experts underestimated our inherent resilience and resourcefulness? Why do they presume fragility in the face of powerful events?" The answers are found in the "professional," personal, and economic benefits to be derived from engagement in the proliferation of a presumed mass need for therapy. In the words of one social commentator, "If you go to the optometrist, you come out with a pair of glasses." If you come across a therapist, or more to the point, if a therapist comes across you, you'll likely find yourself with a syndrome—and an appointment.

The authors comment that as therapists tamper with or even misdirect the mind's natural defenses, they are likely to do more harm than good. Instead, they suggest that the therapy community begin operating on the premise that people will pull together. People will realize that most likely others are far worse off than they are. They will recognize that rather than focusing on the negative aftereffects of something that cannot be changed, they should concentrate on our remarkable capacity for post-traumatic growth. With this far more common outcome, the practitioners will be able to capitalize on the impulses that bring healing and progress in the aftermath of trauma. And, although Sigmund Freud has been largely superseded by modern psychiatric research and practice, the authors fall back on his fundamental wisdom to bring more optimism than pessimism for the long haul:

> The voice of intellect is a soft one but it does not rest till it has gained a hearing.

Ultimately, Sommers and Satel propound that "therapism falters under rational scrutiny." The only remaining question is, when? Will it be sooner—as we call to account the excesses of an almost out-of-control and self-aggrandizing group of "professionals"—or later, when far more harm than good has eventuated? The authors' thoughts coalesce around the idea that "therapeutic 'kindness' is inadvertently [or is it directly?] unkind and disrespectful . . ." and forgets that there is such a thing as right and wrong. Therapism is seen to be at odds with our values. It comes to its brigade post as an adjunct to legitimate psychology, yet it engages in "medicalizing the human condition." This is self-destructive, for the human condition is real; it is not bad; it needs definition and direction, but it cannot itself be eliminated without also eliminating the uniqueness of the human experience.

The practitioners of therapism see virtually all of life as disease. They are able to claim this because there are no perfect people, or perfect circumstances. The rest of us see life as a risk, and the better we are able to deal with that reality without the need to fall back on therapy *or* government, the better off each of us will be.

Perhaps the most cogent observation on the modern practice of psychology, especially mass psychology, was voiced by G.K. Chesterton (1874–1936), English novelist, poet, journalist, and playwright:

> It seems a pity that psychology should have destroyed all our knowledge of human nature.

And perhaps we should we add "common sense."

About the Authors

CHRISTINE HOFF SOMMERS studies feminism and American culture, American adolescents, and morality in American society from her post at the American Enterprise Institute. A former university philosophy professor, she is the author of *Who Stole Feminism?* and *The War Against Boys.* Her professional career has included membership on the Board of Advisors, Center for the American Experiment, and as chairman of the Board of Academic Advisors, Independent Women's Forum. From

1980 until 1999 she was a professor at Clark University. Dr. Sommers earned her BA at New York University in 1973 and received her Ph.D. in philosophy from Brandeis University in 1977.

Sally Satel is a resident scholar at the American Enterprise Institute in the W.H. Brady Program in Culture and Freedom. She is also the staff psychiatrist at the Oasis Clinic in Washington, D.C. Dr. Satel serves on the advisory committee of the Center for Mental Health Services of the Substance Abuse and Mental Health Services Administration. In 2003 she served on the Fowler Commission that investigated sexual misconduct at the U.S. Air Force Academy. Dr. Satel earned a BS from Cornell University, an MS from the University of Chicago and an MD from Brown University. After completing her residency in psychiatry at the Yale University School of Medicine, she was an assistant professor of psychiatry from 1988–1993. During 1993–94 she was a Robert Wood Johnson Health Policy Fellow with the Senate Labor and Human Resources Committee. Dr. Satel has written widely in academic journals on topics in psychiatry and addiction medicine. She has published articles on the cultural aspects and political trends in medicine and science in the *New York Times, New Republic, Commentary, Atlantic Monthly, New York Times Magazine,* and the *Wall Street Journal.* Dr. Satel is author of *PC, M.D.: How Political Correctness Is Corrupting Medicine* and *Drug Treatment: The Case for Coercion.*

Afterword

THE LIFE OF the community is fragile. Our relationships are primarily based on unstated agreements and comprehensions, thus their vulnerability to degradation. The thrust of those agreements is that the members of the community will be good to and for one another—that they will act morally. In *A Defense of the American Constitutions* (1787) John Adams suggested that we must realize how precarious is our hold on virtue. Though it is the foundation of the happiness Thomas Jefferson stated we had a right to pursue when he wrote the Declaration of Independence, Adams understood human limitations and thus the fragility of virtue.

At many points in *First Principles* we have seen myriad authors express an additional sentiment: if we do not have a moral society then we cannot have a free society. In *The Character of Nations* (2000), Angelo Codevilla asks how it was possible during World War II that the German and Japanese people could have cooperated (or even acquiesced) in the insanity of German viciousness toward the Jews, at the treatment by the Japanese of their prisoners of war, and toward the enemies both countries created with their militarism and totalitarianism. How could whole nations become barbarians so quickly after striving so long to become civilized?

The answer lies within us, of course, but ensuring these things do not eventuate or repeat themselves is done through the community of interests we all must understand and implement. We cannot just act responsibly as individuals; we must be able to speak up when our culture devolves into something less than it might be or should be. It is that slippery slope effect that Friedrich von Hayek so eloquently exposes in his books. Failing to act is what allows society to change quickly, often for the worse, when someone invents a shortcut to human perfection.

As the Soviet Union regrouped after World War II, and the Western powers were faced with the possibility of needing to constrain its territorial and political ambitions, the free nations saw two choices—confrontation or containment. The United States championed the latter. We were to lead by example first, and force, if necessary, much later.

George Kennan, the primary architect of President Harry Truman's post-war policy, noted that

> [e]very measure to improve self-confidence, discipline, moral and community spirit [in Europe] is a diplomatic victory over Moscow.

Those things that Kennan outlines in his plan to contain the Soviets cannot be ordained, cannot be reduced to a statute or regulation; they have to be earned (and that, of course, is why they succeed in the first place). They have to be understood to be our *individual* and then *community* responsibility. Virtually the only impediment to making the world work well is ourselves—we know what to do, and how to do it, and why. The only question that remains is, can we?

The human condition can be guided by means of both incentive and command—the proverbial carrot and stick—but neither it nor its effects can be eliminated. Restraining, not stifling that condition is our aim, for the human spirit, the human condition's brighter side, is what has allowed us to achieve all that surrounds us. A successful society also requires that its members be citizens, not subjects, and that requirement demands our time and our effort. Put simply, there is no such thing as a free lunch.

The precariousness of which John Adams spoke, and which the world experiences inevitably, is not quantifiable. It is somewhat akin to Supreme Court Justice Potter Stewart's classic 1964 definition of pornography—"I cannot define it, but I know it when I see it." As a society we need to pull back from the slope that represents the mostly authoritarian and eventually crude shortcuts to societal perfection. Of course, that's an almost impossible order; the slope ordinarily appears neither steep nor slippery. Yet, with care and thought, we can recognize when we begin to slide—whether culturally, socially, governmentally, morally, or economically—and our authors have outlined how we might attempt to act before gravity takes over.

Ultimately, the truth is clear: there is no magic formula to a virtuous society. There are only options and ideas, based in reality, that we can effect before or after we feel the ground moving out from under our feet. Sooner in these instances is almost always better than later. As we observed at the beginning of this book, the concrete facts are these:

If we have a virtuous society it does not matter what form of government we institute.

If we do not have a virtuous society, it does not matter what form of government we institute.

In the first instance, a virtuous people will obey leadership that acts in a moral manner. They will change or defy governance that does not. In the second, no matter how logical and careful, and even comprehensive, are the laws, rules, precedents, practices, or punishments effected to order a conscienceless people, no government can coerce comity. In their debased state the people cannot, or will not, see either what they are doing or what they are causing. Like the citizens of the Confederacy who enslaved themselves by their very actions in prolonging slavery, the venal will be sentenced to misery simply by their vision of life. We don't enforce morality—period. We encourage morals by example, leadership, expectations, teaching, practice, and most importantly, by results. A society cannot be successful with only rules, legislation, police, or bureaucrats—it must have understanding as well. That understanding is gained only as people participate.

IN THE SMALL, modern world in which we live there is no refuge from political reality, and there is no room for innocence. If we do not confront the facts of our social and cultural existence, including the government we choose to order our world, those facts will eventually confront us—at that point we will be at a disadvantage.

Allowing the choice in government to be between corruption and incompetence, in either politicians or bureaucrats, is self-destructive. These aren't the only options, of course, but we often sanction one or the other, or both, by inaction and distance. There are two avenues by which we can begin to avoid some of the consequences of "unsupervised" governance; these paths complement one another. The first is citizen vigilance expressed in watching and assessing the government's purposes and operations; the second is to reduce the size, scope, and stretch of government in order that citizens can more effectively engage in the first effort and experience their own hard-earned freedom. These routes can be negotiated simultaneously, but it requires will and the commitment to become an intentional part (however small) of the governing process itself. Arrival at even this minor level of engagement is often achieved only after bitter experience. The intention of *First Principles* is to help us avoid bitter experience as the starting point for our efforts.

Here is an example of how political process, often as important as substance, has become distorted: Historically, American attitudes toward property rights, sound fiscal management of government resources, and responsible regulation and taxation were not so much subjects of economic policy as of public morality. We knew how to help without doing more harm than good because we observed guidelines founded in moral conduct. Those sinews are being tested today in the fashioning of an authoritarian political correctness that is nothing more than the revival of an older disease—utopianism. Its tools are ancient weapons—the layering of guilt that springs from life's most basic circumstance—inequality—and the promise that parity can be achieved; that there are mechanisms that will rectify mankind's inherent condition. When we attempt to deny inequality's nature, good and bad, our moral views become distorted.

The new barons of social perfection disingenuously, if not dishonestly, refuse to admit that human inequality (found in our varied imaginations, abilities, and personalities) has created all of the progress humanity has experienced throughout history. Rather than work with and through that reality—as humanity has done so well so often—they simply deny inequality's value, using an equalitarian moral cudgel that is false on its face, to subvert rational discussion. There is a truth that needs to be stated: taken to their foundations it becomes clear that freedom and equality are mutually exclusive—if we are to be free, we will not, cannot, be equal. If we are to be equal we certainly cannot be free. This complementary reality can be seen positively or negatively; how we view it determines what kind of society we will choose.

With an ironic twist, the same people who claim inequality is morally wrong then use the fruits of our disparities, the ever-increasing and advancing material well-being we almost universally experience (albeit at necessarily varying rates) when it suits their purpose. Essentially they say, "Well, now that *we've* created all this wealth, we'll use it to make everyone equal." Notice how they take credit for the results achieved by an open society, while concurrently denying its validity.

Of course, in this simplistic manner they dispute any need for progress from where we are; they claim that "this" (whatever "this" is) is enough. Their views are conclusive. As is their right to make economic, cultural, and moral decisions for the rest of us. As was observed earlier, this cadre wants to redistribute wealth that, using their philosophy and schemes, cannot be created.

The fact that utopia in any of its guises has never come to fruition after centuries of effort (with copious use of both carrot and stick) speaks for itself. Those who search for the equalitarian society, when they fail to achieve it, contend that their methods were implemented incorrectly, or insufficiently—they never consider that it is the very theory that is not just flawed but antithetical to human existence. That human beings openly recognize life's inequalities, and work diligently to minimize those that work against us and expand those that work for us is a given. This is the crux of the matter—all inequality is not bad. Einstein's capabilities and achievements, or those of Newton, Michelangelo, Henry Ford, Thomas Edison, Mother Theresa, Winston Churchill, or millions upon millions of lesser mortals, would not, could not spring from an equalitarian society. That each of us appreciates what humanity has accomplished—from the airplane to the zoo, from vacations to vaccines, astronauts to zithers—is unquestioned; that most of us realize those achievements can only be grasped by setting men free from the limits of other human beings is similarly realized. Thus the insistence of the equalitarians is not a siren song. The only hook on which this group can hang its disproved and discredited philosophies is that of the theocratic scold—that each of us and all of us should *want* equality in all things, because that is the only *fair and just* manner of life. Their term for this goal is social justice.

That there is no recognition, much less discussion, of what we would have to give up to go that far backward is the flagrant dishonesty of the equalitarians. They base their claims and assume (without considering human nature in the least) that life will remain the same if the incentive to achieve is removed—actually, not just removed, but punished. That this contention is fallacious on its face seems not to bother them. They do not or will not recognize their own slippery slope—the one that leads to uniformity at the very bottom of existence effected through the only possible means to achieve that end—totalitarian authority.

WHAT CAN THE citizen-reader of *First Principles* do? While there are many avenues to making a difference, the first thing the reader must believe is that he *can* make a difference—not just with his vote, but with his actions. If we believe we cannot make a difference, we most assuredly will not. The tide seems still to be rising against the individual, but the first principles enunciated here are as valid as ever, and probably more necessary to recall in the face of current society's morass of moral relativism—the insistence that any one social choice is as valid as any other. The point of *First Principles* is that all of our choices are decidedly not equal.

Thus, if there is any one thing we can do, it is to formulate not just our own set of values and beliefs, but a common and spoken understanding of why those values and convictions are more estimable than others. The marketplace of ideas will then decide worthiness. Life is not just a series of self-amusing options but a struggle to maintain a semblance of both order and opportunity through sound alternatives—preferences that have withstood the test of time and circumstance and stress. And once our choices are tested and hopefully found worthy, then we must take the next step—to make a difference, even if only by means of our own example, of our own life. It is equally important to realize that if doing more is required to maintain social comity it does not have to be a full-time occupation for any individual; the accumulated small acts of many citizens whether acting individually or as part of like-minded groups will always be enough to carry the day. But those small acts must occur.

The Politics of the Twenty-first Century

AS NOTED IN the introduction to *First Principles*, politics is not the focus of this effort, first principles are. However, the principles we've brought to the fore obviously lead to political activity. That is the junction before you, the reader.

State welfarism—now termed the nanny state—has become the overwhelming purpose of government and produces the bulk of the government's continually increasing size. But welfare programs are often no longer designed to relieve the lot of the poor (in the United States, since roughly 1997 there are more people who receive all or part of their resources from the government than there are taxpayers who support them). They are seen as a device to achieve an ostensible uniformity in life, founded in a monodimensional, politically correct finality: all inequalities must be compensated for. This mantra is then offered as a vehicle to achieve success in electoral politics. One may ask, how has this *Alice in Wonderland* logic been implemented? And one must further consider that if everyone is on the public wagon in this push toward equality, who is left to pull it?

The first step is to recognize that people can be hectored, through claims of the ostensible worthiness of these efforts, into believing they should at least be attempted. Once attempted their validity is thereafter assumed and their franchise grows with time. Those who question these programs are painted as petty or selfish, two words that make any political campaign a longer, more complicated effort. The accusation is easy, proving it invalid more difficult; to do so requires the intellectual attention and integrity of the accuser.

Making people better off sounds fine standing alone. But, it is important in this instance to begin at square one: it is difficult to *make* someone anything—even better off. Before people can achieve something, they have to want it and then work to keep it. If something is given, not earned, it usually has little value to the recipient. It is also difficult to quantify *who* and *how much* better off anyone shall be made; how do we reasonably, fairly, honestly (you choose the adjective) determine where need ends and mere convenience begins—considering those who are asked or forced to give as well as those who are to receive?

The consequence of ignoring these queries is simply futility. In order to make someone better off someone else has to supply the means. What duties fall to the recipient? What obligations can fairly be assessed on the provider? From a global viewpoint the taking may be as manifestly unfair as the giving is unsound. These are not lightly dismissed calculations, for they go to the heart of *everyone's* freedom.

The second avenue for the successful implementation of liberal policy is to foster a feeling of guilt in the self-sufficient over what exists in the world today. This is sometimes not difficult; the world can be a messy place. However, in this case judgment is dishonestly turned on its head—the accusation is that the self-sufficient don't *deserve* all they have, even if they have earned it, simply because there are those who have less. A "moral" indictment is issued for being successful. The reasons and causes of the unequal results, the myriad negative effects of the taking on the self-sufficient, and the benefits derived from equal opportunities that result in valuable but uneven results are, again, plainly ignored in idealistic fantasies. This idealism is also in contravention of the free society's universal social agreement regarding implementing our own opportunity and possibility, and accepting responsibility for ourselves.

Government acts in this field without a rational design or method intended to foster the independence of those to be assisted. As a result of the governing paradigm, there has been taught and learned an incapability and dependence, which then steadily grows on the part of those for whom government has taken responsibility. At this point government efforts morph into "entitlements." When government's actions, for political reasons, ultimately spill over into the middle class (Social Security, Medicare, education, and a million special interest earmarks—from the defense industry to a Peace Garden) that group is no less likely to develop feelings of entitlement than any other—in other words, they feel entitled to their entitlements. And, to ensure there is no misunderstanding of what is intended by these observations, let it be stated again that the discussion of modern government's actions does not revolve around the social safety net—help offered to those who truly cannot help themselves—but it circumscribes the social welfare net, essentially a scheme of income redistribution for political, not civic, purposes.

The welfare state was constructed on the tailings of capitalism's imperfections. As the twentieth century progressed and the contest between capitalism and socialism tilted first intellectually, then practically, and finally universally toward capitalism, the unreconstructed socialists stayed the course to which they were emotionally wedded, irrespective of facts. When the social and economic props were kicked out from under these ideologues, their conceit was de-fanged, but not discouraged. While everyone was looking, this cadre wholly embraced the welfare state, terming their version, as it had always been denoted, the social safety net; but this net was not intended to assist those who could not help themselves; its blueprints were far more grand. In actuality, those who could not help themselves were not the welfare recipients, but the welfare statists. They could not help but expand the safety net until it became the welfare net because they knew they were right in what they said they were doing—helping the helpless, uplifting the downtrodden, raising the hopes of the hopeless. What they really intended was something far greater: material human equality. Only when the attainment of this equality affected them might they begin to think differently. Most importantly, their abject failure in realizing equality through public largesse was rooted not only in the defect of their design, but in the fact that helping was ultimately not their goal, achieving and retaining power was.

If there be any doubt that the need to stay in office is great and the fear of losing office is calamitous—something to be desperately avoided by giving the public all it wants and more, all that can be thought it might need—the description of what the losing politician experiences, and avoids at *our* cost, is aptly described by Robert Traver in *Anatomy of a Murder* (1958). Traver's account puts a face on the politician's wretchedness at being returned to the status of mere citizen:

> I was learning the hard way something that people who have never held public office can perhaps never adequately realize: the feeling of utter forlornness and emptiness that sweeps over a man when he is finally beaten at the polls. And the longer he has been on the job the worse, not better, it is. This morbid feeling is beyond all reason; it is both compulsive and a little daft. One's last friend has deserted him; the entire community has conspired to ridicule and humiliate him; everyone is secretly pointing the finger of scorn and hate at the defeated one.

THERE IS A second area beyond the welfare state where government's continued growth is unrelieved: in increased legislation and regulation—or judicially imposed actions or sanctions—regarding citizen freedom or rights or conduct. These efforts reflect a surety that each life and every enterprise should not only be defined in a general manner that protects all of us from one another, but insists that government must referee our lives. The bureaucrats, legislators, and judges are increasingly convinced that unless they regulate and adjudicate (in a politically correct fashion) the activities and even the rights of individuals, that life will simply disintegrate into chaos or anarchy—or someone at least might feel bad. The vast bulk of our historical success in being a trustworthy, sincere, successful, capable, helpful, etc. society—all managed without such intrusion and oversight—is deemed irrelevant today.

The governing class, by its actions, has also evidenced an intention to make life risk-free in two ways; first, by eliminating personal responsibility for anything that goes wrong, and second, through ensuring the government will make right whatever is judged unjust; it will rectify any inequality. When these designs are conjoined with the nanny state the micromanagers insist we will arrive at utopia.

In these two arenas—the welfare state and the freedom of the individual and the security of his property—government has, with few caveats, taken on a life of its own. The Washington mindset (in particular, but these observations apply at all levels of government) has little to do with electoral constraints or first principles. Thomas Hobbes's behemoth, the philosophical Leviathan we turn to because we supposedly fear a central government less than we fear one another, was demolished as a viable theoretical premise centuries ago—of course, that did not stop utopians from repeatedly resurrecting authoritarianism whenever they felt they could, or should. From the time of the American Revolution forward the freedom and rights of the individual were understood to be more valid than government control of society. Government was to outline the rules—with our consent—not determine the results. These conclusions were reduced to a concrete model by means of our Constitutional experiment. In the twenty-first century we are reversing progress as we allow ourselves through inattention or ignorance to be victimized by government hubris and political perfidy. Thus, by default Leviathan rises again to protect us, as did the immortal phoenix of Egyptian mythology.

> Politics is the art of preventing people from taking part in the affairs which properly concern them. (Paul Valery [1871–1945], French writer and critic)

THERE IS A school of thought that the two most destructive (socially and economically) political impulses in America in the twentieth century were Franklin Roosevelt's New Deal and Lyndon Johnson's Great Society and War on Poverty. They were crafted from false economic premises, launched by the "intellectuals" of those eras, and put into effect through political demagoguery. The noble side of the human condition, by which we fail one another not out of greed and ignorance but out of kindness and arrogance, was strikingly in evidence in both cases. As always, the result of these foolish efforts was the law of unintended consequences coming to full flower—found in the fiscal disaster America faces over the next three decades.

Inertia, in the form of an entrenched bureaucracy, supported by intellectual scolds on the left and an electorate that apathetically returns roughly ninety-eight percent of incumbents to office, allowed little to change as the twenty-first century approached (save the blip of welfare reform implemented by a Republican Congress during the administration of Democrat President Bill Clinton).

In spite of the Democrats' entry into a political wilderness at their own hand during the last two decades of the twentieth century, the political duplicity and fiscal chicanery of the Republicans in the next period ensured the public would equally quickly turn them out of office. Sad for conservatives, but true. The problem, of course, is that although the Republicans were removed from power, what they had wrought—huge increases in "entitlement" spending (the Medicare prescription drug benefit), significant intrusion into local affairs (the No Child Left Behind education initiative and the Homeland Security efforts), and a tepid attempt at Social Security reform that went nowhere—was left in place as they headed for the exit. The fact is that all that was done by them was not undone by the next group, and all that wasn't done, that might have mattered, was left unattempted. Big government just never reforms, never moves back to where it was before suffering the effects of a slippery slope no matter who is in, and who is removed from power.

After the election of 2000, center stage was occupied by an entirely Republican administration and Congress, overwhelmed not by what they could *do*, but by how much they *controlled*, how much they found they liked *being* in control, and how they feared they could *lose* that control if they did not use the government's power and coffers in their efforts to *maintain* control. The result is the series of political disasters that has eventuated. What the Republicans forgot almost as soon as they achieved power was that they were sent to Washington (and many state houses) to change the culture of government. They did that initially in lowering taxes, but then they got the bit in their teeth and began government spending programs that made Democrat proposals seem tame by comparison. It was not long before the electorate had to remind the Republicans of the franchise they were given. What the liberals had not been able to discern philosophically—a reason for the electorate to return them to power—the Republicans essentially handed them on an electoral platter. By 2006 the Republican license was taken away because of their lack of restraint and their perfidious actions. The electorate was reminded that it cannot place much trust in the good intentions of others. What the elected were reminded is if you break that trust, you lose your place in the system.

Government has *no* institutional incentive to either dismantle itself, or, for too many reasons to iterate here, to work more efficiently. No king (or bureaucrat) wishes to reduce the size of his empire, and inefficiency and misdirection expand the scope of government and ensure the public's continued inability to penetrate the fog of any administration. Thus government will not be circumscribed through internal rational assessment no matter how many reformers or experts or consultants or managers claim they can make government run honestly and efficiently. They cannot do that because government does not operate on market principles, or brain power, it runs on politics; it can only be thwarted externally, politically. That did not happen after the Republicans took over in 2001, even with the best intentions and the outright dominion of those who insisted they understood what was wrong with the system. This result occurred because the American electorate, whom those in power actually do fear, sometimes wants to have its cake and eat it too. Who would blame them? Actually, there are many who would point fingers....

Ronald Reagan, even though he understood the reality of politics, preached government retrenchment when he came into office but he accomplished little by the time he had left. He faced a venal Congress, who feared for their jobs, and he could not finish the task alone. He needed the citizens and they seemed (and still seem) to be disconnected from the larger picture. This, of course, was his point in the first place.

> Power corrupts. Absolute power corrupts absolutely.
> Lord Acton

We have attempted not to comment extensively on current politics throughout this book, primarily because they *are* current; this is a text that attempts a more historical and perhaps practical if not philosophical view. However, because the existing political situation fits almost flawlessly into many of the philosophical definitions and examples our authors have offered, the constraints in leaving today's politics to pundits and historians are overcome by circumstances too obvious to ignore.

In the aftermath of the Republican takeover of the national government at the start of the century, the bureaucracy and those in the new ruling political party were mutually supporting—no matter how bizarre and counterintuitive that would seem. The GOP has been campaigning for decades for smaller, less expensive (in all senses) government; indeed, that promise is what brought them to power in the first place. Yet, once in office, they acted exactly as Bertrand de Jouvenel had predicted they would in *On Power* (Chapter 15), his masterful dissection of what happens to people who are allowed to exercise, first, some authority, and then virtually unfettered control. Today, first principles have been ignored—actually sullied—and the entire electorate is scratching its head, either bemused or befuddled at what might happen next (with those on the far left and far right suffering mutual outright indignation, for obviously opposite reasons).

Peggy Noonan, a political columnist who came to be well known writing for Ronald Reagan in the 1980s, observed this paradox of power in a *Wall Street Journal* article (May 11, 2006) using de Jouvenel's comprehension:

> It may take a defeat in November for the GOP to unlearn the lessons of power.
> Power is distancing.... When you've been in Congress for a while, or the White House for a while, you both forget too many things and learn too many things.
> You forget why they sent you. You forget it's not that you're charming and wonderful. You forget it's not you. You become immersed in a Washington conversation.... And you come to forget what [those who sent you] do know. It used to be easy for you to remember that, because it's what you knew too....
> Party leaders are showing a belief in process as opposed to a belief in, say, belief. But belief [ultimately] drives politics. It certainly drives each party's base. One gets the impression party leaders, deep in their hearts, believe the base is ... base. Unsophisticated. Primitive. Obsessed with its little issues. They're trying to educate the base. But if history is a guide, the base is about to teach them a lesson instead.

In *Conscience of a Conservative* (Chapter 18) Barry Goldwater states, "[W]e entrust the conduct of our affairs to men who understand that their first duty as public officials is to divest themselves of the power they have been given." Goldwater's point is that if during the period while they were becoming successful politicians those who were elected did so by means of principle, they must give up the idea that they can force political matters through the use of their newly acquired power; that they can only achieve lasting change by using the merit of those principles they espoused in the first place.

At several points in this book it has been noted that the first consideration for politicians is often, if not mostly, doing that through which they believe they will achieve reelection; most actions become, in campaign parlance, "a sop for the saps." What Noonan and Goldwater see from a distance is that acting in the best interests of the (neither illiterate nor grasping) electorate is as wise and productive, and notable as well as noticeable, a course as any designed to take advantage of that same group's supposed self-interest and venality.

Now that the expected electoral collapse of the Republicans (who are not to be universally conflated with conservatives) has been effected it is clear in hindsight that everyone saw this coming—except, apparently, the players themselves. They seemed not to have learned anything, even though they had every current and historical opportunity to do so. Ryan Sager, in his book *The Elephant in the Room* (2006) asks: "What does a movement do when it's spent decades arguing that the government should have less power, and then it takes control of the government? Does it stick to its principles and methodically find ways to tax less, spend less and interfere less in the lives of Americans? Or does it slowly, but surely—day by day, issue by issue, bill by bill—succumb to the temptations of power and start to wield it toward new ends?" As was observed by Karen Tumulty (*TIME* October 16, 2006) "Every revolution begins with the power of an idea and ends when clinging to power is the only idea left."

Obviously, the Republicans engaged in just the effort described by Sager's sarcasm and decried in Tumulty's rhetorical summersault. Trying to be everything to everyone even closely aligned with big government idealism—and using tax dollars to show their gratitude at being elected, Republican officials thought they could buy the part of the electorate they hadn't won philosophically. Let an historical truth be restated: neither a party nor a politician can buy votes, each must earn them.

Going forward the question is: Were the failures of the Republicans (fiscal failures certainly, but not solely) to recall their principles an aberration, some renascent, even youthful (in terms of the party's tenure in power) exuberance? Or was it a more classic human reaction so often described in the words of the many authors reviewed in this book? The majority of Republican elected officials (thinking and acting as if the voters would only return them to office if they were generous with someone else's tax dollars) were obviously mistaken in their comprehension. The next issue is, will the Republicans be again allowed to control the machinery of governance? Can they regain the people's trust by means of the principles that they still espouse? If they can, will it take two election cycles or the same twenty it took before? Most who observe in this arena hope that conservatives, should they be elected, will not succumb to the magic of power, as they generally did not when they were part of the Republican majority in 1994–2006. The battle between that group and the rest of the party will determine how political influence might be regained in the future.

The electorate may forgive early financial and policy indiscretion, but they will not long tolerate a philosophical and fiscal disconnect (and the thirty to forty-five *trillion* dollar political and fiscal disconnection the United States faces today can only be termed terrifying and enormous). Ultimately, integrity does arrive back at the front door—for integrity is all we really have as human beings. The question of political integrity is now at center stage, and if the Republicans don't recall this, and if the conservatives among the Republicans don't continually act using their principles to keep the government conscious of its obligations, the future is not a bright one for the party, the conservatives within it, or the republic.

There was a shift that began in 1980 with the election of Ronald Reagan, and it was equal in import and size to the shift that began in 1932 with the election of Franklin Roosevelt. Roosevelt was wrong about the economics of governing, but very right about the politics. Reagan was right about both the economics and the politics and the country knew it. The Republicans forgot what Reagan taught them; they were voted out of office in 2006 for two reasons: they did not keep their word, and they did not act on their principles. The question remains: Will those lesser political lights who are to carry on what Reagan started be able to regain the integrity that the society (and the party) needs? The American electorate is ultimately neither as disengaged nor as venal as some fear—as was aptly demonstrated in the 2006 election. We would all do well to remember that, and to act on it.

RONALD REAGAN didn't trust government—not for the obvious reason that there is corruption and intransigence and sheer bureaucracy with which to deal—but because he felt it had lost its franchise. Reagan understood life, and living. He understood the integrity, the virtue, of freedom for the individual. "It is time to check and reverse the growth of government, which shows signs of having grown beyond the consent of the governed," he declared in his first inaugural address. Reagan was politically successful because he comprehended that liberalism's effort to hijack the government's purpose had begun, in the public's eye, to overpower government's true design—which is nothing more than to help order society so individuals may simply be free. Government's purpose is not to solve problems; beyond the mostly petty arbitration that the courts are designed to effect, government's design is to create an atmosphere of liberty in order that the people can resolve their own lives.

Today the liberals suggest to the electorate that they should be willing to give more. The citizens demur, not because they are being forced to do things against their will, but against their judgment. The lack of reasoned discipline in the political arena costs too much—and not just in terms of dollars. The liberals attempt to hector voters into submission. They supposedly mean well, but it isn't just that their theories and plans have proven ineffective; it is also the manner in which they cut off discussion when they begin lecturing that so distances them from others. Upon inspection it seems they have a few ideas, one of which is to force the remainder on the citizenry. As often as this arrogance has been commented upon, and bemusedly decried, criticism of the left's presumed right to preach has been supported primarily by reference to the failures of their ideas when applied, or even forced, on the real world. But even among their own ranks, the effrontery of the liberal's condescension leaves some astonished. James Carville and Paul Begala, two of the architects of Bill Clinton's successful presidential campaigns of 1992 and 1996, put it rather bluntly in their book *Take It Back* (2006) p. 33:

> Many liberals share the conceit that they are intellectually superior.... Argue with a liberal, and before you know it, you'll hear "You're stupid." If he's a little more polite, he'll say, "Your idea is stupid."

Some in Congress feel they have to succumb to liberal attacks or risk loss of an election for being seen as too harsh, uncaring—the tyrant parent. What they forget is the power of their principles. Any fear in stating those ideas is everyone's loss.

THIS IS NOT a book about how responsibility is avoided; it is just the opposite. Our moral understanding is effected through responsible action. Understanding freedom has become confusing for some, partially because of such concepts as political correctness and the distortion and creation of rights that are uncoupled from duties. It was Thomas Jefferson's assumption that it was every *citizen's* responsibility to help correct what was deceitful and specious in society. It did not occur to him to turn to government offices for a solution—and then rest his pen or voice. He knew *only* the citizenry could accomplish the task of rectifying mankind's improper impulses and he expected them to do so, even at the cost of life or limb, freedom or property. He understood the concept of devolution and he expected that his fellow citizens did as well.

Today we often hear in the media of the responsibilities of our elected leaders to us, the citizenry, but we rarely observe any reference to the equal and opposite duty—of each of us as individuals to the idea of our enterprise. That is the essence of *First Principles*, that if we understand and meet our individual duties we need less government, and that which remains will work much better, more effectively, more efficiently. It has been our intent through the works presented here to reaffirm this concept in most of its premises and some of its details in order that the torch and flag be passed on to the next generation—with comprehension, appreciation, and commitment.

Our rights are far more easily lost than they are regained. It is up to *us* to preserve them. We hope the authors we've reviewed have provided the guidance and tools that will foster sensible discussion, and debate that will help effect protection of all that America has achieved. *First Principles* is intended to be used in a re-awakening process in our fast-paced culture. The rest is up to the judgment and care of the citizenry. We need to remind ourselves occasionally that being a citizen is a privilege that must be earned not a status that we inherit. It is for you, the reader, to determine where you fit in.

I cannot do everything, yet I cannot do nothing.

Index of Subject Matter

On governing:

On the Constitution,
  on the imperfections of the U.S. Constitution, 110-111
  on the philosophical and practical content of the Constitution, 110
  on the value of *The Federalist* in explaining and defining the Constitution, 110
  on the obligation and power of the judiciary to keep government within the bounds of the Constitution, 135, 217
  on the goal of equality of result falsely springing from the Constitution's demand for equality of opportunity, 132

On law,
  on its basis in natural rights, 60-62, 123, 426
  on judicial activism, 135, 217

On governance,
  on the necessity of a free society to operate by means of unstated and informal agreements (reciprocity of obligation), 79, 82, 85, 150
  on the conjunction of liberty and responsibility; rights and duties, xvii, xx, 10, 20, 62, 78, 111, 143, 171, 230, 233-234, 249-251, 311, 372, 418, 429, 531
  in the Constitution, xvii
  on the components of ordered freedom, contractual government, 31, 61, 63, 79, 426, 430, 467
  that governing (and economics), above all, is an art, not a science, 405, 429-430
  on the ability of laws, institutions, government, or men to order society; that a moral foundation must first exist, 111, 152-153, 464, 515
  on the utility of precedent as a mechanism for structuring government, 3, 63, 157, 428, 441, 466
  on history's prescriptions, xvi, 25, 28, 148, 393, 439, 441
  on the effects of social science on governing, 27, 235
  on taking government programs and theories to their logical conclusions, 4, 23, 295, 315, 382, 418, 483
  on the nature of the social contract and the consent of the governed, 63, 84, 141
  on egalitarianism, 36, 131-132, 142, 200, 360, 418, 439-440
  that constraints on the citizenry's freedom gradually lead to authoritarianism and then totalitarianism, 86, 137, 152, 194, 274, 307, 420, 457-459
  on the fatal conceit of the political class, 19, 29, 185, 209, 223, 359, 361, 471, 522
  on the nature and value of leadership, xix, 32, 66, 206 *passim*, 236, 260, 263, 266, 274, 276, 353, 366, 397, 421, 431, 451, 459-460, 467, 517, 531
  on the difference between using power and using principle to effect political goals, 214, 527-528
  on the aversion of intellectuals to rely upon personal responsibility to ensure both individual well-being and societal tranquility, 152, 284
  on the rule of law, 1, 6, 28, 79, 123, 130, 192, 236-237, 276, 460
  on the law of unintended consequences, xvii, 16, 131, 185, 228, 235, 282, 287, 295, 304, 308, 330, 345, 373, 404, 438, 461, 524

On government,
  on the first purpose of government: to foster the citizen's ability to defend his person, liberty, and property, 123
  on government as arbiter, not director, of social and economic interaction, xvi, 181, 182, 305, 356, 372-373, 524
  on the disconnection between government activities, and fiscal accountability and free-market discipline and consequences, 28-32, 182, 194, 275, 394-395
  on "unsupervised" government, 237, 395, 517, 526

533

that government has no money except the people's money, 238, 286, 299
on the power and authoritarianism of bureaucracies, 29, 134-135, 142
on the nature of the public servant, 209, 352, 359-360, 375, 522
on politics and the free lunch, 3, 4, 31, 168, 230, 244, 291, 332, 449, 502
on the size, complexity, and distance of government from citizens (centralized government); how citizens lose control of government, 36, 80, 113, 132-133, 135, 300, 305, 371, 395, 517
on reducing the size of government, 396, 530
on the need for a crisis to arise before democracy moves rationally, 303
on making a difference, 4, 520, 531
on "bitter experience" being the starting point for citizen involvement in government, 518
on the sturdiness of a law or policy's continuation once in place, no matter its effects or ill-founded impetus, 165-166, 521, 525
on government distortion of society or social interaction by its efforts; on further government action/interference being an attempt to remedy the mistakes it has previously made, (*see also* the law of unintended consequences), 127, 167, 189, 198, 314, 373, 465
on the increase in government spending, rather than the reduction of previously created debt, as new tax revenues are created by lower taxes, 323 *passim*

On welfarism and "entitlements,"
as a political tool to ensure society is organized in a politically correct fashion, 520
as the cause of the growth of government, 360, 520
on the redistribution of wealth to effect equalitarianism, 14, 26, 124, 178, 238, 250, 284, 308, 328 *passim*, 338, 521
that welfarism is socialism repackaged for the twentieth century and beyond, 7, 123-124, 290, 335, 396-397
on the morality of taking property from some to give to others, 124, 179, 328-329, 343, 383, 386, 519

on the nature, extent, and duration of "entitlements," 4, 30, 120-121, 164, 170, 193, 195, 233, 235, 290, 298-299, 362-363, 373, 386, 397, 502, 522
on the social safety and social welfare nets, 16, 26, 166, 171, 190, 194, 309, 330, 522
welfarism as a political tool to achieve election or reelection, 120, 125-126, 167, 230, 244, 287, 290, 327, 338, 351, 372, 397, 522, 529
on the value of a hand up versus a handout, 30, 166, 170, 375
on the culture of dependency, incapability, 124, 164, 170, 193, 246, 290, 301, 304, 330 *passim*, 361, 522
on making people better off, 382, 521
on the demotion of property's status; its use as a vehicle to attain equalitarian goals, 162
on the moral indictment issued for being economically successful, 521
on "social justice," 200-201, 291, 308, 333, 476, 480, 519, 521

On charity,
that government beneficence and welfare drive out private charitable initiatives and care, 309, 329, 337, 360, 392
on applying private sector business practices to private (or public) sector charitable efforts, 364

Citizens and the citizenry:

On democracy,
that order and the rule of law are necessary antecedents to democracy, 77, 276
on the ascension of democratic rule over the rights of the individual, (*see also* tyranny of the majority), 198, 221
that democracy can become a form of despotism, 130, 134, 142, 210, 215
as a method of removing, and selecting, leaders, 66, 215
on the politician's fear of the electorate, xvi
on retaining power, reelection, by the political class, 29, 209, 218, 305, 521
that the failure of democracy results not in anarchy but totalitarianism, 137, 196

Index of Subject Matter —— 535

on the tyranny of the majority, 24, 123, 130 passim, 142, 432
on repairing the problems of democracy and capitalism without wholly discarding either system, 1-2, 195, 257, 384

On vigilance,
on individual responsibility and personal involvement in governance, xx, 1, 11, 364
on citizen vigilance as the (sole) antidote to government that exceeds the object of its design, 4, 31-32, 133, 135, 143, 148, 194, 208 passim, 363, 441, 517
on the need for an intellectual revolution before a political one (peaceful or otherwise) can occur, 83, 236, 366
on trusting to the good intentions of others, 27, 123, 134, 165, 193, 222, 244, 407, 460, 471, 482, 515-518

On language,
on the meaning of word "liberal" in the U.S. and Europe before and after the Great Depression, 16-17, 234
on the precise use and distortions thereof, 18, 234, 441

On the effects of media and information,
on the amount of information available regarding government and politics; the public's ability to dissect or comprehend it, to not suffer intellectual paralysis, 59, 136, 419
used to increase citizen knowledge, 3, 136
as it affects governing, 21, 128, 136, 237, 269, 397, 531
as it affects politics, 2, 28-29, 67, 120, 125-126, 134, 176-177, 228, 245, 356, 370, 398
exploitation and profit by the media, 33, 35, 183, 321, 342, 440, 497-498, 511
on the human condition and, 7, 419
restraint by the media, 440, 476
the public's trust in, 212, 269

On economic matters:

On economics,
on the necessary conjunction of free-market economics and individual and political freedom, 28, 32, 181-182, 195

on adapting economic policy to man, not man to economic policy, 36, 276, 325, 389-390, 407
on the multiplier effect of capitalistic enterprise, 34, 161, 167, 297
on short term quick economic 'fixes,' that cause long-term ills, 296, 333, 404, 407, 474
as government control of the market increases (taxes and regulations), the economy itself decreases, perversely requiring further government intervention (additional taxes and regulations or the printing of money it cannot collect, thus causing rampant inflation; or both) in order to maintain its current level of activity and income, thus further reducing the economic pie, *ad nauseum* (killing the geese laying the golden eggs), 127, 251, 275, 326 *passim*
on the extension of the Great Depression's effects through government mismanagement of its underlying causes; the resulting growth of the welfare state as a replacement for state socialism, 166-167, 272, 299, 404
on inflation and a sound economy, 112, 272, 275, 283, 287, 300, 332, 353-354, 356, 395, 403, 406
on the nature and effects of government deficit spending, 288, 296, 325, 406

On capitalism, capitalists,
on capitalism's moral foundations, 1, 32, 35
on the necessity of freedom of action *and* consequence for capitalism (or government) to work, 32, 35, 471
on the connection between the differences among individuals and the substance of capitalistic enterprise, 150-151, 160-161, 200-202, 382, 471-472
on human "uneasiness" as the cause of progress, 177, 470
on self-interest as the driver of improvement, 82, 188
on enlightened self-interest, 36, 60, 127, 178 *passim*, 188, 191, 282, 320
on incentive,
as the engine of progress, 6, 26, 29, 31, 35, 123, 191, 244, 275, 376, 464

on the decrease of incentive as taxation and regulation increase, 127, 161, 322, 399

as the demand for equality of result increases, incentive decreases, economic activity declines, 35, 162

on the free market, xv, 129, 169, 175, 275, 282-283, 304, 307, 312, 319 *passim*, 354, 466

on free market discipline, 29, 179, 275, 351, 395, 448

on the rationalization of human activity by means of capitalism's logic, 195, 448

that capitalism creates a higher standard of living operating at its lowest level than collectivist societies create operating at their highest potential, 32-33, 127, 188-189, 337, 340, 345, 373, 475

on what capitalists owe or are owed by society, 34-35

on the activities of thieves and frauds within capitalist enterprise, 33, 182-183, 321

On socialism,
that a totalitarian government (force) is necessary to effect socialism (the welfare state) and to thereafter operate it, 25, 123, 190, 274, 447

that the battle is not between capitalism and socialism (welfarism) but between capitalism and chaos, 35, 37, 475

as a form of economic slavery, 126, 234, 351, 383

that capitalism's wealth cannot be used to achieve socialism's goals, to achieve the welfare state, 163, 327-329, 338-340

on collectivism, 8, 187-188, 434, 459

The human element:

On the human condition,
as the essential element to consider in designing government, 13

on man's imperfectability, 2, 19, 35, 77, 149, 203, 307, 440, 455, 460

on corruption, 20, 26, 32, 66, 84, 120, 195, 276, 313, 344, 352, 356, 459, 487, 517, 526

intellectual, 197, 199, 317

on the distortion of society's relationships through, 3, 466

although perfecting humanity is not possible, striving for such is uniformly beneficial, 152

the human spirit, the human condition's opposite side, 451, 453, 516

on individualism, 19, 24, 25, 27, 31, 130, 132, 137, 139-140, 148, 188 *passim*, 216, 303, 382, 393, 471

the individual vis-à-vis government, 437
and property, 159, 162

on opportunity and discipline, xvi

that human frailties are as likely in the governors, maybe more so, as they are in the governed, 192, 377, 459

on making life risk free, 471, 513, 523-524

on the fragility of life and community, 515

on the emotional response to life's difficulties, 8, 26, 30, 120, 162, 188, 216, 230, 273, 336, 507

Philosophical considerations:

On authority and power,
on the need for authority to control men, but not absolute authority, 60, 148

on government oversight and control of individual conduct, xvii, 111, 148, 205, 522, 530

on theoretical citizen fear of one another and the need for a central authority to protect individuals, 59-60, 127, 524

on the devolution of Constitutional protections through court and Congressional assumption of prerogatives; government institutions and the use of power to protect society rather than the individual, 215, 218, 220, 465, 482

on the fiction of the "will" or "general will" of the people, 80, 125, 207 *passim*, 212, 220, 401

that there is no deified "general will" in the state; that the state is not supreme nor the supreme good, but subordinate to the individual, 149, 212

that government must be given power commensurate with the tasks assigned to it, 62, 223, 363

on gaining political advantage by the use of government's power; how power overcomes the institutions of government, 205, 216, 222, 480

Index of Subject Matter — 537

on the slippery slope of authoritarianism and equalitarianism, 26, 126, 130, 135, 142, 406, 515 *passim*
on the nature and power of those who govern, 192-193, 209-211, 482
that those in authority tend to self-aggrandizement and self-interest, 60, 130, 192, 459, 482
on the necessity of hierarchical systems of authority, 36, 420, 440, 504
on how the roles of private wealth and public authority have been reversed, 163-165, 481-483
on the necessity of changing democratic government from the outside whenever those elected do not adhere to their promises, 198, 525-526

On utopianism and the Enlightenment, utopia's injustice, 9, 188, 301
on the failure to achieve utopia, 9, 188, 325, 456, 519
governance based on what can be thought of versus what can be done, 35, 82-83, 126, 202, 235
on the nature and thinking of the *philosophes* of eighteenth century France, 82-83, 160

On inequality,
as life's most basic circumstance, 25, 36, 306-307, 328-329, 518
as the primary factor of human progress, 25, 33, 35, 82, 149, 328, 518
on the nature of inequality and property distribution, 161, 306, 337
that freedom and equality are mutually exclusive, 518

On freedom/liberty,
and anarchy, 6, 29, 78, 123, 137, 192, 421, 427
as the highest political goal, 37, 139, 148, 216, 221
of choice, xvi, 150, 151
on the difficulty of maintaining, 26, 135, 151, 306, 435, 520
on individual freedom being a natural right, not a contractual agreement or a government grant, 24, 27, 61, 159, 211, 221, 426
on the inverse relationship between the size of government and freedom for the individual, 19, 86, 398

on protecting social gains resulting from, 6, 531
on setting men free from the limits of other men, 519
on the conflict between freedom and security, 127, 361, 450, 452, 455-456, 460-461
that freedom results in unequal material and other results, 25, 160, 337, 383
that freedom is not free, 10, 11, 257
that freedom is not a license but implies duties, 10, 61
that freedom can be frightening, but a lack of freedom is more so, 188

On morality/virtue/ethics,
on the necessity of a moral/virtuous society in order to have a free society, 20, 79, 80, 151-153, 282-283, 389, 515, 516-517
on public morality as the basis for political construction, 140, 440, 517, 531
on public morality guiding economic policy, 518
that virtue cannot be decreed or legislated, 77, 152, 517
on moral relativism (that any one moral choice is not as valid as any other), 20, 132, 144, 422, 520
on the equality of choices; that there are good and bad choices, 18, 277-278, 520

On ideas,
on the marketplace of ideas, 31, 520
on the power, value, utility of ideas, 6, 136, 138, 394
that ideas have consequences, 38, 418
that ideas are more powerful than vested interests, 6, 352, 452, 513
on common sense, xv, 37, 237, 245, 285, 291, 304, 323, 420, 439, 474, 512, 513
on the differences between the French (1789) and American Revolutions, 199-200, 343

Index

accountability,
  bureaucratic, 29, 363, 376
  fiscal, 30, 364
  personal, 14, 164, 193, 363, 377, 418
acquired rights, (see rights, acquired)
Acton, Lord, 37, 148, 187, 195, 216, 250, 526
Adams, John, 21, 38, 234, 244, 515
Adenauer, Conrad, 274
affirmative action, 26
Afghanistan, xx
African Slavery in America, 69
After Liberalism, 15
Age of Reason, 49, 68
Age of Reason, 50, 83-84
Agentry, The, 210
Alexander I, Tsar, 407
Alice in Wonderland, 475, 521
American Revolution, 1776, (see revolution)
anarchy,
  capitalism and, 33, 399
  community and, 390
  freedom and, 6, 29, 78, 192, 427
  Hobbes, Thomas, and, 59
  human connectedness and, 83
  morality and, 77, 132
  rule of law and, 123, 158, 179, 430, 434
  totalitarianism and, 137, 420
Aristotle, 257, 426
Arlington National Cemetery, 10
Articles of Confederation, 17, 110, 113
aspiration, human, (see human striving, aspiration)
Athens, 456
Austria, 381
Austrian School of Economics, (see economics, Austrian School of)
autarky, (see nationalism, autarky)
authoritarian, -ism, 7, 24, 149, 219, 463, 524
  monarchical, 181

Bacon, Francis, Sir, 468
Bailyn, Bernard, 377
Baker, James A., III, xix
Balkans, 450
Bandung Conference, 276
Barzun, Jacques, 37, 38

Basic Economics, 172, 504
Bastiat, Frederic, 172, 185, 235, 281, 328, 337
Bastille, 68
Bay of Pigs, 242
Beethoven, Ludwig, von, 470
Begala, Paul, 530
behaviorists, 28
Bell Curve, The, 253, 379
Benthamism, (see utilitarianism)
Berlin Wall, 284, 390
Bicentennial, American, 9
Big Steel, (see United States Steel)
Bill of Responsibilities, 10, 152
Bill of Rights, 10, 110, 152, 211
  First Amendment, 216
  Tenth Amendment, 217
black market, 407
Black September, 492
blogs, (see Internet)
Bodin, Jean, 157, 325
bourgeoisie, 383
Bozell, L. Brent, 241
Brain Trust, 168
Brandeis, Louis D., U.S. Supreme Court Justice, 165
Britain, (see Great Britain)
Buckley, William F., Jr., 1, 18, 228 *passim*, 366, 441
bureaucracy, bureaucrats,
  control by, 17, 19, 29, 82, 197, 208, 210, 222, 251, 297-298, 305, 322, 344, 353, 449
  courts and, 217
  growth of, 134, 142, 181, 189, 197, 300, 526-527
  nanny state and, (see nanny state, bureaucracy and)
  power and, 208, 210, 243, 339, 366, 378, 386, 389, 523
  rule making and, xvi, 317, 517
  socialism and, 383-384
  state welfarism and, 37, 193, 286, 289, 397, 475-476
  volunteerism and, 359, 364, 372
Burke, Edmund, 19, 31, 67 *passim*, 139, 142, 147 *passim*, 214, 393, 438
Burns, James MacGregor, xx
Bush, George W., 364

Caesar, Julius, 80
Calvin, John, 81
capitalism,
   altruism and, 320
   capital and, 289, 399
   chaos and, 35, 37, 475
   consumer and, 175, 178, 285, 316, 320 *passim*
   definition of, 319
   democracy and, 281-282
   dishonesty within, and distortions of, 32 *passim*, 182, 307, 321, 463
   enlightened self-interest and, (*see* self-interest, enlightened)
   foreign policy and, 262
   freedom and, 27, 290, 303 *passim*
   generally, (*see also* economics; free enterprise, free market), 1, 175, 303, 319 *passim*, 349 *passim*, 447 *passim*
   Great Depression and, (*see* Great Depression)
   imperfections, systemic, 126, 130
   injustice (putative), 336
   invisible hand, 180, 273, 285, 352
   labor, division of, and, 180, 185, 284, 320, 384, 471-472
   living, standard of, (*see* free enterprise, living, standard of))
   mechanics of, 178, 284-285
   monopolies and, 285, 286
   morality and, 1, 385
   multiplier effect, (*see* economic(s), multiplier effect)
   profit and, 320-322, 339 *passim*, 399
   rationalizing human activity and, 195, 448
   redistribution and, 328
   self-interest and, (*see* self-interest, enlightened)
   socialism and, 7, 14, 35, 168-169, 197, 382, 391, 445 *passim*, 447, 475, 522
   transparency and, 329
   welfare state and, 164, 332, 522
Capitalism and Freedom, 161, 239, 314, 337, 367, 371
Capitalism, Socialism and Democracy, 195, 394, 506
capitalists, 32 *passim*
Carville, James, 530
Castro, Fidel, 242, 276
Catherine the Great, 407
Central America, 466
centralization, (*see* government, centralization)
Chamberlain, John, 288, 367
Chamberlain, Neville, 271
Chambers, Whittaker, 229

character,
   individual, 19-20, 130, 134, 440
   national, 328, 340, 345, 455, 515
Character of Nations, The, 515
charity,
   Christian, 391, 473
   public/private, 34, 60, 121-122, 131, 244, 286, 329, 336 *passim*, 364
checks and balances, 42, 60, 79, 111, 131, 143, 198, 203, 208
Chesterton, G.K., 513
Chicago, University of, 303
China, 265, 340, 349, 446, 458, 499, 500
Church of England, 24
Churchill, Winston, ii, xix, 272, 328, 451, 519
Cicero, 157
citizen(s),
   capitalism and, 129, 183, 285, 326, 463
   centralization of government and, 113, 237, 305, 370, 395
   classical liberalism and, 23-24
   community and, 401
   conservatism and, 14-15
   courts and, 216-217
   democracy and, 131, 143, 170, 205, 210, 220
   equality and, 80, 130, 132, 137, 336
   freedom and, 139, 141, 311 *passim*, 521
   generally, xx, 1-2, 10-12, 282, 392-393
   government and, 181, 181, 199, 205, 299-300, 356, 492
   Locke, John, 59-60
   morality, virtue, and, 111, 151-152, 515
   obligations of, 252, 427, 432, 530
   property and, 156, 160, 163, 164
   taxation and, 161, 289-290, 345
   the state and, 132, 406
   vigilance and, 22, 32, 133, 143, 208, 210, 215, 219, 222, 273, 331, 356, 386, 441, 517
Civil War (U.S.), 140, 262
class warfare, 131-132, 133, 142, 336, 341
class, political, (*see* political class, the)
Clinton, Bill, 256, 363, 418, 525
Clinton, George, 110
Codevilla, Angelo, 515
Cold War, xix, 52, 168, 246, 263, 266
collectivism, collectivists, 6, 8, 22 *passim*, 123, 187, 434, 452
   authoritarianism and, 149, 189
   command economy and, 349
   communists and, 481
   economic slavery and, 6, 52, 126, 234, 246, 383
   equality and, 188
   freedom of choice and, (*see* freedom, of choice)

incentive and, 190, 395-396
individual and, 23, 195, 197, 257, 393, 459-460
inflation and, 395
Islam and, 452
justice and, 308-309
managerial state and, 27
preparing for its demise, 231, 303
redistribution and, 308
taxation, regulation, and, 193, 354
totalitarianism and, 25, 149, 191, 391
wartime and, 273, 394
welfare state and, 7, 381, 394-395
colonialism, 276
Colombia, 487
  cocaine trade, 487-488
  Escobar, Pablo, (*see* Escobar, Pablo)
  Medellin, City of, 488
  Pepes, Los, 490
  Violencia, La, 487
Commanding Heights, The, 8, 136, 237, 275, 391
Commerce Clause, U.S. Constitution, (*see* Constitution of the United States, Article I, Section 8)
common law, English, (*see* English common law)
communism, 8, 84, 149, 162, 168, 242, 349, 383, 434, 445
Communism Memorial, Victims of, 232
Communism, Soviet, 38, 187, 262-263, 480 *passim*
Communist Manifesto, The, 22, 445, 464
Communist Party, 350, 480
community, 2, 25, 29, 60, 61, 123, 222, 370, 390, 456, 515
  individual vs. community rights, 393, 395, 515
  private charity and, 336, 360
Confederacy, U.S. Civil War, 517
Congress, U.S., 110, 120, 169, 192, 211, 216, 238, 218, 314, 323 *passim*, 371, 525 *passim*
Conscience of a Conservative, 241, 527
conservatism, conservatives,
  capitalism and, 319, 330
  classical liberalism and, 5, 17, 18, 24, 28, 147, 190, 393
  conservative thought, 5, 9, 147, 439
  definition, 14
  equality and, 150
  fusion, with libertarians, 147
  generally, 7, 227 *passim*, 233-235, 360, 363, 425 *passim*
  Goldwater, Barry, and, 241 *passim*
  intellectuals and, 21, 32, 61, 441

  Kirk, Russell, and, 437 *passim*
  liberal, liberalism (the terms) and, 14
  libertarians and, 147, 152
  morality and, 245, 440
  neoconservatives and, 135, 171, 203, 482
  politics and, 325, 364, 386, 524, 528
  responsibility and, 364-365
  rights and, 26
  terminology, 14-16, 24, 292, 393
Constitutional Convention (1787), 11, 110-113, 236, 326
Constitution of Liberty, The, xx, 22, 80, 196
Constitution of the United States, xvii, 17, 24, 79-80, 130, 159, 211
  Article I, Section 8 [commerce; general welfare; necessary and proper clauses], 91, 217, 313
  drafting, 109
  judicial protection of, 217
  morality and, 199
  original document with amendments, 87
Contract with America, 363, 376
contradiction, law of, 212
Coolidge, Calvin, 272, 330
Cornuelle, Richard, 122, 222, 286, 359, 375, 392
corruption, 20, 120, 356, 459, 466, 492
  bureaucracy and, 26, 339, 530
  education and, 3
  finding, 36
  government morality and, 32, 123, 124, 172, 251, 488, 517
  human condition and, 84
  intellectual, 197, 199, 317
  politics and, 195, 238, 344, 432
  power and, 308, 466
courts, 30-31, 143, 198-199, 216, 314, 427
Cuba, 242, 262, 276, 340, 458
culture of dependency, incapability, 124, 164, 170, 193, 246, 290, 298, 301, 330, 336, 361, 522

Darwinism, social, 181
D-Day, 10
debt, public, 326-327
Declaration of Independence, 11, 65, 71, 110, 175, 250, 369, 515
deficits, fiscal, 237, 288, 297, 326-327, 374
definitions, 39 passim, 409 *passim*
de Gaulle, Charles, (*see* Gaulle, Charles, de,)
deism, 68
democracy, xiv, xx, 129 *passim*, 344, 431 *passim*, 446
  as a control on leaders, 66, 215, 308

bureaucracy and, 198
capitalism and, 467
church/state separation and, 270
Constitution and, 110
definition of, 203
democratic socialism and, (*see* socialism, democratic)
equalitarianism and, 202, 281
freedom and, 7, 192, 209, 427
Greeks and, 456 *passim*
justice and, 141
majority rule and, 142
minorities and, 446
morality/virtue and, 20
order and, 276
power and, 198, 205-207, 215, 221, 401
representative, xvii, 1, 61, 109
rule of law and, 276
socialism and, 190
Democracy in America, 211, 222, 239, 420
democratic socialism, (*see* socialism, democratic)
demagogues, demagoguery, 3, 19, 32, 41, 165, 183, 290-291, 331
dependency, culture of, (*see* culture of dependency)
Depression, (*see* Great Depression)
despots, despotism, 7, 41, 132
determinism, 461
Dewey, John, 273
Dickinson, John, 236
discipline, 4, 167, 195, 201
discrimination, 417 *passim*, 433, 450
dismal science, economics, the 275, 405
diversity, 26
divided government, 218
division of labor, 60, 77, 180, 284, 320, 384-385, 404, 448, 471-472
Dow Jones Industrial Average, 33
draft, military, 207
duty, (*see* responsibility)
Dylan, Bob, i

earmarks (congressional, of federal appropriations), 238
economic illiteracy, (*see* illiteracy, economic)
economic(s), xvi, 14, 28 *passim*, 275, 382, 404, 407, 445, 464, 471, 474
  anarchic nature, 405-406
  as part of the political process, 406
  Austrian School of, 196
  barter system, 405
  borderless, 283
  command economy, 349, 353
  dismal science, the, (*see* dismal science)
  effect on population, 502
  globalization, 284, 404
  living, standard of, (*see* free enterprise, living, standard of)
  multiplier effect, 34, 161, 167, 297, 342, 351
  oppression, 35, 473-474
  slavery, (*see* collectivism; human slavery)
  supply-side, 322
  zero-sum game, 475
Economics in One Lesson, 119, 185, 295, 303, 333
Economics of the Free Society, 172, 281, 480
education, 3, 376-377
egalitarianism, 36, 42, 129-130, 200, 360, 438, 426, 439-440
Einstein, Albert, 403, 472, 519
Eisenhower, Dwight David, 242, 243, 272, 472
elections, 66, 143, 198, 210
electoral power, xv-xvi, 143, 208, 220
electorate, American, 527-528
Elephant in the Room, The, 528
Eliot, T.S., 438
e-mail address (*First Principles*), 12
empiricism, 202-203
England, 24, 63, 163, 175, 354, 394
English common law, 63
English Revolution, (*see* revolution, English)
Enlightenment, 23, 155, 188, 446, 473
  rationalism and, 222, 235, 313, 333, 350, 439
  Scottish, 28, 51
  the "state" and, 149
  utopia and, 82, 83, 126, 355
entitlements,
  administrative expansion of, 30
  as acquired rights, 120-121, 397, 502, 522
  as an obligation, 298, 363, 386
  culture of dependency and, (*see* culture of dependency)
  effect of on citizens, 290, 304
  modern state and, 4, 170, 193, 233, 235
  politics and, 220, 363, 373, 397
  property and, 164
entrepreneur, entrepreneurship,
  as a debtor to society, 34
  character of, 384, 399, 504
  enlightened self-interest and, (*see also* self-interest, enlightened), 320
  government as, 306
  government policy and, 298, 321-322

incentives and, 322, 331, 473
taxation and, 323 passim, 338 passim, 398-399
volunteerism, charitable organizations and, 364
E Pluribus Unum, 38
equal opportunity,
  classical liberalism and, 190
  equal result, equalitarianism, and, 35, 131-132, 382, 418
  government and, 150-151, 193, 328, 339, 434, 472
  individual and, 26, 219, 249, 343, 361, 371, 397
  Libertarians and, 252
  responsibility and, 202, 214-215
  welfarism and, 26, 376, 308
equalitarians, equalitarianism, 14-16, 42, 418, 472, 522
  authoritarianism and, 25, 123-124, 130, 132
  centralization of government and, 135, 395
  Christianity and, 391, 473
  collectivism and, 8
  freedom and, 306, 309
  French Revolution (1789) and, 67, 202
  incentive and, 439
  individualism and, 179, 200, 309, 421
  justice, fairness and, 200, 308-309, 456, 476, 519
  liberal populism and, 15
  Marx, Karl, and, 22
  political correctness and, 26, 36, 194, 235, 421
  property and, 164
  redistribution and, 14
  welfare state and, 306, 385, 397
equality, (*see also* mankind's, inequality is beneficial,)
  and freedom are mutually exclusive, 518
  is undesirable, 200, 421
  of result, 84, 250, 371, 382, 440, 475
Escobar, Pablo Emilio Gaviria, 487 *passim*
  shadow congressman, 488
Essays in the History of Liberty, 148, 187, 216
ethics, situational, 420
Ethics of Redistribution, The, 235, 328, 392
Europe,
  America and, 5, 10, 14, 15, 140, 260, 262
  colonialism and, 276
  definition of liberal, liberalism in, 14-15, 28, 227
  monarchy and, 142
  population, (*see* population)
  Smith, Adam, 175
  socialism and, 126, 168, 313, 346, 355
  Soviet Union, 349
  statism in, 25-26, 277
excellence (human), 418
executive branch of government, 61

Faith and Freedom, 124
family, 245, 273, 377, 472
family planning, 500
Fascism, fascists, 8, 43, 227, 383
fatal conceit, liberal, 19, 209, 361, 527
federal reserve bank/system, 396
Federalist, The, 17, 24, 109 *passim*, 143, 363
  Federalist, The, #10, 104, 131, 472
  Federalist, The, #17, 110
  Federalist, The, #31, i
  Federalist, The, #44, 363
  Federalist, The, #55, 21
  Federalist, The, #70, 143
fertility rates, 499
  replacement fertility rate, 499
  total fertility rate, TFR, 499
feudalism, 448, 463
Fewer, 172, 265, 497
Forbes Magazine, 34
Forbes, Steve, 34
Ford, Henry, 384, 465, 519
Founding Fathers, 20, 261, 392, 472
France, 67-68, 80, 119, 126, 160, 189, 199, 235, 312, 355, 425 *passim*
Franklin, Benjamin, 21, 66, 69, 285
free enterprise, market, (*see also* capitalism; economics) 175 *passim*
  corruption and, 466
  discipline, free market, 30, 179, 275, 314, 351, 395, 448
  dishonesty within, (*see* capitalism, dishonesty within and distortions of)
  government interference with, 307, 311, 313, 319
  Great Depression, (*see* Great Depression)
  human element and, 353, 356
  impetus of, 177, 275, 282
  individual and, 2, 320
  inequality and, 34-35, 201, 202, 330, 336, 345
  international trade and, 185, 272, 283-284, 404
  living, standard of, 33, 127, 161, 189, 328, 345, 373
    effect of taxes on, 251, 339-340
    collectivism vs. free market, 336, 373
    zero-sum economics, 475
  monopoly in, (*see* capitalism, monopoly)

moral society and, 311-312, 395
multiplier effect, (*see* economic(s), multiplier effect)
political freedom and, 28, 129, 281, 304, 306-308, 312, 464, 467
Smith, Adam, (*see* Smith, Adam)
socialism and, 184, 350, 354
safety net, social, 194
taxation and, (*see* taxation)
transparency, 305, 329
welfare state and, 169, 194
free lunch,
entitlements and, 502
human element and, 4, 516
politics and, 3, 31, 168, 244, 289, 331
socialism and, 168-169, 449
free will, 311
freedom, liberty,
anarchy and, (*see* anarchy)
as a right not a grant, 24, 27, 61, 159, 211, 221, 426
as the highest political goal, 37, 139, 148, 216
capitalism and, 304, 464
conservatism and, 440
duty and, (*see* responsibility, duty)
equalitarianism and, (*see* equalitarianism)
extent, 10
"freedom from want," 169
freedom is not free, 11, 257
human condition and, 2, 450
moral society and, 150
of choice, xvi, 151, 274, 306 *passim*, 371, 472
ordered, 29, 36, 60, 63, 77, 85, 252, 427, 432, 467
totalitarianism and, (*see also* totalitarianism), 450
uncontrolled, 420
welfare state and, 176, 306
freedom and equality, 518
French Revolution, (*see* revolution, French)
Freud, Sigmund, 514
friction, as it affects tax dollars, 238, 297, 352
Friedman, Milton, 171, 188, 230-231, 281, 337, 367, 371, 373
From Dawn to Decadence, 37
fusion, in re: conservatism, libertarianism, 147

Gadaffi, Muammar, 213
Gadaffi: The Desert Mystic, 213
Galbraith, John Kenneth, 331-332
Gallop Poll, 212
Gandhi, Mohandas, 274
Gates, Bill, 470, 472

Gaulle, Charles, de, 274
General Welfare Clause, U.S. Constitution, (*see* Constitution of the United States, Article I, Section 8)
general will, (*see* will, general)
Germany, 10, 43, 169, 227, 265, 271, 300, 350, 354, 390, 451, 461-462
East, 390
Olympic Village, Munich, 492
population, 499
West, 390
Gingrich, Newt, 228, 230, 363
Gladstone, William, 145
globalization, economic, (*see* economics, globalization)
Golden Rule, 20, 62, 78, 84, 152, 282, 467
Goldwater, Barry, 166, 228, 386, 527
Gottfried, Paul, 15
government,
centralization, 80, 133, 138, 168, 180, 184, 188, 206, 222, 237, 305, 395
corruption and, 36, 66, 133, 172
deficit spending, (*see* deficits, fiscal)
destructive of state power and/or local rule, 110, 113, 135, 217, 370
emotion and, 9-10, 26, 30, 120, 162, 188, 194, 216, 221-222, 230, 235, 290, 336, 391
hierarchy within, 36, 420, 440, 504
incompetence, 36, 66, 317, 339, 517
intervention, in private lives, 528
one-size-fits-all, 189, 238, 359, 370, 378
power commensurate with its assigned tasks, 223, 363
representative, (*see also* democracy), xv, 1, 25, 61, 109, 157 131, 207-210, 212-213, 308, 398
self-governance, xv-xvi, 7, 12, 18, 60, 82, 158, 199, 370, 437
society of, 482
spending, 323 *passim*
statist, (*see* statists, statism)
totalitarian, (*see* totalitarian, totalitarianism)
unfunded liabilities and, 238, 327
unsupervised, 517
vigilance, citizen, to control, 22, 32, 133, 143, 194, 208, 210, 215, 219, 222, 331, 441, 517
governors, governing class, 120, 135, 148, 156, 160, 168, 212, 523
Great Britain, Britain, 23, 113, 271, 426, 451
prime minister of, 1, 271, 451
Great Depression, 15, 23, 234, 272, 328, 361
acquired rights, entitlements, 120

Index — 545

centralization and, 168
free enterprise and, 15, 120, 448-449
government interference lengthened, 167, 272, 298, 481
individualism and, 166, 328
New Deal, 120, 361, 481, 524
political change during, 227
volunteerism and, 375
Great Society, The, 120, 166, 323, 331, 524
Greeks, 63, 78-79, 141, 455
Grotius, Hugo, 157-159
guillotine, 67, 189, 431
guilt, social, 8, 244, 518, 521

Hamilton, Alexander, i, 17, 109 *passim*
Hammerskjold, Dag, 274
happiness (*see also* uneasiness), 11, 31, 176-177, 249-250, 369, 470-471
  pursuit of, 72, 177, 377
Harding, Warren, 272
Harrington, James, 159
Hart, Benjamin, 124
Hawley-Smoot Tariff Act, 167, 272
Hayek, Friedrich von, xx, 6, 8, 18, 19, 366
  Constitution of Liberty, The, xx, 22, 80, 197
  fatal conceit, of intellectuals/liberals, 19, 29, 210, 361, 471, 530
  Mont Pelerin Society, 228, 230, 304
  Road to Serfdom, The, 6, 136, 153, 187, 197, 234, 295, 337, 363, 508
  slippery slope effect, 515
Hazlitt, Henry, 119, 128, 185, 281, 295, 303, 333
Hegel, Friedrich, 382, 461 *passim*
Heritage Foundation, 255
hierarchy, (*see* government)
Hiss, Alger, 484
historicism, 461-462
Hitler, Adolph, 10, 43, 169, 271, 274, 300, 462
Hobbes, Thomas, 59-60, 84, 127, 157, 162, 211, 524
Hong Kong, 447
Hoover, Herbert, 16
Human Action, 320, 448, 469
human action, 6, 83, 230, 404-405, 471
  economic laws and, 202, 405
human condition, 7, 13, 28, 35-36, 183, 303-304
  corruption and, 488-489
  economics and, 31, 190, 395, 448
  "goodwill towards men" and, 20
  government and, 60, 62, 83, 178, 181, 197, 222, 370, 372
  imperfectability, mankind's, 2, 19, 35-36, 77, 82, 84-85, 149, 191, 203, 235, 440, 455
  making life risk free, 398, 513, 523
  making people better off, 521
  majority rule and, 132
  property and, 61-62, 160-161
  reason and, 83, 202
  regimentation and, xvii, 24-25, 235
  Rome and, 80
  socialism and, 382
  welfare state and, 122, 194
human dignity, 65, 122, 124, 132, 243, 301, 304, 341, 371, 376, 389, 397, 421
human element, 301, 353
human nature, xv, 2, 7, 21, 25, 34, 62, 111, 133, 176, 179, 508
  economics and, 303, 325-326, 331, 336, 382
  happiness and (*see also* uneasiness), 470, 513
  power and, 206, 228, 249, 343-344, 370
  progress and, 209, 383
  welfare and, 397
human rights, (*see* rights, human)
human spirit, 7, 19, 138, 219, 243, 377
  enlightened self-interest and, 60, 128
  equality and, 127, 177
human striving,
  aspiration, 177, 275, 377
  capability, pride, incentive, and, 122, 123, 191, 330, 399, 439
  capitalism and, 178
  disconnection between human experience and government design, xv, 236, 275, 481
  Enlightenment and, 126
  individuals making a difference, xx, 1, 11, 520
  moral society and, 83
  progress and, 176, 201, 383, 453, 456
  redistribution and, 162, 301, 328, 343, 384
Humane Economy, A, 35, 363, 389, 484
Hume, David, 51, 83, 186, 198
Humpty Dumpty, 17
Hurricane Katrina, 510

idealism, idealists, xv, 25-26, 27, 521-522
ideas,
  marketplace of, 31, 520
  value/power of, 4, 136, 138, 257, 352, 394, 417, 452
Ideas Have Consequences, 136, 337, 361
Ideological Origins of the American Revolution, The, 377
illiteracy, constitutional, 291

illiteracy, economic, 180, 213, 291, 331, 333, 407
immigration, 499, 503
imperfectability, man's, (*see* human condition, imperfectability, mankind's)
incentive, 6, 31
  bureaucrats and, 366, 525-526
  collectivism/totalitarianism and, 123, 190, 395-396, 473
  culture of dependency and, 164, 301
  economics, supply-side, and, 322
  equalitarianism and, 26, 34-35, 84, 161, 223
  free market and, 124, 127, 175, 181, 275, 383, 464
  human nature and, 322, 331, 382, 439, 516, 519
  morality and, 32-33
  property rights and, 28-29, 162, 385, 434
  redistribution and, 336
  taxation and, 231, 251, 287, 325, 339, 399
  welfarism and, 244, 376
income, "excess," 337, 342, 399
In Defense of Freedom, 147, 311
In Defense of the American Constitutions, 515
India, 265, 266, 446, 447, 499
individualism,
  action, individual, 404, 520
  character and, 130, 435, 440
  collectivism and, 25, 162, 188, 191, 393, 458, 472
  equalitarianism, equality, and, 132, 195, 216, 474
  fatal conceit (Hayek), and, 19
  freedom of choice and, 306, 463
  government and, 31, 60, 140, 205, 220, 303, 371
  natural rights and duties and, 429, 432, 456
  political correctness and, 26
  tradition and, 148
  welfare state and, 153
Industrial Revolution, 7, 33, 175, 385, 463
inequality, (*see* equality; mankind's, inequality)
inflation, 300, 395
  American Revolution and, 112, 114
  government spending (printing money) and, 272, 275, 332, 351, 406
  government spending, deficit, and, 297, 327
  Keynes, John Maynard and, 288, 332, 351

  monetary system and, 283
  politics and, 333, 353-354, 406
information,
  Information Age, 3
  regarding the amount of, 3, 59, 136, 419-422
initiative, 6, 29, 231, 298, 339
injustice, 9, 123, 139, 200, 431
In Pursuit: Of Happiness and Good Government, 288, 361, 369
integrity, political, personal, (*see* mankind's, integrity)
intellectuals, 441, 456, 464
interests, special, 29, 197, 250, 314
Internet, 3, 136, 190, 322, 432
invisible hand, (*see* capitalism, invisible hand)
Iran, Tehran, American Embassy, 490-491
Iraq, xx, 263-264, 265, 271, 450, 492
Islam, -ism, -ists, (*see also* jihadists; and Muslims), xxi, 78, 222, 260, 263, 265, 266, 276, 452, 491-493
Israel, 447, 491-493
Italy, 43, 51, 451, 492, 499

Jacobins, 44, 70, 178, 400
Japan, xx, 169, 265, 447, 451, 498, 502, 515
Jay, John, 109
Jefferson, Thomas, 515, 531
  Declaration of Independence and, 369
  Paine, Thomas and, 65
  pursuit of happiness, 369, 515
  rights and duties, 249, 531
  Smith, Adam, and, 175, 285
  U.S. Constitution and, 24, 123, 177, 199, 212, 214, 433
jihad, -ists (*see also* Islam), 485
Johnson, Lyndon, 120, 166-167, 172, 245-246, 266, 323, 331, 332, 374, 524
Johnson, Paul, 269, 356
Jouvenel, Bertrand de,
  On Power, 66, 80, 205, 250, 296, 315, 364, 401, 527
  Ethics of Redistribution, The, 235, 328, 335, 392
judicial activism, 135, 217
judicial obligation/power/independence, 135, 143, 198, 208, 216
judicial sanctions, 523
justice,
  capitalism and, 336, 344
  collectivism and, 9
  equality and, 200

freedom and, 306
government and, 123, 151, 182, 431
human condition and, 431
Greeks and, 141, 459
order and, 77
politics and, 250, 256
social, 276, 291, 333, 476, 519

Kant, Immanuel, 211, 382, 461
Keene, David, 23
Keillor, Garrison, 439
Kennan, George, 516
Kennedy, John F., 228, 242, 323, 330, 440
Keynes, John Maynard, 272
   Great Depression and, 404-405
   ideas are more powerful than vested interests, 6, 352, 452, 513
   inflation, spending and, 288-289, 296-297, 332, 351-352
Khrushchev, Nikita, 256
Kirk, Russell, 13, 19, 63, 77, 228, 282, 346, 420
Korea, North, 340, 458, 499
Korean War Memorial, 257

Laden, Osama bin, 490, 493
Laffer, Arthur, 323, 327
Laffer Curve, 323
Lake Wobegon, (*see* Wobegon, Lake)
language, precise use of, distortion of, 15-18
Latin America, 466, 484, 488, 490
Law, The, 119, 172, 185, 235, 328, 337
law of unintended consequences, (*see* unintended consequences, law of)
law, rule of, (*see* rule of law)
leaders, leadership, xix, 5, 24, 66, 158, 206 *passim*, 260-261, 266, 274, 353, 366, 397, 431, 459, 517
League of Nations, (*see* Nations, League of)
legislation, xvi, 17, 30
   bureaucratic power and, 306, 386
   morality and, 77, 124-125
   separation of powers, 198
legislators, 19, 61, 298, 316, 374, 523
legislature, 61, 210
   general will, 207, 219-220, 401
   judicial limits, 135, 217
   limits on, constitution, 80, 199
Lenin, Vladimir, 292, 349 *passim*, 446
Leviathan, Leviathan, 59-60, 127, 148, 524
liberal populism, (*see* populism, liberal)
liberalism or classical liberalism (original, European meaning), 5, 14-17, 24, 28, 190
   fusion, with libertarians, 147
liberals, liberal politicians, liberalism (modern American meaning), 14-17, 256, 439, 530
libertarians, libertarianism, 147 *passim*, 249 *passim*
   fusion, with conservatives, 147
liberty, freedom, (*see* freedom, liberty)
Libya, 213
Lincoln, Abraham, 446
Lippmann, Walter, 272
living, standard of, (*see* free enterprise, living, standard of)
Locke, John, 59, 71, 83, 155, 157, 162, 176, 192, 198, 206, 210
London, 180, 432, 491
Losing Ground, 30
Louis XVI, 70
Luther, Martin, 12, 50

Machiavelli, Niccolo, 69, 480, 492
macroeconomics, 288, 296, 306, 336, 404, 474
Madison, James, 21, 23, 24, 66, 104, 109, 199, 214, 217, 223, 296, 363, 472
Madrid, 491
majority rule, 129, 130 passim, 210
   individual rights vs., 432-433
   tyranny of the majority, 24, 123, 130 passim, 142, 432
making a difference, (*see* human striving)
making life risk free, (*see* human striving)
making people better off, (*see* human condition)
Malthusian Theory, 498, 501
managerial state, 27
Manifest Destiny, 261, 264
mankind's,
   inequality, 25, 482
   inequality is beneficial, 25, 32, 328-329, 345
   integrity,
      intellectual, 18, 38, 195, 437, 485, 510
      political, 79, 212, 249, 394, 398, 521, 529
      personal, 199, 282, 389, 395, 418, 420, 421
Mao Zedong, 274, 349, 462
Marne Salient, 10
Marshall Plan, 265
Marx, Karl, 22, 46, 168, 383-384, 445 *passim*, 463 *passim*, 480
materialism, 418
McDonald, Forrest, 38
McDougall, Walter A., 259, 271, 450, 491
McNamara, Robert, 266
media, mass media,

amount of information presented through, 419
  as it affects governing, xv, 25, 128, 237, 397, 531
  as it affects politics, 2, 28, 29, 67, 120, 125-126, 134, 177, 228, 245, 259, 356, 370, 398
  exploitation, profit and, 21, 33, 183, 321, 342, 500, 511
  human condition and, 7, 419
  integrity, 21, 440
  public's trust in, 212, 269
  restraint and, 356, 440
  to increase citizen knowledge, 3, 136
Medicare, 16, 50, 346, 522
  prescription drug benefit, 135
Memoir on Pauperism, 121
Mexico, 490, 499
Meyer, Frank, 16, 19, 147, 228, 311
Middle East, 263, 265, 276, 490
military draft, (*see* draft, military)
Mill, John Stuart, 37
Minnow, Newton, 440
Mises, Ludwig von, 6, 18, 35, 36, 282, 290, 292, 293, 320, 333, 367, 381, 403, 448, 469, 481
Mississippi River, 113
Modern Times, 269, 356
modernity, 497, 500, 505
monarchy, monarchs, 23, 60-62, 67, 83, 123, 142-143, 158 *passim*, 181, 206 *passim*, 270, 426, 427
money, as a commodity, a means of exchange, and the foundation of a national economy, 283, 405-406
monopoly, (*see* capitalism, monopoly)
Montaigne dogma, 475
Montaigne, Michel Eyquem de, 475
Mont Pelerin Society, 228, 230-231, 304, 306
moral/ethical/virtuous society, 20, 82-83, 518
  freedom and, 473, 515-516
  governing and, 151-152, 199, 311, 530
  justice and, 435
  power and, 80, 261
  public virtue, 80
moral relativism, 20, 46, 132, 144, 291, 422, 520
Mother Theresa, 281, 519
Moynihan, Daniel Patrick, 228, 245, 332
multiculturalism, 26, 46
multiplier effect, (*see* economics, multiplier effect)
Munich, Germany, (*see* Olympic Village)
Murray, Charles, 30, 249, 288, 330, 361, 369

Muslims (*see also* Islam), 446, 485, 490-493
mystics, -ism, 418, 457
Myth of Society, (*see* Society, Myth of)

9/11, 265, 458, 492, 493, 510
1984, 307, 419, 458
nanny state, 194, 222, 317, 472, 520, 524
  bureaucracy and, 26
Napoleon, 180
National Review, 229
nationalism, autarky, 43, 404
nationalization, 275
Nations, League of, 263
nature, state of, 36, 61
Nazi, Nazism, 281, 383, 461-463
Necessary and Proper Clause, U.S. Constitution, (*see* Constitution of the United States, Article I, Section 8)
Negro Family, The Case For National Action, The, 245, 332
neoconservatives, 135, 171, 203, 482
neosocialism, 26, 189
New Deal, (*see* Great Depression, New Deal)
New York, Troy, 37
Nietzsche, Friedrich, 42, 270
Nixon, Richard, 350, 486
Nobel Prize, 230, 303
No Child Left Behind legislation, 135, 189, 525
Noonan, Peggy, 527-528
North Korea, (*see* Korea, North)

obligation, citizen, (*see* responsibility, duty)
Occupational Safety and Health Administration (OSHA), 285
Olympic Village, Munich, Germany, 492
On Power, 66, 80, 205, 250, 296, 315, 344, 364, 401, 527
On The Right, 239, 258
one-size-fits-all government, (*see* government, one-size-fits-all)
oppression, economic, (*see* economic, oppression)
opportunity, (*see also* equal opportunity)
  equality and, 35, 132, 250
  equality of, 151, 190, 200, 219, 250
  freedom and, 201, 329-331, 361, 371
  government and, xvi, 215, 376
  human action and, 6-7, 397, 522
  order and, 77
  progress and, 177, 343
  welfarism and, 26, 193
opulence, 180

ordered freedom, (*see* freedom, liberty; ordered)
Orwell, George, i, 307, 419, 460

Paine, Thomas, ii, 19, 49, 65, 215, 428
Palestinians, 491
Panama, 487
Parables,
  of the fish, 221, 244
  of the talents, 473
Parkinson, C. Northcote, 29, 362
Parkinson's Laws, 29
parliamentary system (democracy), 141-142, 207, 213, 215, 218, 427-429, 476
pathology, 507 *passim*
pathos, 507
Patriot Act, 189
Pearl Harbor, 458
Pepes, Los, (*see* Colombia)
personal responsibility, (*see* responsibility, personal)
philosophes, 82, 83, 160
Pipes, Richard, 62, 63, 155, 207, 290, 312, 432
Plato, 211, 455 *passim*
pluralism, 26, 47
Pol Pot, 274, 462
political class, the, xvi, 28, 31, 212, 251, 286, 327, 333, 345
political correctness, 511, 518, 521, 523, 531
  citizens and, 125, 152, 216, 420
  education and, 3
  equalitarianism and, 26, 132, 138, 194, 219, 235, 314, 386, 472
  responsibility and, 36, 166, 171, 201, 518, 531
  the state and, 86, 219, 475-476, 511
political reality, innocence, 313, 517
polymath, 69, 170, 453, 468
Popper, Karl, 418, 455
population, 497 *passim*
populism, liberal, 15, 22, 230
poverty, 9, 14, 122, 169, 171, 336, 340, 464, 504
  War on, 345, 524
power, 84, 194, 206, 522-523
  effect on those who have it, 130, 482
  government, 305, 482
  will to, 209, 270
powers, separation of, (*see* separation of powers)
praxeology, 367, 412, 471
prescription, historical, xvi, 25, 28, 148, 393, 439, 441
privacy, 163

pro-natalism, 501-502
profit,
  capitalism and, 34, 131, 178, 284, 322, 339-341, 467
  socialism and, 191
  taxation and, 322, 374, 399
progressive, progressivism, 125, 218, 275
proletariat, –ians, 39, 49, 52, 383, 384, 409, 412, 475
Promised Land, Crusader State, 259, 271, 450, 491
property, 28, 155 *passim*, 206, 434
  freedom and, 239, 244, 273, 312
  private,
    capitalism and, 28, 290, 310, 312, 406
    economics and, 385
    eminent domain and, 212
    government and, 22, 28 *passim*, 37
    happiness, pursuit of, and, 369
    natural right to, 61, 406, 434, 437
    politics and, 172, 447
    rule of law and, 192
    security and, 31, 206, 249
    Smith, Adam, and, 176
    socialism, redistribution and, 343, 382, 385, 447
Property and Freedom, 62, 155, 207, 239, 290, 312, 432
protectionism, economic, 404
Protestant Reformation, (*see* Reformation, Protestant)
Prussians, 37
psychology, 507 *passim*
public servant, 19, 209, 315, 344
Publius, 109, 111
Puritans, Puritanism, 23-24, 49, 181
pursuit of happiness, (*see* happiness, pursuit of,)

quality of life, 343, 501
Quest for Community, 364

rationalism, -ity,
  Age of Reason and, 83
  authoritarianism and, 149, 203
  emotion and, 188, 235
  empiricism and, 202
  Enlightenment and, 82, 126, 313, 333, 439
  equality, equalitarianism, and, 84
  French Revolution (1789) and, 204, 222
  idealism and, xv
  Lenin, Vladimir, and, 350
rationalization of human behavior, 24, 195, 354, 448-450, 484

Reagan, Ronald,
    capitalism and, 285
    conservatism and, 1, 228, 245, 246, 386, 529
    debt, public, 327
    leadership and, 6, 10, 526, 530
    president, 86, 185, 187, 221, 243
    supply-side economics, 322 *passim*
    welfare state and, 270 379
Reagonomics, 322 *passim*
reason,
    Age of Reason and, 83
    as a means to truth, 82, 151, 473
    experience and, 236, 257, 430, 440
    force and, 265, 271, 450
    French Revolution (1789) and, 83
    governing and, 13, 235, 456, 530
    human condition and, 83, 202, 236, 456-457
    intellectualism and, 441
    power and, 214, 460
    press, media, and, 440
    socialism and, 202
    utopia and, 200
Reclaiming the American Dream, 122, 222, 286, 359, 375, 392
redistribution, redistributionists, 238 *passim*, 374
    equal distribution, equalitarianism and, 162, 170, 177, 328, 385
    justice and, (*see* justice, social)
    politics and, 14, 190, 238, 251, 301, 522
    social comity and, 124
    socialism and, 22
    taxation and, 193, 251, 328, 339, 374
Reflections on the Revolution in France, 67, 425
Reformation, Protestant, 12, 24, 50, 81
regulation, 288, 308, 314-317, 322, 326, 353, 406, 518
    centralization of government and, 189, 275, 305, 475-476
    of human behavior, 19, 26, 29, 32, 82, 127
    of property, 156, 308
    judiciary and, 198
    monopolies and, 287
    politics and, 185, 195, 250, 272, 275, 317, 465
religion, 265, 270, 419, 435, 439, 452
    as a social element, 19-20, 59, 81, 85
    Calvinism, (*see also* Calvin, John), 39
    First Amendment (U.S. Constitution), 100, 211
    property and, 158
Renaissance, 50, 81

Republicans, 245, 376, 525 *passim*
Republican Congress, 525-529
responsibility, duty,
    as a personal obligation, xvi, xx, 20, 81, 143, 152, 169-170, 230, 274, 377, 421-422, 432, 515
    Bill of Responsibilities, (*see* Bill of Responsibilities)
    capitalism and, 182, 285
    entitlements and, 195, 233
    erosion of, 164, 166, 169-170, 193, 213
    freedom and, xx, 10, 59, 150, 151, 202, 205-206, 372
    government and, 166, 250, 305, 346, 366, 372
    individualism and, 437
    liberalism (traditional European) and, 16, 24
    morality and, 311
    open society and, (*see* society, open)
    ordered liberty and, 252
    political correctness and, 235, 420
    politics and, 193
    welfarism and, 26, 124, 171, 195, 250, 340
revolution, 163, 463
    American, (War of Independence, Revolutionary War), 11, 67, 69, 116, 140, 199, 425, 524
    English, 141
    French (1789), 60, 67, 68, 80, 83, 123, 129, 133, 155, 189, 199, 343, 425
    French (1830), 138
    French (1848), 123, 126, 128, 138
    Russian, 292, 349, 383, 446
righteousness, self-, 209, 276, 281, 287, 342, 373, 471
rights,
    acquired, 120
    alienable, 158-159
    civil, 26
    Constitutional, 199
    historic, prescriptive, 430
    human, 26
    inalienable, 158-159
    individual, 26, 192, 429
    natural, 24, 27, 61, 120, 130, 151, 159, 211, 426, 429-431
    property, 28, 61-62, 434
Rights of Man, The, 428
risk, as an element of life, 398, 471, 513, 523
Road to Serfdom, The, 6, 136, 153, 187, 197, 234, 295, 337, 363, 508
Roberts, Jason, 407
Robespierre, Maximilien, 44, 70
Rogers, Will, 362

Romans, 63, 66, 78-80, 220
Roosevelt, Franklin Delano, 16-18, 524, 529
  Depression, Great, New Deal, and, 120, 166-169, 299, 361, 481
  socialism and, 37, 167, 168, 242
Roosevelt, Theodore, xx, 131, 487
Roots of American Order, The, 63, 77, 158, 282, 346, 420
Roots of Capitalism, The, 288, 311
Ropke, Wilhelm, 18, 35, 281, 325, 341, 363, 389, 480, 484
Rousseau, Jean Jacques, 35, 84, 130, 134, 162, 199, 211, 213, 220, 325, 455
Rube Goldberg, 286
rule of law,
  capitalism and, 336
  freedom and, 6, 28, 276
  government and, 24, 123, 192, 460
  human condition and, 130
  morality and, 1, 36
  responsibility and, 79
Russia, 227, 242-243, 265, 349, 408, 446, 499
Russian Revolution, (*see* revolution, Russian)

safety net, social, 16, 166, 171, 190, 194, 309, 330, 335, 338, 418, 522
Sager, Ryan, 528
St. Lawrence River, 113
St. Thomas Aquinas, 430
Santayana, George, 22, 491
Scalia, Antonin, U.S. Supreme Court Justice, 509
Schopenhauer, Arthur, 461
Schumpeter, Joseph, 195, 394, 445, 484
Scottish Enlightenment, (*see* Enlightenment, Scottish)
Second Treatise on Civil Government, 59, 83, 155, 176, 206
security,
  anarchy versus, 179, 206, 208
  collectivism and, 274, 461
  equality and, 193
  freedom versus, 127, 222, 285, 361, 398, 450, 452, 460-461
  Greeks and, 455-456
  property, distribution, and, 160
self-interest, 188, 319, 391
  enlightened, 36, 60, 82, 84, 127, 178-180, 188, 282, 320
  socialism and, 191
self-sufficiency, 185, 221, 301, 304-305, 309, 371, 376, 392, 397, 521
Sense of the World, A, 407
separation of powers, 42, 61, 79-80, 143, 198, 203, 208, 217

September 11, 2001, (*see* 9/11)
Serengeti Plain, xv
Seurat, Georges, 269
shamans, 457
Shultz, George, 356
Silesia, 173
situational ethics, (*see* ethics, situational)
slaves, slavery, human, 20, 65, 69, 114, 124, 140, 159-160, 234, 456, 517
slavery, economic, (*see* collectivism, economic slavery)
slippery slope of authoritarian or equalitarian government, 26, 135, 406, 515, 516, 519, 525
Smith, Adam,
  capitalism and freedom, 32
  classical liberalism and, 28, 51
  division of labor and, 385-386, 404
  enlightened self-interest, (*see* self-interest, enlightened)
  free enterprise, market, 178 *passim*, 303
  Hobbes, Thomas, and, 60
  invisible hand, (*see* capitalism, invisible hand)
  Keynes, John Maynard and, 288
  Scottish Enlightenment, 28
  self-interest, 188, 319-320
  trade, 284, 404
Smoot-Hawley Tariff Act, (*see* Hawley-Smoot Tariff Act)
social compact, contract, 5, 52, 61, 84, 430
Social Crisis of Our Time, The, 390
social,
  engineer, -ing, 120, 276, 286-287, 308, 399, 471
  justice, 200, 291, 333, 459, 476, 519
  safety net, (*see* safety net, social)
  science, 27
  welfare net, (*see* welfare net, social)
Social Security, 16, 50, 219, 238, 346, 371, 522
social welfare net, (*see* welfare net, social)
socialism, socialists, 381 *passim*, 522
  as an intellectual concept, 37, 284
  capitalism and, 14, 183, 230, 290, 354, 522
  capitalism and chaos and, 35, 475
  Christian charity and, 391
  collectivism and, 8, 22, 197
  demise of, 187, 196, 354, 422
  despotism and, 25, 188, 191
  equalitarianism and, 37, 142, 162, 306, 343, 355, 422
  Europe and, 126
  free lunch and, 449

Germany, East and West, and, 390-391
Great Britain and, 451
Great Depression and, 168
human condition and, 84, 422, 508
individualism and, 191, 193
inflation and, 395, 406
Mont Pelerin Society and, (*see* Mont Pelerin Society)
moral superiority and, 37, 361, 382
Roosevelt, Franklin Delano, and, 37
Russia (Vladimir Lenin) and, 350
slavery and, 6, 126
utopianism and, 394
welfare state and, 7, 23, 37-38, 123-124, 125, 219, 284, 290, 350, 373, 396, 439
zero-sum game and, 475
Socialism, 290, 469, 481
socialism, democratic, 15, 446-447
society,
  closed, 390, 456 *passim*
  open, 2, 24, 191, 259, 273, 275, 291, 336, 341, 390, 455
Society, Myth of, 151
Socrates, 157, 456
South Africa, 446
South America, 466
Soviet Union, (*see* Union of Soviet Socialist Republics)
Sowell, Thomas, ii, 172, 504
Spain, 113, 491, 499
special interests, (*see* interests, special)
speculators, 289
Spencer, Herbert, i
spending, (*see* government, spending)
square one, xv, xvii, 2, 6, 37, 63, 77, 109, 119, 171, 381, 521
Stalin, Joseph, xxi, 274, 349, 462
Stanislaw, Joseph, 8, 275, 349, 406
"starve the beast," (*see* taxation, "starve the beast")
Statecraft, 21
state of nature, (*see* nature, state of)
state welfarism, (*see* welfarism, state)
state, the, 28, 120, 140, 208 *passim*
  as the supreme good, 37, 149
  individualism and, 193
  Roosevelt, Franklin D. and, 37
statists, statism, 24, 220
Stewart, Potter, U.S. Supreme Court Justice, 516
Sumner, William Graham, 170
Sunday on the Island of La Grande Jatte, A, 269
supply-side economics, (*see* economics, supply side)

Switzerland, 447
Sword of Imagination, The, 86

Taft, Bob, U.S. Senator, 228, 230
Take It Back, 530
tariffs, 167, 272, 300, 404, 407
taxation,
  as a disincentive, 231, 251, 275, 287, 296, 297, 322 *passim*, 397-398
  capitalism and, 34, 127, 178, 322 *passim*
  civic obligation of paying, 40, 81
  courts and, 217
  deficit spending and, (*see* deficits, fiscal)
  "entitlements" and, 362, 386
  entrepreneurs and, 161, 286, 322
  flat tax, 324
  freedom and, 239, 244, 287
  Goldwater, Barry, and, 246
  Great Depression and, 167, 299, 449
  Keynes, John Maynard and, 404
  liberalism, liberals, (modern American meaning) and, 17, 22, 236, 309, 328, 354
  lower taxes, 322 *passim*, 525
  political correctness and, 26
  politics and, 29, 124-125, 156, 159, 237, 323 *passim*, 361, 528
  power and, 210, 288
  public administration and, 29, 316, 518
  redistribution and, 193, 251, 309, 328, 337
  revolt against, 112, 345
  "rich," wealthy, taxing the, 331, 341, 398
  security and, 208, 361
  spending, as revenues increase and taxes are lowered, 323 *passim*, 524
  "starve the beast" of government, 325, 366
  U.S. Constitution and, 17, 113, 249
  vigilance, citizen, to control, 32, 289-290
  welfarism, welfare state and, 164, 170, 236, 246, 374, 385-386
Ten Commandments, 40, 155
terrorism, xix, 222, 261, 265-266, 485, 492
Thatcher, Margaret, 1-2, 6, 21, 187, 221, 274, 354
Theory of Money and Credit, The, 292, 333, 403
therapeutic state, 26, 222, 508
therapy, -ism, 508 *passim*
third rail, of politics, 243, 327
Third Reich, 281
Third World, 25, 243, 276, 346, 349, 446, 450, 452

Thurow, Lester, 331
TIME Magazine, 490, 511, 528
Tocqueville, Alexis de, 5, 83, 85, 121-122, 129, 142, 195, 211, 214, 222, 239, 364, 367, 370, 420
totalitarian, -ism,
   as a consequence of a failure of democracy, 86, 137, 452-453
   as a consequence of the demise of monarchies, 270
   capitalism and, 33, 165, 188, 194
   collectivism and, 22-25, 191, 274-275, 447
   democracy and, 198
   human condition and, 149, 153, 307, 447, 459
   inflation and, 406
   information control and, 458
   moral society and, 77, 140, 461
   Plato and, 457, 459
   political correctness and, 86, 420
   redistribution and, 343, 391
   righteousness and, 276
   security and, 460-461
   social engineering and, 471
   standard of living and, (*see* free enterprise, living, standard of)
trade, international, 112, 115, 167, 175, 184, 283, 404, 407
transcendentalism, transcendent order, 418, 437
Treaty of Paris, 116
Treaty of Versailles, 271
Tremlett, George, 213
Treptow, Martin, 10
Trilling, Lionel, 438
Trotsky, Leon, 257
Truman, Harry, 516
Tumulty, Karen, 528
Turner, Ted, 470
Tuskegee Institute, 234
tyranny, xxi, 24, 65, 67, 72-73, 123-124, 135, 220, 309, 471
tyranny of the majority, (*see* majority rule, tyranny of the majority)

U2 spy plane, 242-243
uneasiness, in the human psyche (*see also* happiness), 177, 470
unintended consequences, law of,
   freedom of choice/action as antidote to, 313, 461, 502
   good intentions, theories, and, 38, 131, 157, 228, 235, 287, 288, 295, 524
   government and, xvii, 205, 282, 308, 330, 373, 438
   politics and, 16, 166
   short-term government action versus long-term economic consequences, 404
   "solving" inequality and, 345
Union of Soviet Socialist Republics (Soviet Union),
   central planning and, 189
   Cold War and, (*see* Cold War)
   communism/socialism/collectivism and, 339-340, 349, 351
   controlled society and, 458
   Cuba and, 242
   demise of, 1, 187, 264, 479
   Germany and, 390
   Vietnam and, 262-263
   World War II and, 265
United States Steel, 315
United Student Aid Funds, Inc., 365
"unsupervised" government, (*see* government, unsupervised)
Up From Liberalism, 233, 441
Up From Slavery, 234
utilitarianism, 202
utopia, -ism,
   as a societal goal, 9, 33, 231, 458
   authoritarianism and, 149, 518, 524
   collectivism and totalitarianism as a means to, 185-186, 303, 394
   Enlightenment and, 82-83, 126, 188
   equalitarianism and, 84, 523-524
   human condition and, 382, 441, 460
   persistence of, 284, 480, 518
   Plato and, 457 *passim*
   (political) power of the state and, 28, 172, 194, 206
   using reason to deconstruct, 236, 257, 429, 456 *passim*

Valery, Paul, 524
Victims of Communism Memorial, (*see* Communism Memorial, Victims of)
Victoria, Queen, Victorian age, 142
Vietnam, 262-263, 266
vigilance, (*see* citizen, vigilance)
vigilantes, -ism, 490-491
Violencia, La, (*see* Colombia)
virtue, virtuous society, (*see* moral/ethical/virtuous society)
Voltaire, 51, 186
volunteer, volunteerism, 359 *passim*, 374-375
voting, 132-133, 134, 212, 370, 433, 520
   assumption of power as a consequence of, 212, 216, 276, 292, 378
   as a validation of policy, 332, 502

wage and price controls, 350, 407
Wall Street Journal, 399, 527
War on Poverty, (*see* poverty, War on)
Washington, Booker T., 234
Washington, George, 65, 124, 207, 257
Wealth and Poverty, 35, 161, 237, 296, 319, 395, 400
Wealth of Nations, 32, 60, 82, 127, 175, 188, 284, 321, 385
Weaver, Richard, 337, 361, 366
websites, web addresses,
  First Principles, 18
  Mercatus Center (George Mason University), 378
welfare net, social, 16, 26, 171, 309, 338, 522
welfare programs, purpose of, 372, 396, 520-521
welfare reform, federal, 1996, 30, 165, 218, 363, 374, 376
Wisconsin, 305-306
welfarism, welfarists, welfare state,
  analysis of, 164-165, 191-102, 194, 202-203, 290, 332, 374, 439, 482, 520-521
  emotional appeal of, 8-9, 28, 193, 244
  entitlements and, 120, 195, 290
  equalitarianism and, 162, 189, 235, 308-309, 371, 397, 472
  handout instead of a hand up, 30, 166, 170, 362, 372, 375
  individualism and community, destruction of, 142-143, 153, 162, 193, 250, 304, 397
  Mont Pelerin Society and, 304
  Negro Family, The Case For National Action, The, and, 332
  politics and, 166-167, 171, 386, 476
  property and, 164
  rights/duties of suppliers/recipients of welfare, 120-122, 124, 164, 230, 304, 397
  socialism and, 7, 23, 37, 38, 125, 168, 290
  taxation and, 275, 385-386
  volunteerism/charity and, 361-362, 391-392
Western Civilization, foundations, 1
What It Means To Be A Libertarian, 249, 330
Whigs, 427
wildebeest, 510
Wildebeest Effect, The, xv
will, deified, (in the state), 149

will, general, (of the citizenry), 48, 80, 125, 207-208, 214, 219, 401
will to power, (*see* power, will to)
Wilson, James, 11
Wilson, Woodrow, 218, 263, 266, 272
Winthrop, John, 260
Witness, 229, 293, 401, 479
Wobegon, Lake, 439
workfare, 165, 305, 363
World Trade Center bombing, (*see* 9/11)
World War I, 262, 264, 269, 271, 350
  Germany and, 300, 354, 381
  intellectual reaction to, 480, 481
World War II, xix, 168, 187, 262, 271, 350, 462, 515
  intellectual reaction to, 295, 389, 418
  U.S. capitalism and, 262, 299

YAF, (*see* Young Americans for Freedom)
Yergin, Daniel, 8, 275, 349, 406
Young Americans for Freedom, YAF, 239, 258
YouTube, 17

zero-sum game, -economics, (*see* economics, zero-sum)
Zulu Nation, South Africa, 446

A note regarding particular editions of the books synopsized in *First Principles*

While it is not necessary to read the exact editions of the books synopsized in *First Principles* in order to expand on the knowledge offered here, the editions used in writing *First Principles* are available through the following specific publishers and outlets or through most online booksellers:

Chapter 1
THE SECOND TREATISE ON CIVIL GOVERNMENT John Locke

Prometheus Books
59 John Glenn Dr.
Amherst, NY 14228-2197
(800) 421-0351
marketing@prometheusbooks.com

Chapter 2
COMMON SENSE, THE RIGHTS OF MAN, AND OTHER ESSENTIAL WRITINGS
  Thomas Paine

Meridian/Penguin Group
375 Hudson St.
New York, NY 10014
ecommerce@us.penguingroup.com

Chapter 4
THE ROOTS OF AMERICAN ORDER Russell Kirk

ISI Books
Intercollegiate Studies Institute
P.O. Box 4431
Wilmington, DE 19807-0431
www.isi.org

Chapter 6
THE FEDERALIST Alexander Hamilton, John Jay, James Madison

Liberty Fund, Inc.
Suite 300
8335 Allison Pointe Trail
Indianapolis, IN 46250-1687
(800) 955-8335
www.libertyfund.org

Chapter 7
The Law Frederic Bastiat

Foundation for Economic Education
30 S. Broadway
Irvington-on-Hudson, NY 10533
(914) 591-7230
www.fee.org

Chapter 8
Democracy in America Alexis de Tocqueville

Penguin Putnam, Inc.
375 Hudson St.
New York, NY 10014
ecommerce@us.penguingroup.com

Chapter 9
Essays in the History of Liberty Lord Acton

Liberty Fund, Inc.
Suite 300
8335 Allison Pointe Trail
Indianapolis, IN 46250-1687
(800) 955-8335
www.libertyfund.org

Chapter 10
In Defense of Freedom Frank S. Meyer

Liberty Fund, Inc.
Suite 300
8335 Allison Pointe Trail
Indianapolis, IN 46250-1687
(800) 955-8335
www.libertyfund.org

Chapter 11
Property and Freedom Richard Pipes

Vintage Books (Division of Random House)
1745 Broadway
New York, NY 10019
www.randomhouse.com/vintage

Chapter 12
Wealth of Nations Adam Smith

Prometheus Books
Great Minds Series
59 John Glenn Drive
Amherst, NY 14228
(800) 421-0351
marketing@prometheusbooks.com

Chapter 13
THE ROAD TO SERFDOM Friedrich A. von Hayek

University of Chicago Press
University of Chicago
Chicago, IL 60637
www.uchicago.edu

Chapter 14
THE CONSTITUTION OF LIBERTY Friedrich A. von Hayek

University of Chicago Press
University of Chicago
Chicago, IL 60637
www.uchicago.edu

Chapter 15
ON POWER Bertrand de Jouvenel

Liberty Fund, Inc.
Suite 300
8335 Allison Pointe Trail
Indianapolis, IN 46250-1687
(800) 955-8335
www.libertyfund.org

Chapter 16
THE CONSERVATIVE REVOLUTION: THE MOVEMENT THAT REMADE AMERICA
    Lee Edwards

The Free Press (Simon & Schuster)
1230 Avenue of the Americas
New York, NY 10020
www.simonsays.com

Chapter 17
UP FROM LIBERALISM William F. Buckley, Jr.

Out of print. Used editions are available through most online booksellers.

Chapter 18
THE CONSCIENCE OF A CONSERVATIVE Barry Goldwater

Princeton University Press
Princeton University
Princeton, NJ 08544
www.princeton.edu

Chapter 19
WHAT IT MEANS TO BE A LIBERTARIAN Charles Murray

Broadway Books
Div. of Bantam Doubleday Dell
1540 Broadway
New York, NY 10036
www.randomhouse.com

Chapter 20
LET US TALK OF MANY THINGS William F. Buckley, Jr.

Prima Publishing, Inc.
3000 Lava Ridge Ct.
Roseville, CA 95661
(800) 632-8676
www.primapublishing.com

Chapter 21
PROMISED LAND, CRUSADER STATE Walter A. McDougall

Houghton Mifflin Co.
215 Park Avenue South
New York, NY 10003
www.hmco.com

Chapter 22
MODERN TIMES Paul Johnson

HarperCollins Publishers
10 E. 53rd St.
New York, NY 10022
www.harpercollins.com

Chapter 23
ECONOMICS OF THE FREE SOCIETY Wilhelm Röpke

Libertarian Press, Inc.
P.O. Box 309
Grove City, PA 16127
(724) 458-5861
www.libertarianpress.com

Chapter 24
ECONOMICS IN ONE LESSON Henry Hazlitt

Three Rivers Press, Div. of Crown Publishing
201 E. 50th Street
New York, NY 10022
www.randomhouse.com

Chapter 25
CAPITALISM AND FREEDOM Milton Friedman

University of Chicago Press
University of Chicago
Chicago, IL 60637
www.uchicago.edu

Chapter 26
THE ROOTS OF CAPITALISM John Chamberlain

Liberty Fund, Inc.
Suite 300
8335 Allison Pointe Trail
Indianapolis, IN 46250-1687
(800) 955-8335
www.libertyfund.org

Chapter 27
WEALTH AND POVERTY George Gilder

Institute for Contemporary Studies
720 Market St.
San Francisco, CA 94102
(800) 326-0263
www.icspress.com

Chapter 28
THE ETHICS OF REDISTRIBUTION Bertrand de Jouvenel

Liberty Fund, Inc.
Suite 300
8335 Allison Pointe Trail
Indianapolis, IN 46250-1687
(800) 955-8335
www.libertyfund.org

Chapter 29
THE COMMANDING HEIGHTS Daniel Yergin and Joseph Stanislaw

Touchstone Books, Div. of Simon & Schuster
Rockefeller Center
1230 Avenue of the Americas
New York, NY 10020
www.simonsays.com

Chapter 30
RECLAIMING THE AMERICAN DREAM Richard C. Cornuelle

Transaction Publishers
300 McGaw Dr.
Raritan Center
Edison, NJ 08837
888 999-6778
www.transactionpub.com

Chapter 31
In Pursuit: Of Happiness and Good Government Charles Murray

Institute for Contemporary Studies
720 Market St.
San Francisco, CA 94102
(800) 326-0263
www.icspress.com

Chapter 32
Socialism Ludwig von Mises

Liberty Fund, Inc.
Suite 300
8335 Allison Pointe Trail
Indianapolis, IN 46250-1687
(800) 955-8335
www.libertyfund.org

Chapter 33
A Humane Economy Wilhelm Röpke

Intercollegiate Studies Institute
P.O. Box 4431
Wilmington, DE 19807-0431
www.isi.org

Chapter 34
The Theory of Money and Credit Ludwig von Mises

Liberty Fund, Inc.
Suite 300
8335 Allison Pointe Trail
Indianapolis, IN 46250-1687
(800) 955-8335
www.libertyfund.org

Chapter 35
Ideas Have Consequences Richard M. Weaver

University of Chicago Press
University of Chicago
Chicago, IL 60637
www.uchicago.edu

Chapter 36
Selected Works of Edmund Burke, Volume 2: Reflections on the Revolution in France Edmund Burke

Liberty Fund, Inc.
Suite 300
8335 Allison Pointe Trail
Indianapolis, IN 46250-1687
(800) 955-8335
www.libertyfund.org

THE PORTABLE EDMUND BURKE Isaac Kramnick (Ed.)

Penguin Books
375 Hudson St.
New York, NY 10014
ecommerce@us.penguingroup.com

Chapter 37
THE CONSERVATIVE MIND Russell Kirk

Regnery Publishing
One Massachusetts Ave.
Washington, DC 20001
(202) 216-0600
www.regnery.com

Chapter 38
CAPITALISM, SOCIALISM, AND DEMOCRACY Joseph A. Schumpeter

Harper & Row Publishers, Inc.
10 E. 53rd St.
New York, NY 10022
www.harpercollins.com

Chapter 39
THE OPEN SOCIETY AND ITS ENEMIES Karl L. Popper

Princeton University Press
Princeton University
Princeton, NJ 08544
www.princeton.edu

Chapter 40
HUMAN ACTION Ludwig von Mises

Fox and Wilkes (now part of the International Society for Individual Liberty)
Suite 202
938 Howard St.
San Francisco, CA 94103
www.isil.org

Chapter 41
WITNESS Whittaker Chambers

Regnery Publishing, Inc.
One Massachusetts Ave. NW
Washington, DC 20001
(212) 216-0600
www.regnery.com

Chapter 42
KILLING PABLO Mark Bowden
Penguin Books
375 Hudson St.
New York, NY 10014
ecommerce@us.penguingroup.com

Chapter 43
FEWER Ben J. Wattenberg

Ivan R. Dee, Publisher
1332 N. Halsted St.
Chicago, IL 60622
www.ivanrdee.com

Chapter 44
ONE NATION UNDER THERAPY Christina Hoff Sommers, Ph.D., Sally Satel, MD

St. Martin's Press
175 Fifth Ave.
New York, NY 10010
www.stmartins.com

Acknowledgements

THE FOLLOWING PEOPLE were substantively and editorially instrumental in the preparation and final form of *First Principles*. They are listed here in the order in which they were first involved in this project. Their help was invaluable and necessary; thus with sincere appreciation for their insights, assistance, encouragement, and most of all, their time, I thank each of them:

Stanford Ackley, David Keene, Donald Devine, Ph.D., Jameson Campaigne, Tim Wheeler, Trish Alarie, Joseph Baldacchino, Ph.D., the Ludwig von Mises Institute, Carl Schmidlapp, Dick Olsen, George Winter, Chris Woltermann, Ph.D., Adam Walinski, Henry Hollensbe, Greg Schneider, Ph.D., Paul Erickson, Milton Friedman, Ph.D., George Gilder, Dara Ekanger, Walter McDougall, Ph.D., Ben Wattenberg, Donna Wiesner, Bruce Yuhas, Cathe Kobacker, Charles Murray, Ph.D, Charles King.

About the Author

TOM TRIPP is a political consultant and campaign manager and has held appointments in the Reagan, George H.W. Bush, and Clinton Administrations. A U.S. Army veteran, he is a practicing attorney who also manages business enterprises and serves on educational, corporate, and non-profit boards. He publishes on government, politics, and the law. Mr. Tripp is secretary of the American Conservative Union Foundation and chair of FirstPrinciples.US. He resides in Wilson, Wyoming.

Made in the USA